J.R.D. Heaton.

Skipton; 15th August, 2000

The Art
of the Picture Frame

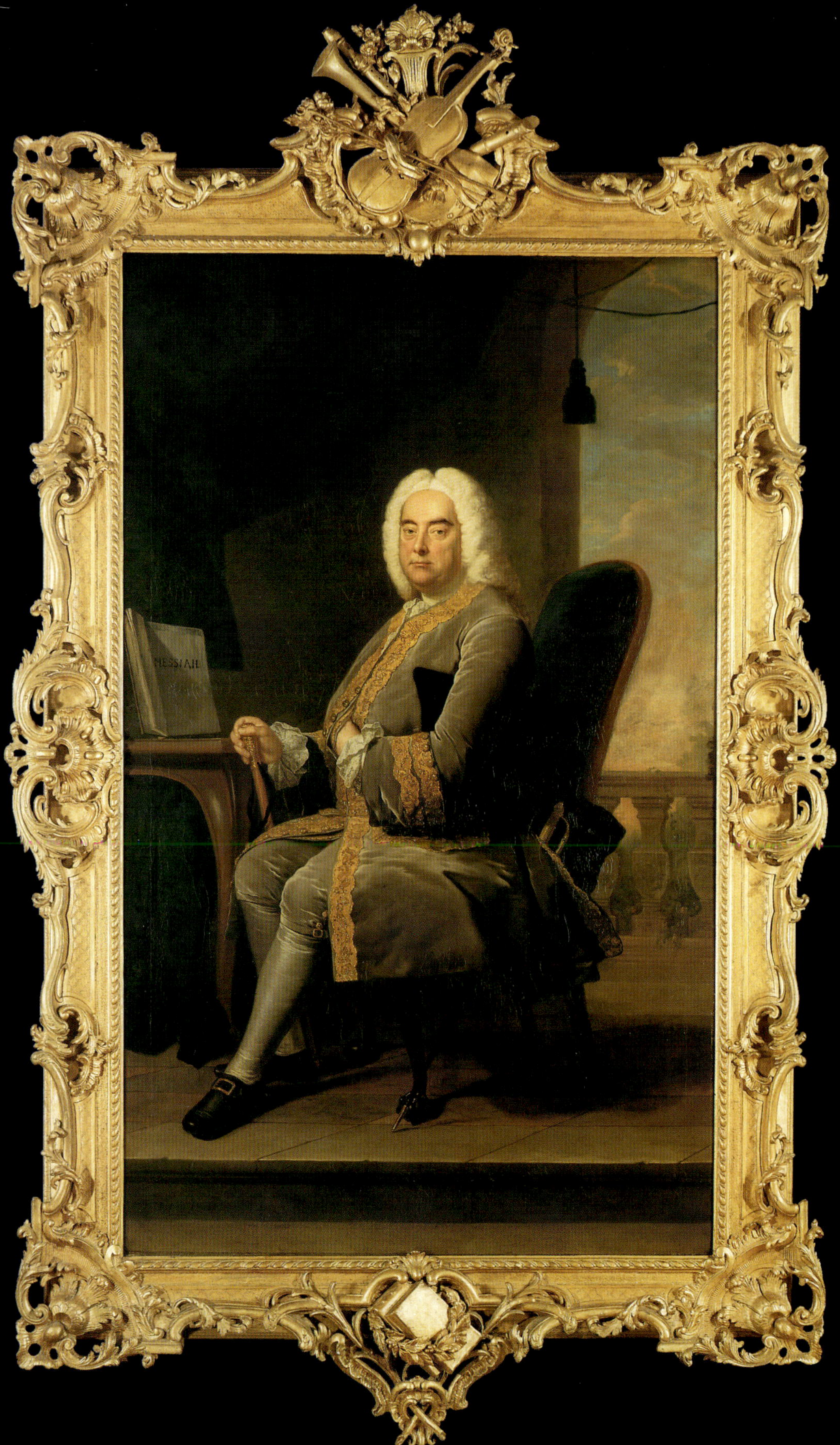
MESSIAH

The Art of the Picture Frame

Artists, Patrons and the Framing of Portraits in Britain

JACOB SIMON

NATIONAL PORTRAIT GALLERY

Published for the exhibition held at the National Portrait Gallery, London, from 8 November 1996 to 9 February 1997

Published by National Portrait Gallery Publications, 2 St Martin's Place, London WC2H OHE, England, 1996

ISBN 1 85514 171 X (cloth)
ISBN 1 85514 172 8 (paper)

A catalogue record for this book is available from the British Library

Project editor: Gillian Forrester
Book designer: Tim Harvey
Cover/jacket designer: Pep Sala
Indexer: Helen Baz
Proof-reader: Luci Collings

Frame sections drawn by Timothy Newbery and computer generated by Neville Bruton Design

Typeset in Monotype Baskerville by Tim Harvey
Printed and bound in Italy on Gardamatt 150gsm by Amilcare Pizzi

All illustrated works are in the collection of the National Portrait Gallery unless otherwise stated.

Frontispiece: *George Frideric Handel* by Thomas Hudson, 1756 (no.37)

Front cover (clockwise from left; details): *Frederick Delius* by Ernest Proctor, 1929 (no.115); *Samuel Pepys* by John Hayls, 1666 (no.18); *George Frideric Handel* by Thomas Hudson, 1756 (no.37) *Sir Edward Hoby* by an unknown artist, 1583 (NPG 1974), *Charles I* by an unknown artist (NPG 4836); *Charles Churchill* by J.S.C. Shaak, *c.*1763-4 (no.53). Back cover (clockwise from left; details): *Kenneth Clark, Baron Clark* by Graham Sutherland (no.119); *Oliver Cromwell* by an unknown artist after Samuel Cooper (no.11); *Victoria, Princess Royal* by Joseph Mordecai, *c.*1900 or later (no.96). The back flap of the jacket for the cloth edition additionally includes a detail of *Henry VII* by an unknown artist, 1505 (no.1).

SPONSORED BY

PAUL MITCHELL
Antique & Reproduction
FRAMES

NATIONAL HERITAGE
ARTS SPONSORSHIP SCHEME

The National Portrait Gallery would like to thank the following for making copyright photographs available:

Arnold Wiggins & Sons Ltd (figs.7, 17); Ashmolean Museum, Oxford (fig.88); Edward Harley Esq. (fig.41); the Fine Art Society (fig.9); Hammersmith and Fulham Archives and Local History Centre (fig.146); the Huntington Library and Art Collection, San Marino, California (fig.12); Magdalene College, Cambridge (fig.130); all rights reserved, the Metropolitan Museum of Art, New York (fig.145); the National Gallery of Canada, Ottawa (fig.40); the Royal Commission on the Ancient and Historical Monuments of Scotland (fig.35); the Trustees of Sir John Soane's Museum, London (figs.23, 63); Woburn Abbey (fig.3); Westminster City Archives (fig.147); Westminster Libraries and Archives (fig.142); the Marquess of Zetland (fig.148).

The Gallery would also like to thank the following for granting permission to reproduce works for which they hold the copyright: Copyright © Mr H.I. Spottiswoode (fig.83); Copyright © reserved Howard Morgan (fig.178). Copyright © (figs. 37, 116, 117, 79, 82, 164).

Figs. 5, 8, 10, 11, 14, 15, 16, 18, 19, 20, 22, 24, 26, 27, 29, 30, 31, 32, 33, 34, 37, 38, 39, 42, 43, 44, 46, 47, 48, 49, 53, 55, 58, 59, 61, 62, 64, 65, 66, 67, 68, 70, 71, 73, 74, 75, 76, 77, 78, 79, 80, 81, 82, 83, 84, 85, 87, 90, 92, 94, 97, 98, 100, 101, 102, 103, 105, 106, 107, 109, 110, 111, 112, 113, 114, 115, 116, 117, 118, 119, 125, 126, 131, 150, 151, 152, 153, 156, 157, 158, 160, 163, 166, 167, 171, 172, 174, 175, 176, 177 and 178 were photographed by Prudence Cuming Associates Limited.

Figs.1, 3, 4, 13, 21, 25, 28, 29, 45, 49, 50, 51, 52, 54, 57, 60, 69, 72, 86, 93, 95, 96, 104, 108, 120, 121, 122, 123, 124, 127, 133, 134, 136,138, 139, 140, 141, 142, 144, 154, 155, 159, 161, 162, 164, 165, 168, 169, 170 and 173 were photographed by A. A. Barnes Photography.

Contents

Foreword

Portraiture, more than most art forms, is a social art, involving a knowledge of how and where portraits hung in order to interpret them. It therefore makes good sense for the National Portrait Gallery to hold a pioneering exhibition which investigates the nature of the relationship between pictures and their frames. It is the frames which retain the evidence of the original circumstances in which portraits were intended to be seen: whether or not they were treated as slightly secret objects hidden behind curtains as in the sixteenth century; or as grand works of interior decoration when the frame might be designed as part of a much larger *mise-en-scène* as in the eighteenth century; or surrounded by nothing more than a thin metal strip as was fashionable in the 1960s.

Once one has been alerted to the significance of looking at frames, it seems odd that so little has been written about the subject before. The frame is after all one of the few things which almost all pictures have in common. Studying them involves a certain amount of technical knowledge as to how they were made. It has a connection to furniture history, since frames cannot be understood independently of their relationship to other aspects of interior decoration. And it ought to be a more prominent part of art history, since it is essential to any understanding of how artists intended their works to be viewed.

Originally the Gallery's exhibition *The Art of the Picture Frame* was planned as a small-scale educational exhibition in the downstairs studio gallery; but as time went by it was clear that it was becoming a very ambitious project, involving a detailed survey of all the frames in the Gallery's collection, undertaken by Jacob Simon, our eighteenth-century curator, with the assistance of a team of volunteers. A catalogue had been planned, which, while it concentrates quite rightly on frames for portraits, is at the same time a remarkably comprehensive and authoritative survey of the subject as a whole. So, when a major exhibition planned for our autumn programme had to be rescheduled, we took the decision that *The Art of the Picture Frame* should be shown in the Wolfson Gallery to a wider public. In retrospect, I regard this as serendipitous, since I think it is important that the Gallery, particularly as it is in receipt of public funding, should show the fruits of recent, pioneering scholarship undertaken by the Gallery and its staff.

The great bulk of the work on the project has been undertaken by Jacob Simon, who has been indefatigable in hunting down documentary material, recording information about the Gallery's frames, supervising his band of helpers, and ensuring that the catalogue is as comprehensive as possible. He quite rightly stresses that the exhibition is only a beginning and that more information will come to light, not least as a result of the exhibition. But it has been a bold undertaking, and I am particularly pleased that it has made such good use of the wonderful resources of the Heinz archive and library, our excellent Registry, the expertise of our conservation studio and, above all, the practical knowledge of our frame conservation studio. In this it has been a model of Museum and curatorial practice.

Charles Saumarez Smith
Director, National Portrait Gallery

Introduction

It was Michael Jaffé who first drew my attention to the importance of picture frames in his classes in the Fitzwilliam Museum, Cambridge. My interest was further encouraged by more than ten years spent working in country houses, first at Temple Newsam House, Leeds, and then at the Iveagh Bequest, Kenwood. But it was not until well into my career at the National Portrait Gallery that the vital importance of the picture frame to portrait painting became clear to the extent that one could begin to link distinctive frame types with particular artists and even identify an artist's work through his or her frames – a process not without its hazards when so many frames have been changed.

Portrait painting is of course only part of the story of painting, but in Britain, at least until the late eighteenth century, it was normally the main part. However this book looks at wider attitudes to the framing of paintings of all sorts and not just portraits. And where helpful it tries to place the story of framing in Britain in the essential context of what was happening on the Continent, especially in France, Italy and the Netherlands.

Style and technique are essential components of this book and the accompanying exhibition. But there is a further intention: to look beyond these questions to matters of choice: how were decisions on framing made by artist, architect, patron or framemaker? The sparsity of information here is not just a matter of the lack of published sources although this is a problem. It is that so little was ever recorded in the first place. As one correspondent told the author when writing of her father's portrait by William Coldstream, 'I remember when Bill Coldstream painted my father they were discussing the framing endlessly – but there is nothing in writing, not even a label on the frame'. The lack of available documentation makes the study of frames more difficult. So little has been published that the researcher is obliged to undertake an inordinate amount of archival work. Every effort has been made to pursue both the obvious and the less obvious sources in the time available but I know that I have only scratched the surface.

I have deliberately chosen to focus on the National Portrait Gallery's collection which is probably the most comprehensive single collection covering the history of framing in Britain over the last five hundred years. This is not to say that there are not finer frames in country houses and in the Royal Collection, especially for the first three hundred years of my subject, and in museums, notably the Tate Gallery, for the next two hundred years. But the National Portrait Gallery's collection is the best display of its kind, arranged in chronological order, and available for permanent study, so that this book will form a guide to the collection and to framing in Britain even after the close of the exhibition.

The choice of the National Portrait Gallery's collection has had a further advantage. In choosing to study five hundred years of framing history, I needed to limit the subject so that it did not expand into a definitive history of the frame in Britain. It is too early in the short history of frame studies to do that. So the exhibition has the deliberate limitation of being a portrait exhibition drawn from one collection. This is the first major exhibition on the subject and not the last. More ordinary frames are shown at the expense of grand country house frames. There is scope for an exhibition of fine frames as superlative works of carving. There is also a demand for an exhibition on the framing of prints, drawings and photographs as I found out in the course of my research.

An explanation of the methods adopted in preparing the exhibition will indicate the limitations of my approach. In the first place it has been necessary to gain an overview of the history of framing in Britain, and here there has been a strong element of opportunism so that I seized on the documentation that came most readily in the belief that it would be enough to inform my discussions. With hindsight this is least true of the sixteenth century. For some other periods where the history of the frame has not been well defined, notably the reign of Charles I and the mid-seventeenth century, the mid-nineteenth century excluding the Pre-Raphaelites and a few other artists, and the first half of the twentieth century, I have ventured a synthesis which relies on contemporary sources as far as possible.

Secondly, the National Portrait Gallery's frames and their context have been studied intensively. Not only have most of the 2,500 frames in the collection been examined, the more important ones off the wall, but also the National Portrait Gallery records have been trawled for information. With the help of a team of volunteers the Gallery's records of the past 140 years have been examined, including volumes of accounts, picture documentation files for individual portraits (the 'Registered Packets'), glass negatives taken in the 1890s and early 1900s and old Gallery photographs, which show the pictures in the frames they then had.

Much of the National Portrait Gallery's collection was stored unframed in the First World War, and the pictures were sometimes put back in the wrong frames after the war. Many of the frames in the collection have been regilt and others have been cut about in the nineteenth century by the fitting of 'doors' in the frames to take glass to protect the pictures from the London atmosphere. It has not been possible (nor was it thought desirable) to restore all the frames to their original condition. This is an exhibition of one gallery's collection, warts and all. To some extent we have tried to make a virtue of the warts in the belief that showing what has happened to the collection is instructive in itself. Hence the conservation of four frames, one painted, one carved, one papier-mâché and one compo as focuses in the exhibition. Hence too the gallery trail, an essential component of the exhibition, which reaches out to examine frames hanging in the galleries. In a way every picture on display at the National Portrait Gallery forms a part of the exhibition.

Research for the exhibition has had a number of benefits, not least the reassessment of several pictures in the collection, in particular the portrait of John Ward, now identified as by Joseph Samuel Webster, and that of Viscount Hardinge, now known to have been begun by G. Clarke and repainted and finished by Sir Francis Grant in 1876. Various pictures have been specially cleaned for the exhibition, many of which were previously unexhibitable, notably the portraits of Henry VIII, Sir Edward Nicholas, the Earl of Strafford, Unknown Woman called the Princess Palatine, William Romaine, John Ward, Benjamin West, John Flaxman, Thomas Phillips and Unknown Man called William Cowper. Not least has been the restoration of pictures to their original frames, usually chosen by the artist, including portraits by John Collier, Arthur Cope, Francis Cotes, John Watson Gordon, Godfrey Kneller, William Hoare, Thomas Phillips and John Russell, some of which are included in the exhibition.

In a project of this kind spread over three years one accumulates many debts of gratitude. I owe an exceptional debt to Paul Mitchell, the exhibition's sponsor, for having the confidence to come forward with the offer of financial support at an early stage and for making available to me his frame archive.

London is arguably the world centre for the trade in period frames and the manufacture of superlative reproductions. I am grateful to many framemakers but most especially to Michael Gregory at Arnold Wiggins & Sons Ltd for discussing frames with me, allowing me access to the archive at Wiggins and notably for agreeing to undertake without charge the conservation of the frame of the Reynolds portrait of Sir Joseph Banks. I am also indebted to Timothy Newbery for his enthusiastic interest and for making the preliminary drawings for the illustrations in the glossary. Contemporary framemakers and gilders who were kind enough to help me included Jim Bradford, Terry Burns, Stephen Carruthers of Artworks, Paul Ferguson, Andy Gizauskas, Nick Hawker and John Jones at John Jones Framing, Anthony Ley of Alexander George Ley & Sons, William Ward and Frank Wenstrum at John Tanous Ltd.

Several artists were kind enough to talk to me on the telephone about their approaches to framing including Maggi Hambling, Derek Hill, Howard Morgan, Humphrey Ocean, Bryan Organ, Tom Phillips, Martin Rose, Leonard Rosoman, Hans Schwarz, John Ward and Alison Watt. Inevitably I have had to limit what I have included in the catalogue. My apologies if the final synopsis does not do full justice to their views.

A number of other individuals have been exceptionally generous to me, notably the Duke of Wellington and the Hon. Christopher Lennox-Boyd for lending me framemakers' account books from their collections, Ian Gow at the National Monuments Record of Scotland, Alastair Laing and Hermione Sandwith at the National Trust, Nicholas Penny at the National Gallery, Charles Sebag-Montefiore, Guy Shaw, curator of the Lennox-Boyd collection, Alice Sielle, daughter of Robert Sielle the framemaker, Michael Snodin at the Victoria and Albert Museum, Georgina Stonor, archivist to the Duke of Wellington and Robert Wenley and Colin Jenner at the Wallace Collection.

Additionally I am grateful to David Alexander, Edwin Becker at the Van Gogh Museum, Amsterdam, Shelley Bennett at the Huntington Art Collections, Chloë Blackburn, Charles Booth-Clibborn, Judith Bronkhurst, Iain Brown at the National Library of Scotland, David Carter, Judy Egerton, John England and John Leighton at the National Gallery, Keith Christiansen at the Metropolitan Museum of Art, Betty Elzea, Christopher Gilbert at Temple Newsam

House, John Harris, Karen Hearn at the Tate Gallery, William Jackson, Elspeth Juda, Mrs James McBey, David Meschutt, John Munday, Evelyn Newby at the Paul Mellon Centre, Charles Noble, formerly at the Royal Collection Trust, Andrew McIntosh Patrick and Peyton Skipwith at the Fine Art Society, Cathy Proudlove of the Norfolk Museums Service, Jacqueline Riding at the Palace of Westminster, Lynn Roberts, John Martin Robinson at Arundel Castle, David Scrase and Jane Munro at the Fitzwilliam Museum, Susan Sloman at the Victoria Art Gallery, Bath, Simon Thurley at the Historic Royal Palaces and Sally Woodcock at the Hamilton Kerr Institute, Cambridge.

I owe a considerable debt to the curators and staff at those collections I studied in some depth namely the National Gallery, the National Maritime Museum, Sir John Soane's Museum, the Tate Gallery, the Victoria and Albert Museum and the Wallace Collection in London, Chevening in Kent, the Fitzwilliam Museum at Cambridge, the City Art Gallery and Temple Newsam House at Leeds, Tabley House in Cheshire, the Walker Art Gallery at Liverpool and the Scottish National Portrait Gallery and the National Gallery of Scotland in Edinburgh.

In producing this book and mounting the exhibition I am also greatly indebted to Tim Harvey, designer of the book, for his unstinting efforts, Pep Sala, designer of the publicity material and Calum Storrie who designed the exhibition with support from Crispin Rose-Innes on the graphics side. I owe a very special debt to my editor, Gillian Forrester, who has worked long and hard on a demanding project to weld the parts of this book into a publishable whole. My thanks also to Peter Funnell, Richard Hallas and Paul Mitchell for reading sections of the book in typescript and making suggestions for its improvement.

At the National Portrait Gallery the exhibition would not have been possible but for the quite exceptional support of Richard Hallas, and his team in the frame conservation studio, notably Stuart Ager and Stephen Williams. Discussion of the frames with Richard Hallas informs almost all the entries in the catalogue section. My thanks also to Sophie Plender and Anne Ablett for their work on individual frames. I am also particularly grateful to Kathleen Soriano in the Exhibitions Office and to Sarah Kemp in the Press Office. In an exhibition like this based on the Gallery's own collection almost every member of staff has been concerned in some way. Those who have been most closely involved in the detailed preparations include Janine Learner who readily took on much of the burden of typing up my manuscript, Penny Dearsley, Kate Holden, Tim Moreton, Carla Preston, Karen Reubens, David Saywell and Jill Springall, to all of whom I am most grateful. The exhibition has also benefited greatly from the indispensable contribution of Margaret Binnie who gave her time to research obscure periodicals and little-known archives; my thanks to her and to all the team of volunteers who helped research the Gallery records: Harriet Atkinson, Annabel Cole, Clare Hillman, Michèle Riley, Lucy Sudlow and James Tuddenham. To all those at the Gallery my warm thanks. At home, Jenny Bescoby's support and understanding has been essential for the realisation of this book. She has seen me live my life for picture frames.

Jacob Simon
September 1996

Bibliography

General Surveys

Bayard, Jane, *Works of Splendor and Imagination. The Exhibition Watercolor, 1770-1870*, exh. cat., Yale Center for British Art, New Haven, 1981 (a very useful essay on the framing of watercolours).

Cahn, Isabelle, *Cadres de peintres*, Paris, 1989 (artists' frames in the second half of the nineteenth century).

Cannon-Brookes, Peter, 'Picture Framing. A Neglected Art', *National Art Collections Fund Review*, 1984, pp.85–92.

Grimm, Claus, *The Book of Picture Frames*, New York, 1981 (a copiously illustrated international survey; the reproductions are clearer in the original German edition, *Alte Bilderrahmen*, Munich, 1978).

Heydenryk, Henry, *The Art and History of Frames*, 1964 (an introductory survey).

Jackson-Stops, Gervase, 'English picture frames and their makers', *The Magazine Antiques*, vol.CXXXIII, 1988, pp.232–47 (based on the introduction to the exhibition catalogue, *Designs for English Picture Frames*, 1987, but with colour illustrations).

Lambert, Susan, *The Image Multiplied*, exh. cat., Victoria and Albert Museum, London, 1987, especially pp.183–93 (for the framing of prints).

Lemoine, Serge (ed.), *Le cadre & le socle dans l'art du 20 éme siècle*, exh. cat., Université de Bourgogne, Dijon, and Centre Georges-Pompidou, Paris, 1987 (the picture frame and the artist in the twentieth century).

Macquoid, Percy, and Ralph Edwards, 'Picture Frames', *The Dictionary of English Furniture*, vol. III, 1954, pp.19–34 (one of the best introductions to English frames before 1800).

Mason, Pippa, 'Framing Prints in England 1640-1820', *Museum Management and Curatorship*, 1992, vol.XI, pp.117–32 (the fullest account of the framing of prints).

Mason, Pippa, and Gervase Jackson-Stops, *Designs for English Picture Frames*, exh. cat., Arnold Wiggins & Sons Ltd, 1987.

Mendgen, Eva, *et al.*, *In Perfect Harmony. Picture + Frame, 1850-1920*, exh. cat., Van Gogh Museum, Amsterdam and Kunstforum, Vienna, 1995 (a wide ranging and accessible examination of artists' frames).

Mitchell, Paul, 'Italian Picture Frames 1500–1825. A Brief Survey', *Furniture History*, vol.XX, 1984, pp.18–27.

Mitchell, Paul and Lynn Roberts, *Frameworks: Form Function & Ornament in European Portrait Frames*, 1996 (a richly illustrated survey published to coincide with the exhibition of the same title).

Mitchell, Paul and Lynn Roberts, *A History of European Picture Frames*, 1996 (a comprehensive survey commissioned by Macmillan for *The Dictionary of Art*).

Newbery, Timothy, 'Towards an Agreed Nomenclature for English Picture Frames: 1530–1795', *International Journal of Museum Management and Curatorship*, vol.V, 1986, pp.357–66.

Newbery, Timothy, George Bisacca and Laurence B. Kanter, *Italian Renaissance Frames*, exh. cat., Metropolitan Museum of Art, New York, 1990 (a survey of eighty-four frames in the Metropolitan's collection).

Newbury, Timothy, 'European "Cassetta" frames from the 15th to the 19th Century', *Museum Management and Curatorship*, vol.XIV, 1995, pp.103–8.

Penny, Nicholas, 'Back to the Wall', *London Review of Books*, 21 September 1995, p.12 (a review of the exhibition, *In Perfect Harmony*).

Roberts, Lynn, 'Nineteenth Century English Picture Frames, I, The Pre-Raphaelites', *International Journal of Museum Management and Curatorship*, vol.IV, 1985, pp.155–72, 'II: The Victorian High Renaissance', *International Journal of Museum Management and Curatorship*, vol.V, 1986, pp.273–93.

Sabatelli, Franco, *et al.*, *La cornice italiana dal Rinascimento al Neoclassico*, Milan, 1992.

Thiel, P.J.J. van, and C.J. de Bruyn Kops. *Framing in the Golden Age. Picture and Frame in 17th-Century Holland*, Zwolle, 1995, English translation of *Prijst de Lijst. De Hollandse schilderijlijst in de zeventiende eeuw*, exh. cat., Rijksmuseum, Amsterdam, 1984 (an excellent survey of ninety-six Dutch seventeenth-century frames).

Verougstraete-Marcq, Hélène, and Roger van Schoute, *Cadres et supports dans la peinture flamande aux 15e et 16e siècles*, Heure-le-Romain, Belgium, 1989 (a systematic, detailed study of the frames of early Flemish paintings).

Techniques in Framing

Ayres, James, *The Artist's Craft. A History of Tools, Techniques and Materials*, Oxford, 1985, pp.133–46 (the best general historical account).

Bigelow, Deborah *et al.*, *Gilded Wood. Conservation and History*, Madison, Conn., 1991, including the following essays: Michael Gregory, 'A Review of English Gilding Techniques. Original Source Material about Picture Frames', pp.109–18; Angela Hückel, 'Picture Frames in the Nineteenth Century', pp.119–26; Mary McGrath, 'Conservation of an Important Eighteenth-Century Frame', pp.357–66.

Cannon-Brookes, Peter, 'An Addendum to Paul Petit: the Role of the Répareur', *Museum Management and Curatorship*, vol.XI, 1992, p.439.

Kirkham, Pat, 'The London Furniture Trade 1700–1870', *Furniture History*, vol.XXIV, 1988.

Mason, Pippa, and Michael Gregory, *Of Gilding. An Essay on the traditional techniques of gilding, silvering and gold beating in England published to accompany an exhibition of craftsmen's tools and picture frames*, Arnold Wiggins & Sons Ltd, 1989 (the best historical account of the gilding process).

Shipounoff, Dimitri, 'La Reparure', *Museum Management and Curatorship*, vol.XIII, 1994 pp.431–4.
Wetherall, Judith, 'The History and Techniques of Composition', in *Gilding and Surface Decoration*, ed. Sophie Budden, papers given at a conference held by the UKIC, 1991, pp.26–9.

Framemakers and Artists

Armstrong, John, 'My Paintings and their frames', *The Studio*, vol.CXVII, 1939, pp.142–5 (Armstrong's account of the framing of his pictures by Robert Sielle).
Bennett, Mary, 'Footnotes to the William Holman Hunt Exhibition', *The Liverpool Bulletin*, vol.XIII, 1968–70, Appendix II, pp.56–64.
Bronkhurst, Judith, 'Holman Hunt's picture frames, sculpture and applied art', in Ellen Harding (ed.), *Re-framing the Pre-Raphaelites. Historical and Theoretical Essays*, 1996.
Buttery, David, 'The Picture Frames of Paul Petit, and Frederick, Prince of Wales', *Apollo*, vol.CXXVI, 1987, pp.12–15.
Cannon-Brookes, Peter, 'Picture Framing. J.M. Whistler's Picture Frames in the Freer Gallery, Washington, in the light of the 1994–95 Whistler Exhibitions', *Museum Management and Curatorship*, vol.XIV, 1995, pp.206–12.
Gilbert, Christopher, *The Life and Works of Thomas Chippendale*, 1978 (figs.310–17 are of frames).
Grieve, Alastair, 'The Applied Art of D.G. Rossetti. 1. His Picture Frames', *Burlington Magazine*, vol.CXV, 1973, pp.16–24.
Harris, Eileen, 'Robert Adam's Ornaments for Alderman Boydell's Picture Frames', *Furniture History*, vol.XXVI, 1990, pp.93–96.
Hayward, Helena, and Pat Kirkham, *William and John Linnell. 18th Century London Furniture Makers*, 1980 (figs.172–6 are of frames).
Heckscher, Morrision H., 'Copley's Picture Frames', in Carrie Rebora *et al., John Singleton Copley in America*, exh. cat., Metropolitan Museum of Art, New York, 1995, pp.142–59.
Horowitz, Ira M., 'Whistler's Frames', *Art Journal*, vol.XXXIX, no.2, 1980, pp.124–31.
Levi, Andrew, and Timothy J. Newbery, 'Picture Frames in the 1986 Reynolds Exhibition Briefly Reviewed', *International Journal of Museum Management and Curatorship*, vol.V, 1986, pp.367–70.
Miles, Hamish, 'Notes on Wilkie's Frames & Framemaker', *Fourteen Small Pictures by Wilkie*, exh. cat., Fine Art Society Ltd, 1981, unpaginated.
Mitchell, Paul, 'Wright's Picture Frames', in Judy Egerton, *Wright of Derby*, exh. cat., Tate Gallery, 1990, pp.272–88.
Murdoch, Tessa, 'Courtiers and Classics. The Gosset Family', *Country Life*, vol.CLXXVII, 1985, pp.1282–3.
Penny, Nicholas, 'Reynolds and picture frames', *Burlington Magazine*, vol.CXXVIII, 1986, pp.810–25.
Simon, Jacob, 'Allan Ramsay and picture frames', *Burlington Magazine*, vol.CXXXVI, 1994, pp.444–55.
Joseph Southall 1861–1944 Artist-Craftsman, exh. cat., Birmingham Museum & Art Gallery, 1980.
Talley, M. Kirkby, *Portrait Painting in England. Studies in the Technical Literature before 1700*, 1981, pp.299–302, 372–3 (for frames on portraits by Mary Beale; also those in the studio of Lely).

Individual Collections

Bazin, Germain, 'Renovation at the Musée du Jeu de Paume, Paris', *Museum*, vol.XIV, 1961, pp.25–35 (setting out the policy for framing pictures in the collection now at the Musée d'Orsay).
Brettell, Richard R. and Steven Starling, *The Art of the Edge. European Frames 1300–1900*, exh. cat., Art Institute of Chicago, 1986 (a survey of seventy-three frames in the Chicago collection).
Chantry, Judith and Kandy Kuhl, 'Pomp and Circumstance. Looking at early English picture frames in the Museum', *The Ashmolean*, no.24, 1993, pp.8–10 (a brief survey of early frames in the Ashmolean Museum, Oxford).
Gilbert, Christopher, *Furniture at Temple Newsam House and Lotherton Hall*, Leeds, 1978, vol.I, pp.240–6 (a survey of some of the more important frames at Leeds).
Jackson-Stops, Gervase, 'Picture Frames at Petworth', *Country Life*, vol.CLXVIII, 1980, pp.798–800, 1030–32.
Jervis, Simon, 'Picture frames and picture hanging at Apsley House', in C.M. Kauffmann, *Catalogue of Paintings in the Wellington Museum*, 1982, pp.17–20.
Laing, Alastair and Nino Strachey, 'The Duke and Duchess of Lauderdale's pictures at Ham House', *Apollo*, vol.CXXXIX, 1994, p.9, fig.9.
Mason, Pippa, 'The Picture Frames', in Tessa Murdoch (ed.), *Boughton House. The English Versailles*, 1992, pp.90–95.
Mason, Pippa, 'Smith's picture frames', in *A King's Purchase. King George III and the Collections of Consul Smith*, exh. cat., The Queen's Gallery, Buckingham Palace, 1993, pp.58–62 (a survey of Smith's Italian frames).
Millar, Oliver, 'Caring for The Queen's Pictures. Surveyors Past and Present' in Christopher Lloyd, *The Queen's Pictures*, exh. cat., National Gallery, 1991, pp.20–22 (a discussion of approaches to framing of the Royal Collection).
Mitchell, Paul, 'Picture Frames in the Cartwright Collection', *Mr. Cartwright's Pictures*, exh. cat., Dulwich Picture Gallery, 1987–8, pp.20–7 (a survey of seventeenth-century frames in the Cartwright collection at Dulwich).
Penny, Nicholas, *Frames*, 1997 (a brief survey of frames in the National Gallery, London).
Sandwith, Hermione, 'National Trust Picture Frame Survey', *International Journal of Museum Management and Curatorship*, vol.IV, 1985, pp.173–8.
Taylor, Gerald, 'Frames on the Tradescant/Ashmole paintings' in Arthur MacGregor (ed.), *Tradescant's Rarities*, Oxford, 1983, pp.327–9.
Thiel, P.J.J. van, 'The Framing of Paintings in the Rijksmuseum since 1800', *Bulletin van het Rijksmuseum*, vol.XXVIII, 1979, pp.159–79, 206–10 (with English summary).
Thornton, Peter and Maurice Tomlin, 'The Furnishing and Decoration of Ham House', *Furniture History*, vol.XVI, 1980.
Tomlin, Maurice, 'Picture Frames at Ham House', *International Journal of Museum Management and Curatorship*, vol.IV, 1985, pp.129–40.

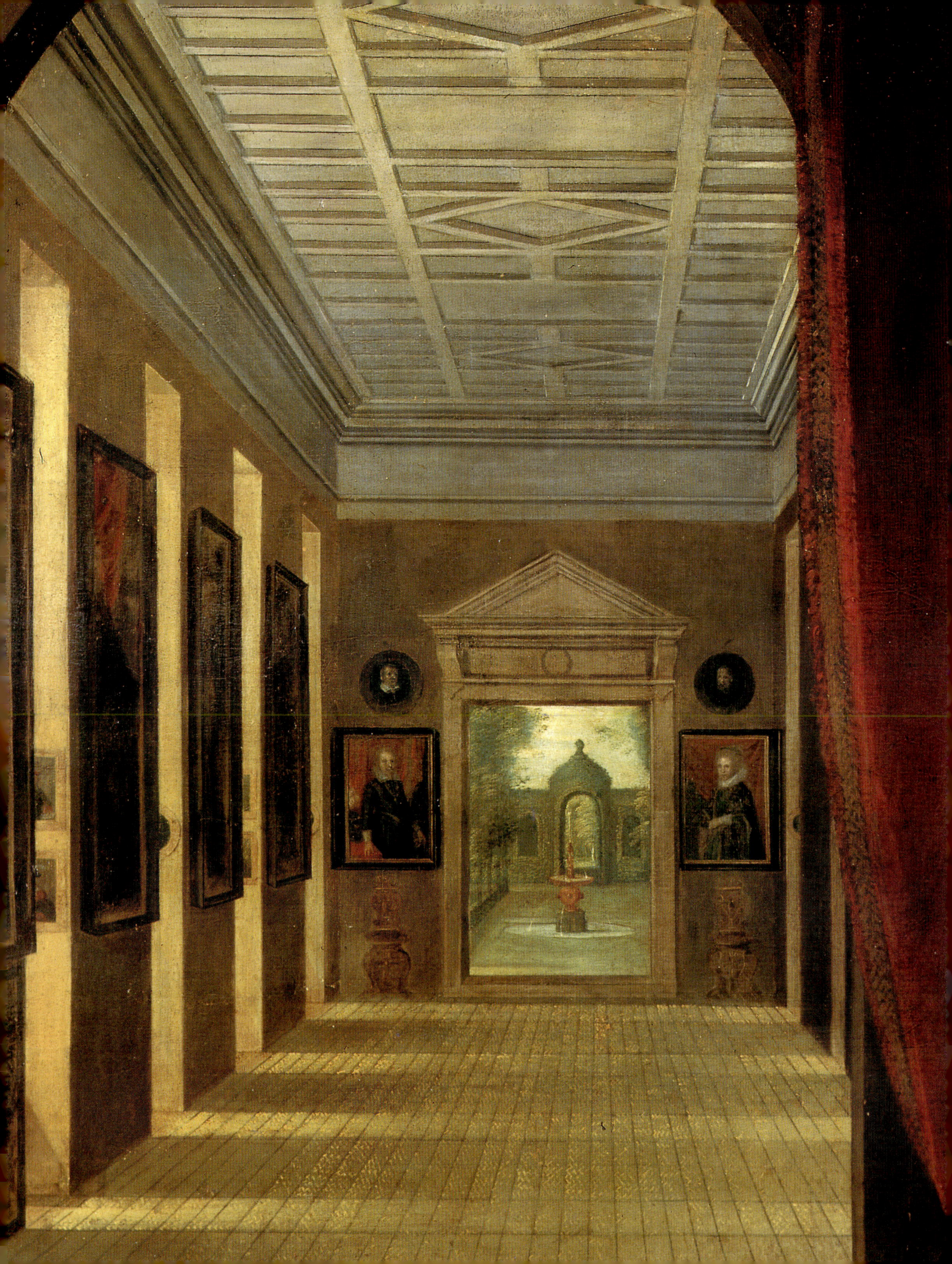

Chapter 1
Attitudes to Picture Framing in Britain and Abroad

Fig.1 (facing page) *Alathea Talbot, Countess of Arundel* by Daniel Mytens (detail), *c.*1618 (Arundel Castle, on loan from the National Portrait Gallery; no.35).

An idealised view of a gallery, perhaps at Arundel House on the Strand in London, hung with portraits in dark frames with gilt sight edges and smaller pictures in gilt frames.

The picture frame has existed for as long as pictures have been moveable. Any moveable painting required a frame to protect it. Even a fixed painting set in panelling needed some sort of framework. The idea of a framing device is older than the picture frame, however, and many early wall paintings and frescoes were given a containing painted or architectural framework.

The frame may have started out as a form of protection but its visual and symbolic purposes soon became equally important. Such purposes are not constant but vary with time and place. The frame separates the work of art from its surroundings and may help focus the viewer's attention. At the same time it can actually unite a work with its surroundings by forming a transition or a link to other works or to the wider setting. The frame can become part of the setting itself when it is designed to fit into an architectural scheme. More obviously, the frame is usually intended to enhance a picture visually and, occasionally, iconographically. Sometimes the frame is used to draw attention to a work as an object of value or reverence; such a frame may not necessarily enhance it in visual terms, but can contribute to its symbolic significance. The frame marks out a picture as a picture, that is as an illusion rather than reality. The many and varied functions of the picture frame will be examined in the following pages. This book will also show how attitudes to framing altered over the centuries, and shaped the development of the picture frame.

In Britain such has been the popularity of portraiture that the history of the picture frame has been first and foremost the history of the portrait frame until well into the eighteenth century. The British liking for portraits was often an object of remark: 'it is amazing how fond the English are of having their pictures drawn', wrote the Swiss enamel painter, André Rouquet in 1754, after a prolonged stay in London.[1] By the 1780s there were more than 110 portrait painters active in London, most of them exhibiting at the Royal Academy, the Society of Artists or the Free Society of Artists.[2] The exceptional number of portraitists at work during this period is explained by the way the market spread so far down the social scale, a phenomenon which was also the subject of comment by Rouquet, who observed, 'as peoples fortunes are more upon a level in England than in any other country, and as the very best painters take only ten or twelve guineas for a bust, this moderate price is no hindrance to the custom of frequently making a present of one's picture'.[3] The scale of demand for portraits in Britain meant that the demand for frames was correspondingly high, and that the production of frames was closely linked to the production of portraits, at least until the end of the eighteenth century. Frames for portraits generally were produced to a specific price just as the portraits were themselves, and often followed standard patterns rather than being specially designed for each commission.

Painted frames and the use of curtains

The story of the picture frame in England begins in the sixteenth century. At this time most paintings were small and the frames simple. Frames do not seem to have been considered objects of great importance and the frames which survive are usually made of oak, fairly simply constructed, and painted or stained black, perhaps with a line of gilding on the sight edge next to the picture, rather in the manner of some of the royal portraits in the National Portrait Gallery (fig.2; see also fig.19; no.3). As early inventories reveal, in the sixteenth century pictures were sometimes protected by curtains, presumably because of

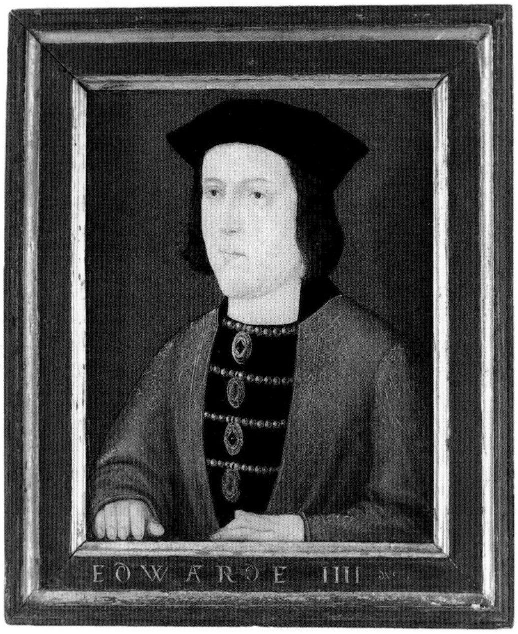

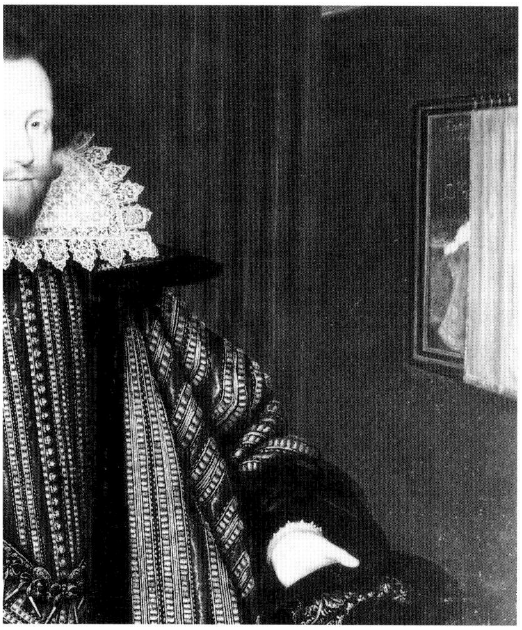

Fig.2 (far left)
Edward IV by an unknown artist, *c.*1540.

Fig.3 (left)
Sir John Kennedy by Marcus Gheeraerts (detail), 1614 (Woburn Abbey).

The portrait in the background is partially covered with a pink curtain fastened by gold rings on a black rod.

Fig.4 (facing page)
Charles II, studio of John Michael Wright, *c.*1660-5 (no.20).

The elaborate gilt frame was made in the 1680s or 1690s, and was not fitted to this portrait until the twentieth century.

their rarity (see fig.3). These curtains were often made of silks such as sarcenet or taffeta, and it is notable that inventories of the period describe the curtains rather than the frames. Most of Henry VIII's pictures at the Palace of Westminster in 1542 had a 'curteyne of white and yellow sarcenet paned together', though the odd picture had a red sarcenet curtain or a green one. At Hampton Court the taste was for green and yellow sarcenet, as the 1547 inventory shows.[4] Curtains may have become more commonly used in the second half of the century, judging from the evidence of inventories.[5] In the Earl of Leicester's collection at Kenilworth almost all the paintings listed at his death in 1588 are described as having curtains, even the 'Two greate Pictures of my Lord in whole proportion'.[6]

In an era of dark wood and painted frames, it was the curtain on the frame which seems to have caught the attention. In his autobiography the poet Lord Herbert of Cherbury recalls being shown a picture by Lord Dorset at Dorset House: 'hee at last brought mee to a Frame covered with greene Taffita and asked mee who I thought was there and therewithall presently drawing the Courtaine shewed mee my owne Picture'.[7] The fashion for picture curtains seems to have waned in England during the reign of Charles I, though the occasional reference – 'Twelve Taphetye Curtaines wth 10 rods, all for pictures', for example – can be found in the valuations of Charles I's goods made after his execution.[8] On the Continent, however, the vogue for picture curtains was more enduring, as painted views of Flemish picture galleries and Dutch interiors suggest.

The introduction of gilt frames

Perhaps the demise of the picture curtain can be traced to the rise of the gilt frame. For a gilt frame is intended for show. The dearth of surviving early seventeenth-century frames means that evidence as to the introduction of gilt frames depends on surviving bills and inventories. Although these documents provide only isolated examples, they do indicate that there was a taste for gilt frames at that time. Leonard Fryer, Queen Elizabeth's Serjeant Painter, was paid £2.12s for 'clere colouringe, guildinge and varnishinge of fyve greate frames for Mappes' in 1598-9. Martin van Bentheim and Henry Holdernes received £3 from Thomas Sackville, 1st Earl of Dorset, for 'painting and gilding the patterne of a frame for a picture' in 1608. And Rowland Buckett, painter-stainer, received £5 for 'gildinge of 8 frames for the pictures that

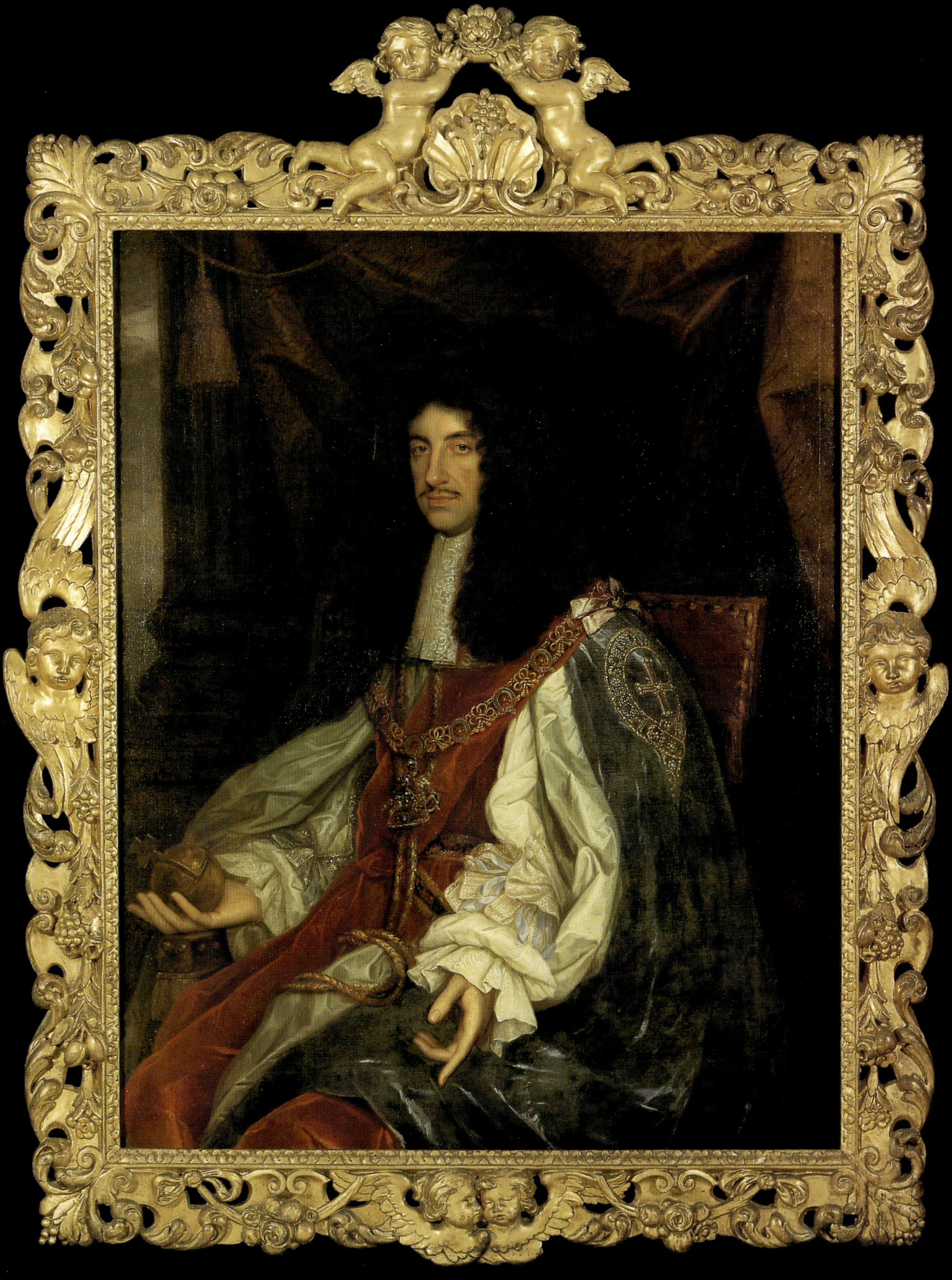

hange in the lower parte of the chappell' at Hatfield House in 1611-12, and a further £4 for a frame 'wrought with blacke and goulde'.[9] Daniel Mytens was paid £32 in 1620 for a portrait of the Earl of Nottingham, made to the king's order, 'with a guilded frame for the same'.[10]

Although gilding was in use earlier in the seventeenth century, it was the activities of Charles I and the court circle in buying the finest pictures abroad which were responsible for bringing about a revolution in English taste. In 1618 Sir Dudley Carleton, Ambassador at the Hague, negotiated with Rubens to buy twelve pictures either by Rubens himself or by Tintoretto, 'all furnished with gilt frames'.[11] In 1628 Charles I's magnificent purchases from the collection of the Duke of Mantua began to arrive in London, some of them already framed. Between 1631 and 1639 there were numerous orders to the Serjeant Painter and to court craftsmen for carving, painting and gilding of frames for Charles I.[12] Such frames could be extraordinarily elaborate. The Serjeant Painter, John de Critz, supplied frames for the set of twelve *Caesars* by Titian in 1631-2, charging £3 each for painting 'in a sadd wallnuttree cullor & guilding over those frames in divers places wth fine gould in oyle and one broad carved edge next all above the picture togeather wth the Maskeheades Festons Draperies the greater Flowers and the lesser flowers the greater & lesser Scrowles & the edges betwixt the flutes all guilt wth fine gold varnished with the best varnish'.[13]

The extent of the popularity of gilt frames outside court circles in the mid-seventeenth century is difficult to gauge. At Newbigging in 1665, in the collection of John Clerk, a Scottish merchant with Paris connections, there were no gilt frames, although many of the pictures were acquisitions of the previous thirty years. In Clerk's collection, black ebony frames dominated, sometimes with added decoration. There were several 'rudish collort wooden frames', a few other coloured frames, one of walnut and one of ivory.[14] In contrast, the inventory taken in the 1680s of the London collection of the actor William Cartwright, which he bequeathed to Dulwich College, reveals that most of the frames were gilt, about a third were ebony, black, black and gold or brown, one was blue and one marbled colour.[15] Although black frames for oil paintings remained in common currency until the mid-eighteenth century, carved and gilt frames, despite their greater cost, became almost universal in fashionable circles.[16]

Why gilt frames?

Gilding was seen as a neutral boundary which enhanced the colours of a painting. An early explanation of the virtue of gilding comes in a letter written by Nicolas Poussin to his patron

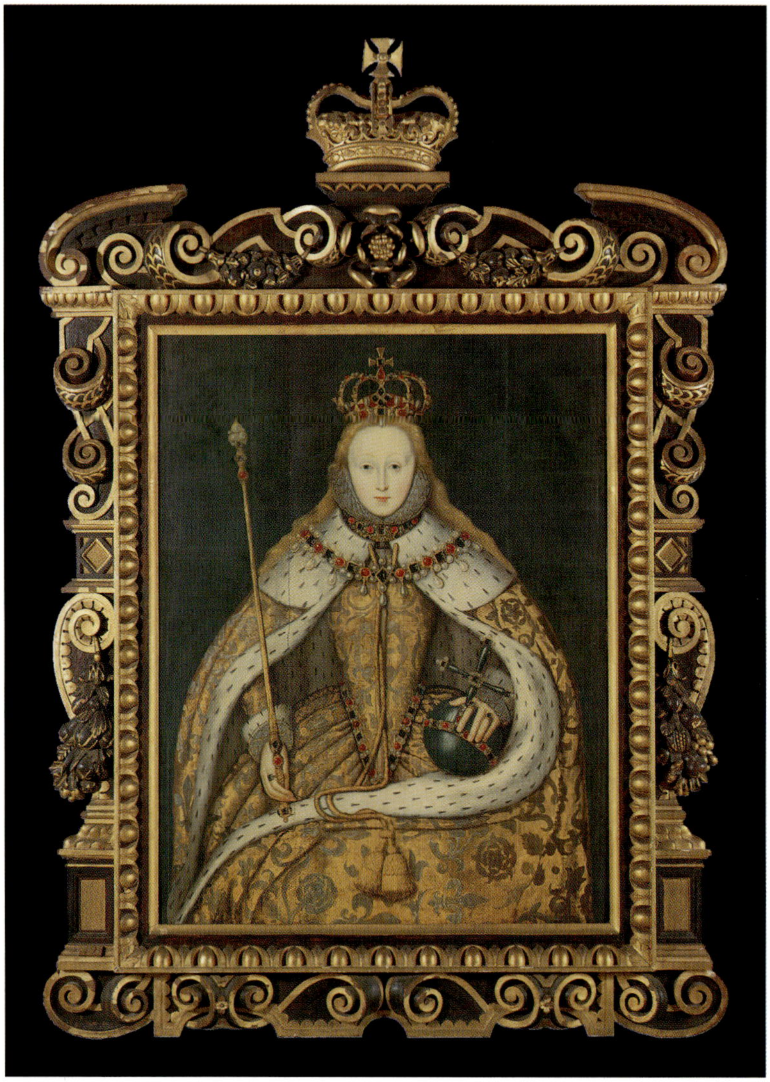

Fig.5
Elizabeth I by an unknown artist, *c.*1600 (no.5).

The Warwick Castle portrait as reframed in the late nineteenth century, before restoration and alteration.

Chantelou in 1639: 'it would be very fitting that the said frame be gilded quite simply with mat gold, for it unites very sweetly with the colours without clashing with them'.[17] In Britain it was not until the nineteenth century that the effect of gilding was taken up in published discussions on pictures. Poussin's idea was echoed by a writer shortly after Turner's death: 'I believe Turner always contemplated the union of the gold of his colour with the gold of his frame, and I know that he enjoyed it, and used to urge the hanging of frames containing his drawings in groups, without intervals between the frames, so that nothing but gold might be seen in connection with the drawing'.[18] In his influential *Hints on Household Taste*, Charles Eastlake advanced the classic explanation that gilding was 'a foil or neutral ground for enhancing the value of colour'.[19] One of the fullest analyses is that of Percy Fitzgerald in the *Art Journal* in 1886:

The fact that the universal taste of mankind for some hundred years has fixed on gold or gilding as the tone or colour for framing paintings with, seems to show that this is the fitting adornment. Gold seems to enrich everything it touches, and set beside colours 'brings them out' with prodigious effect. Another reason may be that every other material offers a colour, but gold is neutral. *It somehow, too, suggests the notion of an abstract boundary or zone between the vulgar surrounding world and the sort of spiritual life of Art.*[20]

The artist and essayist, Philip Hamerton, had expressed rather similar ideas in *The Portfolio* in 1871, adding that 'gold adds to the *splendour* of a work of art more than any other surrounding'.[21]

It was on the Continent that the theory underlying the use of colour and gilding received greatest attention. Goethe's *Theory of Colours*, which was translated into English by Eastlake's uncle, Sir Charles Eastlake, was attacked by the Scottish physicist, Sir David Brewster, for its antipathy to Isaac Newton's optical theories. In the course of a review in 1840 Brewster wrote of, 'certain old gilt frames of pictures, in which the light reflected once or twice from one part of the gilding is again reflected from another part. In this case the depth and richness of the colour is surprising …'.[22] The researches of the French chemist, Michel-Eugène Chevreul, into the effect of different coloured borders were also translated into English and seem to have been the stimulus for a lengthy article in 1854 by the journalist R.H. Patterson in *Blackwood's Edinburgh Magazine* on 'Colour in Nature and Art' in which the use of gilt and coloured frames is discussed in theoretical terms.[23] Chevreul's colour theories appear to have had a limited impact in Britain, however, although they were influential for the French Post-Impressionists later in the nineteenth century.

Reframing and picture hanging

Once the taste for gilt frames was firmly established, questions of reframing and regilding arose. In an interior furnished with even a few gilt frames, black frames would have looked old-fashioned. This discordance must have been felt from an early date, although records of reframing are seldom enlightening as to the nature of the old frame or the reasons for reframing. One therefore has to presume that Sir Edward Dering's placing of an order in 1648 for a 'new frame' for his grandmother's portrait at the same time as he had his wife's portrait painted by Cornelius De Neve, was a matter of fashion rather than necessity.[24] Inventories such as that of William Cartwright's collection, taken in the 1680s, sometimes describe a frame as old or old-fashioned.[25] The oak frame on the early portrait of Richard Foxe, bishop of Winchester, which was owned by the college he founded at Oxford, Corpus Christi, a frame described by George Vertue as painted in imitation of porphyry and signed by the artist, was discarded in 1820 when the picture was reframed.[26] The Warwick Castle portrait of Queen Elizabeth I, now in the National Portrait Gallery (fig.5), had its original frame replaced by a gilt Sunderland frame, probably in the 1680s, and was again reframed in the late nineteenth century. Although there is a lack of documentation for reframing, it is clear from an examination of the surviving pictures that few Elizabethan or Jacobean pictures retain their original frames. In

Dynasties, the 1995 Tate Gallery exhibition of portraits of the period, arguably only eight out of ninety-nine retained their painted frames.[27] As a result of reframing, very few surviving early collections retain their black or painted frames, exceptions being some of the Cavendish pictures at Hardwick Hall, the Tradescant pictures at the Ashmolean Museum and some of the early full-lengths at Berkeley Castle.[28]

Not only pictures in black frames were subject to reframing, however; works in expensive gilt frames were treated similarly. What was stylish to one generation was old-fashioned to the next, and few owners had compunctions about reframing portraits. One of the commonest imperatives was to obtain a uniform appearance in a new interior. Several of the Van Dycks now or formerly in the Spencer collection at Althorp were reframed in Sunderland frames in the 1670s or 1680s. For Houghton Hall and Kensington Palace in the 1720s, William Kent made careful drawings showing how he wanted to reframe and position all the old masters and portraits to match his new interiors (see fig.132) and similarly, a generation later, in the 1760s, Robert Adam drew up schemes for Kedleston where the framing and placing of the pictures is vital to the balance of the setting. Reframing in order to match pictures to interiors seems to have been as actively pursued in the nineteenth century. At Buckingham Palace in 1851 Prince Albert had all the paintings in the Picture Gallery reframed in matching frames ('all the pictures have been framed & re-hung which makes them look beautiful', Queen Victoria noted with pride in her *Journal*).[29] In the twentieth century the grand reframers have often been museums, as will be shown below.

If interiors influenced the frame, the reverse could also be true. In a grand interior the placing of the gilt frame against the wall greatly influenced the appearance of the room and could determine the colour-scheme. Despite her close friendship with the Duke of Wellington, Mrs Arbuthnot could not countenance the Duke's plans for the Waterloo Chamber at Apsley House: 'He is going to hang it with *yellow* damask, which is just the very worst colour he can have for pictures and will kill the effect of the gilding'.[30] In the eighteenth and early nineteenth centuries blue and red were favourite colours for showing off pictures in gilt frames. A visitor to Houghton describing the Saloon designed by William Kent said it was 'filled with ye finest Painting all in rich gold frames and so close to one another that we could see but little of ye hangings behind wch were all of Genoa Damask, or figured velvets'.[31] In 1759 Lady Caroline Fox wrote to her sister Lady Kildare about the gallery at Holland House, 'I have fitted up the gallery with blue paper, gilt borders, and a few good pictures'.[32] And in 1838 a critic of the new National Gallery wrote, 'The proper ground for showing pictures to advantage is red; deep crimson hangings would harmonise and enrich the *ensemble*'.[33] The unity of the whole was William Morris's concern in a speech in 1891: 'No picture ... is complete unless it is something more than a representation of nature ... It ought to be ornamental. It ought to be possible for it to be part of a beautiful whole in a room, or church, or hall'.[34]

The rise of the exhibition frame

Both the foundation of the Royal Academy in 1768 and the increase in public exhibitions were to have a profound influence on the framing of pictures (see fig.6). Although it was not until the early nineteenth century that wide, rich frames became almost universal, complaints of 'massy gold frames' encumbering the Academy walls were being made as early as 1781, when it was said that 'the carver rather than the artist deservedly claims our attention'.[35] Frames continued to get wider and deeper over the next generation for a number of reasons. One was the fashion for a heavier, more masculine, style of architecture in the Regency period, so different from the delicacy of the architectural language of Robert Adam and James Wyatt. Another was the introduction of composition, a plaster mixture known as compo, as a means of reproducing ornament, since it gave framemakers the

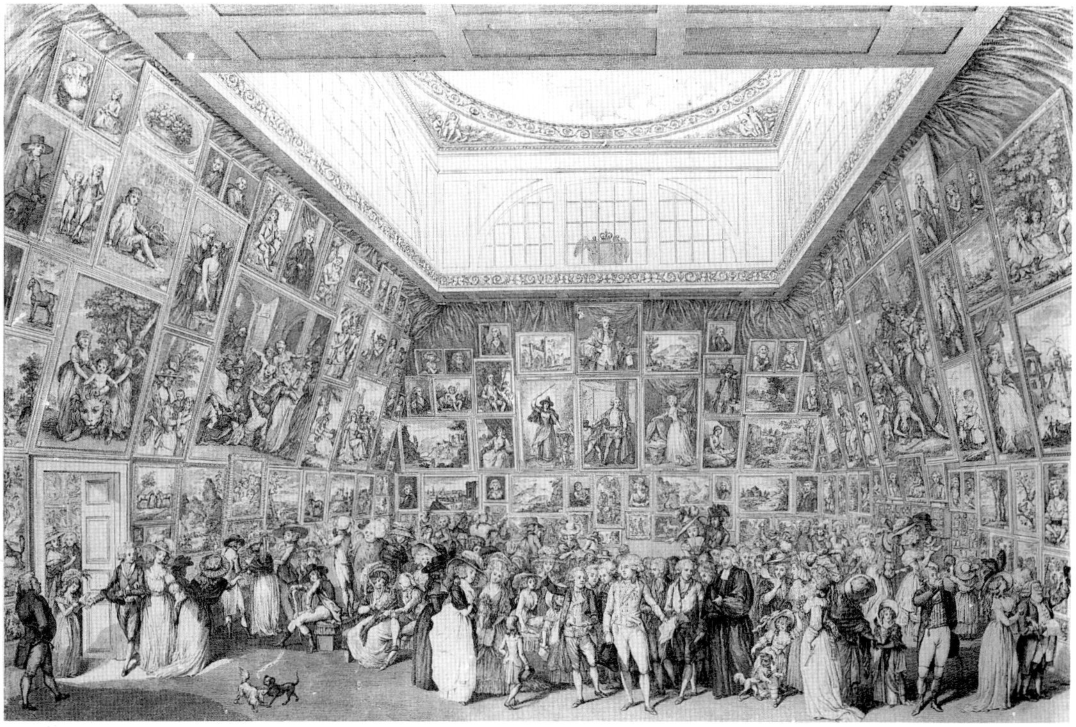

Fig.6
The Exhibition of the Royal Academy, 1787 by P.A. Martini after J.H. Ramberg, engraving (British Museum, London).

This engraving depicts the Great Room at Somerset House with more than 370 paintings and miniatures vying for attention.

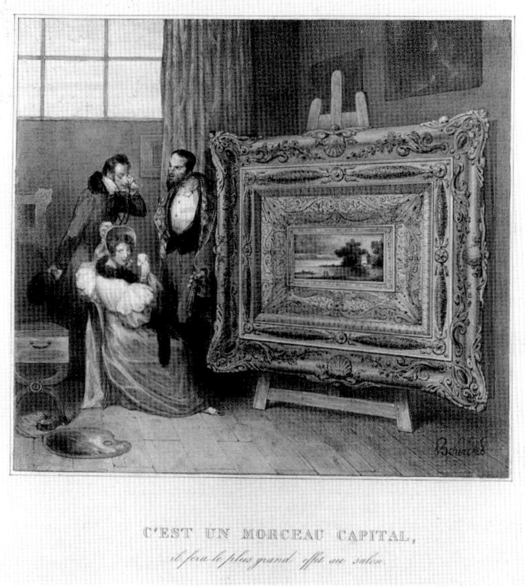

Fig.7
'C'est un morceau capital, il fera le plus grand effet au salon' by Bourdes, colour lithograph (Arnold Wiggins & Sons Ltd).

In Paris as in London, the extravagant size of exhibition frames was the subject of ridicule.

scope for much more elaborate decoration at reasonable cost. But the primary reason for adopting showier frames at exhibitions seems to have been that they were considered an effective means of attracting public attention (see fig.7).

Heavy frames were said to encourage buyers, both of the old master paintings flooding into Britain during the Napoleonic wars, and of the modern masters on the walls of the Royal Academy. In 1804 the dealer William Buchanan wrote to his agent in Rome, 'It is wonderful how much better pictures sell by being in handsome, rich, deep frames. I have mentioned before that English purchasers are much led by first impressions, and often buy upon the impulse of advantage as a handsome frame'.[36] And in 1828 the genre painter Thomas Uwins, writing from Italy, made clear his opinion about selling pictures: 'I know the importance of first impressions. I believe frames pay more than pictures'.[37] It would however be a mistake to regard the need to sell a picture as the sole moving force behind large frames. The activities of collectors in the first half of the nineteenth century suggest that there was a prevailing ethos in Britain (not shared to such an extent in France) that wide frames were *de rigeur* from an aesthetic point of view. In the 1820s, for example, George IV had the frames on the Canalettos in the new gallery at Windsor Castle widened to four-and-a-half inches by the carver and gilder, Joseph Crouzet,[38] while in the 1840s the Prime Minister Sir Robert Peel was prepared to widen the frames on works acquired for his gallery at Drayton Manor.[39]

The taste for such frames was laid at the doors of successive presidents of the Royal Academy, judging from contemporary comments. W.H. Pyne in his *Royal Residences* of 1819 wrote of the 'well applied margins for picture frames' and 'the splendid notions we now possess', attributing the new style to Benjamin West: 'he had the spirit to set the example to the English, in the public exhibition at Somerset House, of the advantage of placing pictures in wide and richly ornamented frames'.[40] While James Northcote, in conversation with James Ward, identified Sir Thomas Lawrence as the culprit: 'To be sure, the flaring gaudiness of our exhibitions has gone its utmost length, not only in the pictures, but in the frames as well; 'tis Lawrence who has brought up this fashion of having such expensive frames'.[41]

Such large frames could cause problems for the hanging committee of the Royal Academy as R.R. Reinagle complained to John Constable in 1833: 'The frames, confound them, have tortured us, and have in a very great many instances operated to exclude many pictures from very favourable situations ... . It is a Mania ... that of overframing pictures; which seems to rage more on our Walls than any where else.' The cause of this outburst was the size of frame on Constable's heath scene, which prompted Reinagle to plead with his old friend, 'Now My good fellow, pray order another frame not to exceed 5 inches & ½ at the back & 6 inches in front for your picture'. Reinagle proposed a limit on frame sizes: 'A regulation is now indispensable and all must in future abide by it'.[42]

Although miniature painters exhibiting at the Academy had been limited to one-inch frames in 1791 and to two or two-and-a-half inches in 1837,[43] it was not until 1847 that a resolution regulating picture frames, put forward by Thomas Uwins, was adopted by the Royal Academy Council: 'None but gold frames can be admitted', with the added warning, 'where space is scarce great breadth in the frames as well as projecting Mouldings, will frequently prevent the possibility of a picture obtaining the situation it merits'.[44] The Liverpool Institute had insisted on frames being gilt, bronzed or in fancy wood since at least 1838 while the Royal Scottish Academy introduced a rule stipulating gilt frames in 1839.[45] So widespread did rules on frame sizes and gilding become in Britain and abroad that Charles Dickens felt obliged to write from Paris in 1856 to ask his old friend, Daniel Maclise, about the framing of his portrait by Ary Scheffer (fig.8), requesting him to ascertain the Royal Academy's regulations: 'Will you kindly tell me what width of frame the laws of the Medes allow?'

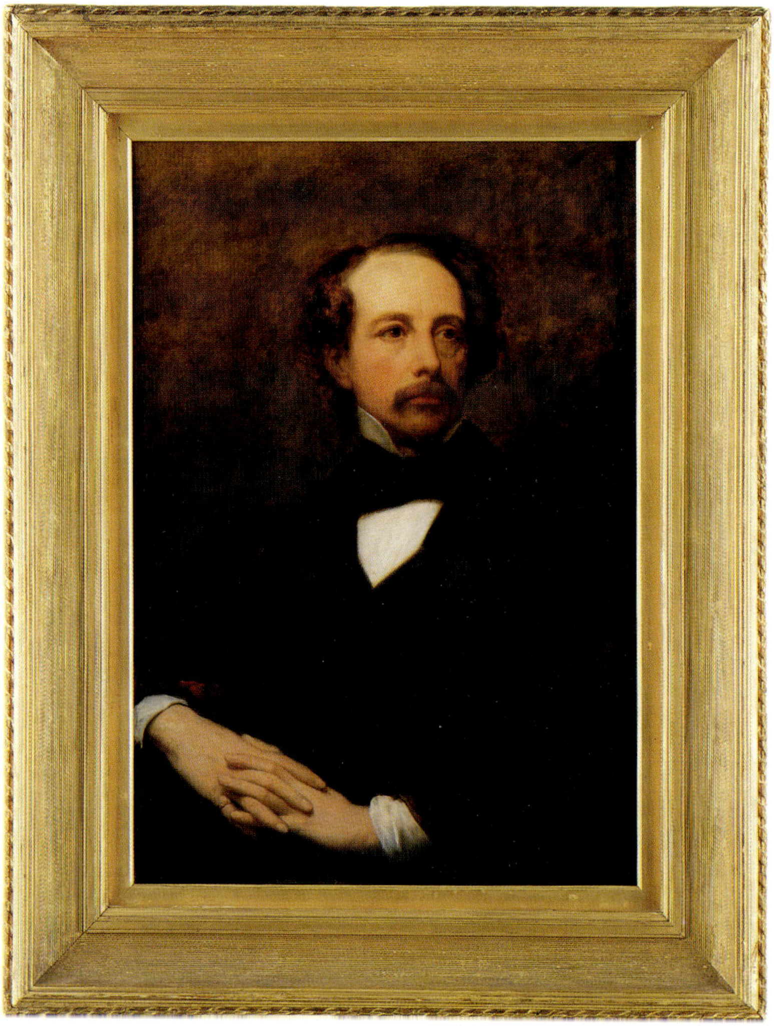

Fig.8
Charles Dickens by Ary Scheffer, 1855 (no.77).

Scheffer had the portrait framed in Paris in 1856 for exhibition at the Royal Academy, London.

The reaction against compo

Large richly ornamented frames only became economically possible, it has already been suggested, with the increase in use of compo in framemaking in the early nineteenth century. The economics of the process are explored in greater detail in Chapter 6.

Given the fragility and poor design of some compo frames, it is perhaps surprising that the use of compo did not become the subject of widespread public debate until the second half of the century. The concerns voiced by the critic Percy Fitzgerald in 1886 are typical:

How unpleasant, too, look the huge frames of old paintings of thirty or forty years ago, whose outline bends and waves in what was thought graceful 'scroll work', and 'volutes' swelling out at the corners, and all wrought in elaborate 'composition'! The edges, having no strength, generally chipped off, revealing the white material beneath.[46]

It was perhaps Charles Eastlake, later Keeper of the National Gallery, who was most influential in questioning the framing practices of the time, first in an article of 1864 in the *Cornhill Magazine*, where he complained that 'rococo scrolls and tortuous nonentities ... which pretend to be the result of so much labour are chopped out by the dozen out of the meanest material', and later in his seminal book, *Hints on Household Taste*, which went through four editions between 1869 and 1878.[47]

Eastlake felt that the fussiness of compo frames distracted the eye. He recommended that the outer part of the frame should be made of oak or some other tough wood. And he suggested that gilding 'ought to be laid directly on the wood, without any intervening composition; and if any ornament in relief is attempted, it should be carved in the solid material. The effect of oak-grain seen through leaf-gold is exceedingly good, and the appearance of *texture* thus produced is infinitely more interesting than the smooth monotony of gilt "compo"'. In recommending the use of oak and the application of gilding directly on to the wood, Eastlake was reflecting the practice of artists like Rossetti, Watts and Whistler (see nos.79, 83), whose experiments with gilding and decoration had brought new construction methods and a new vocabulary to picture framing.

White frames and the revolt against gilding

In 1873 Whistler wrote to his friend, the collector George Lucas, ' ... I wish this also to be clearly stated in Paris that I am the inventor of all this kind of decoration in color in the frames; that I may not have a lot of clever little Frenchmen trespassing on my ground'.[48] Whistler was a bridge between avant-garde artistic circles in London and Paris, and his gilt oak frames with added painted decoration were novel and influential. The French, however, did not 'trespass' on this ground, but chose to challenge the hallowed assumption of more than two centuries that pictures frames should be gilt.

It was in Paris in the late 1870s that white frames and coloured frames began to be widely used by Edgar Degas, Camille Pissarro and other Impressionists. 'The most original aspect of these revolutionaries', wrote the journalist Jules Clarétie in 1881, 'is the surrounds of their works, which are white. Gold frames are left to old painters, tobacco-chewing daubers, opponents of light paintings'.[49] Such frames were being used by 1877 when a play, *La Cigale*, at the Théâtre des Variétés in Paris, featured an Impressionist painter, Marignon, presenting a painting on stage with a white frame.[50] These experiments led rapidly to the use of red frames, green frames and frames of other colours. 'Gold is chimerical metal which ill accords with the simplicity of certain scenes', wrote the author Jules Champfleury in 1882, recommending green frames for landscapes, vermilion for dramatic scenes and pale grey for a representation of a woman.[51]

Why were such frames so popular? Artists such as Pissarro and Seurat were encouraged to experiment by the colour theories of the chemist, Michel-Eugène Chevreul, who had carried out research earlier in the century to determine the best colour to co-ordinate a frame with its picture.[52] But part of the thrill of such frames was the challenge they made to accepted norms. In direct reaction to the innovations of the Impressionists, the Paris Salon changed its rules for its exhibitions in 1884 to forbid white and

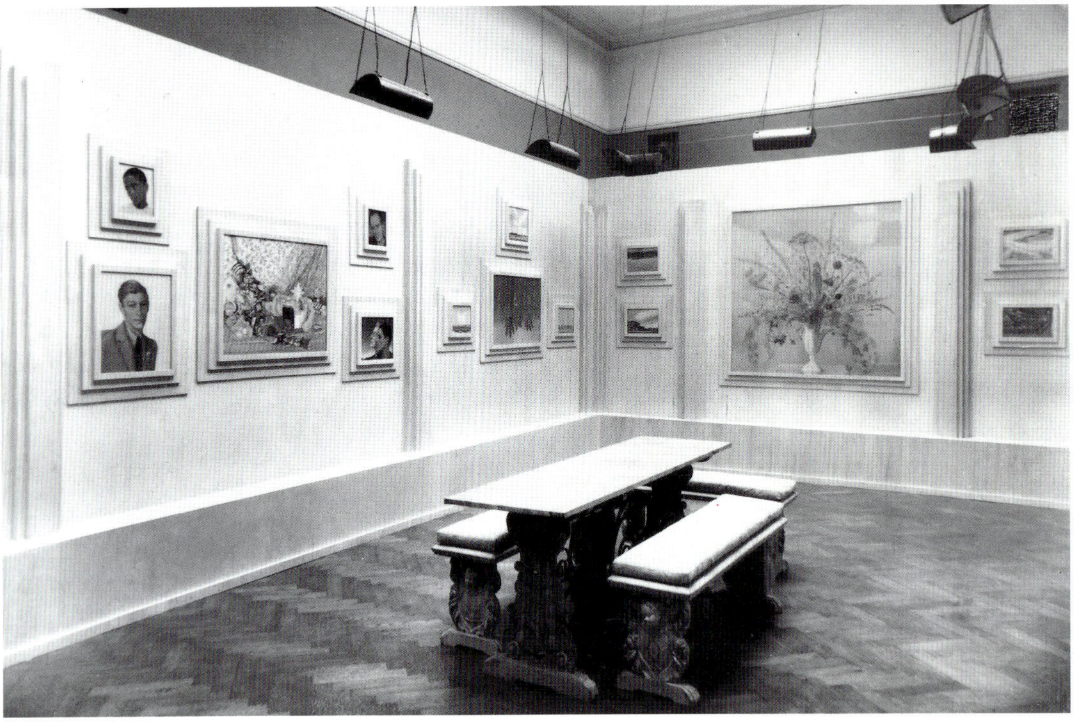

Fig.9
The Gluck Room, created by the artist for her exhibition at the Fine Art Society, 1932. The stepped 'Gluck' frame was patented by the artist.

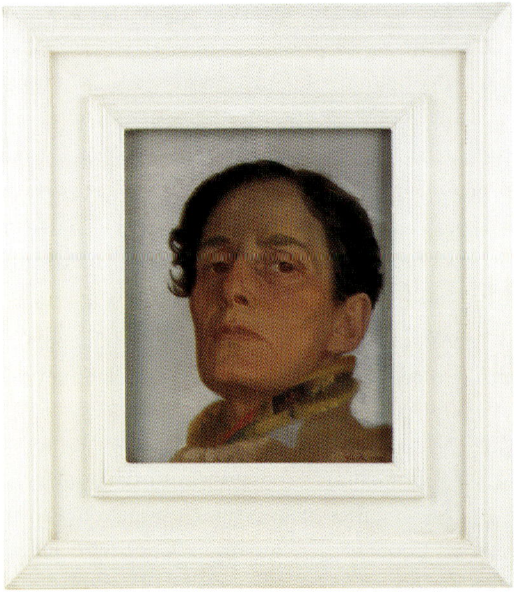

Fig.10
Self-portrait by Gluck, 1942 (no.117).

The white Whistler frame, made by Rowley Frames, was used by the artist in the 1940s for her smaller pictures in preference to the 'Gluck' frame.

coloured frames: 'Les Ouvrages seront encadrés, à l'exclusion de toutes autres, dans des bordures dorées, noires ou en bois naturel foncé'.[53]

Such concerns were not restricted to Paris. In 1899 Thomas Eakins felt obliged to check whether the Carnegie Institute in Pittsburgh had 'a hard and fast rule that frames must be gold'. He wanted to use a dark wood frame to harmonise with a portrait, but, if necessary, he wrote, 'I could still have the frame gilded or gold painted temporarily for exhibition purposes but I always protest against the barbaric splendour of new gold frames which injure all paintings'.[54] Eakins's caution was fully justified, judging from Mrs Havemeyer's experience in New York in the 1880s, when she lent her Degas pastel to the National Academy of Design, only to find that 'the delicate grey and green frame had been generously treated to a thick coating of brilliant gold bronze'.[55]

In Britain it was young artists, such as John Lavery and Sidney Starr, in touch with Impressionism and the avant-garde in France, who experimented with white frames.[56] As early as 1883 Whistler put his Venice etchings in 'exquisite white frames' for his exhibition at the Fine Art Society, though he kept to gilt frames for his paintings.[57] Also in 1883 the Paris dealer Durand Ruel was exhibiting Pissarro's pictures in London in white frames.[58] By the turn of the century such frames were sufficiently common in fashionable circles for Joseph Crawhall to write to his dealer, Alexander Reid, simply requesting him to send 'two frames, white of a good

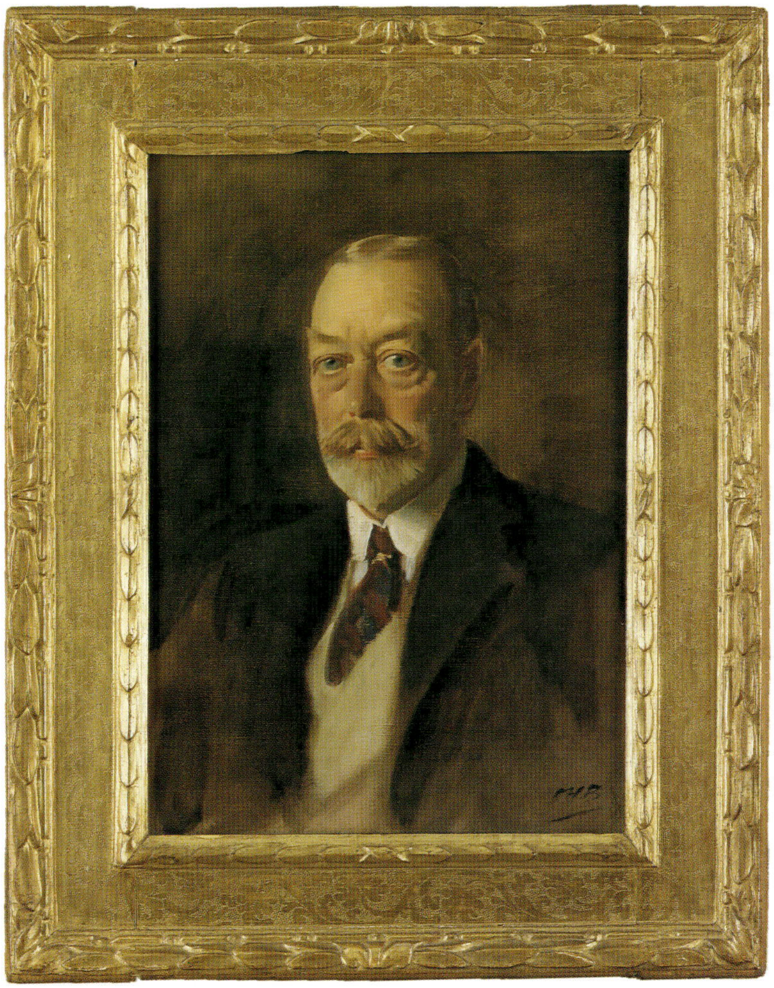

Fig.11
George V by Sir Oswald Birley, *c.*1935 (no.116).

In an early seventeenth-century Italian *cassetta* frame chosen by the artist.

design'.[59] Artists like Augustus John, William Orpen and C.R.W. Nevinson used white Whistler frames in the 1910s and 1920s, and as late as 1932 Gluck created a special white 'Gluck' frame for her Fine Art Society exhibition (fig.9). Before and after the Second World War Ivon Hitchens used distinctive off-white frames for his poetic landscapes.[60]

It was not until 1920 that the Royal Academy removed its ban on coloured frames, and as late as 1930 the Royal Scottish Academy had a rule against white frames.[61] The Royal Academy was reacting to pressure from artists, but at the same time the relaxation of the rules encouraged framemakers to experiment so that within a year Bourlet's was promoting 'new patterns coloured to meet the conditions laid down for the guidance of artists sending in other than gilt frames'.[62] In the order books of Alfred Stiles & Sons, a leading London firm working for many artists of the younger generation, references to white and coloured frames became frequent in the 1930s.[63] The prejudice against white and coloured frames remained in official quarters: in 1933 the Art Institute of Chicago removed all the white frames from the Impressionist and Post-Impressionist paintings given it by Frederick Bartlett, despite protests from the donor.[64] And it was not until 1964 that the Royal Academy finally abandoned its recommendation that frames of extravagant colour should be avoided.

The taste for old frames

While some British artists were experimenting with white frames, long after they had ceased to be a matter of controversy in Paris, others, usually portrait painters, were trying out period frames on their pictures. 'I have found a charming old frame ... which I hope you will approve of', wrote John Singer Sargent to an American patron about a portrait commission in 1895.[65] And in 1899 it was said of the Royal Academy exhibition, 'there is a noticeable display of old frames, for which there is now a great demand'.[66] Such an approach was not wholly new. The taste for old frames had developed in the 1820s and 1830s, when revival styles began to become fashionable. The Leicestershire collector, Henry Payne, told William Etty in 1832 that he would 'much prefer having a fine old french carved frame, fresh gilt, to a new composition frame, as I am not partial to the latter and the frames in my Drawing Room ... are chiefly carved and of superior quality'.[67] A few years before, Benjamin Dean Wyatt had offered the Duke of Wellington 'very fine old carved oak French Picture Frames' to suit the revival style of the Waterloo Gallery at Apsley House.[68]

In the twentieth century artists have sometimes bought old frames and then had canvases made to size. Such was Sir Oswald Birley's practice (see fig.11) and on occasion James Gunn's and Russell Flint's.[69] For his most treasured paintings, James McBey would use superlative period frames to be hung in the panelled drawing room below his studio.[70] The practice continues to this day, witness Humphrey Ocean's choice of an English late seventeenth-century frame from the National Portrait Gallery store for his portrait of Viscount Whitelaw in 1993.

The Duveen frame

To find a portrait such as Thomas Lawrence's *'Pinkie'*, his full-length of Sarah Barrett Moulton, in a superlative French Louis Quinze revival frame (fig.12) may come as a surprise to British eyes used to seeing Lawrence portraits in rather different frames. But just as Sargent was offering an American patron 'a charming old frame' to enhance her portrait, so dealers such as Joseph Duveen were reframing old masters and English portraits to suit them to the taste of rich collectors. Such activity was not restricted to Duveen's sales to American clients – some of the pictures now at Kenwood, sold by Agnew's to the rich brewer, Edward Cecil Guinness, later Lord Iveagh, are in frames of this sort – but the chief market was American.

The style of frames supplied by Duveen for the Italian renaissance pictures in the Metropolitan Museum, New York, has been well characterised by Keith Christiansen:

all the frames were based on period models but the proportions were usually 'sturdier' and the gilding more brash. They were, however, of extremely fine quality. Duveen had a good idea of what his clients would like and in one case he had two frames made for a Holbein portrait so that if one proved unsuccessful another would be ready. In the case of Altman's Dutch and Flemish paintings of the seventeenth century, the frames are all reproduction Louis XIV frames, but of a quality that in some cases actually surpasses most period frames. ... Thus, with later pictures he seems to have given his clients 'better-than-period' frames rather than vulgar, over-done models. My guess is that most of the English pictures either got good English or French frames ... [71]

At one stage Joseph Duveen was using the framemakers Vannoni in France and Emile Remy in London to make some of his frames.[72] The frame on Thomas Lawrence's *'Pinkie'* was a favourite model which was often used for English portraits and crops up by name in the cables sent between the Duveen offices in London, Paris and New York. In 1925 when George Romney's *Mrs Francis Burton* was sold by Duveen to the collector Henry Huntington in California, Duveen (London) requested a 'Pinkie frame' from Duveen (Paris), explaining in a later cable that they were quite aware that the thirty by twenty-five inch frame was not really a 'Pinkie' frame, but a Régence one, but they were using this term as it was generally used by the New York office when speaking of a French frame.[73]

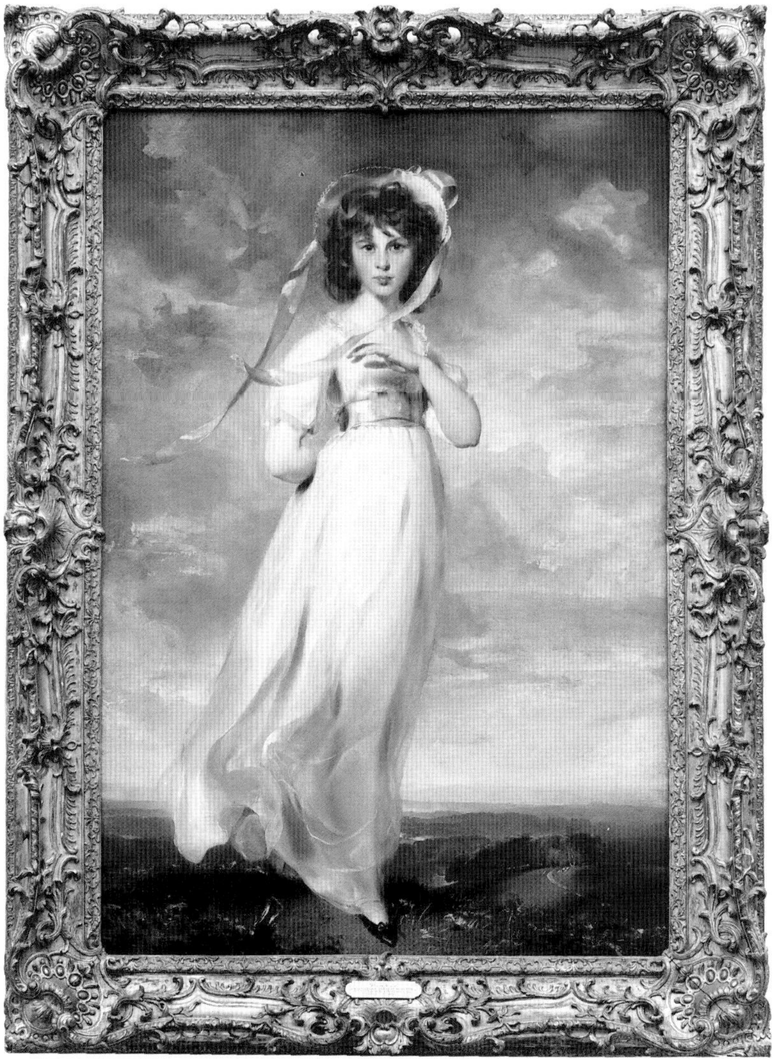

Fig.12
Sarah Barrett Moulton ('Pinkie') by Thomas Lawrence, 1794 (Huntington Library and Art Collection, San Marino, California).

The 'Duveen' frame was probably made in 1910 at the time the picture entered the collection of Lord Michelham.

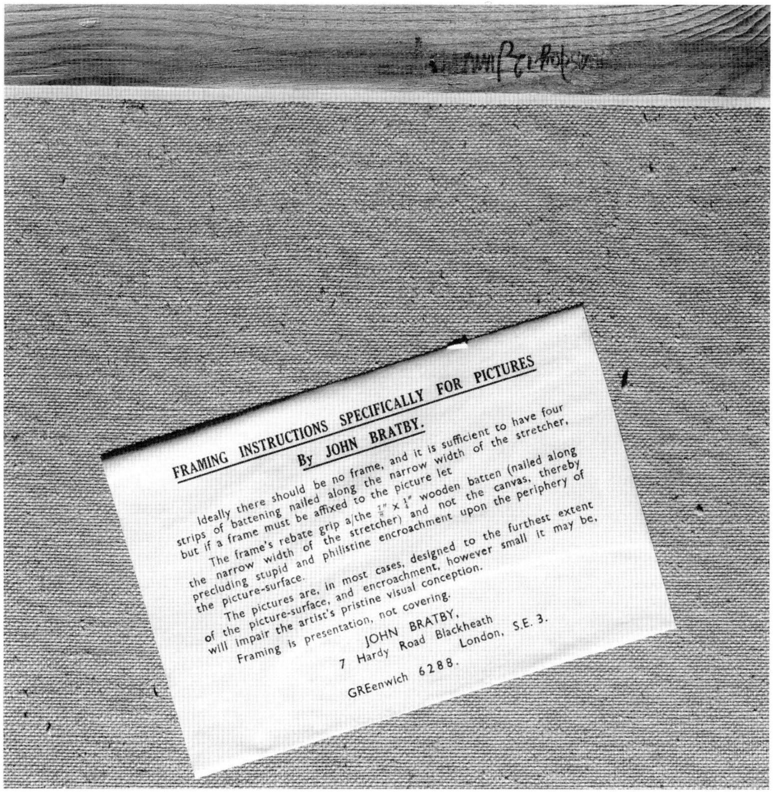

Fig.13
John Bratby's strictures against framing, recorded on a label fixed to the back of his portrait, *Brian Rix and his wife, Elspet Jeans*, 1967 (no.121).

Frames valued and devalued

In the 1930s, 1940s and 1950s many paintings passing through the auction room were so cheap that it was worth buying them for their frames, a practice adopted by frame dealers such as H.J. Spiller and Arnold Wiggins, as many a Christie's price list shows, and by institutions including the National Portrait Gallery where a former director, David Piper, has recorded how in his early years curators would 'snap up for ten or twenty pounds deplorable copies ... for the sake of the fine original carved frames that housed them'.[74]

Carved frames were prized but nineteenth-century frames, and in particular compo frames, despised. Writing in 1938, J.B. Manson, Director of the Tate Gallery, denigrated 'the debased taste of the Victorians' and claimed that the national galleries were 'disfigured by frames that are not only in the worst possible taste but are actually destructive of the pictures they adorn'.[75] And even as late as 1966 attitudes had hardly changed, as is apparent from the Tate Gallery's apologia for its then plans to knock down its 1890s portico facing the Thames: 'The old façade is rather like the massive frames of the period. It pays impressive tribute to art, yet eventually becomes a burden to it'.[76] Yet as an editorial in *Apollo* magazine asked in reply, 'Could it not be argued that Victorian frames admirably suit Victorian pictures?'[77]

Fortunately most of the Victorian pictures at the Tate have in fact kept their frames but this has not always been the case elsewhere. Such was the general attitude that frames were even discarded for the value of their gold. A scrap merchant known in the London art trade as 'Burner' Bagnell would come round with his son, Horace, to collect frames for their gold content, piling them up in the back of an open lorry.[78] In York the City Art Gallery curator, Hans Hess, is said to have sold some damaged old frames which were then burnt for their gold content in the late 1950s,[79] and it is reported that in France during the Second World War many French museums 'bought frames to preserve them from the Germans who burnt all they could get hold of to recover the gold'.[80]

The frame abandoned

Perhaps the ultimate radical idea in framing was to have no frame at all, a scheme not only espoused by artists but also by some museums. John Bratby, an artist of the 1950s 'kitchen sink' school, actually took the trouble to paste framing (or rather anti-framing) instructions on the back of his pictures, explaining his attitude (fig.13): 'Ideally there should be no frame. ... The pictures are, in most cases, designed to the furthest extent of the picture-surface, and encroachment, however small it may be, will impair the artist's pristine visual conception'.

What lay behind moves to abandon the frame? Even a brief study of the undercurrent of ideas of the time suggests that there were two main streams of thought. There were some, usually artists, who, like Bratby, explained their concerns in terms of the impact of the frame on the pictorial space, while others, often museum curators or owners, regarded the matter in a more symbolic way, arguing that the frame imparted values by its very existence or that it was one of the externals interfering with appreciation of a picture for its own sake.

The impact of the frame on the pictorial space has been variously interpreted by artists.[81] Bratby regarded it in terms of encroachment on the picture surface. Piet Mondrian in 1943 claimed to be the first to bring the painting forward from the frame, rather than set it within the frame. He noted that 'a picture without a frame works better than a framed one and that the framing causes sensations of three dimensions. It gives an illusion of depth, so I took a frame of plain wood and mounted my picture on it. In this way, I brought it to a more real existence'.[82] For American Abstract Expressionists such as Morris Louis with his very large paintings of the *Veils* series in the 1950s, there was a concern to avoid restricting the pictorial space: 'not compressing the painting by bringing in the pressure of pre-existent outside edges but expanding it and taking it out, causing its pictorial space "to leak through – or rather, to seem about to leak through, the framing edges of the picture into the space beyond"'.[83]

The idea of a frame imparting values by its very existence is a recurring one. For Gertrude Stein, 'the need that a picture exist in its frame, remain in its frame was over'. Her famous portrait by Picasso was intentionally left frameless in 1906: 'A picture remaining in its frame was a thing that always had existed and now pictures commenced to want to leave their frames ... '.[84] In the case of Mark Rothko's late dark paintings of 1969 and 1970 it has been claimed 'their representational allusion to landscape or seascape is consistently reinforced by the narrow framing band that surrounds each of the paintings'.[85] A generation grown accustomed to viewing a certain sort of painting without frames could have its perceptions influenced by the existence of even the most residual framing device.

This same generation could also countenance displaying works in museums with their frames removed, arguing either that the frame imparted unacceptable values or that it influenced perceptions in a way which distracted attention from the object itself. In Italy, at the Palazzo Bianco museum in Genoa, reconstructed by Franco Albini in 1951, and at the Museo Correr in Venice, the work of Carlo Scarpa a decade later, Italian renaissance and baroque old masters were displayed shorn of their frames on screens and bare walls. At the Palazzo Bianco the guiding principle behind the renovation was based on the tenet that the 'setting ... would consider the piece of art for the sake of art only, free from any external interference'.[86] The notion of the 'spurious frame' was defined as one 'in an idiom different from that of the time to which it belongs', and the dogma was applied to the collection: 'For moral as well as educational reasons, the process of elimination from the exhibition rooms was directed with particular energy against spurious items – one picture, many pieces of furniture, and a large number of frames'.[87]

In America the campaign against the frame has been restricted to a limited number of modern art museums. William Rubin, Director of Paintings and Sculpture at New York's Museum of Modern Art in the 1970s and 1980s, has condemned the gilded frame as so much 'eye-catching fluff', actively detrimental to the appreciation of the picture within. Hence his controversial decision to apply simple narrow mouldings to works by Cézanne, Van Gogh, Gauguin and Seurat in place of their period frames.[88] And at other venerable New York institutions, removing frames has proved controversial. 'It came as a great shock to me', the dealer and collector Heinz Berggruen has said,

> *when I learnt that the Guggenheim Museum had decided to take off its frames and show pictures naked, so to speak. They felt that a picture has to stand by itself and should not be embellished. I thought it was an unwise decision. The pictures looked bare and no longer had their previous character. When I learnt that the frames were to be taken off the Klees I gave to the Metropolitan Museum, I protested violently.*[89]

The extraordinary difficulties experienced by

museum staff in reframing modern pictures is well documented by the case of the Van Goghs in the Stedelijk Museum in Amsterdam. In the 1930s plain modern frames of a fairly uniform simple profile were used for many of the pictures. In the 1950s very narrow protective strips of pine became the fashion, a sort of minimalist frame described by one critic as suitable for a 'third-class funeral'. In the 1980s quite wide plain gilt frames were tried out. And more recently, in 1990, wide flat coloured frames, re-creating Van Gogh's own experiments, have been employed without real success. Each generation of curators has wished to try its hand, just as dealers and private owners have changed the frames on the Van Goghs they have owned.[90]

Museum attitudes today

In writing about the framing of Van Gogh's work Louis van Tilborgh has divined a sad truth:

There were almost as many new frames as new owners, for it is unusual for the frame to be retained when a picture changes hands. It is the only part of a painting that a new owner can alter in order to make an acquisition truly his own. The more expensive or important a work the greater the desire for change.[91]

To return to the problems of framing old masters, curators and collectors have to decide whether to accept the frame in which a work comes to them or to select another more pleasing frame (necessarily a subjective judgement) or a more historically accurate frame (apparently an objective judgement but one which time often proves to have been more subjective than was first thought).

Does one listen to Gervase Jackson-Stops, who wanted to promote a greater tolerance towards frames that are not coeval with their pictures? 'We must hope', he wrote in 1987, 'that the days are over when seventeenth-century Dutch landscapes would be automatically torn out of their carved and gilded eighteenth-century frames and given expensive new wave-moulded ebony surrounds held to be more in keeping with the artists' original vision'.[92] The experience at Dulwich Art Gallery is instructive. Many of the smaller paintings are in frames which to modern eyes are too large. But the experiment of Sir Gerald Kelly after the Second World War in reframing four major Spanish paintings in Spanish frames of seventeenth-century type, though individually pleasing, disrupted the appearance of rooms filled with uniform frames.[93] At the Wallace Collection, *The Laughing Cavalier* by Frans Hals stands in solitary isolation in a recent black ripple frame among a sea of gilt frames in the main gallery. And at the National Gallery, London, another Hals, *Young Man holding a Skull*, appears in an even more arresting black ripple creation but one which is not at ease with its surroundings.

The difficulties of framing are particularly acute in a museum setting, as Nicholas Penny has explained, using the example of Nicolas Poussin's *Worship of the Golden Calf* in the National Gallery:

The urge to divorce an old picture from a later frame is often greatest in the very circumstances in which history should be most respected, for it is the interior of the modern museum which exaggerates any incongruity. Were the frame which surrounds the Poussin to retain a cornice above it, consoles beside it and chairs beneath it, all carved and gilt in a style to match, it might, paradoxically, be more easily dissociated from the painting within it. Today, the frame demands attention because it is out of sympathy with both the painting and its setting.[94]

In the case of British portraits, the tendency among dealers and museums has been to choose a frame which is earlier than the picture. Instead of a heavy Lawrence frame, a Maratta might be chosen. In place of a Maratta frame, something of more rococo character could be deemed suitable. And a running pattern might be preferred to a centre-and-corner frame. At the Wallace Collection, Reynolds's full-length portrait of Mrs Elizabeth Carnac has had a late seventeenth-century panel frame put on in place of the Maratta frame visible in old photographs. At the Tate, Gainsborough's *Madame Baccelli* has been given a splendid and pleasing rococo frame of twenty years earlier than the picture (see no.39).

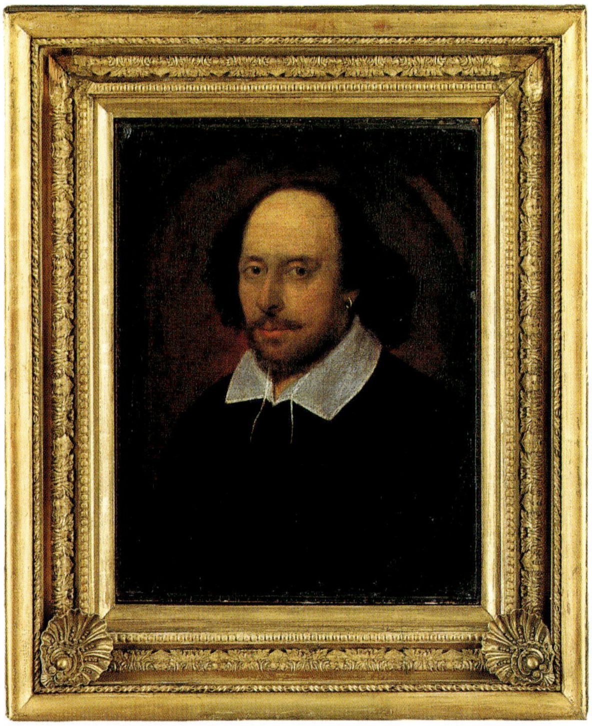

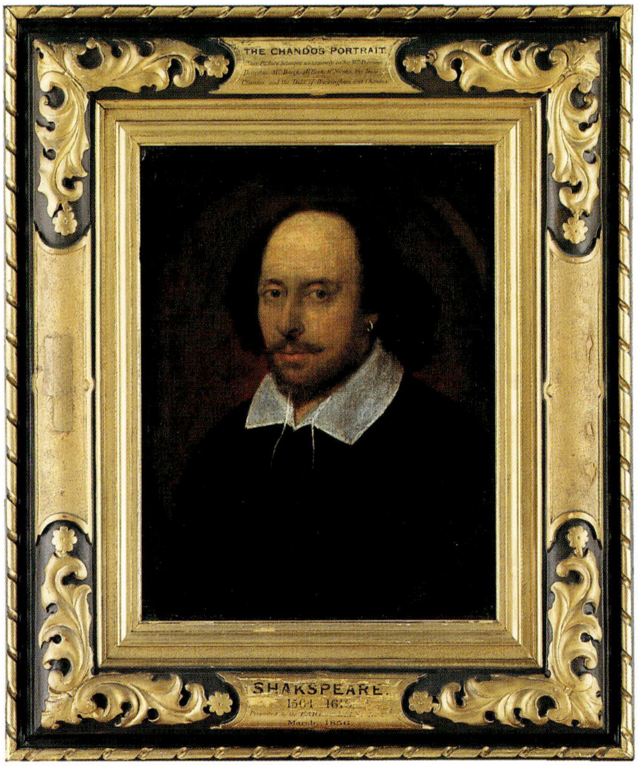
THE CHANDOS PORTRAIT
SHAKSPEARE.

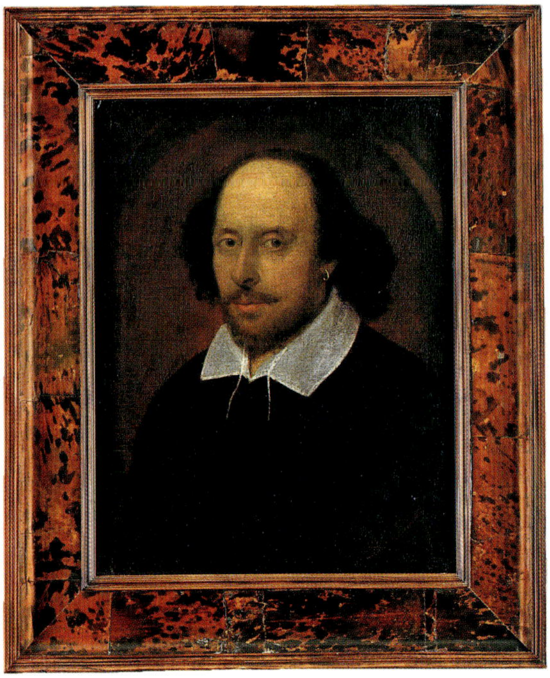

Fig.14 (facing page, top left)
William Shakespeare ('The Chandos Portrait') by John Taylor, *c.*1610 (no.97).

The portrait is shown in the eighteenth-century Maratta frame in which it came to the National Portrait Gallery in 1856. The corner shells (two of which are missing) were added in the early nineteenth century when the frame was reduced in size.

Fig.15 (facing page, top right)
The same picture reframed by Foord & Dickinson for the Gallery in 1864 in a mock seventeenth-century frame which focuses attention on the frame at the expense of the picture. In the 1950s or 1960s the frame was removed and the picture placed within a velvet-lined case.

Fig.16 (facing page, below left)
The same picture reframed by John Davies for the Gallery in 1983 using an old tortoiseshell frame. Though not a period frame, it seems to enhance the scale of the picture and its sense of colour.

And at the National Gallery in London almost all the large Reynolds and Gainsboroughs have been reframed over many years in frames of a style earlier than the picture. At the National Portrait Gallery there has been an unwritten policy to replace the more outspoken 'country house' frames when out of period with the picture with something simpler and closer in date to the picture. So the portrait of the Lord Belasyse by Gilbert Jackson has lost its extraordinary overmantel frame, that of Samuel Butler its spectacular rococo frame and that of the 3rd Earl of Burlington its frame in the Empire style. In the nineteenth century, almost all the Tudor portraits were put into uniform black-and-gold frames on acquisition (see no.102). Something is gained in visual unity as a result, but the rich history of a picture's former owners may be lost. Furthermore, there is a tendency for the 'museum' frames of previous generations to be seen as candidates for replacement, as the taste of curators changes. The National Portrait Gallery's first acquisition, the portrait of William Shakespeare, is onto its fourth frame (see figs.14-16).

How then should one tackle the subject of framing in museums today, and for that matter in private collections? Firstly there is a need to accept that there may be more than one valid approach. If, for example, some great museums and collectors have decided to adopt a uniform framing method, whether the rococo frames of the Elector of Saxony in the 1740s or the narrow mouldings of the Museum of Modern Art in the 1980s, then this results in a clear aesthetic whether one likes it or not. But in most situations a less dogmatic approach will be appropriate, one which is based on research, experience and a clear rationale. Though much reframing goes on in museums, few have publicly explained what they are about. The most detailed exposition, expressed with great clarity, is that of Germain Bazin, published in 1961, setting out the approach to the Impressionist collections then at the Jeu de Paume and now at the Musée d'Orsay in Paris. More recently Pieter van Thiel has described the approach to framing adopted at the Rijksmuseum in Amsterdam.[95]

The foundation of any framing policy should be an informed understanding of the museum's collection. What can one observe from a close study of the frames themselves? And what can one learn from a study of the history of the painting? Is the frame perhaps original and who may have chosen it and why? If the frame is later what can it tell one about the history of the picture? Is it a pattern used elsewhere in the same collection or other collections? Once one has an understanding of the present frame, and of the collection in which it sits, one can go on to ask if there is a case to reframe a picture or whether it would be better left as it is, whatever its faults.

If the decision is to reframe, whether an old master or a more modern work, is one to try to find something historically accurate (and does one have the knowledge), or is a pleasing frame the criterion? And whatever the preference, should one try to find a period frame, if one can be found at the right price, or is it better to have a frame made? There are only so many original seventeenth-century Italian frames or French Louis XV frames which have survived to cut about to fit to one's pictures.

Our knowledge of the history of picture framing is in its infancy. As research continues, attitudes to framing and re-framing will continue to evolve. The spate of publications on the history of framing not surprisingly excites interest in the subject. Such publications should instil caution as well as confidence.

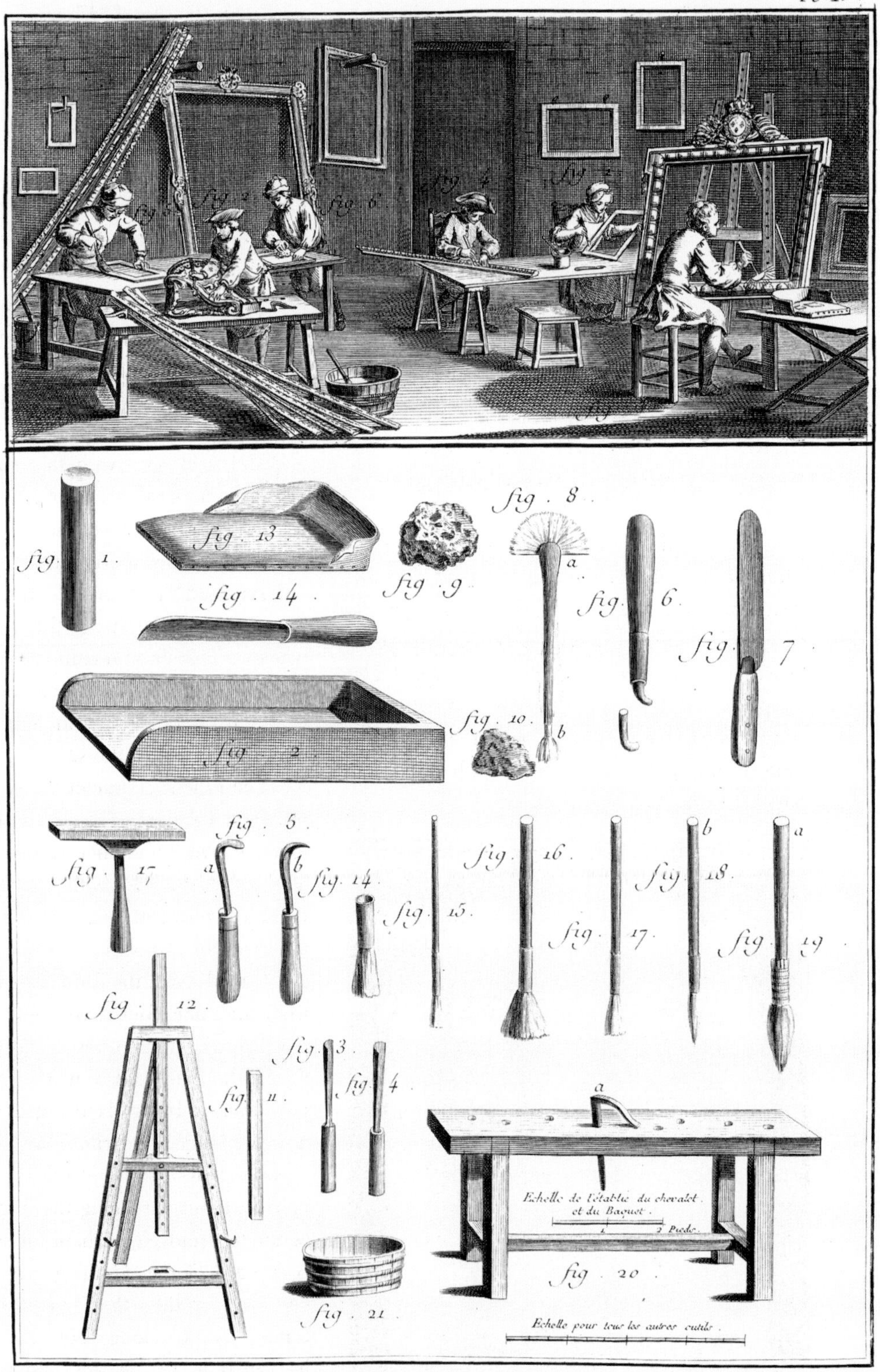

Doreur, Sur Bois.

Chapter 2
The Techniques and Practice of the Framemaker

Have you ever considered in the early history of painting, how important also is the history of the frame maker? It is a matter, I assure you, needing the very best consideration. For the frame was made before the picture. The painted window is much, but the aperture it fills was thought of before it.[1]

John Ruskin was lecturing about early Florentine art, but his remarks apply as much to the Wilton Diptych or the Despencer Retable, which were among the very few early English panel paintings to survive. The Wilton Diptych in the National Gallery, London, an exceptional image of Richard II probably painted shortly before his death in 1399, is made up of two oak panels, each with a frame carved out of the same piece of wood as the painted panels themselves.[2] The Despencer Retable in Norwich Cathedral, an altarpiece of about the same period, has an elaborate frame, richly ornamented with inset glass panels bearing coats of arms.[3]

Fig.17 (facing page) *Doreur, Sur Bois (The Gilder on Wood)*, engraving, 1763 (Arnold Wiggins & Sons Ltd). From Diderot's *Encyclopédie*, showing gilding equipment and stages in the process of gilding. The frame on the easel in the scene at the top is in the course of being water gilded.

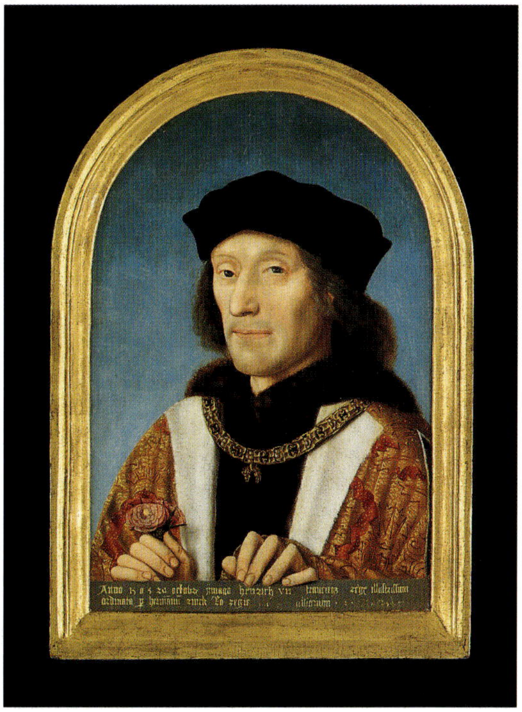

Fig.18
Henry VII by an unknown artist, 1505 (no.1).

Oak frame integral with the panel.

So few early devotional pictures painted in England survive (owing to the destruction wrought at the Dissolution of the Monasteries and in the Civil War), however, that the starting-point of this study is the portrait in the sixteenth century. Even then portraits were still very much rare luxury items. The earliest in the National Portrait Gallery is that of Henry VII painted in 1505 and, like the Wilton Diptych, its frame is of oak and is integral with the panel (fig.18). It is one of a very small group of arch-topped English portraits of the early sixteenth century, of a type more commonly found in the Low Countries, characterised by an arched roll moulding and a flat sloping sill giving the impression of a window. This illusion is further enhanced in the portrait of Henry VII by the way his fingertips project over the painted inscription that appears immediately above the sill.

The salient characteristic of these early oak frames is that they were prepared with the panel, and the panel was then painted in the frame. The same is the case with a subsequent development: the engaged or grooved frame popular in the first half of the sixteenth century (figs.2, 19, 20). For this type, the frame was made separately from the panel, but it was designed so that the panel fitted into grooves cut in the edge of the frame, the four sides of which engaged with the panel before being fixed together with wooden dowels. Once the frame was assembled and decorated, it was very difficult to remove the panel without damaging the frame. If the panel had to be removed, perhaps for conservation, the back edge of the retaining grooves usually was cut away, rather than risk disassembling the frame by knocking out the dowels. This happened in the distant past with two of the three original frames of this sort at the National Portrait Gallery, and with one of the two at the Society of Antiquaries, London.[4]

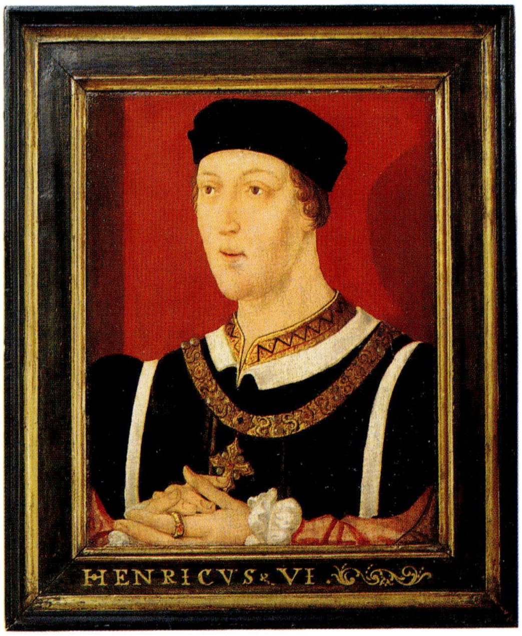

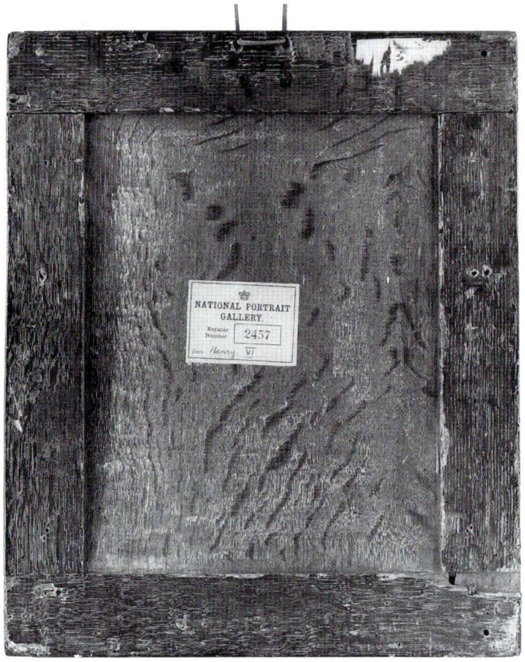

Fig.19 (far left)
Henry VI by an unknown artist, *c*.1540 (no.2).

Oak frame engaged with the panel.

Fig.20 (left)
The back of the frame, made up of four lengths of oak fixed at the corners by wooden dowels, with the oak panel fitting into grooves cut in the sides of the frame. Note the two hanging holes at top centre, through which a leather cord has been strung.

Engaged frames of this sort are fairly simple in cross-section, and fixed at the corners with a dowelled lap joint. They were normally painted. The main frieze, the flat area of the frame, is sometimes decorated with lettering. The sight edge moulding next to the painting is slightly raised and is often gilt. The back edge, furthest from the painting, is usually more prominent and may sometimes be partly gilt.

A further stage in the development of the frame occurred when the frame came to be made independently of the painting. A portrait no longer had to be painted in its frame, but could be fitted from behind once the painting was complete. In Flemish painting this method was introduced before 1520 and had become the norm by the mid-century. English portrait painters followed suit, perhaps finding the independent frame more convenient for the larger panels in use by the 1540s. Once the frame no longer needed to be made at the same time as the painting's support the intimate relationship between the two was broken. Payments such as that made by the Company of Cathay in 1576 confirm that the frame was made independently of the picture: 'Paid Cornelius Ketel, payntar … for making a great Picture … £5, and the Joyner for a frame and case for it … 13s.4d'.[5]

As yet no detailed study of English frames has been made to match that carried out in Belgium in the 1970s and 1980s, charting changes in frame construction, profile and decoration over the course of two centuries of Flemish painting.[6] It would appear that most frames in England were painted or stained black, or perhaps dark brown, with a few more expensive frames being finished in colours or marbled. Framing in the sixteenth century was conservative. It was the patronage of Charles I and his court which was to bring about a revolution in framing. Painted frames continued to be made but with the great difference that they were normally carved and gilded as well.

Painted frames in the time of Charles I

The 1620s and 1630s were years of tremendous activity as Charles I, the Duke of Buckingham, the Earl of Arundel, the Marquis of Hamilton and other members of the court circle acquired pictures in large quantities. The arrival of the Gonzaga collection from Mantua in and after 1628, the greatest single acquisition ever made for the Royal Collection, brought a flood of orders for fine frames. It is clear from contemporary accounts and inventories and from the relatively few surviving frames of the period that many of these frames were carved, gilded and painted, apparently with the low-relief carving gilded and the backgrounds painted. A few very early survivals such as the frames at Knole on the De Critz portrait of Thomas Sackville, 1st Earl of Dorset of the early 1600s and the full-length of James I by Daniel Mytens of *c.*1621, suggest that carved, gilded and painted frames had already begun to come into fashion earlier in the century.[7]

In the Royal Collection it was Charles I's own acquisitions, whether of old master paintings or commissioned portraits, which were the most richly framed. In the inventory of 1639 most of the paintings by Mytens and Van Dyck are described as having carved and gilded frames, as are the Mantua pictures by Titian, Andrea del Sarto, Raphael, Correggio and Giulio Romano.[8] Several of the frames are additionally described as 'whited' or blue.[9] The compiler of the inventory, Abraham van der Doort, often left open the question of the degree of gilding, only occasionally specifying the frame as 'all over guilded' or 'some part guilded', and it is probable that colour of some sort featured on many of the frames. If one turns to the King's Works accounts it is clear that many of the carved and gilded frames made for Charles I were partly painted in restrained colours such as stone colour, timber colour, 'sadd lute colour' (a dark clay or cement colour) and 'sadd wallnut-tree colour'.[10]

While the published accounts do not include payments for frames painted white or blue, frames of this sort do occasionally survive in collections of the period. At Knole the frames on the copies of the Raphael Cartoons, probably painted in the 1630s, are carved and gilded with a black background which seemingly was off-white originally, while the frame on the Van Dyck full-length portrait of Lady Frances Cranfield, wife of the 5th Earl of Dorset, is one of a number in the collection which has some traces of an old blue background beneath later gilding.[11]

The carved frame

The reign of Charles I saw the rise to prominence of the carved and gilded frame, a taste which continued through the Civil War and became the norm in fashionable circles after the Restoration. The greater demand for frames and the fashion for more elaborate frames turned framemaking into a significant business so that by 1660 John Evelyn could deem the gilding of frames as a trade worthy of being included among those he lists as 'curious'.[12]

Framemaking at the time was a partnership between the joiner, the carver and the gilder. The basic framework was the task of the joiner. In 1632 the Joiners' Company of London emerged triumphant from a lengthy dispute with the Carpenters' Company, so establishing the right of joiners to make picture frames, among other forms of furniture.[13] In practice the power of the craft guilds, or Livery Companies as they were called, to regulate trade diminished with time. Many carvers and gilders, at least in the eighteenth century, worked outside the guild system, including leading figures such as William Hallett and Thomas Chippendale, and the last restrictive laws were withdrawn in 1856.[14]

The limitations of the role of the joiner in framemaking by the mid-eighteenth century are described in Campbell's *The London Tradesman*:

> *There are a set of Joiners who make nothing but Frames for Looking Glasses and Pictures, and prepare them for the Carvers. This requires but little Ingenuity or Neatness as they only join the Deals roughly plained, in the Shape and Dimensions required. If the Pattern chosen for the Frame is to have any large Holes in it, these they cut out in their proper places, or, if it is to have Mouldings raised in the wood, they plant them on; but they leave the Carver to plant on the rest of the Figures. But we have said enough of this Trade, who is no more than a cobbling Carpenter or Joiner.*[15]

Before the carver began work the raised parts of the frame were fixed on the sub-frame. 'All Figures that rise above the Plain [*sic*] of the Frame are glued on; that is, suppose a Figure is to rise two Inches above the Plain of the Frame, in that Case a Piece of Wood of that Height, and of the Bulk of the Figure designed, is glued on'.[16]

During the second half of the seventeenth century oak was replaced as the normal wood used in frame construction by pine, which was easier to work. In France oak remained the standard, but French craftsmen working in England seem almost always to have used pine. Occasionally other woods were used for the most intricate carving. Limewood was favoured by Grinling Gibbons and other virtuosi carvers of the late seventeenth century for elaborate undercut naturalistic woodcarving. Boxwood was sometimes employed, especially in the late eighteenth century, for small-scale intricate details such as the laurel leaves on the frame of the self-portrait by George Stubbs (see fig.97; no.49).

Methods of construction varied considerably in the seventeenth century with various types of lap joints in use (see fig.198). It was only in the late seventeenth century that the familiar mitre joint fixed with tapering keys at each corner became common (fig.200). The mitre has sometimes been criticised as lacking the strength of a lap joint since it required precise cutting and the fixing of end grain to end grain. Nevertheless the mitre proved a very satisfactory method of construction, and it remained in use until the early nineteenth century when the increased size of frames, and especially their greater depth, were responsible for the introduction of the use of large corner blocks to give strength to the frame. In frames of great depth, the weight could be reduced by making the back edge and sight edge separately from the main body of the frame (see fig.193). Other types of fixing were sometimes used, including the butterfly key (fig.201).[17]

Although these construction details can be valuable for understanding and dating picture frames, they were rarely given any thought by the customer at the time since it was the work of the carver and the gilder which commanded the greatest attention. The changing styles of the carver will be the subject of Chapter 3. The finishing of the frame, usually by gilding or silvering, is described below.

Oil gilding

'The gilding with oil is the most easy and cheap, as well as the most durable kind; and, therefore, is mostly applied to common purposes. It is performed by cementing the gold to the ground, by means of fat oil.'[18] This account by Robert Dossie in 1758, from *The Handmaid to the Arts*, one of the fullest descriptions of the gilding process in the eighteenth century, reflects a long-standing preference in England for oil gilding over water gilding. Oil gilding was the standard process for picture frames in the seventeenth century, supposedly on account of its durability, although by the end of the century water gilding was coming into fashion. The essential differences between the two types of gilding are in technique and appearance. Both types of gilding require the use of a gold size to serve as an adhesive for the gold leaf: in oil gilding the size is oil based, in water gilding it is wetted immediately before gilding. Oil gilding has to be left matt whereas water gilding can be burnished to give it a high sheen.

The gold leaf used was extremely thin. Improved techniques allowed it to be beaten into leaves 290,000th of an inch in thickness by the mid-nineteenth century.[19] The finished leaves were placed into books of twenty-five sheets of gold, each three-and-a-quarter inches square. By alloying the gold with other metals, different colours could be obtained: 'The deeper colours are alloyed with copper, the middle colours with silver and copper, and the paler golds with silver only'.[20] Taste in gilding has varied, as Robert Dossie, writing in 1758, recognised: 'The full yellow is certainly the most beautiful and truest colour of gold: but the deep reddish cast has been of late most esteemed from the caprice of fashion'.[21] Gold leaf can commonly be obtained in about a dozen colours ranging from pure gold at twenty-four carat and almost pure red golds of twenty-three or twenty-three-and-a-quarter carat to white gold of only five carat. In the nineteenth century the colours were described as 'fine gold, red, pale red, extra deep, deep, orange, lemon, deep pale gold, pale, pale pale, deep party, party and white'.[22]

Fig.21
Gilding equipment, including a gilder's tip for picking up gold leaf and a gilder's cushion, bordered on three sides to protect the gold leaf. From the trade catalogue of Hamilton & Co., 1876.

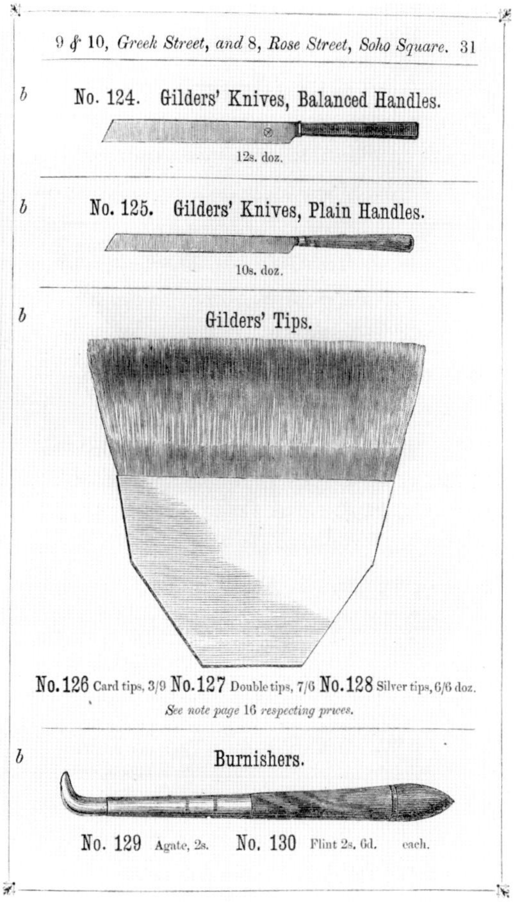

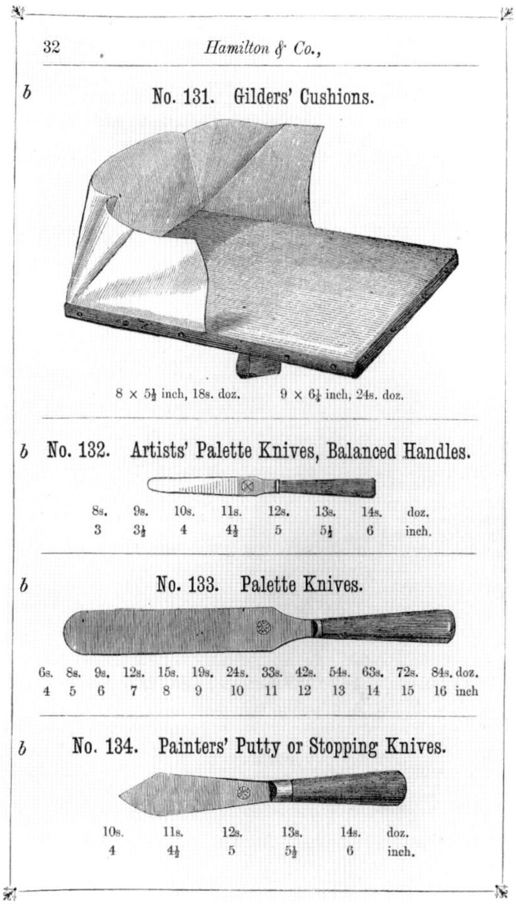

With most carved frames a layer of gesso was applied to the frame as a preparation for the gold size. The gesso was made by adding 'whiting', usually chalk, to a hot size. It was then applied to the frame: 'Size over your Frame once with it, then add more Whiting, until tis of a reasonable consistence and thickness: With this lay it over three or four times, as you find it deserves, granting it time to drie sufficiently before every turn'.[23] This account by John Stalker and George Parker, published in 1688 in their *Treatise of Japaning and Varnishing*, is the fullest early description of a process which has varied little over the centuries. After smoothing down, the dried gesso surface was ready to receive the gold size.

The gold size for oil gilding was traditionally based on linseed oil, which was thickened by allowing it to stand until it became as thick, or fat, as possible. Stalker and Parker recommended exposing it to the sun for five or six months. Finely ground yellow ochre was then added, and sometimes also a little vermilion, to make gold size. Thomas Sheraton in his *Cabinet Directory* of 1803 makes a distinction between japanner's gold size, which could be ready for gilding in four hours or less after application, and house painter's gold size, which was based on a thicker oil and frequently took twenty-four hours before being in a state fit to receive the gold, adding that 'the longer it is in drying, the greater lustre in gilding will be produced'.[24] Such niceties in the final appearance of the gilding had long been recognised, and were partly a matter of fashion. If a thinner, faster-drying size is used, Robert Dossie advised, in 1758, 'the gilding is also rendered … less shining and glossy; which is esteemed a perfection in this kind of gilding: though, taking away the prejudice of fashion, I should think the most shining the most beautiful; and of the strongest effect'.[25]

The size was brushed onto the frame, taking

care to 'pass the brush into all the hollows and cavities' of the carving, 'for where the size fails to be laid on, the gold will never take ... '.[26] For the greatest perfection the size was left to dry and the frame then sized a second time or even a third time. When the final coat was almost dry to touch but still just tacky the gold was applied. The gold leaf was placed on a gilder's cushion and cut to size with a gilder's knife, and then the fragile sheet picked up with a brush of fine hair known as a gilder's tip (see fig.21). The tip was passed lightly across the gilder's hair, neck or face to pick up enough moisture or grease to hold the gold leaf, and the leaf was then laid on the frame. Once dry the surface was brushed over with a soft brush to take off any loose fragments of gold. If any part had been missed, it would be resized if necessary and the process repeated. Finally the gold was smoothed with a soft leather cloth.

Water gilding

Water gilding did not become commonly used in England for picture frames until the late seventeenth century. Sir Godfrey Kneller, the leading portrait painter, charged the Earl of Salisbury £2.10s for a 'burnisht freame' in 1694 and £2 for a 'burnisht gold frame' in 1699.[27] Burnished gold always implies water gilding, for oil gilding could not withstand the polishing process of burnishing. 'As to lustre and effect,' wrote Thomas Sheraton in 1803, 'it has doubtless the advantage of oil gilding, but is attended with much more trouble and expense'.[28] At its finest water gilding was a time-consuming and demanding process which required the skills of an experienced gilder. In France gilding was usually done to a particularly high standard, and Jean Felix Watin in his manual on painting and gilding, first published in 1773, identified no fewer than seventeen steps in the gilding process.[29]

Before gilding the frame had to be prepared by applying gesso to the surface of the wood. The gesso was made by boiling down the finest white parchment to form a size to which whiting was added until it came to the consistency of strong cream, according to Sheraton,[30] who also recommended that, 'With this mixture, the work to be gilded must be covered 5, 6, 7, 8, or 9 times according to the nature of the work', allowing each coat of whiting to dry before the next was applied. Before the final coat was quite dry, the surface was wetted and smoothed over and then could be reworked 'to recover the out-line of the mouldings', as is described in more detail below. At this stage the frame was sometimes described as 'in the white'.

The parts of the surface to be burnished were once again smoothed and polished with a fine wet rag, and then a yellow ochre, mixed in the parchment size, was laid on the frame. The ochre was chosen to be near in colour to the gold, and a little vermilion or red lead might therefore be added. 'This ... method is to give the appearance of gilding to the deeper and obscure parts of the carving, where the gold cannot, or is not thought necessary, to be put'.[31] At this point the frame was 'in the yellow'. It is rare to find records of frames being supplied in this state but 'Yellowed frames to Shew Pictures' were lent to George Romney by his framemaker, William Saunders, among them 'a frame Carv'd & yellowed for Spinning Wheel', supplied in 1785 for the picture now at Kenwood of *Lady Hamilton at the Spinning Wheel*.[32] In this case, apparently, the frame was only gilded when the picture found an owner.

Next, two or three coats of a gold size for burnishing, known as the bole, were applied to the gessoed surface. Bole is a soft greasy-textured clay, the colour of which varied according to its source. A dark red, favoured for the rich warm colour it imparted to the gold, was used for French frames in the seventeenth and eighteenth centuries, and on much Huguenot work in England.[33] A lighter pink bole is also found on frames made in England in the eighteenth century, while greyish-blue or even black boles were sometimes used in the nineteenth century. The strength of the gold size was varied according to the time of year, since in winter it would dry more slowly. And there were dangers in

Fig.22
Kenneth Clark, Baron Clark by Graham Sutherland (detail), 1963-4 (no.119).

Overlap in the burnished gold leaf treated as a decorative feature.

attempting the work in times of hard frost, 'for your Whiting will be apt to peel off, the Gold and Silver-size will freez in laying on, not to say any thing of other misfortunes that attend the unseasonable operation'.[34] Thomas Chippendale experienced such difficulties in January 1768 when he wrote to Sir Rowland Winn, his patron at Nostell Priory in Yorkshire, explaining that 'all the picture frames are Carv'd and now Gilding, they would have been finishd by this time had not the frost come on so very severe'.[35]

The frame was now ready for gilding. It was placed almost upright so that the excess of the gilding water used to wet the surface of the bole could run off. The water usually contained some thin size and sometimes a little alcohol. The gold leaf was cut and applied with a gilder's tip in the same manner as for oil gilding, the surface of the frame being progressively wetted as gilding proceeded. 'If your work be sufficiently moist,' Stalker and Parker wrote, 'you'l perceive how lovingly the gold will embrace it, hugging and clinging to it, like those inseparable friends, Iron and the Loadstone'.[36] The leaf was attracted as the water was rapidly absorbed by the bole. It was held in place by the tackiness of the wetted surface. Each sheet was allowed to overlap the previous one by about one-eighth of an inch to avoid breaks in the surface, as can be seen on the frame of Graham Sutherland's portrait of Kenneth Clark (fig.22). Any parts that had been missed had to be gone over again, as Stalker and Parker described: 'Cut some leaves of gold into small pieces, ... wet the unguilded parts, and take up bits of gold proportion'd to the places that stand in need of it; this last performance we call, Faulting'.[37]

Faults in gilding could also be rectified by applying a second layer of gold leaf to the frame, a process known as double gilding. This method was especially popular in the nineteenth century when 'all the best work that is flat, such as the broad insides to picture frames, spandrills, flat looking-glass frames, &c, are double gilt; and this is done to give the work a better colour and more solid appearance'.[38] Once the underlying bole had sufficiently hardened, which could take twenty-four hours, depending on the time of

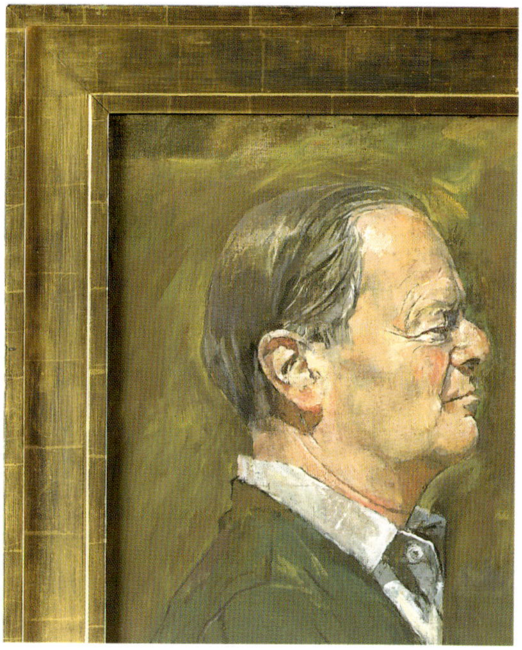

year, the gilding might be burnished by polishing the surface with a dog's tooth, or an agate or flint burnisher made for the purpose, until the gold acquired its full gleaming intensity.

There were two further related processes, both of which involved applying a size to the areas left unburnished. Because water gilding was more vulnerable than oil gilding, unburnished areas would be protected by sizing: 'that which is not burnisht', wrote Stalker and Parker, 'must be matted or secured with Size, Seed-Lac varnish, or Lacker, if you desire it deep-colour'd'.[39] Often a weakened mixture of the parchment size was used, to which a little vermilion might be added. Secondly, the appearance of the gilding could be enhanced if the hollows of the carving, including such features as the veining of the leaves and foliage, were set off with a lacquer, which might be made up with the Dragons Blood and Saffron of Stalker and Parker's recipe, or with the egg-white size containing red lead mixed with vermilion, yellow ochre or burnt sienna, as described by Dossie.[40]

The contrast between burnished and matt areas was one of the most notable features of water gilding, as was widely recognised: 'leave the ground of the carving untouch'd, and some other parts which you shall think fit; which being

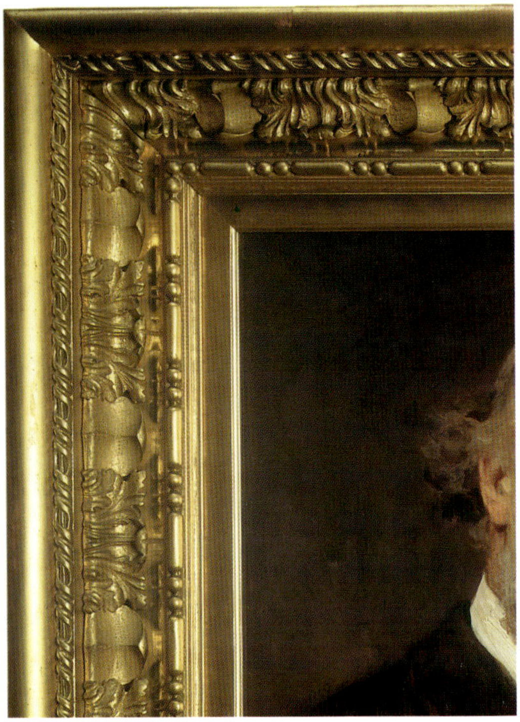

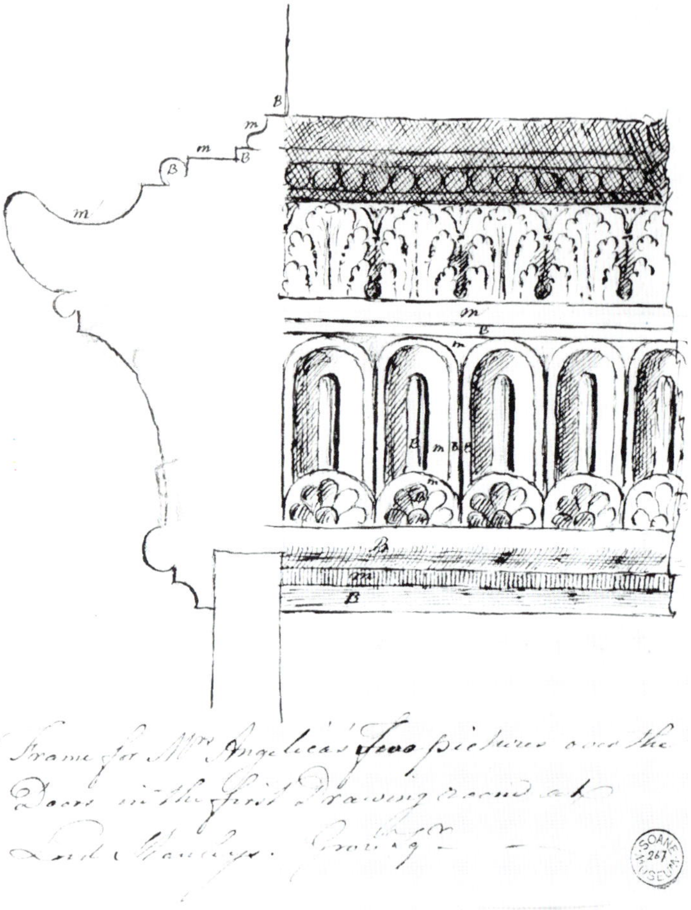

rough, if compar'd with the other, will set off and beautify that which is burnish'd'.[41] Thomas Chippendale's watercolour design of 1767 for a picture frame for Nostell Priory is inscribed, 'N.B. The coloured part is burnish'd Gold the other part all Dead',[42] and Robert and James Adam in *c.*1775 made drawings such as that for Angelica Kauffmann's overdoors at Lord Stanley's (fig.23) which are annotated 'B' and 'm' to indicate areas to be burnished or left matt.

The choice between oil gilding and water gilding, or between matt and burnished gilding, has always been partly a matter of fashion and partly one of need. 'Mouldings full of small members, and work full of ornaments, are generally gilt in oil, while broad flat surfaces and plain beads and hollows are gilt in water, and sometimes in oil' according to the guidelines in one nineteenth-century gilders' manual.[43] The small-scale ornament used by Sir Thomas Lawrence in framing his later portraits did not lend itself to burnishing so it is hardly surprising to find him writing to a patron in 1828 to the effect that a good frame would usually be unburnished. For the same reason many early eighteenth-century frames with small-scale running patterns were oil gilt. In contrast, the wide C- and S- scrolls of rococo frames (see fig.123) lent themselves to burnishing as did the smooth hollows and the tongues between the acanthus leaves of Carlo Maratta frames (see fig.24). In the second half of the twentieth century burnished gilding has become a fashionable way of finishing a frame, often done so as to emphasise the decorative quality of overlapping sheets of gold leaf (see fig.22).

Silvering

Another favoured finish in the seventeenth century was silvering, applied in much the same way as gilding. Silver had to be lacquered to prevent it tarnishing, and often a lacquer or varnish of yellow or brown colour was used to give the impression of gold. As Stalker and Parker described the process in 1688: 'If you …

Fig.24 (above left)
Sir Oliver Lodge by Sir George Reid (detail), *c.*1907 (no.90).

A reflection of the carving can be seen in the burnished hollow of the frame.

Fig.23 (above right)
Design by Robert and James Adam, *c.*1775 for a picture frame moulding for overdoor paintings by Angelica Kauffmann at Derby House (Sir John Soane's Museum, London).

Annotated with 'B' and 'm' to indicate burnished and matt gilding.

Fig.25
William Shenstone
by Thomas Ross
(detail), 1738 (no.27).

The ornament has been worked in gesso, notably the modelled low-relief work, the cross-hatched corner motifs and the punched background.

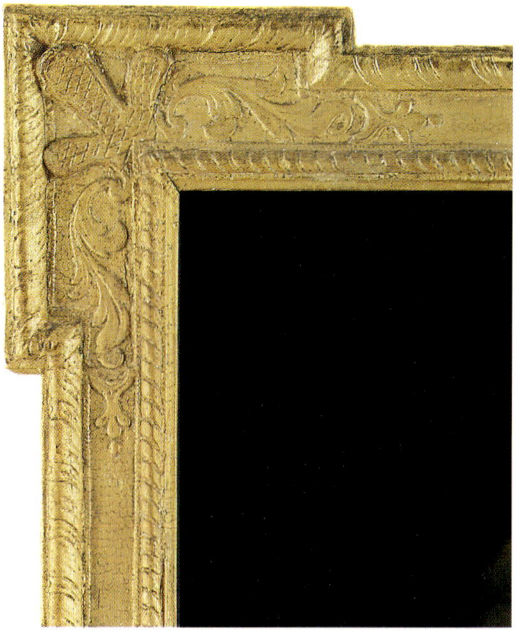

Fig.26
George Frideric Handel by Thomas Hudson
(detail), 1756 (no.37).

Much of the surface ornament has been worked in gesso, the thickness of which is apparent at a number of old damages.

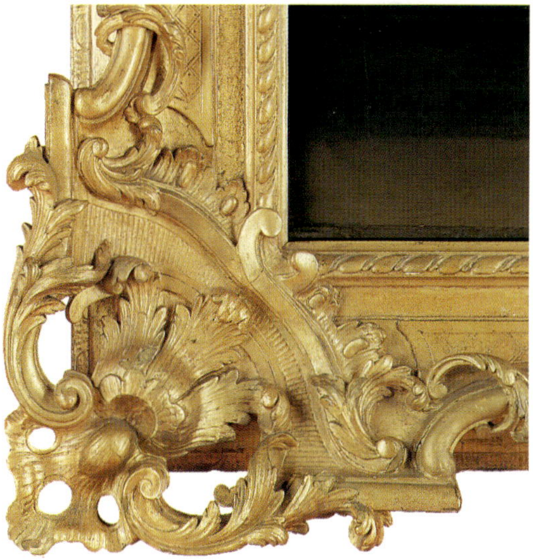

have graced your Lacker with a true gold-colour ... unless narrowly surveyed, twill put a fallacy upon and deceive curious discerning eyes'.[44]

An old lacquered silvered frame can have the appearance of very gentle gilding but only too often such frames have been subsequently gilded for reasons of taste or to make good tarnished silvering. The silver can sometimes be detected where the later gilding has been chipped or damaged. Nowadays regilded silver frames are occasionally stripped to reveal the silver, as with the frame on Kneller's portrait of John Dryden (fig.33), or resilvered, but the modern use of a clear varnish rather than of a coloured lacquer means that such frames lack the appearance of gilding which was often intended. It is difficult to find silvered frames in anything resembling their original condition, but a rare surviving set of Elizabethan portraits at Parham House, Sussex, reframed in the late seventeenth century, retain their carved and silvered 'Lely' panel frames.[45]

Silvering was undoubtedly cheaper than gilding for the silver leaf cost so much less.[46] While silver has been called 'the poor man's gold',[47] it was used for lacquered frames in the best circles. When Samuel Pepys gave a portrait by Kneller to Oxford University in 1702 he wrote that he had done his best towards it, adding,

Nor lett its comeing in a lackered frame lead you to thinke otherwise ... But I was ledd to it by the advice of Sir G. Kneller's owne man, in consideration of its first luster being nothing inferiour to that of gold, and its being for ever kept soe (when time shall tarnish it) at the twentieth part of the charge and trouble that gold will. An observation confirmed by 40 yeares experience of my owne.[48]

By 1758 the practise of lacquering silvered frames to give them the effect of gilding was described by Dossie as 'now greatly disused'.[49]

Working in the gesso

Early descriptions of the gilding process make it clear that much of the surface detail of the frame could be worked in the gesso, or whiting, thus restoring the intricacies of the carving obscured by successive coats of gesso. 'In the next place, with an instrument called a Gouge, no broader than a straw, open the veins of the Carved work, which your Whiting has choakt and stopt up', wrote Stalker and Parker in 1688.[50] Late seventeenth-century frames such as that on Kneller's portrait of Dryden (fig.33) were treated in this way. Rather different in effect is the unusual frame on the William Shenstone portrait of 1738 (fig.25) where almost all the ornament is worked in the gesso: punching, cross hatching and modelled patterns.

By the mid-eighteenth century, following the French example, this process had been taken much further so that some carvers relied on retooling in the gesso for much of their effect. R. Campbell in *The London Tradesman* in 1747 went so far as to say,

'*There are two Sorts of Carving upon these Kinds of Frames: One Sort of them is carving in the Wood entirely, ... In the other, the Figures are first roughly cut out in the wood, then the whole is covered with two or three coats of Whiting, to the Thickness of a Quarter of an Inch; when this is dry, the Carver wets the Whiting with a Brush, then finishes his Figures, by making such Flourishes in the Whiting as is agreeable to his Pattern*'.[51]

The magnificent frame on Thomas Hudson's 1756 portrait of Handel is worked in this way (fig.26) but the gesso is more like a one-sixteenth of an inch thick than Campbell's overestimate of a quarter of an inch.

The French word used to describe work done according to this process, *reparé*, might accurately be translated into English as retooled or finished in the gesso, but French *immigrés* working in London sometimes rendered it in English as 'repaired' which is potentially misleading. The bills of the Huguenot carver, Paul Petit, contain entries of this kind. In 1739 with Henry Joris he charged the Prince of Wales £160 for 'a Picture Frame Carved in ye Grandest Manner with boys and Roman Eutropheus Richly Ornamented Neatly repair'd and gilt in Burnish gold' and in 1740 £70.10s for 'two very large picture frames Carved with ye Coronet and Crest Richly Ornamented Neatly repair'd & gilt in oyl gold'.[52] Such frames could be finished in either burnished water gilding or oil gilding.

Papier-mâché

As early as 1671 the scientist Robert Boyle had drawn attention to the use of papier-mâché in picture framing, 'Though Paper be one of the commonest Bodies that we use, yet there are very few that imagine it is fit to be imployed otherwaies than about Writing, or Printing, ... without dreaming that Frames for Pictures and divers fine pieces of Emboss'd work ... may ... be made of it.'[53] Boyle went on to give a description of the manufacture of papier-mâché and the pressing of ornament in papier-mâché and specified that it could be finished in gold or silver leaf.

In the seventeenth century papier-mâché was only occasionally used in picture framing and even then was generally limited to pressed ornaments of the sort one finds on one of the portraits in the National Portrait Gallery (see fig.27). It was not until the mid-eighteenth century that papier-mâché came into its own in frame-making and interiors.[54] In 1751 Lady Luxborough explained the process, which was evidently still a novelty, to her friend William Shenstone:

I am assured that the paper carvings are quite as beautiful, and more durable, than either wood or stucco; and for ceilings infinitely preferable .... They adorn chimnies and indeed whole rooms with them, and make picture-frames of them. The paper is boiled to mash and pounded a vast while, then it is put into moulds of any form. ...[55]

A much more detailed explanation is given by Robert Dossie in *The Handmaid to the Arts* in 1758.

The carver and gilder, Duffour, probably Joseph Duffour (see fig.28), advertised himself as the 'Original Maker of Papie Máchie', and already by 1749 he was called by Mrs Delany 'the famous man for paper ornaments like stucco'.[56] Another supplier, Peter Babel, is described in Mortimer's *Universal Director* of 1763 as 'One of the first Improvers of Papier Mache Ornaments for Ceilings, Chimney-pieces, Picture-frames,

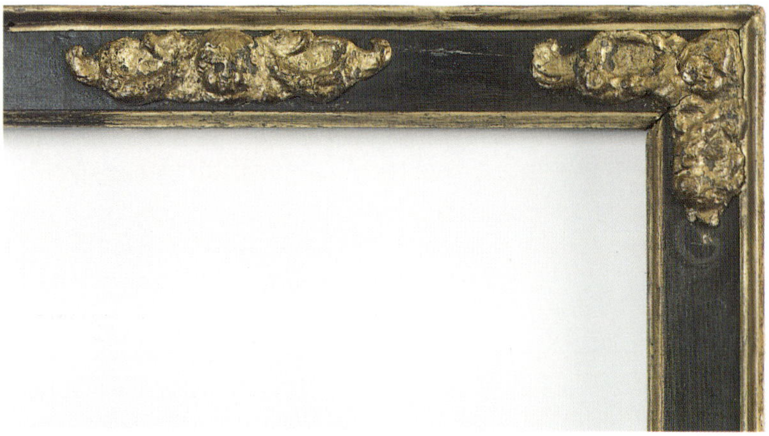

Fig.27
Unknown woman, called Elizabeth, Princess Palatine by an unknown artist (detail of frame only), *c.*1630 (no.9).

The papier-mâché ornament was pressed in moulds and then gilded.

Fig.28 (right)
Trade card of Duffour, probably Joseph Duffour, carver and gilder, and supplier of papier-mâché, *c.*1750–65.

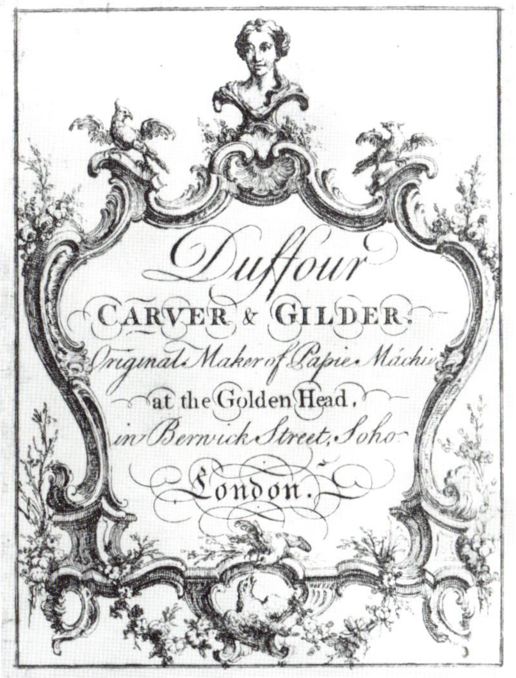

Fig.29 (far right)
William Romaine by Francis Cotes (detail), 1758 (no.38).

Damaged papier-mâché ornament on a wooden frame.

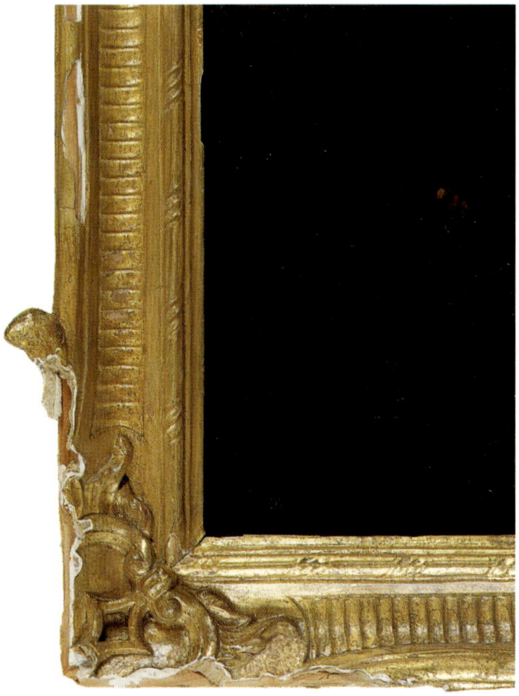

&c. an invention of modern date, imported by us from France, and now brought to great perfection'.[57] That the invention was closely associated with France is confirmed by the frontispiece of Thomas Johnson's engraved book of designs of 1758, dedicated to the Grand-President of the Anti-Gallican Association, which incorporates a cherub setting fire to a scroll inscribed *French Paper Machee*.[58] Even top-of-the-market firms such as Linnell and Chippendale supplied some decorative ornament and borders in papier-mâché. The relative cheapness of papier-mâché undercut the market for carved work, prompting one Bath carver and gilder, Thomas Smith, to advertise in 1761: 'He engages to perform in Wood any Sort of Papier Machée Ornaments, and at the same Price'.[59]

Surviving frames in papier-mâché are few perhaps because they were easily damaged, as one of the few examples in the National Portrait Gallery's collection demonstrates (see fig.29). It is said that looking-glass frames in papier-mâché are difficult to tell,[60] but a papier-mâché picture frame is usually recognisable by its appearance. While the frames can be quite three-dimensional and richly ornamented, the detailing tends to be rather heavy, lacking the freedom of a carved frame, and the parts can seem rather out of proportion one to another, especially when a rococo corner detail suitable for a three-quarter length portrait is applied to the much smaller frame of a half-length.[61] The papier-mâché detail, once it had been stamped out, was laid onto a wooden framework so that the use of papier-mâché may not now be obvious from behind.

It is no coincidence that the heyday of papier-mâché in the eighteenth century was the period from 1740 to 1770, coinciding with the ascendancy of the rococo. Papier-mâché was very convenient for reproducing the intricacies of the rococo style and competed keenly on price if not on quality. Although it continued to be used for architectural ornament, papier-mâché did not prosper in the Robert Adam era later in the century as a material for picture frames. It was not until the mid-nineteenth century that papier-mâché came into its own again.

Composition frames

If the use of papier-mâché forms an interesting footnote in the history of framemaking, the introduction of compo, a composition of glue and

Fig.30
Captain Sherard Osborn by Stephen Pearce (frame only), *c.*1857.

A compo frame before restoration; the white compo and the pine base are visible in areas of old losses.

whiting or plaster, revolutionised the framing of pictures. Not only did its use change the appearance of frames, it also killed off the carved frame which had been the dominant form for more than 150 years. Compo was said to be at least eighty per cent cheaper than carving.[62] Within a generation of its introduction in the late eighteenth century, Thomas Martin could write, 'There are only eleven master carvers in London, and about sixty journeymen (though at one time there were six hundred), many of the latter are now very old. … Of about 150 persons, who call themselves carvers and gilders, the greatest number are gilders only … [many] never saw a carving tool in their lives'.[63]

The use of made-up materials such as compo was hardly new. In Italy mixtures of sawdust and glue had been used in castings for frames as early as the fifteenth century and *pastiglia* (paste work) was a feature of many frames,[64] while in England a recipe for a paste of glue and whiting, 'fit to mould or raise Carved work on Frames for Guilding', appeared in Stalker and Parker's *Treatise of Japaning and Varnishing* in 1688.[65]

Compo began to be used extensively in picture framing in the late eighteenth century. An early reference in the Hatfield House accounts in 1781 refers to 'A very large size picture frame, enricht with composition mouldings, and gilt in burnisht gold compleat, containing $23\frac{1}{4}$ feet' at £8.12s'.[66] The essential difference between compo and the various mixtures of gesso, paste or whiting which had long been popular was the use of considerable quantities of glue and resin. Linseed oil was another standard ingredient. No more whiting was added to the hot mixture than was necessary to make a stiff dough. Owing to its flexible nature, while still warm compo could be moulded to the profile of a picture frame. Once it had cooled and set firm it could be gilded in much the same way as gesso.

The introduction of compo is sometimes associated with Liardet's cement, an oil-based stucco patented by John Liardet in 1773 and used by Robert Adam and his brothers for external work, but this stucco was quite different to the paste compo used in picture framing.[67] Various other patents for oil- and water-based stuccos and cements were taken out between 1765 and 1796 but none of these has yet been identified with compo.[68]

The heyday of the compo frame was the nineteenth century. The use of compo had a considerable impact on frame design. Its relative cheapness allowed for larger, more richly ornamented frames, and encouraged the development of the taste for elaborate swept frames and for ornamenting surfaces with a maze of small-scale compo ornamental scrolls and leaves.

Compo could be made up according to one of the many recipes or, in London at least, by the early nineteenth century it could be bought ready-made 'soft from the press'.[69] It was especially appropriate for use on frames, as nineteenth-century handbooks explained: 'The composition ornament … is exceedingly pliant and supple, and may be bent into almost any form without breaking or injuring it; it is this property which makes these ornaments so convenient; as they may be applied to the round, the flat, or the hollow parts of a frame, with almost equal ease'.[70] Compo came to be used very widely by gilders and framemakers but they

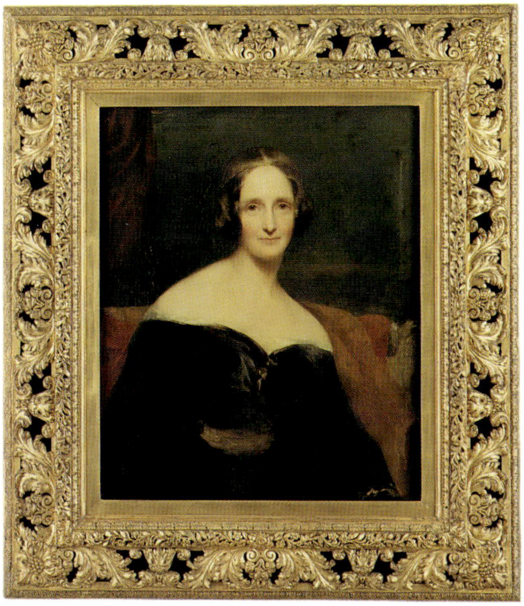

Fig.31 (right)
Mary Shelley by Richard Rothwell, exhibited 1840 (no.68).

A papier-mâché frame made by C.F. Bielefeld, the ornament applied to a wooden framework; the frame is slightly later than the picture.

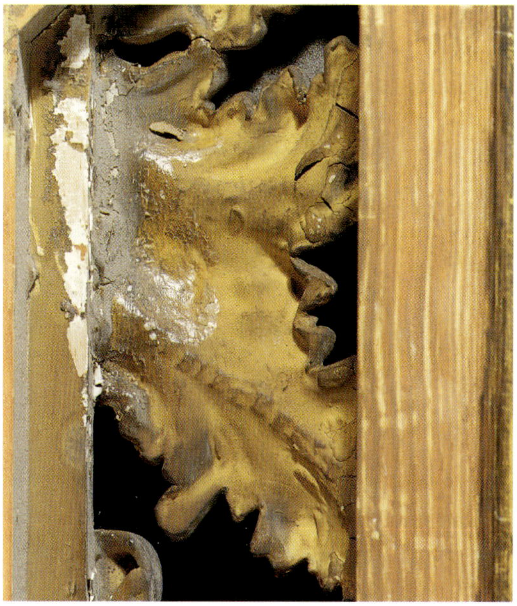

Fig.32 (far right)
Detail of the back of the frame showing C.F. Bielefeld's stamp as impressed in the papier-mâché.

depended on the superior skills of the carvers who cut the finely detailed boxwood moulds which were used for pressing and producing the compo ornament. It was possible to purchase made-up twelve-foot lengths of frame mouldings in compo, produced in factories and supplied by frame wholesalers, which only required cutting to size, fitting together and finishing to meet the needs of the cheaper end of the considerable market for frames in Victorian Britain.[71]

Whatever the cost advantages of compo, its fragility was a failing (see fig.30). 'A very slight shock', wrote Philip Hamerton in 1871 of the ornaments used on frames, 'is sufficient to break them off, for the paste becomes exceedingly brittle with time; and if there is any extra heat – as, for instance, if you hang a picture near a chimneypiece – the mouldings are apt to curl up and detach themselves without the help of any shock whatever'.[72] Sending compo frames to exhibitions was a real problem: 'Those who suffer most from the extreme perishableness of the frames commonly in use are the ordinary crowd of artists, whose pictures are frequently refused at the exhibitions, and are sent from one exhibition to another. ... The frames of pictures declined at the Academy are *always* damaged ... '.[73]

Even the best compo frames are liable to shrinkage when the compo dries out, as can be recognised from the fine cracks in the ornament, but well-made compo frames, if treated with respect, have proved extremely durable.

Papier-mâché in the nineteenth century

'Bielefeld's Improved Papier Mâché Picture Frames ... to be had at the Works, 15, Wellington St North, Strand', advertised Charles Frederick Bielefeld in 1840.[74] In the nineteenth century technical advances allowed papier-mâché to be used much more widely in furniture and architectural decoration. It was employed for the throne canopy in the House of Lords, for the laurel-leaf friezes in galleries at the British Museum and even for a prefabricated patent waterproof papier-mâché village of ten houses exported to Australia.[75] Papier-mâché was used by Jennens & Bettridge and other Birmingham firms for a wide range of small articles such as trays, tea-caddies and letter-racks, but also for chairs and even beds and wardrobes, usually 'japanned' to give a deep black finish which could be painted or inlaid with mother-of-pearl.[76]

In picture framing there can be no doubt that Bielefeld was the leader. He went into business with a Mr Haselden in the 1830s but soon

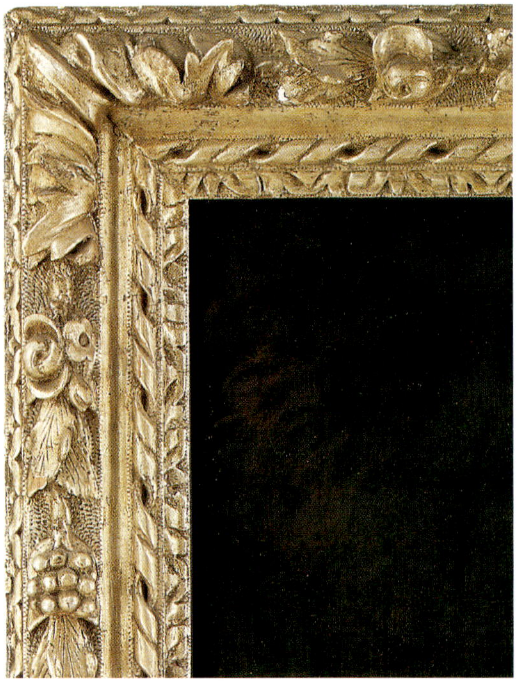

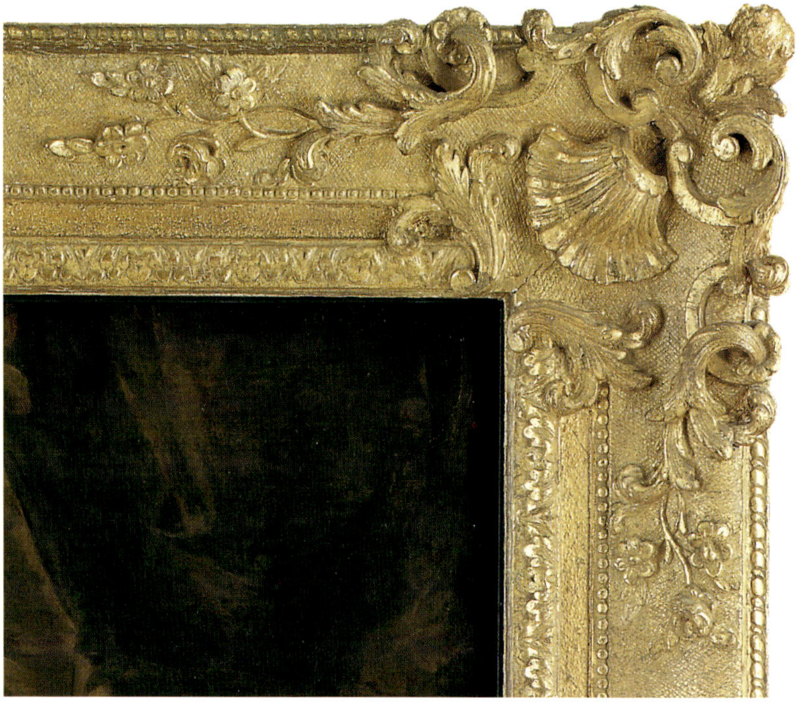

Fig.33 (above left) *John Dryden* by Sir Godfrey Kneller (detail), 1693 (no.19).

The zig-zag scored lines, or hazzle, enliven the flat surface beneath the carved leaves.

Fig.34 (above right) *A Club of Artists* by Gawen Hamilton (detail), 1735 (no.30).

The corners and the curved sides are cross-hatched. The narrow flat band next to the sight edge is sanded.

went his own way, setting up his new papier-mâché works, built to the design of Sydney Smirke, in Wellington Street, London, in 1839 (smoke from the works brought objections from local residents who also complained about the 'hordes of vagabond boys' employed there).[77] Always a good publicist for his work, Bielefeld benefited from a series of articles and promotional puffs in the *Art Union*, *The Builder* and the *Illustrated London News* in the 1840s and early 1850s, and issued several illustrated catalogues of his papier-mâché ornament and furniture.[78] At one stage he employed a workforce of not less than one hundred.[79] But his success was short-lived: he was bankrupt by 1861 and died in 1864, though his business continued in other hands until the mid-1870s.

As Bielefeld's catalogues show, his frames were assembled from pressed parts which were priced individually so that a frame like that on the portrait of Mary Shelley (fig.31) was made up from seven different elements. The large leaves are stamped with the words 'CF BIELEFELD LONDON' (fig.32). Though this frame was built on an open framework, others are much closer to contemporary compo frames in appearance. It was claimed in the *Art Union* in 1842 that papier-mâché frames had several advantages over compo, apart from appearance: 'they are cheaper: being about two-thirds of the cost ... ; next, they will not "chip" in carriage; and next they are so much lighter in weight ... '.[80] Despite Bielefeld's claims, there was some feeling that papier-mâché did not form such a good foundation for gilding as wood or composition, nor did it retain a firm hold of nails or screws.[81] For whatever reason, the use of papier-mâché in framemaking did not prosper beyond the 1860s.

Surface effects

Over the centuries various techniques have been used to animate flat areas on gilt frames. Scoring, punching and sanding were methods popular in the seventeenth and eighteenth centuries. A hazzle, that is a zig-zag scored line, is often found on the flat areas of late seventeenth-century frames (see, for example figs.33, 129), and a more methodically applied cross-hatched ground can be seen on some mid-eighteenth century frames such as that on *A Club of Artists* (fig.34). A technique found on much gilt furniture of the Queen Anne period, the use of a small circular ring

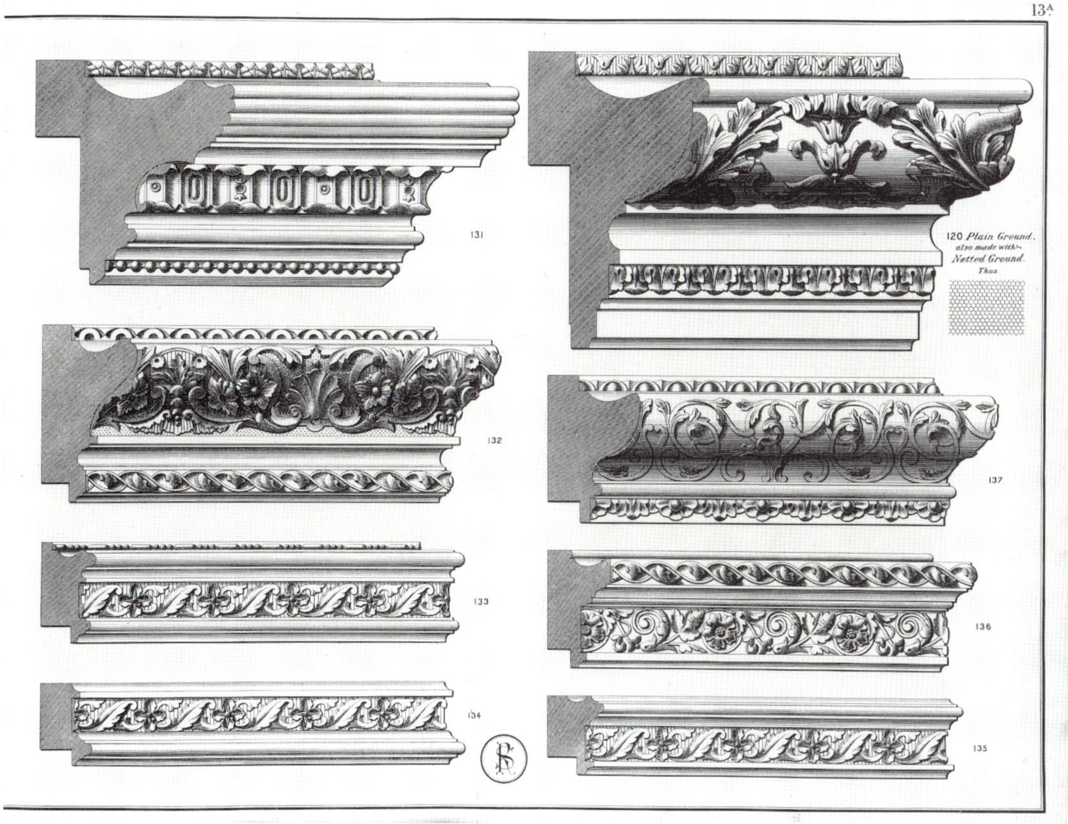

Fig.35
Frame mouldings including a detail of a 'netted ground', illustrated in the trade catalogue of 'RS', an unidentified London framemaker working in the 1880s (Royal Commission on the Ancient and Historical Monuments of Scotland).

punch, pressed into the gesso after gilding to create a random pattern of tiny circles in the background to the carving, is found on running pattern and other frames of the period (see fig.25). In the 1720s the use of a sanded ground became common, achieved by laying sand, fine or coarse, onto a prepared sized surface before gessoing and gilding; this is primarily a technique used on picture and mirror frames and in particular frames in the William Kent style, such as the Kit-cat portrait of Jacob Tonson (fig.133).

In the nineteenth century the introduction of compo brought occasional complaints about the harsh effect of gilding on plain plaster. It is not surprising, then, to find the techniques of the eighteenth century revived. Scoring was frequently used to lend life to the surfaces on which compo ornament was laid, usually by means of a fine regular cross-hatched network of incised lines, easily applied while the whiting was still freshly laid. Another traditional method occasionally employed was the use of a punch to decorate and animate plain background areas. Thomas

Fig.36
Edmund Lyons, 1st Baron Lyons by George Frederic Watts (detail), 1856-7.

Woodgrain as a decorative feature, achieved by gilding directly on to a flat oak surface.

Phillips evidently favoured this approach for the wide curving surfaces of his frames of the 1820s and 1830s (see no.64), though the detail of the wide shallow punching he favoured, so different from work of the previous century, is readily obscured by later regilding. A complete innovation was the application of a fine hexagonal mesh, or netted ground, to the surface of the whiting before setting (see fig.35).[82] The mesh seems to have been cut slightly larger than the area to be decorated, stretched and then set on the gessoed surface after which the edges would be trimmed. Once it was dry it could be gilded in the usual way.

The reaction against compo frames, signalled by the Pre-Raphaelites, brought a renewed interest in surface effects. Gilding directly on to the wood, at first oak (see fig.36), but later deal and other timbers, became an essential feature of many frames. As Charles Eastlake wrote, 'The effect of oak-grain seen through leaf-gold is exceedingly good, and the appearance of *texture* thus produced is infinitely more interesting than the smooth monotony of gilt "compo"'.[83] By the 1880s Rough Deals, as they were called, in the form of roughly cut cheap timber which was then gilded, began to appear in commercial framing catalogues (see fig.37).[84] The experiments in this direction by the Scottish Impressionist, Arthur Melville, were roundly condemned by one critic in 1883: 'if he cannot electrify you with his picture he will at least strive to transfix you with the frame which seems to be composed of four stray railway sleepers, caught wild, mitred, stained black and clamped together'.[85]

Although gilding remained the normal finish for picture frames, at least until after 1900, there was a greater willingness to consider other approaches for economy or for effect. In 1841 David Ramsay Hay, one of the leading Edinburgh decorators and framemakers, submitted a quotation to the Royal Scottish Academy for supplying a frame at £7.10s in lacquer or Japan, £10.15s in gold powder or bronze and £14 in real gold leaf, and he was then asked to estimate for using Dutch Metal.[86] Dutch Metal and Schlag leaf are types of foil usually made of copper alloyed with zinc, a cheap substitute for gilding which was liable to turn green through corrosion unless varnished. At the top end of the market the cushion frame on Herkomer's portrait of Robert Baden-Powell demonstrates how successfully a copper leaf of this kind can be used to create a rich effect (fig.114). There was also a whole range of frames, categorised as 'German Mouldings', which were 'used for common work, and for those whose means will not allow them to order gold frames'.[87] These were silvered and lacquered to look like gold, or sometimes finished in imitation rosewood, oak or mahogany and were known for their cheapness. By the early years of the twentieth century a wide range of finishes were being used commercially: old gold, antique gold, bronze gilt, green and gilt, green bronzed, green ivory tipped, imitation walnut, walnut and gilt are all descriptions from H. Morell's 1910 catalogue, though some of these may have been used for drawings or prints rather than for paintings.[88]

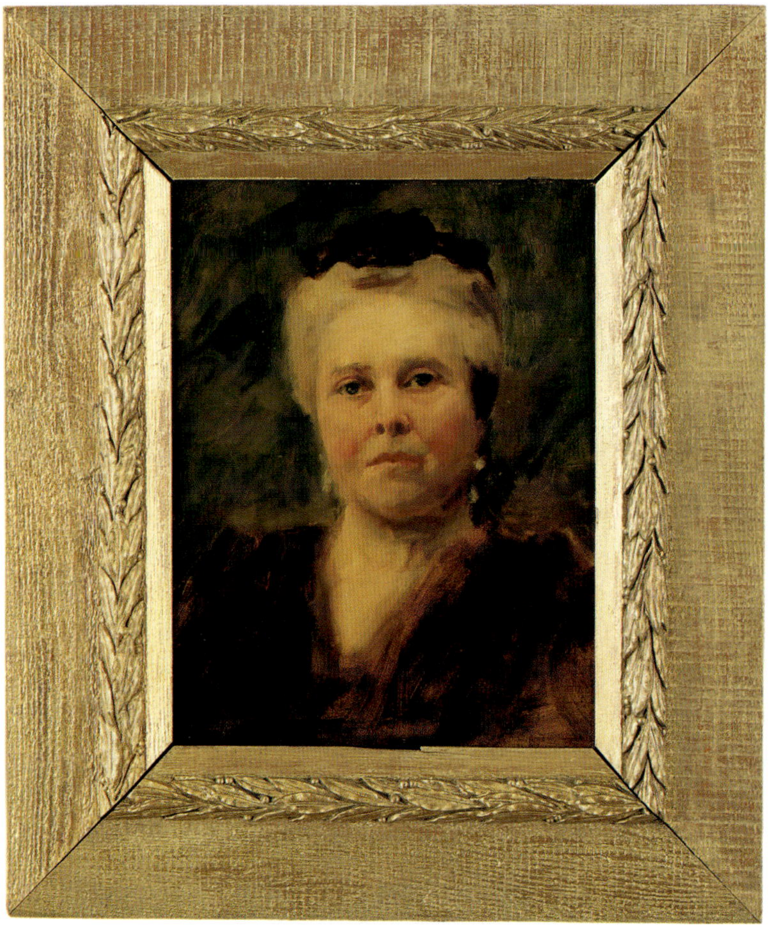

Fig.37
Victoria, Princess Royal
by Joseph Mordecai,
*c.*1900 or later (no.96).

Roughly cut timber, known as Rough Deals, finished in imitation gold leaf for decorative effect.

Fig.38
Sir John Summerson by Leonard Rosoman (detail), 1984 (no.127).

Overlap in the oxidized silver leaf treated as a decorative feature.

The twentieth century

Even before the Royal Academy relaxed its insistence on gilt frames in 1920, a range of plain and painted frames was being tried elsewhere for effect. Polished or stained wood frames of dark colour had been allowed at the Paris Salon since 1884 and frames of this type were used in London by artists such as William Nicholson in the early 1900s. White frames also became popular in the 1910s in the hands of Augustus John, C.R.W. Nevinson and other artists of the new generation, as has already been mentioned. These innovations led on to experiments with painted and textured surfaces, whether brushed, glazed, rubbed or 'antiqued'.

In the 1930s the use of canvas flats or slips between the frame and the picture became common. Alfred Stiles & Sons Ltd worked for many leading artists and their records are revealing: Ivon Hitchens had frames supplied in 1936 and 1937 with grey canvas and unbleached calico flats, John Piper had frames with 'no.6 linen flats' in 1939 and Graham Sutherland a 'green velvet flat to show 3/4″' the same year.[89] But when Harold Speed suggested a frame with a canvas flat to the National Portrait Gallery in 1942 for his portrait of Lord Grey of Falloden, claiming that it would give 'a light silvery tone that I feel very much improves the colour (particularly the darks) of a picture – takes the stuffiness out of it', his approach was rejected in favour of something more traditional.

A post-war innovation, probably dating to the 1950s in the work of framemakers like Alfred Hecht, who made frames for both Graham Sutherland and Francis Bacon, has been the use of gold leaf and other metal leaf finishes in a decorative manner. Sutherland's portrait of Kenneth Clark of 1963-4 uses burnished gold, allowing the leaf overlap to be seen and the dark ground to show through (see fig.22), Leonard Rosoman's full-length portrait of Sir John Summerson of 1984 (fig.38) and Maggi Hambling's head of A.J.P. Taylor (no.131) have frames in oxidised silver leaf. Other metal leaves which have been used to effect include palladium, platinum and aluminium.

Over the past thirty or forty years approaches to framemaking have continued to develop. Metal frames such as the welded-corner aluminium frame created by Robert Kulicke for the Museum of Modern Art, New York, in 1960 have come into fashion and gone out again.[90] Hardwoods such as ramin from Indonesia and Malaysia, and obeche from West Africa, have found favour for commercial framing, since they have a fine grain that can readily be worked and which lends itself to a variety of surface finishes. However, much of the best work continues to be done in traditional woods such as oak, ash, cherry and pine, depending on current fashion and availability. The range of materials and techniques now in use undoubtedly is wider and more varied than ever before.

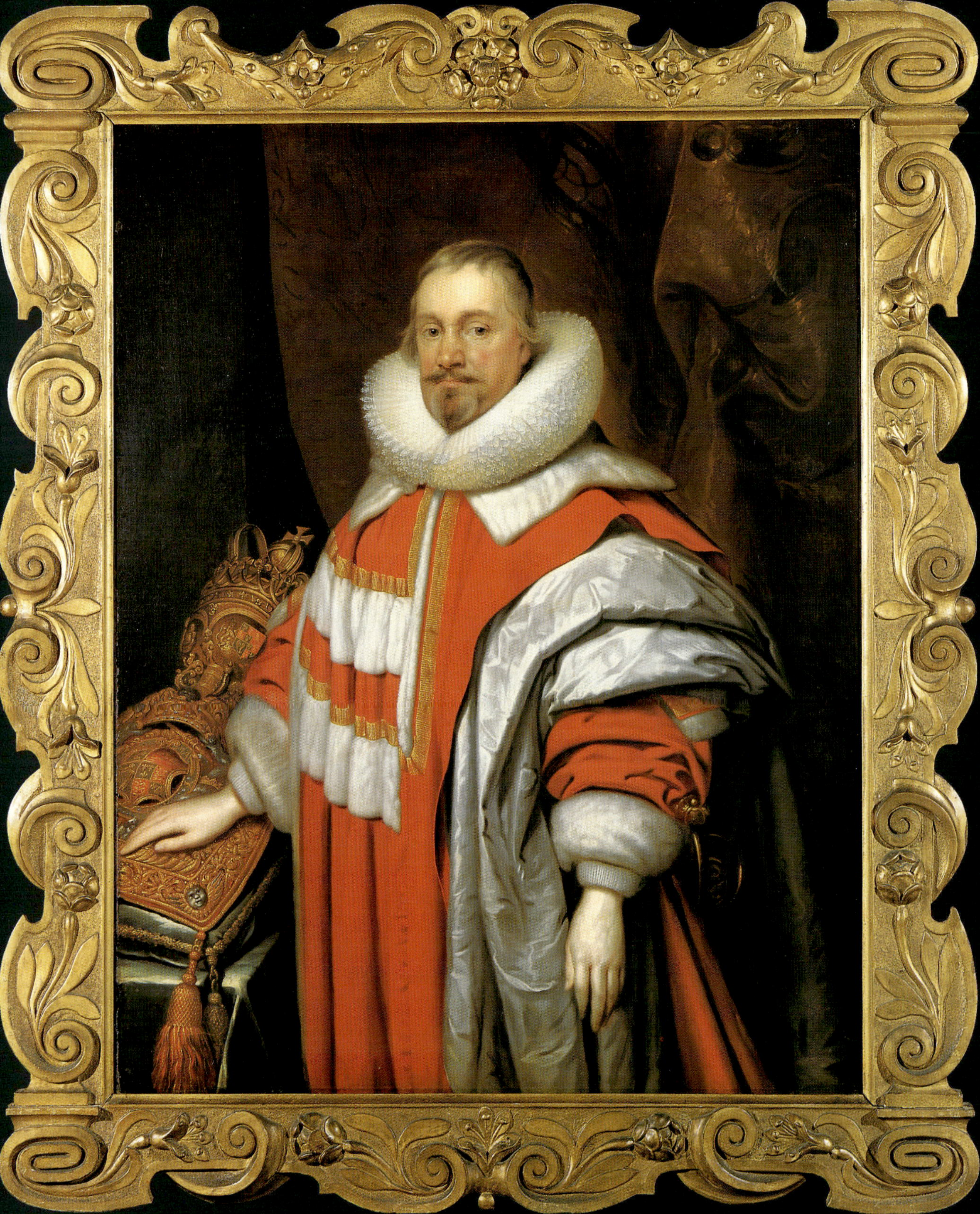

Chapter 3
The Development of the Picture Frame

Fig. 39 (facing page) *Thomas Coventry, 1st Baron Coventry* by Cornelius Johnson, 1639 (no.6).

A carved and gilded frame in the Italianate manner popular in the 1630s.

Over the last five hundred years picture frames have gone through some remarkable changes in style. Frame styles are dictated by taste and fashion rather than function; they sometimes reflect architectural taste closely, notably in the cases of Palladian, or Kent, and neo-classical frames, but also draw on other sources. Others are more decorative – the leaf and foliage pattern frames of the late seventeenth and early eighteenth centuries, the rococo and some nineteenth-century frames; these may relate to contemporary interiors in their ornamentation without being strictly architectural in character. A few frame styles are non-architectural, most obviously the Sunderland frames of the seventeenth century with their fantastic organic forms.

The main frame types have as a rule each remained in use for forty or fifty years before going out of fashion. At any one time, at least during the ascendancy of the carved and gilded frame in the seventeenth and eighteenth centuries, three or four styles were usually current. There were perhaps four new types each century, but a style once introduced was sometimes elaborated into richer forms before being abandoned, and, as a result of these changes in decoration, a single frame style can often be found in several different guises. Whatever the changes in style, however, the underlying frame profiles were slower to change, as the sections illustrated in figs.180-97 show.

Tudor frames

In the sixteenth century ownership of paintings was restricted to the most wealthy. Interiors were often richly decorated, either panelled or adorned with fabric or tapestry. Moveable pictures had their part to play as important decorative features in certain areas, most commonly in galleries,[1] but with their simple frames, often painted black, they made a much less significant contribution to the overall scheme of things than did the splendid paintings with richly carved and gilt frames in the collections of the next century.

In their use of materials, notably oak, and in constructional techniques, Tudor picture frames can be related to contemporary panelled interiors and to what furniture of the period survives, although in form and function, of course, the picture frame is different. In form the frame has a slightly raised inner moulding bordering the picture, a flat frieze or panel in the middle, and a prominent stepped outer moulding next to the wall. In function the frame is a container for the picture – hence the description 'box frame' or the Italian word for this frame type, *cassetta*, meaning a box or case. The frame serves to protect and isolate the picture from the outer world. The type is traditional, international, and entirely appropriate to its purpose.[2]

To what extent was a frame in the sixteenth century intended to go beyond its function in protecting the picture and to serve as a showpiece? At the time if the frame is described at all in inventories or bills it is usually simply as wood, wainscot (i.e. oak) or painted. A frame of 'woode all gilt about the border' and another 'black ... parcell gilt' (i.e. partly gilt) were in the Earl of Leicester's collection at Leicester House at his death in 1588.[3] The few references in Henry VIII's inventories to elaborate frames of 'black ebonet [i.e. ebony] garnished with silver' and 'wood gilt with burnished golde' do not allude to picture frames at all but to embossed velvet or sculpted images.[4] Many pictures were kept covered by curtains, as we have seen in Chapter 1, so that in collections such as that of Henry VIII, where most of the pictures had white and yellow or green and yellow silk paned curtains, it must have been the curtains rather than the

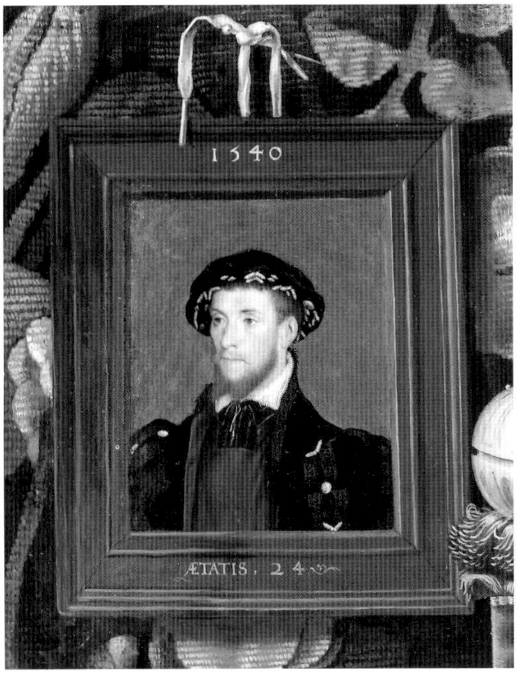

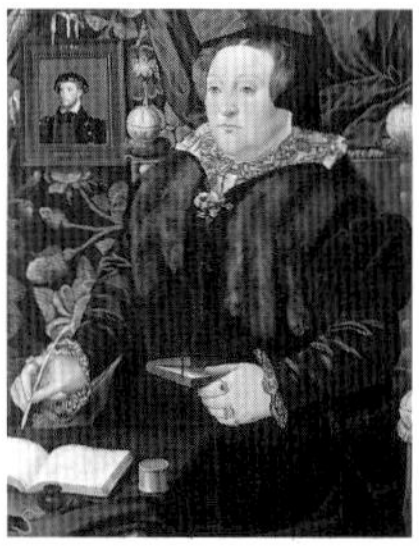

Fig.40 (detail, left; whole image above) *Thomas Fiennes, 9th Baron Dacre*, detail from the portrait of *Mary Neville, Baroness Dacre* by Hans Eworth, *c.*1555 (National Gallery of Canada, Ottawa).

The portrait of Baron Dacre bears the date 1540 and is hung in the manner of the time by a ribbon in the top of the frame.

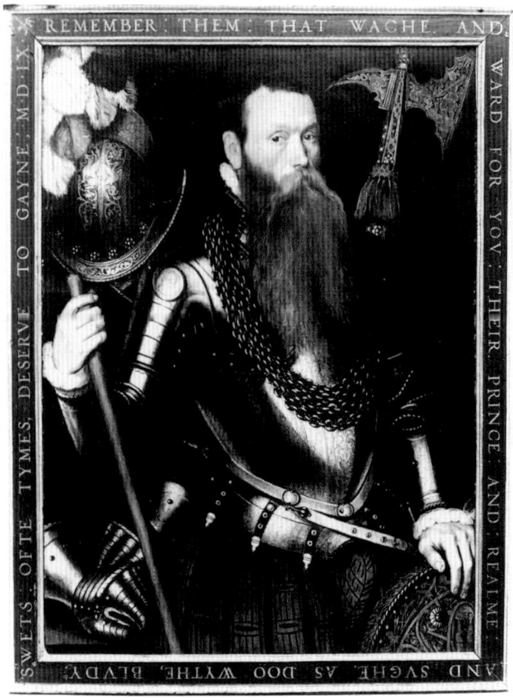

Fig.41 (below left) *A Gentleman, traditionally called Vaughan of Tretower*, Netherlandish School, 1560 (Edward Harley Esq.)

This detail shows the original inscribed frame, but not the outer moulding added later.

frames which attracted attention. Judging from surviving frames (see nos.2-3) and from contemporary visual evidence, pictures were generally hung by a cord or ribbon strung through paired holes in the centre top of the frame (see fig.40).

There were, however, two types of picture frame which must have been intended for show: those which were painted or marbled in rich colours and those which were prominently inscribed with lettering round the frame. Painted frames are known from contemporary descriptions but most have since been destroyed. Charles I had a set of 'nyne old heades' of early kings and queens from Edward III to Henry VIII in frames all painted red and gilded with the exception of one which was painted blue.[5] He also owned a portrait of Henry VII with a frame of black and green. A portrait of Bishop Foxe at Corpus Christi College, Oxford, was described as having a frame 'of Oak imitated like Porphery or Elitropean (the ground blew but first green)'.[6] Such richly marbled frames are rarely found now but the effect can be guessed at from the decoration of extant Elizabeth church monuments. More common are the frames with elaborate inscriptions running round the frieze either identifying the sitter or propounding a moral text, usually in gold capital letters on a black ground. 'REMEMBER THEM THAT WACHE AND WARD FOR YOV THEIR PRINCE AND REALME AND SVCHE AS DOO WYTHE BLVDY SWETS OFTE TYMES DESERVE TO GAYNE M.D.LX.' reads the inscription round the imposing portrait of a gentleman, traditionally called Vaughan of Tretower, providing a date of 1560 for the portrait, though not identifying the sitter by name (fig.41).[7] Most frames of this type date to the period 1560-1620. It would be satisfying to believe that the very existence of such inscriptions encouraged later owners to retain the frames, however old-fashioned they may have come to seem.

Even after the rise to fashion of carved and gilt frames, black frames of one form or another remained common, though their profiles changed with time. There were many in the collection of Charles I, including waved ebony frames on pictures from Germany.[8] Frames made from ebony, a tropical hardwood imported into Europe, were expensive owing to the cost of the veneer, and were generally used for framing precious paintings of small size. The Earl of Northumberland was buying ebony frames regularly during the 1630s and 1650s.[9] In 1678 a description of a 'waving engine' for making ripple frames. Black frames began to go out of fashion in the seventeenth century, but survived well into the eighteenth century. As late as 1762 Joseph Wright of Derby was supplying his provincial customers with 'Black & Gold' frames.[12]

The age of Charles I

When Rubens visited England in 1629 he said he had 'never seen such a quantity of pictures by great masters as in the palace of the King of England and in the gallery of the late Duke of Buckingham'.[13] Since the early 1610s English connoisseurs had been actively acquiring old master paintings abroad. In a life of Titian published in Venice in 1622 the five key players were identified as Prince Charles, the Duke of Buckingham, the Marquis of Hamilton and the Earls of Pembroke and Arundel.[14] Some of the pictures collected abroad came with frames while others were framed in London. In the case of the Royal Collection, with the accession of Charles as king in 1625 the emphasis of the King's Works, the organisation responsible for carrying out building and related work for the king, changed dramatically from outdoor works to indoor schemes, including painting interiors, making pedestals for sculpture and, notably, the carving and decorating of picture frames.[15] From 1628 to 1639, the last year of the Works accounts before the dispersal of the court, elaborate carved and gilded picture frames made numerous demands on the royal purse.[16]

During Charles I's reign, London was very open to continental artistic influences, particularly by way of the Low Countries. Painters working in England such as Cornelius Johnson, Daniel Mytens and Van Dyck had extensive knowledge of what was happening on the Continent. Agents including Balthazar Gerbier and Nicholas Lanier travelled widely there on behalf of the great collectors, acquiring paintings and arranging such picture framing as may have been required either abroad or in London.[17] Those actually involved in producing frames in England had their own continental links. The

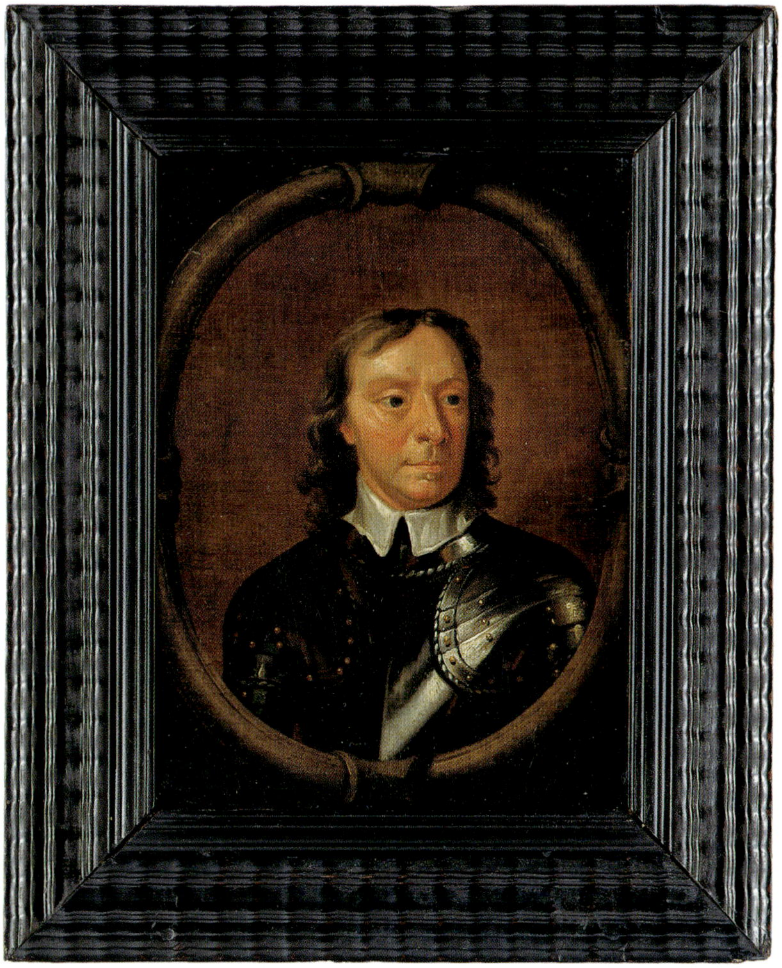

Fig.42
Oliver Cromwell by an unknown artist, perhaps eighteenth century, after Samuel Cooper (no.11).

An ebonised ripple frame probably of the seventeenth century.

mouldings for ebony frames appears in Joseph Moxon's *Mechanick Exercises*.[10] At Ham House the Green Closet to this day retains a mix of pictures not unlike that described in the 1677 inventory: 'Nynteine pictures with guilt frames. Therttie eight of black Abinie frames'.[11] The fashion for ebony led to the use of cheaper fruitwood and softwood frames stained black and polished to look like ebony. The ebonised frame on a portrait of Oliver Cromwell in the National Portrait Gallery, though not original to the picture, shows how such pictures might have been framed (fig.42). Another portrait, formerly identified as the Princess Palatine (fig. 27), has a frame which incorporates an early form of papier-mâché; this material was sometimes used in the mid-seventeenth century for stamping out motifs which were then gilded and applied as decoration to the corners and centres of flat artist and frame supplier, George Geldorp, German by birth but trained in Antwerp, was a close friend of Van Dyck. The Serjeant Painter, John de Critz, who decorated many elaborate frames for the King, sometimes worked closely with his brother-in-law, the Netherlandish sculptor, Maximilian Colt. Two other members of the King's Works, the painter, Matthew Goodrich, and the carver, Zachary Taylor, whose names are often linked in the royal accounts, sometimes acted as sub-contractors to Nicholas Stone, English by birth but trained as a sculptor in Amsterdam.[18] And, of course, Inigo Jones, the influential King's Surveyor, was one of the most widely travelled and cosmopolitan figures at Charles I's court.

The wealth of frames which survive from the 1630s fall into two related groups. Firstly, there were the Italianate frames which were decorated with paired volutes, scrolls, foliage and floral buds. This type reflects an international style of which the Venetian Sansovino frame, named after the sixteenth-century architect Jacopo Sansovino, is the best-known manifestation. In England this style flowered in the 1630s but had no successor. In contrast were the auricular frames of the period which were essentially organic in their ornament and based on stylised animal and marine forms, an English manifestation of the international taste for the auricular style. They are the forerunners of the Sunderland frames of the second half of the century.

In 1621 the Duke of Buckingham's agent, Balthazar Gerbier, arranged for two great frames to be made in Venice 'after the Italian fascion' for Titian's great *Ecce Homo* and Tintoretto's *The Woman Taken in Adultery*.[19] The considerable appeal of Venetian pictures to the English may explain why the Sansovino frame seems to have been particularly influential as a style. Pictures were also being imported from France, Spain and the Low Countries: those offered by Rubens to Sir Dudley Carleton in 1618 were described by him as having gilt frames.[20] But few gilt frames of the period from these countries are known, so that it is difficult to judge how far other continental patterns were of influence in England.

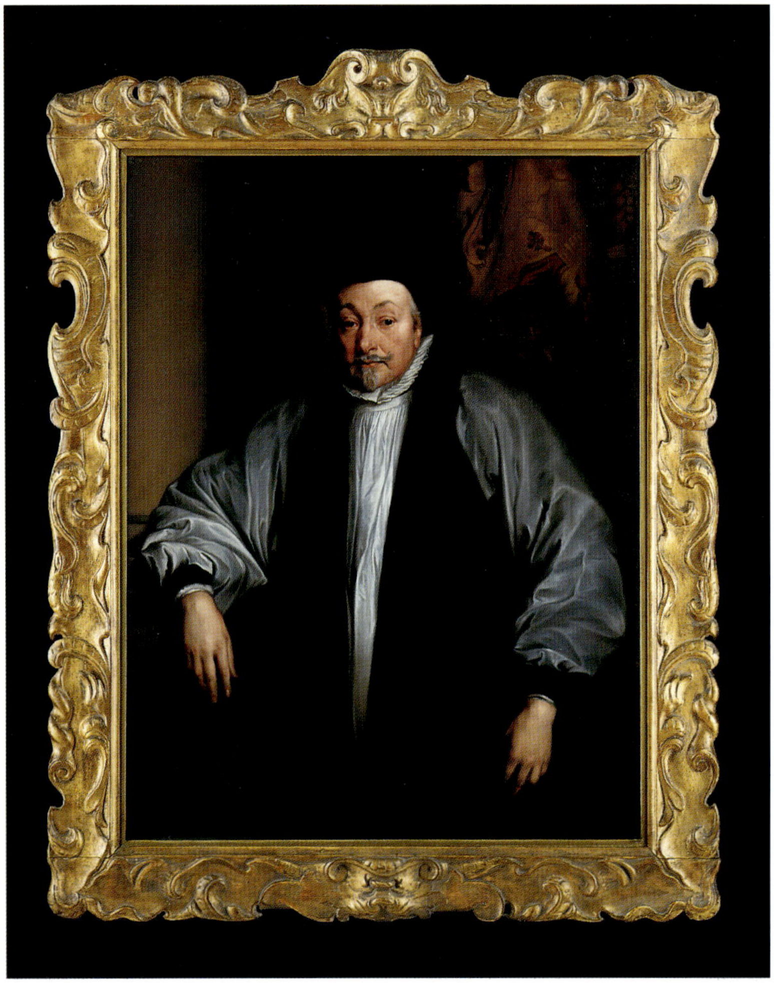

Fig.43
William Laud, after Sir Anthony Van Dyck, *c.*1636 or later (no.12).

An early auricular frame crowned by a stylised lion mask.

The spectacular frame on Cornelius Johnson's 1639 portrait of the Lord Chancellor, Lord Coventry (fig.39), relates closely to the Sansovino frame in its use of curving scrolls which typically are tightly packed as spirals at the corners and paired as volutes at the centres. It differs, however, in the preponderance of stalks, leaves and flowerbuds ornamenting the intervening spaces. This style is found on the Earl of Middlesex's copies of the Raphael Cartoons at Knole which probably date to the late 1620s or 1630s, and it was also apparently used by one of the most active collectors of the period, the Marquis of Hamilton.[21] Another classic pattern of the 1630s, to be found at Knole on the Van Dyck of Lady Frances Cranfield painted shortly before her marriage in 1636, retains the paired volutes of the Sansovino style but otherwise relies for its effect on a harmonious arrangement of waving foliage, meeting at fleur-de-lis shaped corners.[22] This most serene of types is also found on the Van Dyck studio head of Queen Henrietta Maria at Ham House and on other contemporary portraits.[23]

It may seem strange that in the 1630s, at a time when Inigo Jones was embracing the classicism and clarity of Italian renaissance architecture, English patrons should choose to put their pictures into auricular frames, some of the most fantastic and anti-classical frames ever found in Britain. But Jones himself used the auricular style for some decorative details and the style was fashionable internationally and familiar at court through contemporary silver and engravings. At their most extreme these picture frames are organic in the nature and use of their ornament, hence the name 'auricular', or 'of the ear'. Within the diverse range of auricular frames of the period, three distinctive patterns can be found, all probably originating in the 1630s. For ease of reference they are identified here by the differing mask types which usually crown these frames: the lion, the grimacing man and the owl.

There can be little doubt that one of the starting-points for frames of this kind was the idea of an animal skin, as exemplified by the lion mask and paws found in a highly stylised form on the top of frames such as that on the Van Dyck studio portrait of Archbishop Laud of *c.*1636 or later (fig.43). Such features can also be found in rather different form on Italian so-called 'Pitti Palace' frames of the same epoch.[24] The sides of the Laud frame are like a flat skin, the edges of which are irregular and curling. The concept of using an animal skin as a framing device is also found in English portrait engravings of the 1630s, in some contemporary silverware and at a later date in church monuments.[25]

The second auricular frame type of the 1630s and 1640s, with a scroll-topped mask of a grimacing man as the crowning feature, has a monster mask at the bottom, and stylised foliage and other organic ornament liberally applied to the intervening surfaces. It can be found occasionally on the work of Cornelius Johnson, notably the portrait of the Duke of Lauderdale at Ham, and on other contemporary portraits.[26] The frame now on Jacob Huysmans's portrait of Thomas Chiffinch (fig.44), with its motif of paired dolphins at top and bottom, is an unusual variant on the type. More typical is the full-length frame now on Peter Nason's portrait of Oliver St John on loan from the National Portrait Gallery to the British Museum.

Too little is known of contemporary working practices to ascertain whether each of these auricular frame styles originated with a particular workshop or artist. Examples of the third type, characterised by an owl-like crowning mask and eagle heads and wings on the frame sides are found on the portrait of Lord Edward Fitzgerald, on loan to the National Portrait Gallery, and at Claydon House, Knole and in the Tradescant Collection in the Ashmolean Museum, Oxford.[27]

The outbreak of the Civil War in 1642 led to

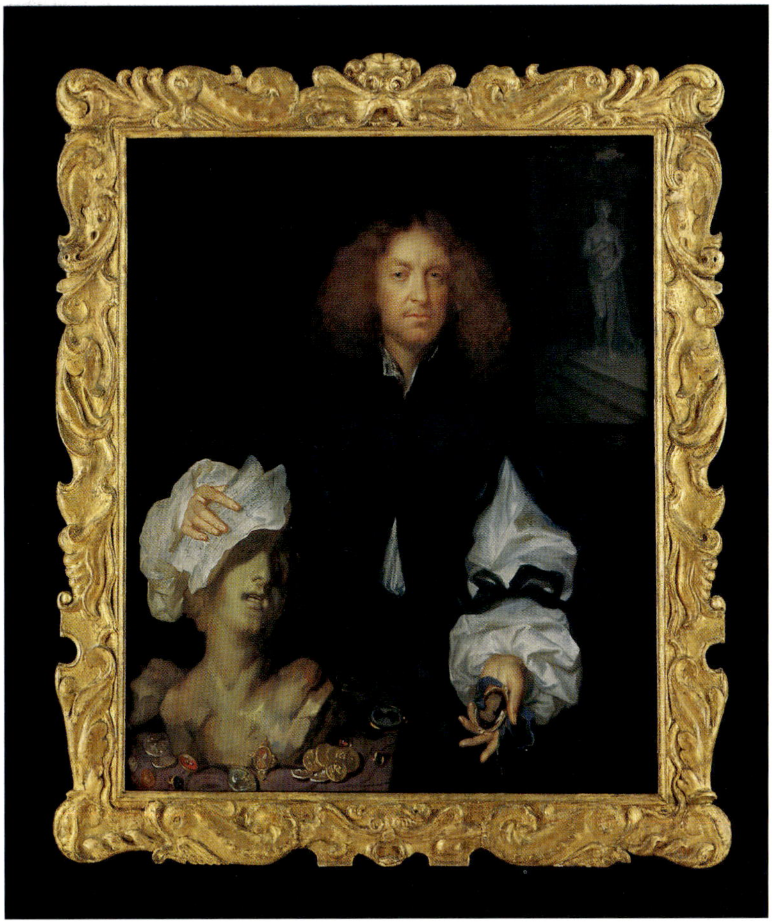

Fig.44
Thomas Chiffinch by Jacob Huysmans, *c.*1655-60 (no.14).

An unusual early auricular frame, altered to fit the picture.

the dispersal of the great English collections, and many works were acquired by collectors on the Continent. Another consequence of civil war was that some of the finest artists of the period chose to look abroad for patronage. In England, these momentous changes brought about the destruction of the culture built up by Charles I and his court. There was also an impact abroad which went rather further than the obvious enrichment of a few great collections. Many of the Marquis of Hamilton's pictures ended up in the Archduke Leopold Wilhelm's gallery in Brussels, for example, and the frame on one of Hamilton's old masters, almost certainly an English frame, was thought sufficiently remarkable by the Archduke's court painter David Teniers to be given a place of great prominence in his view of the Archduke's collection in 1651.[28] It was not only pictures which left the country, however. Cornelius Johnson, one of the leading portrait painters in London, moved to Holland in 1643. His portraits of Jasper Schade and his wife of 1654 are among the earliest works known to have been framed in Holland in the auricular style; though the carving is more fluid than the frames in this style on Johnson's English portraits of the 1630s, the language is essentially similar.[29] The significance of such links remains to be determined but the idea that it was Dutch frames of this sort which formed the starting-point for English Sunderland frames of the 1660s and 1670s is no longer tenable given the strength of

Fig.45
Arthur Capel, 1st Earl of Essex, and his wife Elizabeth by Sir Peter Lely, *c.*1653 (no.15).

An early Sunderland frame with ornament of a marine nature.

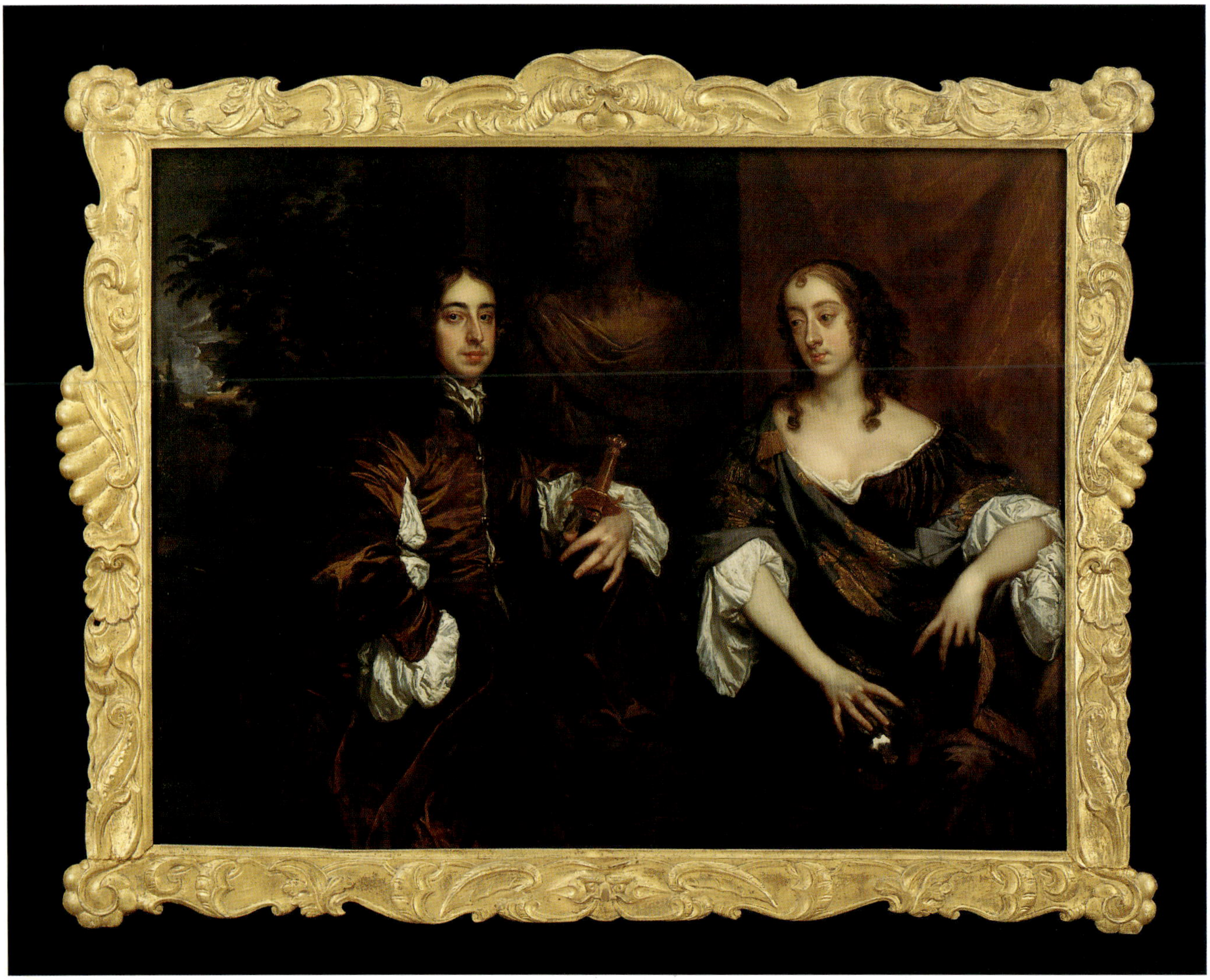

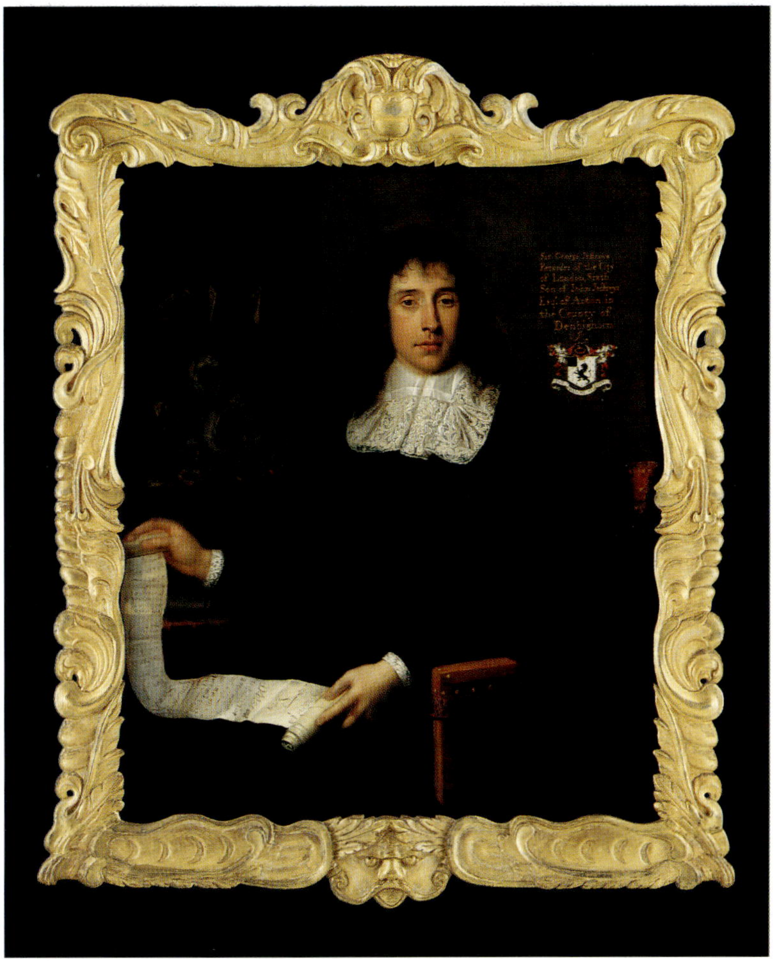

Fig.46
George Jeffreys, 1st Baron Jeffreys ('Judge Jeffreys') by John Michael Wright, 1673 (no.17).

A fully developed Sunderland frame of typical form with irregular sight edge.

the auricular tradition in picture framing in England.[30]

The Sunderland frame

The Sunderland frames, fashionable from the 1650s to the 1680s, are a further manifestation of the auricular style first seen in the reign of Charles I. The Sunderland pattern takes its name from Robert Spencer, 2nd Earl of Sunderland (1640-1702), many of whose pictures at Althorp are framed in the style, but the term is probably a nineteenth-century one.[31] In the seventeenth century most bills simply refer to carved and gilded or richly carved and gilded frames but it is clear that artists and craftsmen categorised the pattern as 'leatherwork'. The name occurs as a 'leatherwork gilt frame' in the accounts for Mary Beale's portraits in 1677 and 1681, and as a 'guilt leatherworke frame' in the executorship accounts of Sir Peter Lely in about 1680.[32] The term also appears in the accounts of Grinling Gibbons in 1697 and 1701,[33] and continued in use until as late as the mid-eighteenth century when James Dryhurst charged the Foundling Hospital for an ornament of 'Shield & Leatherwork' for the bottom of the frame made for Charles Brooking's *Flagship before the Wind*.[34] By this date the ornament appears rococo in character. In the case of Mary Beale, her leatherwork frames at £3.10s were the most expensive she used, reflecting the amount of labour involved in an elaborately carved frame. What does the description 'leatherwork frame' imply? The frames were clearly of wood and not of leather but, as H. Avray Tipping explained of this type of carving in his book on Grinling Gibbons, 'its appearance of being made out of a material that could easily be cut, bent and rolled made it retain ... the name of "leather work"'.[35]

If the forerunners of the Sunderland frame looked to animal skins for their inspiration, it was the oceans that provided the source for the sea-monster-and-shells pattern favoured by Sir Peter Lely and others in the 1650s and early 1660s. This design is found at the National Portrait Gallery on Lely's large double portrait of the Earl and Countess of Essex (fig.45), his three-quarter length of the Earl of Shaftesbury and his half-length of the Earl of Sandwich (fig.90). There are stylised nautilus shells at the frame corners, scallop shells near the centre of the sides, fantastic masks of a sea monster at the top of the frames, and a winged monster at the bottom. Somewhat similar monsters can be found on portrait engravings published in England in the 1630s, such as those by John Payne,[36] and on the engraved cartouches published in Amsterdam by Johannes Lutma in the 1650s.[37] The Dutch prints coincide with the growing popularity of frames in the auricular style in Holland, and were more influential on Dutch frames than their English counterparts.

In its fully developed form in the 1670s the Sunderland frame achieved a bewilderingly complex appearance, incorporating highly stylised patterns of flowing stalks, leaves, fronds and scrolls, centred at the top on a cartouche, or scroll, and at the bottom on an animal mask or other grotesque mask. A good example is the frame on John Michael Wright's portrait of Judge Jeffreys of 1673 (fig.46). In no other English frame type does the inner sight edge cut into the space of the picture in such an irregular way. Though the overall effect appears wild and capricious, examples of this type usually conform to one consistent overall pattern so that frames on full-length portraits, despite their grander scale, can be related element by element to their smaller equivalents. The pattern remained in common use until the 1680s. In a few houses where the type became firmly established as a house style, such as at Kingston Lacy, it continued to be copied into the eighteenth century. In collections where Sunderland frames are grouped together in a single room the effect can be remarkable, for example, at Ham and Althorp.

Cushion frames

Much more modest in character than the Sunderland frame was the cushion frame of the Commonwealth period, an English pattern without obvious continental parallels. Normally only two or two-and-a-half inches across and of a flattish rounded section (see fig.183), cushion frames were carved with distinctive leaf patterns in very slight relief running from a clasped leaf motif at the centre of each side to the corners. Four or five patterns are found, all belonging to the period 1640-70. The commonest is the 'tulip' pattern of half-open bulbous buds strung on a twisted rope. It is found on Lely's portrait of Sir Edward Nicholas of 1662 (fig.47) and on the portraits of William Cartwright and his last wife, Jane, by John Greenhill at Dulwich Picture Gallery. Two other common types are known, both popular in the 1650s. Firstly, there was a waving pattern of twisting leaves and beads-on-a-string used for portraits of all sizes, including the whole-length Honthorst portrait of the Queen of Bohemia of 1642 in the National Gallery, London. The second, a pattern of compact overlapping leaves, is found on John Greenhill's self-portrait at Dulwich, and in altered form at the National Portrait Gallery on the portrait of the 3rd Earl of Southampton. There were also other less common types, notably a pattern with tightly spaced leaves featuring a central pod or button which was used for the portrait of the Earl of Strafford (see fig.47) and for the Ashmolean Museum's De Critz portrait of John Tradescant the younger and his wife of 1656.[38] These cushion frames seem to be found most often on the works of lesser portrait painters such as John Greenhill, Gerard Soest and Henry Paert. The sort of patron going to these artists – affluent, but not necessarily wealthy – probably would not have wanted to commission a Sunderland frame at twice the cost, and in any case, may have considered the style too elaborate.

Gerard Soest's work has the added interest that he often inscribed the back of the canvases with details of the commission. One of his portraits, for example, a head of a man painted in 1667, was inscribed by him with the cost of the picture at £3, and the frame at 16s.[39] At this price the frame would have been a cushion frame or an even simpler type. References to 'halfe Round Gilded frames' and 'lesser halfe Round Gilded frames' at prices of only 7s and 5s appear in John Norris's account to the Duchess of Lauderdale in 1673, and to a 'round guilt frame' at 14s in the Lely executorship accounts,

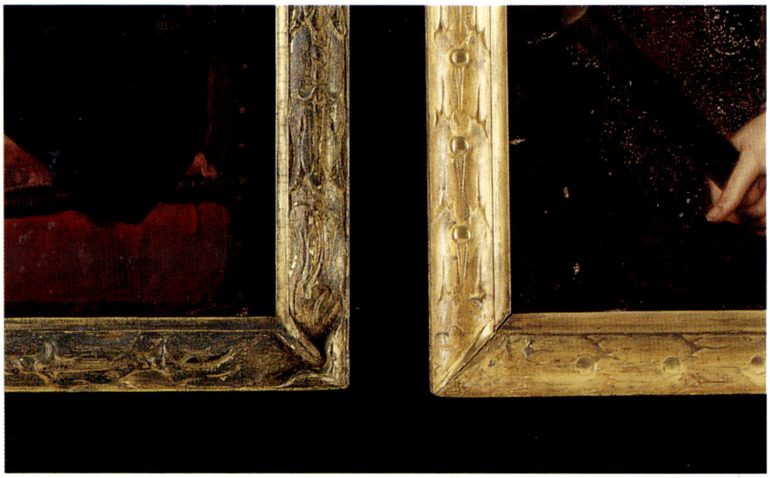

Fig.47 (below) *Sir Edward Nicholas* by Sir Peter Lely (detail, left), 1662 (no.7).

Thomas Wentworth, 1st Earl of Strafford, after Sir Anthony Van Dyck (detail, right, the painting during conservation), *c.*1633 or later (no.8).

Two cushion frames, the 'tulip' pattern on a twisted rope (left) and another pattern with tightly packed leaves (right).

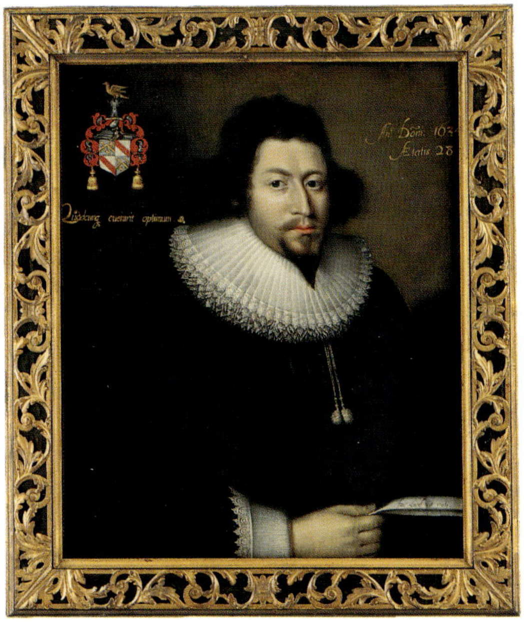

Fig.48
Bulstrode Whitelocke, by an unknown artist, 1634 (no.10).

A black-and-gold frame, perhaps of eighteenth-century date, with applied gilt carving on a black backframe, altered to fit the picture.

and these descriptions may refer to frames of a cushion type.[40]

Mention should also be made of the black frames with applied gilt carving introduced in the 1630s, and in use until the early eighteenth century. The frame on the portrait of Bulstrode Whitelocke (fig.48) is ornamented with intricately carved and gilt scrolling foliage, and acanthus leaf corners, applied to a flat black backframe for effect. This pattern is found in a limited number of collections, sometimes as a house style. In its classic form with scrolling foliage the pattern was used on some of the panels by Polidoro da Caravaggio at Hampton Court, acquired by Charles I in 1638.[41] The style continued to find favour in the late seventeenth and early eighteenth centuries in a limited number of collections, and is found for example at Althorp, Dunham Massey, Lanhydrock and Petworth.[42]

The age of the baroque

There is no such simple thing as the baroque frame, but rather a series of different frame types more or less closely related to the styles of mouldings found in late seventeenth- and early eighteenth-century interiors: the architecture of Wren and his contemporaries or, more properly, the woodwork of the carvers who worked in the city churches and at Hampton Court, Chatsworth and many country houses.

The frames of the period also drew on broader, international, influences. When Charles II returned to England in 1660 at the age of twenty-nine after many years spent in France and Holland he brought with him a more cosmopolitan approach. Many of the new picture frame patterns introduced over the next generation in England were derived from models in widespread use internationally. They were often inspired by styles developed in France and in particular those introduced at Versailles under the Sun King, Louis XIV. These patterns were brought to England either directly or sometimes via Holland by *emigré* craftsmen either attracted by the opportunities for employment in England or forced to flee France following the revocation of the Edict of Nantes in 1685.

New forms were evolved alongside the Sunderland frames and the cushion frames of the Restoration: the bunched leaf or oak-and-acorn frame, various running foliage patterns, and the Bolection frame. Later, gadrooned frames, panel frames and centre-and-corner frames came into fashion. There was a rich choice available to the artist sending work out ready framed. In 1681 Mary Beale, a middle-rank portrait painter with a diverse clientele, was using five different styles for her paintings. This wealth of choice was symptomatic of a society with higher expectations than in the past and one in which many more people now had the means to indulge in such inessentials of life as having their portrait painted. These changes did not pass unnoticed. As John Evelyn expressed it when the King died in 1685, 'Charles II loved planting and building, and brought in a politer way of living which passed to luxury and intolerable expense'.[43]

The frames of the baroque period share certain characteristics. Their chief ornament is naturalistic in origin, whether of large leaves, bunches of fruit or acorns, or scrolling foliage. This ornament is usually set in a running or repeated pattern covering much of the surface of the frame. The result is a substantial frame with a richness of effect, especially when there are several bands of carving, and a harmonious rhythm which engages the eye.

The earliest of the new types were the bunched leaf frames, sometimes known as oak-and-acorn frames from the bunches of oak leaves and acorns often found on them (laurel leaves, berries, fruit and flowers also commonly occur). Such frames were probably introduced soon after the Restoration and enjoyed great popularity until the 1690s. Samuel Pepys used the style for the portraits in his library (see fig.130) and many of Sir Peter Lely's later portraits were framed with this type. In origin the style is French. Although frames of this sort are often called Louis XIII in France (the King died in 1643), many French frames of the type belong to the 1660s and 1670s. In quality these frames are usually much finer than their English counterparts, more densely and crisply carved, and with the leaf pattern reversing at a central rosette.

On English frames the bunches of leaves are normally arranged so that they run from the top centre out to the corners, then down the sides and into the bottom centre. Occasionally other configurations are found, but usually on frames which have been altered or were made in a provincial workshop or at a later date by a craftsman who did not fully understand the frame type. A study of carved door, overdoor and window surrounds in country houses of the period clearly shows that the bunches hang on ropes with their leaves pointing downwards. This feature can be found at Ham House, Castle Ashby and Stapleford Park, and these examples also demonstrate how closely picture frames of this type relate to contemporary interiors.[44] The oak-and-acorn frame seems to have been characterised at the time by its bunches of leaves, judging from bills for architectural decoration and from the occasional frame description. Richard Cleare's architectural work at Coleshill in 1662, including 'Bunches of leaves and berryes' at 4s per foot does not survive, but John Bullimore's carving at Ham House in 1673 – 'bunches of leaves about ye dores' – is a conspicuous feature of the Marble Dining Room.[45] In

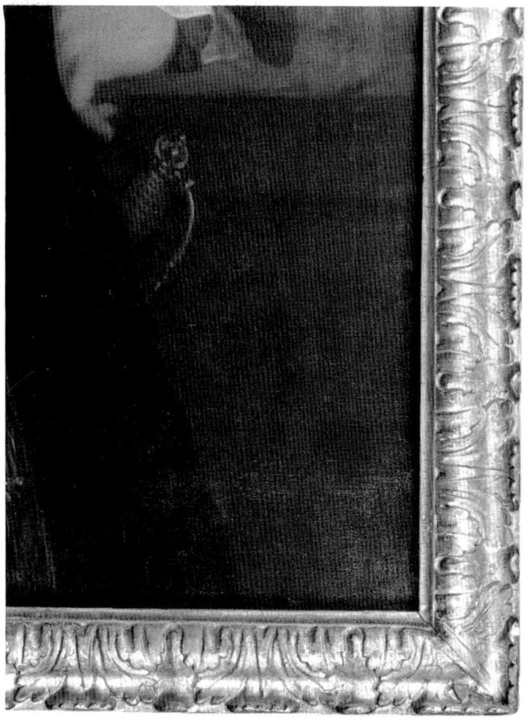

Fig.49
Dr Richard Mead by Allan Ramsay and studio (detail), 1740 (no.24).

A Bolection or raffle leaf frame of the late seventeenth century.

1681 Mary Beale was using 'bunched gilt frames' supplied by Norris at £1.10s each for some of her smaller portraits.[46] At Whitehall Palace in 1686 William Emmett provided a large overmantel frame with two enrichments consisting of 'oak leaves & acorns' at 2s.6d per foot; this presumably was a bunched leaf frame.[47]

One of the most attractive types of the later seventeenth century was the Bolection frame, commonly known in its day as the raffle leaf frame. It relates particularly closely to Italian leaf frames of the mid-seventeenth century and to English architectural interiors of the late seventeenth century. The term Bolection derives from the Bolection moulding commonly found in interiors of the period; this distinctively shaped convex moulding curves up from the picture and back to the wall (see fig.49). Although it can be found plain it is usually decorated with large 'raffle' leaves at right angles to the moulding. When used in interiors the raffle leaves often took the form of a large acanthus leaf but the term means no more than a serrated leaf or one with cut edges, perhaps deriving from the French *érafler*, to scratch or graze.

At Ham House raffle leaves are found in

several of the interiors, supplied by John Bullimore in 1673, for example the thirty-three feet of 'great rafle leaves' framing the alcove in the Duchess's Bedchamber.[48] In 1681 Mary Beale had three picture frames from Norris, which are described as 'Raffle leaf gilt frames' or 'Narrow raffle leaf'; at £1 each they were cheaper than the bunched leaf frames supplied by the same maker.[49] At Combe Abbey in 1685 Edward Pearce charged £2.17s for a larger picture frame ornamented with 'Great Raphild leaves' and other carving.[50] The Bolection picture frame could take more than one form: the standard raffle leaf frame such as that now on *Dr Richard Mead* (fig.49), the twisting leaf of the frame now on Gerard Honthorst's *Frederick of Bohemia* (National Portrait Gallery), or the more elaborately carved frames of the late 1690s or early 1700s found on some contemporary flowerpieces and landscapes, such as the frames for the Monnoyers at Boughton House which were carved by René Pelletier, closely reflecting the designs of the Huguenot Daniel Marot and probably intended as overdoors.[51]

Another popular style, the gadrooned frame, was in fashion between about 1690 and 1725. These frames are easy to use, and reuse, since the repeated pattern lends itself to later adaptation; they are also easy on the eye, and seemingly appropriate for framing pictures of many periods, as their repeated use in the Royal Collection would confirm. Gadrooned frames take their name from the French architectural term *godron*; they are ornamented with a series of gadroons, or convex-shaped ridges set in a decorative pattern. On picture frames the gadroons are normally raking, that is, set at an angle radiating out from the central leaf motif of each side of the frame. This baroque form was used primarily on picture frames, silverware and church monuments, most frequently from the 1680s to the 1720s. Its impact in England seems to have been due to the influx of Huguenot refugees from France in the late seventeenth century, and to the work of French-inspired designers such as Daniel Marot who worked both in Holland and England after leaving France.

The type is also known in framemaking terms as a raking knull frame ('knull' meaning ridge), for when the raking gadroons catch the play of light, they are at once the most striking feature of the frame, especially if burnished, as occasionally happened. The gadrooned frame is essentially a portrait frame and is most often found on full-length and three-quarter length pictures. It occurs on many of Sir Godfrey Kneller's later works. At four inches, the frames are wider than the average for the period. The raised gadroons on the top edge are undercut by a deep hollow carried back to the outer edge of the frame, which typically is decorated with a pattern of little twisted leaves and rosettes or florettes (see fig.186). Sometimes the gadrooning is more delicate in scale, as on Kneller's portrait of Sir Christopher Wren (fig.50), and this is normally the case whenever the style has been used for smaller pictures such as Philip Mercier's Brownlow family conversation piece of 1725 at Belton House. Although gadrooning went out of fashion in the 1720s as baroque styles retreated, it did not disappear altogether. Benjamin West's frames of the 1770s have a richly gadrooned top edge and the style is occasionally found on other frames of Maratta profile for its richness of effect.[52]

One of the commonest and most enduring baroque styles was the running pattern frame

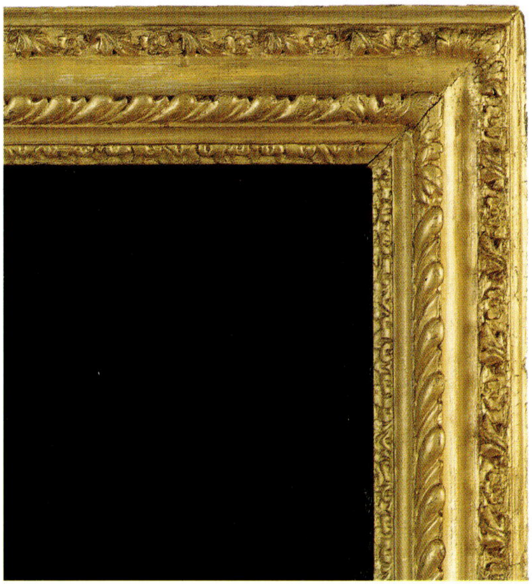

Fig.50
Sir Christopher Wren by Sir Godfrey Kneller (detail), 1711 (no.25).

A gadrooned frame.

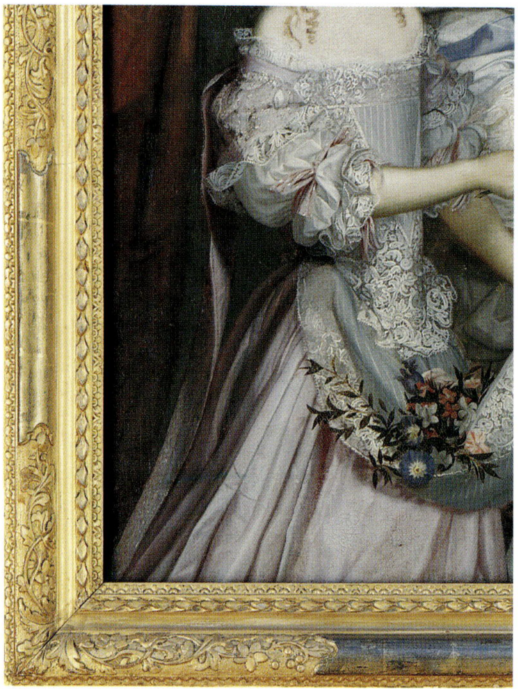

Fig.51 (far left)
John Christopher Pepusch by Thomas Hudson (detail), *c.*1735 (no.21).

A finely carved running pattern, French in inspiration, dating to the 1670s or 1680s.

Fig.53 (left)
Sir Robert Viner and his Family by John Michael Wright (detail), 1673 (no.23).

A panel frame.

carved in low relief with leaves and flowers or with scrolling foliage, sometimes with the addition of strapwork. This sort of ornament can be found on many of the subsidiary mouldings in interiors of the period either in isolation or in combination with other patterns. Such frames came into fashion in the 1670s and in one guise or another remained popular until as late as the 1740s. One of the earliest in the National Portrait Gallery's collection is the frame of the 1670s or 1680s found on Thomas Hudson's later portrait of J.C. Pepusch (fig.51); it is densely carved with a rich pattern of leaves and florettes and is close in quality and design to French prototypes of the period. An even more elaborate frame of exceptional richness, now fitted to a portrait of William III after Sir Peter Lely, probably dates to the 1690s (fig.52). A much simpler and less expensive type used in the late seventeenth and early eighteenth centuries was the panel frame, such as the one found on John Michael Wright's group of the Viner family (fig.53), where the extent of the carving is reduced by the introduction of plain panels. The modern description sometimes used for this style, a 'Lely' frame, is a misnomer because the type did not really become popular until after Lely's death in 1680.

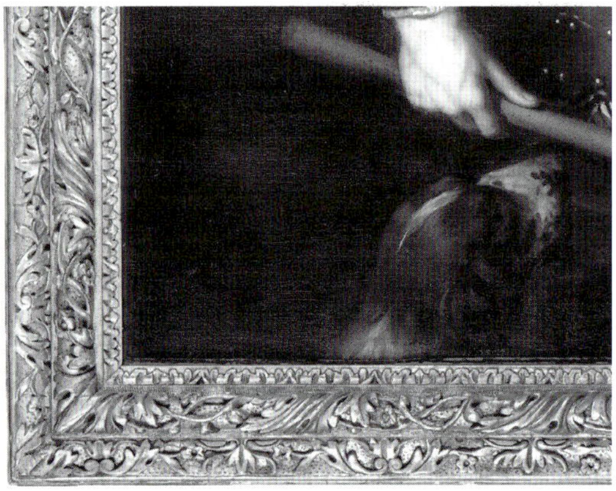

Fig.52 (below left)
William III, after Sir Peter Lely (detail), 1677 or later (no.22).

A very fine reverse section pattern of the 1690s with undercut foliage carving.

In the first half of the eighteenth century running pattern and other frames with prominently carved centres and corners became common. Thomas Pelletier supplied a 'three quarter frame with corners and middles raised' for Boughton in 1707.[53] Almost thirty years later in 1736 Gerrard Howard charged Jacob Tonson junior £11.18s for six large carved and gilt frames with 'Rais'd Corners & Middles'.[54] Pelletier's frame may have been in the manner of some of those which appear in Daniel Marot's engravings, with grand applied carving at the centres and corners but otherwise rather plain. Howard's frames at almost £2 each were not expensive and are likely to have had simple

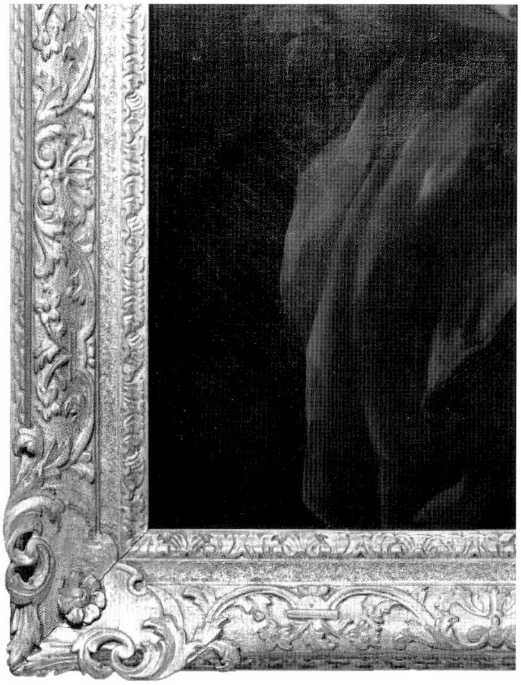

Fig.54
William Jones by William Hogarth (detail), 1740 (no.32).

A running pattern frame with small-scale pierced foliage corners.

corners, perhaps with running foliage sides of the type found on Hogarth's slightly later portrait of William Jones of 1740 (fig.54). A frame of the quality of that on Gawen Hamilton's *A Club of Artists* of 1735 (fig.34) with its exceptional French-inspired carving would have been much more expensive to produce and is quite unusual. Much more common are the frames featuring slightly raised corner panels with a rosette set between foliage scrolls like the Hogarth; by about 1740 these scrolls were normally pierced, a prelude to the lighter frames of the rococo.

The William Kent frame

Of all the styles used in Britain, the most distinctively British is the Kent frame, named after the architect William Kent, a frame type which relates intimately to Palladian architecture. In its classic form with projecting square corners, raised inner and outer architectural mouldings (the outer normally egg-and-dart) and flat main section decorated with sand or an architectural pattern, the Kent frame is instantly recognisable (see fig. 55).

The Palladian style saw its first flowering in Britain in the 1620s under Inigo Jones who not only knew the architecture of Andrea Palladio at first hand, but also owned many of the Venetian architect's drawings. The rebirth of Palladianism in the eighteenth century was marked by the publication in 1715 of the first volume of Colen Campbell's *Vitruvius Britannicus* and by the appearance in the same year of the initial part of the first translation into English of Palladio's *The Four Books of Architecture*.

As a framing device for pictures, the revived Palladian style probably first made its influence felt in the form of fixed surrounds for overmantels and decorative elements in the interiors of the early 1720s. Perhaps the earliest documented instance of the use of the style for moveable pictures is its introduction at the hands of William Kent at Kensington Palace and Houghton Hall in 1725 and 1726 respectively, for both of which he produced designs to show how the pictures were to be framed and hung (for Houghton, see fig.132).[55]

The Kent frame is the only important style in Britain named after an architect rather than an artist or collector. In Kent's own day the names given this frame type reflect its architectural origins. 'Architrave' frame is the term used by the framemakers John Howard, for his work for Houghton in 1729, and Gerrard Howard, for the Kit-cat Club frames in 1733 (see fig.134), and by the portrait painter, Arthur Pond, in his account book from 1737.[56] 'Tabernacle' frame is the description used by such leading Palladian architects as Lord Burlington and Roger Morris in their architectural drawings, by the framemakers John Green and Paul Petit in 1734 and by John Hele in 1737. In the next generation, Chippendale also used the term 'tabernacle' frame, as did Bradburn and France in 1762 and Robert Adam in 1773.[57] 'Palladian' frame is not found until the nineteenth century and 'Kent' frame seems to be a more modern invention.[58]

Palladian frames were often not given a specific name, however, but were described in architectural terms. Thus James Richards, the Master Carver in the Office of Works, carved a chimney frame for Sir William Strickland in 1726 or early 1727 at a cost of £6: 'For Carving another frame, wth an archatrive enricht, and other moldings and flowers, a frize wth Eagles Hds and festoons of Oak Leaves, and foliages, A peice of Ornamt for ye top of ye frame wth a scallop shell and scrowles, and 2 side scrowles to ye frame wth ornamts'.[59] In 1739 William Linnell supplied Richard Hoare with a pair of elaborate frames for £13.12s: 'For making and carving a pair of half length picture frames very neatly carved, with a Venus head and feathers at top and foliage on each side, foliage at bottom, and a double French shell in the middle drops of old fruit and flowers all down the sides pelmets. Lapping over the mouldings top, bottom and sides, all the mouldings carved and key fret in the sandings'.[60]

The frame style promoted by Kent at Kensington Palace and by other pioneers proved to be highly influential. It was taken up by architects and carvers, led by Henry Flitcroft, James Richards and John Howard who all had strong connections to the Office of Works, which undertook building work at the royal palaces and on government buildings. The style received further promotion through the publication of Kent's own *Designs of Inigo Jones* (1727), James Gibbs's *Book of Architecture* (1728) and Isaac Ware's *Designs of Inigo Jones and Others* (1731), as well as through the more popular architectural books of Batty Langley.[61]

Palladian frames are found in many variations: simplified without projecting corners, sometimes even reduced to a band of egg-and-dart as on the Foundling Hospital frames;[62] enriched with real shells on the sandings or with architectural or heraldic motifs replacing the sandings; and elaborated with crestings, pediments or scroll tops containing a mask, coronet or shell. At the hands of second-generation Palladian architects, men such as Isaac Ware and John Vardy, picture frames became both freer and richer, breaking away from the strict language of Palladianism. Even freer still are the highly enriched picture and mirror frames produced by carvers such as Samuel Norman, sometimes incorporating elements of the rococo while retaining the basic architectural framework of the Palladian style. By taking in such elements the style survived the dominant fashion for the rococo in the 1750s and 1760s, only to be killed off by the lighter, more graceful classicism of Robert Adam. In the introduction to the first number of their *Works in Architecture*, published in 1773, Robert and James Adam claimed, 'The massive entablature, the ponderous compartment ceiling, the tabernacle frame, almost the only species of ornament formerly known, in this country, are now universally exploded'.[63]

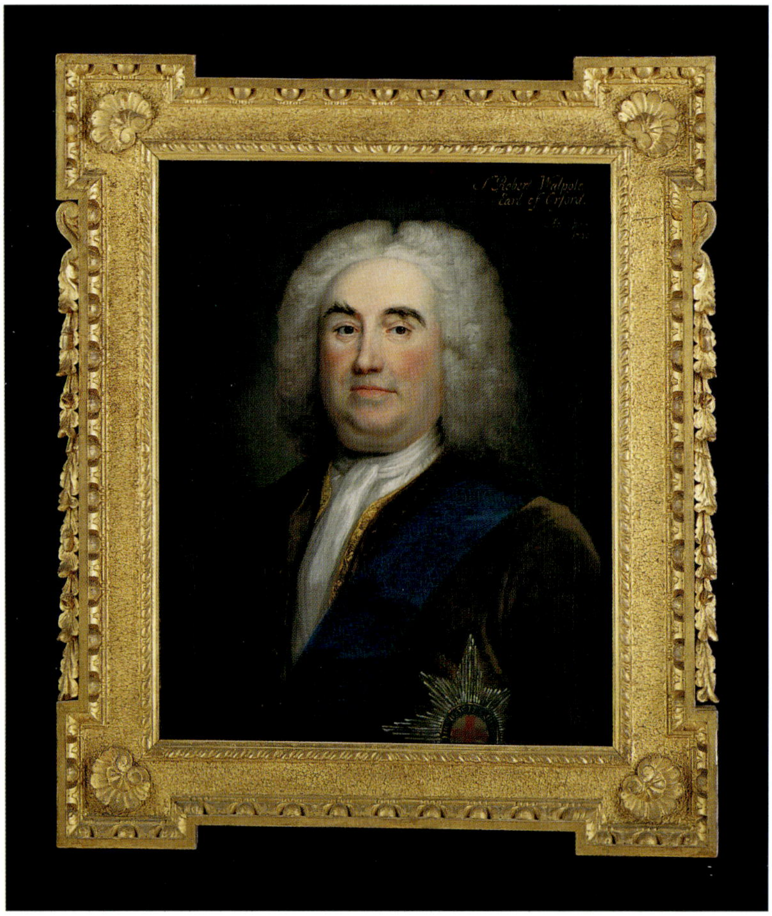

Fig.55
Robert Walpole, 1st Earl of Orford by Arthur Pond, 1742 (no.28).

A Kent frame, or 'architrave gold frame', of a type made for the artist by Gosset.

The rococo

When André Rouquet attacked the French rococo style characteristic of the reign of Louis XV in 1754 he was writing as a Swiss artist long resident in London: 'a taste so ridiculous and whimsical, when applied to objects susceptible of

Fig.56
A Picture Frame and Table by M. Lock and H. Copland, 1752, etching. From *A New Book of Ornaments* (Victoria and Albert Museum, London).

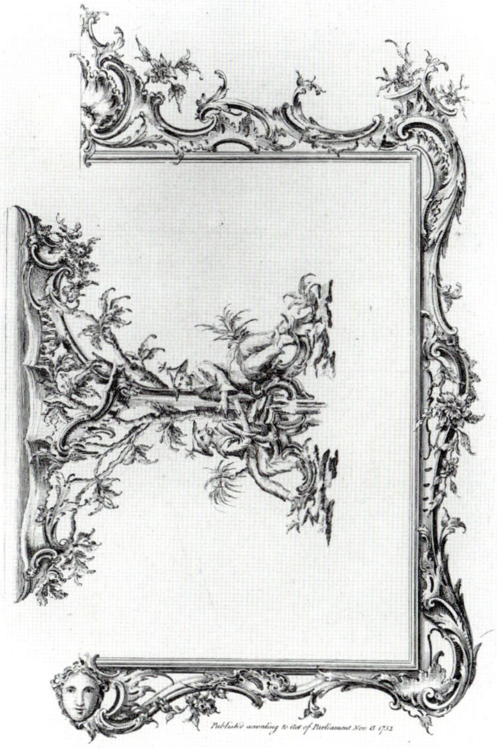

symmetry, has reached as far as England, where it everyday produces, as it does elsewhere, some new monster'.[64] The rococo had been popular in England since the late 1730s but only achieved its full flowering in the 1750s and 1760s, as exemplified by the plates of Thomas Chippendale's *Director* and other contemporary publications. It is a style which the architect Isaac Ware, referring to the characteristic C-scrolls and counter-curves, described as consisting of crooked lines like C's and reverse C's.[65] The term 'rococo' is a later one, which did not come into use until the nineteenth century.[66] In England at the time such frames were generally described as being in the French taste or as swept frames (an allusion to their sweeping curves). Thus William Linnell charged Richard Hoare £3.13s in 1742 for 'a chimney frame in the French fashion' and £5.10s in 1753 for 'a large sweept picture frame',[67] while Samuel Norman billed the Earl of Egremont £8.18s in 1762 for alterations to a 'Large French Picture frame, with Sweep'd Corners & middles, curiously Carved in Large manner'.[68]

The 1740s and 1750s were a time of war and intense rivalry with France, and things French were objects of both admiration and derision. As Isaac Ware put it, the French were 'a frivolous people whom we are to apt to imitate'.[69] Apart from the influence of French Huguenot carvers working in England, such as Paul Petit, Jean Antoine Cuenot and Isaac Gosset, there were many French pattern books and engravings readily available in London.[70] The picture framemaker James Pascall was advertising the sale of Simon Gribelin's pattern books in 1738, while the carver Gideon Saint kept a scrapbook of Régence-style French engravings and English rococo designs.[71] Occasionally one can point to likely borrowings from engraved sources such as Lock and Copland's picture frame (fig.56) which may have been the starting-point for the heavy rococo frame on William Hoare's portrait of the Earl of Chatham (fig.57).

Picture frames in the rococo style could reach amazing heights of elaboration as demonstrated by the fantastic frames made for Frederick Prince of Wales in the 1740s.[72] The frames used by portrait painters for their work are less extravagant, but are nevertheless often fine and distinctive examples from the workshops of leading rococo framemakers. Both Francis Cotes and his rival, William Hoare, used special rococo patterns to frame their pastels as did

Fig.57
William Pitt, 1st Earl of Chatham, by William Hoare and studio, 1754 or later (no.39).

A rococo frame of the 1750s or 1760s.

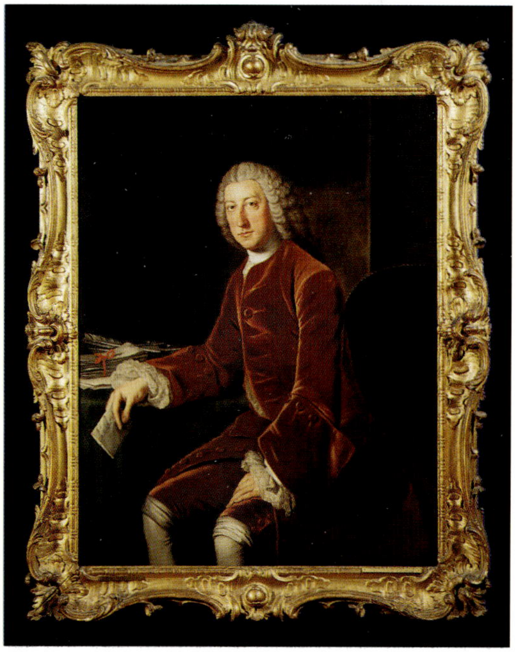

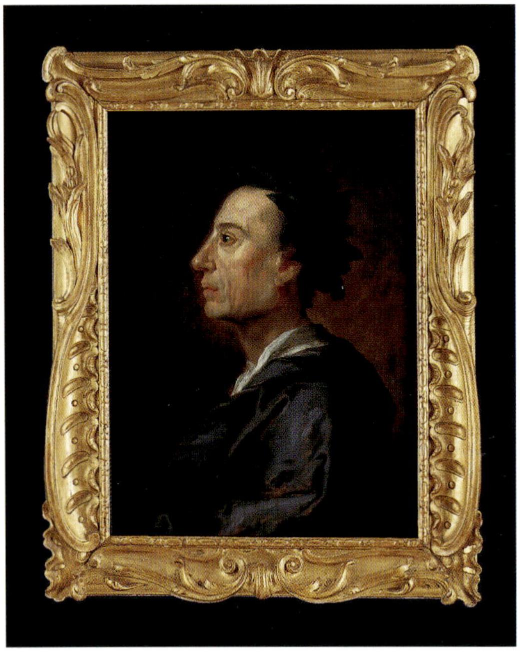

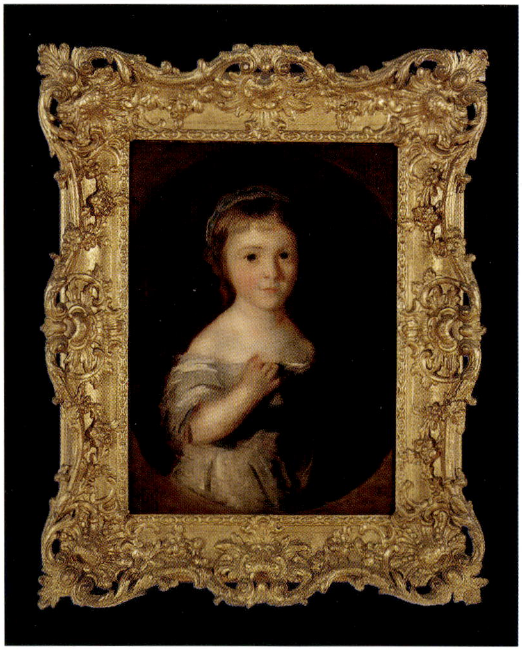

Fig.58 (far left)
Alexander Pope, by Jonathan Richardson, *c.*1737 (no.31).

A rococo frame of unusual design, perhaps intended for a pastel.

Fig.60 (left)
Georgiana Spencer, Duchess of Devonshire by Sir Joshua Reynolds, *c.*1761 (no.40).

An elaborate rococo frame of the 1750s or 1760s in the Huguenot manner.

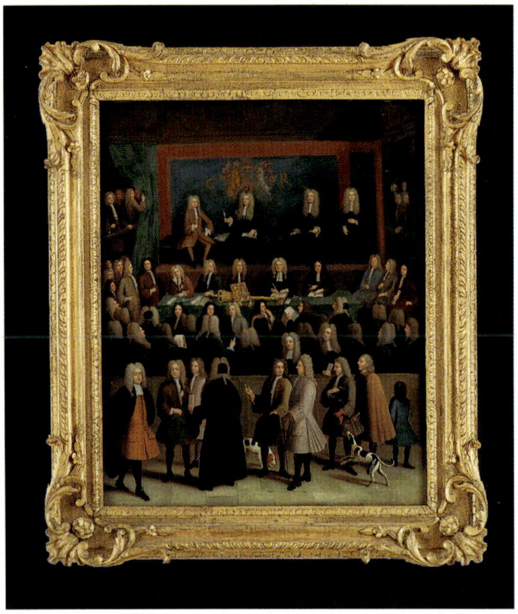

Fig.59 (below left)
The Court of Chancery in the Reign of George I by Benjamin Ferrers, *c.*1725 (no.34).

An ogee-sided frame of *c.*1750 with open rococo corners.

Thomas Hudson and Allan Ramsay for their oils; these artists' frames will be discussed in greater detail in Chapter 4.

Extravagant designs such as the extraordinary water rush pattern on the frame of Jonathan Richardson's portrait of Alexander Pope (fig.58) are rare on portraits. Much more typical is the little Highmore of Samuel Richardson (no.33), with its C-scroll corners, or the French-inspired ogee-section frame on Benjamin Ferrers's *The Court of Chancery* (fig.59), a widely used pattern in the 1750s which has been described as 'rococo only at the corners'. Frames made by French Huguenot craftsmen tend to be more organic, sculptural and three-dimensional than their English counterparts which in comparison are formalised and linear, and make use of trailing arrangements of flowers and leaves. The frames on two portraits by Reynolds, *The Duchess of Devonshire* and *Sir Joseph Banks* (figs.60, 61) illustrate the two very different traditions.

The Carlo Maratta frame

The Maratta frame is an Italian style which takes its name from the last of the great Roman baroque painters, Carlo Maratta, who was active in the late seventeenth and early eighteenth centuries. In Italy especially the pattern is usually known as a Salvator Rosa frame after the Italian artist to whom the design is attributed. The Maratta is found in one form or another in the great Roman galleries – the Colonna, the Pallavicini, the Spada and the Doria-Pamphili palaces.[73] Occasionally in the inventories of Roman collections the frame style is specified so that, for example, a picture by Nicolas Poussin in

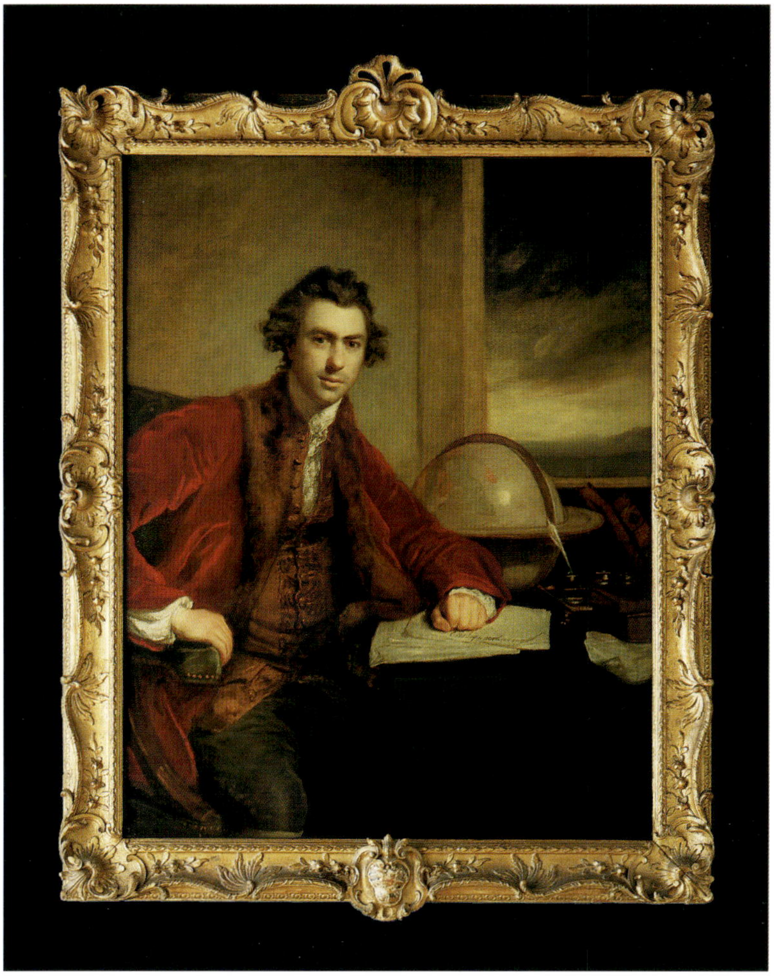

Fig.61
Sir Joseph Banks by Sir Joshua Reynolds, 1773 (no.41).

A rococo frame of the 1760s in the English manner.

the Dal Pozzo collection is described in 1740 as having a frame 'fatta à modello di Salvatore Rosa'.[74] The style was current in Britain by 1750, reaching the heights of popularity in the 1760s and 1770s, and remaining in wide use until the 1790s. In no other country outside Italy was the Maratta taken up with such gusto as in Britain, and in the late eighteenth century it became a particularly British style for picture framing.

The British visiting Italy on the Grand Tour, an increasingly popular activity in the early eighteenth century, often wintered in Rome and it was there that many tourists expected to sit for their portraits and sometimes to acquire paintings and sculpture to bring home. The Maratta style must have been familiar to those who examined the pictures in Roman palaces and especially to the increasing numbers of British artists who studied in Rome, including Charles Jervas, Allan Ramsay, William Hoare and Joshua Reynolds.[75] It was, however, presumably the frames on Italian pictures imported into Britain which provided the immediate model for the Maratta style, probably in the 1740s.[76] The British were peculiarly susceptible to Italian and in particular classical models, witness the popularity of the Kent frame in the Palladian style at a time when the late baroque and the rococo were the dominant modes on the Continent. Unlike the Kent style, the Maratta does not have close links with contemporary architecture: it is a framemaker's style and not an architect's.

Distinctive in profile with a deep front hollow and a prominent outward curving top edge undercut by a back hollow (see fig.190), the Maratta frame is also distinctive in decoration, typically having a band of carved Maratta ornament, sometimes also called Carlo ornament, of acanthus leaves and tongues (or shields) placed in the depth of the front hollow or along the sight edge. The hollows and the tongues are often found burnished (no.90 is an excellent late nineteenth-century example; see fig.24). In the frame's simplest form the Carlo ornament is omitted, as with the frames of John Russell (see no.45). In its enriched version the plain tongues are replaced by shells and the plain top edge is sometimes carved with gadroons (see fig.96). But regardless of the form of decoration, the basic profile remains much the same.

In England one of the earliest references to the style is in Joseph Duffour's bill of March 1752 for a gilt 'Carlomarat' frame with eighteen feet of moulding in the 2nd Earl of Egremont's accounts at Petworth House.[77] Maratta frames were used by William Hogarth in 1751 or before for his 'Marriage à la Mode' series (National Gallery, London),[78] by Francis Cotes for his pastels, including his *Elizabeth Gunning* (fig.62), and apparently by John Wootton for his landscapes as early as 1749.[79] The earliest reference in Joshua Reynolds's pocket books occurs in 1757.[80] In contemporary accounts the style normally appears described as a Carlo Maratt frame, sometimes spelt Marat or Maratti. Very occasionally a reference to a Salvator Rosa frame

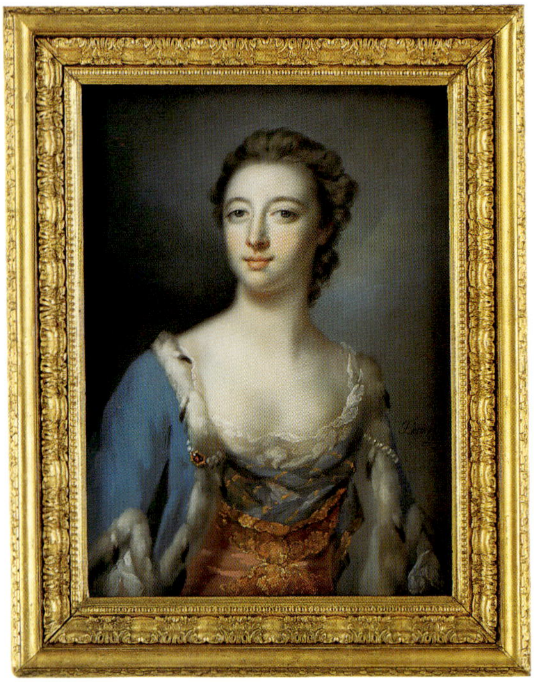

may be found, as in the notebooks of the collector, Edward Knight.[81]

The Maratta was widely used for portraits by Reynolds, Gainsborough and the young Lawrence, though not by some artists of the older generation such as Allan Ramsay or Thomas Hudson. The style was not universally liked ('I don't like that Carlo Marat frame for a portrait', wrote Lady Kildare to her husband in 1762), but nevertheless it found very widespread acceptance.[82] It was also used for landscapes, though perhaps less commonly, and in this context the top edge is sometimes found sanded, as in some of the frames on paintings by Sawrey Gilpin and William Marlow. Maratta frames in enriched form, with the tongue of the Carlo ornament replaced by a shell and the top edge carved in gadroons (the so-called 'raking knull') were produced in the 1770s, and can be found on the work of Benjamin West and some other artists. 'To a broad bold rich burnish gold whole length frame carv'd with knull and hollows, rich foliage, leaf and stick for yr. Graces picture by Sr. Joshua Reynolds', reads Thomas Vials's bill to the 3rd Duke of Dorset in 1771 for an enriched Maratta frame costing twenty-five guineas.[83]

The Maratta frame remained remarkably popular in the face of competition from more neo-classical frame types, and was used until the 1790s. But a change of attitude is already apparent in a letter written in 1772: 'The picture frames are not of *Carlo Marratti* kind, they are at present not the Taste'.[84]

Fig.62
Elizabeth Gunning, Duchess of Hamilton and later of Argyll by Francis Cotes, 1751 (no.42).

A Maratta frame of a pattern used by Cotes.

Neo-classicism

To attempt to identify a representative neo-classical frame type would be misleading for there are several frame styles which reflect one aspect or another of neo-classicism over the period 1760-1820, sometimes having little more in common than their rectilinear outlines and their use of some sort of neo-classical ornament.

The birth of the neo-classical picture frame in France has been traced to the frames carved in 1760 for the Marquis de Marigny, Mme de Pompadour's brother, and exhibited at the Salon in 1761.[85] The provenance of the neo-classical style in England is less simple, however. The rococo had never held such sway as on the Continent, and both the William Kent and the Carlo Maratta picture frame, classical styles if not neo-classical, were already in use in 1760. In the field of architecture, Robert Adam claimed 'to have brought about in this country, a kind of revolution', without having 'trod in the path of others'.[86] In his *Works in Architecture*, published jointly with his brother James, commencing in 1773, Adam also claimed to have adopted 'a beautiful variety of light mouldings' and to have been able to seize 'the beautiful spirit of antiquity, and to transfuse it, with novelty and variety'.

Despite Adam's claims there were others who had helped pioneer the taste for neo-classical architecture, notably the architects James 'Athenian' Stuart and William Chambers, though they lacked Robert Adam's skill as a self-publicist. Nevertheless, in interior decoration and furniture design Adam's influence was highly significant. As early as 1761 picture frames in the neo-classical taste were being made to his design by Sefferin Alken for the Painted Breakfast Room at Kedleston Hall.[87] Adam's severely classical seat furniture for the gallery at Croome

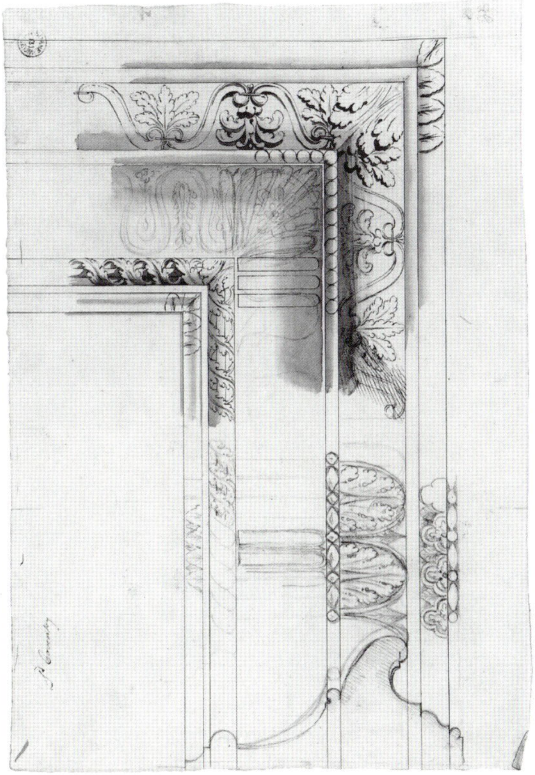

Fig.63
Designs by Robert Adam, 1764, for the picture frame of Allan Ramsay's portrait of the 6th Earl of Coventry (Sir John Soane's Museum, London).

The frame as made follows the top design closely.

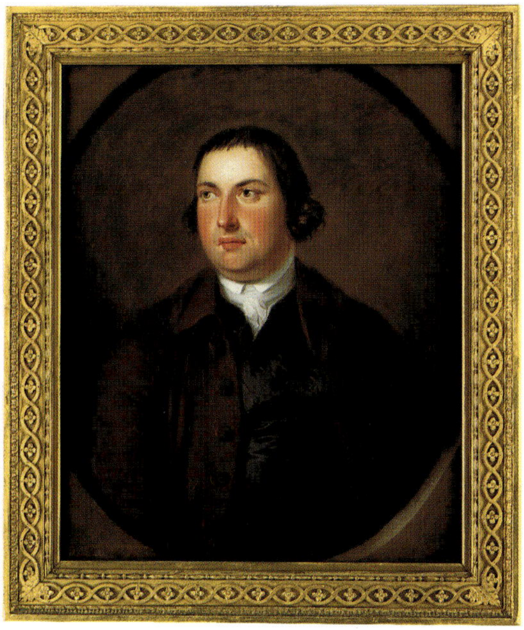

Fig.64
Charles Churchill by J.S.C. Schaak, *c.*1763-4 (no.53).

A neo-classical frame, probably of the 1770s, with open guilloche fretwork.

Court in 1763, with fluted legs and fluted frieze, was followed by picture and mirror frame designs in a related style (see fig.63).[88] His innovations were rapidly taken up by others, as an elaborate picture frame designed by Thomas Chippendale for Nostell Priory in 1767 demonstrates.[89] Chippendale's frame is shallow in profile with a fluted frieze, paterae corners and waterleaf top edge, all features which can be found in neo-classical picture frames in the 1770s and 1780s (see fig.189).

Francis Cotes's portrait of the Earl of St Vincent (fig.94), painted in 1769, shows how quickly the idea of a fluted frame was taken up by fashionable portrait painters. In profile, however, like some other early neo-classical frames, the frame more closely resembles the Maratta style. This is especially evident when a comparison is made with neo-classical patterns such as the frame now on J.S.C. Schaak's portrait of Charles Churchill (fig. 64) with its flat frieze and slightly raised outer edge. It is generally the case that neo-classical frames chosen by portrait painters such as George Romney, Joseph Wright of Derby, John Downman and Hugh Douglas Hamilton (figs.87, 98, 155) are relatively plain in style, with their ornament limited to a few simple features to avoid great expense.

For more elaborate patterns one must look to special designs such as that on George Stubbs's self-portrait (fig.97) with its rich laurel-leaf top edge and fluted sides, a pattern chosen to suit the taste of Josiah Wedgwood, or the frame on John Opie's portrait of Mrs Delany (fig.121), designed by Horace Walpole and decorated with elaborate swags of trailing flowers, a rare example of the French neo-classical taste in English frames of the period. Both these frames belong to the 1780s when neo-classical frames were taking on a variety of new forms. The simplest of these are the ribbon-and-reeded frames: the classic 'Morland' frame (see fig.65), named after the artist George Morland, or the much flatter frames of Romney such as found on his portrait of William Paley (fig.98).[90] Rather richer are the laurel leaf frames found on the work of Stubbs, and on Guy Head's portrait of John Flaxman (fig.66).

The frames of the 1790s and early 1800s with their deeper profiles herald the second phase of neo-classicism, when the lightness and fussiness of Robert Adam was pushed aside by a bolder, more masculine taste. Nowhere can richer or

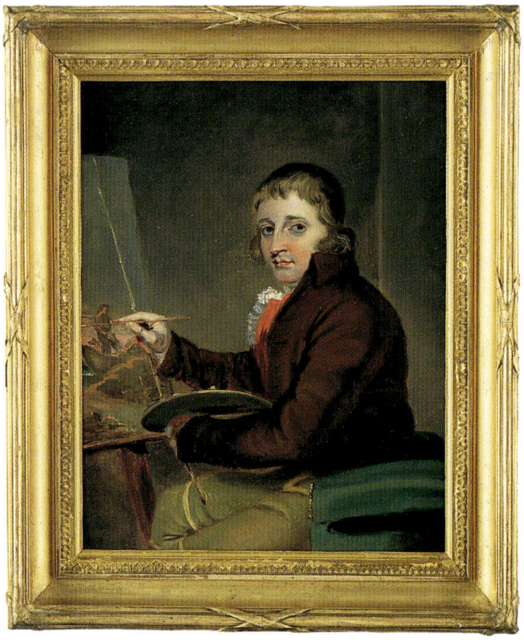

Fig.65 (above left)
George Morland by John Raphael Smith, *c.*1792 (no.57).

A Morland frame with a ribbon-and-reeded top edge.

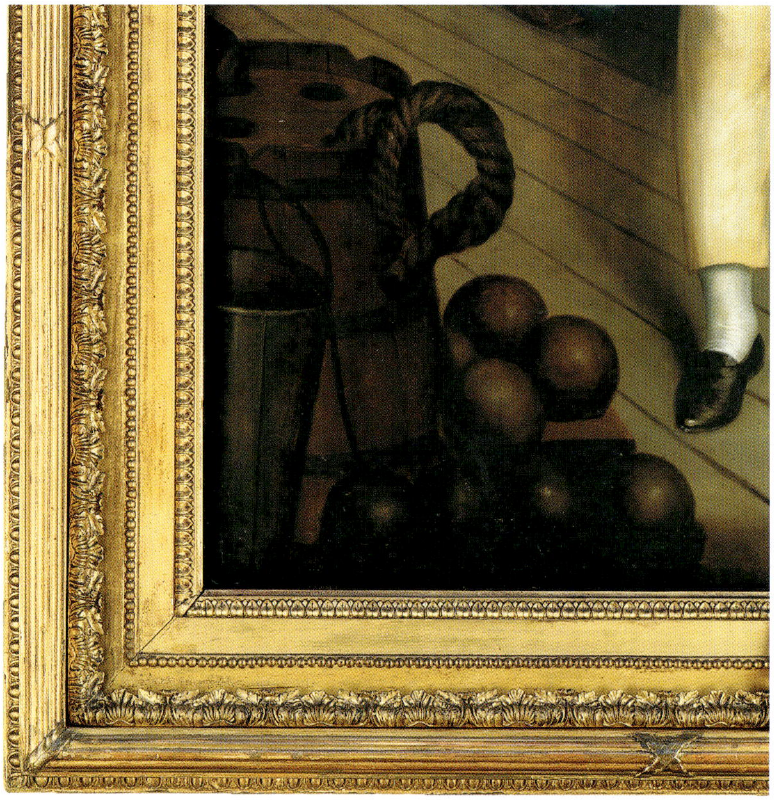

Fig.67 (above right)
Horatio Nelson, Viscount Nelson with a Midshipman by Guy Head (detail), 1798-9 (no.56).

A heavy ribbon-and-reeded neo-classical frame, probably made *c.*1801-5 by John Brydon shortly before the portrait was given by Nelson to Emma Hamilton.

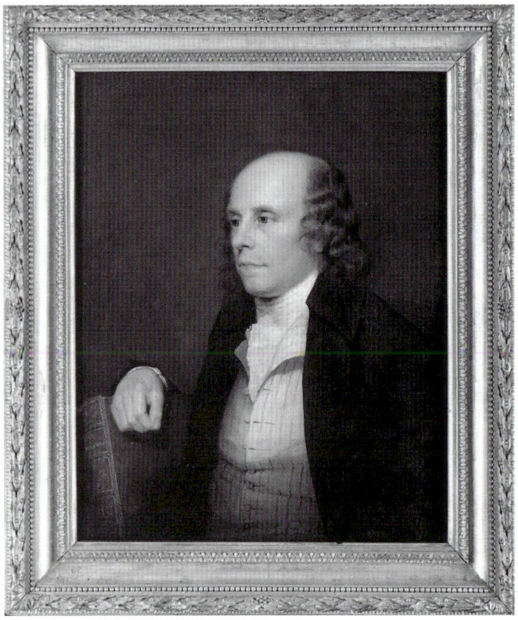

Fig.66 (left)
John Flaxman by Guy Head, 1792 (no.55).

A neo-classical frame with a laurel-leaf top edge.

finer frames of the period be seen grouped together than at Southill, a house which was remodelled by Henry Holland in the 1790s for Samuel Whitbread, a member of the Prince of Wales's circle.[91] At the National Portrait Gallery the very deep frame on Guy Head's portrait of Nelson, dating to the early 1800s, with reeded top edge and a residual band of Maratta ornament in the depth of the frame, is an exceptionally severe example (fig.67). Much more typical is Thomas Phillips's self-portrait (fig.68), again with reeded top edge, but with extensive ornamentation on the frame's curved sides. The rise in the use of pressed composition ornament in preference to carving meant that it became easier to produce lengthy runs of elaborate ornament relatively economically.

This taste for heavier richer frames is reflected in contemporary accounts. In 1812 John Smith charged the Prince Regent £75.12s for a pair of 'superb frames' for half-length portraits of George I and George II; these frames were '5½ [inches] wide richly ornad with Carv'd Foliage corners & Shells, fluted hollows & 5 rich Mouldings'.[92] Thirty years before, a frame for a picture on this scale would have been only three or four inches wide and would have had three mouldings at most. For patrons who did not want new frames, existing frames might be enlarged to give them more weight. John Smith, for example, charged the Earl of Uxbridge £9.3s in 1812 for regilding a three-quarter length Maratta frame and adding foliage corners and shells, while for another collector, John Pedley,

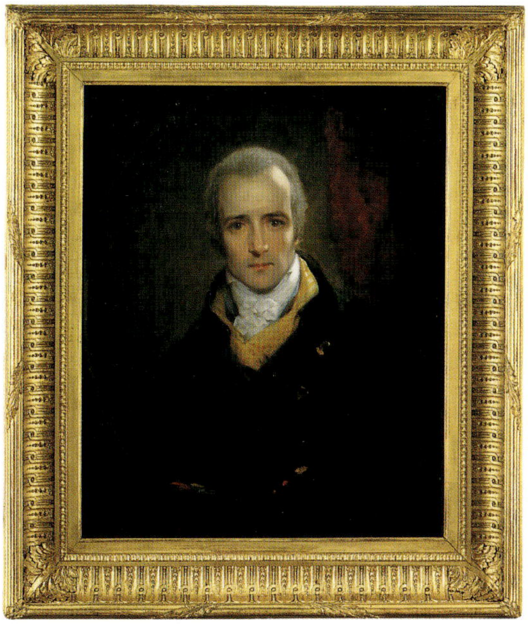

Fig.68
Self-portrait by Thomas Phillips, 1802 or 1803 (no.63).

A neo-classical frame of a pattern used by Phillips, an early example of a frame extensively ornamented in compo.

he made a substantial addition measuring three inches wide and more than five deep to a large frame, adding corners and various mouldings at a cost of £9.8s.[93]

The French Empire taste, which made use of such classical motifs as the anthemion and lotus for frame ornaments (as represented, for example, on the Bonnemaison Raphael copies at Apsley House), never caught on in England, no doubt because links between the two countries were severed by war. However an earlier French introduction, a Louis XVI pattern of the 1780s, found a readier reception: the classic fluted frame with tightly cut flutes on the curved frame sides and guilloche or other ornament filling the narrow flat top edge. The frame on Beechey's portrait of Thomas Hope (fig.69) was of this type until it was altered. The style was revived first in the mid-nineteenth century in France, and subsequently in Britain.

Despite these aftercurrents, the importance of neo-classicism as a force in framing was on the wane by the 1810s, and the Grecian classicism of the architects Robert Smirke, William Wilkins and Decimus Burton had little impact on fashions in picture framing, where taste had moved on to a range of revival styles.

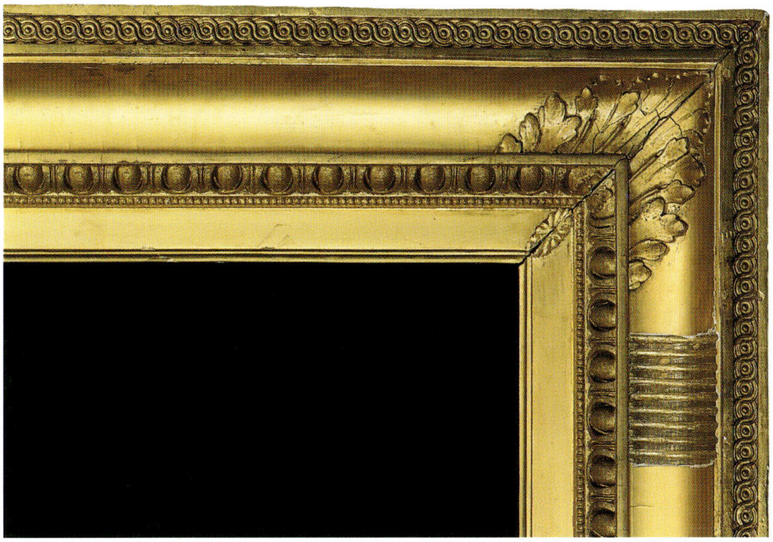

Fig.69
Thomas Hope by Sir William Beechey (detail), 1799 (no.58).

The original fluting of this neo-classical frame has recently been revealed at one corner beneath a smooth later layer of gesso covered in fine linen. The acanthus mitre leaves are also later.

Revival styles in the nineteenth century

It is equally due to the artists of France to acknowledge, that their elegant fancy furnished the English frame-makers with examples for tasteful and gorgeous patterns which now add so much grandeur to the walls of our modern picture galleries and noble apartments.[94]

When W.H. Pyne paid his handsome tribute to the 'artists of France' in 1819, Britain and France had been at peace for several years after almost a generation of war. The perennial French influence on English taste had been renewed in the form of the Louis Quartorze revival in interior decoration, a style which saw its full flowering in George IV's Ball Room at Windsor Castle in the 1820s and in the London club houses and town houses of the period, including notably the Duke of Wellington's Waterloo Gallery at Apsley House.[95] From the Louis Quartorze to the Louis Quinze seems to have been but a step in the minds of the time, so that rococo revival interiors such as the White and Gold Room at Petworth House, dating to the late 1820s, were created in the same epoch as interiors in the more masculine Louis Quartorze taste.[96] Both these styles are reflected at some remove in the picture frames of the period.

'Sir Thomas Lawrence pattern or Swept' advertised P. Garbanati in the 1840s when promoting the virtues of his ornamental gilt frames.[97] The Lawrence pattern was straight-sided with small-scale ornament, often in the Louis Quartorze or Régence taste, while the swept frame favoured broad curves with centre and corner motifs in the rococo or Louis Quinze taste. The ledgers of the leading framemaker, John Smith, show that the rococo taste had begun to come back into fashion in framing in the 1810s. 'Sweep sided' frames were being supplied as early as 1812. It is of particular interest that towards the end of the decade such an influential figure as the Earl of Yarmouth, the close friend of the Prince Regent, should be choosing to use both antique frames and revival patterns: an 'Old carved french frame' for a Dutch picture in 1819 and 'A large handsome Frame … sweep sides and back edge with rich french middles and corners' to be made for an unspecified picture of three-quarter length size in 1817.[98] By the 1820s and 1830s advertisements such as Joseph Garbanati's for 'A Choice Collection of French Carved Picture, Chimney & Pier Frames' were not uncommon.[99] The francophile George Hayter, later to become history painter to Queen Victoria, used an icing-cake French rococo frame of the 1740s for his own youthful self-portrait (fig.70). In comparison, the modern rococo frame on his portrait of Lord Hatherton is quite modest in structure and ornamentation. Such rococo revival patterns became more elaborate in the 1830s, but their prominent curving top edge and corner projections meant that they were vulnerable to accidental damage.

It was probably as much for practical reasons as a matter of taste that most artists used straight-sided frames. As views of the Royal Academy and the Paris Salon demonstrate, by the second half of the century the overwhelming majority of pictures are in straight-sided frames. Indeed, the regulations of the Salon discouraged circular or unusually shaped pictures, insisting that they should be framed as a rectangle.[100]

By the mid-nineteenth century certain styles of frames started to be identified by name in advertisements and bills, notably the Lawrence frame, the Collins pattern and the Alhambra frame. All three types were straight sided. The Lawrence frame was of a broad ogee section and ornamented with a small-scale all-over foliage and scroll pattern as seen on Lawrence's portrait of George Canning (fig.103). It was used by Sir Robert Peel for the portraits he commissioned for his gallery at Drayton in the 1840s, such as F.R. Say's *Earl of Ellenborough* (fig.125). As late as 1865

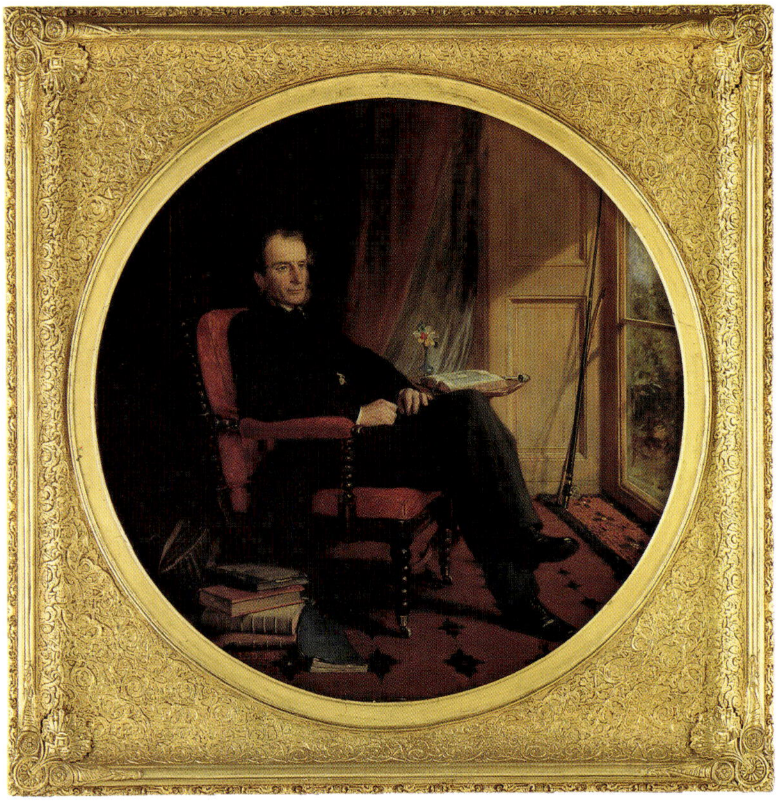

Fig.71 (above) *Charles Kingsley* by Lowes Cato Dickinson, 1862 (no.78).

An Alhambra frame with elaborate Moresque ornament formed out of compo in the spandrels.

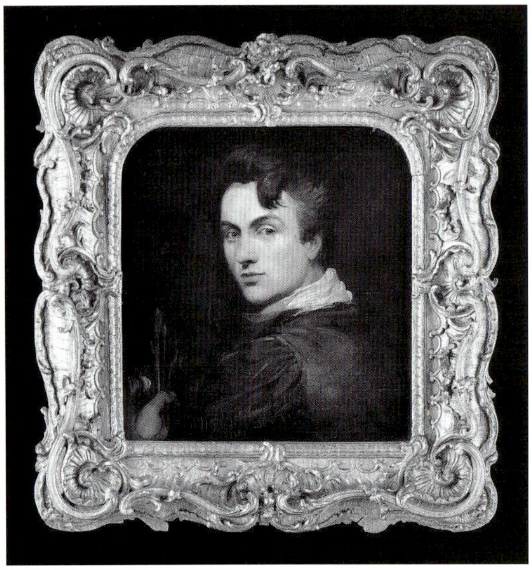

Fig.70 (left) *Self-portrait* by Sir George Hayter, 1820 (no.66).

A mid-eighteenth century French rococo frame, reused by Hayter for his self-portrait.

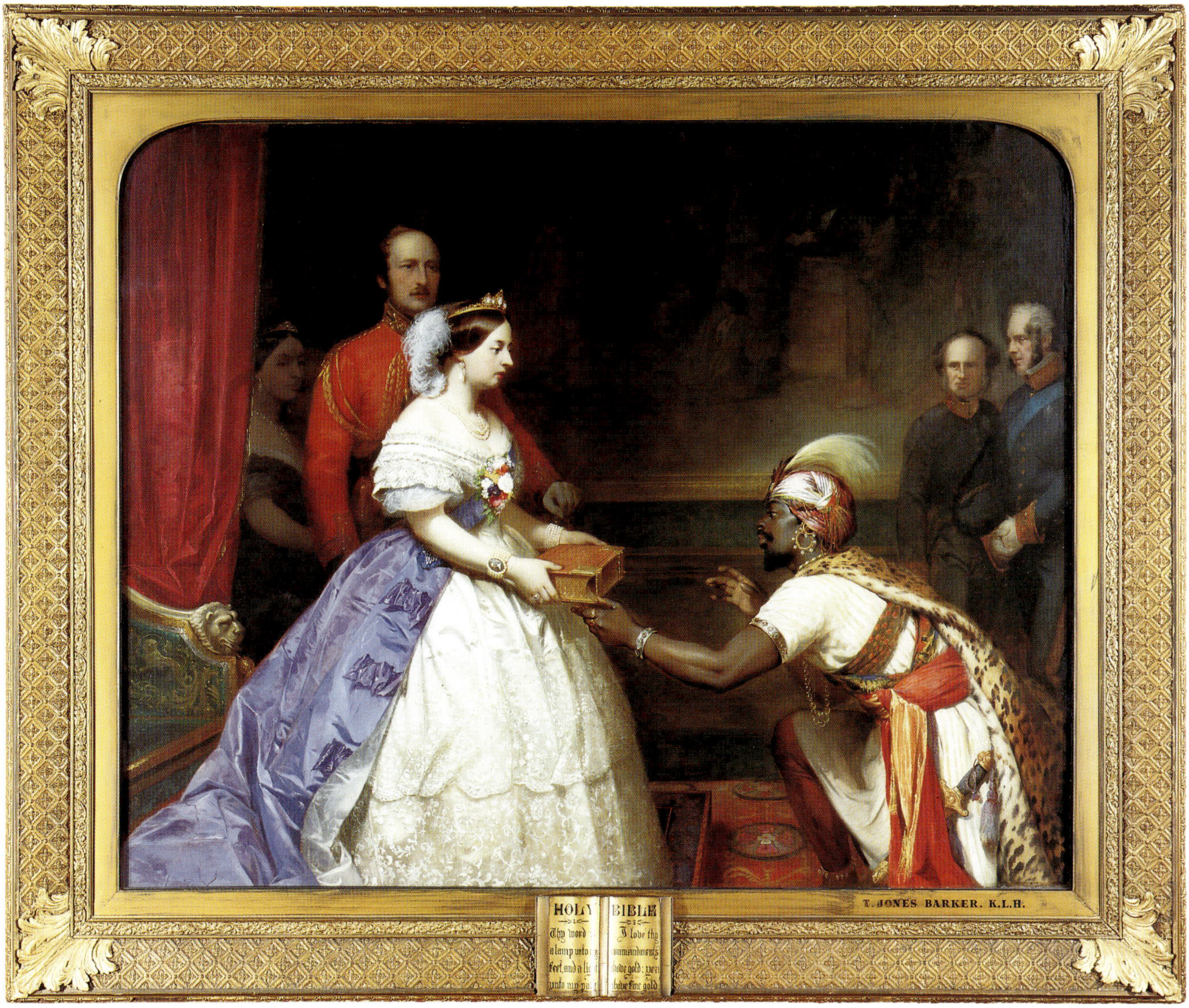

Fig.72
The Secret of England's Greatness by Thomas Jones Barker, *c.*1863 (no.76).

A handsome frame with a broad sloping cushion ornamented with a diaper pattern in compo, and inset with an open Bible; made by Criswick & Dolman.

'Lawrence gold frames' were being supplied to Queen Victoria.[101] The heavy section was a response to the weightiness of Thomas Lawrence's style with its broad expanses of dark paint and strongly modelled features; these frames were seen by Lawrence as the essential counterpart to his pictures, as is explained in Chapter 4. By contrast, the Collins pattern is lighter in scale. It is characterised by a prominent convex cushion with a running ornamental foliage pattern, usually with wide, spreading, flat shell or scroll corners which occupy the whole width of the cushion but do not project beyond. The type may have been named after the landscape painter, William Collins, who used the style for framing pictures such as his *Early Morning, Cromer* of 1845-6 in the Tate Gallery. E.W. Cooke was using Collins pattern frames for some of his sea-pieces in the late 1840s.[102] The third of these frame types, the Alhambra pattern, may be a little later in date. An extraordinarily rich example can be found on L.C. Dickinson's portrait of the novelist, Charles Kingsley, of 1862 (fig.71). In its more typical form, the Alhambra pattern had a convex main hollow, decorated with a very fine small-scale all-over shallow abstract surface pattern and a prominent rounded top edge on which the corner motifs are planted. The surface pattern of the Dickinson frame is in the Moresque style of the Alhambra at Granada but later other ornamental patterns came to be popular.[103] Like the Collins pattern, the Alhambra was a well-understood frame type which remained in use until at least the 1910s but is now forgotten.[104]

The mid-nineteenth century is marked by the diversity of available patterns. Antiquarianising frames incorporating elements relating to a distant past were sometimes used, as, for example, the frame made for the portrait of 'Bess of Hardwick' in 1865 for the National Portrait Gallery (fig.120). A taste for small-scale abstract or geometric patterns, perhaps encouraged by the publication of books such as Owen Jones's *The Grammar of Ornament* (1856), is evident in some of the most striking frames of the period, including T.J. Barker's *The Secret of England's Greatness* and *The Relief of Lucknow* (figs.72 and 73). More common were the English seventeenth-century revival patterns such as the bunched leaf frames favoured by Henry Wyndham Phillips (see fig.74) and by the Scottish portrait painter, Sir John Watson Gordon. Also common were French classical revival patterns, notably the fluted frames used extensively by the Marquess of Hertford for his old masters in the late 1850s (these now form part of the Wallace Collection) and by a few portrait painters, including George Richmond and Alessandro Ossani. The renaissance revival, probably encouraged by the acquisitions made by the National Gallery and the South Kensington Museum in the 1860s, was taken up by artists in the Pre-Raphaelite circle such as Burne-Jones and Strudwick, and also by some portrait painters. The frame on the copy of

Fig.73
The Relief of Lucknow by Thomas Jones Barker, 1859 (no.75).

A trophy frame ornamented with flags and cannons, commemorating one of the key events of the Indian Mutiny in 1857.

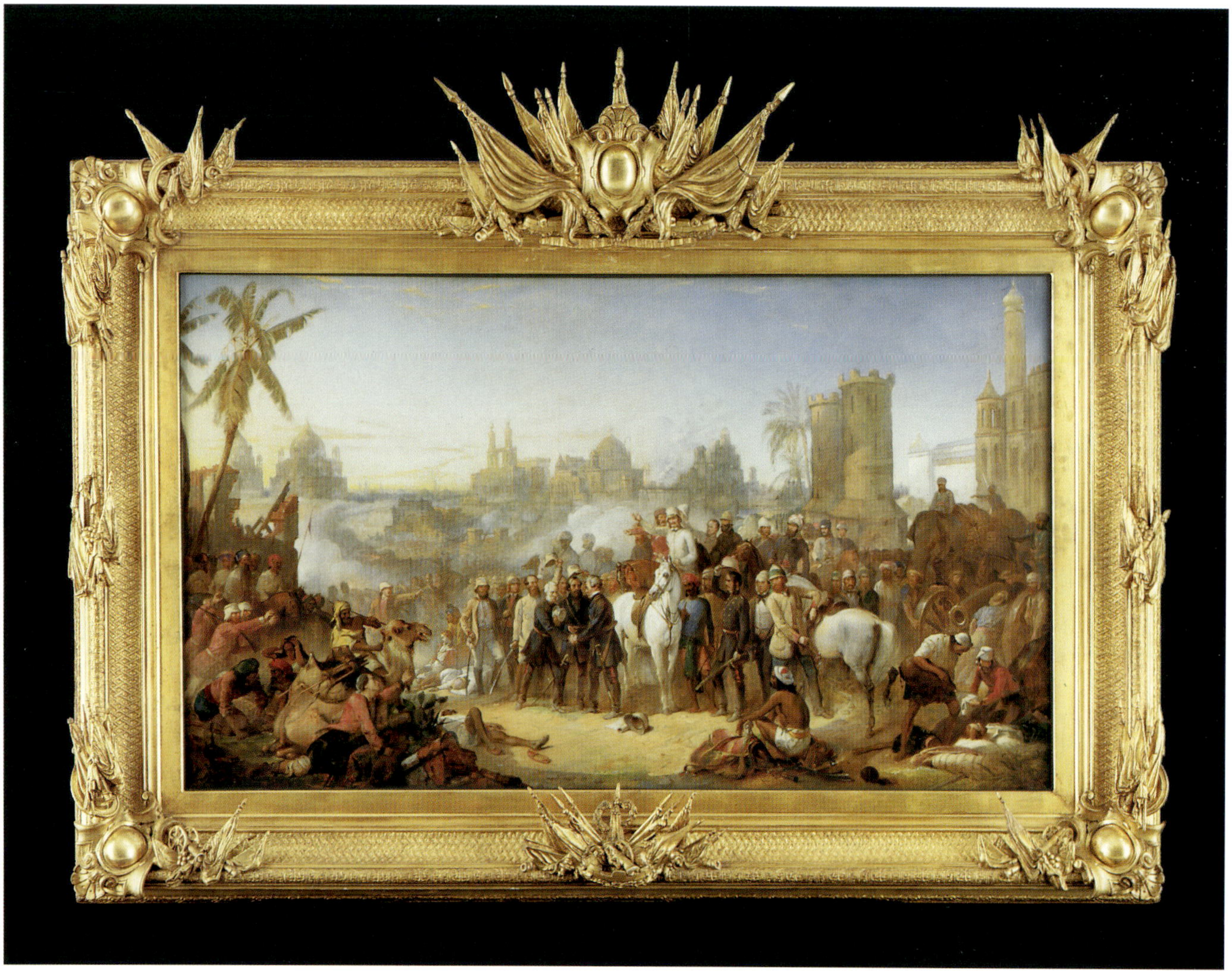

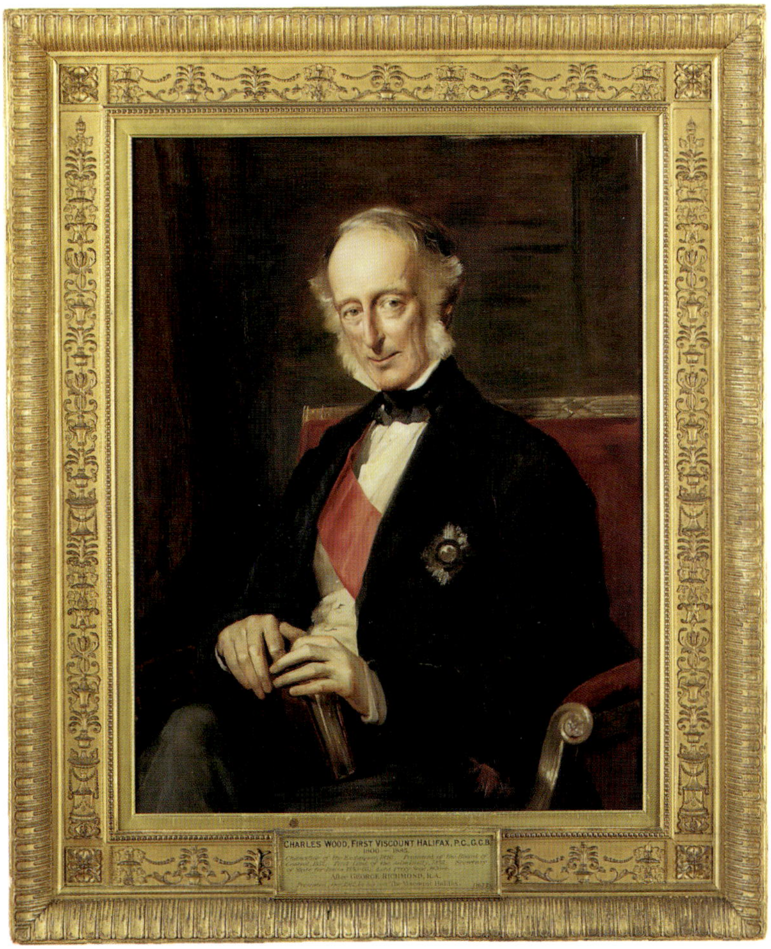

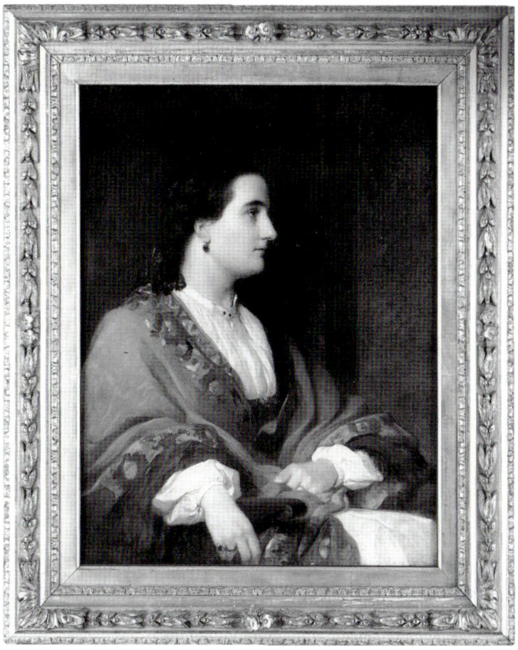

Fig.75 (above)
Charles Wood, 1st Viscount Halifax by Anthony de Brie after George Richmond, *c.*1912 (no.86).

A renaissance revival pattern made by Chapman Bros.

Fig.74 (above right)
Lucie, Lady Duff-Gordon by Henry Wyndham Phillips, 1851 (no.71).

In a seventeenth-century style frame of a pattern used by Phillips.

George Richmond's *1st Viscount Halifax* is a late example of the style (fig.75). But alongside this interest in the Italian renaissance there were other stirrings which flowered in the experiments of the Pre-Raphaelites, Watts and Whistler.

Artists' frames from Watts to Whistler

Of course, for the frame to be in perfect harmony with the painting, it must be designed by the artist himself. This has been done by Mr. Burne Jones, Mr. Alma Tadema, and Mr. Whistler, but is, of course, a rather expensive process, and, if a proper selection of patterns were kept in stock by frame-makers, should be unnecessary, except in the case of very special works of art.[105]

Luther Hooper's account of picture framing written in 1883 reflects the widespread concerns of the period for a better standard of framing. While the Pre-Raphaelite frame has attracted the greatest attention, there were other artists' patterns of the period, including the Watts and the Whistler frame which were taken up more widely, and none more so than the Watts frame.

The Watts frame, named after George Frederic Watts, one of the most individual artists of the period, achieved a remarkable popularity and, though based on Italian prototypes, became in its adapted form, a quintessentially British frame type (see figs.76, 77). By the 1880s it was so universally accepted that Luther Hooper could single out the Watts frame: 'Fully one-third of the pictures at the various exhibitions for some years past have been framed in mouldings of this pattern in its various sizes, and it is indeed the only pattern of a really satisfactory character for wide frames in the market'.[106] A generation later one of the National Gallery trustees, Robert Benson, numbered the Watts frame as one of the 'poor designs used without discrimination' at the Gallery, complaining that 'The "Watts" frame appears 13 times in one room on pictures by Reynolds, Gainsborough, Romney, Lawrence, Opie, Hoppner and Millais'.[107] At the National Portrait Gallery the style was the frame of choice for late nineteenth-century portraits, and one

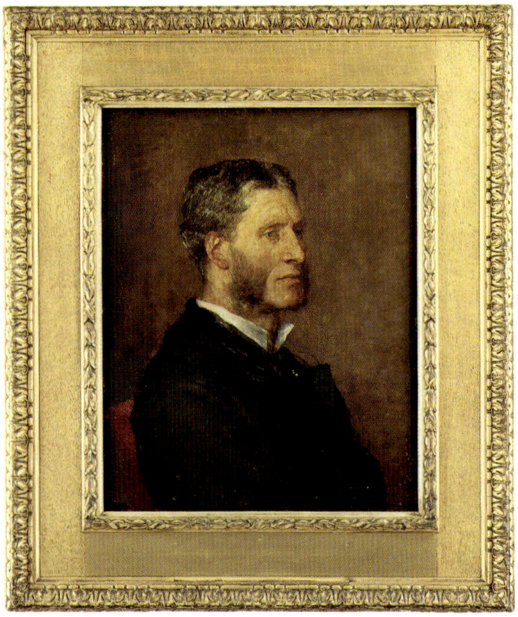

Fig.77 (left)
Matthew Arnold by George Frederic Watts, 1880 (no.80).

A Watts frame made by W.A. Smith of a pattern frequently used by Watts.

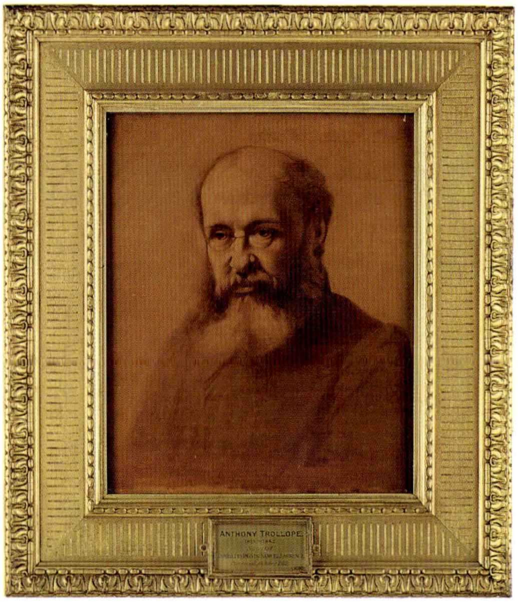

Fig.78 (below left)
Anthony Trollope by Samuel Laurence, *c.*1864 (no.87).

A fluted Watts frame of a pattern used by Laurence.

Fig.76 (facing page)
Dame Ellen Terry by George Frederic Watts, *c.*1864 (no.79).

An enriched Watts frame of a pattern used by Watts in the mid-1860s with punchwork on the flat frieze.

artist was told that it was the only pattern which would enable her picture to be hung harmoniously with others of the same period.[108]

In its classic form with a main wide flat frieze, gilt directly onto the oak, and raised inner and outer mouldings in compo, the Watts frame was taken up by several leading artists. Millais, for example, made it his own for his later portraits, such as his *Lord Salisbury* (no.88), to the extent that references to 'Watts pattern frames with Millais pattern front mouldings' appear in the National Portrait Gallery framing bills in the 1890s.[109] Some artists preferred to use the design with variations. Ford Madox Brown called the enriched version with punched leaf decoration on the frieze a 'Venetian' pattern (see fig.110). Samuel Laurence used a rather absurd fluted version (see fig.78) while D.G. Rossetti, Frank Holl and George Reid all had their own preferences.

Does the credit for the type belong to Watts? He had studied in Italy in the mid-1840s and was familiar with Italian frame styles, occasionally using old Italian frames on his works in the 1850s. Both he and Rossetti were using Watts frames by the mid-1860s but it is difficult to document earlier examples or to pinpoint the introduction of the style precisely. It has been suggested that two of the standard components of the Watts frame, the gilding directly onto the wooden surface of the flat of the frame so that the oak grain shows through, and the use of vertical butt joints in the flats instead of mitres, are first found in 1861 in Rossetti's work.[110] Various frame types are mentioned in some detail in Rossetti's correspondence but not the Watts frame, and, in the absence of contrary evidence, it is reasonable to accept that the Watts frame by its very name was an innovation of G.F. Watts, whether or not the idea of gilding directly onto the oak was Rossetti's. The two men knew each other well in the late 1850s and early 1860s and no doubt will have discussed picture framing as a subject of mutual interest.

The heyday of the grand artists' frame was the half-century from 1850 to 1900 which saw not only the experiments of the Pre-Raphaelites but also the grandest efforts of Leighton, Alma-Tadema and Burne-Jones, and the aesthetic frames of Whistler and Albert Moore. The Pre-Raphaelite's interest in picture framing, and in particular the frame patterns used by Rossetti and Ford Madox Brown in the 1860s and 1870s, are described in more detail in Chapter 4. These frames were not the only ones to attract attention at the time. Charles Eastlake, in his *Hints on Household Taste* in 1878, drew attention to the 'practice with many artists of the rising English school to design their own frames for the pictures

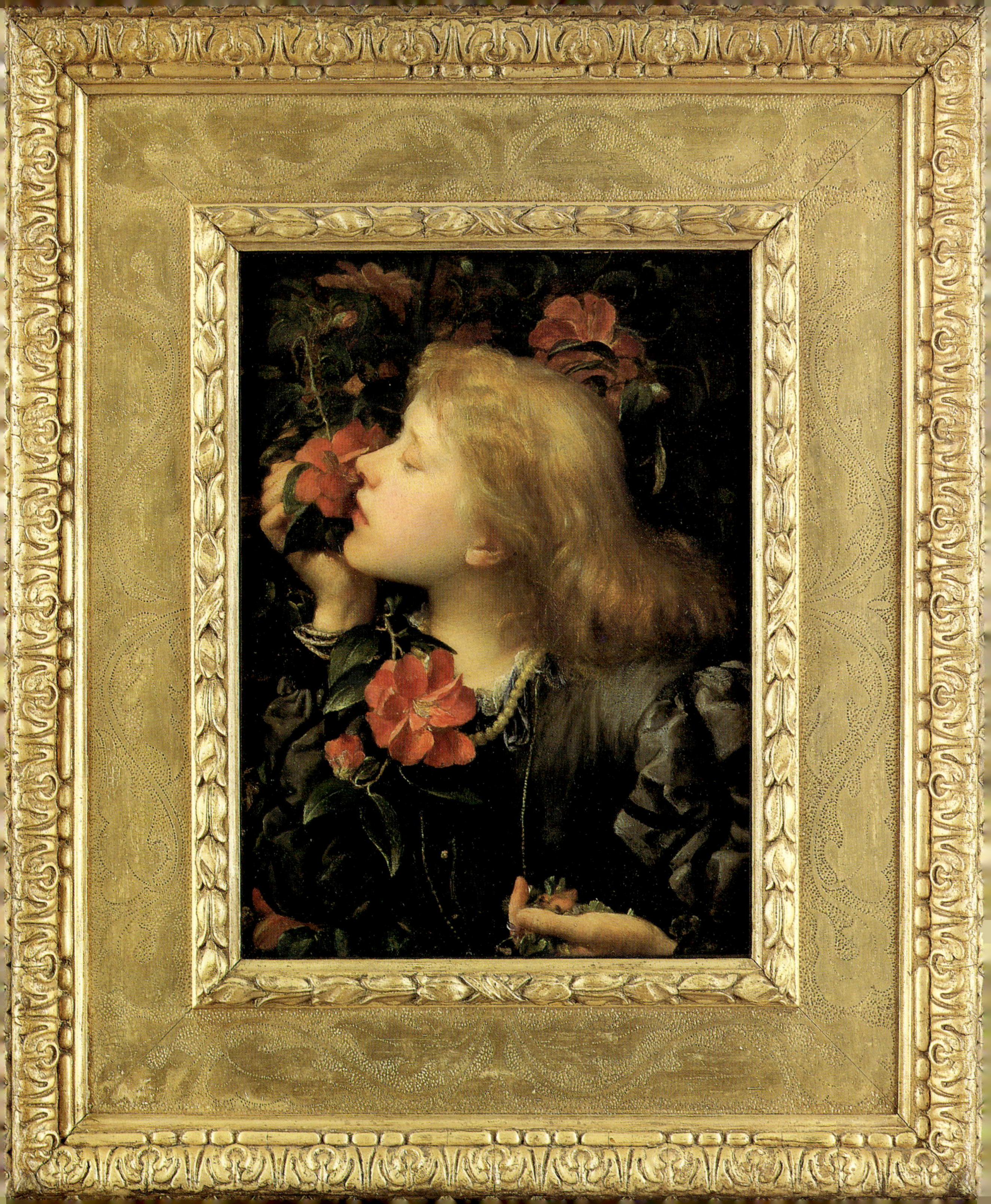

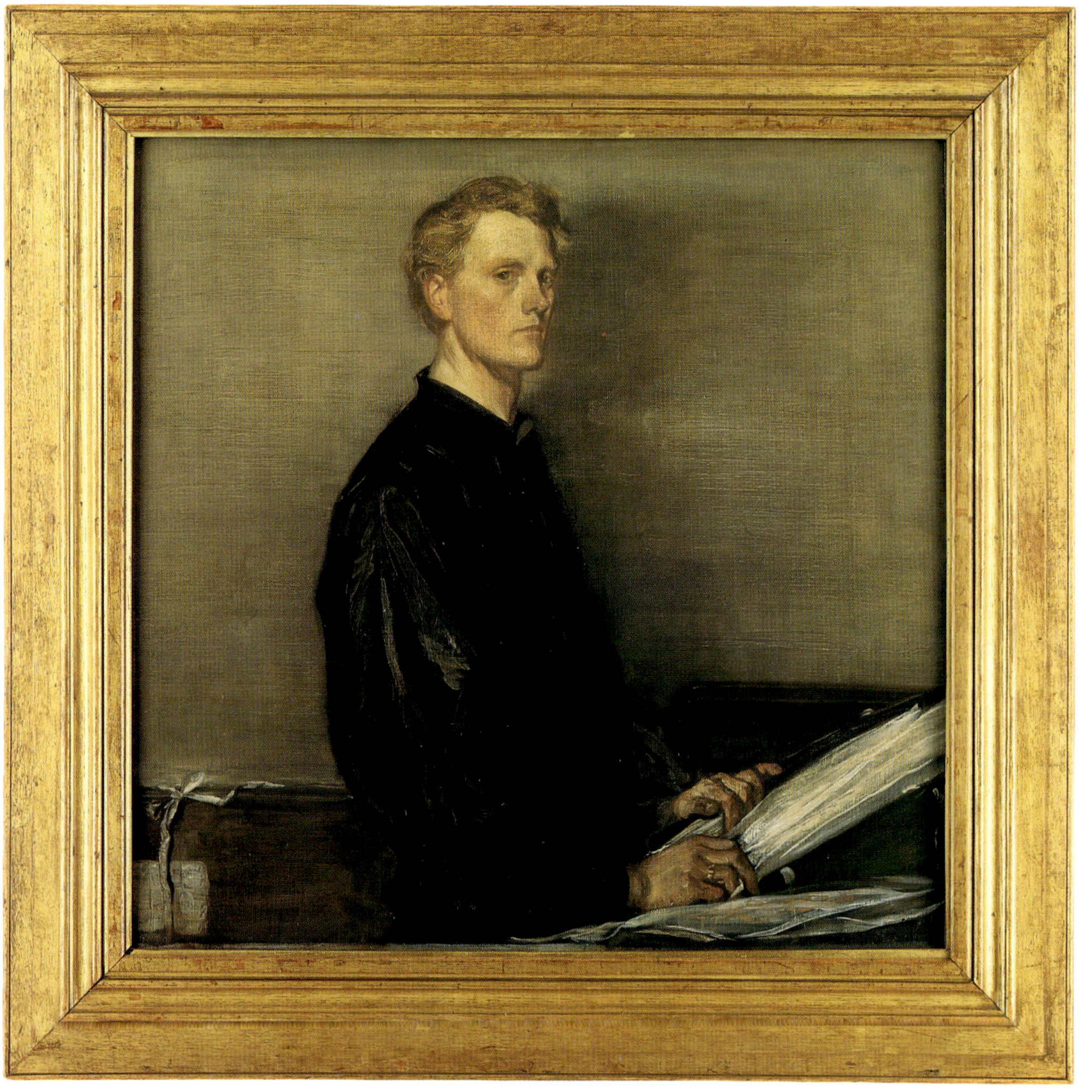

Fig.79
Self-portrait by Charles Haslewood Shannon, 1897 (no.105).

A wide reverse-section frame, gilt directly on to the oak, of a pattern used by Shannon.

they exhibit'.[111] Such frames were much in evidence at the exhibitions at the Royal Academy, the Old Water-Colour Society and, from 1877, the Grosvenor Gallery, and a few exhibition reviews paid special attention to the frames on view. In a long article in *The Architect* in 1869, Phené Spiers discussed the frames on many of the Academy exhibits, picking out for special comment works by Alma-Tadema, Leighton, Albert Moore, Edward Poynter and Val Prinsep among others.[112]

A feature of many artists' frames was the use of ungessoed wood. Eastlake commended the effect of oak grain seen through leaf gold as 'exceedingly good', and it has been suggested that the gilding on oak grain, whether for flat or reeded frames, became particularly associated with the Grosvenor Gallery where many of the most 'advanced' artists exhibited in the late 1870s and 1880s.[113] Such frames were normally fairly plain in appearance, relying on the oak grain for their effect rather than on any applied ornament, and were widely used over the next generation. Herkomer's *Lord Kitchener* (fig.113), Blanche's *Aubrey Beardsley* (no.104) and Shannon's *Self-portrait* (fig.79) are three examples of the 1890s in the National Portrait Gallery's collection.

The most influential artists' frames of the late nineteenth century were those designed by Whistler. Shortly after the artist's death, his biographer described how he was 'never content with the stock patterns of the frame-maker, but

Fig.81 (right)
Thomas Hardy by William Strang, 1893 (no.103).

A Whistler frame with a prominent reeded cushion.

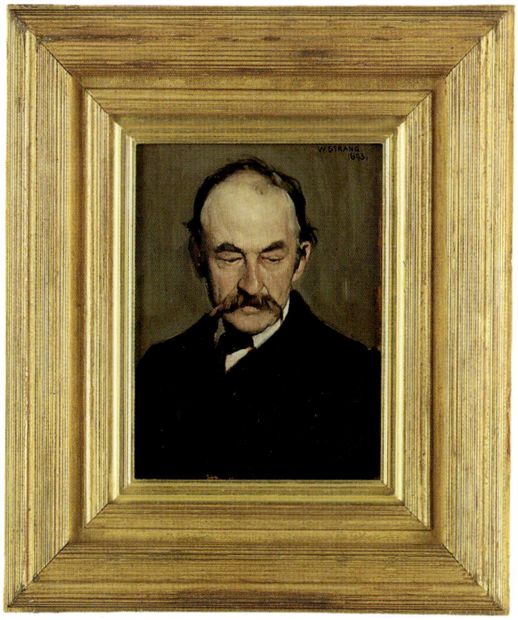

designed his own mouldings. ... All his frames are extremely simple in style, and it is interesting to trace through the years the changes which he developed, not only in the mouldings, which were mostly arrangements of fine reeds, but in the colour of the gold used'.[114] From the 1870s he used two classic types, both with delicately reeded mouldings and usually gilt directly onto the oak. The simpler of the two has inner and outer bands of parallel reeded lines set close together, separated by a wide flat which the artist himself sometimes decorated in paint. J.S. Sargent's portrait of Coventry Patmore, painted in 1894, has a plain frame of this type (fig.80). The other style, more often used by Whistler for his smaller pictures, has inward sloping sides with parallel reeded lines set close together – as many as fifteen on the main slope of the top cushion. The portrait of Thomas Hardy painted by William Strang in 1893 is framed in this style (fig.81). Not only were these frames widely influential in Whistler's lifetime, but they continued to be used for many years after his death.

Fig.80
Coventry Patmore by John Singer Sargent, 1894 (no.106).

A Whistler frame, gilt directly onto the oak, made by C.M. May.

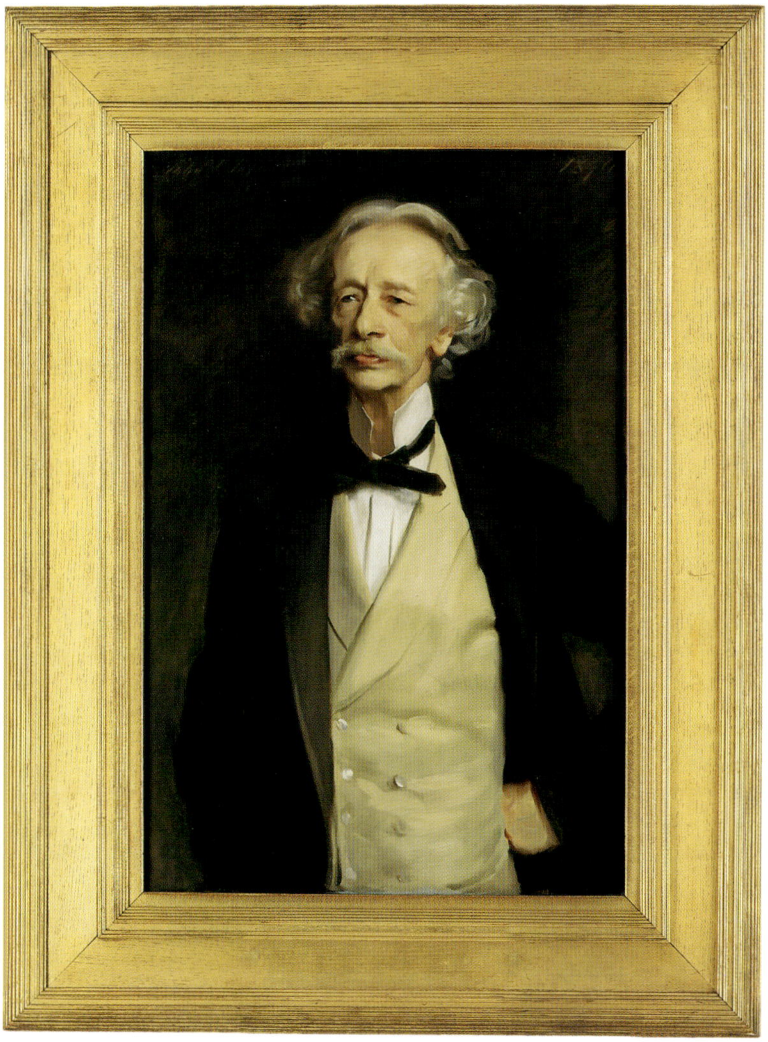

The twentieth century

From the late nineteenth century until the end of the First World War some of the most interesting frames were being made for portraits. Many younger artists were painting smaller pictures and experimenting with new frame styles. Compo frames remained popular: William Nicholson's two standard patterns of these years were in gilt compo, albeit in novel designs.[115] There was, however, a shift to polished wood – Nicholson's *Max Beerbohm* of 1905 (National Portrait Gallery) is an example – and a return to carved frames such as the superlative French-inspired frame on Sir John Lavery's great group of George V and his family of 1913 (fig.83). New revival styles – the Italian 'Pitti Palace', the Dutch ripple and the Spanish reverse pattern, all highly distinctive seventeenth-century styles – were used by painters such as Arthur Cope, Augustus John, J.S. Sargent, Luke Fildes and

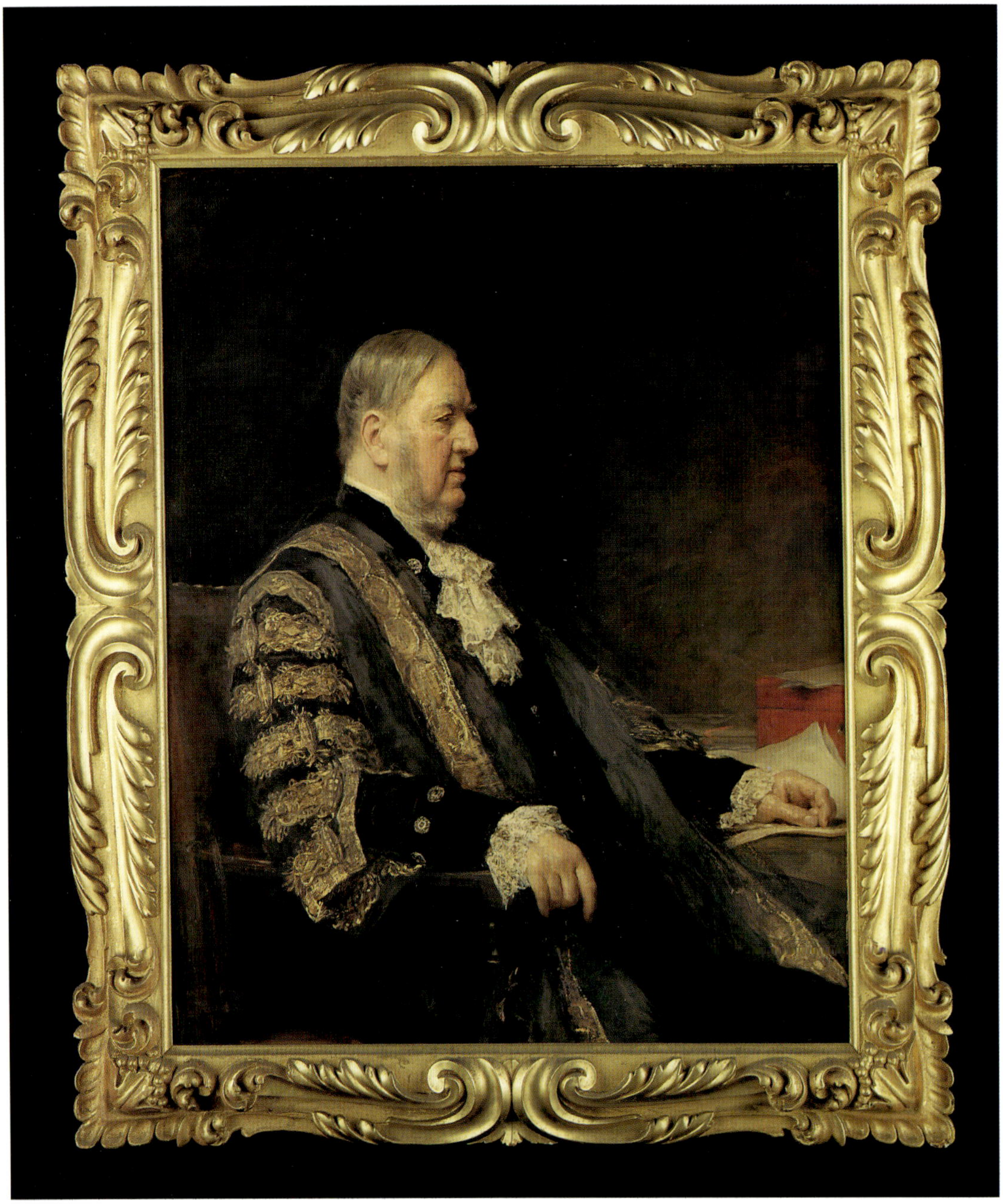

Fig.82
Sir William Harcourt by Sir Arthur Cope, 1904 (no.109).

An Italian 'Pitti Palace' revival frame of a pattern used by Cope.

Philip de Laszlo (see figs.82, 117, 118; nos.108, 114). These frames were produced to a high standard, often being carved, and were much closer in spirit to the originals than the compo revival styles of the previous century. The Watts frame ceased to be widely used and if there was a standard frame type it was the Whistler frame, which can be found on Augustus John's work, on C.R.W. Nevinson's in the 1910s, and on Gluck's as late as the 1940s (see fig.10).

The War Artists of the First World War included William Orpen, Henry Tonks, Philip Connard, and younger painters such as Wyndham Lewis, Paul Nash, Stanley Spencer and Henry Lamb. An indication of the frames used by these artists, many of them specially ordered despite the supposed need for war-time economy, is provided by the records of the Ministry of Information and the new Imperial War Museum.[116] In 1918 the Ministry was ordering brushes, colours and frames from the Chenil Galleries for 'Major Sir William Orpen ARA' including 'Best White Enamel 6″ Whistler Frames' ('always 6″ says Chenil'). Other artists' patterns are mentioned over the next year: gilt oak Whistler pattern, Sargent oak pattern for drawings, 'Strang' pattern one-inch oak and a Philpot special oak pattern with rosewood edges. Revival styles include a 'Panel Pattern Frame' and a Spanish moulding frame, burnished gilt with black panels. More unusually, Charles Holmes wanted his *Two-year-old Steel Works* framed in a similar style to Carpaccio's *St Ursula* in the National Gallery, London.

If the framing of the Great War pictures brings one era to a close, the Royal Academy's abandonment in 1920 of its rule insisting on gold frames opens another. The painted and polished wood frames of the 1920s and 1930s are often of simple section, and reduce the elaborate mouldings of the past to their essentials: a sloping side of an uninterrupted single curve or a flat section with simple raised inner and outer edges. The frame on Nina Hamnett's portrait of Osbert Sitwell (fig.85) is a particularly attractive example. In the 1930s pictures were often given an inner slip of canvas or linen, separating the frame from the canvas.[117] Apart from the simplicity of their forms, such frames often relied on the subtlety of their surface finishes for their attraction. This is borne out by the ledgers of a leading firm of framemakers, Alfred Stiles & Sons Ltd of Hammersmith. The gold-toned Dutch patterns, the Sargent oak gold and the Birkett Foster gold frames gave way to polished and painted frames: 'polished black rubbed slightly red' for Derwent Wood in 1925, 'wood parts to be green' for Russell Flint in 1930, 'stained special pink' for C.R.W. Nevinson in 1931, 'stone grey & slight pink smooth finish' for Ivon Hitchens in 1934.[118] There was also another tradition, exemplified by the reproduction frames in subdued tones popularised by Bourlet's and much used until recently.

In 1940 Stiles won the contract for the supply of War Artists frames in the Second World War.[119] Suiting the economy of the times, a single pattern was used for most pictures, a simple moulding frame of traditional section. But to suit the taste of the time these frames were normally finished in a warm off-white dragged or mottled painted finish, as can be seen in the galleries of the National Maritime Museum, Imperial War Museum and many provincial museums.

After the war new framemakers brought new ideas to bear. There were three notable trends, the return to gilt or silver-leaf frames, the introduction of simple narrow aluminium frames, and, more recently, the use of polished wood frames of flat or geometric section. The renewed enthusiasm for gilt frames was encouraged by framemakers such as Alfred Hecht and Robert Sielle, but using flatter or simpler sections than in the past, forsaking ornament for surface

Fig.83
The Royal Family at Buckingham Palace by Sir John Lavery (detail), 1913 (no.111).

A French rococo revival frame, perhaps made by Emile Remy.

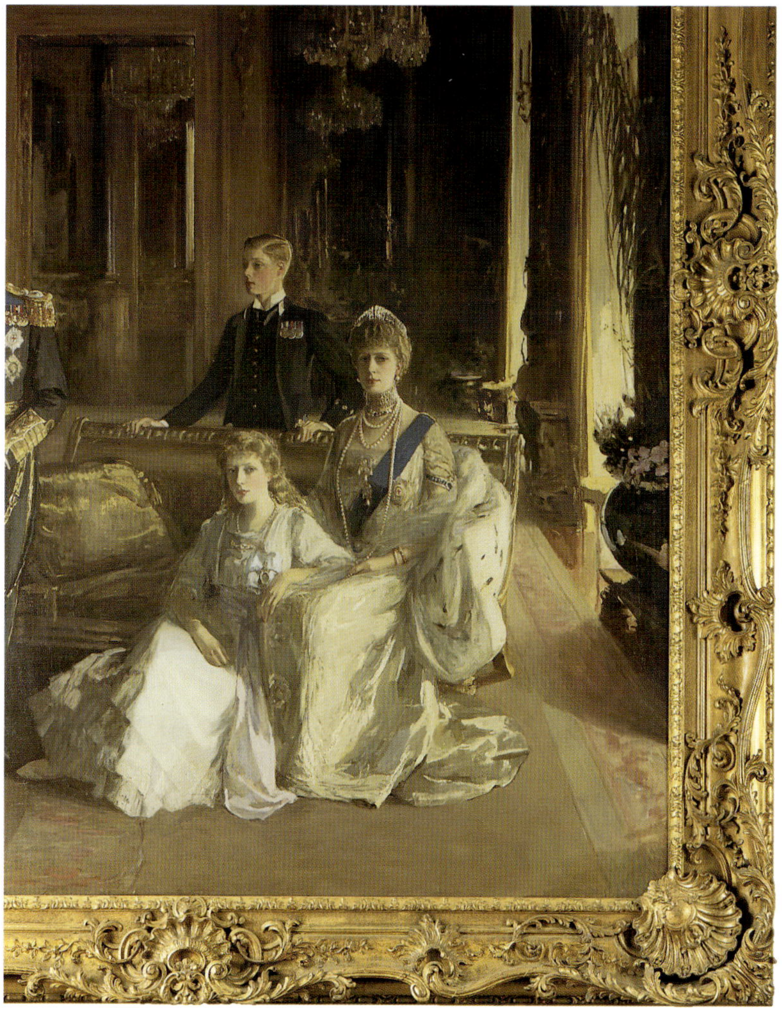

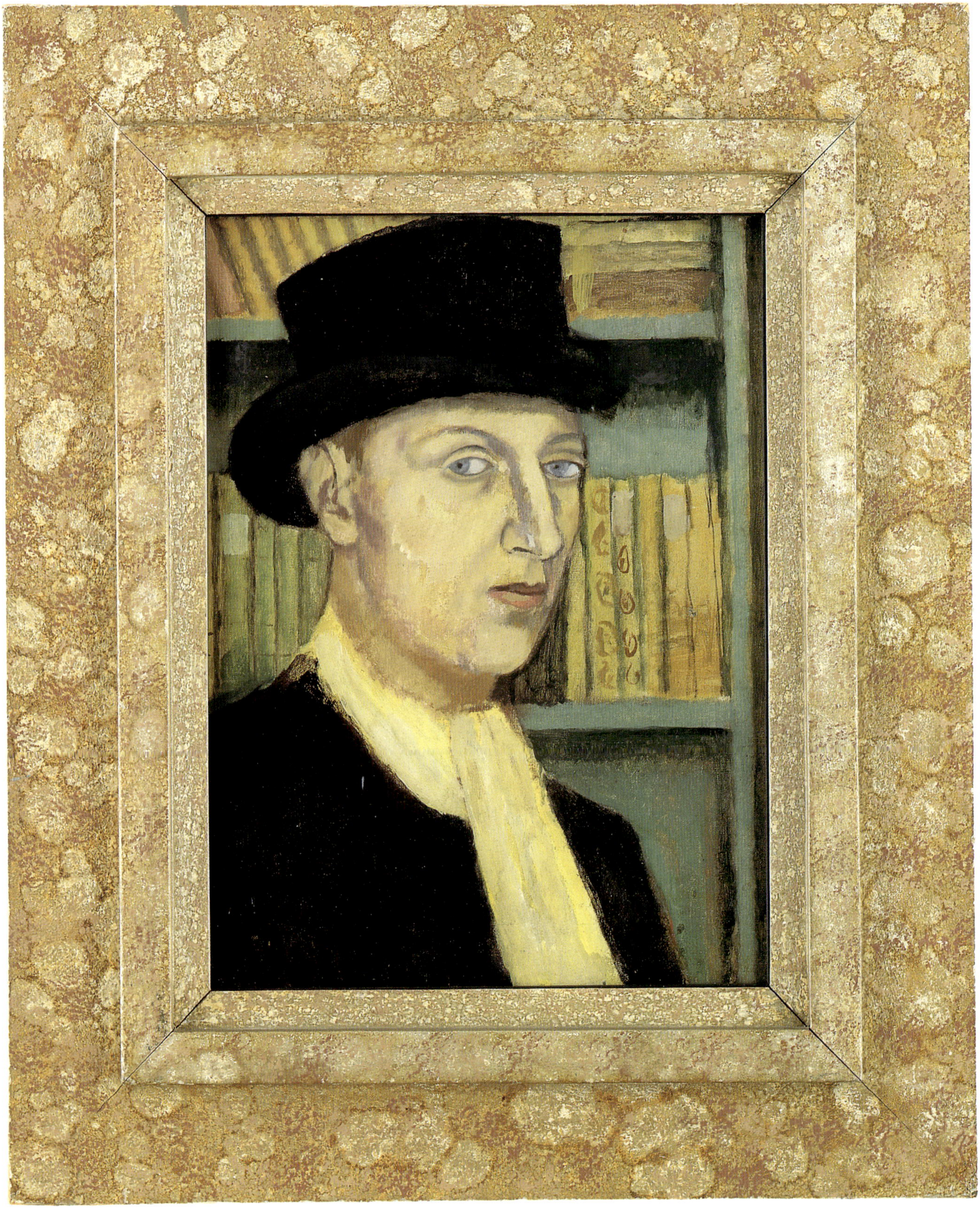

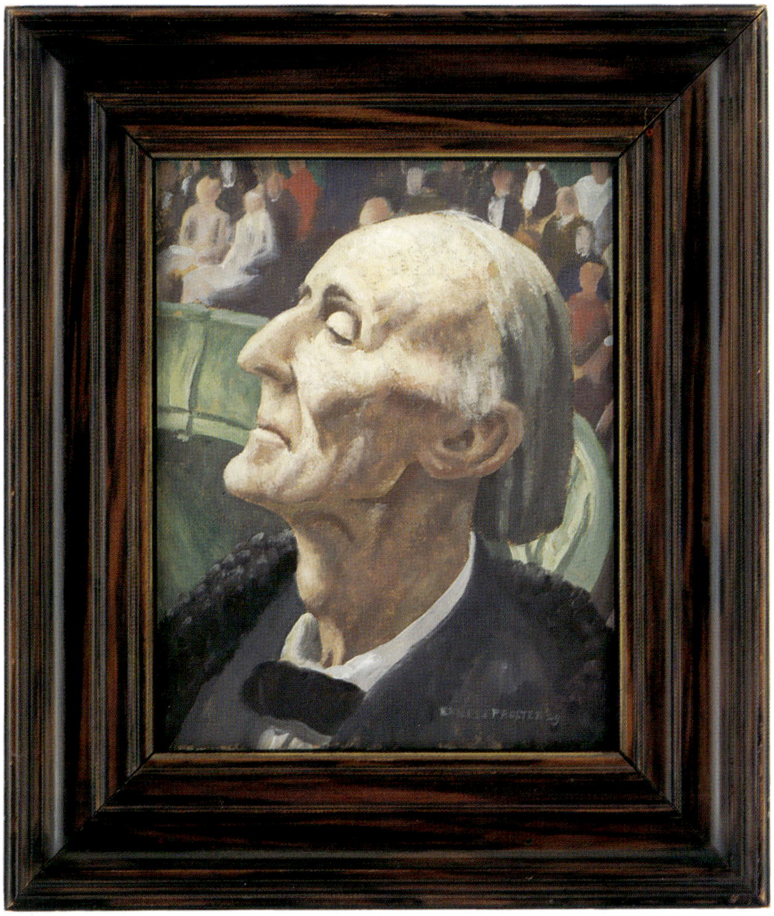

Fig.84
Frederick Delius by Ernest Proctor, 1929 (no.115).

A simulated rosewood frame.

Fig.85 (facing page)
Sir Osbert Sitwell by Nina Hamnett, *c*.1915-18 (no.112).

effects. What was once achieved by accidental wear and tear – the rubbing away of the surface to reveal the colour of the bole or the overlap of the sheets of gold leaf – was now arrived at by design. Graham Sutherland's portrait of Kenneth Clark (fig.22), painted in 1963-4, has a box section with flat raised inner and outer edges, burnished in gold, but with the dark grey bole used to offset the brilliance of the gold. Two recent frames by Nick Hawker, a silvered reverse section for Leonard Rosoman's portrait of Sir John Summerson with an oxidised finish (fig.38, and a flat silvered frame for Maggi Hambling's portrait of A.J.P. Taylor (no.131), where the overlap between the leaves of silver is treated decoratively, show what can be done with less expensive materials. Like much of the most successful modern work, these frames have simple profiles, relying for their effect on their quality of finish.

Perhaps as a reaction to the minimalist aluminium frames of the 1960s and 1970s, there has been renewed interest in using substantial polished wood sections whether flat, rounded or angular. Sometimes such frames are polished to reveal the wood grain, sometimes stained dark or to a particular colour. To take three examples from the last ten years, Tom Phillips's *Iris Murdoch* has a flat frame made by Andy Gizauskas, stained to a dark brown of similar intensity to the background of the picture (no.128), Alison Watt's *Queen Elizabeth the Queen Mother* has a reverse section stained to an off-white to take up the tonality of the portrait (no.130), while Tom Wood's *Alan Bennett* is framed in a polished ash cushion made for the artist by Alwyn Turner (National Portrait Gallery).

Recently a certain self-consciousness has crept into framemaking as is evident in the incorporation by artists of real objects into their frames: football studs in Humphrey Ocean's frame for his portrait of the soccer player, Daniel McGrain (Scottish National Portrait Gallery), cutlery in the frame of Jasper Johns' *Dancers on a Plane* (Tate Gallery), apparently referring to the multihandiness of Indian deities, and microphones and records around the frame of Howard Morgan's *Golden Gate Triptych*.[120]

As we near the end of the twentieth century it is possible to look back at the frames of the last hundred years and to see tremendous changes both in style and technique, changes as great as in any previous century. The renewed interest in picture framing in our time holds out the promise of further change in the future.

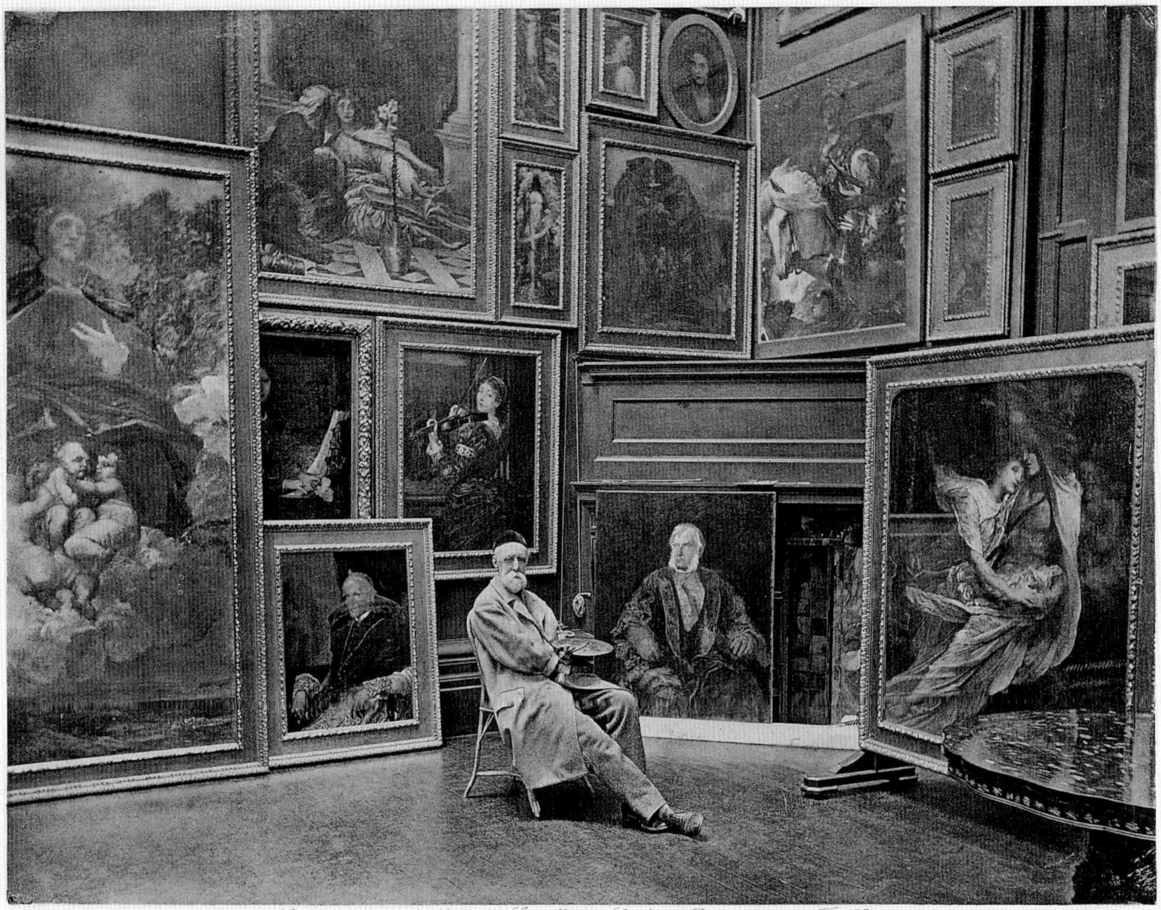

J. P. Mayall Photo. London published by Sampson Low Marston Searle & Rivington 188 Fleet St. Park Lane Studio...London

G. F. WATTS R.A.

Chapter 4
The Artist and the Picture Frame

The framing of portraits was generally an essential part of the business of the portrait painter, a business which by the late eighteenth century had become highly developed and competitive.[1] To earn a living, portrait painters had to produce a constant stream of portraits, as many a successful artist complained, and as a result there was a continual flow of work requiring framing. Most leading artists took trouble over how their paintings were framed and presented, and this was necessarily the case with portrait painters, since their sitters usually expected to take away their pictures complete with a handsome gilt frame, unless the portrait was an especially grand one, or was intended to be hung in a special position. Examination of artists' sitter books and accounts which refer to framing confirms that most portraits were sent out framed. Clearly the artist's role was often central, but it is difficult to ascertain the precise nature of their involvement because decisions on framing were usually made face-to-face and so went largely undocumented. It is therefore exceptional but all the more illuminating when evidence does survive, as in the cases of George Stubbs ('Mr. Stubs approves so much of this model ... that he will adopt it for his first enamel picture of the largest size'), Thomas Lawrence ('A good frame ... should be sufficiently broad and rich, but the ornament ... composed throughout of small parts') and J.R. Herbert ('I designed a frame a few years ago which goes by my name').[2]

Fig.86 (facing page) *George Frederic Watts in his gallery at Little Holland House* by J.P. Mayall, photogravure. From F.G. Stephens, *Artists at Home*, 1884.

Behind Watts is his portrait of Cardinal Manning, above his head is Lady Lindsay of Balcarres, both in Watts frames, and to the right, unframed, is the 7th Duke of Devonshire.

Although the 'Herbert' frame is hardly a household name, there are other more familiar patterns which are linked to individual artists. The Carlo Maratta frame, an imported Italian model, became a generic term for a frame type used in Britain in the late eighteenth century. The Lely panel frame is a modern designation for a late seventeenth-century frame type, and is something of a misnomer, since it does not seem to have become fashionable until after the death of Sir Peter Lely. But when a pattern became known by an artist's name in or soon after his lifetime – the Lawrence frame, the Watts frame or the Whistler frame – we are on firmer ground in suggesting that the artist had a part, probably the leading one, in the introduction of the frame. It is the exception, however, to find an artist actively promoting a style associated with their name as Gluck did with the 'Gluck' frame which she patented in 1933 (see fig.9).[3]

Much more common is the situation where a frame type is now recognised as being generally or uniquely associated with a particular artist and hence has come to be known by the artist's name, in the way the simple neo-classical 'Downman' frame is named after the portrait painter and draughtsman, John Downman (see fig.87). This process of identifying patterns associated with particular artists is a vital one. The frame styles of Rossetti, Watts, Whistler, Alma-Tadema and Leighton are characteristic and well known. But those of Francis Cotes, George

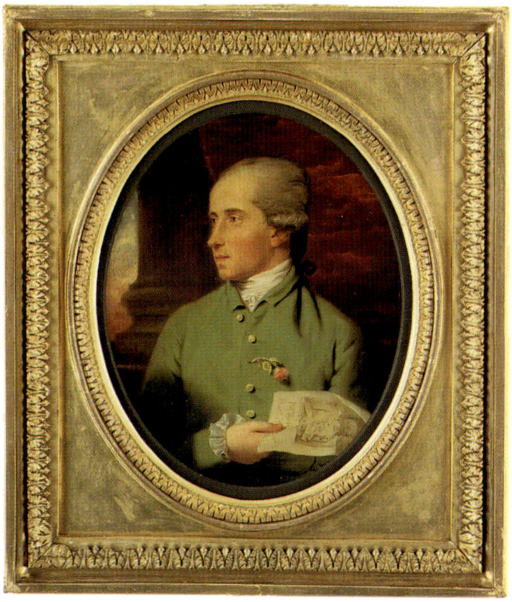

Fig.87 (right) *Benjamin West* by John Downman, 1777 (no.50).

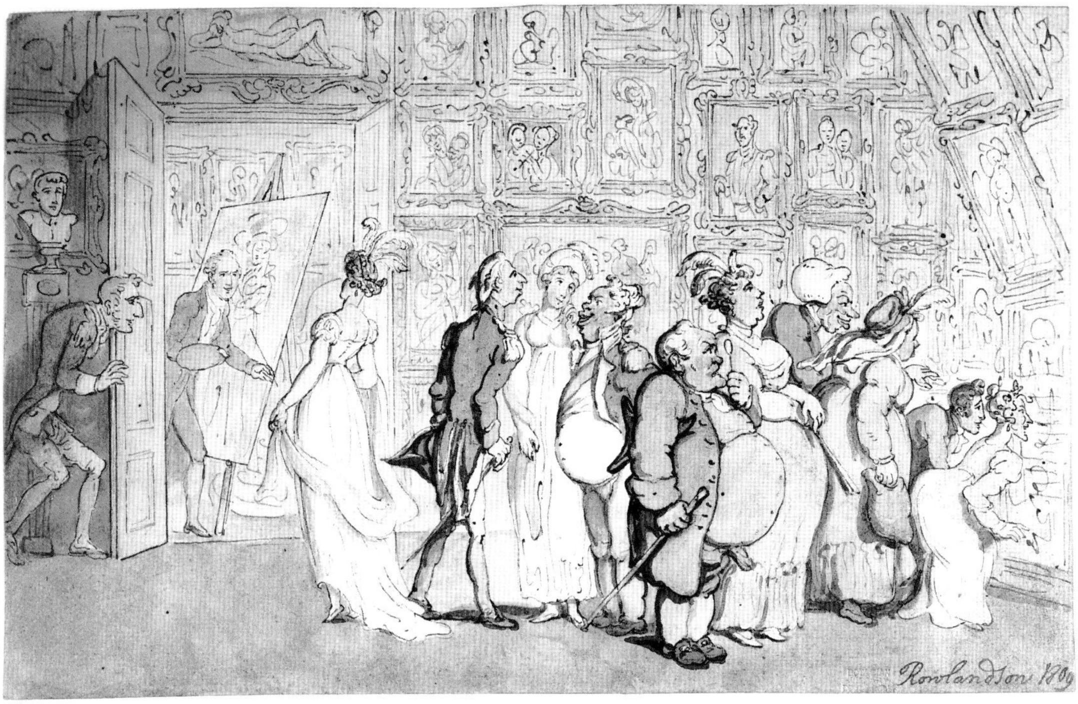

Fig.88
The Portrait Painter's Showroom by Thomas Rowlandson, 1809 (Ashmolean Museum, Oxford).

An imaginary view of a painter's showroom.

Romney and Thomas Lawrence are just as distinctive once one learns to recognise them. The process is a rewarding one because it enables the spectator to come to some understanding as to which frame patterns were chosen by the artist, which by the patron and which are later introductions. Only with this sort of knowledge can one hope to understand collections of British paintings and the taste of the artists and patrons which they represent.

Artists and their patrons

'Every portrait painter in England has a room to show his pictures, separate from that in which he works. People who have nothing to do, make it one of their morning amusements, to go and see these collections'. So wrote André Rouquet in *The Present State of the Arts in England* in 1754, after more than twenty years spent as a miniaturist working in London.[4] Some or probably all of the portraits to be admired in the showroom by a casual visitor or, more importantly, a potential patron, were exhibited framed (see fig.88). The accounts of George Romney's framemaker regularly refer to frames made for pictures in the showroom.[5] Romney's showroom was said to contain 'a large display of the portraits of well-known characters, painted at various periods of time',[6] while that of Joshua Reynolds was described as 'a splendid gallery for the exhibition of his works'.[7] The practice of having a showroom was certainly well established by 1734 when John Smibert, who had recently emigrated to America, wrote to an old patron in Scotland that his father-in-law had built him 'a large & handsome painting room & showroom'.[8] Here a sitter could see not only a selection of portraits by the artist but also examples of the frame patterns he was currently using.

The importance of the frame was widely acknowledged. The use of 'large Gold Frames' by the crayon painters George Knapton, Arthur Pond and William Hoare was one of the features George Vertue particularly commended in 1742 when writing about the vogue for pastel portraits.[9] In 1786 a lesser artist, Andrew Rymsdyk, was advertising 'the most fashionable frame that ever was invented' as a feature of his small portraits, while the frames offered with Matthew Boulton's 'mechanical paintings' were described as 'elegant and shewy'.[10] Artists were very aware of how important a frame was in selling a picture. Rossetti wrote to Ford Madox Brown in 1874 about the sale of one of Frederick Leyland's pictures by Frederic Leighton: 'His big Leighton fetched – what do you think? £2,677! and the thing is really bad even of its own kind! I believe that flash frame he put on it did the job!'[11]

Confirmation that most portraits, and many other pictures, were sent out framed can be obtained from surviving account books and studio records. The earliest British artist whose use of frames is documented is Mary Beale, a competent portrait painter in the Lely manner. The notebooks kept by her husband Charles Beale for 1677 and 1681 show that just over half her work was sent out ready framed.[12] In the case of Arthur Pond, whose very detailed account books survive for the period 1734-50, almost all his portraits are recorded as being sent out framed, as was commonly the case with pastels which were difficult to transport unless protected by a frame.[13] Two other pastel portraitists of the period, William Hoare and Francis Cotes, also sent out most of their work in this medium ready framed. For painters in oils in the late eighteenth century, there is the evidence of George Romney and James Northcote. In Romney's case an examination of one of his studio ledgers shows that in 1789 over seventy per cent of his portraits were sent out framed, a proportion which seems to be typical of his work in this decade.[14] An analysis of Northcote's account book indicates that in his first year in practice after his return from Italy in 1780 almost ninety per cent of his portraits were being sent out framed.[15]

In the nineteenth century several account books mentioning framing survive. Between a third and a half of James Ward's animal paintings and portraits were sent out framed by the artist in the 1810s and 1820s.[16] In the case of the marine painter, E.W. Cooke, the great majority of his seascapes went out framed in the period 1833-78.[17] The Scottish portrait painter, Colvin Smith, had almost eighty per cent of his portraits framed before dispatch in the years 1833-44.[18] An examination of the frames of other painters such as Francis Grant, George Richmond, G.F. Watts, J.E. Millais and Hubert von Herkomer confirms that the great majority of portraits were sent out framed. Painters in other genres might expect to send out their pictures ready framed but the evidence here still needs to be explored more carefully.

As Val Prinsep told Albert Moore in 1871, 'purchasers are only too glad for artists to choose their frames'.[19] Some patrons were willing to trust implicitly in the artist's judgement, as was Lord Whitworth to whom William Mulready wrote about a picture in 1816, 'I ... have as your Lordship desired, got such a Frame as I think best adapted to it'.[20] Another patron, R.J. Spiers of Oxford, told William Etty in 1846, 'With regard to the frames for these three, you will oblige me by ordering for them just such frames as you prefer, whether flat or otherwise, but I should like good ones'.[21]

Artists could expect to be asked to advise on framing. Hogarth was called upon to make recommendations on the framing and hanging of his large painting, *Paul before Felix*, at Lincoln's Inn in 1748.[22] John Shackleton, Painter to the King, was obliged to produce a design for a frame for the British Museum Trustees in 1762, to help them decide on the framing of his portrait of George II.[23] And Colvin Smith was asked to advise on the appropriate width of frame for a portrait of Lord Lauderdale: 'I have seen a very fine old frame, but before I conclude my bargain for it, I wish to know what width the Frame should be to look handsome. The frame I allude to is about 10 inches or a foot wide'.[24]

The artist was often expected to make the arrangements for framing. 'At 11 send the frame maker to Col. Geakle's', noted Joshua Reynolds in his sitter book in 1755.[25] 'General Stuart Desires that as soon as his Picture is put into his Frame and finished we must let him know that he may look at it', noted George Romney's studio assistant in 1787.[26] 'I gave orders to have the Frame to our Deane's Picture put on', wrote Charles Jervas to his patron, Lord Harley, in 1724 about his portrait of Dean Swift.[27]

Some artists seemed to prefer to leave the

framing arrangements to the sitter, however, doing no more than provide advice and recommend a framemaker. In 1792 Henry Raeburn sent his compliments to Miss Bruce, sister of Professor John Bruce, advising her that he had sent home her mother's portrait, adding, 'If she wishes to have a frame made for it he will send Mr. Liddell the Frame Maker to wait on her',[28] and in 1814 he advised another client that his portrait of George Buchanan 'should not be sent to a frame maker's shop for fear of accidents, 'tis enough that the measure of it be given'.[29] Despite this apparent distancing by Raeburn from the business of framing, his portraits are readily recognisable by their distinctive frame types and on occasion he is known to have arranged framing for his sitters.

Raeburn's avowed reticence may have been a response to the difficulties involved in framing. Not all patrons were easy to please, witness a curt letter William Etty received in 1838: 'My dear Sir, I find the frame is much too large – be so good as order a moderate priced one from your frame maker. I am Yours &c. J. Fairlie'.[30]

Requests from patrons for frame patterns out of the ordinary were another potential source of difficulties. In 1767 Gainsborough had to get a frame made from a drawing sent him by the MP, Richard Stevens, and on receipt of the framemaker's bill he felt obliged to apologise to Stevens, 'I think it a dear one, but he says the trouble he had in working after a limited scale and pattern in Drawing occasioned the additional charge'.[31] A few years later in 1778 Robert Edge Pine faced similar complaints from David Garrick about the cost of frames made to a pattern which Garrick had apparently used some years before for his portrait by Nathaniel Dance. Pine explained that it was 'a pattern I had never before seen, and consequently could not inform you of any price for it ... I charge you what the maker charged them at ... if you think them dear I must beg you to observe that oval frames are much more expensive than square ones'.[32]

The considerable expense of frames meant that they were a cost to be reckoned with. In the seventeenth and eighteenth centuries the frame was normally the responsibility of the patron, charged separately from the picture. Only those artists routinely selling their portraits framed, as pastel painters did because of the fragility of the medium, found it expedient to fix on an inclusive price. When William Hoare set up in Bath in 1738, for example, he charged five guineas for his pastel portraits or eight guineas framed and glazed.[33] The introduction of annual exhibitions, at the Society of Artists in 1760, and in 1769 at the Royal Academy, led to a new situation. Some artists produced uncommissioned work which they hoped to sell at one of the annual exhibitions in London or, from the early nineteenth century, in the provinces, and in this case artists had to find the frames and then hope to recoup any outlay if and when they sold their work. An entry in the Council minutes of the Royal Academy before the 1779 exhibition records that Edward Penny would send in a whole-length portrait 'if he can get a frame'.[34] In the 1830s the Old Water-Colour Society provided frames to those of its members who had been voted one of the yearly premiums.[35] In 1901 Pollak & Co were advertising 'Gold Frames lent on hire for Exhibitions', but how common the practice was of hiring frames remains uncertain.[36] It was probably much more usual for an artist to keep frames for reuse, a practice which even the first President of the Academy, Sir Joshua Reynolds, adopted, as his pupil James Northcote recalled: 'Sir Joshua's frames went year after year; one frame in particular, I remember, had gone so often that it might almost have found its way to the Exhibition alone'.[37]

Was the frame included in the exhibition price or not? Disputes could arise if there was ill-feeling or misunderstanding. Joseph Wright of Derby instructed the secretary of the Society of Artists in 1774 that 'the picture of *The Earth Stopper* is to be delivered to Lord Hardwicke without the frame. The shabby price his Lordship is to pay for it will leave no room for his Lordship to expect the frame with it'. Wright claimed that the picture was 'exhibited in an old Italian moulding frame which I have had by me for many years and keep for the use of the exhibition'.[38]

Fig.89
Joseph Chamberlain by Frank Holl, 1886.

In a Watts frame chosen by Holl.

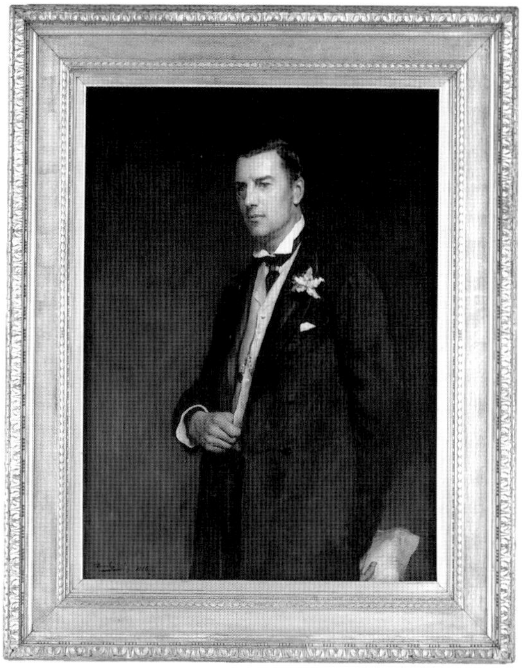

Some artists, such as the landscape painter, William Daniell, included the frame in the price, a practice which Joseph Farington specifically noted when Daniell increased his prices in 1805.[39] The alternative approach, to charge separately, was noted by Philip Hamerton: the successful artist, he wrote in 1871, 'can easily stipulate, and often does so, that the frame shall be a separate transaction between the purchaser and the frame-maker'.[40] This was the practice of the landscape painter Thomas Creswick. Writing to the Preston industrialist, Thomas Miller, in 1858 to offer him a picture, he explained that the price of seventy guineas did not include the cost of the frame: 'I find so many differences of opinion about frames that I never sell my pictures with them'.[41]

The most common practice, at least in the nineteenth century, was to treat the price of the frame as an extra for commissioned portraits and paintings but to include it for uncommissioned paintings exhibited at the Royal Academy with a view to sale. The rule for exhibiting watercolours at the Old Water-Colour Society, at least initially, was that the price should not include the frame, leaving the purchaser the option of buying drawings framed or unframed.[42] Confusion could arise, however, when the situation was not made absolutely clear at the outset of a commission. When the Newcastle collector, James Leatheart, complained to Albert Moore in 1871 about the extra charge he had made for a pair of fine frames from Foord & Dickinson, Moore was obliged to explain his practice: 'when pictures are bought in their frames, the latter are included in the purchase – but in the case of commissions the price named only refers to the picture & the frame which is eventually made, is paid for by its possessor'.[43] Moore enlisted the support of Watts and Leighton in his cause but still lost his patron as a result of this disagreement.

It is not surprising, then, that when Watts was approached two years later by the politician, Sir Charles Dilke, he was careful to explain his practice: 'I have made it a rule not to provide frames to portraits unless it is desired I should do so and then the price of the frame is extra. This does not apply to a picture bought after it is complete as the frame is then part of it and considered in the price …'.[44] He went on to ask Dilke for a further five guineas on top of the three hundred he had already paid for a portrait of John Stuart Mill. Watts's attitude must have seemed tight-fisted to Dilke, all the more so when there were other artists who took a different approach. Frank Holl, when selling a portrait of Chamberlain to Dilke in 1885 (fig.89), wrote: 'You are only indebted to me for the picture viz. 350 gs … I never make any charge for the frame'.[45]

This issue has not gone away in the twentieth century, as a letter from Lawrence Gowing to the Director of the National Portrait Gallery in 1982 shows: 'I always invoice the frames of portraits, which have been fluctuating so wildly in price, separately to the purchaser'.[46]

Artists and their framemakers

'It is evident that F. and D. are the only frame makers', wrote Rossetti in 1876.[47] At this period Foord & Dickinson were the favoured framemakers of many leading Victorian artists: Rossetti, Leighton, Whistler and Burne-Jones, to name but a few. Leading artists have almost always chosen to go to the best specialist framemakers, and at any one time there were only a limited number of really competent businesses to choose from. This is not to say that a wide range of framemakers did not work for artists but rather that a limited number of firms often secured a disproportionate part of the business. In the eighteenth century, for example, Isaac Gosset was favoured by William Hogarth, Allan Ramsay, William Hoare and Thomas Gainsborough. In the nineteenth century it was not only Foord & Dickinson which attracted numerous artists, but also Joseph Green, later trading as W.A. Smith, and Criswick's, later Dolman's. Their clientele is described in more detail in Chapter 6. In the early years of the twentieth century Chapman Bros were used by Sargent and Orpen, and after the First World War, Alfred Stiles by Mark Gertler, Ivon Hitchens and Graham Sutherland among others. Since the Second World War two or three framemakers have played a leading role; Alfred Hecht framed the work of Sutherland and Francis Bacon, while more recently, Nick Hawker at John Jones has worked with Leonard Rosoman and Maggi Hambling.

It seems likely that framemakers were chosen largely on the basis of their reputations. 'Sir T. Lawrence came home with me & we had conversation respecting his business with Tijou, the Frame Maker', noted Joseph Farington in his diary in 1816, and he later referred to Lawrence settling Tijou's account.[48] By the early 1820s Lawrence's very considerable business had been transferred to George Morant of New Bond Street. Rossetti's claim that Foord & Dickinson were 'the only frame makers' was made in exasperation with another maker, L. Bertram, whom he ventured to try after a disagreement with Foord's manager, Richard Williams. Rossetti became anxious to return to Foord's, whose quality was reliable. 'In seeing Williams', Rossetti told his studio assistant, 'you might make some approach towards my giving him another order, but in a light and trifling manner, and try and get from him some expression of regret for the cause of the split'.[49]

In the eighteenth century artists working outside London, if their clientele was a sophisticated one, might prefer to get their work framed by a London maker. 'I wait for its frame from London', wrote William Hoare to his constant patron, Henry Hoare, in 1760.[50] William Hoare used Isaac Gosset to frame his pictures, as did another Bath portrait painter of the period, Thomas Gainsborough.[51] Artists working in Bath sometimes found it convenient to use their framemaker as an agent to receive payment in London. William Hoare wrote to the Hon. Charles Yorke, the Attorney-General, in 1762, 'Mr Gosset has the Account of the Pictures I have had the favour to do for you, & I will desire him to wait on you', and again in 1764 thanking him for paying Gosset for various pictures.[52] At a later date the Edinburgh landscape painter Alexander Nasmyth had many of his paintings framed in London, probably because he used the Royal Academy as a showcase for his work. Just as Hoare and Gainsborough relied on Gosset as a London agent, so Nasmyth depended on his framemaker, William Cribb, when it came to dealing in London. Writing from Edinburgh in 1826, he offered Cribb pictures at a reduced price, 'as you and I have had many and I hope may have more dealings'.[53] There were of course many capable makers working outside London, especially in the nineteenth century, and on occasion the trade was in the other direction, as the Manchester framemaker, Charles Rowley, was proud to point out in his autobiography: 'I made some fine frames for Rossetti, and so saved him much over London prices'.[54]

The working relationship between artist and whichever framemaker he or she chose to use was a vital one. A good framemaker was important to an artist for there was so much he could do. The framemaker could come to know the artist well, and might have the entrée to his or her premises. 'At breakfast Mr. Coward called to measure a frame', noted Constable in his diary in 1824.[55] Several years later in 1832 Constable wrote to his friend and fellow-artist, C.R. Leslie: 'Mr. Smith of Bond Street has just been here. He has just carried home the magnificent frame for your picture of the "Grosvenor Gang" – it is in it & fits beautifully. I told him I hoped he had not hid an atom – he said he had not'.[56] The necessity of a reliable framemaker is very apparent from Constable's correspondence with another friend, John Fisher, in 1823. Constable was obliged to use a framemaker chosen by Fisher's father for a particular picture, and complained: 'I am stopped in its progress by the wretched Smith, who has & will plague me to death with the frame, how vexing it is to be involved again with these wretches whom I had long ago turned adrift – for worthlessness, lies, and ingratitude'.[57]

What passed between artist and framemaker is seldom recorded, however, because most dealings were face-to-face. Instructions were occasionally written on the back of a work, however, as with an anonymous pastel of Capel Hanbury's daughter in the 1740s: 'To be framed and glazed. To be sent to Mr Capel Hanbury in the Privy Garden, & you will receive 7 Gui & half, & the Carriage as usual'.[58] P.J. de Loutherbourg was not content merely to recommend Robert Cribb to a patron, Mr Dunnage, in 1808, but insisted on writing to Cribb particularly requesting him to follow an existing pattern 'in every respect'.[59] But if the artist were not so precisely fixed on a particular pattern, he might be glad to give general directions and then rely on the framemaker's judgement as Edward Bawden, the watercolourist, did with Alfred Stiles in 1957:

The frames I should like to be white, with besides a thin gold edge if possible, but nothing very elaborate; also, as for the inner slip you generally give me, could it please be plain white or off-white, perhaps canvas, but not with any coloured stippling or fancy finish. I think that the plainer the frames are the better they might be. However, I am sure you will do something attractive ... [60]

There must have been many conversations of this kind between artist and maker of which we have no record.

'As to when I shall be able to send the pictures to you I can say nothing. I write to my framemaker from time to time, in as strong language as I can comfortably use, but there is no result'. So John Strudwick told one patron in 1896.[61] It was in the painter's interest to keep a good working relationship with his framemaker. Such a relationship was even more obviously in the framemaker's interest because a successful artist could bring a steady flow of relatively unproblematic business for what were usually standard frame patterns. Most complaints by artists related to the quality of their framemaker's work or to speed of delivery. To read of 'pictures stolen by the framemaker', in correspondence between John Smibert and his fellow artist, Arthur Pond, in 1744, is quite exceptional.[62] Much more typical is Leighton's cry, 'I suppose that horrible framemaker must have sent at least *part* of the frame by that time', when proposing to an important patron that he should shortly come to see a picture in its frame.[63]

Exceptionally in the case of Rossetti, correspondence dating from 1876 survives to show both the artist's and the framemaker's point of view. In response to Rossetti's criticisms, his then framemaker, L. Bertram, responded in no uncertain terms:

I have the frame now before me and fail to discover the slightest fault in it, every possible pains was bestowed on it from beginning to finish, there is not one spot of lacquer on it and is not gilt with inferior gold but the very best procurable. The punched design on the flat I consider the best I have ever done in my life, in fact, the frame is a perfect specimen of good workmanship and materials of unsurpassed quality. ... You cannot get a better go where you may.[64]

Whatever the concerns of the artist, it was important for the framemaker to receive regular payment. In 1676 John Michael Wright told a patron, Sir Walter Bagot, that 'before Christmas I allwayes make even my accounts with my Carvers, gilders, Joyners, and Colourmen, etc'.[65] When Charles Beale, Mary Beale's husband, received a loan of £100 in 1681, being 'in so great distress for money to pay severall Importunate Debts', the largest amount he paid out, other than for the rent, was £20 to John Norris, his wife's framemaker, 'in part of the Account betwixt us'.[66]

An artist and his framemaker would settle accounts at intervals. For this purpose it seems that some sort of frame book was normally kept. There is a passing reference in Sir William Beechey's account book in 1816, 'credited in the framebook', but Beechey's frame book, like almost all others, is lost.[67] The only leading portrait painter whose frame books do survive is George Romney; his frames have already been described in Chapter 3. Apart from recording interesting details as to the frame patterns used, these frame books and the associated documentation show that moneys for frames might be collected by either artist or framemaker and that there was an annual settling of accounts between the two men.[68] Arthur Pond's account book from 1734 to 1750, though not a frame book, does show that he made fairly regular payments on account to Gosset, his framemaker, usually two or three times a year, so that the outstanding balance was kept in check.[69]

An artist could expect a cut from his framemaker's takings, as Joseph Farington explained to Sir George Beaumont in 1806:

Sir George desired me to tell Him explicitly whether painters derived any profit from frames. I answered Him witht. hesitation, that it had ever been the case since I knew the profession; that Sir Joshua Reynolds and all others had an allowance from the frame maker, but that the price to others was not encreased by it, as that allowance was deducted from the common profit of the frame maker. It was what may be called a trade allowance.[70]

Thus in the annual settling of accounts between George Romney and his framemaker, William Saunders, in the years 1783 to 1792, a 'Discount of frames delivered' is often specifically listed, amounting to as much as sixteen per cent, typically 10s on a half-length, 18s on a three-quarter length, £1 on a large three-quarter length and £1.9s on a whole-length, quite considerable sums.[71] In rather similar manner, C.R. Leslie was charged a discounted price of nine pounds for a nine guinea frame, an allowance of just under five per cent, by John Smith & Son in 1837.[72]

Not surprisingly, such payments were seldom acknowledged publicly. Beaumont's direct question to Farington in 1806 was sufficiently unusual for Farington to note it in his diary. A discount or allowance was not an artist's exclusive prerogative, however, for any professional person might expect some financial recognition for introducing new business. It is only in the rare instances when one has access to the financial records of those in the business does the system become apparent. Thus the paintings restorer, R. Brown, of Alpha Road, Regent's Park, benefited from passing frame orders to William Paley in the 1810s and 1820s,[73] while the artists' colourmen, Charles Roberson & Co, offered three different prices in their catalogues: wholesale, retail and professional, a system which favoured artists among others until it was abandoned in 1920 after complaints of abuse.[74]

On occasion the relationship between artist and framemaker could blossom into one of friendship. William Marlow is called 'my worthy friend' by the framemaker, Thomas Vials, in his will in 1780,[75] while Gainsborough painted the portrait of Isaac Gosset, who was to be present at his funeral in 1788, as one of 'those friends he most respected'.[76] In the nineteenth century George Richmond and his son, William Blake Richmond, were close friends of the framemaker James Henry Chance. Chance bought one of the son's early works and later sat to him for his portrait; he also owned a self-portrait by the father which he inscribed, 'one of my best friends'.[77]

Artists and their frames

Although artists have often taken an interest in framing, there are few extant records of their wishes for the frames of their pictures before the late eighteenth century. In the case of continental artists, some earlier sketches for frames exist, for example by the Italian painters Filippo Lippi, Luca Cambiaso and Pietro da Cortona,[78] and occasionally an early frame designed by an artist is known, such as Durer's elaborate setting for his painting, *The Adoration of the Holy Trinity*,

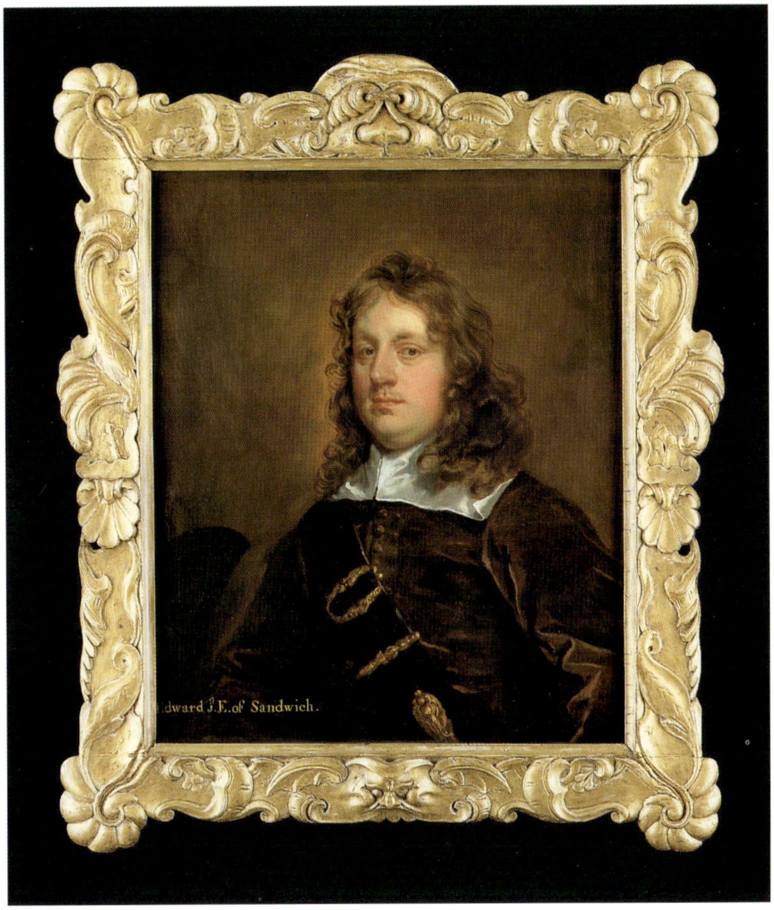

Fig.90
Edward Montagu, 1st Earl of Sandwich by Sir Peter Lely, *c.*1659 (no.16).

which was executed by Veit Stoss.[79] Occasionally, too, the attitude of an artist is documented. Poussin, according to one of his patrons, 'always requests that his paintings be given quite simple frames with no burnished gold'.[80] In Britain it is possible to document the interest of artists in the appearance of picture frames from the late eighteenth century, when their involvement with framing increased. This documentation can be supplemented by observation of the frame types which can be associated with individual artists by identifying recurring patterns. It is the visual evidence of the surviving original frames which often provides the readiest insight into an artist's intentions.

Whatever the artist's taste, he or she had to match the means and wishes of his or her patrons. Most portrait frames sent out by artists were produced to a price. The 'artist's frame', if we can call it that, usually avoided elaborate carving or highly detailed finishing, and was produced by the carver and gilder to an acceptably high standard for a set price; it was a product for a general market, albeit a relatively sophisticated one. Patrons wanting more elaborate frames or with their own ideas would usually arrange their own framing.

The seventeenth century

There is little documentary evidence of the attitude of artists to picture frames in Britain in the seventeenth century but a letter from John Michael Wright, written in 1676 to Sir Walter Bagot, does reveal both the extent and the limitations of his role:

'Yo^{r} frames ... are richer than the first patterne I shewed you ... but my Lady Wilbraham comming hither caused her's to bee made broader and richer ... wch occasioned that I did the like to all yo^{rs} that they might not bee inferiour to any in that Country'.[81]

It is evident from her husband's notebooks that another artist of the period, Mary Beale, could provide her sitters with a range of frame types – bunched gilt, leatherwork gilt, raffle leaf, stick gilt and ebony, as they were termed – but beyond naming the frames, these records provide no evidence as to her attitude or taste.[82] On the present known evidence it is not possible to associate specific patterns with particular artists at this period.

That Van Dyck sent out some of his portraits with frames during his stay in London is shown by the bill he submitted to Charles I in about 1638, where two of the portraits of the king are listed as framed and other frames are mentioned as outstanding from a former account.[83] There is a portrait of Charles I at Ham House which appears to be that described by Van Dyck as 'Le Roi vestu de noir au Monsr Morre, avecq sa mollure', 'Morre' being William Murray, later Earl of Dysart, owner of Ham. The superb carved and gilt frame on this portrait, if it is indeed the original supplied by Van Dyck, provides an indication of his taste in framing.[84]

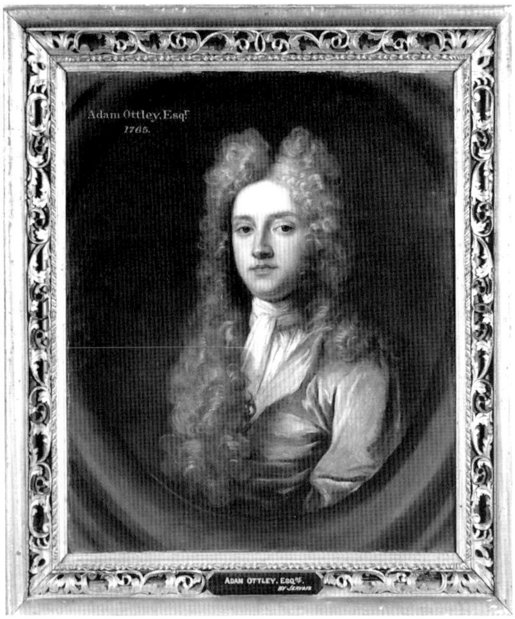

Fig.91 (left)
Adam Ottley by Charles Jervas, *c*.1715 (National Library of Wales).

In the case of Sir Peter Lely, many more pictures survive in what may be their original frames, and a limited number of extant bills record frames being supplied with pictures.[85] Two of Lely's early family groups, *The Perryer Family*, 1655, and his *Lord and Lady Southampton* of *c*.1660 have exceptionally rich frames for the Commonwealth period, but without documentation it is difficult to associate them with Lely.[86] We are on more certain ground with the Sunderland pattern used on many of his pictures in the 1650s and early 1660s, including his *Earl and Countess of Essex* (fig.45) and his smaller *Earl of Sandwich* (fig.90). This sea-monster-and-shells pattern is found so often on his work of the period, and more often on his work than on other artists', that it is possible to suggest that the type was much favoured by him.[87] The quality of Lely's frames should not surprise us; he had trained in Holland, he owned paintings by Van Dyck and was by far the most cosmopolitan and sophisticated artist working in England during the Commonwealth.

After the Restoration, several different patterns, including the fully developed Sunderland frame with cartouche and serrated sight edge, can be found on Lely's work and it seems that other artists of the period, such as John Michael Wright and Mary Beale, were using a rather similar range of frames. In the case of Sir Godfrey Kneller, we know the names of his framemakers, the sort of patterns he used and that a good number of pictures were sent out ready framed, but it is not possible to link individual patterns specifically with Kneller rather than with other artists.[88]

The eighteenth century

It is not until the early eighteenth century, with the work of Kneller's pupil, Charles Jervas, that a frame type can be associated with some confidence with a particular artist. Jervas began to use an Italianate frame of Maratta profile with applied carving of scrolling leaves in the hollow (see fig.91) following his return to London in 1709 after almost ten years in Paris and Rome. This pattern is different from the frames generally in use in England at the period and can better be compared with contemporary Italian frames of Bolognese and Venetian origin.[89] The hollow is stained black, so showing up the applied carving to great effect (rather in the manner of the flat black-and-gold frames originating in the seventeenth century; see fig.48).[90]

In the early 1740s George Vertue singled out the use of 'large Gold Frames' in discussing the work of the pastellists, George Knapton, Arthur Pond and William Hoare.[91] Most pastels were sent out ready framed (hence the importance of an attractive frame as a selling-point), and most have been left in their frames ever since. The first type to become fashionable, a Palladian frame with distinctive shells ornamenting the projecting corners, was used by Pond and Hoare and later by Knapton's pupil, Francis Cotes, almost as if it were the expected uniform for a pastel in the 1740s (it can also sometimes be found on oils; see fig.55). In his journal Pond called frames of this kind 'architrave gold frames', and his source of supply was given as 'Gosset' – although it is not clear to which member of the family of framemakers Pond was referring.[92]

Relatively few of Pond's works have been traced but the many by Hoare in this pattern

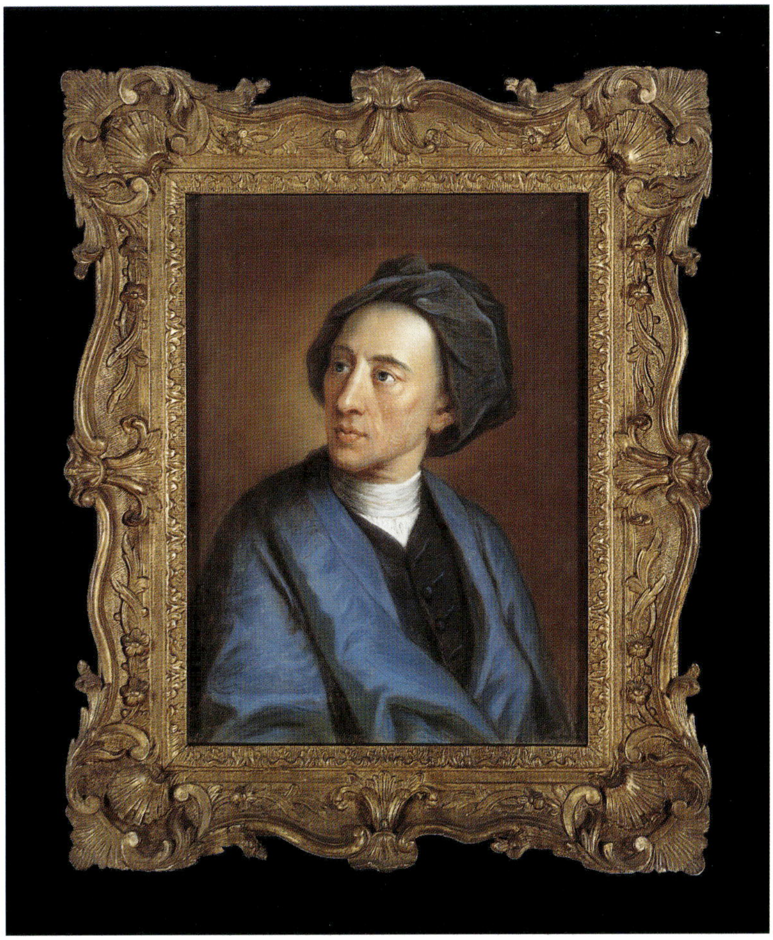

Fig.92 (above)
Alexander Pope by William Hoare, 1740 or later (no.43).

Fig.93 (right)
Thomas Pelham-Holles, 1st Duke of Newcastle by William Hoare, *c.*1752(?) (no.44).

date to the 1740s and 1750s. Hoare also used a distinctive rococo frame (see fig.92) on his pastels from the 1750s as well as a more ordinary Maratta pattern (see fig.93) with a crisply cut small-scale acanthus-and-tongue Carlo ornament in the scoop. His rococo frame, French-inspired and sculptural in quality, is just what one might expect from Isaac Gosset, who is known to have supplied many of his frames.

Like Hoare, Cotes appears to have offered his patrons a choice between three different styles for his pastels: an English Palladian pattern, a French-inspired rococo frame and an Italianate Maratta model, a demonstration of the range of fashionable styles in the 1750s. His rococo pattern is an anglicised version of the type favoured by the French-trained pastellist, Jean-Etienne Liotard, who was in London from 1753 to 1755.[93] Cotes's Maratta pattern (see fig.62), an early example of the use of the style in England, is distinguished by the denseness of its carving so that the Carlo ornament completely fills the hollow, and the tongues at the ends of each run come very close to the corners. In the 1760s when Cotes turned to oil painting in earnest he continued to use the Maratta style, but often preferred a handsome fluted frame (see fig.94) of neo-classical appearance with the ribbon-and-reed of the sight edge and the fluting in the hollow worked in the gesso in the French manner.

In the middle years of the eighteenth century it became quite common for artists to use distinctive frame patterns for their work. Highmore, Hudson, Ramsay and Wright of Derby all seem to have developed their own framing styles although the subsequent passage of more than two centuries has seen the loss of many original frames. Not all portraits were sent out in frames of distinctive patterns (indeed the proportion may have been half or less at times), nor were all such patterns exclusively associated with one particular artist, but nonetheless we can with some confidence associate certain recurring patterns with particular artists.

A detailed analysis of Allan Ramsay's work suggests that from the late 1740s he used two

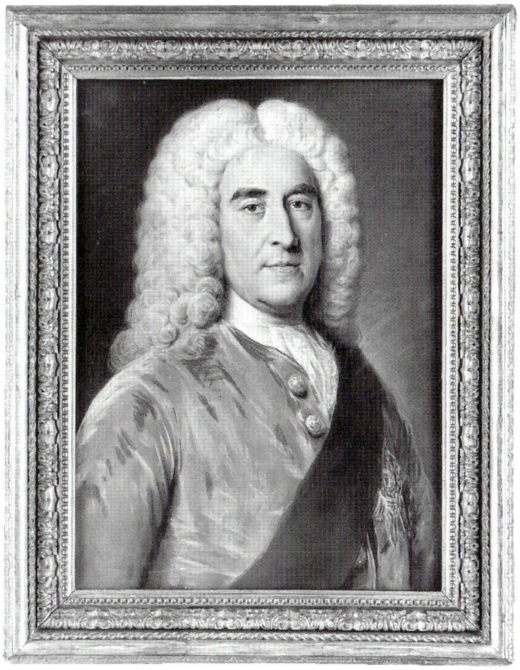

frame types for his smaller portraits (that is, those measuring thirty by twenty-five inches or less), and that one in five of these portraits retain their frames.[94] One of his preferred types, a full-blown rococo style, seems to have been used almost exclusively by Ramsay; the other is of a much more common pattern which was widely used at the time (see fig.59). In view of the fact that it has not been possible to identify a standard pattern on Ramsay's three-quarter length portraits, those measuring fifty by forty inches, it might seem that patrons were more inclined to have their own frames made for these pictures, but judging from the output of Ramsay's rival, Thomas Hudson, this was not necessarily the case. For with Hudson it is much easier to identify standard patterns on his three-quarter lengths such as that of Sir Peter Warren (fig.95). This rococo frame type is one of several found on Hudson's portraits of the 1750s. Can its use be seen as a response to Ramsay's choice of a distinctive rococo frame in the late 1740s?

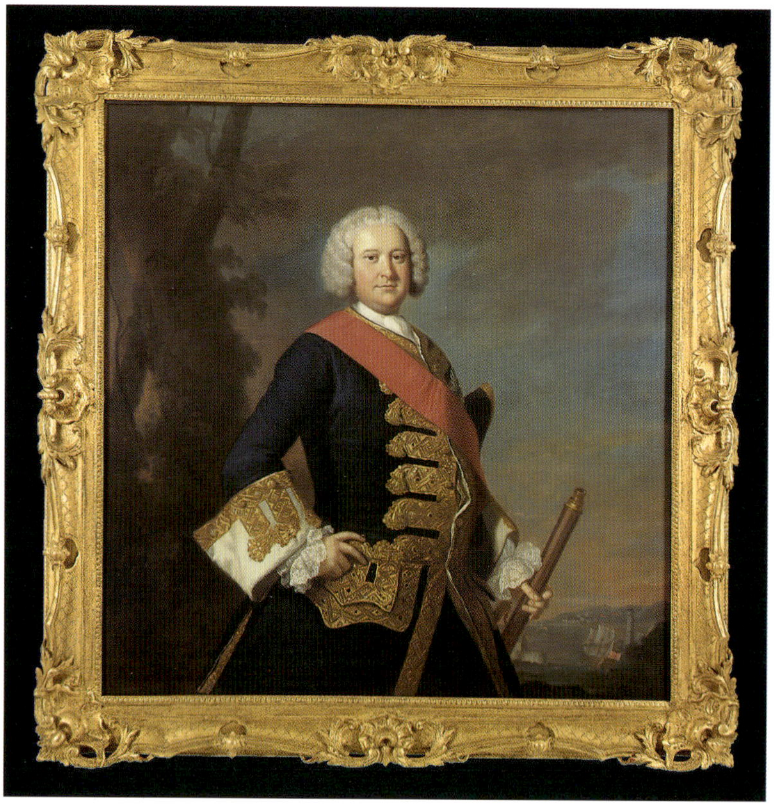

Fig.95 (above)
Sir Peter Warren by Thomas Hudson, *c.*1751–2 (no.36).

It need not surprise us to find Hudson's pupil, Joseph Wright of Derby, choosing to use a rococo pattern not unlike Hudson's in the first few years of the 1760s. He then moved on to using Maratta patterns in the mid-1760s and neo-classical frames in the late 1770s. Wright of Derby's frames were examined in some detail by Paul Mitchell in the run-up to the 1990 Tate Gallery exhibition.[95] Mitchell found that more than half Wright's later frames were of one predominant streamlined neo-classical pattern with distinct but clearly related variations. As Mitchell has said, 'The particular significance of these frames is that they were evidently devised between Wright and his framemaker exclusively for him'.

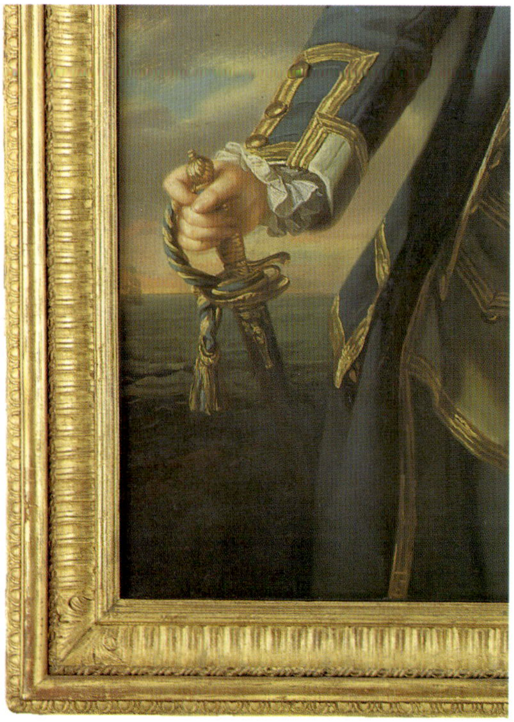

Fig.94 (left)
John Jervis, Earl of St Vincent by Francis Cotes (detail), 1769 (no.47).

What was the extent of the artist's role in the design of frames in the later eighteenth century? Of Sir Joshua Reynolds, Nicholas Penny has suggested that he 'certainly exercised his taste in the selection of his frames, but surely not his genius in the design of them', adding, 'There is every reason to suppose that his attitudes were typical – otherwise they would surely have provoked more comment'.[96] On present evidence this is a fair analysis. In the late eighteenth century, it is likely that most artists' frames were chosen as a result of discussion between artist and framemaker.[97]

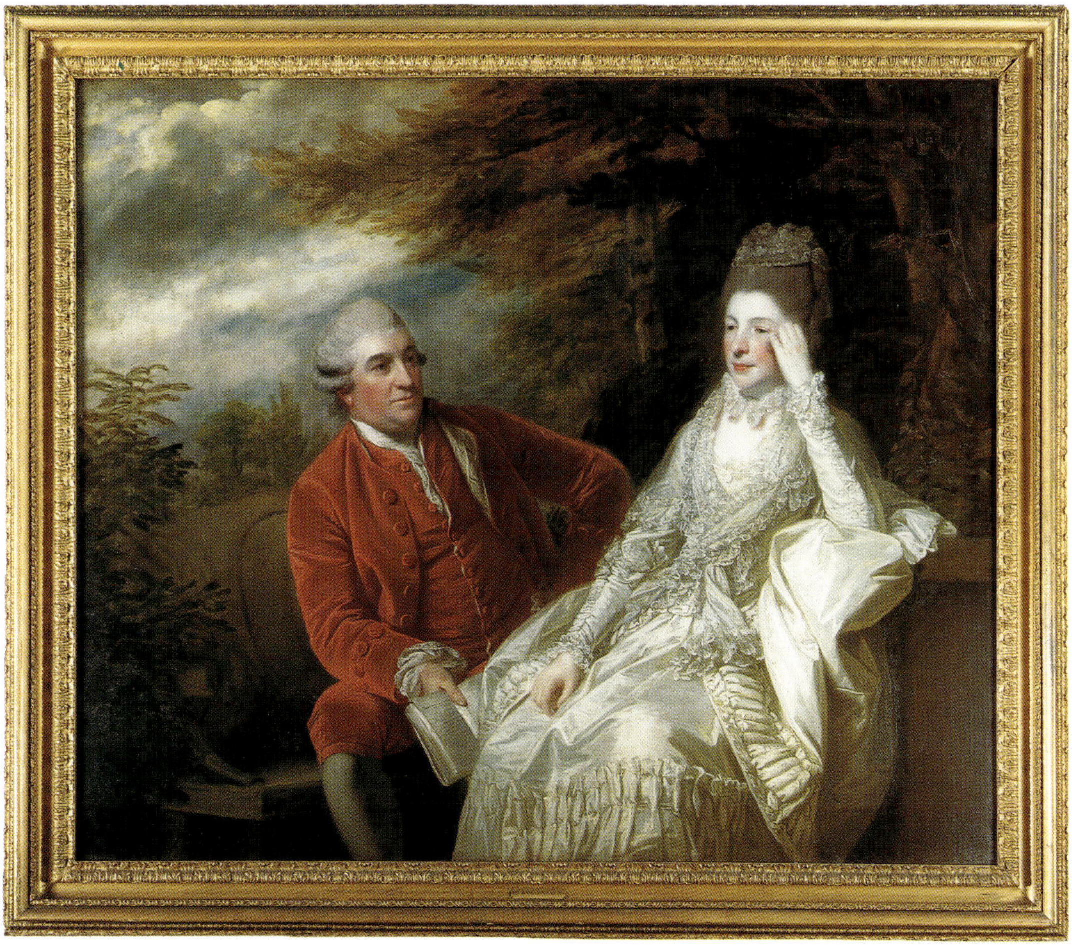

Fig.96
David Garrick and his wife Eva Maria by Sir Joshua Reynolds, 1773 (no.48).

Reynolds has generally been associated with the Maratta style and indeed many of the pictures at the Royal Academy's great Reynolds exhibition in 1986 had frames of this type, as a survey carried out by Nicholas Penny shows.[98] Reynolds's pocket books confirm that he was sending out pictures framed in the style by the late 1750s and the evidence is that he continued to favour the Maratta for much of his career. By the 1770s, as Penny has observed, the Maratta frame was more deeply modelled, heavier and richer in effect. In the double portrait of David Garrick and his wife (fig.96), a shell replaces the plain tongue of the Carlo ornament which, unusually, sits on the sight edge. The Maratta style was adopted for the framing of Reynolds's state portraits of George III and Queen Charlotte following his appointment as Painter to the King in 1784.[99] But by this period many of his pictures were being framed in other more neo-classical mouldings, whether by Reynolds or his patrons.

Penny has described how many of Reynolds's frames were replaced by Edwardian dealers with Palladian and rococo patterns of the 1740s and 1750s which better complied with contemporary notions of the Georgian style. To sound a cautionary note, however, almost all the Reynolds's on display at the National Portrait Gallery were put into their Maratta frames in the 1960s and 1970s, so that they should comply with more modern notions of a Reynolds frame. The pictures of celebrated artists like Reynolds have changed hands much more often than the works of lesser artists and as a result are more likely to have lost their original frames as successive owners have adjusted the appearance of the picture to their taste.

If Reynolds has been linked with the Maratta style, Gainsborough has sometimes been associated with the rococo. However, while Gainsborough's works of the 1750s are often found in rococo frames, his portraits from the 1760s onwards seem to have been framed in Maratta patterns as a norm. The occasional reference linking Gainsborough with Isaac Gosset suggests that this well-known Huguenot maker may have produced many of his frames.[100] It is possible that Gainsborough took special trouble over the framing of his landscapes. In the 1770s and 1780s he seems to have adopted two unusual styles, an ogee-profiled frame with a heavy top edge of large-scale linked husks, such as found on his *Going to Market* of *c*.1770 (Iveagh Bequest, Kenwood House), and a more neo-classical type also to be found on a landscape at Kenwood, his *Greyhounds Coursing a Fox* of the late 1780s.[101]

It is extremely rare to be able to trace the evolution of a frame pattern in any detail, and the documentation relating to the creation of George Stubbs's preferred frame style of the early 1780s (a type which is found on his self-portrait; fig.97) provides particularly valuable insights into the role of Stubbs and his patron in the framing process. The type was produced for Josiah Wedgwood, who had commissioned Stubbs to produce work on his large Wedgwood enamel plaques.[102] Wedgwood first writes from Etruria to his partner Thomas Bentley in London on 28 October 1780 about the framing of his large 'family piece' painted on panel, depicting himself, his wife Sarah, and their seven children:

Mr. Stubs is likewise very desirous of seeing my picture framed & wishes me to write for one today to be sent down as soon as possible, but it will not do to write to a frame maker to send a frame of such & such dimensions; I must trouble my dear friend to look in Leicester square or at some other frame makers & chuse a pattern for me. It must be … not less than 6 or 7 inches broad … I have put down my idea of a section on the other side, but it is not meant to bind your choice for ten to one I should alter mine if I saw a variety, & as you know the subject of the picture I leave the choice entirely to your good taste …

A week later Wedgwood writes again in response to a letter from Bentley, who had visited the framemaker, Thomas Vials, in Leicester Square:

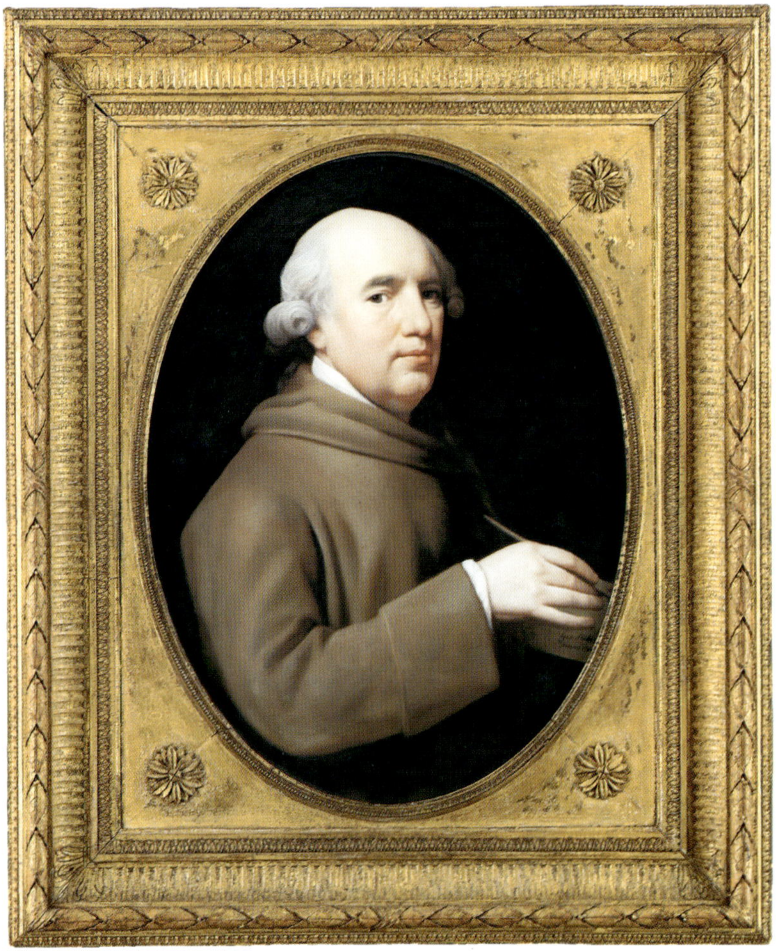

Fig.97
Self-portrait by George Stubbs, 1781 (no.49).

Before this reaches my dear friend he will have reciev'd a model of a picture frame a little alter'd from the section in my last & I think for the better. Mr. Stubs approves so much of this model (though he had not the least hand in designing it) that he will adopt it for his first enamel picture of the largest size …

Wedgwood goes on to discuss the idea of having 'a simple flat unpolish'd part of some breadth' next to the picture, as being less distracting than a 'prominent & glaring one'. He also refers to gilding as '*matt & polish*', probably matt and burnished water gilding, and states that Stubbs, though he did not mention it before, 'has a great objection to that kind of gilding, & prefers the oil gilding'. He asks for a model of a few inches of whatever the pattern Bentley and Vials decide upon so that Stubbs may 'see & chuse for himself', and he refers to the fluting in the model he had sent Bentley as being not deep enough but in the right place with respect to the beads, 'that is the center of the flutes are in a line with the center of the beads'.

A further week passes before the final letter in which Wedgwood requests Bentley to send a few inches of the frame which had been intended before he sent his own model, 'as it is most probable I may prefer the model you had fixed upon to my own'. In the event not only did Stubbs use the chosen pattern for 'his first enamel picture of the largest size', but he also adopted it for various of his enamel plaques of the early 1780s.

No correspondence of this kind survives in the case of George Romney, but his work is exceptionally well documented owing to the survival of his framemaking books in the Fitzwilliam Museum, Cambridge, which provide an unusual insight into the methods of a portrait painter who liked to use a variety of neo-classical mouldings.[103] 'Allwood's Carving Book', as it is inscribed, provides details of the frames Thomas Allwood made for Romney's portraits from 1775 to 1781. Many of the frames are specified by the name of a sitter who had previously used the pattern, thus 'Mr Bucks pat$^{\underline{n}}$', 'Mr Sullivan's pat$^{\underline{n}}$', 'Lord Gowers pat$^{\underline{n}}$', 'Capt Beards pattern'. Allwood's account includes an entry for 'A ¾ around Lord Gowers P^{t} in the Shew Room' (a three-quarter frame was for a picture size thirty by twenty-five inches), which indicates that at least one of these patterns was on display in Romney's showroom. Some frames are described more specifically: 'A ¾ fluted frame', 'A ¾ new pat$^{\underline{n}}$ with Reeds and Rib$^{\underline{ns}}$ crossing' (the reeds and ribbons pattern becoming a favourite), 'A ¾ frame with Rib$^{\underline{ns}}$ in the Corners and Middles', 'A ¾ with a Vine frett', 'A ¾ frame new pat$^{\underline{n}}$ with Oval inside'.

When William Saunders replaced Allwood as Romney's framemaker in 1782 a new 'Frame makers Book' was started. Saunders worked for Romney throughout the 1780s and 1790s. The early accounts are in the name 'Eade & Saunders' and specify most of the frames as being of profiles A, B or C (what those profiles were is not described), sometimes including further details such as the entry for 17 October 1782 for 'a ¾ picture frame 3 members carv'd & gilt in Burnish Gold husks beads & Ribbond & Stick of the profile B' at two guineas, or that on 31 October for 'a ¾ picture frame 3 members carvd small strap close beads and plain strap with stalks on top round of profile C & gilt in Burnish Gold', which was more expensive at two-and-a-half guineas. Evidently the starting-point, at least for the framemaker, was the profile of the frame; the decoration could be varied at will within certain limits. Saunders could also provide frames for whole-length portraits to the same profiles; such a frame made to profile A for the Earl of Derby cost £9.15s.6d in 1783. Only twice is a Maratta frame mentioned and indeed such frames rarely occur on Romney's work of the 1780s, although they remained popular with some portrait painters. The neo-classical frame on his portrait of William Paley (fig.98) still has on the back the maker's label of William Saunders. Its reeded sight edge tied by ribbons and the ribbed top edge are hallmarks of the Romney frame in the 1780s.

The distinctive nature of Romney's patterns make it possible to suggest that the artist played a significant part in the choice of the frames, in collaboration with his framemaker, especially in

Fig.98 (right) *William Paley* by George Romney (detail), 1789-90 (no.52).

A Romney frame, made by William Saunders.

the cases of Lord Gower's frame and of the other frames which were made for pictures in his showroom. The fact that there is little change in appearance between the frames made before 1782, presumably by Allwood, and those made by Saunders afterwards, indicates that the dominant consideration in their design was Romney's taste for neo-classical frames of fairly chaste appearance.

The work of artists producing pastels and other small-scale portraits is usually to be found in the original frame, and so often do one or two familiar types recur that one can readily identify the frame patterns preferred by these artists. In the 1780s and 1790s the leading pastel portraitist, John Russell, was using a plain but handsome scoop frame of Maratta section with pearl sight edge and ribbon twist beneath the top edge (see fig.99), turning to a slightly heavier variant with Carlo ornament on the sight edge for his large late pastels of the mid-1790s and early 1800s. John Downman's small-scale portraits of the 1780s, drawn in a distinctive combination of pencil, chalk and watercolour, frequently retain their flat neo-classical 'Downman' frames, which are plain, apart from a V-tooth sight edge and waterleaf next to the top edge (see fig.87). Hugh Douglas Hamilton, an Irish artist who worked in London and Rome, produced small-scale chalks and oils for much of his career. He kept his frame style up-to-date so that one can tentatively link a specific style with each phase of his work, his most neo-classical frame (see no.51) being found on his Roman portraits of the 1780s.

By this time many artists were using distinctive patterns for their pictures. It is possible to see two related influences at work. Firstly, the eighteenth century witnessed the elevation of the professional status of the artist. The use of distinctive frame types can be seen as a signal of the artist's assertion of individuality. Secondly, the rise of the Royal Academy's annual exhibition to a central position as a showcase for both leading and lesser artists evidently prompted all artists to consider the presentation of their work much more carefully. As Paul Mitchell has said of Joseph Wright, by using a special frame Wright was advertising 'the individuality of his pictures'. Mitchell goes on, 'It is not too much to assume that this novel design must have deliberately helped to single out his work among that of other artists on the walls of his patrons' houses as well as in the prestigious Royal Academy and Society of Artists exhibitions'.[104] It was not only Wright whose work was singled out in this way: all leading artists were striving for attention.

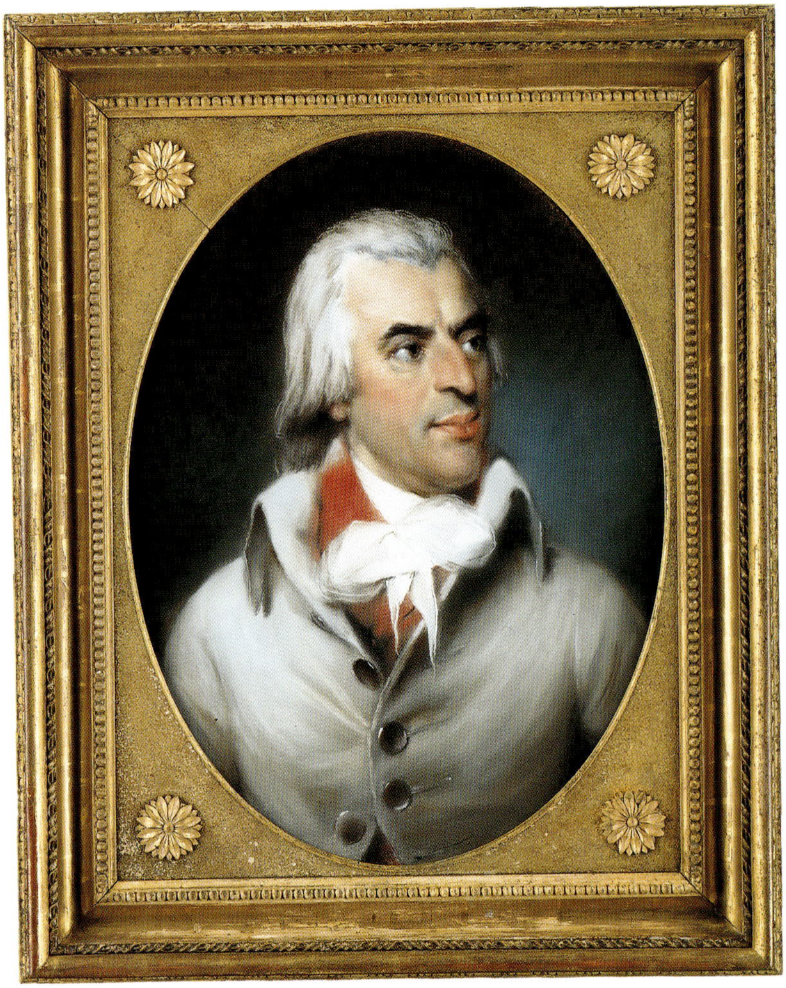

Fig.99
Arthur Young by John Russell, 1794 (no.45).

A generation later, in 1819, the painter and author, W.H. Pyne, attributed the leading role to Benjamin West: 'it is due to Mr. West, the venerable president of the Royal Academy, to state that he had the spirit to set the example to the English, in the public exhibition at Somerset House, of the advantage of placing pictures in wide and richly ornamented frames'.[105] The highly enriched form of the Maratta frame adopted by West in the 1770s, with enriched

Carlo ornament of acanthus-and-shell, and a gadrooned or raking top edge, can be found on many of his large pictures in the Royal Collection and elsewhere.[106] In the next decade West moved on to using more neo-classical frames but still of considerable richness.[107]

The nineteenth century

If any one person can be seen as influential in the shift in taste to heavier frames in the early nineteenth century it was Sir Thomas Lawrence. Painter to the King at the age of twenty-three in 1792, knighted in 1815 and President of the Royal Academy in 1820, Lawrence was the acknowledged leader of his profession. His influence on picture frame style was not welcomed by his older contemporary, James Northcote, who complained to James Ward of the 'gaudiness' of the frames introduced by Lawrence, as has already been noted in Chapter 1.[108]

Lawrence used a variety of frame types during his career. The four frames discussed below belong to successive decades from the 1790s to the 1820s. Though not the only patterns favoured by Lawrence, they are found on many of his pictures and epitomise the changing taste of the period. Each type found favour with Lawrence for a period of ten years or so, judging from surviving examples; they are almost like a uniform, marking the pictures as 'Lawrence' in a way which must have helped make his work stand out at the annual Royal Academy exhibitions. Those Lawrences not now in such frames seem either to have been reframed at a later date in reaction against the artist's taste for heavy frames, or were framed by the sitter rather than artist in the first place.

The remarkable thing about the earliest of the four Lawrences, the portrait of Sir Graham Moore of 1792 (fig.100), is the traditional nature of its Carlo Maratta frame. The frame was hand carved at a juncture when mass-produced compo mouldings were beginning to undermine the carver's trade. Though broader than the Maratta frames of the 1750s and 1760s, it is otherwise not unlike those used by Francis Cotes or the young Reynolds. Indeed the pattern is very like one adopted by Reynolds for his full-length state portraits of George III from 1785 onwards.[109] When Lawrence succeeded Reynolds as Painter to the King in 1792, he not only kept to this Maratta pattern, with its prominent pearl sight edge, but also took on the king's framemaker, William Adair, to frame some of his private work as well as his state portraits.

Lord Castlereagh (fig.101) of 1809-10 is quite different and represents a transition towards the styles of later decades. It has deep scoop sides decorated with interlacing husk-and-guilloche, top edges with flat gadrooning, and heavy applied corners of shell-and-foliage. This pattern, with minor variations (the guilloche sometimes replaced by a French leaf, or a boss substituted for the shell corner), is found on numerous works by Lawrence of the 1800s and, in modified form, on pictures by other artists. The effect is bold and massy, giving great weight to the containing corners, at least on small pictures like the Castlereagh portrait, and sharply focusing the eye inward by means of the decoration running at right angles to the sides of the frame. The introduction of compo encouraged the taste for deeper and wider frames because the cost of

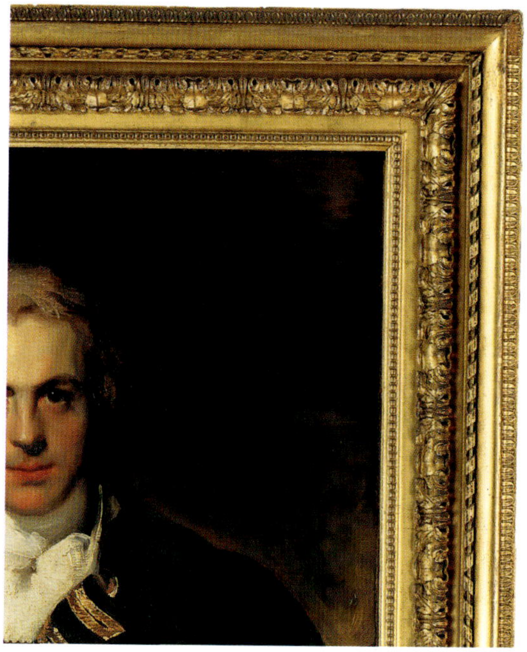

Fig.100 (right) *Sir Graham Moore* by Sir Thomas Lawrence (detail), 1792 (no.59).

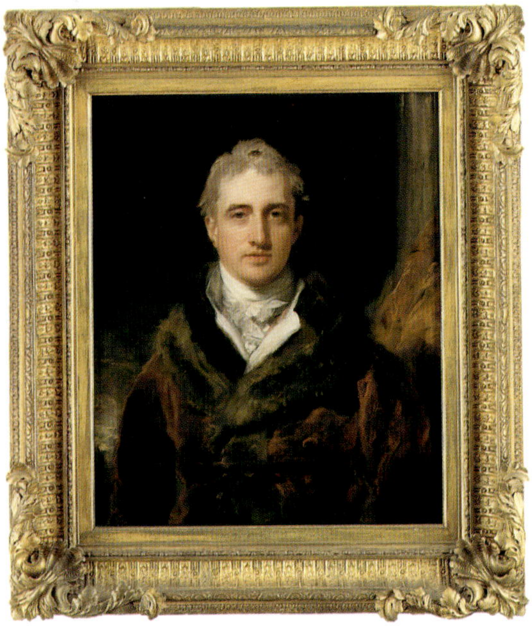

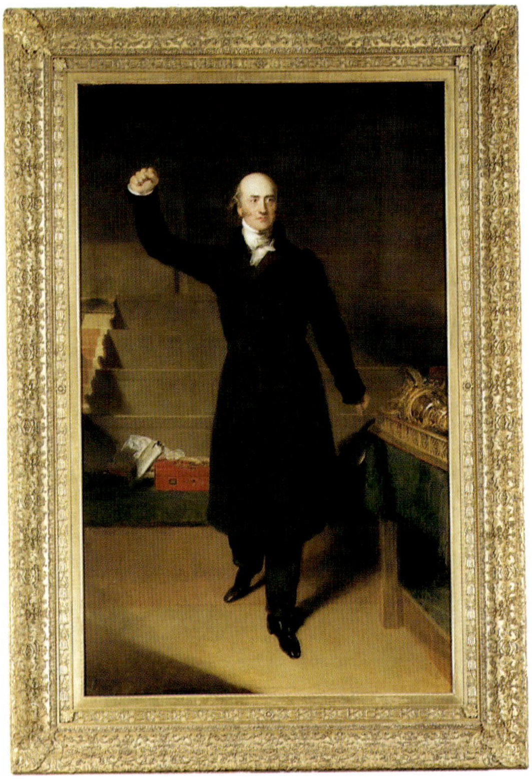

Fig.101 (far left)
Robert Stewart, 2nd Marquess of Londonderry (Lord Castlereagh) by Sir Thomas Lawrence, 1809–10 (no.60).

Fig.103 (left)
George Canning by Sir Thomas Lawrence, 1825 (no.62).

The frame was probably made by George Morant.

moulded ornamentation was much cheaper than that of carving, as has been noted above.[110]

The freedom which compo gave the framemaker is even more apparent in the styles which followed. In Lawrence's *George IV* (fig.102) of about 1814 the corners are much less prominent and the emphasis now is on surface pattern, in this case a motif of scrolling leaves which was a common feature in Regency decorative design. This sort of design, usually applied to an ogee section with a matt oil gilt surface enlivened by punching, was widely influential, and was taken up by Lawrence's rival, Thomas Phillips (see fig.105), among others. The inner frieze of stylised leaves and acorns is another innovation, taken from contemporary decoration in furniture and architecture. Lawrence's framemaker in 1816 was Michael Tijou who also worked for other portrait painters such as James Northcote.

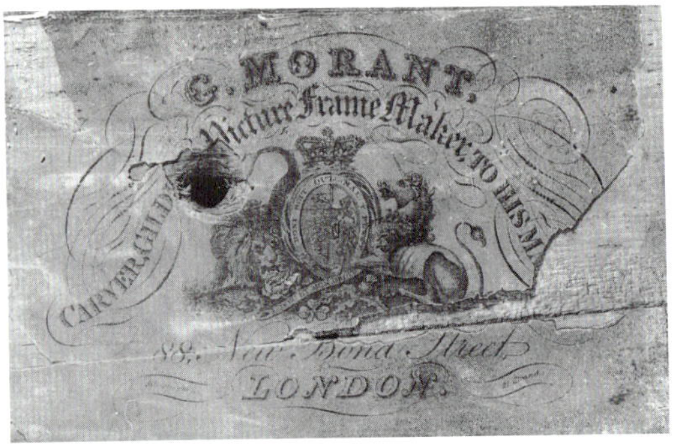

The frame on Lawrence's full-length portrait of George Canning of 1825 (fig.103) takes the design a stage further but significantly reduces the prominence of the corners and eliminates the centre ornaments. This type was used in one guise or another for portraits of all sizes but is most commonly found on Lawrence's full-lengths and half-lengths of the 1820s, including for example, his portrait of Lord Liverpool of 1827 (National Portrait Gallery, on loan to the National Gallery). The Liverpool frame is almost identical to the Canning and still bears the label of George Morant, the interior decorator, carver and gilder, and Lawrence's framemaker of the 1820s (fig.104). The small-scale ornament on the cross-hatched ogee sides takes inspiration from the French Régence style of the early eighteenth century but the motifs here are used as a repeating surface pattern and so are quite different in effect to the sculptural nature of the French prototype.

Lawrence's attitude to picture framing at the time is very clearly set out in a letter dated 13 October 1828 to Mrs Benjamin Gott of Leeds, who had suggested a narrower frame for her portrait

Fig.102 (facing page)
George IV by Sir Thomas Lawrence, *c.*1814 (no.61).

Fig.104 (left)
Label of George Morant on the reverse of *Lord Liverpool* by Sir Thomas Lawrence, 1827.

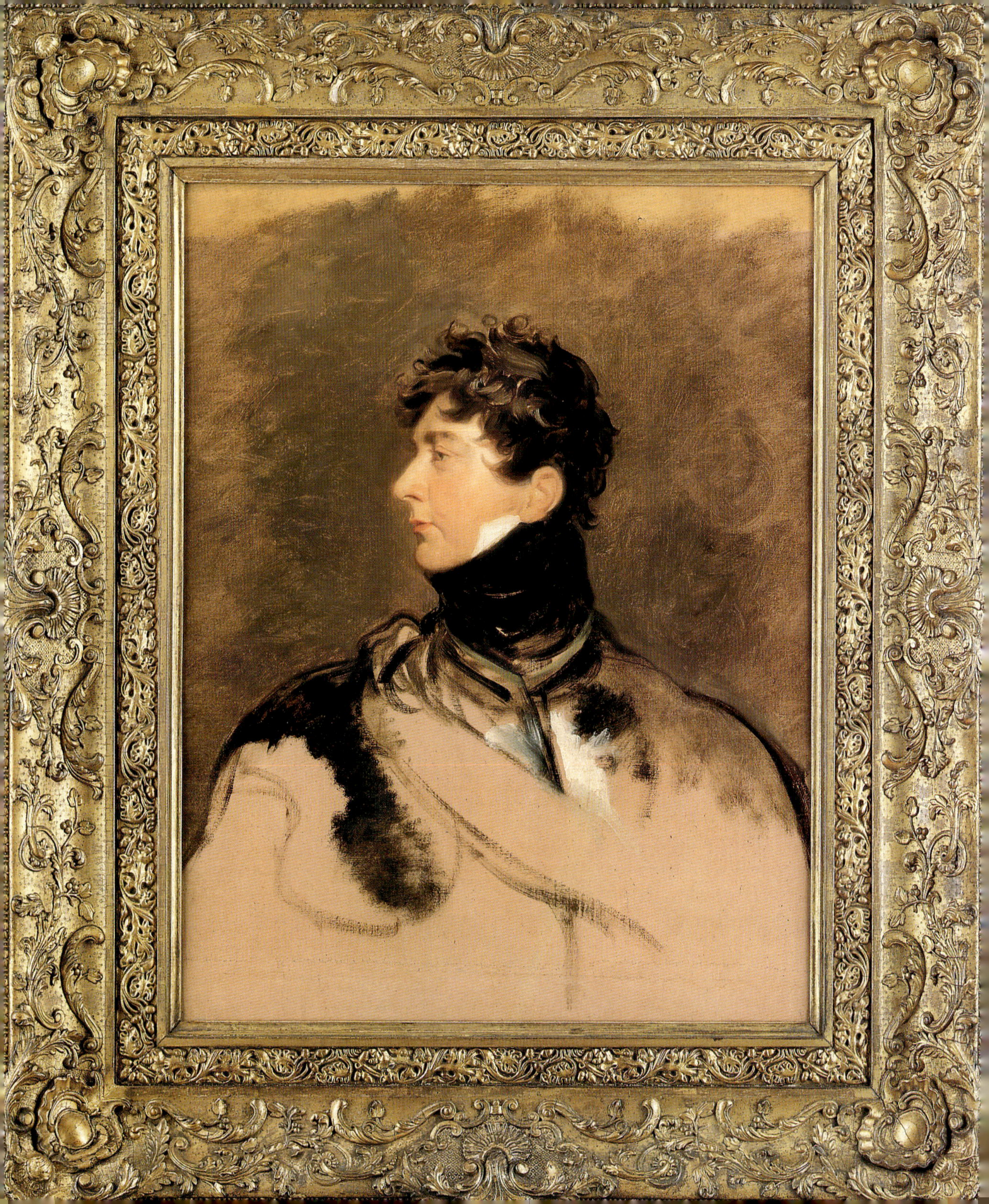

and that of her husband than Lawrence wanted.[111] Lawrence put forward several basic precepts:

'the comparative richness of the frames … has been adopted with not the remotest view to their impression on the eye as mere splendid decoration'

'the pattern has been selected by me'

'its dimensions [are] determined solely with a view to the advantage of the Pictures'

'a frame which is 'very plain and very narrow' is unbecoming, as is one which has 'large obtrusive Ornaments in the Centre, and corners'

'A good frame … should be sufficiently broad and rich, but the ornament of that richness composed throughout of small parts, and usually it should be unburnished'.

Lawrence went on in his letter to Mrs Gott to argue for a wide frame, describing some of his recent portraits:

You may remember, My dear Madam, the portrait of Sir Walter Scott which is not a whole length tho' it is something more than the Bishop's half length. The breadth of the moulding of that frame is 12 inches – the moulding of the frame of Sir Ashley Coopers is 10 inches. The breadth of the moulding of your intended frame is 9 inches. Will you suffer it to be 7 inches or between that and six? Less than six would I am certain be injurious to the Picture …

The portrait of Scott, painted for George IV, is still in the Royal Collection. The frame Lawrence described added twenty-four inches or almost half to the fifty-two-and-a-half inch width of the portrait, an extreme ratio. In the event, however, Lawrence was forced to give way over the framing of Mrs Gott's portraits and accepted that she would use a narrower frame than he would like.

Whether the fashion for heavy frames can really be laid at Lawrence's door is difficult to prove. But such was certainly the perception of many of his contemporaries, as Northcote's comment suggests. John Constable, when on the hanging committee of the Royal Academy, found that the excessive size of the frames gave him considerable trouble; an exhibitor he remonstrated with on this point defended himself by saying that his frames were made exactly on the pattern of those of Sir Thomas Lawrence, leading Constable to reply, 'It was very easy to imitate Lawrence in his *frames*'.[112]

Lawrence's influence can be seen by examining the work of two other leading Royal Academicians, Thomas Phillips and David Wilkie. Many of Phillips's frames relate to the type that Lawrence was using in the 1810s (see fig.102) but have bolder corners; while Lawrence abandoned this style, Phillips continued to use it for the rest of his career so that his frames of the 1830s (see fig.105) are much like those of twenty years before. Wilkie liked 'a frame with rich corners & then more plain in the middle';[113] his frames are more varied than Phillips's but in his later work he usually favoured the small-scale ornament of Lawrence's frames of the 1820s while giving greater prominence to the centre

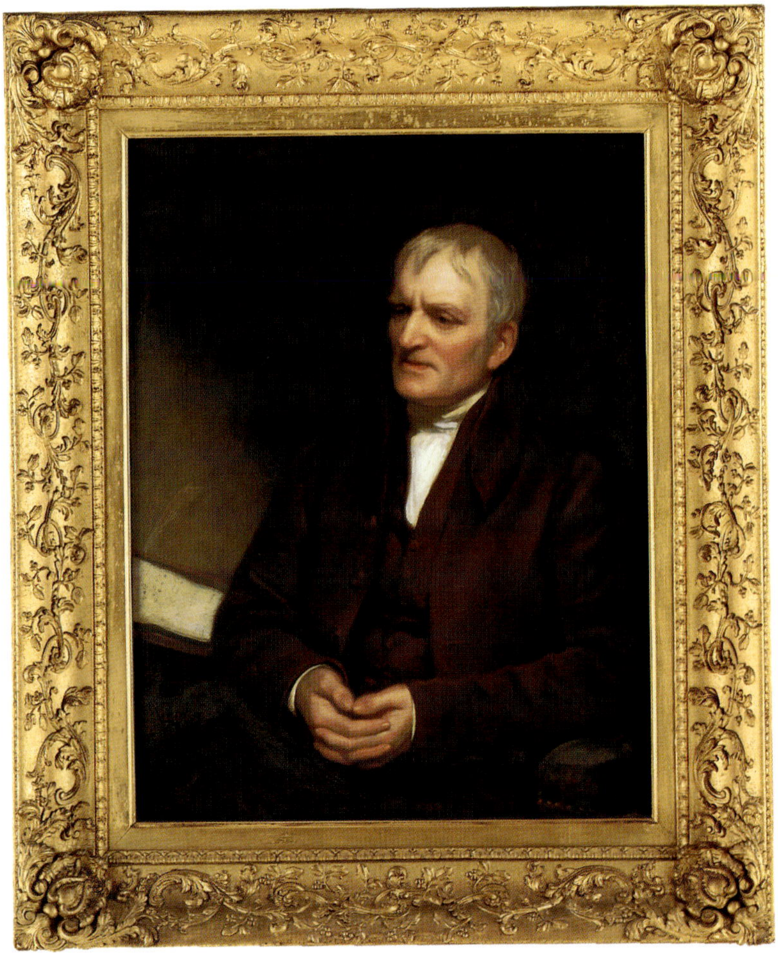

Fig.105
John Dalton by Thomas Phillips, 1835 (no.64).

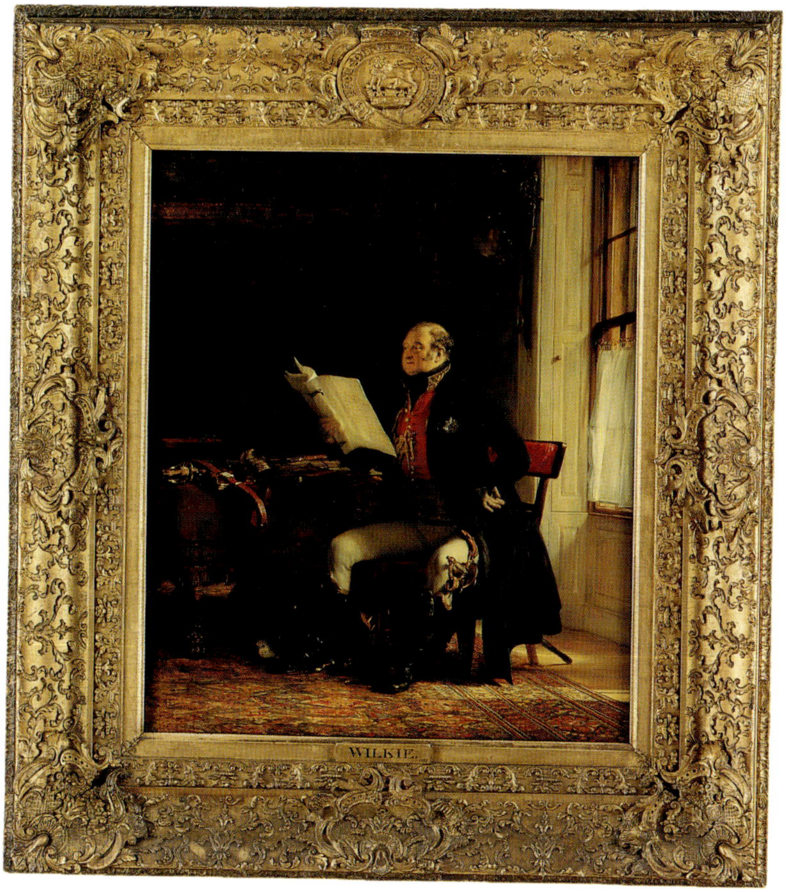

Fig.106
Frederick, Duke of York by Sir David Wilkie, 1823 (no.65).

and corner motifs, as in his portrait of the Duke of York (fig.106).

In the first half of the nineteenth century, the increasing interest taken by artists in the framing of their work is very evident from surviving correspondence. The practice of using one or more special frame patterns was widespread, almost as if it were a necessary part of the artist's relationship with his public to have a style of his own to offer.

There are various references to framing in John Constable's correspondence. 'The frame is my own invention', he wrote to John Fisher in 1823 about a favourite picture which he was in the process of dispatching.[114] A drawing in the Fitzwilliam Museum shows in very schematic form a design for a frame by Constable, probably intended for a version of *The White Horse* in 1819.[115] Those of Constable's pictures which retain their original frames suggest that his taste in framing was fairly conventional. Turner's interest in frames has yet to be explored in detail, but the story of his framing three of his pictures with twisted rope immediately before the opening of an exhibition in Rome in 1828 is well known.[116]

The very detailed interest that artists of the period could take in framing is apparent in the correspondence of William Etty. For the secretary of the Scottish Academy in 1829 he provided a sketch showing his proposals for the framing and hanging of his enormous *Judith* triptych which the Academy was in the process of acquiring. Etty had already arranged the framing of the centrepiece in a pattern he was then using for sending his work to the Royal Academy. 'With respect to the frame to the next Picture', he wrote of the right wing, 'I should recommend that it should match with the other in Pattern and in size and breadth, and that on the inside, and next the Picture a *Flat* of *the same Character* as that of the Judith should intervene between the Frame and the Picture, *all of which must be seen* and *none of* it cut off by the Rabbit, which may be easily managed by having Slips nailed around the Picture … '.[117]

In the case of John Martin, in 1842 he provided Benjamin Hicks, the Lancashire entrepreneur who purchased his visionary painting, the *Celestial City*, with a design for a frame at Hicks's request:

I have purposely departed but little from ordinary frames as the makers generally fail in representing my intentions. I only desire to impress that the flat next the picture should be not less than 2 & ½ inches broad. The bead is the common egg and anchor, and the corners of some tight and elegant scroll shell and leaf pattern of which there are already many varieties for you to choose from. In the centre of the frame at the top should be a dove surrounded by rays … [118]

Like Etty, Martin was providing advice for the owner rather than actually supplying the frame; like Etty, he insisted on a broad flat next to the picture. With the exception of the central motif of a dove Martin was prepared to see stock ornament used on the frame and had evidently had difficulty in getting his ideas made up in the past. It required a determined artist, like Rossetti or

Whistler in the next generation, to work with a framemaker on an unfamiliar pattern.

A most interesting instance of an artist taking a controlling interest in the framing of his pictures involves John Rogers Herbert, whose work became well known to the Pre-Raphaelites. In 1849 he wrote to his patron, Thomas Miller of Preston, about his picture, *Lear disinheriting Cordelia*:

It occurs to me that the frame which would best suit the Cordelia should be one not having much bold ornament about it, but small and in low relief. I designed a frame a few years ago which goes by my name, and is certainly better than those we are accustomed to see in our exhibitions.[119]

Miller evidently consented, for less than two months later Herbert wrote again, 'You will see that I have slightly illuminated the frame for the purpose of carrying out the colour of the picture and which to my eye serves both frame & picture'. The artist himself added the finishing touches to the frame, which was probably of the type he had already used for his *Sir Thomas More and his Daughter* of 1844 (Tate Gallery) and *St John the Baptist preaching to Herod* of 1848 (Penrhyn Castle).[120]

The landscape painter, Thomas Creswick, told Thomas Miller in 1858: 'I find so many differences of opinion about frames that I never sell my pictures with them – for my own part I do not think they can be too simple'.[121] This did not mean that he did not have his own preferred frame styles, however, for he went on to tell Miller of a frame he had just had made for another patron which he particularly liked. Equally reticent was G.F. Watts, whose claim to a patron, 'my judgement on frames is worth nothing; I never give one on the subject', appears to have been made through a wish to avoid problems rather than by way of lack of interest.[122] The celebrity of the 'Watts' frame as the best known of all Victorian frame styles has already been discussed in Chapter 3.

Perhaps the least recognised frames of the mid-nineteenth century are those of portrait painters. It is however relatively straightforward to analyse their taste since many portraits remain in their original frames. At the height of his success in the 1850s and 1860s, Sir Francis Grant, President of the Royal Academy, was using at least four different patterns in varying styles for his work, including a French Régence revival frame (see fig.107). His slightly younger contemporary, George Richmond, favoured a fairly simple but high quality frame with corner detailing worked in the gesso for his fashionable large chalk portraits (see no.85), while preferring to use classical patterns for his oils, either a rather traditional fluted frame or a more elaborate Italian renaissance revival pattern decorated with arabesques in low relief.

Fig.107
George Bingham, 3rd Earl of Lucan by Sir Francis Grant (detail), 1855 (no.72).

One of four distinctive patterns used by Grant, and made by William Thomas.

The most distinctive nineteenth-century frames are those used by the Pre-Raphaelites, who were among the earliest artists to take a controlling interest in the design of their frames. In the early years many of their frames were one-offs, designed for specific pictures, and often inscribed with verses or decorated with ornament relating to the subject matter, leading one reviewer to attack these pictures for their 'golden glories, fanciful scribblings on the frames, and other infantine absurdities'.[123] 'I have designed a frame for Charles' painting of "Lilies", which, I expect, will be acknowledged to be the best frame in England', wrote John Everett Millais in 1851 about his frame for Charles Allston Collins's

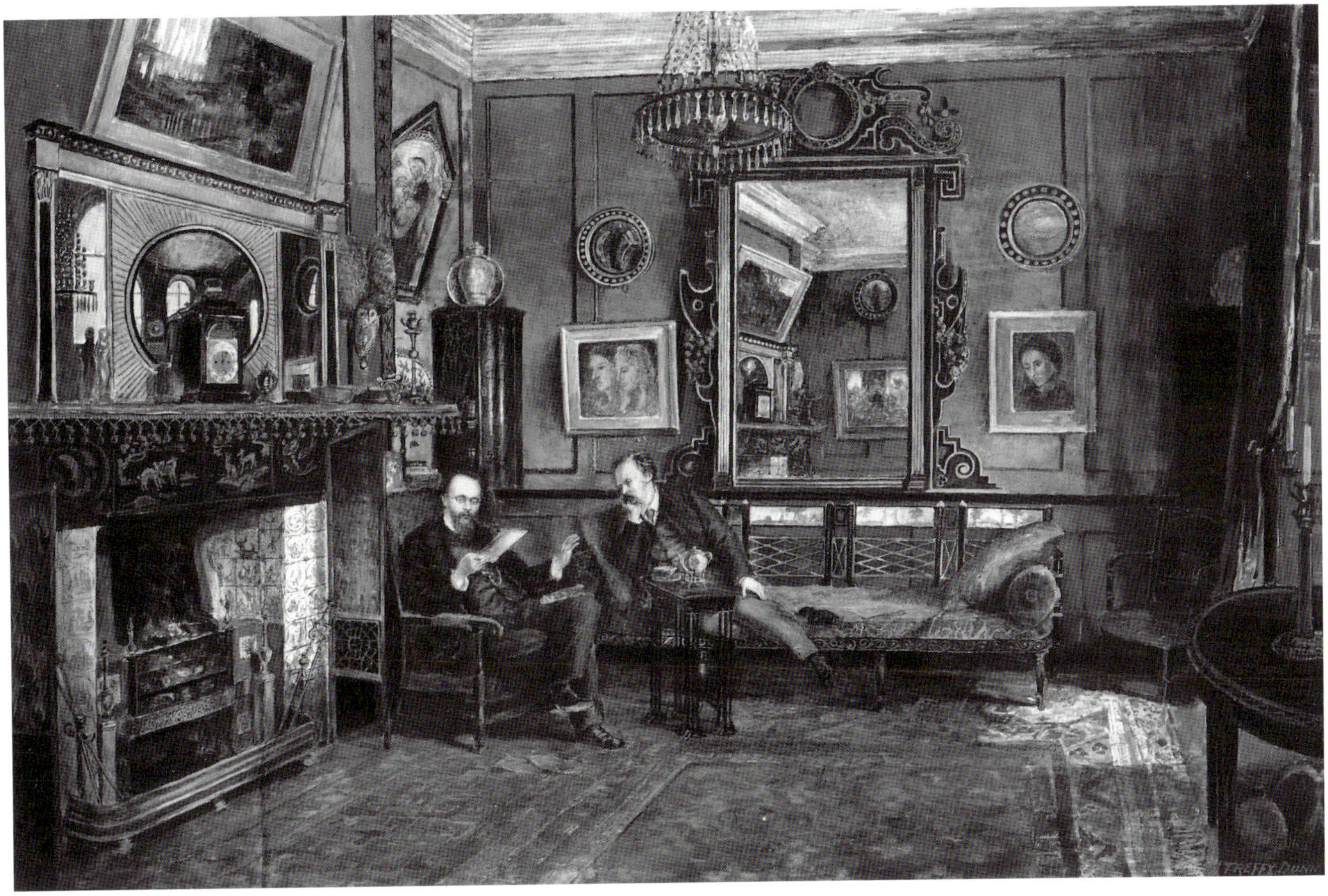

Fig.108 (above)
Dante Gabriel Rossetti and Theodore Watts-Dunton by Henry Treffry Dunn, 1882.

Rossetti's sitting-room at his house in Cheyne Walk, Chelsea, with his pastel of his sister and mother (fig.109) hanging to the left of the large mirror.

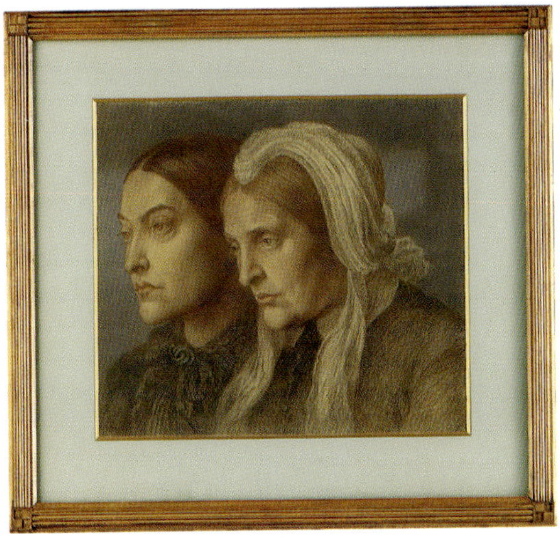

Fig.109 (right)
Christina Rossetti with her mother Frances Rossetti by Dante Gabriel Rossetti, 1877 (no.83).

painting *Convent Thoughts* (Ashmolean Museum, Oxford).[124] Edward Burne-Jones had a vision of a 'glorious curly-wurly frame, a piece of wholesale upholstery' which he wanted for a picture in his collection, a putative Giorgione, 'to make it shine like a jewel as it is … '.[125]

William Holman Hunt continued the practice of designing individual frames for most of his paintings, but Dante Gabriel Rossetti and Ford Madox Brown moved towards the use of a limited range of standard patterns of their own design in the 1860s. Rossetti favoured a frame of triangular section decorated with semi-circular indentations, which Brown also used, calling it 'Rossetti's thumb-mark pattern'. Another classic pattern used by both painters had a flat reeded border inset with decorative squares at the corners and roundels on the sides, ornaments of the 'chefs-square and wheel kind' in Rossetti's words (see fig.109).

'I am particular as to the frames for my pictures', Ford Madox Brown told Sir Charles Dilke in 1872, recommending a 'Venetian' pattern 'much liked now by friends of mine' for his portrait of Henry Fawcett with his wife (fig.110). So confident was Brown that he told his framemaker, Joseph Green, 'to employ all or any of my patterns, as it might spread a taste for a different kind of thing from the debased article now in use'.[126] Indeed the reeded pattern was widely used, notably being taken up by Rossetti's friend, Frederick Sandys (see no.84). It was Whistler who took the development of reeding as a framing device to its ultimate form and, as has been discussed above, his patterns became standard models, which are found, for example, at the National Portrait Gallery on the work of William Strang in 1893, J.S. Sargent in 1894 and Gluck as late as 1942 (see nos.103, 106, 117).

Whistler's interest in picture framing was probably stimulated by Rossetti, whose neighbour he became in 1863. Like Rossetti he took a proprietorial interest in his pictures, even going to the extent of reframing his earlier works, at his own expense if necessary, as he did with one of his most exquisite early paintings, *The Balcony*. 'Look also at the matter of the little Balcony', he wrote to its then owner, John Cavafy, in 1879, 'I borrowed it several times from your Father – and each time I worked upon it and added to its worth. … In the end I also ordered for it a new frame – and elaborately painted and ornamented it – and again the mere price of the frame was refused when Ford and Dickinson sent in his bill'.[127] The depth of Whistler's interest is apparent from a letter he wrote in 1873 to his close friend, George Lucas: 'You will notice and perhaps meet with opposition that my frames I have designed as carefully as my pictures – and thus they form as important a part as any of the rest of the work – carrying on the particular harmony throughout'.[128]

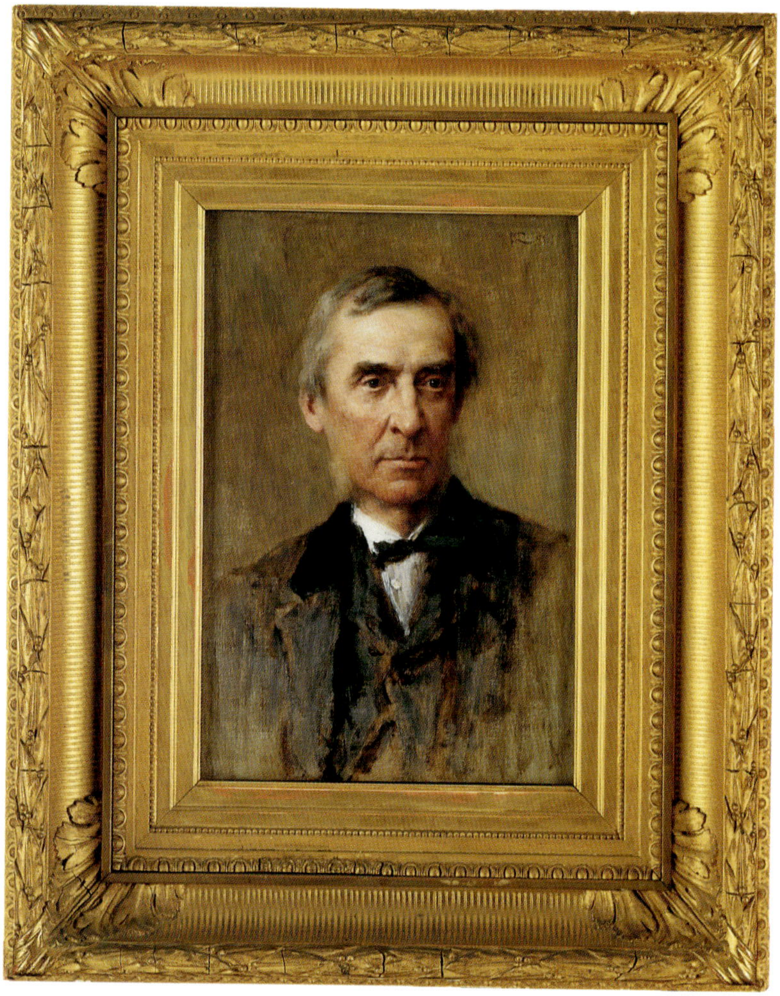

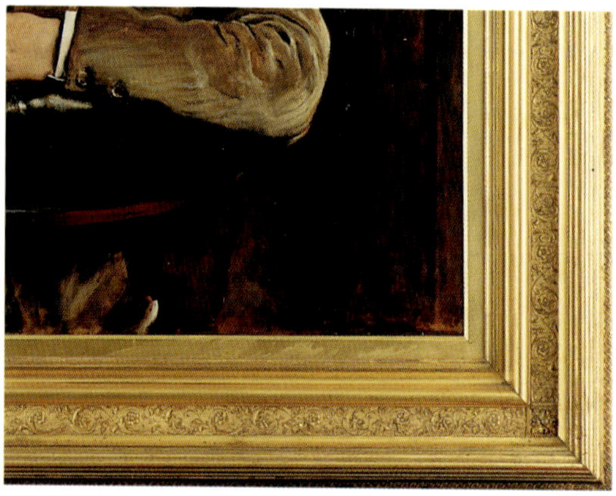

Less well known than the frames of the Pre-Raphaelites are those of artists of the next generation, such as Frank Holl, George Reid and Hubert von Herkomer, all born in the 1840s. Both Holl and Reid used a Watts frame for some of their portraits, but both men offered alternatives, in Holl's case a top-heavy reeded frame for his larger portraits with an inset frieze of renaissance arabesques (see fig.111), and in Reid's a range of traditional patterns depending on the size and nature of the portrait (see fig.112). Like Holl, Herkomer is best known for his subject pictures, which have their own distinctive frames. His portraits are all much on the same bold scale and instead of offering his sitters a choice of frames, he seems to have sent almost all his portraits out in a standard pattern, at first using a very heavy oak frame with gilding directly on to the wood (see fig.113), a style he

Fig.112 (above)
James Froude by Sir George Reid, 1881 (no.89).

A fluted frame with laurel leaf top edge.

Fig.111 (left)
Sir William Schwenk Gilbert by Frank Holl (detail), 1886 (no.91).

Fig.110 (facing page)
Henry Fawcett and Dame Millicent Fawcett by Ford Madox Brown, 1872 (no.82).

A Watts frame of 'Venetian' pattern probably made by Joseph Green.

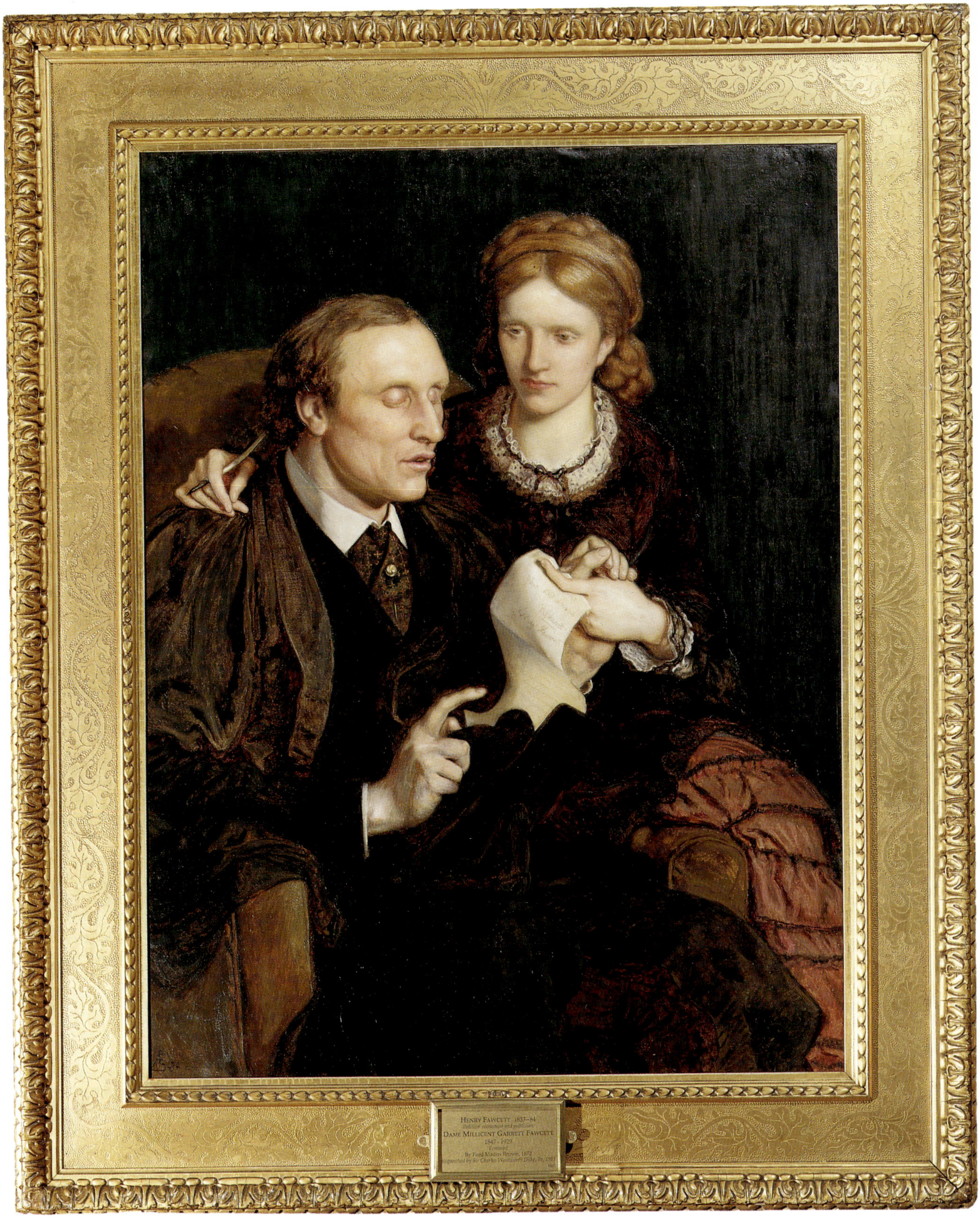

HENRY FAWCETT 1833–84
DAME MILLICENT GARRETT FAWCETT
1847–1929
By Ford Madox Brown, 1872

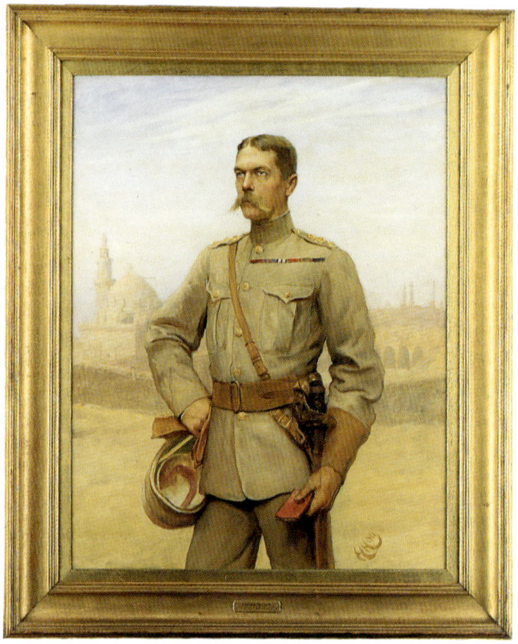

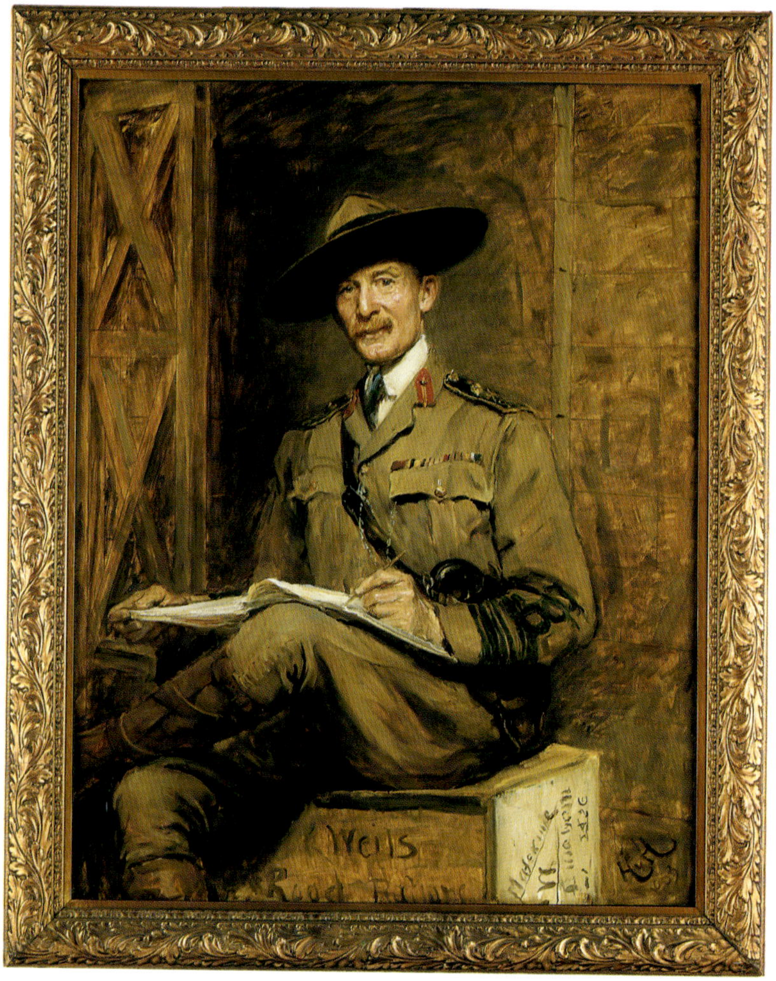

favoured until 1902, and thereafter adopting a lighter cushion frame decorated with a running foliage pattern (see fig.114). The contrast is remarkable and may indicate that in some circles at least, the emphasis on using gilding directly onto the oak and other aesthetic effects was starting to wane by the beginning of the twentieth century.

The twentieth century

Indeed, the fashion for using a limited range of distinctive patterns was in retreat by the Edwardian period. A greater diversity of choice is apparent in the frames of the leading portrait painters of the next generation, such as John Singer Sargent and Sir John Lavery, and the slightly younger Philip de Laszlo. While certain patterns still recur, such as those on Lavery's *Sir Lionel Cust* (fig.116) or De Laszlo's *Jerome K. Jerome* (fig.117), the range of frames used by these artists has become much greater and the designs richer.

It may seem surprising that it is far from easy to document the attitude of the artist in the twentieth century. This is in part because so little has been collected and published. It is also indicative of a shift in the artist's concern to take into account the context or the wider setting of the picture as much as the frame. At one level this is reflected in the approach of the society portrait painter, Philip de Laszlo, who claimed to choose his frames before beginning his pictures: 'I believe that the frame is an integral part of the picture and must be there from the beginning. If it is added at the last moment after the picture is finished there is always the risk that it may not agree with the character of the work'.[129] Some other portrait painters such as Oswald Birley and James Gunn would choose an antique frame and then have a canvas made to size.[130]

If De Laszlo hoped to suit picture to frame, Gluck's wish was to suit frame to setting by means of her stepped frames of the 1930s: 'One day, feeling quite despairing, I took a lump of plasticine and started trying to make something very simple which, if possible, could be part of any wall on which it might be placed, and in doing

Fig.114 (above) *Robert Baden-Powell, 1st Baron Baden-Powell* by Sir Hubert von Herkomer, 1903 (no.93).

Fig.113 (above left) *Horatio Kitchener, 1st Earl Kitchener of Khartoum* by Sir Hubert von Herkomer, 1890 (no.92).

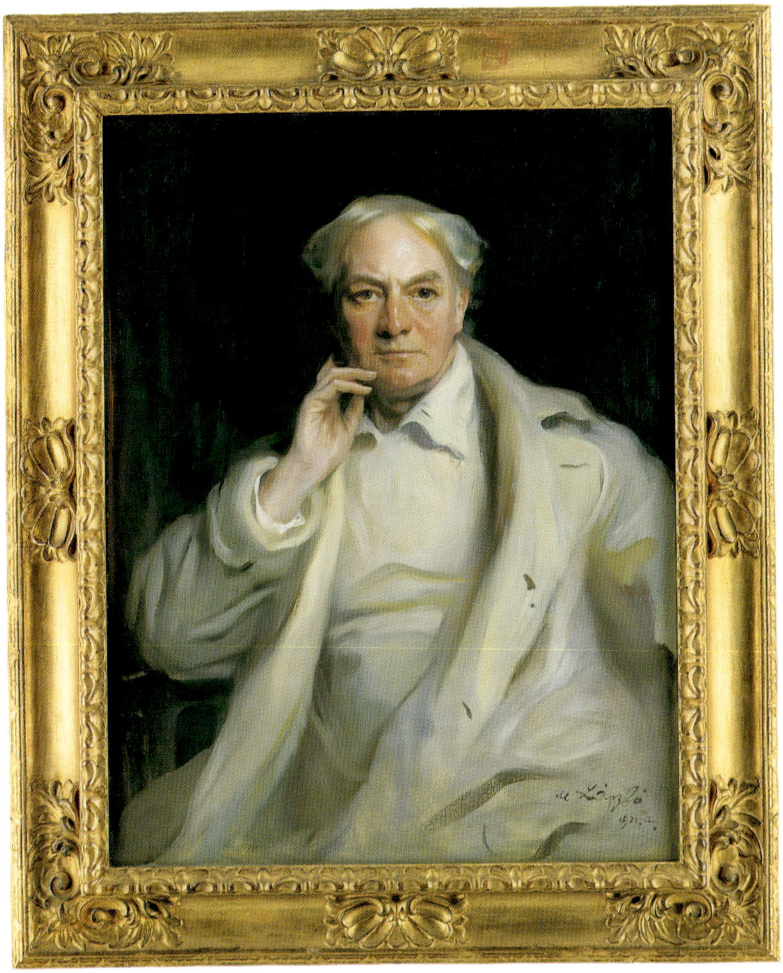

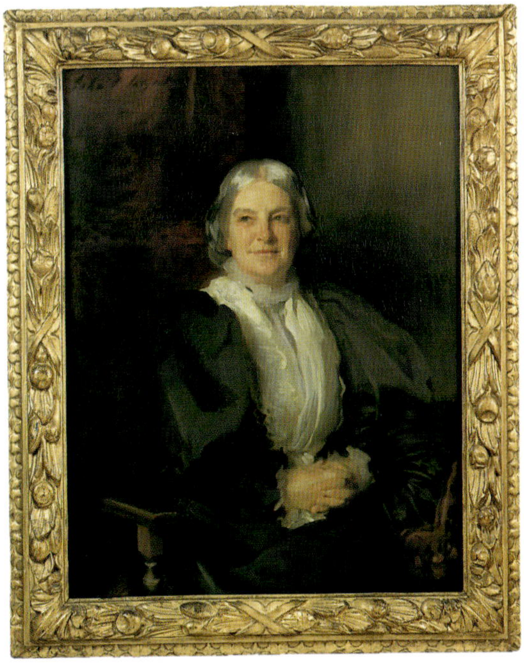

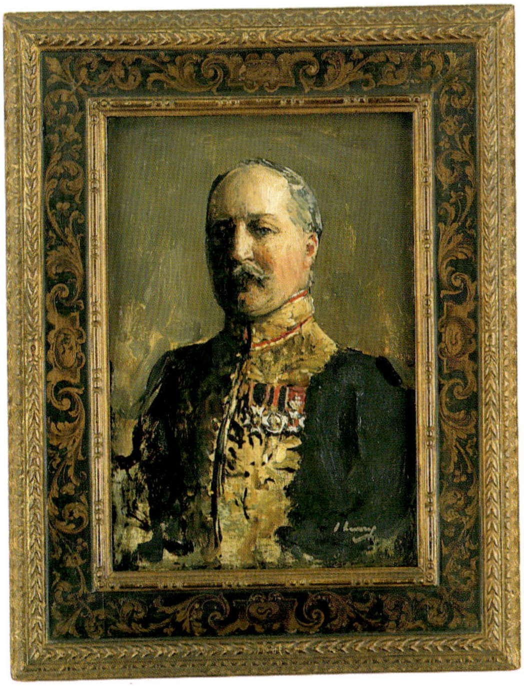

Fig.117 (above)
Jerome K. Jerome by Philip de Laszlo, 1921 (no.114).

A Spanish-style reverse section frame made by Emile Remy.

Fig.115 (top right)
Octavia Hill by John Singer Sargent, 1899 (no.107).

Fig.116 (above right)
Sir Lionel Cust by Sir John Lavery, 1912 (no.110).

A renaissance-style frame made by Emile Remy.

this I suddenly realised that what has now become the Gluck frame was the only solution'.[131] In the twentieth century generally, the concept of the artist's frame in terms of frame patterns associable with individual artists is a more flexible one, however. Although there are frame types associated with painters such as Augustus John (see fig.118), Graham Sutherland (see fig.22) and Howard Morgan (see no.132), to choose three very different artists from succeeding generations, the use of standard patterns has become less common for portraits as frames have increasingly been treated as one-offs in an age when the portrait is no longer the central concern of most leading artists.

How far does the interest of the artist in framing really extend today? The doyenne of London's West End gallery owners, Lilian Browse, cannot recall any artist talking about frames, and indeed, the modern practice of dealers arranging the framing of an artist's work for exhibition implies a shift in control away from the artist. In the experience of one leading framemaker, John Jones, painters may sometimes have little idea of what they want or what is appropriate for their work. Many artists want a framemaker or a dealer who will sort out the framing of pictures

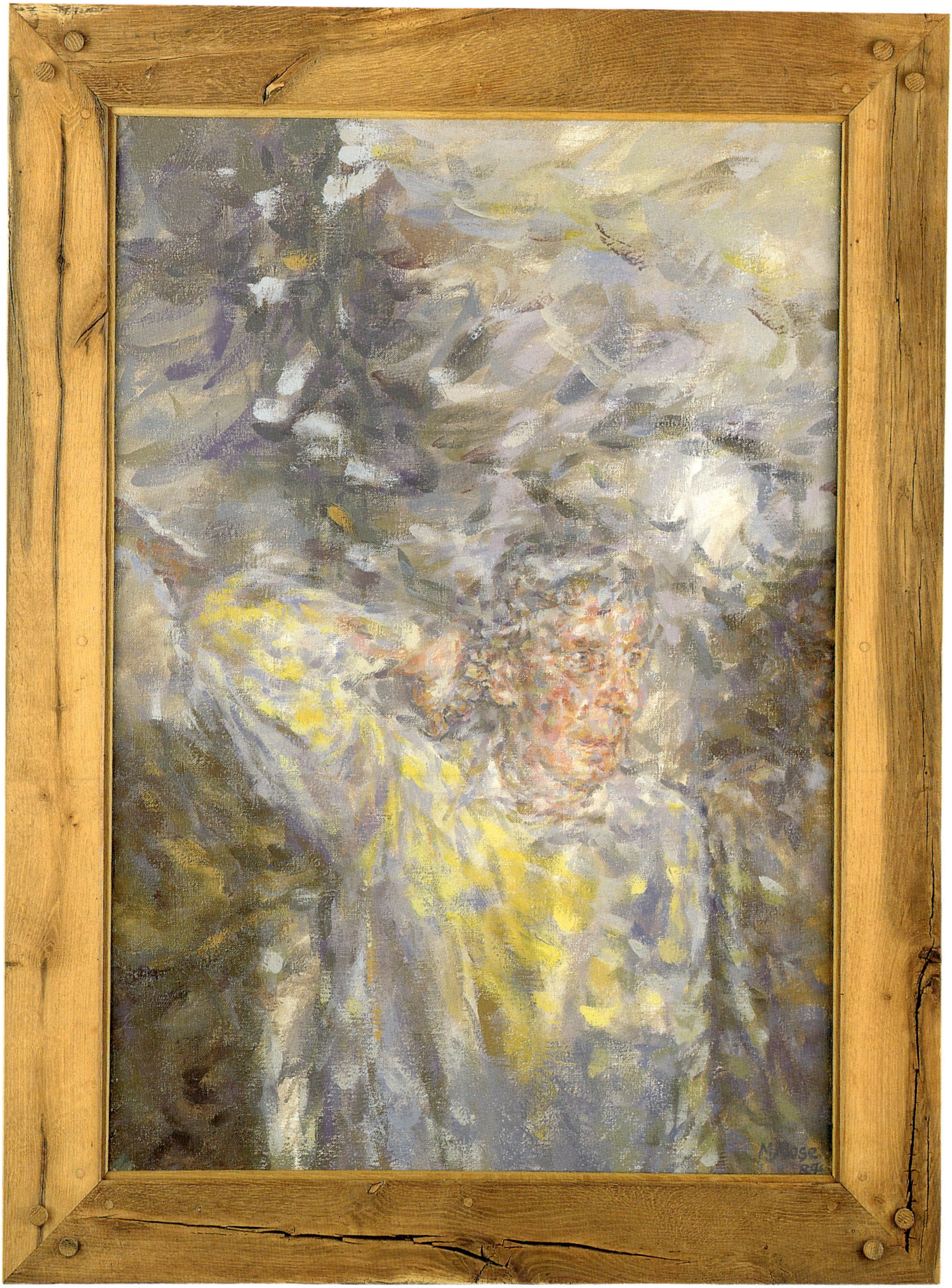

Fig.118 (right)
Francis Crittall by Augustus John, 1919 (no.113).

A Dutch-style reverse section ripple moulding frame of a type used by John among others.

Fig.119 (facing page)
Sir Michael Tippett by Martin Rose, 1989 (no.129).

A frame of reused old English oak made by Edward Pontefract to the artist's specification.

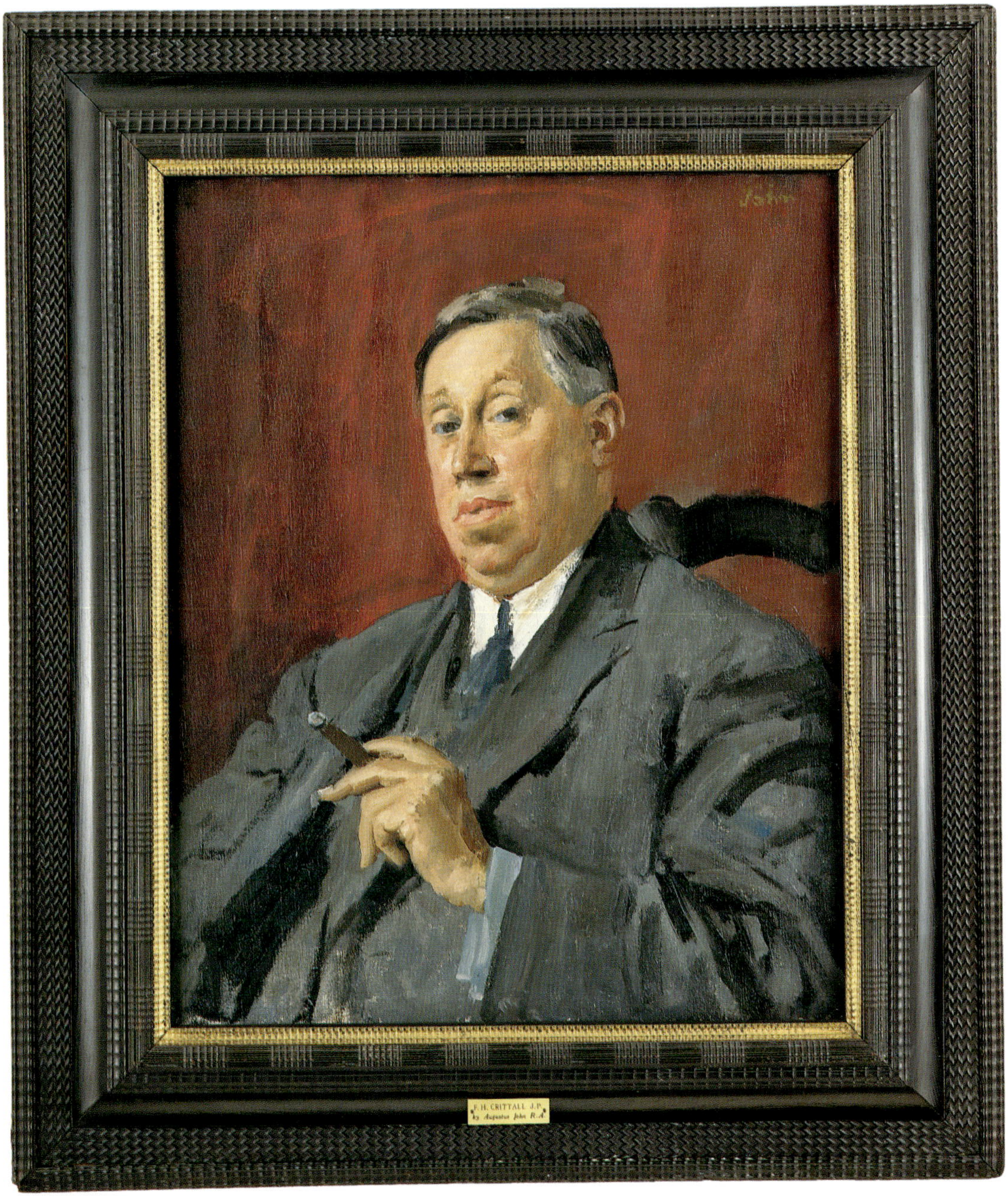

on their behalf, just as many patrons want to buy work which is ready framed. That said, there are as many artists who take a keen interest in the subject. When it comes to a public commission, the National Portrait Gallery's experience is that most artists will take special care over the picture frame. For some such as Tom Phillips or Leonard Rosoman, it is primarily a matter of selecting a frame which does most for a picture visually. For others such as Martin Rose, Humphrey Ocean and Hans Schwarz (see fig.119 and nos.125, 126) the frame can take on certain additional symbolic qualities. The age of artists persistently using one or more stock frame patterns may be over but in its place there has arisen a more thoughtful approach among some artists, who will give great consideration to the framing of each individual work on its own merits.

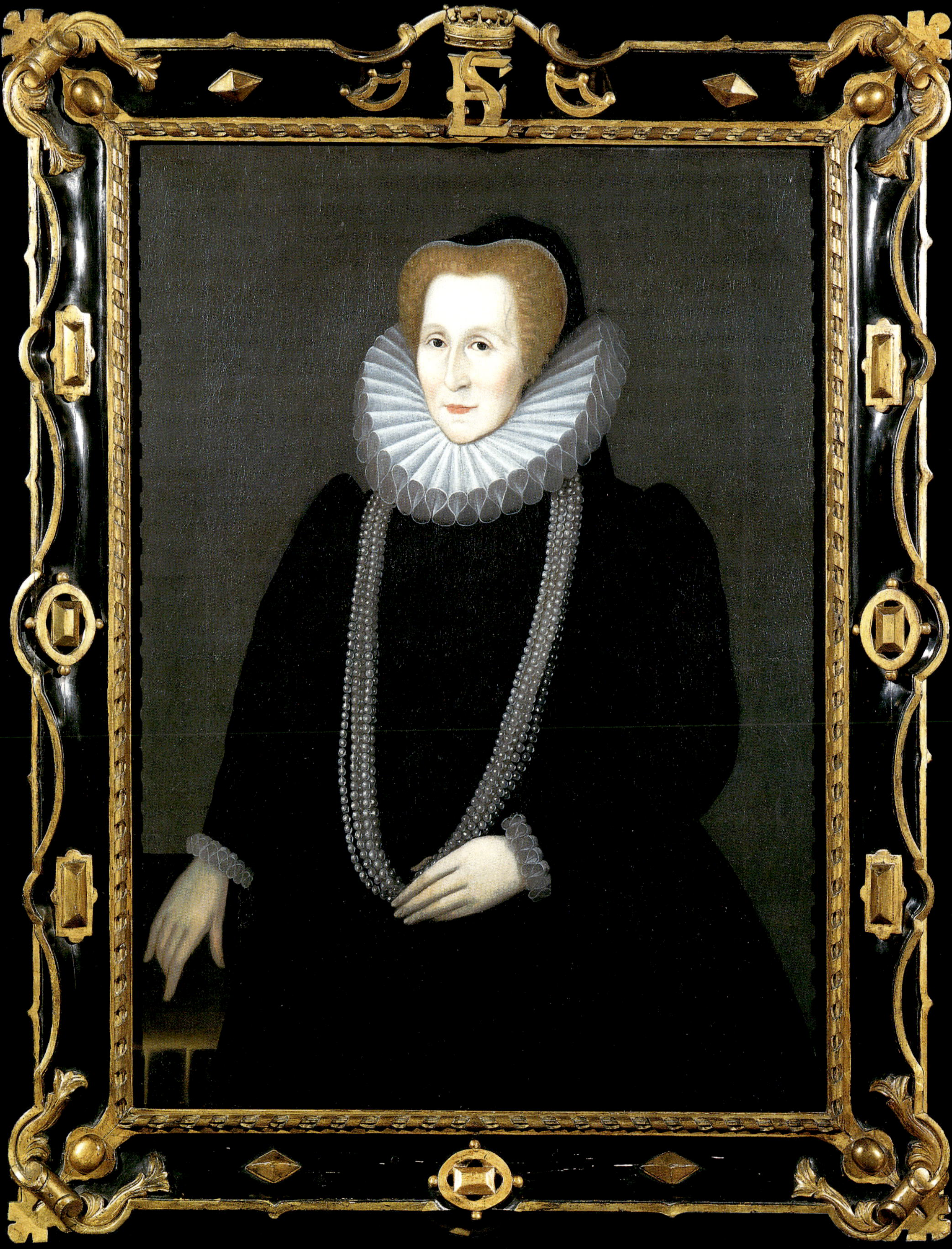

Chapter 5
Patrons and their Advisers

Fig.120 (facing page) *Elizabeth Talbot, Countess of Shrewsbury* by an unknown artist, *c.*1600 (no.98).

An 'Elizabethan' frame made by Henry Critchfield in 1865 to the instructions of George Scharf, Secretary of the National Portrait Gallery.

Few patrons had the strong determined ideas of Anthony Ashley Cooper, 3rd Earl of Shaftesbury, the philosopher–Earl of the early eighteenth century who considered that in all the arts 'plainness and simplicity are the most becoming and are the greatest perfection'. In the face of the fashion for gilt frames he determined to have very simple frames to accord with his aesthetic theories, and wrote from Naples in 1712 about the framing of the *Judgement of Hercules* by Paolo Mattheis, 'there will be no need either of a carved gilded or otherwise expensive frame; it must be plain and of dark colour'd or black Wood, not shining'.[1]

And few patrons had quite the confidence of Horace Walpole, who commissioned gothic and other revival style frames for his extraordinary villa at Strawberry Hill in Twickenham, collected pictures with frames by Grinling Gibbons and William Kent, and who even designed a frame in the new French neo-classical style for a portrait of Mrs Delany (see figs.121, 122).[2]

This chapter looks at the role of the patron in the framing of pictures, and that of his or her advisers, whether architects, dealers or artists. The survey extends to include institutional patrons such as the Foundling Hospital and the British Museum in the eighteenth century, and examines some of the attitudes which influenced the advice given to patrons on framing. Whatever the advice, it was of course ultimately the patron's choice which mattered, and in the face of strongly held opinions even as distinguished an artist as Sir Thomas Lawrence had to beat a graceful retreat, as he did in the case of one of his sitters, Mrs Gott, who refused to have frames as wide as he desired. In the face of her intransigence, Lawrence concluded, 'I shall now only pray that the other pictures be brought up close to them, so that the effect of greater breadth of gilding may still be retained'.[3]

Patrons and their frames

There are certain great houses – Ham from the seventeenth century, for example, or Boughton from the late seventeenth and early eighteenth centuries – where picture framing has taken on a highly distinctive character which reflects the history of the house and the taste of successive owners. Many of these frames are more elaborate than the average portrait frame. If one can recognise such a thing as the 'artist's frame', as suggested in Chapter 4, can one also identify a 'patron's frame' or what one might call 'the country house frame'? If there is such a type, it is to be recognised by one or more distinguishing features: its extra richness and expense, its architectural character or its relationship to the interior design scheme, its individuality, whether a matter of distinctive style or of particular ornamentation with armorial devices or trophies, and finally its differences from the artist's frame. Many of the frames in the National Portrait Gallery are artists' frames. But some – the trophy frames on the portraits of Handel and Mrs Delany (see frontispiece and fig.121), the carved frames on *Lord Coventry*, *Charles II* and *Joseph Banks* (see figs.4, 39, 61), and the compo frame on F.R. Say's portrait of Lord Ellenborough (fig.125) – are clearly, in this characterisation, country house frames. Some of these pictures – the *Handel* for example – may originally have hung in the patron's London house, and now that the great town houses of the eighteenth and nineteenth centuries are no more such pictures have often come to enrich country house collections.

The 9th Duke of Norfolk rebuilt Norfolk House in St James's Square in the 1750s and fitted out the interior in the most spectacular manner, choosing to reframe many of the family portraits, such as that of the Countess of Arundel (fig.123), in a uniform rococo style. Norfolk House, however, has long since gone and the pictures are now mostly at Arundel Castle. A somewhat similar fate met Sir John Fleming Leicester's gallery of modern British pictures in Hill Street, Mayfair, which was opened to the public in 1818, apparently under the supervision of his frame-maker, Michael Tijou. At Sir John's death in 1827 his executors sold up the London house in the face of financial difficulties and the few pictures which were saved from the sale were moved to the family's country seat, Tabley in Cheshire.[4]

It is thus to the country house that one turns for the finest frames, at least for those dating from the seventeenth and eighteenth centuries: Knole for the extraordinary carved frames of the 1620s and 1630s originally in the Earl of Middlesex's collection, Berkeley Castle for rare painted frames of the early seventeenth century, Ham House for a varied array of elaborate carved frames, most especially from the 1630s to the 1670s, Boughton for its superb late seventeenth-century Huguenot frames and eighteenth-century Palladian frames, Felbrigg and Arundel for their rococo frames, and Southill and Tabley for the finest neo-classical and early nineteenth-century frames. These are but a few from the great wealth of such houses. All these collections reflect the taste of the grander or richer collectors, aristocratic patrons for the most part, whose families had sometimes commissioned portraits for generations and who may also have collected old master paintings.

For the nineteenth century the situation is rather different, as many of the finest frames are

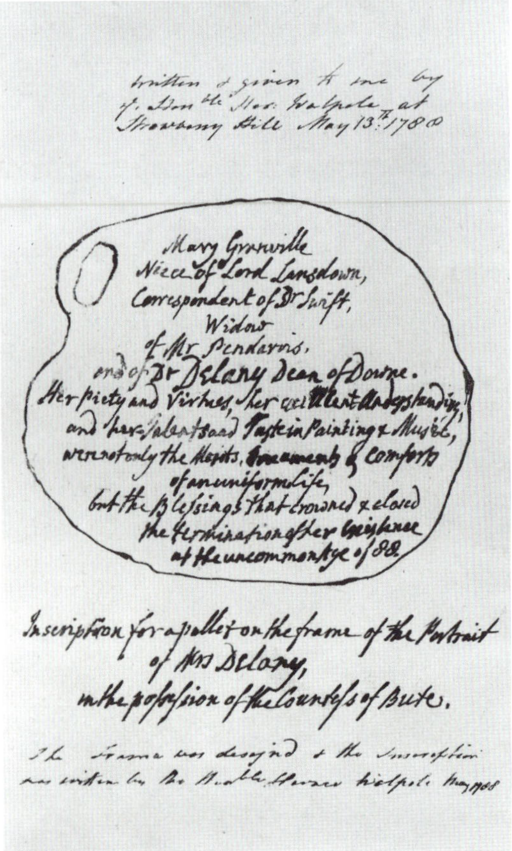

Fig.122 (below left) Horace Walpole's draft for the memorial inscription on the frame of *Mary Delany* by John Opie (fig.121).

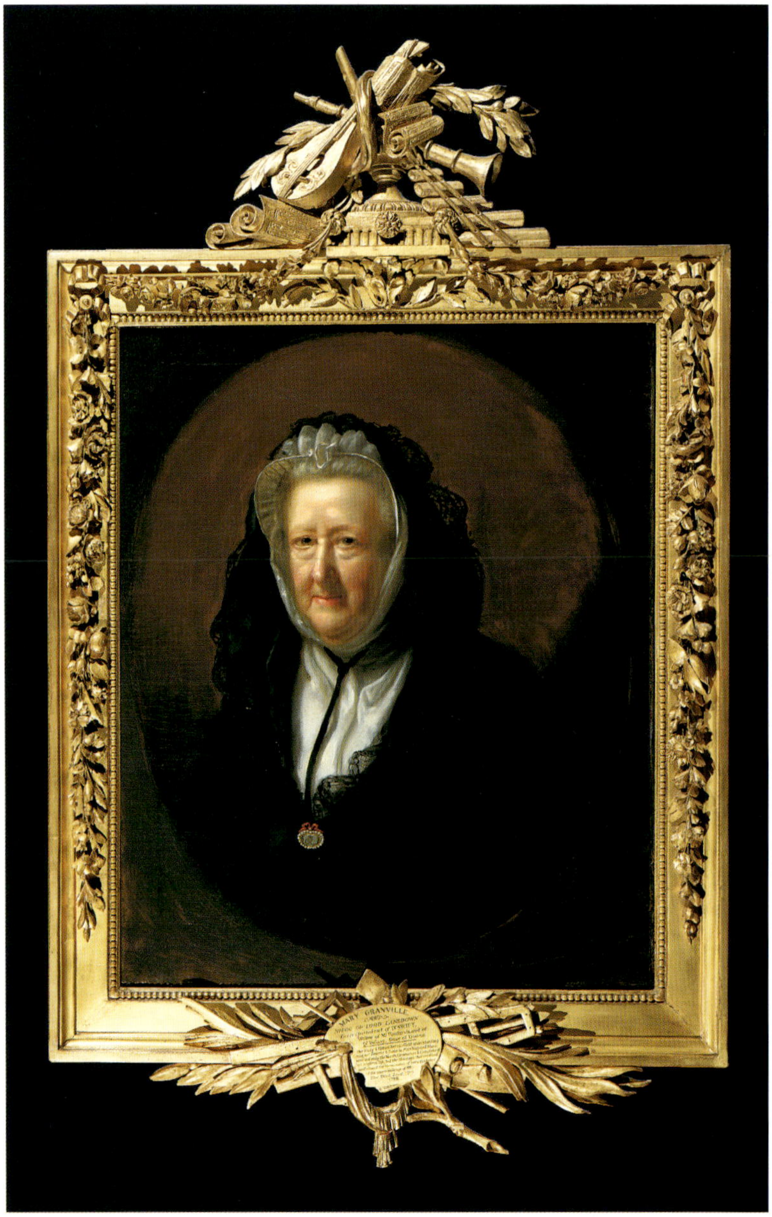

Fig.121 (below) *Mary Delany* by John Opie, *c.*1782 (no.54).

The frame was designed by Horace Walpole for Lady Bute in 1788.

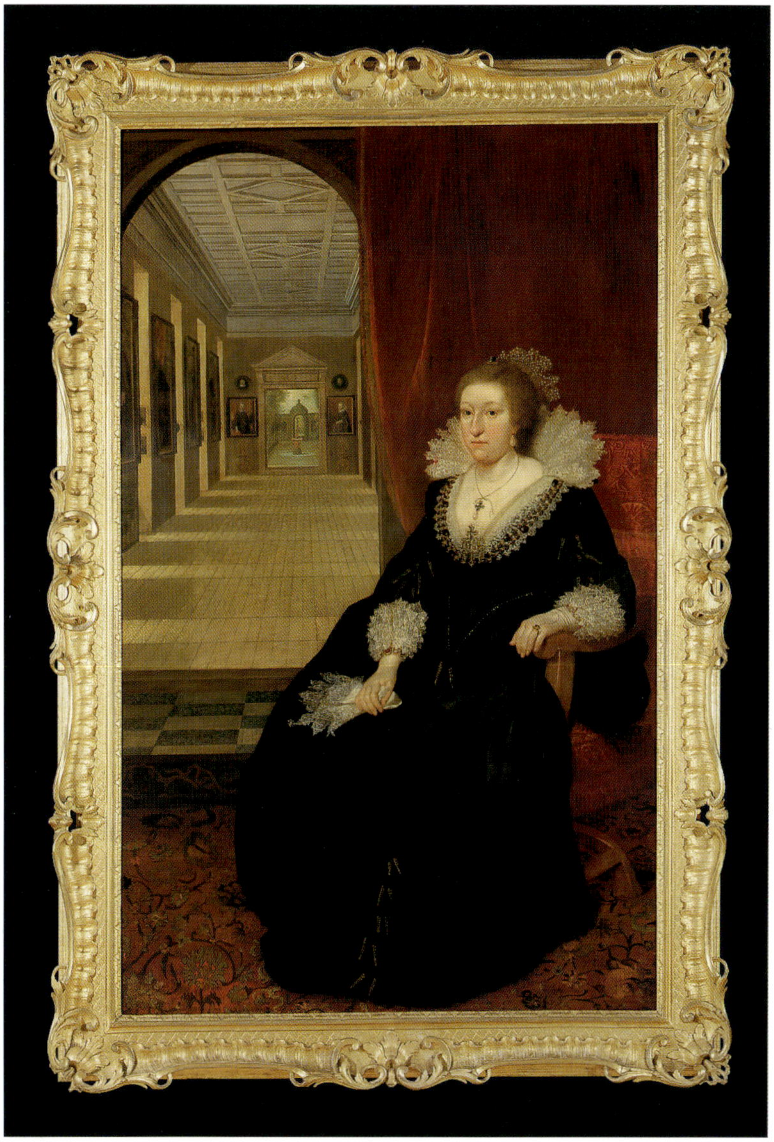

Fig.123 (above)
Alathea Talbot, Countess of Arundel by Daniel Mytens, *c.*1618 (no.35).

The portrait was reframed in the 1750s.

in museums. One of the most exciting aspects of London public collections is the sequence of great gifts and bequests of the period: the Bourgeois bequest at Dulwich, Sir John Soane's Museum, the Wellington Museum at Apsley House, the Turner bequest, the Robert Vernon gift and Sir Henry Tate's collection at the Tate Gallery, the collections of the 3rd and 4th Marquesses of Hertford at Hertford House, now the Wallace Collection, and the Sheepshanks, Townshend, Ionides and Jones collections at the Victoria and Albert Museum. Taken together, they provide a remarkable conspectus of nineteenth-century framing styles.[5]

As far as the evidence has been collected it would seem that the Sheepshanks and Vernon collections, both formed over a relatively short period of time, obtain their remarkable homogeneity in style from the preference by many patrons and artists at the period for frames with all-over small-scale compo ornamentation. Both John Sheepshanks and Robert Vernon (fig.124), the former a cloth manufacturer, the latter an army contractor, bought many pictures which were framed by the artists themselves. For example, E.W. Cooke's ledger in the Royal Academy Library shows that in 1836 both collectors purchased pictures from Cooke with frames, Vernon acquiring *Undercliff Cave* (Tate Gallery) in a frame by Wyatt, and Sheepshanks the *Antiquary's Cell* (Victoria and Albert Museum) in a frame, now lost, by Criswick & Ryan. But on occasion both men arranged their own framing. Sheepshanks used Foord as framemaker when he acquired Turner's *Venice from the Canale della Giudecca* (Victoria and Albert Museum).[6] Vernon's Turners at the Tate Gallery stand out from pictures of comparable date in the Turner bequest, which suggests that they too may have been framed by patron rather than artist. When acquiring a work by J.C. Horsley in 1839, Vernon refused the frame, claiming 'that is not

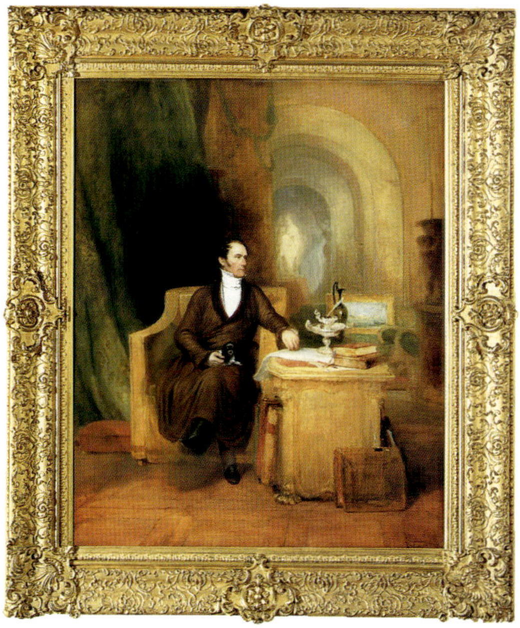

Fig.124 (right)
Robert Vernon by George Jones and Henry Collen, 1848 (no.70).

Vernon gave his collection of modern British paintings to the National Gallery in 1847.

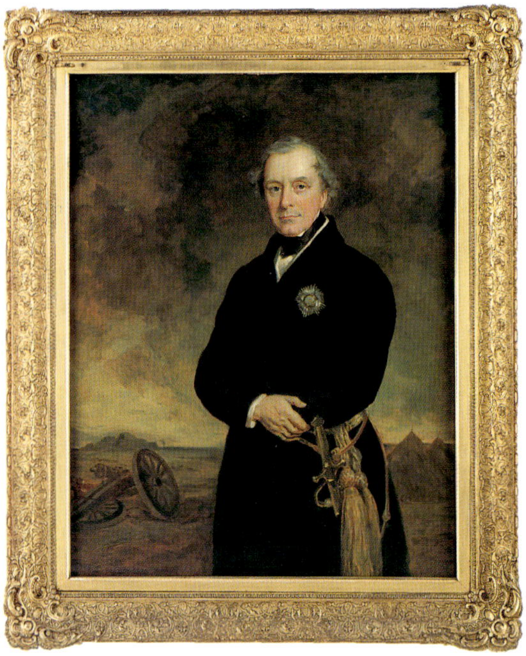

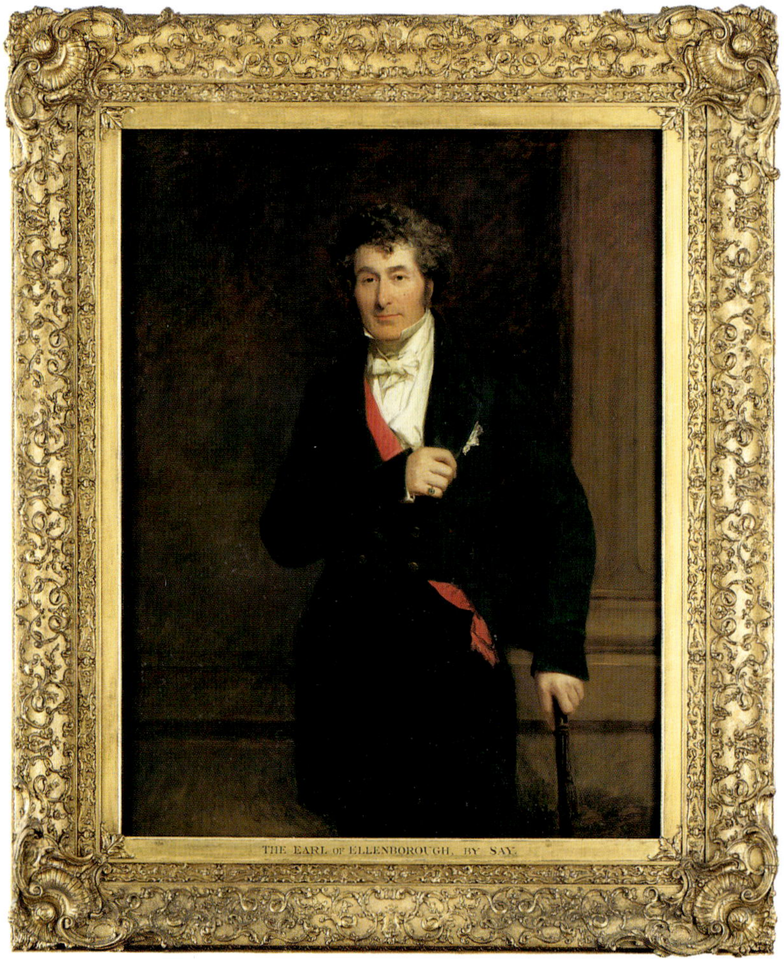

my pattern of frame'.[7] What was this pattern of Vernon's? There is some evidence that he had a predilection for a frame with an inward sloping cushion finished in small-scale foliage or arabesque ornament, a popular style at the period, found also on many of the Sheepshanks pictures.

In contrast, the Tory Prime Minister, Sir Robert Peel, who collected portraits as well as old masters, persisted in using the frame style established by Thomas Lawrence in the 1820s when he added a gallery of eminent statesmen and celebrities of his day at his country house, Drayton Manor in Staffordshire, in the 1840s. Peel's portrait of Lord Ellenborough (fig.125) is one of a set of six painted for him by F.R. Say in the mid-1840s. While Say the artist showed a preference for rococo revival frames, Peel the patron, actually using the same framemaker as Say, kept to the more severe Lawrence manner. The role of Peel's adviser, John Seguier, in matters of framing is described in more detail below, but it is clear that Peel's was the dominant taste. In a somewhat similar way to Peel, a politician of a later generation, W.H. Smith, accepted Millais's choice of a Watts frame for his portraits of Disraeli and Lord Salisbury (no.88) as the model for the small group of portraits of his political contemporaries that he commissioned or bought from Edwin Long, Hubert von Herkomer, W.W. Ouless and Lawrence Alma-Tadema in the last ten years of his life. The single-minded approach of Peel or Smith in framing portraits, many of which now belong to the National Portrait Gallery, may be compared to that of the Gallery itself, where the tendency in the nineteenth century was to frame a few pictures as one-offs, such as the portrait of 'Bess of Hardwick' (see fig.120), but to adopt a range of unelaborate standard patterns for use on most portraits (see figs.126, 127).

Two collectors with a liking for French eighteenth-century fine and decorative arts indulged in reframing their pictures in the French taste. At Hertford House the 4th Marquess had almost a hundred pictures reframed in the late 1850s by W. & P. Evans using a standard fluted pattern with large acanthus mitre leaves somewhat in the

Fig.125 (above)
Edward Law, 1st Earl of Ellenborough by Frederick Richard Say, *c.*1846 (no.69).

Framed by Robert Thick in the Lawrence manner for Sir Robert Peel.

Fig.126 (above left)
Henry Hardinge, 1st Viscount Hardinge by Sir Francis Grant, 1876 (no.100).

Framed by Henry Critchfield in the Lawrence manner for the National Portrait Gallery.

French manner.[8] In the case of John Jones, whose collection came to the Victoria and Albert Museum, he had most of his English nineteenth-century pictures, by artists such as W.P. Frith and Thomas Webster, framed in the Louis Seize revival style by J. & W. Vokins.[9] It is hoped that a closer study of the frames in these and other nineteenth-century museum collections may lead us to a better understanding of collectors of the period as well as of their collections.

Attitudes of patrons to framing

'The picture must have a very handsome French frame; I don't like that Carlo Marat frame for a portrait. Let it be bespoke after some handsome frame at Richmond House'.[10] So wrote Lady Kildare to her husband about the framing of his portrait by Allan Ramsay in 1762. It is rare to gain an insight into a patron's attitude to matters of style in quite this way since surviving correspondence on framing generally keeps to the more mundane subjects of price, quality and delivery. This is as much the case with institutional patrons as with private individuals. In the National Portrait Gallery's copious records it is quite exceptional to find letters like that of the Director, Charles Holmes, who wrote in 1912 to the artist Milly Childers about her father's portrait (fig.127), telling her that 'a "Watts" pattern was the only one which would enable the portrait to be hung here harmoniously with the other pictures of the same period', or that of his successor, Henry Hake, to another artist, Harold Speed, in 1942, rejecting the use of canvas slips: 'I am not very anxious to start the canvas fashion in frames because nearly all the frames in the Gallery are of carved wood'.[11]

The starting-point for Lady Kildare's letter to her husband was the understanding that it was Lord Kildare as the sitter, rather than Allan Ramsay as the artist, who would arrange the framing of the portrait. This was a common attitude amongst great country house owners in the seventeenth and eighteenth centuries. Lord Glenorchy, who became 3rd Earl of Breadalbane, commissioned portraits from Highmore, Pickering, Seeman, Ramsay, Hudson, Catherine Read and Gainsborough over a period of thirty years and, judging from his account books, normally arranged his own framing, firstly with William Waters and then from 1764 with another London maker, Crawford of Compton Street.[12] A fellow Scottish peer, the 2nd Duke of Montrose, paid the Edinburgh portrait painter, Sir John Medina, for frames as well as portraits in 1710 but subsequently, when commissioning portraits from Kneller, Aikman and Richardson in London, preferred to turn to the king's framemaker, John Howard, for most of his frames, rather than to the artist.[13]

When it came to framing old master paintings the situation was rather different. There was, of course, no artist to consult but instead a dealer selling the picture or an agent acting for the collector. The vast majority of patrons expected to reframe old masters on acquisition. This was often a matter of necessity, since pictures frequently were imported without their frames, as were the superb French and Italian paintings in the Orleans collection in the 1790s.[14] Such pictures may have been brought into Britain without frames because those managing the trade either knew that the old frames would

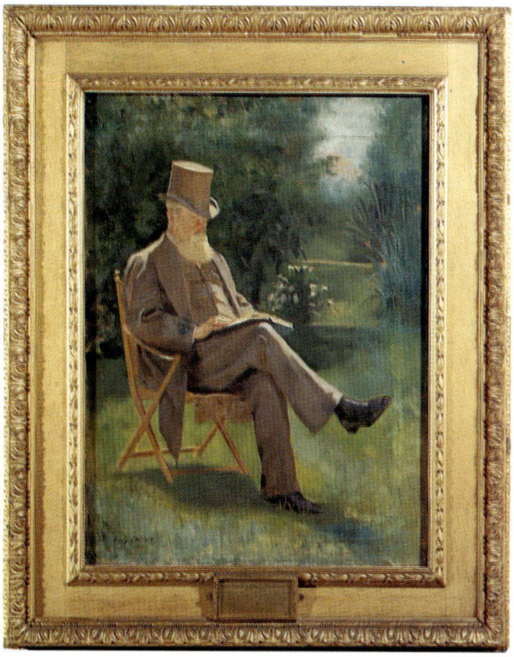

Fig.127 (right) *Hugh Childers* by Emily Childers, 1891 (no.101).

Framed by Francis Draper in a Watts frame for the National Portrait Gallery in 1912.

in any case be likely to be discarded by the new owner or believed that new frames would help sell the pictures.[15] The result is that almost all the old master collections formed in the Napoleonic era in Britain, including for example those of Sir Francis Bourgeois at Dulwich Picture Gallery or the Duke of Wellington at Apsley House, have heavy frames of the period. The patron who was willing to leave pictures in old frames was the exception; it has been suggested that Henry Hoare and his successor Colt Hoare at Stourhead deliberately kept good French frames in the rococo style to set off as grace-notes against the more sober Maratta frames of the larger paintings.[16]

Reframing pictures on acquisition was one tendency. Another was the regilding of frames either on acquisition or when rehanging works in a new interior. As a result most old frames have been regilded at least once, and often several times. In France and Italy, perhaps because of the superlative quality of much of the original water gilding, but more probably because regilding was not the fashion, old frames are much more likely to have been left untouched. Of course there could be practical reasons for regilding: the London atmosphere in the nineteenth century was very damaging to gilt surfaces, and to pictures generally, which is why glazing of pictures became so prevalent. But there was also a pronounced taste for new gilding for its own sake, which contrasts with the vogue nowadays for mellow or artificially distressed surfaces. In 1781 George Selwyn wrote to Lord Carlisle about his pictures, 'I shall propose that the frames of yours may be gilded, as mine will then be, anew'.[17] And in 1852 when Sir James Kay-Shuttleworth held a housewarming party at Gawthorpe Hall, newly decorated by J.G. Crace, he reported that 'the Dining Hall with all the Pictures in their newly Gilt Frames (uncovered) looked very handsome'.[18] There are persistent references to regilding frames at the National Portrait Gallery in the Gallery's records throughout the late nineteenth and early twentieth centuries. At the National Gallery in 1914 one of the Trustees, Robert Benson, bemoaned the fact that even fine original frames had 'almost all been re-gilt, wholly or partially, in the early Victorian style, upon a white ground instead of red'.[19] The result, of course, of regilding is a loss of detail, especially if a frame is regessoed during the process (see fig.128).

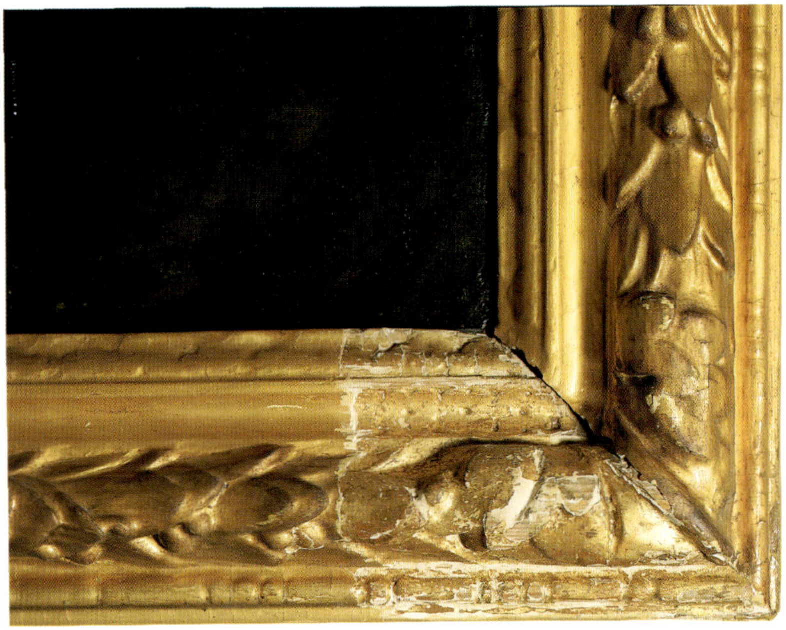

Fig.128
James Scott, Duke of Monmouth, studio of Sir Godfrey Kneller (detail), *c.*1678.

The original gilding and the details of the carving have been partially revealed by chipping away the later layers of gesso and regilding.

How widely appreciated the niceties in gilding techniques that could be achieved in France or Italy were is not clear. For most patrons' purposes what could be done in London was more than adequate. But from the seventeenth century onwards it was to Paris that those with connections and resources occasionally turned for craftsmanship of the highest order. When Lord and Lady Burlington sat to William Aikman for their portrait in 1723, Aikman's patron 'commission'd a fine frame from Paris'.[20] For a portrait painted in London to be framed in Paris was unusual, even though pictures purchased on the Continent by British collectors might be framed there, as were the Duke of Buckingham's in 1621 or the Earl of Upper Ossory's in the 1760s.[21] It was not until the nineteenth century that the habit of going abroad, usually to Italy, for the finest carving and gilding became more common. In 1850 William Bankes wrote from Florence to his sister about 'three gloriously carved frames' which he had sent to England for the Spanish Room at Kingston Lacy.[22] By 1855 the National Gallery was going to the framemaker, Ugo Baldi, in Florence, in search of the best quality carving and gilding at lower prices than could be found in London. As the Director, Sir Charles Eastlake, reported to the Gallery Trustees, 'The pictures purchased in Florence have been left there in order to have a frame made for one, and the old frames of the others repaired and regilt; the art of frame-carving being practiced with great ability in Florence'.[23] Two years later the National Gallery's great Pollaiuolo altarpiece, the *Martyrdom of Saint Sebastian*, was framed in Florence to fine effect in a tabernacle frame.[24] The fashion did not endure, probably for the reason that the artist John Strudwick put to a patron in 1896: 'I used to have my frames from Florence ... but I found it troublesome dealing with people so far away, they so often made mistakes'.[25]

Some artists and patrons found it easier to go to continental craftsmen working in England than to send their orders abroad. A French framemaker, Emile Remy, who set up business in London in 1904, later advertising himself as a 'Specialist in Restoration and Reproduction of Antique Gilding', met with a ready reception.[26] Not only did artists such as Sir John Lavery and Philip de Laszlo turn to him (see nos.110, 114) but he was also recommended to the National Gallery in 1916, perhaps by the collector, Robert Benson, who had prepared a report on framing at the Gallery a few years before.[27] Benson's report encouraged the Gallery to take the next step, which was to acquire antique frames, following the fashion set by artists in the 1890s.[28] One such collection was purchased from Cassirer in 1935 and old frames have continued to be acquired by the National Gallery, the National Portrait Gallery and other museums both in Britain and abroad.[29] This approach has of course been taken one stage further in recent years so that if original frames are not available, reproductions are often made to period patterns as far as they are understood.

All this is a far cry from the attitudes of the past where a single pattern, the so-called 'livery' frame, might be chosen to frame a whole collection. In some cases, Sunderland frames of the seventeenth century were adopted as house styles, as already mentioned.[30] And sets of pictures such as those hung by George I in the gallery at Kensington Palace or by Jacob Tonson in the pavilion he built for the Kit-cat Club were uniformly framed. Portraits in libraries hanging above the bookcases seem to have been particularly prone to reframing, as at Narford Hall, Chesterfield House, Kingston Lacy and Saltram.[31] Nevertheless, the reframing *en masse* of an existing collection has not been common in Britain, and where it has taken place, it has not always worked very satisfactorily. Prince Albert's reframing of all the pictures in the grand Picture Gallery at Buckingham Palace in the 1850s was already being denigrated early this century by Lionel Cust, Surveyor of the collection under Edward VII, and in recent years has been undone by the purchase of old frames for the pictures.[32] These pictures, then, are certainly in their third frames and some of them may have seen even more reframings in the course of almost four centuries of matching pictures to palaces and decorative schemes.

Artists and framemakers as advisers

'William Seguier began to study the Art, but not having energy, he gave it up, turned Connoisseur, a much easier profession, and though without education or common knowledge, from sheer native tact, soon rose to confidential situations'.[33] Such was the artist Benjamin Robert Haydon's somewhat jaded assessment of the leading adviser to collectors in the aftermath of the Napoleonic Wars. It was a common practice to retain an agent or adviser of some sort to take on the detailed arrangements of bidding at auction, picture restoration and framing. Most such advisers were failed artists, as Haydon implied, although painting restorers (who were usually artists) and framemakers sometimes assumed the role.

The Royal Collection has from the time of Charles I employed a Surveyor or Keeper of Pictures, who has more often than not, at least until this century, been an artist. So the minor sculptor Abraham van der Doort was made responsible for Charles I's collection, arranging conservation and framing on occasion, and making a highly detailed inventory of the collection in the late 1630s, in which frame descriptions formed an important part.[34] The arrangements for the Royal Collection have varied with the personalities involved so that, for example, at the end of the seventeenth century, the Surveyor of Pictures, the obscure portrait painter, Frederick Sonnius, appears to have been somewhat overshadowed by William III's framemaker, John Norris, an energetic man whom Vertue actually calls 'picture keeper'; together with the king's Dutch secretary, Constantijn Huygens the younger, it was Sonnius and Norris who hung the king's new gallery at Kensington Palace in 1695, as Huygens recorded in his diary.[35]

A collection which rivalled that of Charles I was the Duke of Buckingham's. The artist Balthazar Gerbier, who travelled extensively on the Continent on his behalf, generally arranged for the framing of the pictures he bought for the Duke. In Venice in 1621 he caused 'two great frames ... to bee mayde and karven after the Italian faschion' for two very large pictures by Titian and Tintoretto, while three years later he arranged for another Titian, this time purchased in Paris, to be delivered to York House in London, 'to my father-in-law, who will put it in a frame'.[36] At a time when important pictures were beginning to be framed in London in quantity, a man such as Gerbier, highly aware of continental tastes in framing, would have been in an influential position.

This was collecting at an international scale. At a more modest level later in the century, there were some patrons such as Samuel Pepys who were sufficiently sure of themselves to be willing to rely on their own taste, if necessary with some advice from the framemaker. Pepys was not a collector on a grand scale but he was a patron of some sophistication, close to the cross-currents of fashionable court taste. In 1669 at the framemaker, 'one Norris in Long-Acre', he was shown 'several forms of frames to choose by; which was pretty, in little bits of mouldings to choose by', as he noted in his diary.[37] When he had his own portrait painted by John Hayls in 1666 (fig.129) he noted down both the cost of the portrait at £14 and the frame at 25s. His library was hung with portraits over the bookcases (see fig.130), seemingly framed in uniform bunched leaf frames of the type found on Hayls's portrait. Much later in 1702 when framing a portrait of Dr John Wallis by Sir Godfrey Kneller to give to the University of Oxford, he wrote about consulting Kneller's 'owne man', probably his studio assistant rather than his framemaker, about using a silvered frame.[38] Revealingly, Pepys describes the advice he received as 'confirmed by 40 yeares experience of my owne'. Rather more typical than Pepys was the lawyer Sir John Perceval, who employed a Dutch artist and restorer, Gasper Smitz, to make arrangements for work on his pictures, as a letter he received from Smitz in 1685 reveals: 'As to the frames, I am confident that they cannot but please you, since I am sure they are much the best that I have seen or had done for me, and I gave a better allowance to my gilder that the colour might be as good and glorious as could be made ... if you have an occasion for any

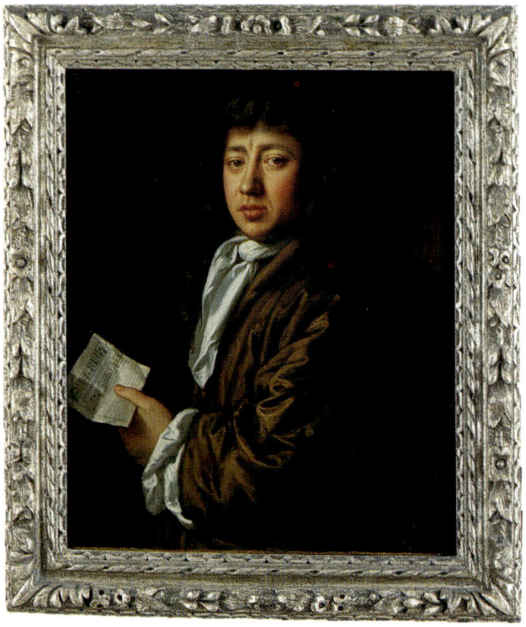

Fig.129
Samuel Pepys by John Hayls, 1666 (no.18).

The portrait is apparently still in its original silvered bunched leaf frame.

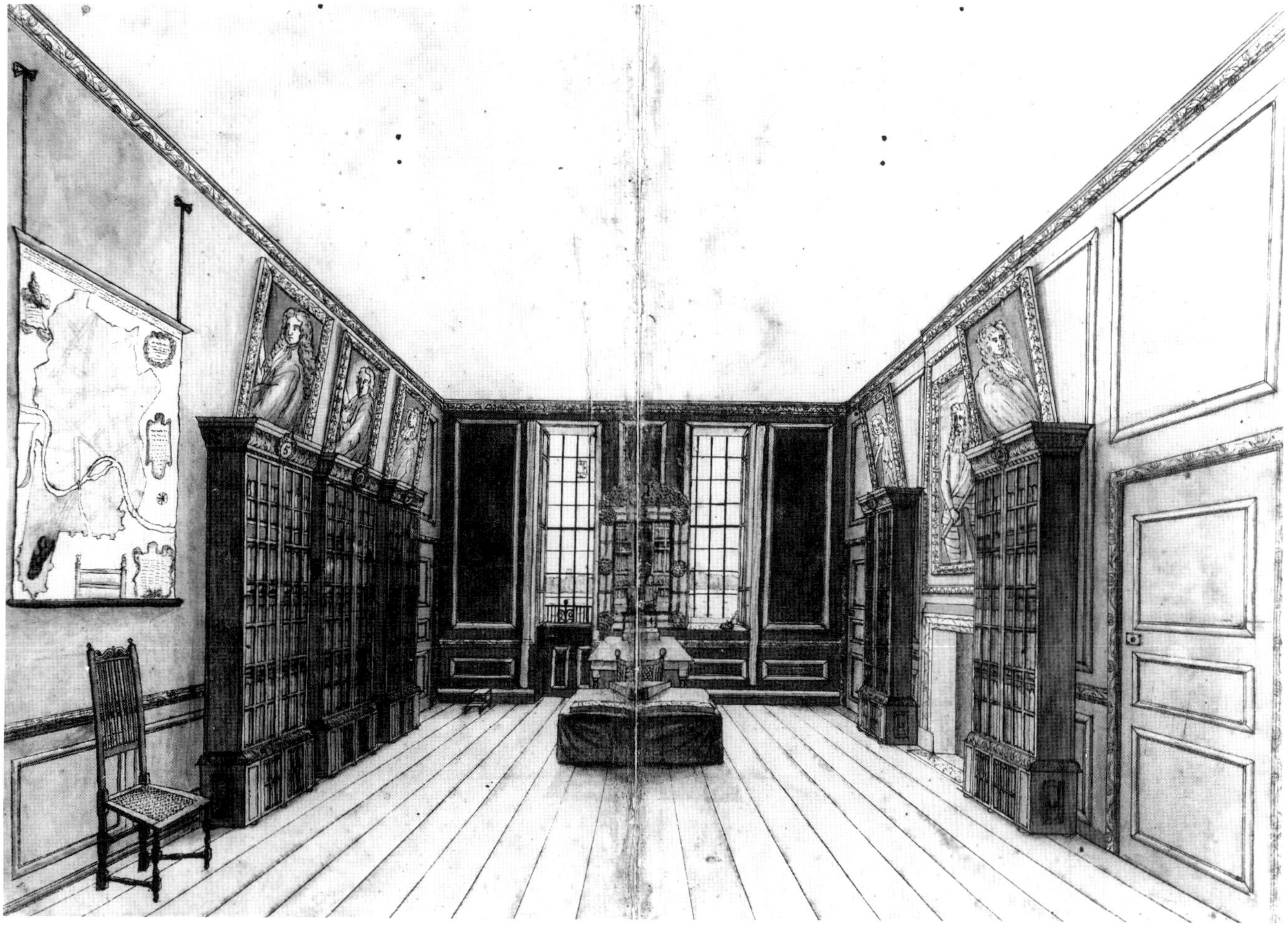

Fig.130 (above) Samuel Pepys's library by an unknown artist, *c*.1693 (Magdalene College, Cambridge).

Pepys's library in his house in Buckingham Street overlooking the Thames was hung with portraits in matching frames. His own portrait by Hayls (fig.129) appears over the bookcase at the left.

other kind of pictures ... or frames of any sort, let me but have the measure ... and I doubt not but to send them to you to your satisfaction'.[39]

Many minor artists were willing to undertake conservation and provide a general service of this kind. In 1756 the Trustees of the newly founded British Museum chose the portrait painter and print publisher, Arthur Pond, to restore the wall-paintings at Montagu House and then asked him to arrange the framing of the oil paintings. Thus originated the earliest type of 'museum' frame in England (see fig.131). Even a leading artist would take on the framing of pictures for a favoured client, as Sir Joshua Reynolds did for the Duke of Rutland, who was forming a collection on his advice. 'I have order'd very handsome frames to be made for them, at ten guineas each, and very broad, which I think gives a picture a more consequential air', Reynolds told the Duke in 1787 when framing Nicolas Poussin's *Seven Sacraments*, five of which still remain at Belvoir Castle.[40]

In the early nineteenth century the wealth of old master paintings flooding into Britain brought exceptional opportunities for collectors. The greatest adviser of the epoch was the Surveyor of the King's Pictures, William Seguier, as the ever caustic Benjamin Robert Haydon made clear: 'His King does nothing without Mr. Seguier's advice. At the B. Gallery he is keeper, hanger, judge, secretary, & factotum. At the National Gallery he is director & every private collection is under his controul, his management, & his protection'.[41] Not only did Seguier advise George IV and hang the exhibitions at the British Institution (or Gallery), he did indeed, with the help of his younger brother, John, have the management of many of the most important private collections. Both brothers had begun life as artists but found the business of working as experts and restorers of pictures more profitable. While William was the better known, his brother, John, was not without influence. John had the responsibility for framing and hanging the Daniel Mesman collection in the Fitzwilliam Museum under the terms of Mesman's bequest in 1834.[42] After William Seguier's death in 1843 it was John who took on the direction of the Duke of Wellington's collection, being paid for arranging pictures at Apsley House in 1845.[43] The detailed interest he took in the hanging and framing of pictures can be seen from his correspondence with another celebrated collector, Sir Robert Peel, to whom he wrote in 1848 about pictures recently purchased for Drayton Manor, including a portrait of Lord Granville by Hoppner: 'The frame of this picture, about a four inch moulding, looks rather mean for so good a picture. I think it should be enlarged to make it suitable to the other half length pictures at Drayton'.[44] It appears that the Seguiers had links with two leading firms of framemakers, Thomas Temple until his bankruptcy in 1839, and thereafter his successor in business, Robert Thick.[45] Probably through William Seguier's influence, Thick was appointed the National Gallery's framemaker in 1840, and he also did work for Wellington, Peel and other Seguier clients. One or other of the Seguier brothers might receive a small cut from Thick from the business thus generated, so that one finds that £3.6s was 'deducted for Mr Seguier' from the £139.5s received by Thick from the Earl of Burlington in 1841.[46]

On occasion, when an owner reposed exceptional trust in an individual, the framemaker would assume the wider role of providing advice and acting as agent. A case in point from the late eighteenth century is Edward Foxhall, a friend of Sir John Soane, who acted for William Beckford of Fonthill. Foxhall made frames for the collection, witness the entry in George Romney's ledger in October 1789: 'The Picture of Alderman Beckford sent to Font Hill the care of Mr. Foxhall who made the Frame'.[47] But he also undertook much of the furnishing of Fonthill and acted extensively as Beckford's agent in purchasing works of art and commissioning pictures, exciting a good deal of animosity among artists in the process.[48] Such was Beckford's reliance on Foxhall that at his death in 1815 he could write, 'I haven't failed to perceive and feel the horror of the loss of Foxhall'.[49]

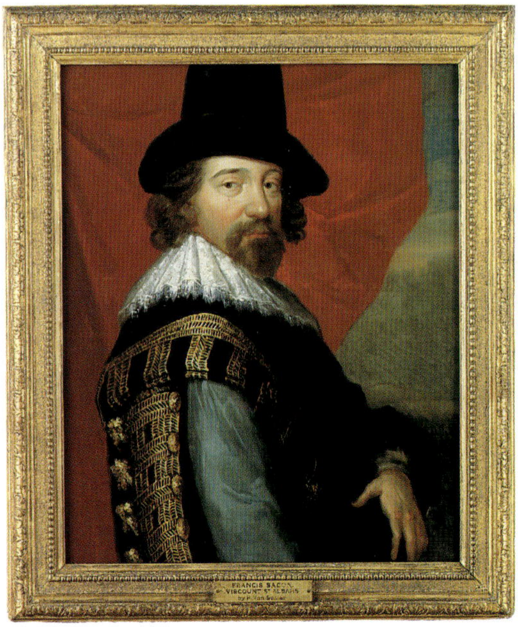

Fig.131 (left)
Francis Bacon, Viscount St Alban
attributed to John Vanderbank, *c.*1731 (no.29).

Framed in a simplified Palladian style for the British Museum in 1758.

The role of the architect

'My Lord Duke having appointed you to be his carver, I desire you will wait on Mr. Flitcroft and take his direction for such things as are wanted in the way and I make no doubt but you will perform the work in the best manner and with all possible dispatch'.[50] So wrote the Duke of Bedford's agent to William Linnell, carver and gilder, in 1749, giving him instructions to take orders from the architect, Henry Flitcroft, for carving work, including picture frames, at Woburn Abbey and elsewhere. In the eighteenth century under the influence of William Kent the role of the architect came to be one of great importance in the design and layout of all aspects of interiors, including picture framing. Thirty years after Flitcroft set to work at Woburn another architect, Robert Adam, called on the

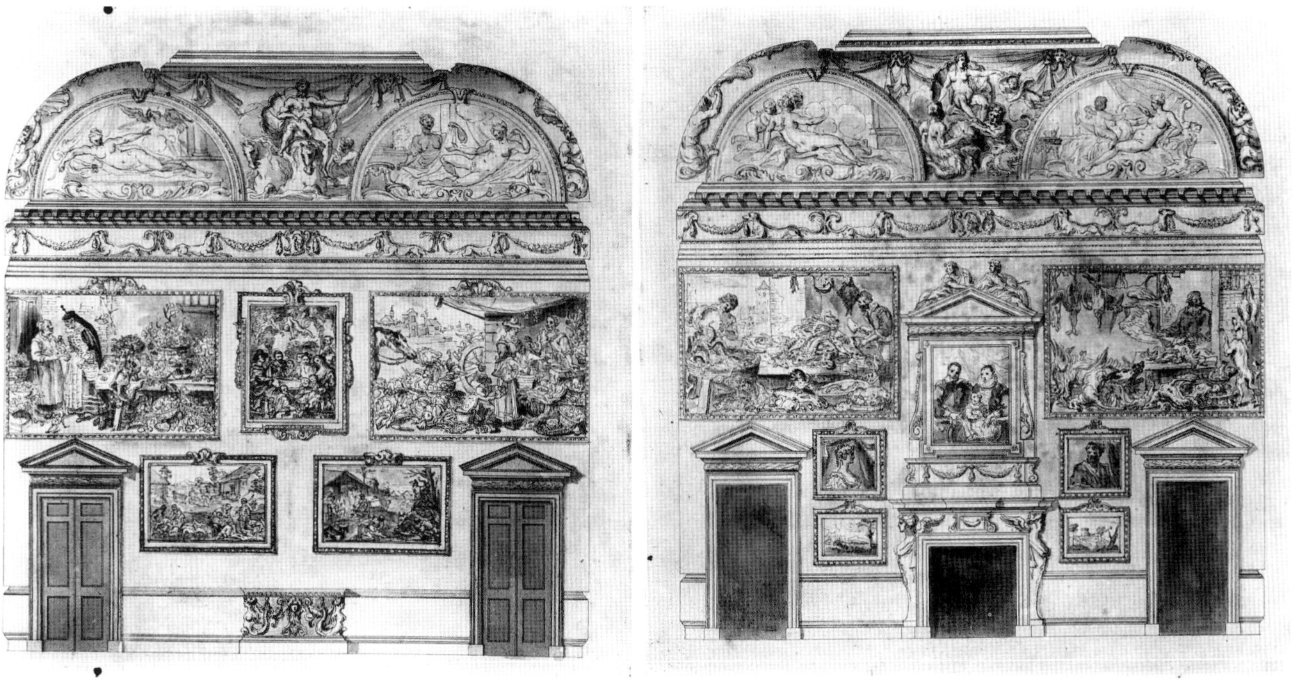

Fig.132
Designs by William Kent, 1725, for the Saloon at Houghton Hall (Private Collection).

bluestocking Mrs Montagu to make alterations at her house, as she reported to a friend: 'He came at the head of a regiment of artificers, an hour after the time he had promised: the bricklayer talked about the alterations to be made in a wall; the stonemason was as eloquent about the coping of the said wall; the carpenter thought the internal fitting up of the house not less important; then came the painter, who is painting my ceilings in various colours, according to the fashion'.[51] Though there is no mention of picture frames here, Robert Adam designed numerous frames for other clients and had many a carver among his 'regiment of artificers'.

Even before the age of Kent and Adam, architects were expected to be able to take charge of the fitting-out of interiors, to approve craftsmen's accounts and to give advice on practical matters. Sir Roger Pratt, architect of Clarendon House in the 1660s, made careful notes, for example, on the cost of gold leaf and of gilding mouldings so that he would know what a craftsman should charge.[52] William Winde, a slightly younger contemporary of Sir Christopher Wren, wrote to Lady Bridgeman, his patron at Castle Bromwich Hall, in 1686, 'I shall by ye first opertunity send downe the Joyners Desines wch I have corrected where it was necessary', and some years later he was anxious that another joiner, Robert Aiscough, should 'doe 3 or 4 inches of a sorte' of moulding as a sample and set out his prices.[53] While it was the joiner who produced the designs and samples, it was the architect who was responsible for approving and correcting his work as necessary. Whether these mouldings would have been used for picture framing is not known, but it was generally the responsibility of the joiner to produce frames. In 1685 Winde wrote to his patron, Lord Craven, at another great house, Combe Abbey, suggesting that a set of four great landscapes could be hung on the staircase: 'And if your Lordshipp likes the proposalls, there may frames for them and some other Pictures ... be made on the place (whilst the workmen are here) at reasonable rates'.[54]

With the advent of the Palladian style at the hands of Colen Campbell, William Kent and Lord Burlington, pictures came to be seen as an integral part of the appearance of interiors. At Kensington Palace Kent's responsibility for the entire appearance of the new Drawing Room is evident from his bill submitted in 1727: 'For drawing the sides of the Drawing Roome with all the Pictures sketcht in proper Colours designing

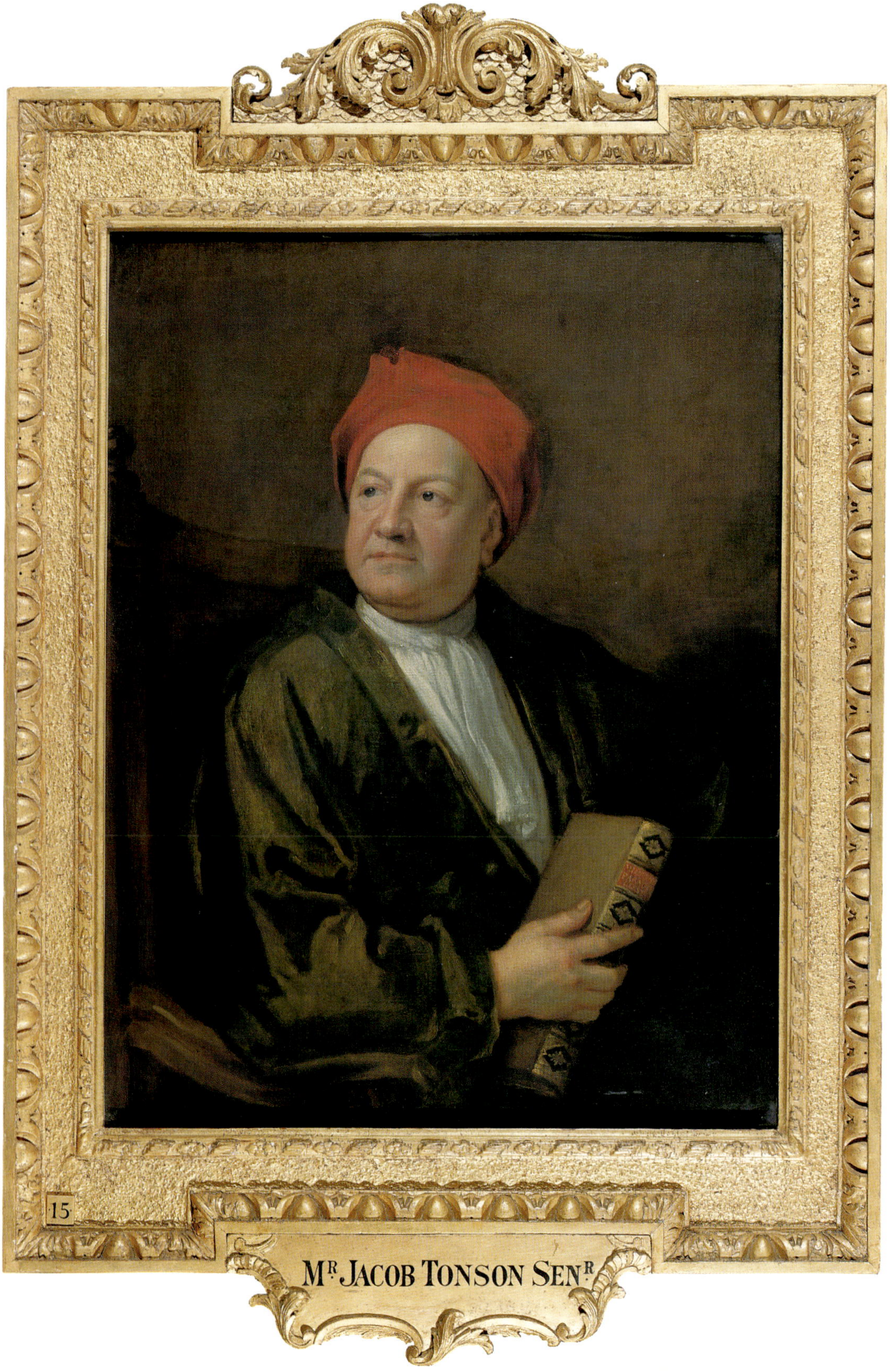

Fig.133
Jacob Tonson senior by Sir Godrey Kneller, 1717 (no.26).

One of a set of forty-one identical frames made by Gerrard Howard in 1733. The portraits were given to the National Portrait Gallery by the National Art Collections Fund in 1945 and now hang at the Gallery and at Beningbrough Hall, Yorkshire.

& drawing the mouldings & ornaments for all the picture frames, glasses, etc.'.[55] This design does not survive but an almost contemporary design for the Saloon at Houghton Hall, the house of the Prime Minister, Sir Robert Walpole, shows the kind of detailed drawing Kent produced (fig.132). For the Gallery at Kensington Palace, Kent's bill specifies 'the frames drawn with ornaments at large', that is that full-scale designs were produced.[56] The Gallery has recently been restored and rehung so that the vital contribution of Kent's frames to the appearance of the room can now be appreciated once more.[57]

A few years later when Jacob Tonson junior wanted to rehouse the Kit-cat Club portraits which had been give to his uncle, the publisher Jacob Tonson senior, Secretary of this Whig dining club, he employed the minor architect, Henry Joynes, with his experience as Clerk of the Works at Kensington Palace, to build a new pavilion for him at his house at Barn Elms. More than forty pictures, representing Sir Robert Walpole and other leading Whig politicians and writers, were framed by Gerrard Howard, the king's framemaker, in 'architrave' frames, that is frames in the Kent style, at a cost of two guineas each (fig.133). Whether the distinctive frames were designed by Joynes or chosen in consultation with Howard is not recorded, but the pictures and their frames, double hung as recorded in a contemporary plan, must have created a very powerful effect.

It became common practice for architects working in the Palladian style to produce drawings for interiors showing pictures in frames as features ornamenting and articulating the walls

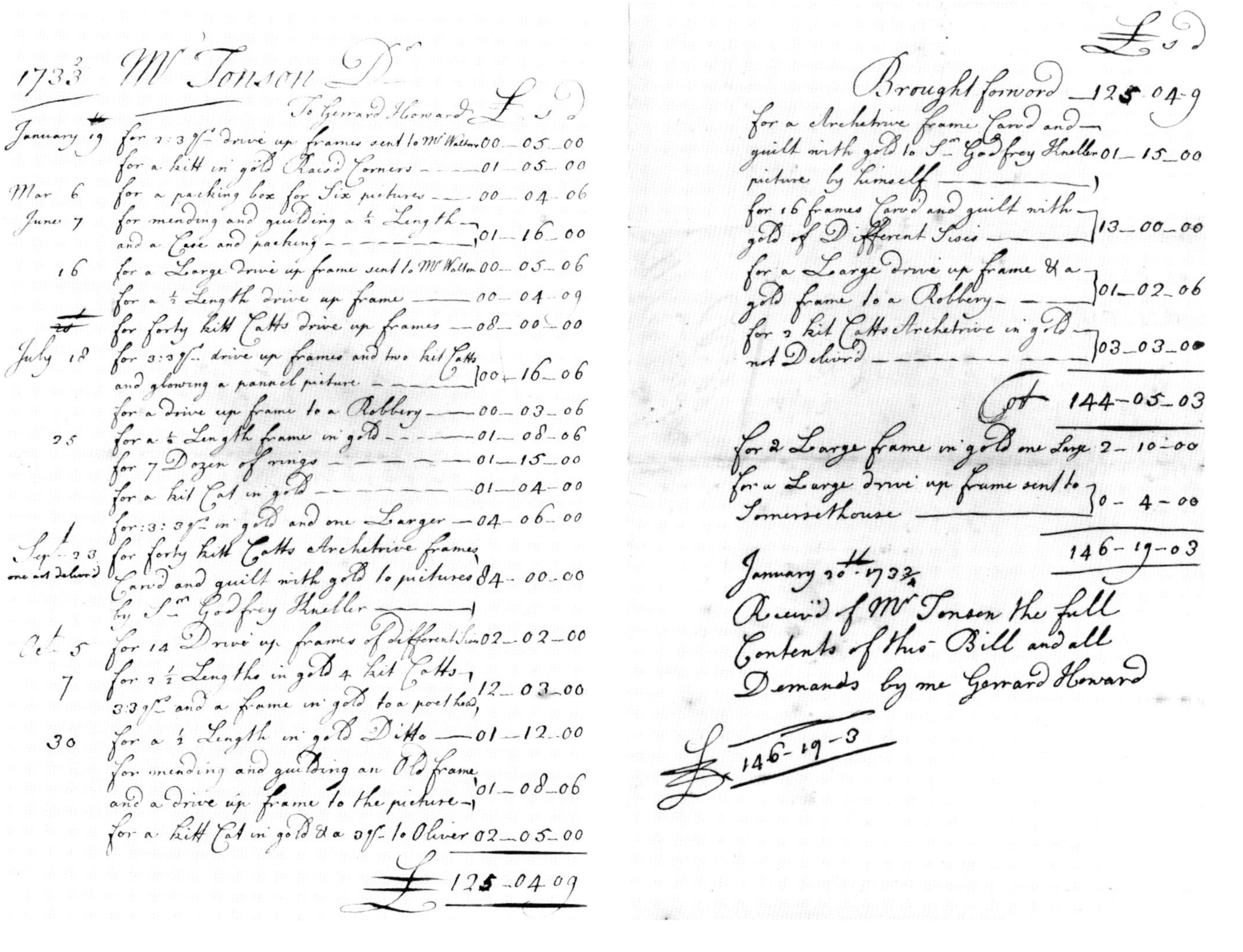
1733 Mr Tonson Dr
To Gerrard Howard £ s d
January 19 for 2 : 3 qr drive up frames sent to Mr Walton 00 – 05 – 00
for a kitt in gold Raised Corners — 01 – 05 – 00
Mar 6 for a packing box for Six pictures — 00 – 04 – 06
June 7 for mending and guilding a ½ Length and a Case and packing — 01 – 16 – 00
16 for a Large drive up frame sent to Mr Walton 00 – 05 – 06
for a ½ Length drive up frame — 00 – 04 – 09
20 for forty kitt Catts drive up frames — 08 – 00 – 00
July 18 for 3:3 qr drive up frames and two kit Catts and glewing a pannel picture — 00 – 16 – 06
for a drive up frame to a Robbery — 00 – 03 – 06
25 for a ½ Length frame in gold — 01 – 08 – 06
for 7 Dozen of rings — 01 – 15 – 00
for a kit Cat in gold — 01 – 04 – 00
for 3:3 qr in gold and one Larger — 04 – 06 – 00
Sept 23 one not Delivrd for forty kitt Catts Archetrive frames Carv'd and guilt with gold to pictures by Sr Godfrey Kneller 84 – 00 – 00
Oct 5 for 14 Drive up frames of Different Sizes 02 – 02 – 00
7 for 2 ½ Lengths in gold 4 kit Catts 3:3 qr and a frame in gold to a poet head 12 – 03 – 00
30 for a ½ Length in gold Ditto — 01 – 12 – 00
for mending and guilding an Old frame and a drive up frame to the picture 01 – 08 – 06
for a kitt Cat in gold & a 3 qr to Oliver 02 – 05 – 00
£ 125 – 04 – 09

£ s d
Brought forword 125 04 9
for a Archetrive frame Carv'd and guilt with gold to Sr Godfrey Kneller picture by himself 01 – 15 – 00
for 16 frames Carv'd and guilt with gold of Different Sises 13 – 00 – 00
for a Large drive up frame & a gold frame to a Robbery 01 – 02 – 06
for 2 kit Catts Archetrive in gold not Delivrd 03 – 03 – 00
Tot 144 – 05 – 03
for 2 Large frame in gold one Large 2 – 10 – 00
for a Large drive up frame sent to Somersethouse 0 – 4 – 00
146 – 19 – 03
January 20th 1733/4
Receiv'd of Mr Tonson the full Contents of this Bill and all Demands by me Gerrard Howard
£ 146 – 19 – 3

Fig.134
Gerrard Howard's invoice for framing Kit-cat Club portraits for Jacob Tonson junior, 1733 (National Portrait Gallery).

The largest sum, £84, is for forty Kit-cat architrave frames. An earlier charge of £8 was made for forty 'drive up' frames, meaning stretchers.

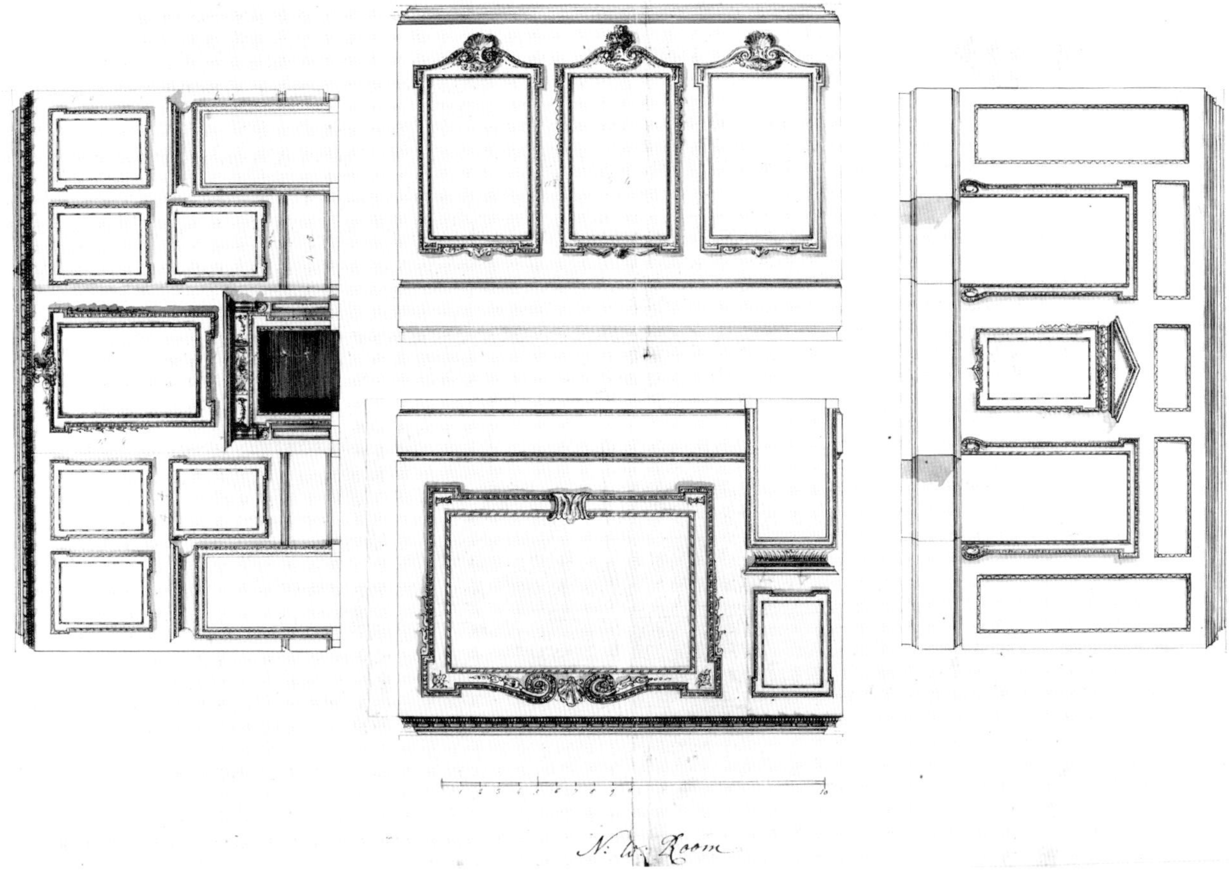

Fig.135
Design for the North West Room, Wolterton Hall, Norfolk, by Thomas Ripley, *c.*1739 (The Lord Walpole).

of the major state rooms. Thus Thomas Ripley, Comptroller of the King's Works, provided designs for Wolterton Hall for Lord Walpole, youngest brother of Sir Robert Walpole, showing his ideas for framing and hanging the pictures (fig.135), and he then took charge of hanging the newly framed pictures in Lord Walpole's absence abroad, as he reported to him in July 1739: 'I took all the pictures and frames out of the cases and see the frames put all together and the picktures safe put in them. They are hung up in their proper places ... The Queen's pickture does mighty well over the Chimney in the Dineing Room ... The French King did not do well at the East End between the late & present King. I have therefore put the late King in the middle, King Charles the first on one side and the present King on the other side of him. The frames being all of a size and make, that End of the Room looks mighty well ... '.[58] Such close involvement at different stages of the process is rarely documented; in this case, only the chance of the owner's absence abroad allows for these details to be recorded.

At Woburn, Henry Flitcroft, Ripley's successor as Comptroller of the King's Works, worked with the carver William Linnell, whose letter of appointment to work for the Duke of Bedford in 1749 has already been quoted. As a highly experienced carver and designer, Linnell was given a good deal of latitude by Flitcroft. Linnell was asked to produce 'some drawings for picture frames over the two chimneys at Oakley', a secondary house on the Duke's Bedfordshire estates.[59] The production of such drawings provided the opportunity for Flitcroft as architect and the Duke as patron to influence the final appearance of the frames.[60] The process is illustrated by the drawings Linnell produced for the carving in the pediments at Woburn. Here Flitcroft advised on the basic concept but left Linnell to make the detailed designs under his supervision, as he indicated in a letter to the Duke's agent: 'I have desired the carver to call on me … who may make a proper scetch at large of it to show His Grace'.[61]

It was not only private patrons who took advice on the framing of pictures. At the Foundling Hospital the governors turned to their architect, Theodore Jacobsen, for help in 1750, directing that Andrea Casali's altarpiece for the chapel should be framed 'in such a manner as Mr Jacobsen shall direct'.[62] At the Middlesex Hospital, where the governors were faced with a choice of designs for a large frame for R.E. Pine's portrait of the Duke of Northumberland in 1764, they decided to postpone a decision until their architect, James Paine, could be consulted.[63]

The interest of the architect could extend to the details of execution. William Chambers visited Isaac Gosset and Robert Ansell to order picture frames and mirror frames for the Duke of Marlborough in 1774, venturing to suggest to the Duke that Ansell's pier glass frames and tables could be 'Gilt of two coloured Gold wh. is very beautiful & gives a fine Effect to the ornaments'.[64] Chambers went so far as to call himself 'a very pretty Connoisseur in furniture' in a letter asking Viscount Melbourne that he should have the opportunity of approving Thomas Chippendale's designs for furnishing Melbourne House in Piccadilly, 'as I think from his small Drawings that some parts may be improved a little'.[65]

The close relationship between architect and framemaker continued in the first half of the nineteenth century. Sir John Soane designed a new shop front in Cavendish Street for his friend the carver and gilder, Edward Foxhall, and later took Foxhall's son into his office as a draughtsman.[66] J.B. Papworth produced designs for the framemaker, George Morant, both for his house at Hendon and his new shop in New Bond Street.[67] Sir Sydney Smirke used C.F. Bielefeld's papier-mâché ornament extensively in his interiors, notably in the British Museum Reading Room and in Sir Robert Peel's portrait gallery at Drayton Manor, and he also designed Bielefeld's new manufactory in Wellington Street, off the Strand.[68] But there is no evidence that the professional relationships of this period extended to the design of picture frames. By the time the gallery at Hertford House, the home of the Wallace Collection, was built in the 1870s, the great age of private picture collecting and of building private galleries was waning. The few significant new collectors of old masters and eighteenth-century British portraits, industrialists and businessmen such as Edward Guinness, later Lord Iveagh, or Herbert Stern, later Lord Michelham, were wont to take advice from their dealers, notably Agnew's and Duveen, who would arrange such framing as was required.[69] The day of the artist and the architect as adviser was largely over.

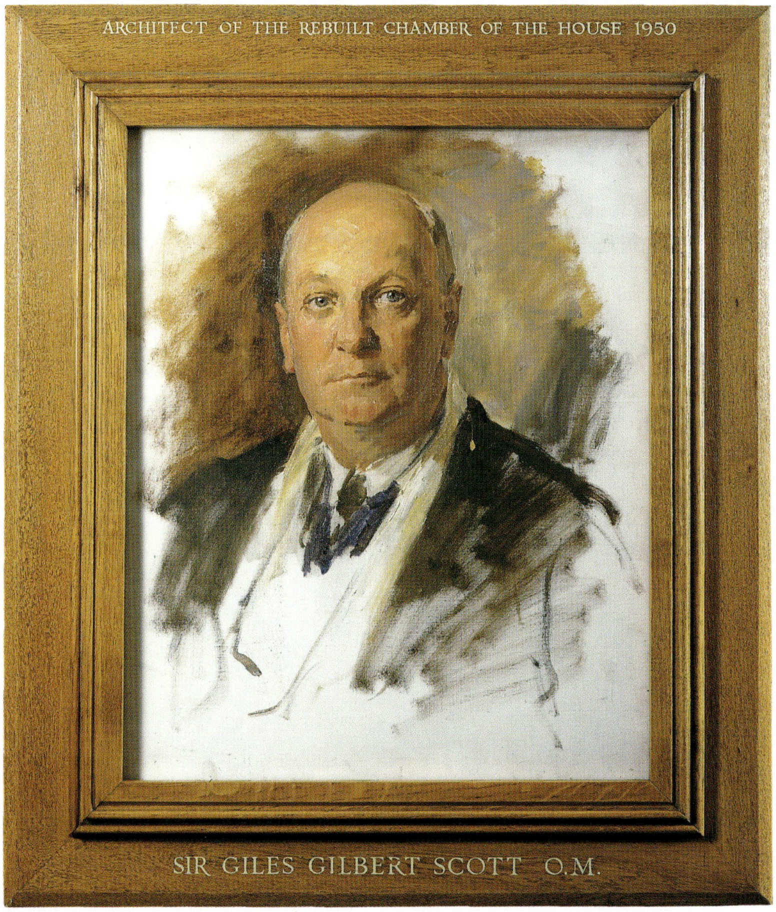

Fig.136
Sir Giles Gilbert Scott by Reginald Grenville Eves, 1935 (no.122).

Reframed in 1979 in the House of Commons 'Gilbert Scott' oak used for the rebuilding of the House of Commons chamber after the Second World War. An unusual modern example of reframing for a particular location.

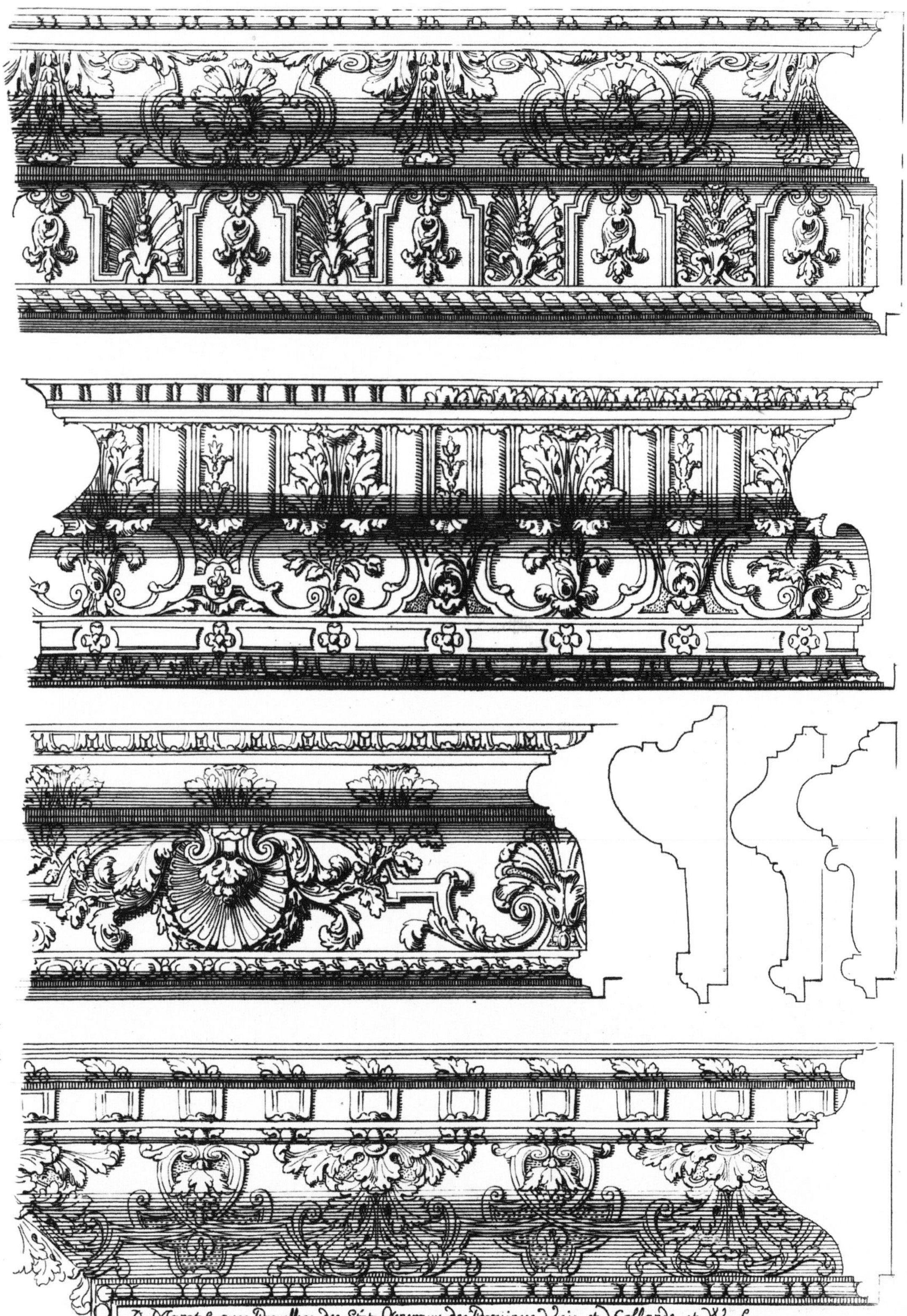

D Marot f. avec Previlege des Etats Generaux des Provinces Vnie„ et d Hollande et W. f.

Chapter 6
Framemakers and the Business of Framemaking

Framemaking became a specialist business in the mid-seventeenth century. By 1660 John Evelyn could specify the gilding of frames as a skilled occupation worthy of note.[1] A century later the framemaking trade was sufficiently developed for Joseph Collyer, in his *Parent's and Guardian's Directory*, published in 1761, to be able to divide framemaking into three separate branches, the looking-glass and picture framemakers, whom he describes as 'a set of Joiners, who make these Frames for the Carvers', the glass and picture-frame carvers themselves, and the print framemakers, whose work he calls 'a different trade'.[2]

Although these specialist framemakers dominated the business, even the finest firms of furniture makers in the eighteenth century, such as Thomas Chippendale or William Linnell, would make and supply frames to their clients as part of their wider business. Thus, when Sir Rowland Winn of Nostell Priory wanted his cabinet pictures reframed in 1768, Chippendale was glad to oblige, providing forty-one frames for £63.10s as part of his complete house furnishing service, which extended not only to the supply of the finest furniture but also to the provision of curtains and blinds, the hanging of India paper and damask, and the furnishing of the servants' quarters.[3] William Linnell's provision of 'a large picture frame very neat ... with an eagle at the top, festoons down the sides and mozaiks at the bottom, all very richly ornamented' at £25.18s for the Duke of Bedford in 1752 seems expensive for a single picture frame but needs to be seen as part of a larger commission for carving work worth more than £350.[4]

Fig.137
Designs by Daniel Marot for four picture frame mouldings, *c.*1700. From Marot's *Nouveaux Livre d'Ornements* (Victoria and Albert Museum, London).

Quite apart from these furniture-making firms, there were virtuosi carvers who produced frames on occasion, often of great elaboration, but who were not specifically picture framemakers by trade. In the seventeenth century Grinling Gibbons was so revered that John Evelyn could call him 'the greatest Master, both for Invention, & rareness of Worke, that the world ever had in any age'.[5] Much of Gibbons's finest work, including picture frames sprouting fruit, corn and birds, is still at Hampton Court and Windsor. When Gibbons died in 1721 he was succeeded in the post of 'Master Sculptor and Carver in Wood' to the King's Board of Works by James Richards.[6] In his capacity of carver Richards produced some of the finest overmantel frames and decorative work in the Palladian interiors of the 1720s and 1730s, often working under the supervision of architects including William Kent and Roger Morris. He was also responsible for the Royal State Barge, a work of consummate craftsmanship, carved to Kent's design for Frederick, Prince of Wales, in 1731-2.

It was another great carver, Paul Petit, who took on the double gilding of the Prince's Barge, though he is probably best known for the outrageous frames he produced for the Prince in the 1740s, *tours-de-force* of gilded woodwork which quite overwhelm the pictures they contain.[7] In the next generation Sefferin Alken, a member of the Alken family of sporting painters, worked extensively for Robert Adam as a specialist carver in the neo-classical style. His interior carving work was not limited to fine picture frames. For Lord Coventry at Croome Court, Alken produced superb bookcases for the library (now in the Victoria and Albert Museum) as well as the frame for Coventry's picture by Allan Ramsay (see fig.63).[8] Subsequently Alken worked with Sir William Chambers and carved the frame to Joshua Reynolds's large picture, *The Marlborough Family*, in 1778, a frame of the highest quality that was most probably made to Chambers's design.[9]

Work of the sort Petit or Alken produced met the needs of the top end of the market:

patrons who wanted superlative work and were willing to pay accordingly. The great run of business, however, was for more modest frames, finely finished but less elaborately carved, of the kind which artists supplied to clients with their portraits in the normal course of events. They were made by dedicated framemakers at a price suited to the pocket of a wider clientele. It is these specialist firms which are of vital importance in the history of framing portraits. Much of our information about picture framing derives from their activities, and the following survey is largely concentrated on their work.

The picture framemaker

In the reign of Charles I, the earliest period for which there is much surviving evidence, the supply of fine frames seems to have been produced principally by the king's carvers, gilders and painters, notably Zachary Taylor, John de Critz and Matthew Goodrich, and by George Geldorp, an artist working for those in the immediate court circle.

If more elaborately finished frames were required prior to this time they would be painted and gilded by the king's Serjeant Painter – George Gower in the 1580s, Leonard Fryer in the later 1590s and John de Critz thereafter – or by other artists such as the obscure Martin van Bentheim or the better-known Rowland Buckett, who both worked in the reign of James I.[10]

John de Critz, together with his assistant, Matthew Goodrich, was responsible for painting and gilding numerous frames for Charles I, many of which had been carved by Zachary Taylor. Goodrich seems to have been a painter of some ability and one who was held in high esteem by Inigo Jones. For the Crown he decorated the new chapel at St James's Palace and various interiors at Somerset House, providing numerous frames for pictures including those by Van Dyck. He also helped decorate the interior of Inigo Jones's new church of St Paul in Covent Garden in 1631-2, painted and gilded the staircase at Ham House in 1637-8, and later worked at Wilton House.[11] He provided picture frames for the Duchess of Buckingham in 1632 and, with Zachary Taylor, a frame for the Earl of Middlesex in 1639 at the not inconsiderable cost of £12.[12]

George Geldorp, a native of Cologne, came to London in about 1623 where he was active not only as a portrait painter but also as a dealer, copyist and collector over a period of forty years. He was working for the Earl of Salisbury in 1626, supplying pictures and frames for Hatfield,[13] for the Earl of Middlesex in about 1636, framing and copying the work of Van Dyck,[14] for the Earl of Northumberland from 1638 to 1642[15] and the Earl of Lothian in 1649,[16] a notable roll-call of leading patrons. His bills are always in French, of an anglicised nature: 'les carved fraems d'orre', and his prices suggest work of considerable elaboration: 'ung autre bordure tout dore pour la bergeere de Mr van dyck' cost Lord Middlesex £6.10s. How much of the framing work Geldorp actually undertook himself is not known, but in 1626 his wife was responsible for gilding seven frames for Lord Salisbury: 'pour la dorure de 7 bordures que ma femme a dorée pour l'or et ouvrage'. At the Restoration he helped track down those of the king's pictures that remained in the country, and was rewarded with the appointment in 1662 of picture mender and cleaner to the king.[17]

Picture framing after the Restoration was dominated by the Norrises: Henry and John, presumably father and son. They worked extensively for artists, the nobility, and in later years the Crown. Henry Norris first appears in the accounts of the Duke of Northumberland in 1655 as 'Norris the Joyner' and again in 1658 as 'Henry Norris', supplying picture frames, cases and picture stretchers.[18] John Norris worked for the Duke in 1667, providing stretchers and mending frames,[19] and for the Duchess of Lauderdale in 1673, probably supplying some of the Sunderland frames which now ornament the Long Gallery at Ham House. In 1669 Samuel Pepys had visited 'the frame-maker's, one Norris in Long-Acre'.[20] By 1677 Mary Beale was referring to 'old Mr Norris', which must be Henry

Norris, and 'young Mr Norris', probably John Norris, although a reference in 1681 to Thompson Norris suggests that the business extended to other members of the family.[21] In 1682 Henry Norris is described as Keeper of the King's Pictures and in 1689 John Norris was appointed Joiner to the Privy Council and thereafter worked on a variety of commissions for the Crown.[22] George Vertue called John Norris 'frame maker & picture keeper at Court in King William & Queen Anns Time' and noted how in the disastrous Whitehall Palace fire in 1698 few or none of the pictures in his care were burnt 'tho' large & weighty'.[23] He also recalled how Norris promoted the career of Charles Jervas, a pupil of Kneller's, by lending him any picture in the Royal Collection to copy. John Norris also worked for the Duke of Dorset, supplying old master paintings as well as picture frames, for the Earl of Salisbury, framing portraits by Wissing, and for numerous other prominent patrons including Sir Stephen Fox, for whom he provided frames, picture stretchers and some paintings from 1675 (the payment may be to his father) until 1703 when the name of John Norris junior, presumably his son, first occurs.[24]

Among other leading framemakers of the time were John Smith, who framed pictures by Lely, John Le Sage, who worked for Kneller and also at Hampton Court, and William Emmett, René Cousin, Jean Pelletier and his sons, who likewise worked at Hampton Court and at other royal palaces. Some, like John Smith, were primarily framemakers; others, including most of the French carvers, who were Huguenot refugees from France, produced carved and gilded woodwork and mouldings for interiors as well as picture frames.[25]

John Norris was succeeded as the king's framemaker by John Howard in 1714, and he in turn in 1727 by his son, Gerrard Howard, who held the post until 1752.[26] By this time there were many more framemakers at work in London but nevertheless the influence of Howard, father and son, must still have been considerable. They are known to have worked for Sir Robert Walpole, the Prime Minister, whose collection of old masters at Houghton was one of the most important of the period, Earl Fitzwalter, a member of Walpole's circle, and Jacob Tonson, nephew of the publisher, for whom Gerrard Howard framed up the Kit-cat Club portraits in 1733 (see figs.133-4).[27] The frames for the numerous full-length portraits of the king presented to ambassadors and governors going abroad were the prerogative of the king's framemaker, bringing the Howards into contact with Sir Godfrey Kneller and his successors as Painter to the King: Charles Jervas, William Kent and John Shackleton.[28] John Howard also carved the gilt frames for the Gallery at Kensington Palace 'according to Mr Kents design', probably among the earliest, and certainly some of the finest, frames in the Kent style.[29] He died in 1746 'at his House in Newport Street', having acquired 'a handsome fortune' through 'the Business of Picture Frame Making'.[30]

Another prominent framemaker patronised by the Crown was William Waters, who like the Howards worked for some very eminent patrons, including Queen Caroline, Earl Fitzwalter, the Earl of Breadalbane and Charles Wyndham.[31] He may also have made frames for Charles Jervas at some stage.[32]

One of the remarkable features of framemaking in the mid-eighteenth century was the significant role played by Huguenot framemakers, such as Paul Petit, René Stone, Isaac Gosset and his brothers Jacob and Gideon. They were mainly second generation members of French Protestant families who had come to England to seek refuge from persecution in France. Their work was more sculptural in nature than that of most of their English contemporaries, being both bolder and more naturalistic than the type of formalised trailing ornamentation so often favoured at the period. Of this group of Huguenot framemakers, Paul Petit's creations for Frederick Prince of Wales have already been discussed. Joseph Duffour, a French Catholic, also worked for the Prince but his main business was as a leading London framemaker. He appears to have made frames for Thomas Hudson, the most fashionable

London portrait painter in the late 1740s and early 1750s, and is probably the 'Duffour' who advertised as a maker of papier-mâché (see fig.28).[33] René Stone, who like Duffour and Isaac Gosset had his workshops in London's Berwick Street at the heart of the French quarter in Soho, succeeded Gerrard Howard as the king's framemaker in 1752 and in turn at his death was succeeded by Gosset in 1774. Stone is still an obscure figure while Gosset is well known, especially for his work for leading artists: William Hogarth, Allan Ramsay, William Hoare and Thomas Gainsborough.[34] In 1751 George Vertue praised Gosset's skills as a modeller of portrait profiles in wax and refers to frame carving as his original business, adding that 'he still undertakes carving for persons that are willing to pay him well for his labours – which can be managed under his care'.[35] Vertue also mentions Gosset's uncle, Matthew (who was living in Berwick Street as early as 1716), and a brother, probably Gideon but possibly Jacob Gosset, all of whom were carvers. Isaac Gosset gave up his appointment as the king's framemaker in 1785 at the age of seventy-two, but lived on until 1799.

A framemaker of great importance in the late eighteenth century for his wide-ranging contacts and the quality of his work was Thomas Vials of Great Newport Street, and later of Leicester Square, who was active from the mid-1750s until his death in 1781, when his business passed to his nephew, William Beaumont.[36] 'Mr Vial's is more amongst the Great, more Elegant in Taste and I guess in price', wrote William Constable's agent about an order for a table frame for Burton Constable, providing an indication of the high reputation Vials enjoyed.[37] The 'great' presumably numbered the 3rd Duke of Dorset, who ordered a very rich frame for his full-length by Joshua Reynolds in 1770 at a cost of twenty-five guineas and had numerous smaller pictures by Reynolds framed by Vials during the rest of the decade.[38] Vials was conveniently close to Reynolds's studio in Leicester Square, and this proximity perhaps encouraged the artist to turn to him for the finest carved frames. Reynolds ordered frames from Vials for his two Dilettanti Society groups at a cost of twenty guineas each, though a dispute over the bill meant that the frames went unpaid for years.[39] Vials also produced a frame pattern for Josiah Wedgwood in 1780 which George Stubbs took up with enthusiasm for his large enamels.[40] Vials had close links with other leading artists. In 1764 he had framed two pastels by Catherine Read for James Grant of Grant, and also two drawings by William Marlow.[41] Both Marlow and Sawrey Gilpin used Vials as a contact address in the exhibition catalogues of the Society of Artists, Marlow from 1764 to 1780 and Gilpin in 1768 ('At Windsor, enquire at Mr. Vial's').[42] Vials supplied the frames for Gilpin's pictures at Calke Abbey and was responsible for packing Gilpin's pictures at the Society of Artists exhibition.[43] His links with Marlow were even closer for he calls the artist 'my worthy friend' in his will, naming him an executor and bequeathing him £100. Vials left considerable leasehold property and other assets, requesting to be interred in Clapham churchyard in the same grave as his late wife.[44]

In the late eighteenth century the increased number of leading framemakers meant that the significance of the role played by the framemaker to the king was much reduced, although William Adair, who succeeded Isaac Gosset in office in 1785, came from a leading family of framemakers. Other notable London makers of the period were Thomas Fentham, who traded from the Strand for many years, Solomon Hudson, who carried out work to Robert Adam's design, retiring from business in 1793, and William Cribb, sometimes described – on meagre evidence – as Sir Joshua Reynolds's framemaker, who eventually turned to print publishing.[45]

The nineteenth century has only just begun to be seriously explored by those interested in the history of framemakers. Some framemaking firms were still small in size and lasted no longer than the lifetime of the master craftsman. But others were sufficiently substantial to endure most of the century, if not as family concerns, then by bringing in new partners or by selling the goodwill to a successor in business. Even

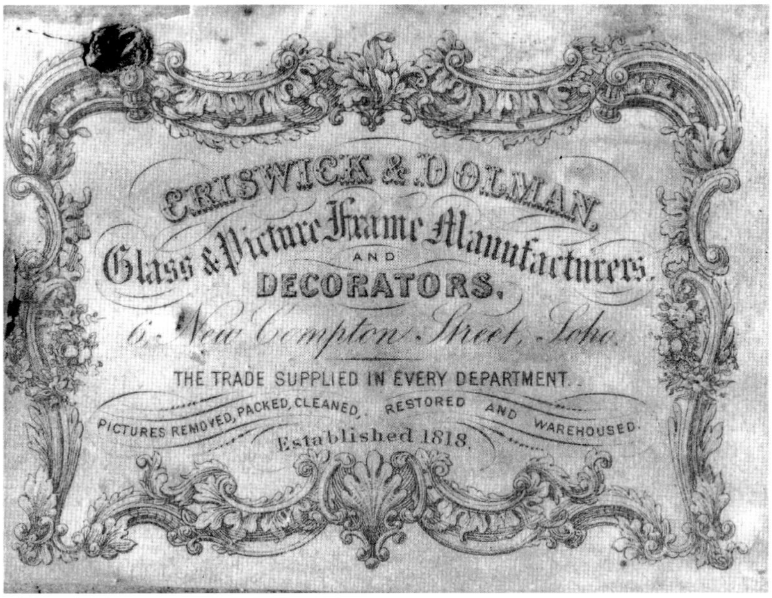

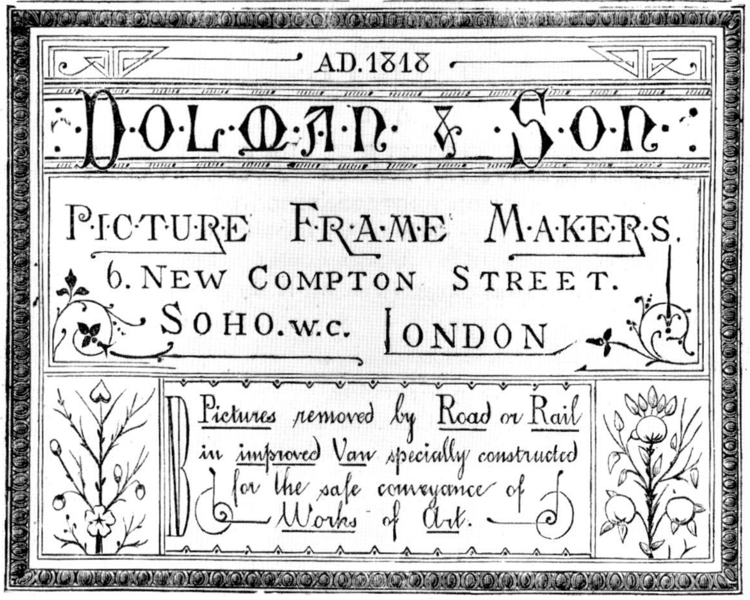

Fig.138 (top)
Label of Criswick & Dolman on the reverse of *The Secret of England's Greatness* by Thomas Jones Barker (no.76).

Fig.139 (above)
Advertisement for Dolman & Son. From *The Year's Art*, 1881.

framemakers in leading positions could meet with problems in the competitive London market, however. Thomas Temple, a framemaker of forty years' standing with a clientele of the greatest in the land, was made bankrupt in 1839. His business went to Robert Thick and then to Henry Critchfield, and it was Critchfield who told the sorry story of two framemakers in royal employ: 'Thick was ruined by excess of work at Windsor Castle. Henderson, previously employed at Windsor Castle, not being able to gain payment in time, cut his throat in despair'.[46] Difficulties with payment were common, though usually leading to bankruptcy rather than suicide.

A leading firm, with a reputation for fine quality work at competitive prices, was Criswick's, which went through various transformations. Established in 1818 as J. Criswick, the business traded successively as Criswick & Ryan (by 1836), Criswick & Leppard (1842-53), James Criswick (1854-6), Henry Criswick & Co. (1857) and Criswick & Dolman (1862-76).[47] The firm traded for eighty years from no.6 New Compton Street, finally in 1879 becoming Reginald Dolman & Son in which guise it lasted until 1919, a remarkable record of stability in a trade where few businesses lasted more than a generation or two. At first Criswick's also manufactured elaborate looking-glass frames, as a surviving catalogue of the 1840s shows. But from an early date they made frames for artists including E.W. Cooke, William Frost and Thomas Jones Barker, while Sir Lawrence Alma-Tadema and Sir Hubert von Herkomer were among clients in later years. The handsome frame for Barker's *The Secret of England's Greatness* (see fig.72) bears the label of Criswick & Dolman (fig.138).

It was trouble at the National Gallery which helped establish the dominant position of the firm, now trading as Dolman & Son, at the end of the century. Henry Critchfield, the National Gallery's framemaker of many years, was exposed for double-charging by claiming to be working at both the National Gallery and the National Portrait Gallery, then situated in South Kensington, at one and the same time.[48] The National Gallery sought recommendations for a successor to Critchfield from two artists, Alma-Tadema putting forward the name of Dolman, and Philip Hermogenes Calderon that of James Guillet. Dolman's won the contract on price, and later went on to add the newly opened Wallace Collection to their list of clients, though it was as 'Frame Makers to the National Gallery' that they advertised (see fig.139) until the demise of the firm in 1919.

While the Criswick–Dolman business took on a broad range of top-of-the-market clients, two other firms, Joseph Green and Foord & Dickinson, specialised in the most demanding and innovative work for artists, numbering Rossetti, Holman Hunt, Ford Madox Brown, Watts, Leighton and Whistler among others. Joseph Green had set up in business in Charles Street, now Cavendish Street, in the shadow of Middlesex Hospital in 1801, and he and his son, also named Joseph, carried on trading until 1870.[49] The Greens did work for William Etty and Daniel Maclise in the 1830s and 1840s, and acted as forwarding agents for the Royal Scottish Academy,[50] but it is not until the next generation when the younger Green worked for Rossetti, Holman Hunt and Ford Madox Brown that the firm became the first to have strong links with the Pre-Raphaelites. Brown's Fawcett portrait (fig.110) was probably framed by Green. He had earlier encouraged Green to use his patterns as widely as possible.[51] Green died or retired in 1870,[52] the business becoming Joseph Green & Co. in 1870 and passing to William Augustine Smith by 1872.[53] Holman Hunt referred to the firm as 'Green of Charles Street' as late as 1877, so the business may have kept up the Green name.[54] Hunt described the firm as possibly the best gilder and maker, saying that 'one of the men there carves in after hours', a further recommendation in an age when most framemakers only dealt in compo frames.[55] Many of Green's more fastidious artists moved away when the business changed hands, but Smith continued to work for artists, including G.F. Watts, John Strudwick and Edward Stott. The business became Smith & Uppard in 1889 and was acquired by James Bourlet & Sons, another old established firm, in 1899.[56]

Smith's loss of customers was Foord & Dickinson's gain. The business had been founded in 1829 by George Foord, who was framer to the Old Water-Colour Society, and at his death or retirement, Eliza Foord had continued trading in her own name (see fig.140) until in 1858 the firm was renamed Foord & Dickinson on James Dickinson becoming a partner.[57] John Ruskin used Foord from 1844 until 1879, most especially in mounting the Turner drawings in

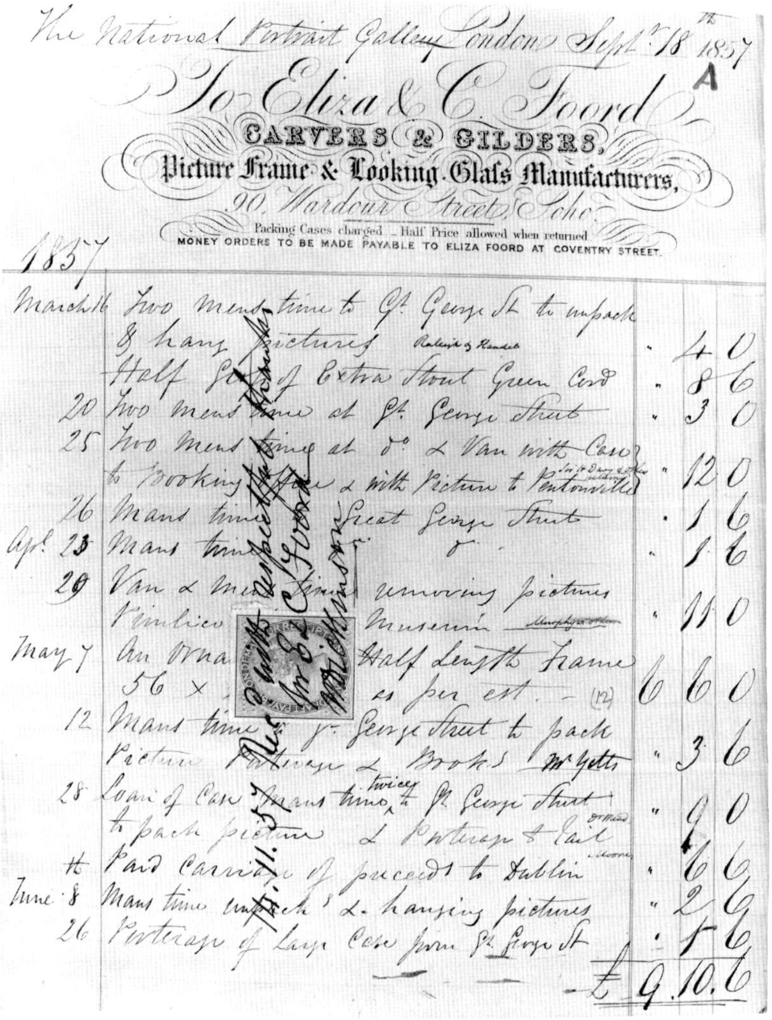
The National Portrait Gallery London Sept. 18 1857
To Eliza & C. Foord
Carvers & Gilders,
Picture Frame & Looking-Glass Manufacturers,
90, Wardour Street, Soho.
Packing Cases charged _ Half Price allowed when returned
MONEY ORDERS TO BE MADE PAYABLE TO ELIZA FOORD AT COVENTRY STREET.
1857
March 16 Two mens time to Gt. George St to unpack & hang pictures . 4 0
Half ... of Extra Stout Green Cord . 8 6
20 Two mens time at Gt. George Street . 3 0
25 Two mens time at do & Van with Case to Booking office & with Picture to Pentonville . 12 0
26 Mans time Great George Street . 1 6
Apl 23 Mans time do . 1 6
29 Van & Mens time removing pictures Pimlico Museum . 11 0
May 7 An Ornamental Half Length Frame 56 x ... as per est. 6 6 0
12 Mans time Gt. George Street to pack Picture Porterage & Books . 3 6
28 Loan of Case Mans time twice to Gt. George Street to pack picture & Porterage & Cart . 9 0
Paid Carriage of proceeds to Dublin . 6 6
June 8 Mans time unpack & hanging pictures . 2 6
26 Porterage of Large Case from Gt. George St . 1 6
£ 9.10.6

Fig.140
Eliza & C. Foord's invoice for framing, packing and hanging pictures for the National Portrait Gallery, 18 September 1857 (National Portrait Gallery).

The most expensive item is the charge of £6.6s for an 'Ornamental Half Length Frame' for a portrait of William Lenthall acquired in 1857.

the National Gallery in the 1850s, 'with good help from Richard Williams of Messrs. Foord's'.[58] In their role as one of the National Portrait Gallery's framemakers from 1857 to 1869, the firm used revival patterns to frame pictures such as Ramsay's portrait of George III (no.99), and this work is in contrast to the many frames in the latest advanced styles Foord's made for the Grosvenor Gallery exhibitions from 1877 to 1890. When Mr Williams, by now manager at Foord's, was shown the 1877 exhibition, he viewed it with a true professional's eye: 'But it is a fine lot of frames!', he exclaimed, completely ignoring the pictures.[59] Rossetti, Sandys, Leighton, Burne-Jones, Whistler and John Collier were all Grosvenor Gallery artists and were all framed by Foord's. The firm was always known as Foord's of Wardour Street until 1899 when it moved to nearby Berwick Street, a year before the business was sold, becoming G. Minns & Co. in 1900.[60]

Other prominent Victorian makers included James Henry Chance, proud of his distant relationship to John Linnell, who did work for George Richmond, Lowes Cato Dickinson and Alessandro Ossani (see nos.85, 78), and William Thomas, framemaker to Queen Victoria and other members of the royal family, who also worked for Sir George Hayter and Sir Francis Grant, both royal warrant holders (see no.67; fig.107).

There were of course significant firms trading outside London, such as William Freeman in Norwich and James Wyatt in Oxford in the first half of the century, Charles Rowley in Manchester, D.R. Hay and Aitken Dott in Edinburgh and John Kesson in Aberdeen, to name but a few.

The end of the century saw a number of important new firms emerge. Francis Draper worked extensively for the National Portrait Gallery from 1884 and later for the National Gallery and the Royal Family; he claimed a wide range of official appointments (see fig.141) and on a more personal note he was described by Sir Charles Holmes, Director of the National Portrait Gallery, as 'best of fellows and framemakers', after an afternoon spent trout fishing together! Charles Mitchell May, later trading as C.M. May & Son, called himself 'English & French Picture Frame Maker', advertising his 'thoroughly competent workmen English and French'.[61] If he was responding to the taste led by Rossetti and Whistler for the finest craftsmanship and gilding he seems to have succeeded for May worked extensively for John Singer Sargent whose frames featured 'the finest water gilding' according to a National Gallery report of 1914.[62] May's frames for Sargent's portraits of Coventry Patmore of 1894 (fig.80) and Sir Frank Swettenham of 1904 (no.108) are good examples. May went out of business in 1922 and his mantle was assumed by his rival, Chapman Brothers of Chelsea, a firm which not only worked for Sargent but also for William Orpen and a number of other leading artists.

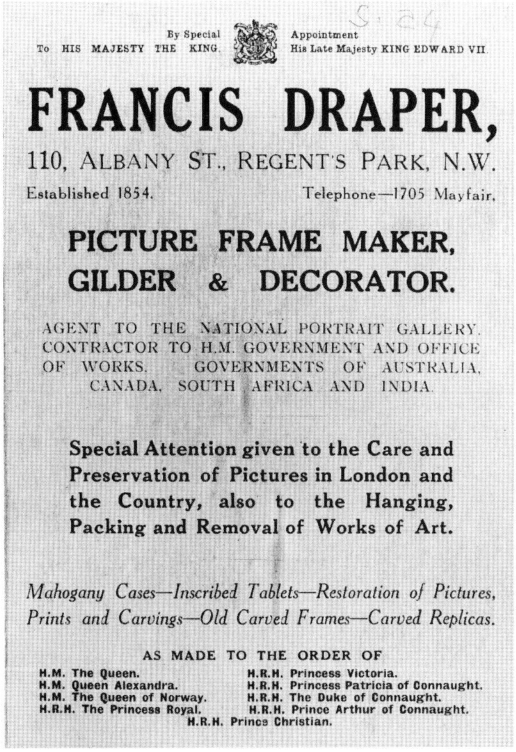

By Special Appointment
To HIS MAJESTY THE KING. His Late Majesty KING EDWARD VII.

FRANCIS DRAPER,

110, ALBANY ST., REGENT'S PARK, N.W.

Established 1854. Telephone—1705 Mayfair.

PICTURE FRAME MAKER, GILDER & DECORATOR.

AGENT TO THE NATIONAL PORTRAIT GALLERY. CONTRACTOR TO H.M. GOVERNMENT AND OFFICE OF WORKS. GOVERNMENTS OF AUSTRALIA, CANADA, SOUTH AFRICA AND INDIA.

Special Attention given to the Care and Preservation of Pictures in London and the Country, also to the Hanging, Packing and Removal of Works of Art.

Mahogany Cases—Inscribed Tablets—Restoration of Pictures, Prints and Carvings—Old Carved Frames—Carved Replicas.

AS MADE TO THE ORDER OF

H.M. The Queen. H.R.H. Princess Victoria.
H.M. Queen Alexandra. H.R.H. Princess Patricia of Connaught.
H.M. The Queen of Norway. H.R.H. The Duke of Connaught.
H.R.H. The Princess Royal. H.R.H. Prince Arthur of Connaught.
H.R.H. Prince Christian.

Fig.141 (right) Label of Francis Draper on reverse of *Joseph Conrad* by Sir William Rothenstein (National Portrait Gallery).

The portrait was probably framed on acquisition in 1925.

Soon after the outbreak of the Second World War the Ministry of Information obtained quotations from three well-known firms, Alfred Stiles & Sons, J. Tanous and C.H. West, for the framing of works by official war artists.[63] Stiles got the job, and as a result was able to retain most of his staff during the war years. For the war artists Stiles provided a standard economy moulding with a mottled paint finish. But before the war he had produced gilded, painted and stained frames for artists including Vanessa Bell, Duncan Grant, Mark Gertler, Eric Ravilious, Gilbert Spencer and Graham Sutherland. The business had been established in 1870 and then refinanced in 1919 with the Fine Art Society as the majority shareholder.[64] Stiles continued trading until 1963. After the war the most remarkable new businesses were probably those of Alfred Hecht and Robert Sielle.[65] These framemakers came from different backgrounds; the former a German immigrant who had tried metal-broking and the textiles business, the latter a First World War fighter pilot and former show dancer. Both men worked extensively for leading artists until the early 1980s.

Advertising and the search for custom

The first imperative for any framemaker was to procure patronage. This might come through personal recommendation or from advertising. Many recommendations will have been by word of mouth in the ordinary course of business, but written record does survive on occasion. James Cullen, the entrepreneur and cabinet maker who often sub-contracted work, was approached in 1777 by Sir John Dick, who 'wanted a Carver to carve some frames – to know if Mr Cullen has any person he could recommend'.[66] Some years later, in 1808, the landscape painter, Philip James de Loutherbourg, wrote to his framemaker, Robert Cribb, at no.288 Great Turnstile, Holborn, saying he had recommended him to 'an intimate friend of mine, Mr Dunnage'. De Loutherbourg was most anxious that Cribbs should rise to the occasion: 'I must request particularly of you, Sir, to do it in the very best manner possible, as Mr. Dunnage on my account has been so polite to take my recommendation in preference to employing a person who has formerly worked for him'.[67] Artists must always have been prime sources of recommendations for framemakers, especially in London where so many portrait painters were at work, lending all the more force to Justus Moser's observation in 1767 that the master of a furniture-making workshop 'keeps in touch with people of taste and visits artists who might be of assistance to him'.[68]

If the sheer quantity of framemakers' advertisements and trade cards is any indication, advertising must also have been an important source of new business. What was the customer looking for? Attitudes changed with time. Trade cards, often found in the form of a letter, bill or receipt, provide a mine of information for the eighteenth and early nineteenth centuries (see fig.143), while advertisements are the essential source for the Victorian period and the early twentieth century.

'In the latest fashion' is the framemaker's constant refrain, so that one finds Robert Hulton promoting his frames as 'Made after ye Newest Faishion & in ye Nicest Manner' in about 1739 and Richard Fletcher claiming to work in the 'neatest and newest Taste' in the 1770s.[69] The late eighteenth and early nineteenth centuries evidently saw speed of service as a selling-point: 'Three Quarters Kit-Cats and Half-lengths may be had in a Minute's Notice for Ready Money'

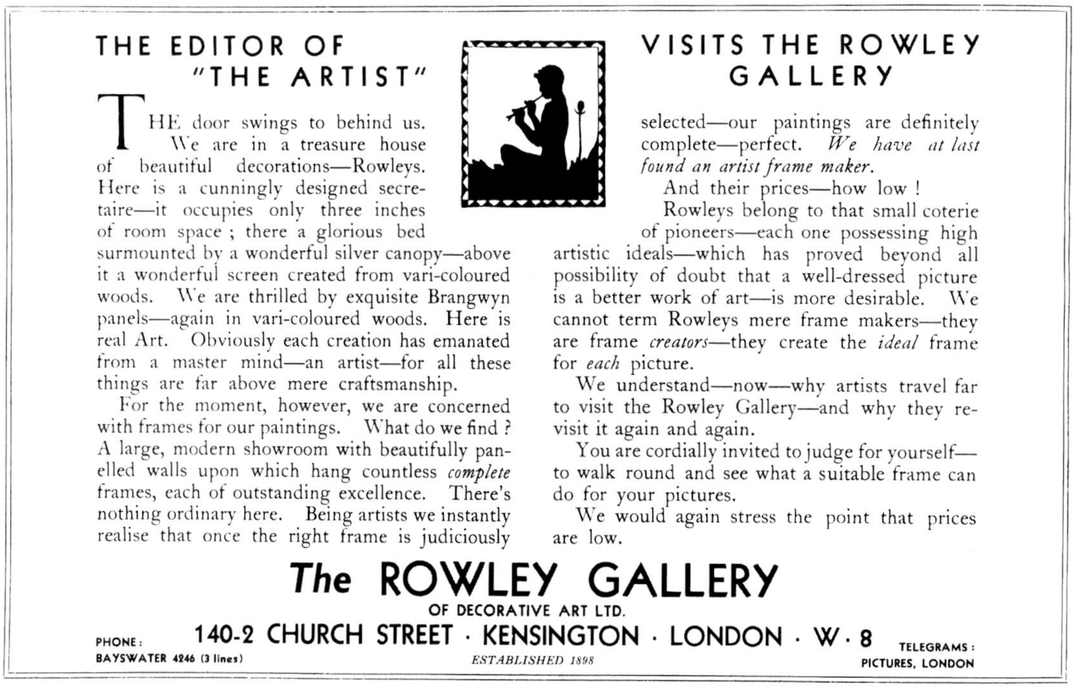

Fig.142
Advertisement for the Rowley Gallery. From *The Artist*, March 1934 (Westminster Libraries and Archives).

Founded in 1898, the Rowley Gallery sold marquetry panels, silver leaf furniture, picture frames and other decorative items. The Rowley Gallery undertook framing work for the National Portrait Gallery from 1930 to 1935 and made frames for Gluck, including her self-portrait of 1942 (fig.10).

Fig.143
Trade card of Charles Mathyson, picture framemaker, *c.*1760-70.

Apart from supplying frames for pictures, looking-glasses and prints, Mathyson also advertised his services as a restorer of pictures and prints.

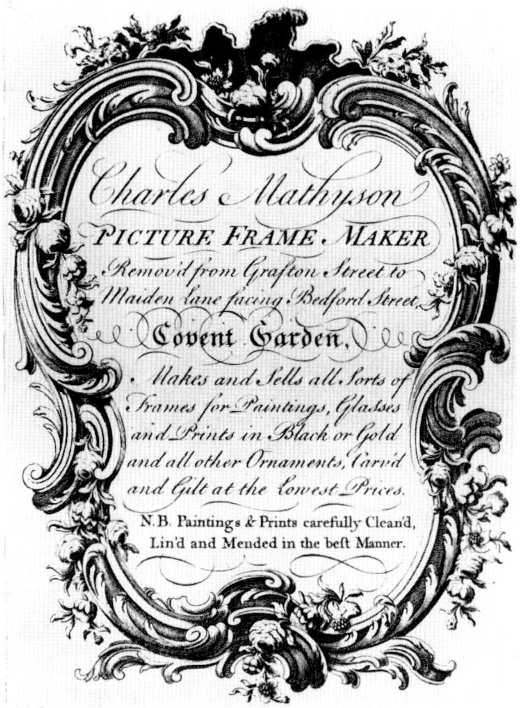

according to Adrian Maskens, 'Old Frames New Gilt on the Shortest Notice' claimed Thomas Merle in 1826. At the same epoch the sale of ready-made mouldings was being promoted: 'Supplies country cabinet makers etc. with mouldings of any length or pattern' in the words of John Farley's trade card in 1785, 'Mouldings of Different Patterns and Lengths for the Conveniency of exportation' according to Thomas Merle in 1826.

The introduction of machine-made mouldings in the nineteenth century, supplied by wholesalers in lengths, brought intense competition on price which is reflected in contemporary advertisements. In the *Art Union*, one of the most widely circulated art periodicals of the 1840s, it is not uncommon to find three or four bitter rivals advertising on the same page. Charles McLean of no.181 Fleet Street claimed 'the very best gilt frames at prices never hitherto attempted ... 10,000 Frames ready for immediate delivery. All goods taken back, if not approved of, in three months'. He gives the prices for ten sizes of 'highly-ornamented Gilt Frames', ranging from 11s for a twelve by ten inch picture to 90s for a fifty by forty inch. These prices were closely matched by C.J. Eckford, who operated from a few doors further along at no.15 Fleet Street. Both men offered a 'Sheet of Drawings', showing their frames with sizes and prices, and Eckford offered to send his sheet 'Gratis and free of postage to any part of the United Kingdom'.[70] C.F. Bielefeld, the papier-mâché framemaker, offered a whole volume of ornament designs, almost a thousand in number, and with an eye to supplying papier-mâché for interior decorative features he described it as 'bound complete, for the architect'.[71] Bielefeld was a master of self-publicity, exploiting the periodicals of the time with stories of his new papier-mâché manufactory and the superior quality of his products.[72]

At the end of the nineteenth century the emphasis of many framemakers shifted from price to the range of services on offer. For example, Smith & Uppard advertised 'Special Designs made to order' and Foord & Dickinson 'Artists' own Designs made up', not infrequent claims at a period when so many artists designed their own frames.[73] H. Morell, a firm which went for the wider market, claimed the largest stock in the United Kingdom, and issued their own catalogue, price one shilling: 'New Edition of Pattern Book, containing all the Newest Designs. 160 Pages. Just Published' reads their 1902 advertisement.[74] Such substantial catalogues were unusual although for many years James Bourlet & Sons issued an illustrated trade brochure featuring a range of traditional designs.

Advertisements of one kind or another provide a fascinating but partial glimpse into the framemaking trade. Some of the better firms, and probably many of the smaller ones, never seem to have advertised. And such advertisements can only tell one side of the story – the framemaker's rather than the customer's.

The choice of frames and the spread of ideas

How were frames chosen and ordered by the customer? And how did the framemaker keep abreast of fashions in framing and ensure that his range of patterns met his customer's ideas?

In the case of Robert Cribb's frame for Mr Dunnage's picture by De Loutherbourg, the pattern was specified by the artist to match a previous one. Many frames, if not most, were made to match earlier orders or existing patterns. George Romney's framemaker in 1780, Thomas Allwood, referred to his frames by the names of Romney's previous sitters, so for example in July that year he supplied, 'A half length the patn of Mr Sullivans frames, for Mrs Barrow'.[75] Many leading artists, such as Francis Cotes and William Hoare in the eighteenth century or G.F. Watts and Hubert von Herkomer in the nineteenth century, sent their portraits out in one of a very limited range of frame patterns, so that the maker knew very well what was expected. 'This frame can be repeated at any time quoting the number 30.886', reads R. Dolman & Co.'s label on the back of the frame of Herkomer's portrait of Sir George Goldie (National Portrait Gallery).

On occasion a frame would be made to the customer's own pattern. Carving an unfamiliar design from a drawing could cause problems even for an experienced framemaker, as Gainsborough found out when ordering a frame for the MP, Richard Stevens, in 1767.[76] If the framemaker was not supplied with a drawing then an actual frame or frame sample might be copied, as in the case of Henry Tonks's order to Chapman Bros in 1919 for a 'Special handmade English gilt reeded oak frame 7″ wide, to copy of a pattern frame'.[77]

If the customer did not have a clear idea in mind he would have asked the framemaker for advice. When Samuel Pepys visited Norris, the leading framemaker, in 1669 he was shown 'several forms of frames to choose by; which was pretty, in little bits of mouldings to choose by'.[78] One can be confident that he was looking at a range of the most fashionable frames. For a more distant customer a design might be sent, as when Isaac Gosset wrote to Robert Dingle in 1755 supplying 'a scetch of a frame and a Carlomaratt patern'.[79] This sketch has not survived, but it may have been of the nature of the design by John Linnell in the Victoria and Albert Museum for Castle Howard, showing two alternative treatments for a neo-classical frame in the French manner.[80] Rather different in intent is Chippendale's carefully finished wash drawing for a neo-classical frame for a painting by Guido Reni at Nostell Priory, which accompanied an estimate sent to Sir Rowland Winn in 1767.[81] Drawings of this kind rarely survive, but their use is often referred to in accounts for frames, such as that sent by William Linnell to William Drake in 1749 for '6 half-length picture frames, compleat by drawing'.[82]

Not infrequently one comes across a reference to a frame in a new pattern or new fashion. Thomas Allwood made a frame with reeds and ribbons crossing for one of Romney's smaller portraits in 1777 which he called a new pattern.[83] Henry Hue charged the Duke of Montrose 16s in 1714 for 'a frame of new fashion finely Carved and Gilded'.[84]

How were these new ideas introduced? There were leaders in taste who might be copied or emulated. In 1686 the Duke of Somerset ordered panelling, mouldings and picture frames from the joiner Thomas Larkin 'according to those in his Majesties new lodgings in Whitehall'.[85] The work at Whitehall Palace for James II had been carried out under the supervision of Sir Christopher Wren. The role of the architect was usually an important one, as shown in Chapter 5. To look at one leading firm of carvers and gilders in the eighteenth century, the Linnells, is to see how craftsmen came into contact with changing architectural taste: William Linnell worked closely with Henry Flitcroft at Woburn in the late 1740s and his son John Linnell with Robert Adam on various commissions in the 1760s.[86]

This was one way in which the ideas of architects and designers might be spread. Another was through engravings and pattern books, some of which were imported from abroad. When Wren visited Paris in 1665 he made a point of bringing back with him a collection of engraved designs: 'I have purchased a great deale of *Taille-douce* [engravings] that I

Fig.144 (facing page) 'Large Mouldings for Pannels or Picture Frames by Mr Gibbs'. From Batty Langley's *Ancient Masonry*, 1733-6.

Three frames in the Palladian style by James Gibbs featuring friezes ornamented, in (from top to bottom) Greek key, Vitruvian scroll, and guilloche.

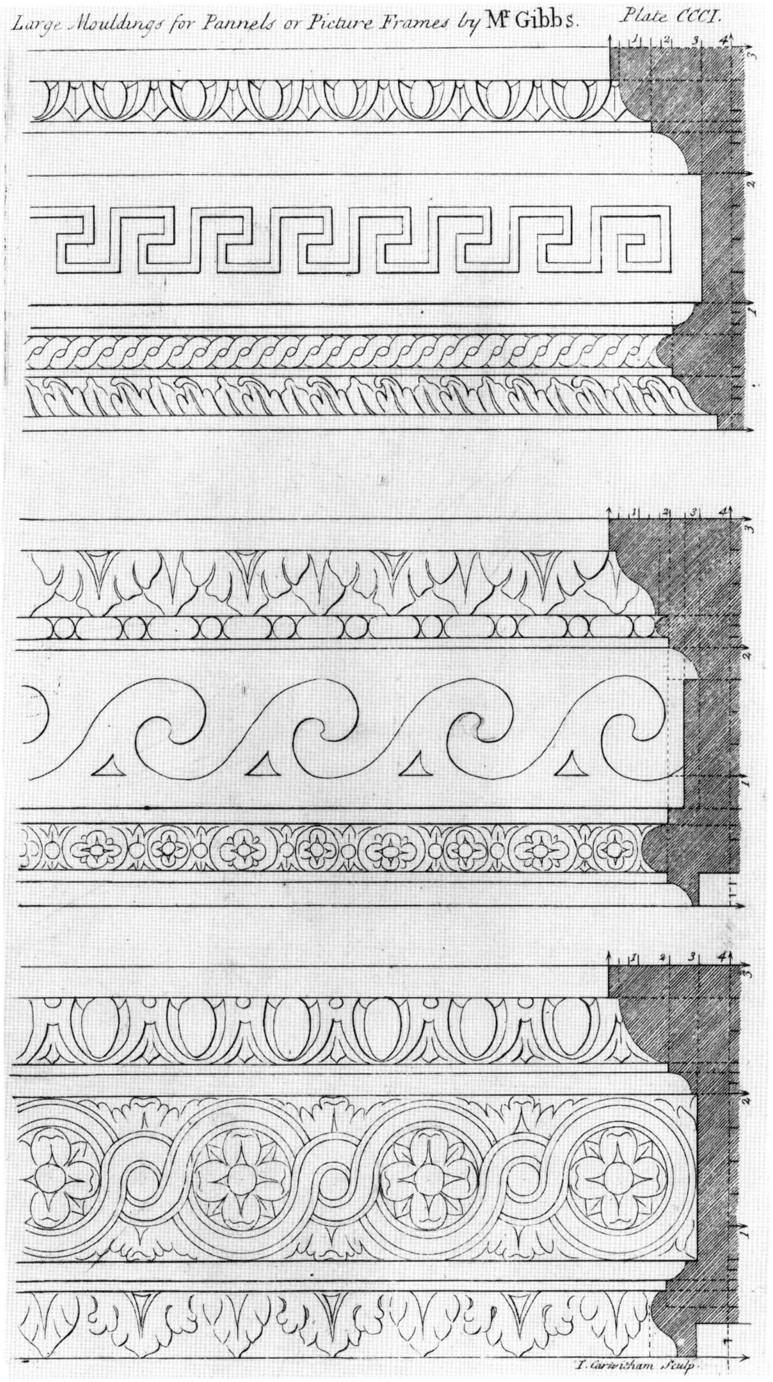

might give our Countrymen Examples of Ornaments and Grotesks, in which the Italians themselves confess the French excell'.[87] The importance of engraved designs as a source for craftsmen is manifest in the work of another architect, Daniel Marot, French by birth but who worked for William III in Holland and England. His *Nouveaux Livre d'Ornements* of *c.*1700 contains various rich designs for picture frames (see fig.137) which being in the French manner proved especially popular among Huguenot carvers working in England.[88] The finer architectural books would have had a limited circulation, being more likely to be found in a gentleman's library than on a carver's bench. But there were those who produced cheaper editions with the lower end of the market in mind. Batty Langley, for example, published a stream of popular architectural books in the 1730s and 1740s, which typically were described on the title page as being intended not only for gentlemen but also for 'Masons, Carpenters, Joyners, Bricklayers, Plasterers, Painters, &c'.[89] His *Ancient Masonry*, issued in weekly parts between 1733 and 1736, included 459 plates; no.301, entitled 'Large Mouldings for Pannels or Picture Frames by Mr Gibbs' (fig.144), will have reached a far wider audience than James Gibbs's own select publications.

The most important publication of the next generation was Thomas Chippendale's *The Gentleman's and Cabinet Maker's Director*, a remarkable collection of some two hundred plates including several of picture and mirror frames, which went through three editions between 1754 and 1762, the first edition being purchased by more than two hundred cabinet makers, carvers, joiners and craftsmen. His engraved designs pack in as much ornament as possible, leaving the craftsman and patron to select such details as suited their individual taste and budget. A plate in Ince and Mayhew's *Universal System of Household Furniture*, published in parts from 1760, is annotated: 'Designs of Picture Frames, the Ornaments of which may be extended to suit any siz'd Picture'.[90]

To find a collection of engraved designs kept by an eighteenth-century carver and gilder is extraordinarily rare but just such a resource survives in the form of Gideon Saint's carving scrapbook in the Metropolitan Museum, New York, with 290 engraved designs and 162 drawings. Gideon Saint, a Huguenot carver born of French parents, kept a workshop 'at the Golden Head in Princes Street, near Leicester Fields', that is Leicester Square. He advertised that he made 'all sorts of Sconces, Girondoles, Chandeliers, Brackets, Tables, Chimney-Pieces, Picture Frames, &c'. His scrapbook, arranged in twelve different sections by type, one of which features picture-frame mouldings, includes both engraved and manuscript designs. The earliest are French engraved designs, mainly Régence in character, from the previous generation, the work of Berain, Boulle, Mariette, Pineau and Roumier, which were still influential but becoming old-fashioned. Next are the latest English engravings in the fully fledged rococo style, published by Matthias Lock, Henry Copland and Thomas Johnson (see fig.56), the largest number of which are taken from Johnson's *New Book of Ornaments* of 1758. These would have been useful as design sources for elements of Saint's own work. Almost contemporary in date but perhaps belonging to the early 1760s are a group of English rococo pen-and-wash designs including a standard range of rococo frame patterns (see fig.145), each numbered for reference. These are probably patterns which Saint actually used although few of them are likely to have been made by him exclusively since they were widely in demand at the time. Lastly there are a small number of extra designs in an up-to-date neoclassical style. The scrapbook is a graphic document of how the eighteenth-century carver worked, as Morrison Heckscher has suggested.[91] Firstly it shows how craftsmen 'mined' published collections of engravings for ideas, cutting up volumes and rearranging the contents by type of object, to provide a book of anonymous designs which could be shown to potential clients. Secondly, the two full-scale drawings of decorative motifs in the book, both for picture frames, are of a sort which would actually be used by the craftsman in laying out a frame for carving.

The demise of the carved frame in the late eighteenth century as ornament in compo became popular led to the carver's drawing becoming a thing of the past. A very wide range of ornament could now be called up from stock moulds without having to rely on a carver's familiarity with a particular pattern. The ledgers of John Smith, a leading framemaker and subsequently a picture dealer, provide an extraordinary insight into practices in the early nineteenth century.[92] They reveal the superior nature of his clientele, which included the Prince Regent, the Earl of Yarmouth and Lord Byron. More intriguingly the ledgers show how Smith regularly identified his ornament by framemakers' names. Thus for Lt-Col. Addenbrooke in 1812 he produced two 'handsome frames', richly ornamented with 'Temples bands, My Corners, Egg M[ouldin]g with inside oval Turn'd Spandrils enrich'd with Blundels Dolphin ornament'. Temple was presumably the leading maker, Thomas Temple, and Blundell probably William Blundell. Elsewhere he refers to 'Blundells bead', 'Moselys corners', 'Pratts shell', 'Bowers corners', 'Derby corners', 'Smarts corners', 'Touzets bubble', 'Blundells flat laurel', 'Jacksons rich shell moulding', 'Greens foliage', 'Freemans Grecian leaf', 'Jacksons egg', 'Jacksons frilled edge', 'Woodburns corners' and 'Leaders corners', a veritable panoply of ornament, named for the most part after framemakers. There was no copyright in ornament and it seems that Smith borrowed patterns as he required from other framemakers in order to keep up to date. The process of assimilation has not been established conclusively, but it seems probable that Smith made drawings of ornament he liked as a point of reference, or may even have had the chance to take plaster casts, and then had boxwood moulds carved up for permanent use for pressing out compo ornament as required. Presumably other leading makers did likewise, with the result that much the same range of ornament could be found at each of the leading establishments.

The organisation of the workshop

In the eighteenth century the framemaker's workshop would have been organised to meet the different needs of the joiner, carver and gilder. In 1763, at William Linnell's, a carver and gilder who made some frames, the workshops

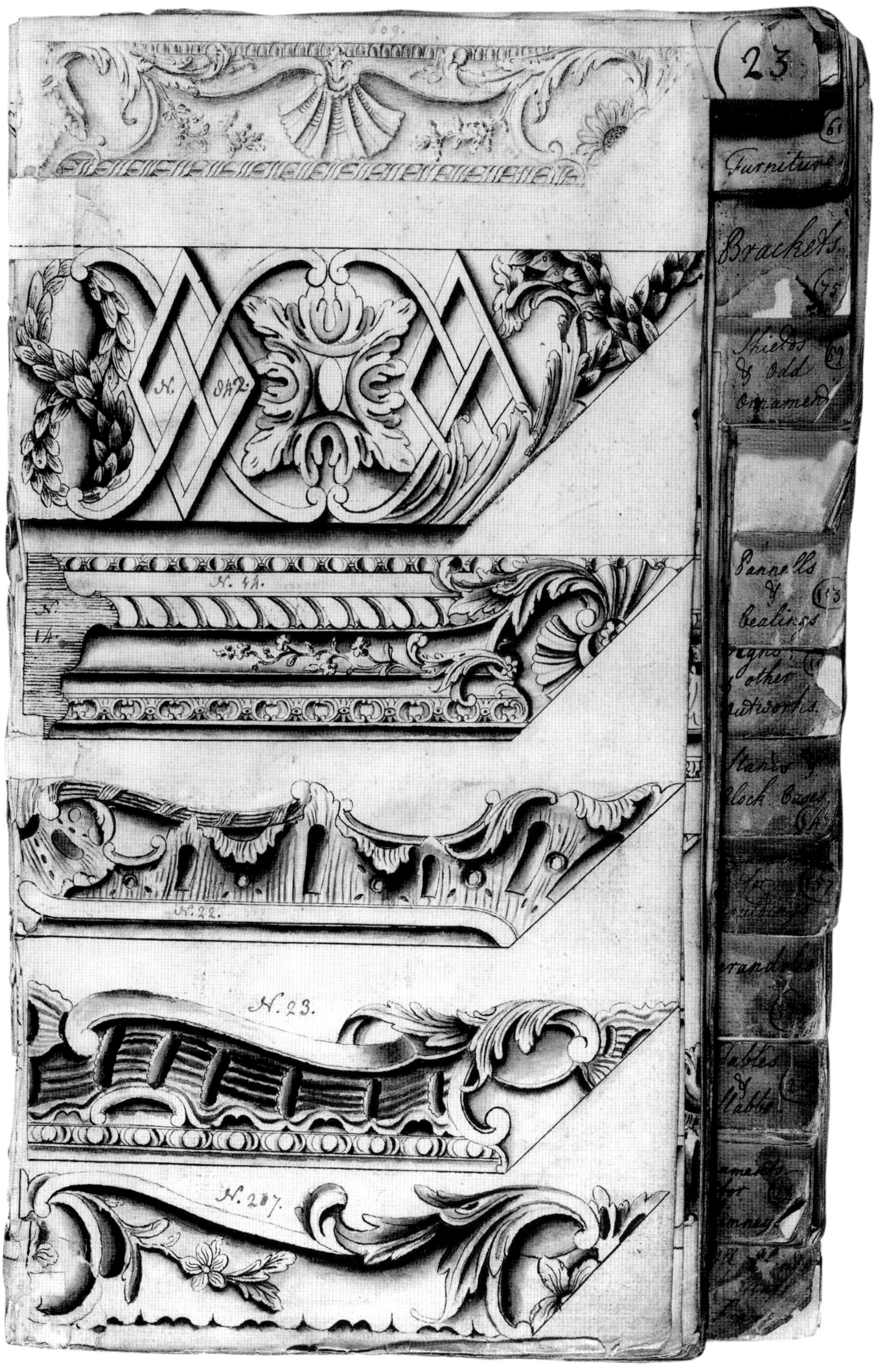

Fig.145
A page in Gideon Saint's scrapbook of ornamental designs, *c*.1760 (Metropolitan Museum of Art, Harris Brisbane Dick Fund, 1934 [34.90.1]).

The scrapbook is arranged in twelve sections, each with a finger-tab. This page is one of many devoted to picture frame mouldings and shows English rococo pen-and-wash designs. Each frame is numbered for reference and shows a length running from the centre to the corner of the top side. Design no.23 is close to the frame on Highmore's portrait of Samuel Richardson (no.33).

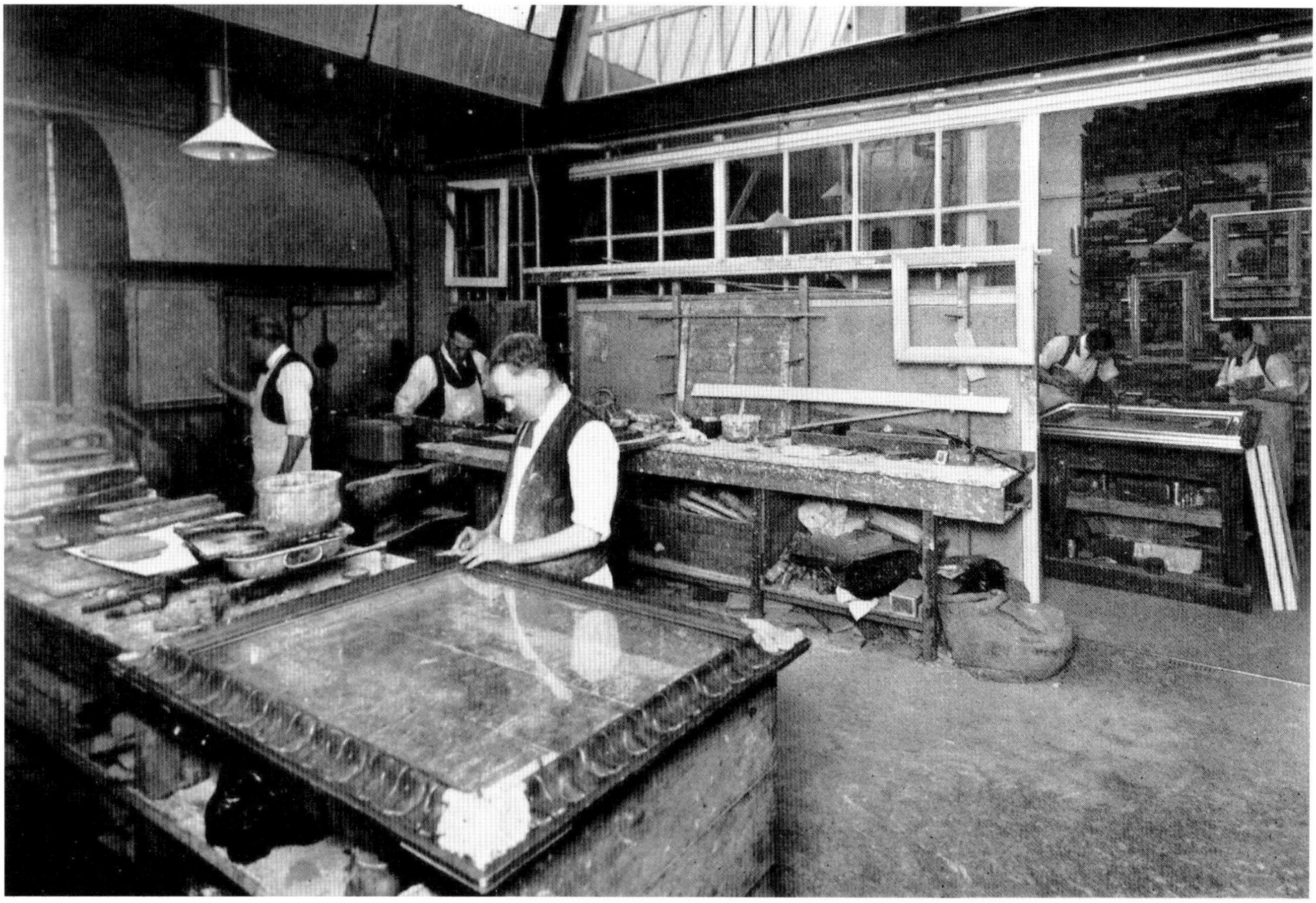

covered three floors at no.28 Berkeley Square, comprising a showroom, office, glass room and joinery shop on the ground floor, cabinet making and upholstery apparently on the first floor and the carving and gilding shops at the top of the building.[93] Even in a smaller workshop, each area had its own requirements. Gilding, for example, needed a clean atmosphere in which sawdust from the joinery department would not settle on the gold size, and an even temperature, since the sizing and gilding process could be adversely affected by extremes of heat or cold. Although carving and gilding were carried out separately, many carvers were also gilders. John Lord, who worked for Samuel Norman before moving from London to South Carolina in the mid-1760s, could claim to have been employed 'doing all the different parts of his business at the Shop of Mr Norman, Carver and Gilder to her Majesty'.[94]

Framemaking in the eighteenth century was a time-consuming business because of the many processes: joinery, carving, whitening, gold sizing, gilding and finishing. The various techniques and their refinements have been described in detail in Chapter 2. Despite subsequent changes in the methods of producing frames, workshops have continued to be organized along similar lines into the twentieth century, and as recently as 1931 a large concern like Alfred Stiles & Sons had premises divided into the Machinery and Joinery Workshop, the Mounting and Whitening Department, the Gilding Shop, and the Showroom (see fig.146).[95]

An occasional practice, rarely documented, was the sub-contracting out of work when a framemaker was unable to cope with the volume of business or found it more profitable to buy-in certain types of work. For example, Samuel Norman, a leading carver and gilder who produced picture frames on occasion, sub-contracted out some of his work to William Long, a carver and gilder with his own business

Fig.146
The premises of Alfred Stiles & Sons showing the Mounting and Whitening Department with the Gilding Shop beyond. From *Town and Country News*, 13 November 1931 (Hammersmith and Fulham Archives and Local History Centre).

in Long Acre.[96] Especially revealing is the ledger of another sub-contractor, Robert Tull, a minor carver and gilder who lived in the parish of St James, Westminster, until his death in 1758.[97] His ledger covers the last five years of his life. Although he carried on his own business as a framemaker, working for the artist Catherine Read and for patrons such as Lawrence Dundas and the Earl of Carlisle, it is his work as a sub-contractor to several leading framemakers of Huguenot origins which is of special interest. According to his ledger, Tull worked for a Mr Gosset, either Isaac Gosset or one of his brothers, a Mr Cunot, who is presumably Jean Antoine Cuenot of Warwick Street, Golden Square, and a Mr Pettet, presumably Paul Petit. Much of Tull's work was fairly slight but is of great interest, since it provides evidence that even minor components of frames could be contracted out. Gosset was charged 6d for 'carving the edges of a small frame', 1s for 'sizing 2 large frames and gould sizing a large broad one', 1s. 3d for 'mending a common frame and packing one up' and 3s. 2d for 'guilding a large frame at home'. Cuenot and Petit were both charged for carving but not for gilding, Petit paying 12s for 'carving a 3/4 frame with Shellworke'. Another important customer, Mr Wright, paid for frame components such as a 'long peace of a half length' at 14s and for other bit work including 'repearing part of the frame and whitening a peice over again' for 9s. 6d and 'guilding a large Glass frame in burnish'd 9 books & 1/2 at 5s a book' for £2.7s.6d. Robert Tull's work as a sub-contractor may have been rather ordinary, judging from his prices, but nevertheless it formed a significant part of his business in 1753 and 1754.

Frames were usually priced on the basis of time spent and materials used. The larger businesses normally kept ledgers in which the costs are broken down in some detail. Some of the

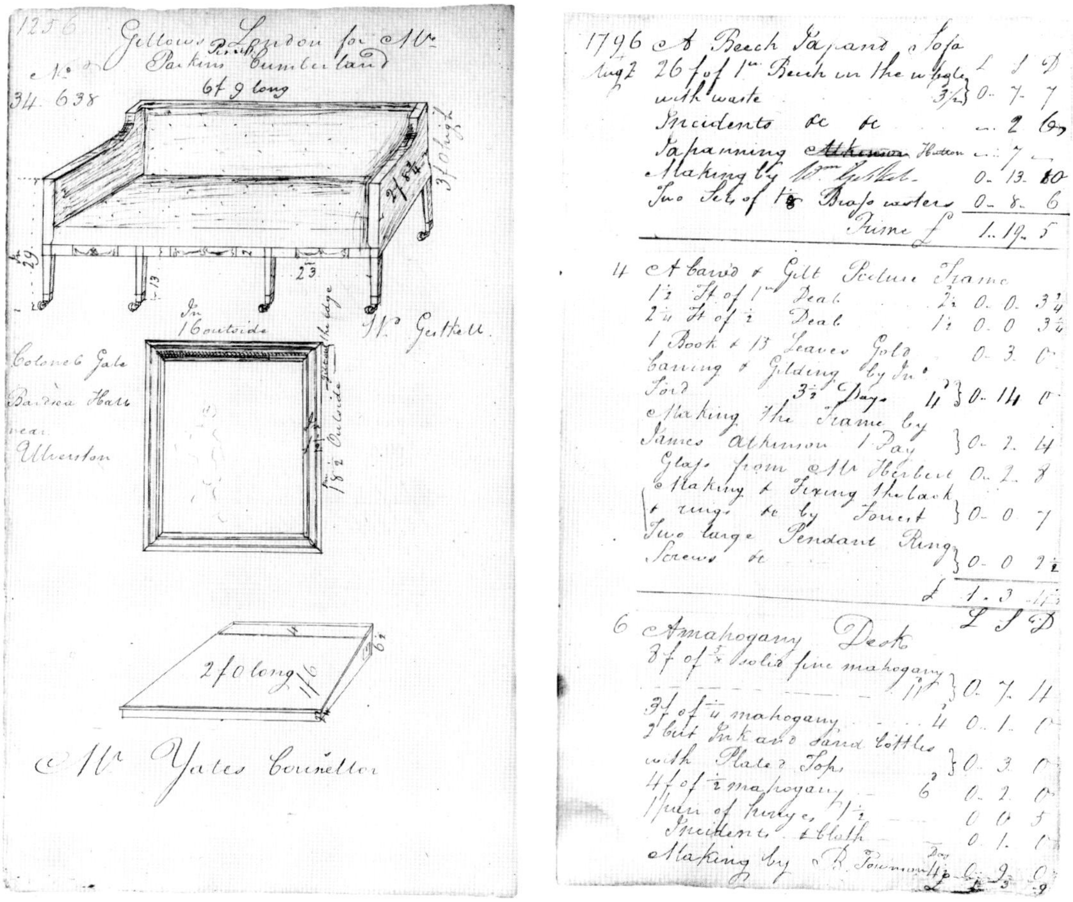

Fig.147
An opening in Gillow's ledger, August 1796 (Westminster City Archives).

Gillows of Lancaster and London made all sorts of furniture. The ledger entry for 4 August gives a detailed breakdown of the costs for making a carved and gilt picture frame.

entries in the books of John Smith are very specific. He charged Philip Rawlings £16.16s for a 'handsome sweep sided frame' in 1812, noting down his own costs as £12.4s made up of twenty-seven days' work at £7.3s, woodwork at £1.2s, compo ornaments at £1.18s, fourteen books of gold leaf at £1.6s, and other materials at 15s. For Lord Charles Townshend in 1827 he made a frame for William Collins's *Scene at Folkestone*, noting that gilding the frame in oil and burnished gold took four days and seven hours, and required twelve whole books of gold and twelve leaves of another book.[98] Gillows of Lancaster even named the craftsmen in their ledgers. For example, in 1796 they charged one of their local customers, Colonel Gale of Bardsea Hall, £1.3s.4½d for a relatively simple carved and gilt picture frame (see fig.147), calculating the making of the frame by James Atkinson at 2s.4d for a day's work, the carving and gilding by John Ford at 14s, or three-and-a-half days at 4s a day, the glass at 2s.8d from Mr Herbert, the making and fixing of the back and rings by Forrest at 7d, two large pendant ring screws at 2½d, and other materials including gold leaf at 3s.6½d.[99]

In pricing frames allowance was made for the time-consuming process of using burnished gold in place of oil gilding. Isaac Gosset quoted four guineas for a burnished frame, and three for one gilt in oil, when he wrote with his prices to a patron in 1755.[100] John Constable recommended paying an extra pound for burnishing an egg moulding 'which will much enhance the beauty of the frame', bringing the price he asked for to seven guineas.[101]

Picture hanging and other services

The framemaker usually provided a wider range of services than the making of frames. Almost all firms would arrange the packing and dispatch of both pictures and frames. 'Honoured Sir', wrote John Le Sage to Sir Justinian Isham in 1685, 'I have this day delivered into the Carrier at the Ram in Smithfield eight frames with the three pictures from Mr Nellers all safely packt up in flower Boxes and the Carrier has promised to take a speciall care in delivering of them'.[102] In the nineteenth century, framemakers such as Joseph Green and Michael Tijou acted as packers and forwarding agents for the many provincial exhibitions.[103]

Hanging pictures was another important service. William France took infinite care with Sir Lawrence Dundas's pictures when they were hung in his London house in Arlington Street in 1764 (see fig.148), 'attending every weekday from the 17 to the 29 March' in order to 'find proper Places, and putt up' pictures, including the provision of 'very large brass headed nails with carved heads ... to suit the weight of the pictures' and 'green silk line for the Pictures'. Later the same year France billed Dundas for putting up 'Canvas & Cateridge paper behind your 8 Large Picture Frames, to prevent the frames and Nails scratching the Damask, when they shall be hung on it'.[104]

Other framemakers offered a similar service. Rather more unusually, Francis Draper, the National Portrait Gallery's framemaker, was paid 1s. 6d for 'Draping portrait of "Queen" with black cloth' at Queen Victoria's death in 1901.[105] Perhaps it is not surprising that some early nineteenth-century framemakers, notably George Morant and William Thomas, also advertised their services as interior decorators.

There were other facilities which some framemakers offered. Picture restoration was one of these. William Waters charged Lord Glenorchy 10s in 1740 for 'a Stretching frame Cloth & lining your Lordships picture a half length', one of many paintings he treated.[106] Framemakers were widely used for restoring pictures in the seventeenth and eighteenth centuries but one correspondent in the *Gentleman's Magazine* in 1764 was against the practice; he recommended avoiding 'colourmen or framemakers, for I should as soon give them a commission to make me a suit of clothes, as to mending my pictures'.[107]

Other framemakers trespassed into the dealer's province, including 'Cribb', probably William Cribb, who bid on behalf of Lady

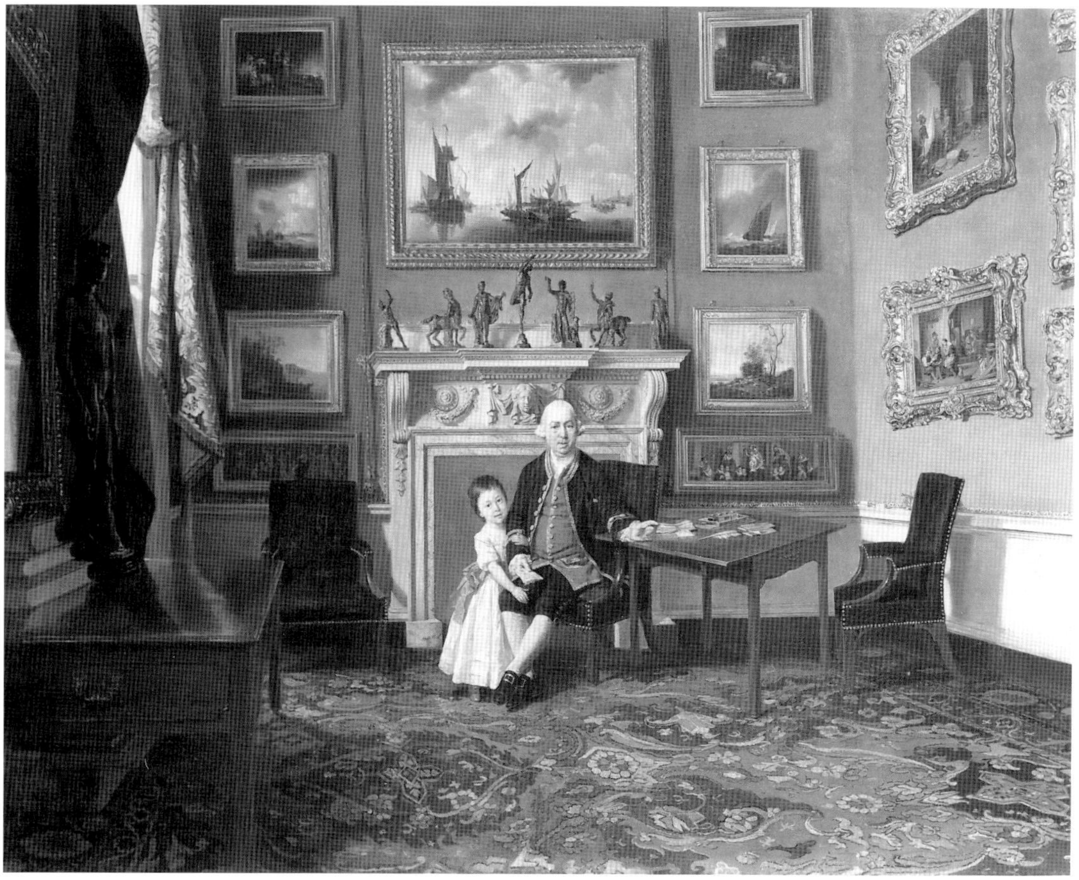

Fig.148
Sir Lawrence Dundas with his Grandson by Johan Zoffany, 1769-70 (The Marquess of Zetland).

The Library, or Pillar Room, at no.19 Arlington Street was among the rooms hung by William France in 1764. Zoffany has taken the liberty of bringing together pictures from other rooms in the house for the purposes of this view, but has otherwise painted a fairly faithful representation. Many of the pictures can be recognised including, for example, over the chimney-piece, the Van de Cappelle sea-piece now in the National Musem of Wales. The frames appear to be English except for those in the French rococo style. The brass-headed nails used by France are clearly visible above some of the frames.

Inchiquin at Sir Joshua Reynolds's sale in 1796,[108] and John Smith, who turned from framemaking to dealing by stages. Smith sold Rubens's *Chapeau de Paille* to Sir Robert Peel for £2,725 in 1824 and between 1829 and 1842 published the celebrated Smith's *Catalogue Raisonné of the most Eminent Dutch, Flemish and French Painters.* Foord & Dickinson not only framed Edward Lear's work but exhibited it for sale at their premises in Wardour Street in the 1880s, leading Lear to christen his framemakers 'Foord's of Wardoff Street', because they warded off the wolf from the door.[109]

Finally in this survey of framemakers' activities, a mention should be made of the provision of art supplies to amateurs and country house owners. In 1778, for example, Thomas Fentham sent John Grimston of Kilnwick in Yorkshire a small case containing '3 dozen of Middletons Pannels & a Book of Leaf gold [and] some parchment ye same as I use [to make size]'.[110]

The cost of frames

'Frames may be carried up to a great expence' wrote William Hogarth in 1748 when asked to advise on the framing of his *Paul before Felix* for the Hall at Lincoln's Inn.[111] This was at a period when some extraordinarily rich and expensive frames were being produced, often costing as much or more than the picture, and Hogarth was probably aware of the frames made by Paul Petit for Frederick Prince of Wales at a cost of as much as £160 for a single frame.[112] Lord Bateman bought elaborate frames in Paris in 1742 for portraits by Robert Tournières at a cost of 300 livres, which he remarked on as 'intolerable dear ... everybody says there never were 2 such frames made in Paris'.[113]

Old master paintings were often expensively framed, perhaps as a reflection of the superior status such pictures enjoyed in the eighteenth and nineteenth centuries. Pietro da Cortona's

Coriolanus cost £74 to frame for Holkham Hall in 1757.[114] This practice of drawing attention to the most valuable old masters by giving them the richest frames reached its apogee in the early nineteenth century. Benjamin West's remark that the Duke of Wellington's Correggio and Giulio Romano 'ought to be framed in diamonds' need not be taken literally, but it epitomises the attitude of the time.[115]

Modern pictures could also be given expensive frames. In 1769 Gainsborough's whole-length of Garrick at the Stratford Shakespeare Jubilee was provided with a frame costing £74.4s compared with the £63 the artist had been paid for the picture.[116] The frame for J.S. Copley's great canvas, *The Siege of Gibraltar*, was rumoured to have cost four hundred pounds, 'a greater sum, we believe than was ever given before for a similar article', though the Guildhall records suggest that it was intended that it should cost no more than £130.[117]

Such prices were exceptional. Until the mid-twentieth century most picture frames cost a few pounds and sometimes only a matter of shillings, but nevertheless significant sums of money at the time. It is instructive to look at the cost of frames made in one of the most frequently used sizes, namely the thirty by twenty-five inch half-length portrait (sometimes called a three-quarters at the period, from its use of about three-quarters of a yard of canvas). For this size Mary Beale in 1677 and 1681 charged £1, £1.10s or £2 according to style.[118] Even cheaper were plain black frames with a gilt sight edge. Such frames, costing 16s, were being used for the work of William Aikman in 1725 and Joseph Wright of Derby as late as 1762.[119] The same price was charged by Gerard Soest for a frame, finish unspecified, in 1667.[120] In the eighteenth century gilt frames became the norm. Allan Ramsay charged two-and-a-half guineas for a rococo swept frame and two guineas for a simpler corner frame.[121] Reynolds normally charged three, three-and-a-half or four guineas, and Romney much the same.[122] With Reynolds's pupil, James Northcote, we come to a transition point. At the outset of his career his frames were two-and-a-half or three guineas; fifty years later in the late 1820s the figure was more like five or six guineas.[123] The heavier, richer frames of the later period were more costly in both time and materials, though Northcote's frames were cheaper than Sir Thomas Lawrence's which were done to an especially high standard. At the other extreme the advent of machine-made mouldings meant that mass-produced frames of meaner design could be sold very cheaply. In 1844 P. Garbanati advertised thirty by twenty-five inch frames of four-inch width for £1.6s, five-inch at £1.10s and six-inch at £2.[124] Such prices were exceptionally low.

The simpler taste in framing of the late nineteenth and twentieth centuries served to keep prices down for even the better quality frames. G.F. Watts charged five guineas for the 'Watts' pattern in 1873.[125] William Orpen was using six-inch wide Whistler frames finished in white enamel at £5 each in 1918.[126] Costs rose sharply for a period after the First World War so that a gilder's wage, 9d an hour in 1912, stood at 2s. 3d in 1920, according to Francis Draper, the National Portrait Gallery's framemaker.[127] In the late 1930s, however, the fairly simple frames used by Graham Sutherland, Gilbert Spencer and Ivon Hitchens for paintings of about twenty-four by twenty inches, one size down from the standard thirty by twenty-five inch, were still costing only £2, £2.10s and £3.10s.[128] It was not until after the Second World War that prices began to go up sharply. For the best part of three centuries the prices charged by leading artists for their frames had remained remarkably stable.

Another measure of price was the cost per foot of the frame. It is rare to find patrons as clear-headed as George Washington in America who was ordering frame moulding by the foot in 1797: 'Let it cost one dollar a foot. I do not want high price frames'.[129] In England frames could be expensive. Josiah Wedgwood in 1780 thought 12s a foot 'considerably more than I had any notion of' when procuring a specially designed frame from a top London framemaker for a work by George Stubbs.[130] In the 1760s Edward Knight, one of the great collectors of the period, kept a tight control of his costs: 'Orderd of Mr.

Brunnett a Frame ... not to exceed 7s a foot'.[131] Even 7s a foot was expensive and implied a price of more than £6 for a three-quarter length fifty by forty inch portrait. More normal was the price of 5s a foot for a four-inch wide oil gilt frame in the Maratta style (actually noted as an 'S.R.' or Salvator Rosa frame), which Knight ordered from 'Gosset' in 1772. Frames for smaller pictures, with their narrower mouldings, would cost less per foot as would those with simpler carving. Most of Knight's orders were costed at 2s.6d, 3s or 3s.6d a foot. It should be added that Knight was exceptional in his interest in the cost per foot. Accounts of the period were usually reckoned in terms of the cost per frame.

The practice of calculating framing at a rate per foot was more commonly adopted in work done for architectural interiors since most interior carving was calculated in this way. At Hampton Court and Whitehall Palace in the 1680s and 1690s overdoor and overmantel frames, carved but not gilded, were typically costing between 2s.6d and 3s.6d a foot at the hands of leading carvers such as William Emmett. A frame with more enrichments, or members (as runs of carved work were described), or with more elaborate carving would have been more expensive. Emmett charged 3s.10d a foot for framing with two enrichments at Whitehall Palace which quite exceptionally he describes as 'painfully wrought'.[132]

Most of the fixed frames at Whitehall had two or three enrichments. Some of the free-standing work done under Robert Adam's direction for Lord Coventry at Croome Court in the 1760s had as many as four or even six enrichments. Sefferin Alken charged 25s a foot for 'A frame to Picture 6 Members very Richly Carv'd', or £22.10s for eighteen feet, a figure which did not even include the gilding, which came to a further £10.[133] In 1789 the frame supplied by Richard Lawrence for Benjamin West's altarpiece painting in the Royal Naval College chapel at Greenwich cost the quite remarkable figure of 50s a foot.[134]

In all this discussion about the price of frames it must not be forgotten that patrons will generally have looked at the price of the picture before considering the cost of the frame. Lawrence's frame for the chapel at Greenwich may have cost £145 but West's painting came to £1,200. The price of paintings, and notably portraits, increased greatly as the professional status of the artist improved in the late eighteenth century with the foundation of the Royal Academy. Van Dyck asked Charles I £34 for his portrait ready framed in 1638, of which £30 seems to have been for the picture and £4 for the frame. In contrast, G.F. Watts could charge Sir Charles Dilke £315 for a portrait in 1873 and a further five guineas for the frame.[135]

In the seventeenth and eighteenth centuries the frame could cost as much as half the sum a minor artist could command for a portrait. At the outset of his career James Northcote charged five or six guineas for a thirty by twenty-five inch portrait and a further two-and-a-half or three guineas for the frame. By the end of his career his own fee had gone up to twenty guineas making even the increased cost of five guineas for a frame in the 1820s seem rather less significant.[136]

Turning to the present day, it is intriguing to look at five paintings commissioned and framed by the National Portrait Gallery in the mid-1990s: Howard Morgan's *Antoinette Sibley* (no.132), Tai-Shan Schierenberg's *Lord Carrington*, Martin Yeoman's *Sir James Black*, Philip Harris's *Sir Anthony Dowell*, and Peter Edwards's *Kazuo Ishiguro*. The prices of both paintings and frames have of course increased dramatically so that these frames have cost the Gallery between £681.50 and £1,880 each. But taken as a proportion of the cost of the paintings, the sums range from seven to thirty-one per cent, and are comparable to those of the past. Though the hand-carved frame of Morgan's *Antoinette Sibley* was the most expensive to produce, it was the least costly as a proportion of the portrait's cost.

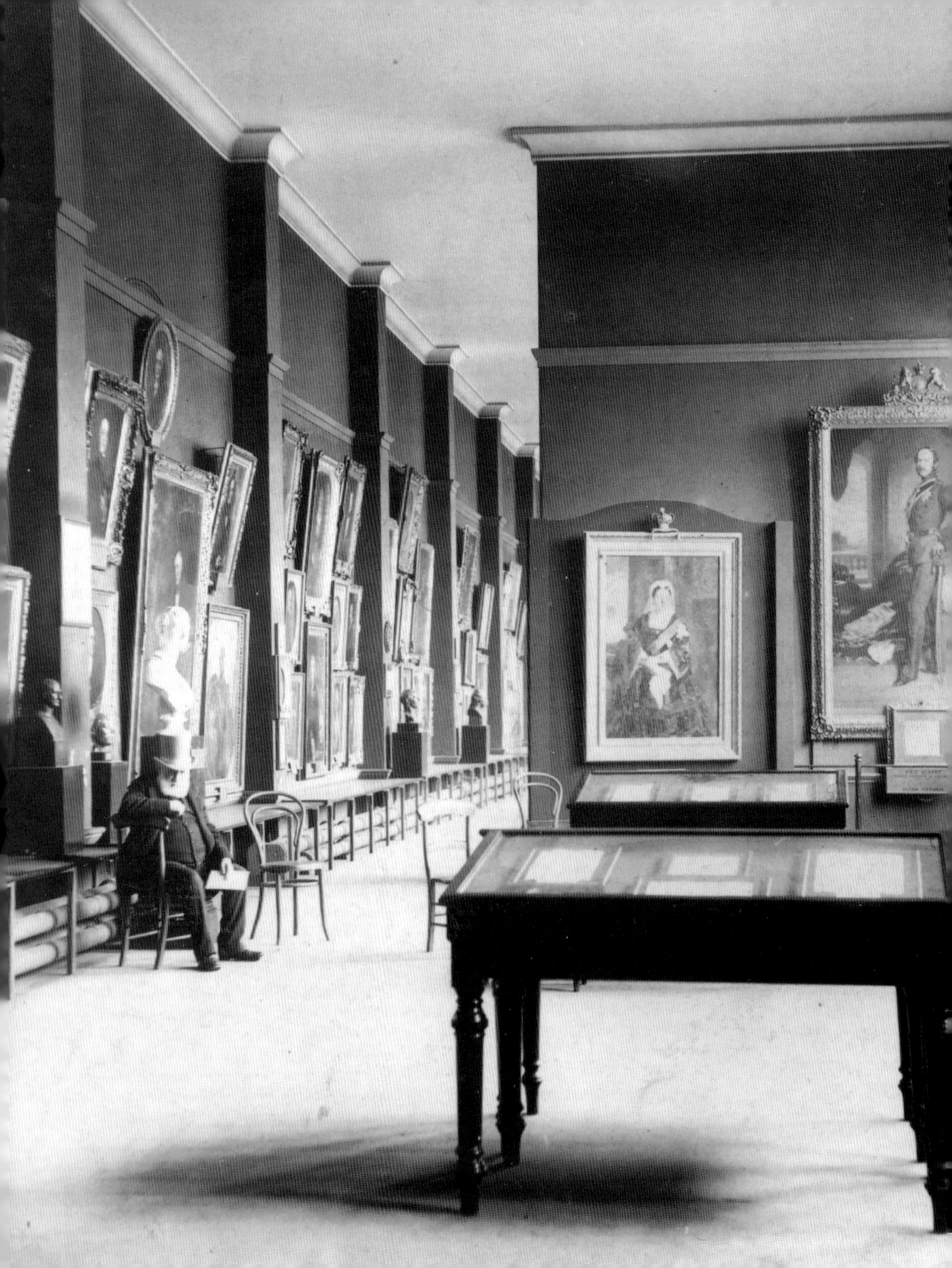

A Survey of Picture Frames in the National Portrait Gallery

These frames are some of the more significant in the National Portrait Gallery collection. The arrangement is approximately chronological, in terms of the date of the frames, rather than of the portraits. The frames are original to the pictures unless otherwise indicated.

Each entry takes the form of a description of the portrait, with dimensions given height before width in centimetres followed by inches in parentheses; a technical description of the frame, with the width of the frame given in inches as is conventional; and a discussion of the frame. Technical terms are explained in the Glossary, pp.206-209.

Gilt frames are in oil gold in whole or part unless stated; the use of water gilding is generally noted. It should be assumed that frames made before the mid-nineteenth century have been regilded at some stage unless reference is made to the gilding being original. Gilding directly onto the wood is noted; other frames will have been gessoed before gilding.

Construction methods have been recorded where evident. Mitred and keyed frames have tapering feather keys (see fig.200) unless stated. The use of blocks to strengthen the corners of nineteenth-century frames is noted but not the placing of blocks along the frame sides.

The frames in the collection of the National Portrait Gallery which are on display at Beningbrough Hall and Bodelwyddan Castle have not been examined in detail for technique. These are nos.21, 36, 40, 43, 54, 70, 81 and 82.

The National Portrait Gallery's framing bills are kept in the National Portrait Gallery Archive in a series of nine volumes, entitled 'Duplicates of Accounts', for the period 1856 to *c.*1930, and in the Registered Packets for individual pictures acquired since *c.*1930. Reference is sometimes made to Gallery correspondence which usually will be found in the relevant Registered Packet.

Fig.149 (facing page)
The National Portrait Gallery at South Kensington, one of a set of photographs taken by Praetorius and Messrs Wood & Co. shortly before the Gallery's removal from its second home, 1885 (detail). The Gallery's first Director, Sir George Scharf, can be seen seated. Conspicuously displayed are the portraits of Queen Victoria and Prince Albert.

1 [figs.18, 180]
Henry VII (1457–1509)
By an unknown artist, dated 1505
Oil on panel, 42.5 × 30.5 (16¾ × 12), arched top
NPG 416

Oak, integral with the panel, with an applied outer moulding of softwood along the arched top (the grain of the wood and the nail fixings are visible under X-rays), gessoed and water gilt, the later black paint on the outer moulding removed in 1972 and regilt. 1⅛ inches wide.

This is the earliest painting in the National Portrait Gallery's collection. The frame is integral with the panel painting, being made out of a single piece of oak, but for an applied softwood moulding forming the outer element of the arched top. The gilding is modern. According to the inscription above the sill, the panel was painted for Herman Rinck, agent of the Emperor Maximilian I. It is the work of an unknown Netherlandish artist (the old attribution to Michel Sittow does not appear tenable).[1] The panel is probably the portrait of Henry VII which belonged to the Emperor's daughter, Margaret, and was recorded as being in her palace at Malines in 1516 when it was described as having 'une couverture paincte de vermeil', or a cover painted in red.[2] The back of the panel is indeed red but the three old inserts in the panel do not appear to be related to a cover for the portrait.[3]

1. I owe this observation to my colleague, Catharine MacLeod.
2. Roy Strong, *Tudor and Jacobean Portraits*, 1969, pp.149–50. Strong reproduces a detail from an x-ray of the picture as pl.291.
3. These wooden inserts are at the top (1⅝ inches wide), 2¾ inches below the top (15/16 of an inch wide) and 7½ inches below the top (1 inch wide). It is possible that the top insert is in the position of old hanging holes for the portrait. The other two inserts may have been made to prevent the panel splitting at its weakest point.

2 [figs.19, 20, 181]
Henry VI (1421–71)
By an unknown artist, *c.*1540
Oil on panel, 31.8 × 25.4 (12½ × 10)
NPG 2457

Painted and gilt oak, mitred lap joint with corner dowels visible in the frieze, the outer gilt moulding and on the back face of the frame, the inner moulding and the hollow of the outer moulding gilt, the rest of the outer moulding black, the frieze brown with the original gilt lettering, HENRICVS VI, *much of the paint renewed, a pair of hanging holes at the top centre pierced through the back and top edge of the frame. 2⅜ inches wide.*

This is one of a group of panels painted in about 1540 by an unknown artist known for the cast shadows in his portraits. Both the frame and panel are of oak. The frame is an engaged or grooved frame, with panel fitted into grooves in the side of the frame (see fig.20). The frame is held in place by wooden dowels at the corners. To find a frame like this with its grooves intact is unusual; those on the companion portrait of Edward IV in the National Portrait Gallery have been cut away, but a similar portrait of Edward IV at the Society of Antiquaries retains the original grooves.

3 [fig.150]
Henry VIII (1491–1547)
By an unknown artist, *c.*1535–40
Oil on panel, 57.2 × 42.5 (22½ × 16¾)
NPG 1376

Painted and gilt oak, mitred lap joint with dowels, the top 9 inches of the back of the frame and the corresponding area of the back of the panel painted over with a yellow orpiment and white chalk mixture probably in the sixteenth or seventeenth centuries, possible traces of scribe lines at one corner on the reverse of the frame, two partly filled hanging holes on the reverse at top centre, further holes at top left and top right, probably recent but possibly associated with old fixings such as for a picture curtain. 2¾ inches wide.

Like the frame on the portrait of Henry VI (no.2), this is an engaged frame made of oak, held together by corner dowels, although the original retaining grooves holding the panel painting in place have long since been cut away at the back. The portrait is from an unidentified Anglo-Flemish workshop and appears to have been painted in the frame, judging from the ridges of paint at the edge of the portrait. This has been confirmed by chemical analysis which shows splashes of the white underpaint used on the panel occurring on the extreme inner edge of the frame.[1] The same analysis suggests that the frame has been decorated five times. The original finish was a combination of gilding and what appears to be a type of graining. At a later date the graining was varnished black, leaving the gilding intact. The whole frame was subsequently twice varnished black all over. The frame was probably given its present graining and gilding in the nineteenth century.

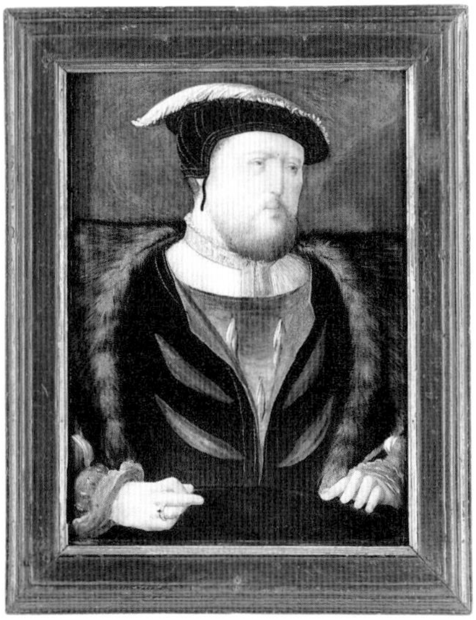

no.3; fig.150

What was the frame like originally? The areas that are gold today were originally gilded. The main part of the frame had a semi-translucent dark layer of paint laid directly over a white ground. It is uncertain precisely how this layer would have been painted, but it may have been a form of graining, or possibly tortoiseshell or marbling. It is made up of a mixture of azurite blue and fine-particled red and brown ochres. The whole frame including the gilding was finally given a clear varnish. The picture was probably hung by a ribbon or cord through holes pierced through the back and top of the frame.

1. A pigment analysis was undertaken in 1996 by UCL Painting Analysis Ltd, report no.c891.

4 [fig.151]
Edward VI (1537–53)
By William Scrots, 1546
Oil on panel, 42.5 × 160 (16¾ × 63)
NPG 1299

Painted oak, mitred and pegged lap joint, the surface of the frame refinished in black in the late eighteenth century or the nineteenth century, obliterating the signature of the artist on the frame recorded by George Vertue in 1713.[1] 1 9/16 inches wide, 2 inches deep.

The round notch at the right of this frame marks the original position of an iron viewing device which pulled out to allow the anamorphosis to be seen from the correct position to avoid distortions in the image. The photograph reproduced here is taken from this position and includes a view of the side of the frame, showing the lap joint at top and bottom. The exceptionally deep but relatively narrow frame, with various grooves and slots in the underside, is explained by the need to accommodate the viewing device.

1. See Roy Strong, *Tudor and Jacobean Portraits*, 1969, pp.88–9.

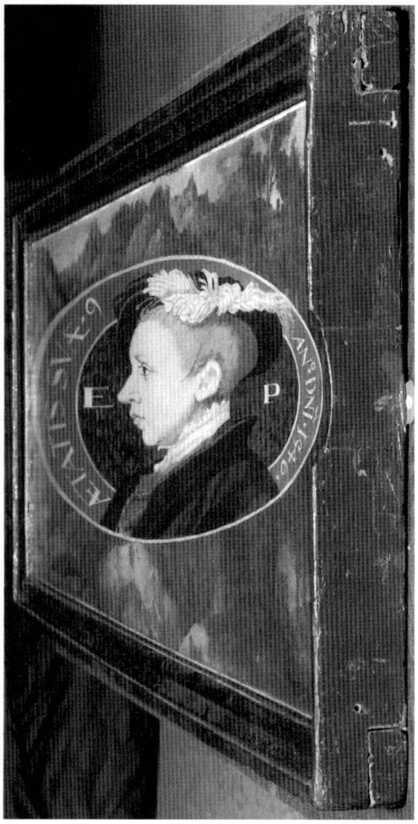

no.4; fig.151

5 [fig.5]
Elizabeth I (1533–1603)
By an unknown artist, *c.*1600
Oil on panel, 127.3 × 99.7 (50⅛ × 39¼)
NPG 5175

Carved, stained and gilt pine, lap joint with a horizontal join at front, vertical at back, the carving planted on to a backing frame. Soon after acquisition by the National Portrait Gallery in 1978 the frame was stripped and reduced in size at top and bottom centre before regessoing, regilding and refinishing. Fig.5 shows the frame before alteration. The main frame is 5½ to 9½ inches wide.

This portrait, which originally hung at Warwick Castle, is in its third frame. It may have originally had a painted frame of flat profile, conceivably a grander version of the one on the portrait of Henry VIII (no.3). It was probably in the 1670s or 1680s that it was given the Sunderland frame which can be seen on the portrait in photographs taken at the National Portrait Exhibition in 1866;[1] this frame was of the type found on the portrait of Judge Jeffreys (no.17). After the fire at Warwick Castle in 1871, the portrait was reframed again, probably as part of Anthony Salvin's reconstruction, and given pride of place in the Great Hall. The design and manufacture of this frame is yet to be documented.

The frame is an elaborate nineteenth-century variation on the Sansovino style popular in Venice at very much the time the portrait was painted in about 1600, but it is heavier and more grandiose than its Venetian prototypes. Such one-off romanticising of a royal portrait was not uncommon in the nineteenth century. At Charlecote, George Hammond Lucy reframed his portrait of Queen Elizabeth in 1836 at the considerable cost of £43.10s. In 1872 Sir Gilbert Scott gave the Westminster Abbey portrait of Richard II a magnificent new frame, made by Clayton & Bell to his design at a cost of £57.15s.

1. A photograph of the picture in its frame, taken at the National Portrait Exhibition at the South Kensington Museum in 1866, is in the Picture Library at the Victoria and Albert Museum.

6 [fig.39]

Thomas Coventry, 1st Baron Coventry (1578–1640)
By Cornelius Johnson, signed and dated 1639
Oil on canvas, 126.4 × 100.3 (49¾ × 39½)
NPG 4815

Carved and gilt oak, chamfered on the top rear edge, mason's mitre, the carved decoration raised above a sanded ground which is probably of later date, the rear of the frame built up with pine at the bottom and on both sides. 3¾ to 6 inches wide.

This Italianate frame with its scrolls and volutes is an important survival from the 1630s, a decade when a wide range of fine frames began to be made in England to satisfy fashionable taste in court circles. The type is an anglicised version of the Sansovino frames popular in Venice, as discussed above on p.52. This portrait of the Lord Keeper, Lord Coventry, was sold at auction in 1970 with an identically framed portrait of his wife, also by Cornelius Johnson, now in Sheffield City Art Gallery. The frame type is found with a black background, perhaps originally white, on the set of early copies of the Raphael Cartoons at Knole and in variant form on another picture at Knole, the full-length of Mary Curzon, wife of the 4th Earl of Dorset. The type can also be seen framing a painting of *Cain and Abel* by Cantarini as depicted in David Teniers's painting at Petworth of the Archduke Leopold Wilhelm's collection at Brussels in 1651.[1]

1. See also Chapter 3, n.28.

7 [figs.47, 183]

Sir Edward Nicholas (1593–1669)
By Sir Peter Lely, 1662
Oil on canvas, 124.5 × 100.3 (49 × 39½)
NPG 1519

Carved and gilt pine, mitred lap joint with bevelled edge, the frame grained or similarly finished, perhaps in the nineteenth century, but now perished revealing the original gilding in places. 2⅜ inches wide.

This recently cleaned portrait of Sir Edward Nicholas, Secretary of State under both Charles I and Charles II, was seen by George Vertue in or before 1731 at West Horsley, the Nicholas family house, along with copies by Henry Paert of portraits of three other Royalist leaders, Lord Capel, Lord Northampton and Sir William Compton, all of which came to the National Portrait Gallery in 1908 with similar cushion frames.[1] This portrait is exhibited with the frame from the portrait of Lord Capel which is similar in design to the Nicholas but of rather better quality. This type of cushion frame is discussed in more detail on pp.56–7.

1. See Arthur Oswald, 'West Horsley Place, Surrey', *Country Life*, vol.LXXXV, 1939, p.332.

8 [fig.47]

Thomas Wentworth, 1st Earl of Strafford (1593–1641)
After Sir Anthony Van Dyck, *c.*1633 or later
Oil on canvas, 124.5 × 108 (49 × 42½)
NPG 2960

Carved and gilt pine, mitred and pinned lap joint with bevelled edge, later water gilding on the berries and the centre and corner ribbons, three pairs of holes in the top edge, perhaps for hanging the picture, the most substantial being in the centre, 3 inches apart. 2⅞ inches wide.

This recently cleaned portrait, a mid-seventeenth century copy of Van Dyck's portrait of one of the leading statesmen of Charles I's reign, is almost certainly in its original cushion frame since the picture's canvas and hence its frame is not a standard size. The pattern of overlapping leaves with a central berry or pod is one of those discussed above on p.56 where reference is made to an identical frame on a portrait of 1656 in the Ashmolean Museum, Oxford. A somewhat similar framework of overlapping oak leaves and acorns can be found on P. Lombart's engraving of Van Dyck's portrait of the 3rd Earl of Arundel.

9 [fig.27]

Unknown woman, called Elizabeth, Princess Palatine (1618–80)
By an unknown artist, *c.*1630
Oil on canvas, 76.5 × 63.5 (30⅛ × 25)
NPG 543

Pine painted black with gilt applied papier-mâché winged cherub heads and a gilt sight edge, mitred lap joint with bevelled edge, the joints not mirroring the adjacent corners but turned through ninety degrees. The outer gilt moulding is a later, probably nineteenth-century addition, which fits over and under the back edge of the original frame; this moulding appears to have been fitted at the same time as the papier-mâché ornament was repaired in compo and regilt; it hides the original black back edge and the original hanging holes, 3 inches apart, which pierce the top edge of the frame. There is no rebate for the picture except for a nineteenth-century build-up on the back of the frame; there are traces of old canvas impressions and nail holes on the back of the frame. 2 13/16 inches wide (3 3/8 inches with later outer moulding).

A rare survival of a mid-seventeenth-century frame type produced for showy effect at minimum expense. The frame has gilt winged cherub heads at the centres and corners which must have been produced in a mould using an early form of papier-mâché. An area of old damage reveals paper with lettering printed in a black gothic type. The cherub heads have lost much of their detail, as with other early papier-mâché frames, and have been repaired in compo. The use of papier-mâché in framemaking in the seventeenth century is discussed above on pp.40–1. It is not possible to be sure that the frame is original to the picture, which was given to the British Museum as a portrait of the Princess Palatine, apparently by Dr Andrew Gifford (see no.29) in about 1758.

Other examples of this frame type are to be found at Knole (*Heraclitus* and *Democritus* by Moreelse, perhaps of the 1630s, the flats of the frame now sanded but originally painted blue), the Ashmolean Museum, Oxford (five portraits, mainly of the 1650s, from the Tradescant Collection), the National Portrait Gallery (*John Fletcher* and *Lord Herbert of Cherbury*, on loan to Montacute, both frames fitted in the 1960s), and at Snowshill Manor (*Portrait of a Dutch Gentleman*).[1]

1. For the variations in profile and construction, see Macgregor (ed.), *Tradescant's Rarities*, Oxford, 1983, p.327–9.

10 [fig.48]
Bulstrode Whitelocke (1605–76)
By an unknown artist, dated 1634
Oil on canvas, 76.2 × 63.5 (30 × 25)
NPG 4499

Pine painted black, mitred and keyed, the keys renewed, with applied gilt carving which has been renewed at the bottom from the left corner to the centre and in some other small areas, the outer convex moulding gilt but apparently originally painted black. The frame slightly reduced in size by Riccardo Giaccherini when acquired in 1983. 3 3/8 inches wide.

This portrait of the Parliamentarian and writer, Bulstrode Whitelocke, framed soon after acquisition in 1966 in a carved silver gilt reverse section panel frame, was subsequently reframed in 1983 in this black-and-gold appliqué frame with gilt carved foliage ornament applied to a flat ebonised back frame, a style popular in the seventeenth and early eighteenth centuries.[1] The central motif and the use of flat gilt fillets to contain the running foliage carving are unusual features and may indicate an eighteenth-century date for this frame.

1. See above, pp.56–7.

11 [fig.42]
Oliver Cromwell (1599–1658)
By an unknown artist, perhaps eighteenth century, after Samuel Cooper
Oil on canvas, 22.2 × 16.5 (8 3/4 × 6 1/2)
NPG 588

Veneered pine, mitred and pinned lap joint, the joints not mirroring the adjacent corners but turned through ninety degrees, the veneer of an ebonised red hardwood, the sight edge of rosewood, the frame altered and the rebate perhaps enlarged. 1 15/16 inches wide.

This frame is not original to the picture, but the thickness and style of the ebonised hardwood ripple mouldings, applied to a pine back frame, suggest that it may be seventeenth-century in date. The use of ebony frames in England at the period is discussed in more detail on pp.50–1.

12 [figs.43, 182, 199]
William Laud (1573–1645)
After Sir Anthony Van Dyck, *c.*1636 or later
Oil on canvas, 123.2 × 94 (48 1/2 × 37)
NPG 171

Carved and gilt oak, chamfered at the back, mason's mitre, the upper part of the lion mask planted, the original back frame in pine with a mortise and tenon joint with the projecting tenon fixed with two pegs at each corner, apparently all in original condition except for a later additional build up to allow for glazing and backing of the picture; three pairs of holes, perhaps for hanging, in the top edge of the back frame at distances between 1 3/4 and 3 1/4 inches apart. The frame 3 to 5 inches wide, 7 inches at top cresting.

This fine auricular frame of mid-seventeenth century date, original except for the later surface, has a stylised lion mask at the top and another more grotesque mask at the bottom. By identifying the upturned rounded forms on either side of the lion mask at the corners as paws, a reading of the top of the frame as a highly stylised representation of a lion's skin is possible. The mask at the bottom is tied through the eyes as if by a cord fixed to the substrate of the frame. The capricious ornament of the sides of the frame derives ultimately from the idea of an animal skin with irregular curling edges, as discussed above on p.53.

The frame of this portrait of Archbishop Laud can be seen in an old photograph of the Gallery taken in 1911, and may be original. Another Van Dyck, the portrait of Margaret Lemon at Hampton Court, has a frame of this type although not necessarily original. A particularly fine example can be found on the early Lely of Lord and Lady Dacre, sold Christie's, 19 November 1982, lot 79, and a variant of the type on another early Lely of the Countess of Dysart at Ham House (one of four of this pattern at Ham). Other examples in the National Portrait Gallery include a frame in store from a mid-seventeenth century anonymous portrait of the 1st Earl of Craven, the frame on Jacob Huysman's portrait of the 1st Duke of Lauderdale of *c.*1665, and the frame which has been fitted to the anonymous portrait of Sir John Ray.

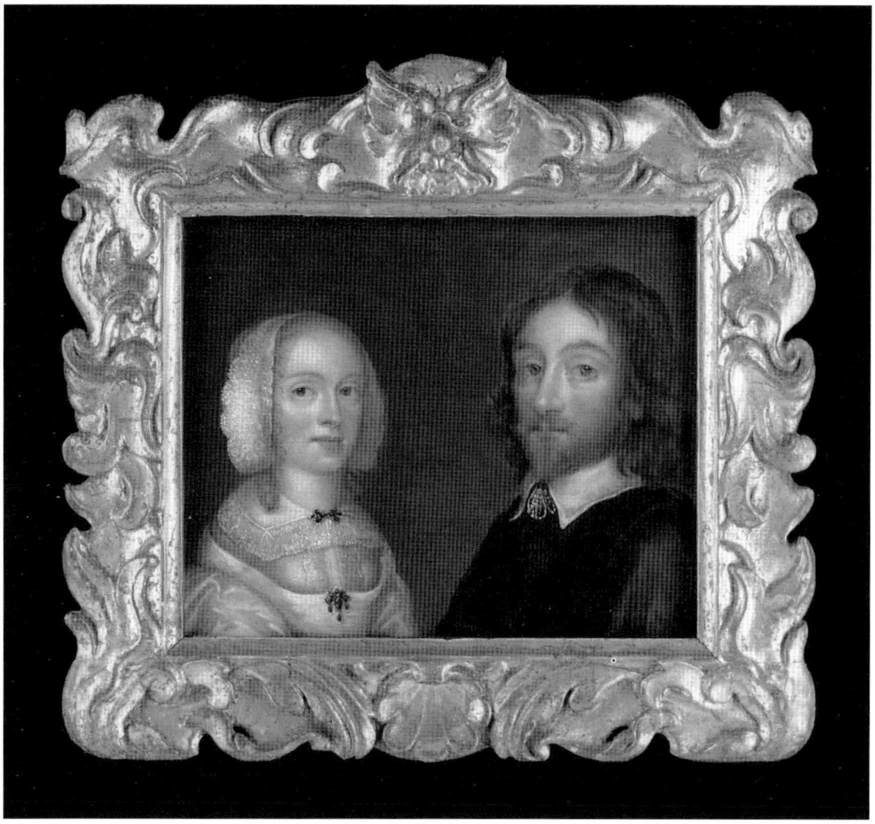

no.13; fig.152

13 [fig.152]
Sir Thomas Browne (1605–82) *and his wife, Dorothy* (1621–85)
Attributed to Joan Carlile, *c.*1641–50
Oil on panel, 18.4 × 22.9 (7¼ × 9)
NPG 2062

Carved and gilt oak, lap jointed mason's mitre, the owl mask damaged at the top, the frame surface regilt with traces of bronze powder and lacquer. 1½ to 2 inches wide, 2¾ inches at top cresting.

Many small portraits were framed in auricular or Sunderland frames in the mid-seventeenth century including the copies after Van Dyck attributed to Theodore Russel in the Brown Gallery at Knole and some pastels of the Restoration period. The frame on this portrait of the Royalist politician and writer, Sir Thomas Browne, is an early example belonging to the 1640s and certainly original to the portrait. It is of fine quality with a rather satisfying tight rhythm to the carving though the surface has been renewed. It does not follow one of the standard auricular patterns identified on p.53. At the bottom, two branches spring from the corners to surround the central shell. At the top, an owl-like mask provides a large-scale centrepiece. The frame is of oak, chamfered on the rear like the chamfered oak panel of the portrait; it retains its original hanging holes pierced through from the back of the frame to the top edge for a cord or ribbon (see fig.40).

14 [fig.44]
Thomas Chiffinch (1600–66)
Attributed to Jacob Huysmans, *c.*1655–60
Oil on canvas, 113 × 93.3 (44½ × 36¾)
NPG 816

Carved and gilt oak, chamfered at the back, mason's mitre, the top and bottom of the frame extended by 1⅞ inches at both corners, the sides by 2⅜ inches at the bottom, the back frame replaced, the tips of the mask at bottom centre replaced. 3¾ to 4¾ inches wide, 5¾ inches at top cresting.

A superb auricular frame of individual character with grotesque masks at top and bottom set between dolphins with open mouths seemingly engulfing the corner ornament of the frame. It was acquired by the National Portrait Gallery in the mid-1970s and slightly enlarged on all four sides to fit the picture. The marriage of frame and picture may not always seem appropriate, and is always a matter of opinion, but in this case the sense of movement in the frame seems undeniably to suit the dynamic nature of this portrait of the collector and connoisseur, Thomas Chiffinch.

The basic pattern of the sides of the Chiffinch frame links it to a group of auricular frames of the 1630s and 1640s, characterised by a mask of a grimacing man at the top of the frame, as discussed above on p.53. Examples of the type can be found on the work of Cornelius Johnson, for example, his *2nd Lord Herbert*, 1635 (Powis Castle), *Anne Peyton*, 1636 (with Lane Fine Art, 1994) and the *Duke of Lauderdale*, 1642–3 (Ham House), and on George Geldorp's full-length *Sir Arthur Ingram*, *c.*1638–9 (Temple Newsam House). Another full-length of the type, Peter Nason's *Oliver St John*, 1651 (National Portrait Gallery, on loan to the British Museum), is a recent marriage of picture and frame.

15 [fig.45]
Arthur Capel, 1st Earl of Essex (1631–83) *and his wife, Elizabeth* (1636–1718)
By Sir Peter Lely, *c.*1653
Oil on canvas, 123.8 × 166.4 (48¾ × 65½)
NPG 5461

Carved and gilt oak, irregularly chamfered at the back, mason's mitre, the pine back frame lap jointed with bevelled edge, though with the top and bottom ends of the side timbers removed, some guide lines visible at bottom corners, the extremities of the carving planted at the corners and at the main projections on the sides, the remains of fittings for hanging in the form of a U-pin and holes at left and a cord at right. 4½ to 6¼ inches wide.

This sea-monster-and-shells pattern, an early type of Sunderland frame, was favoured by Peter Lely and some other artists in the 1650s. It is found on a large scale on no.15 and on Lely's portrait of Sir John Cotton and Family (Manchester City Art Gallery), as a three-quarter length on the Lely studio *Charles II* at Ham House and as a half-length (see no.16).[1] In each case the same basic elements are repeated, as described on pp.55–6. Other Capel family portraits, which once hung in the Great Library at Cassiobury, including the portrait of Mary Capel and her sister (Metropolitan Museum, New York), have similar frames.

1. The portrait of the Cotton Family is reproduced with frame in Oliver Millar, *Sir Peter Lely 1618-80*, exh.cat., National Portrait Gallery, 1978, no.30.

16 [fig.90]

Edward Montagu, 1st Earl of Sandwich (1625–72)
By Sir Peter Lely, *c.*1659
Oil on canvas, 76.2 × 63.5 (30 × 25)
NPG 5488

Carved and gilt oak with slight chamfer at back, mason's mitre, the back frame replaced, the gilding distressed showing the gesso. 3¾ to 5 inches wide, 6 inches at top cresting.

This portrait of the Admiral, Edward Montagu, created Earl of Sandwich in 1660, has an early Sunderland frame very similar to that on no.15, but on a different scale.

17 [fig.46]

George Jeffreys, 1st Baron Jeffreys (1645–89)
By John Michael Wright, signed, 1673
Oil on canvas, 121.3 × 101 (47¾ × 39¾)
NPG 6047

Carved and gilt oak, the back roughly cut with a slight chamfer, mason's mitre with signs of repair, the top cresting of one piece, the back frame replaced. 3¾ to 5 inches wide, the bottom mask 6½ inches.

This is a fine example of the Sunderland frame in its fully developed form with an irregular sight edge, which was popular in the 1670s, as discussed above on pp.55–6. The type is found on other examples of Wright's work, for example his portraits of Mrs Herbert at Claydon, Colonel John Russell at Ham (a portrait of 1659 in a slightly later frame) and Sir John Corbet at the Yale Center for British Art, New Haven, as well as on the work of other artists, especially that of Sir Peter Lely as at Althorp, Ham and Kingston Lacy.

Many Sunderland frames of this type were made by the leading carver and gilder John Norris. He supplied the first of the frames for Wright's 'Fire Judges' for the Guildhall in 1671, in a heavy variation on the design. The frame on this portrait of Judge Jeffreys remains undocumented, however.

18 [figs.129, 184]

Samuel Pepys (1633–1703)
By John Hayls, 1666
Oil on canvas, 75.6 × 62.9 (29¾ × 24¾)
NPG 211

Carved and silvered pine, mitred, partly resilvered. 4 inches wide.

As recorded in his diaries and correspondence, Samuel Pepys took a great interest in all matters affecting the appearance of his apartments, and this concern extended to picture framing. This portrait was painted for him by John Hayls in 1666 for £14, and Pepys paid an additional twenty-five shillings for the frame on 16 May. Many of Pepys's books and frames were damaged in the Great Fire of London later the same year, and in his diary on 19 September he lamented the loss of some of his books, adding, 'Most of my gilt frames are hurt, which also troubles me, but most my books'.

This type of bunched leaf frame can be seen on all the portraits in a drawing of Pepys's library of *c.*1693 (fig.130). Silvered frames of this kind were common at the period and were lacquered to give them the appearance of having been gilded, and to prevent them from tarnishing. The surface of the frame has suffered over the years; it was partly regilded in 1881 and 1895, and in 1956 the peeling gilding was cleaned off down to the original silver surface, damaged areas were resilvered and the frame finished in a clear coat of lacquer. Despite some loss of detailing the frame is close to that depicted in Pepys's library and may be the original.

19 [fig.33]

John Dryden (1631–1700)
By Sir Godfrey Kneller, signed, 1693
Oil on canvas, 124.5 × 101 (49 × 39¾)
NPG 2083

Carved and silvered pine, mitred and keyed, the frame slightly reduced in size, perhaps by ½ inch, as indicated by the former keys cut through at the mitres, the surface stripped, regessoed, reworked, resilvered and toned. 5¼ inches wide.

A silvered bunched leaf frame of a style introduced in the 1660s (see no.18) and rather old-fashioned by the time this portrait was painted in the 1690s. Although the frame is of fine quality, its surface has been stripped and renewed and the corners slightly cut making it unlikely that the frame is original to the picture.

20 [fig.4]

Charles II (1630–85)
Studio of John Michael Wright, *c.*1660–5
Oil on canvas, 126.4 × 101 (49¾ × 39¾)
NPG 531

Carved and gilt pine, the top frame with a mason's mitre, the back frame lap jointed at top and butt jointed at bottom, the rebate enlarged at top and bottom, some of the carving renewed possibly including the top flower held by cherubs. 4¼ to 6 inches wide, 11 inches at top cresting.

An exceptional frame of the 1680s or 1690s, in an idiom associated with Sir Christopher Wren's woodcarvers, with cherubs on either side of a shell at the top, more cherubs on the sides and at the bottom, swags of fruit and festoons on ribbons at the top and sides, and additional swags at the bottom. At some stage the frame has been stripped, repaired, regessoed and regilt and in the process much of the original surface detail has been lost.

The purpose of this frame is not known but presumably it was made for an important picture. Very similar but even finer frames, each surmounted by a crown, graced portraits of William III and Queen Mary formerly at Cullen House, Banffshire.[1] The frame of no.20 appears to have come to the Gallery on the portrait of Charles I's physician, Sir Theodore Mayerne, which was a copy after Rubens made in the late seventeenth century or early eighteenth century.

1. Sold on the premises by Christie's, 22 September 1975, lot 479.

21 [fig.51]
John Christopher Pepusch (1667–1752)
By Thomas Hudson, *c.*1735
Oil on canvas, 127 × 102.2 (50 × 40¼)
NPG 2063

Carved and gilt, mitred. 4½ inches wide.

This richly carved running pattern of leaves, paired florettes and husks is a very fine French-inspired design of the 1670s or 1680s. The high quality of the carving suggests a leading London framemaker, perhaps of Huguenot origin. Frames of this type can be found in the Royal Collection and elsewhere.[1] On acquisition in 1924 this rather old-fashioned portrait of the court composer J.C. Pepusch was, however, in a centre-and-corner frame; when and why this frame was changed is not recorded.[2]

1. The frame type can be found on the Lely and studio three-quarter length, *James II when Duke of York*, *c.*1665, completed later (Royal Collection, Millar no.240, print from old negative including frame in National Portrait Gallery Archive); the Lely half-length, *2nd Duke of Newport*, dated 1676 (Christie's, 26 March 1976, lot 59); the Simon Verelst half-length, *Lady Willoughby*, perhaps of the 1680s (Grimsthorpe Castle), and the Lely half-length copy, *William Wycherley* (National Portrait Gallery; the frame cut down).
2. Duplicate of Accounts, vol.IX, p.36.

22 [fig.52]
William III (1650–1702)
After Sir Peter Lely, 1677 or later
Oil on canvas, 124.5 × 99.7 (49 × 39¼)
NPG 1902

Carved and gilt pine, reverse section, mitred, the cushion on which the top edge carving sits is punched as is the background of the back edge carving, the flat areas to either side of the top edge cushion are hazzled. The condition of the corner ribbons suggests that the corners have been repaired. 4 inches wide.

This exceptionally fine reverse section frame of the 1690s with its enrichments on both the top and back edges must have been expensive to produce owing to the considerable work involved in the undercutting of the leaves and tendrils and the other carving. It presumably came from the workshop of a leading carver, perhaps of Huguenot origin. Very closely comparable are the frames on John Closterman's *Taylor Family* of 1696 (National Portrait Gallery, on loan to Beningbrough Hall) and on Francesco Solimena's *Virgin and Child with Figures* (Fitzwilliam Museum, Cambridge), the latter a later marriage of picture and frame.

The frame now on the portrait of William III appears to have come to the Gallery on L.F. Abbott's late eighteenth-century portrait of Admiral Viscount Hood, on the evidence of a photograph made from an old glass negative. It was subsequently used to frame the portrait of Sir Christopher Wren (no.25).

23 [fig.53]
Sir Robert Viner and his Family
By John Michael Wright, signed and dated 1673
Oil on canvas, 144.8 × 195.6 (57 × 77)
NPG 5568

Carved and gilt pine, mitred and keyed, the keys modern and the mitres probably reshot, the two panels on each side and the husks next to the sight edge burnished on a black bole, the ground of the foliage punched. 4½ inches wide.

A panel frame of a type popular from the 1680s until the 1710s. As is usual with this style, the curved profile out of which the running foliage pattern was carved corresponds with that of the panels. The frame appears to be an early example of the style, made for a particularly wealthy patron, the goldsmith Sir Robert Viner, in whose family the picture remained until acquired by the National Portrait Gallery. The frame was clearly made for the picture, but the mitres apparently have been opened and reshot in the twentieth century. The surface of the frame was refinished in the nineteenth century; this work may have caused some loss of detail in the leaves and flowers, and the inappropriate water gilding on the panels and elsewhere was probably done at the same time.

24 [figs.49, 185]
Dr Richard Mead (1673–1754)
By Allan Ramsay and studio, signed and dated 1740
Oil on canvas, 126.4 × 101 (49¾ × 39¾)
NPG 15

Carved and gilt pine, mitred lap joint with bevelled edge, the surface renewed. 2¾ inches wide.

This portrait of the collector and court physician, Dr Mead, has a Bolection frame of a type popular in the late seventeenth century, as discussed above on pp.58–9. It is not known when it was fitted to the picture.

25 [figs.50, 186]
Sir Christopher Wren (1632–1723)
By Sir Godfrey Kneller, signed and dated 1711
Oil on canvas, 124.5 × 100.3 (49 × 39½)
NPG 113

Carved and gilt pine, mitred and pinned lap joint with bevelled edge. 4 inches wide.

The gadrooned frame on this portrait of Sir Christopher Wren, visible in old photographs, was removed from the picture, probably for storage during the First World War. It was subsequently swapped for a late seventeenth-century frame, then on L.F. Abbott's portrait of Admiral Viscount Hood but now on a Lely school portrait of William III (no.22). It has recently been restored to the Wren portrait.

Gadrooned frames of this reverse section (fig.186), with twisting leaves and florettes on the back edge and an undercut gadrooned top edge, were commonly used from the late seventeenth century onwards, as described above on p.59. They are found on many of Kneller's portraits, including for example, his full-length portrait of the Earl of Oxford, 1714 (National Portrait Gallery), and that of the Earl of Londonderry, *c.*1720 (Chevening). The gadrooning of the Wren frame is on a particularly delicate scale.

26 [fig.133]
Jacob Tonson senior (1655–1736)
By Sir Godfrey Kneller, signed and dated 1717
Oil on canvas, 91.4 × 71.1 (36 × 28)
NPG 3230

Carved and gilt pine, mitred and keyed, the flat roughly sanded, the top and bottom corner projections planted, the cresting of scrolling foliage on a fish-scale ground, the bottom tablet in the rococo style, conceivably a later addition, inscribed MR JACOB TONSON SENR. *3⅞ inches wide (8¼ inches with the top cresting).*

One of a set of forty-one identical architectural or 'architrave' frames in the Kent style made for the Kit-cat Club by Gerrard Howard, the King's framemaker, in 1733 at a cost of two guineas each. On 23 September Howard charged Jacob Tonson junior £84: 'for forty Kitt Catts Archetrive frames, Carv'd and guilt with gold to pictures by Sr Godfrey Kneller' (see fig.134). The bill is marked 'one not deliver'd', but the order was presumably subsequently completed because the account, which covers the period from 19 January to 30 October 1733, was paid in full on 20 January 1734. The bill also includes under 30 October 1733 a charge of £1.15s 'for a Archetrive frame Carvd and guilt with gold to Sr Godfrey Kneller picture by himself' (presumably the small self-portrait which came with the Kit-cat portraits to the National Portrait Gallery) and a charge of £3.3s 'for 2 kit Catts Archetrive in gold not Delivr'd' (that is, presumably, not delivered on 23 September but subsequently supplied). The bill also includes references to 'drive up frames', that is stretchers for the canvases.

The members of the Kit-cat Club, a Whig political dining club, had their portraits painted by Kneller for presentation to the club secretary, the publisher Jacob Tonson senior, over a period of more than twenty years from about 1697. Contrary to what is sometimes said, there is no evidence as to how they were originally framed or displayed, or indeed if they were framed at all, but when Tonson's nephew, Jacob Tonson junior, received the portraits he determined to rehouse them in a new pavilion adjacent to his house at Barn Elms on the Thames at Barnes. Tonson junior employed as his architect Henry Joynes, Clerk of the Works at Kensington Palace, who used various Office of Works craftsmen to build the new pavilion, and it was perhaps through Joynes that Howard came to be employed on the frames. A contemporary record of how the pictures were arranged at Barn Elms shows a double hang almost throughout. Most of the portraits are double hung to this day, half of them at the National Portrait Gallery and the others at Beningbrough Hall, Yorkshire.

27 [fig.25]
William Shenstone (1714–63)
By Thomas Ross, signed and dated 1738
Oil on canvas, 75.9 × 56.5 (29⅞ × 22¼)
NPG 4386

Gilt pine, the ornament worked in the gesso and water gilt over a black bole except for the oil gilt cross-hatched corners (perhaps restored), the ground punched, hazzle-work next to the sight-edge gadrooning and the top edge, the sub-frame lap jointed with strips of timber applied to the sides of the sub-frame to create the stepped corners. 2⅜ inches wide (3⅛ inches at corners).

This portrait of the twenty-four-year-old William Shenstone, creator of the celebrated landscape garden at the Leasowes near Birmingham, was probably painted while he was still in residence at Oxford or soon after he had returned home. Thereafter Shenstone rarely strayed far from the Leasowes, taking delight in his schemes for his garden and house, and those of his friends and neighbours.

This frame is presumably the work of a local cabinet maker, working to Shenstone's instructions, which would explain the non-standard construction and the unusual combination of a Kent frame, albeit a rather delicate one, with ornament of the sort to be found on mirror frames of the 1720s. There is an emphasis on economy of effect, with much of the decoration worked in the gesso, and the distinctly old-fashioned punched ground.

28 [figs.55, 187]
Robert Walpole, 1st Earl of Orford (1676–1745)
By Arthur Pond, signed and dated 1742
Oil on canvas, 63.5 × 50.8 (25 × 20)
NPG 6085

Carved and gilt pine, mitred and keyed, the corner projections planted, the heavily sanded frieze and the pendant oak leaves and acorns at the sides oil gilt but much of the rest of the frame water gilt on a plum bole. Markings on the top of the frame perhaps left by a former cresting. 3⅜ inches wide, 4⅜ inches at the corners.

This portrait of Robert Walpole was painted in 1742, probably soon after his defeat and resignation as prime minister. It is not recorded in Arthur Pond's account book, which has no entries for the period November 1742 to March 1743, but an earlier payment of eight guineas is entered under Walpole's name on 28 August 1740 for a pastel portrait of his illegitimate daughter, Maria Walpole, still at Houghton, and a further £2.12s.6d for a 'Gold frame & plate glass'.[1]

Pond's account book contains numerous references between 1737 and 1748 to 'architrave gold frames', a style we would call a Kent or Palladian frame with projecting 'ear' corners ornamented with shells and oak leaf and acorn pendants down each side. Most if not all of these frames were made for Pond by 'Gosset' (probably Isaac Gosset or his brother Gideon), the recipient of large payments on account from Pond in the years 1735 to 1749. The type is also found on the work of William Hoare and Francis Cotes and is discussed above on pp.92–3.

1. Louise Lippincott, 'Arthur Pond's Journal of Receipts and Expenses, 1734–1750', *Walpole Society*, vol.LIV, 1991, p.254. The frame cost £1.11s.6d and the glass £1.1s.

29 [fig.131]

Francis Bacon, Viscount St Alban (1561–1626)
Attributed to John Vanderbank, *c*.1731
Oil on canvas, 76.5 × 63.2 (30⅛ × 24⅞)
NPG 520

Carved and gilt pine, mitred with narrow keys, narrow rebate, fine grade sand on the flat, damaged at bottom right corner, oil gilt except the plain surfaces which are water gilt. 3½ inches wide.

When the British Museum transferred some seventy portraits to the National Portrait Gallery in 1879 at least seven came in architectural frames of this unusual pattern.[1] The Museum was established in 1753 in Montagu House and three years later selected the artist Arthur Pond, in competition with Andrea Casali, Andien de Clermont and a Mr Anderson, to restore the Montagu House wall paintings. It was a short step to giving Pond the additional responsibility of cleaning and framing the oil paintings in the collection, a task which passed to his assistant, Thomas Black, at his death in September 1758.[2]

This portrait of James I's Lord Chancellor, Francis Bacon, was one of a group given to the Museum by its assistant librarian, the Revd Dr Andrew Gifford, which the Trustees in November 1758 ordered to 'be delivered to Mr Black to be cleaned repaired and framed where wanting'. Thomas Black received payments for his work of £33.6s in September 1759 and £17.18s in November 1760.[3]

The frame type was probably established while Arthur Pond was responsible for the collection and is a very early example of a 'museum' frame chosen to be relatively inexpensive yet practical and sightly. Though still architectural in character, it lacks the projecting corners of the Kent frames made by Gosset for some of Pond's own work (see no.28), and the carving of shell and leaf on the top edge is quite shallow. It is possible that the frames were made for the British Museum by Gosset but the Museum accounts are unrevealing, since payment was not made directly to the framemaker, while Pond's own account books only cover the years to 1750 and his executorship papers are no more helpful.[4]

1. The following National Portrait Gallery pictures retain British Museum frames of this type: Richard Baxter (NPG 521), called Duke of Monmouth (NPG 556) and called Sir William Walker (NPG 577). Four other frames of this kind have been removed from their pictures. Kent frames of different patterns but perhaps made for the British Museum are found on some larger portraits at the National Portrait Gallery.
2. The account by J.R. Fawcett Thompson and F. Gordon Roe, 'Some Oil Portraits in the British Museum', *Connoisseur*, vol.CXLVII, 1961, pp.114–18, 189–95, can be supplemented from the following sources: British Museum General Meeting Minutes (vol.I, p.90); British Museum Committee Minutes (vol.I, pp.133–4; vol.II, pp.407, 437–8, 439, 466, 468, 475).
3. British Museum General Payments (29 September 1759, 28 November 1760).
4. Arthur Pond executorship papers (British Library, Add. MS. 23,725).

30 [fig.34]

A Club of Artists
By Gawen Hamilton, 1735
Oil on canvas, 87.6 × 111.5 (34½ × 43⅞)
NPG 1384

Carved and gilt pine, mitred and keyed, cross-hatched ground, burnished water gilding, partly renewed (perhaps when the frame was restored by Wiggins in 1956), over a deep plum bole on the hollow and gadrooning of the back edge, the flat scrolls, fillets, flat parts of the shells, heights of the flowers and sight-edge leaf. 5¾ inches wide.

Gawen Hamilton's portrait of himself and his fellow artists at the King's Arms in New Bond Street was raffled for his benefit in 1735 when it was won by Joseph Goupy.[1] The painting is said to have been sold by Goupy to his patron, Frederick Prince of Wales, but in all probability it was retained by Goupy since it appeared in his sale in 1765. The frame is undoubtedly the original and, if not chosen by Hamilton before the raffle, it would have been arranged by Goupy afterwards, perhaps with a view to a sale to the Prince of Wales, who was known for his taste in elaborate frames. Whoever had the frame made, the result is exceptionally heavy for a picture of this size: English but in the French manner with strongly modelled centres and corners and of very fine quality despite the later refinishing of the surface.

1. John Kerslake, *Early Georgian Portraits*, 1977, pp.340–2. See also Jacob Simon, 'New Light on Joseph Goupy (1689–1769)', *Apollo*, vol.CXXXIX, February 1994, pp.15–18, and Ilaria Bignamini, 'George Vertue, Art Historian, and Art Institutions in London, 1689–1768', *Walpole Society*, vol.LIV, 1991, pp.29–30.

31 [fig.58]
Alexander Pope (1688–1744)
By Jonathan Richardson, *c.*1737
Oil on canvas, 61.3 × 45.7 (24 1/8 × 18)
NPG 1179

Carved and gilt pine, mitred and keyed, the flat background areas sanded, the incised panels worked in the gesso, the C- and S-scrolls slightly concave and perhaps originally burnished, the frame regilt with consequent loss of detailing, the rebate enlarged at left and right to take a larger picture than the present one. 3 1/2 inches wide.

This remarkable rococo frame with its shell crested top, dominant C- and S-scrolls and sides ornamented with water rushes and rocaille ornament, is a powerful but rather uncomfortable design. The frame might seem to have been carefully chosen to suit the subject, with the leaves of the rushes echoing Alexander Pope's bay wreath; it is, however, not original to the picture, and may date to about 1750.

Very similar to the *Alexander Pope*, but of higher quality, are the frames on a set of five pastels by William Hoare, size twenty-four by seventeen inches, from Ditchley Park, Oxfordshire, sold at Sotheby's, 24 May 1933, lots 48–52, of which the portrait of Sir Watkin Williams Wynn is now in the National Museum of Wales. The pattern may have originated as a de luxe frame for pastels which in the mid-eighteenth century were often given exceptionally rich frames. So unusual is this particular design that the portrait of Pope was once shown at the National Portrait Gallery with its frame upside down, giving it a remarkable top-heaviness.

32 [fig.54]
William Jones (1675–1749)
By William Hogarth, signed and dated 1740
Oil on canvas, 127 × 102.2 (50 × 40 1/4)
NPG 5734

Carved and gilt pine, mitred and keyed, the punching of the ground obscured by regilding. 4 inches wide.

This traditional running pattern of foliage and strapwork with shell-and-leaf sight edge and narrow sanded flat is of a type found on frames of the 1720s and in slightly different form as early as the 1690s. The corners, however, clearly date the frame to the 1740s. The shaped panels, rosettes and pierced foliage scrolls are typical; less usual is the way the scrolls end at the corners in paired outreaching leaves.

Hogarth's portrait of the mathematician, William Jones, was formerly part of the large series of eighteenth-century portraits at Shirburn Castle, Oxfordshire, commissioned by the Earls of Macclesfield. There is nothing to suggest Hogarth's involvement in the framing of the picture and it may be that the 2nd Earl, both Hogarth's and Jones's patron, chose a rather traditional pattern in keeping with his other portraits. Jones's wife, Maria, was the daughter of the leading carver, gilder and framemaker, George Nix, an acquaintance of Macclesfield's, but there is no published evidence to support his involvement in the frame.

33 [figs.153, 188]
Samuel Richardson (1689–1761)
By Joseph Highmore, signed and dated 1750
Oil on canvas, 52.7 × 36.8 (20 3/4 × 14 1/2)
NPG 1036

Carved and gilt pine, mitred and keyed, much regilt, the corner rosettes replaced in 1961 in carton pierre. 3 1/4 inches wide.

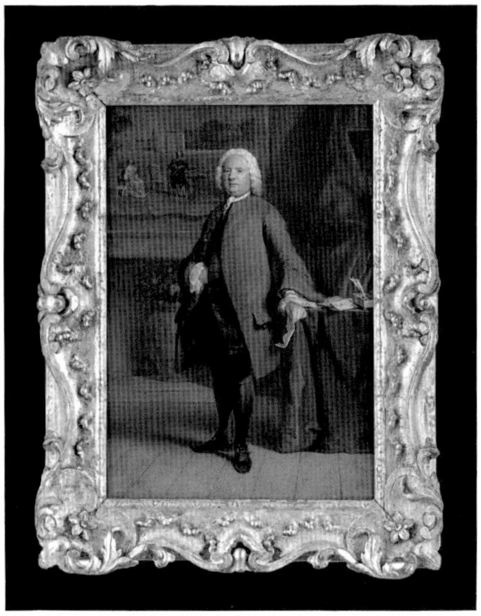

no.33; fig.153

Highmore painted this little portrait of the novelist Samuel Richardson between June and November 1750 for Richardson's admirer, Lady Bradshaigh of Haigh Hall, Lancashire. The frame is a scaled-down version of the sort found on many of Highmore's paintings of the period. In the background of the portrait is a view of Haigh Hall, probably that painted for Richardson in 1750, and perhaps by Highmore himself, framed in the rococo style. In the 1740s and 1750s Highmore used a number of distinctive frame types: the corner pattern found on his *Pamela* series of 1743–4, which recurs on a portrait of the Wyndham brothers of 1743 (Christie's, 14 July 1994, lot 27), and various more rococo patterns such as those found on his portraits of Mrs Iremonger, 1745 (Sotheby's, 18 November 1992, lot 55), Samuel Richardson, 1747 (Worshipful Company of Stationers), and Henry Stebbings, 1757 (National Portrait Gallery). The frame on no.33 has been heavily regilded so that much of the detail of the rocaille ornament and the mouldings has been lost, but conservation work to remove the later regilding was initiated in 1996.

34 [fig.59]
The Court of Chancery in the Reign of George I
By Benjamin Ferrers, *c.*1725
Oil on canvas, 75.6 × 63.2 (29 3/4 × 24 7/8)
NPG 789

Carved and gilt pine, mitred and keyed, the corners planted, fine grade sand on the flat, the oil gilding original and rather friable. 3 3/4 inches wide.

With its ogee section, finely gadrooned top edge, and corners of stylised shells and rosettes set on a sanded ground between C-scrolls overlaid with foliage, this is an English version of a French frame type. The style found favour from about 1745 to 1770 and as such this frame is later than the picture. With its straight sides, the type has been aptly described as 'rococo only at the corners'. Although apparently flowing out of the sides, these corners would have been made separately, as the hair-line cracks in the frame confirm. The pattern was a popular one, and probably was used by several workshops. It is found on various portraits by Allan Ramsay of the period 1747–67,[1] and on the work of Reynolds, Gainsborough and other artists.[2]

1. Jacob Simon, 'Allan Ramsay and picture frames', *Burlington Magazine*, vol.CXXXVI, 1994, p.447.
2. For example, see Nicholas Penny, 'Reynolds and picture frames', *Burlington Magazine*, vol.CXXVIII, 1986, p.822, fig.55.

35 [figs.1, 123]
Alathea Talbot, Countess of Arundel (1590–1654)
By Daniel Mytens, *c.*1618
Oil on canvas, 207 × 127 (81 1/2 × 50)
NPG 5293

Carved and gilt pine with extensive working in the gesso on the sight edge, back edge and the ground, the corners mitred and keyed, the C-scrolls at the centres and corners water gilt over a dark bole as are the concave sweeps and the inner flat fillet. Reduced in size at the quarter points of the frame at top and bottom (unlike the identical frame on the portrait of her husband (NPG 5292) which appears intact). 5 3/4 inches wide.

This portrait of Alathea Talbot, the wife of the collector Earl of Arundel, is doubly interesting: for its rococo frame, possibly the work of Jean Antoine Cuenot, and for the representation of a Jacobean gallery in the background of the picture, perhaps an idealised vision of the gallery of Arundel House on the Strand in London. Hanging in the gallery can be seen fourteen pictures: four full-lengths and two three-quarter lengths in simple black frames with gilt sight edges, a pair of heads in dark brown circular frames and, in the window embrasures, six small pictures in straight-sided gilt frames.

This rococo frame is one of many of the pattern found on family portraits in the collection of the Duke of Norfolk at Arundel Castle, Sussex, and appears to belong to one of the two building campaigns of the 9th Duke of Norfolk: from 1753 to 1756 at Norfolk House in St James's Square and after 1762 at Worksop Manor, Nottinghamshire, when damage caused by a fire was made good.[1] Many of the pictures were subsequently moved to Arundel Castle. At Norfolk House most of the portraits were on the ground floor. The maker responsible for the frames on the first floor, one of the most resplendent sequence of rooms in London, was Jean Antoine Cuenot, a carver of French origins.[2] Cuenot charged, for example, £18.3s.2d for 'carving two picture frames, with heads, shells festoons &c' and another £8.12s for gilding; the frames were for the Red Room, and were apparently larger and richer than the one on this portrait of Lady Arundel.[3] No accounts for frames for the ground floor or for Worksop have been published, but an attribution of no.35 to Cuenot's workshop is feasible.

1. John Martin Robinson, 'Antiquarian Taste at Arundel Castle – III', *Country Life*, vol.CLXXIII, 1983, p.333.
2. Desmond Fitz-Gerald, *The Norfolk House Music Room*, 1973, pp.26–34.
3. A copy of Cuenot's bill is in the Furniture Archive at the Victoria and Albert Museum.

36 [fig.95]
Sir Peter Warren (1703–52)
By Thomas Hudson, *c.*1751–2
Oil on canvas, 135.9 × 132.1 (53 1/2 × 52)
NPG 5158

Carved and gilt pine, mitred, the surface refinished and the sight edge altered. 5 1/4 inches wide.

This frame type was favoured by Thomas Hudson in the 1750s. With its wide, spreading centres and corners, inset cross-hatched panels and swept sides with concave top rail and applied clasps at the pierced mid-points, the style is a somewhat gauche English translation of French frame types of the period. Indeed, Hudson's five-week visit to Paris and the Low Countries in August 1748 may have encouraged him to adopt new frame styles at a time when his chief rival in the London portrait market, Allan Ramsay, had recently introduced a French-inspired frame of his own.[1]

The frame on this portrait of the Louisbourg hero, Admiral Sir Peter Warren, has had its sight edge replaced by a lamb's tongue instead of the more usual gadrooning. It is one of three portraits of the Admiral which Hudson painted in 1751 or 1752 at a total cost of £114.19s, according to a payment made by his widow after his sudden death in July 1752; this sum probably included the frames.[2]

Other portraits by Hudson in this frame type include two three-quarter lengths, *Cornelius Dutch*, 1756 (Apothecaries Hall; frame payment to Hudson), and *Lady Oxenden*, *c.*1756 (Private Collection), the half-length *Unknown Man* (Sotheby's, 3 April 1996, lot 46) and the large *Family of Sir William Courtenay*, 1756 (Powderham Castle). The type was used in a much grander form on Hudson's portrait of Handel (no.37). Somewhat similar frames can be found on seascapes by Hudson's close acquaintance, Samuel Scott. The framemaker who can most closely be associated with Thomas Hudson is Joseph Duffour, a leading carver and gilder of French Catholic extraction. His name occurs in Hudson's bank account in 1751 and again in 1752–3, and he was probably the 'Duffour' paid for repairing the frame of Hudson's *Benn's Club of Aldermen* for the Goldsmiths' Company in 1762.[3]

1. See above, p.94.
2. Information about this payment supplied by Julian Gwyn, 11 October 1977.
3. Hudson's bank account was at Coutts & Co. For the Goldsmiths' picture, see Ellen Miles and Jacob Simon, *Thomas Hudson 1701–1779*, exh.cat., Iveagh Bequest, Kenwood, 1979, no.52. Samuel Scott's large views at Felbrigg may have been framed by Duffour; see *Felbrigg Hall, Norfolk*, guidebook, 1987, p.15. A payment of £25 to 'Duffour' occurs in William Windham II's account book in the Norfolk and Norwich Record Office (information via Alastair Laing).

37 [frontispiece and fig.26]
George Frideric Handel (1685–1759)
By Thomas Hudson, signed and dated 1756
Oil on canvas, 238.8 × 146.1 (94 × 57½)
NPG 3970

Carved and gilt pine, mitred and keyed, much of the surface detail worked in the gesso. At top, violin and bow, tambourine, lyre, three wind instruments and sheet music; at bottom, three bound volumes of music. 7½ inches wide with prominent centres and corners projecting 2½ inches and trophies at top and bottom, projecting 14 inches and 10 inches respectively.

This splendid frame in the rococo style, with its trophies of musical instruments, and scores at top and bottom, was designed for Hudson's full-length picture of Handel, showing the composer in old age. The portrait was painted in 1756 for Charles Jennens, librettist of *Messiah*, a rich man with a taste for ornate rococo interiors. There is, however, no evidence that the frame was designed for a particular location, since the portrait hung first in Jennens's London house and then at Gopsall, his country house in Leicestershire.

The trophy at the top of the frame is based on a French engraving by Jacques Dumont after Jacques François and Marie Blondel, a source which the French carver, Jean Antoine Cuenot, used for the Music Room at Norfolk House, completed the very same year as the Handel frame (this room is now in the Victoria and Albert Museum).[1]

The basic elements of the design are, however, found on a more modest scale on some other Hudson portraits of the 1750s, such as his *Sir Peter Warren* (no.36); these features include the prominent stylised shell centres, the piercing of the sides at the quarter points, the inset panels scored with a mesh of diagonal lines, and the sanded flat next to the gadrooned sight edge. The vocabulary suggests that Hudson's usual framemaker may have been responsible for making the frame to Jennens's order. What evidence there is as to his identity points to Joseph Duffour (see no.36), another carver and gilder of French origin.

1. See Desmond Fitz-Gerald, *The Norfolk House Music Room*, 1973, pl.40. For Cuenot's work for Norfolk House, see also no.35.

38 [fig.29]
William Romaine (1714–95)
By Francis Cotes, signed and dated 1758
Oil on canvas, 124.5 × 99.1 (49 × 39)
NPG 2036

Pressed and gilt papier-mâché on pine, mitred, the sight edge cross-banding worked in the gesso, all the papier-mâché gessoed before gilding, the centre and corner scrolls and inset lozenges originally burnished as revealed by tests, other areas perhaps originally water gilt but largely regilt in oil. 2¾ inches wide (4 inches at the corners).

By the 1750s papier-mâché was beginning to be used more commonly for picture frames, as is discussed above on pp.40–1. This frame of the 1760s is probably not original to Francis Cotes's portrait of the evangelical divine, William Romaine, which appears to have been acquired by the Gallery in another frame.[1] In its damaged state (see fig.29), it is clear that the frame was constructed by applying a layer of papier-mâché to the pine carcass; the papier-mâché was then gessoed and gilded. Though the sight edge twisted ribbon, worked in the gesso rather than papier-mâché, is not unlike that on another Cotes portrait, that of Lord St Vincent (no.47), the main body of the frame is altogether less substantial than most other frames of the period and the lozenge motif set between C-scrolls at the centres and corners seems a rather uncomfortable feature.

1. Francis Draper's bill for repairing the frame of the Romaine portrait on acquisition in 1924 refers to 'making up missing carving on 4¼″ carved corner O.G. frame'.

39 [fig.57]
William Pitt, 1st Earl of Chatham (1708–78)
By William Hoare and studio, 1754 or later
Oil on canvas, 126.4 × 101 (49¾ × 39¾)
NPG 1050

Carved and gilt pine, mitred and keyed, two layers of burnished water gilding over much of the surface, one on a yellow bole, the other plum, and oil gilt on top resulting in much loss of detail; the tops of the foliage carving damaged in various places. 4¼ inches wide, 5¾ inches at centres of sides, 7½ inches at top cresting.

This handsome rococo frame with its bold swept sides, rocaille carving and heavy sculptural centres and corners, is a striking design of the late 1750s or early 1760s. In its boldness and rhythm it is a simplified version of an engraved design published by Lock and Copland in 1752 (fig.56). The type does not appear to have been taken up widely but is found on a small number of portraits of the period including Allan Ramsay's *Sir William Guise* of 1761 (Guise Family), Joshua Reynolds's *Sir Charles Saunders* of 1765 (National Maritime Museum), and, on a smaller scale, Richard Brompton's *Charles Graham* of 1769 (Sotheby's, 10 July 1996, lot 48). Closely related in style is the frame now on the rather later Gainsborough full-length, *Madame Baccelli* (Tate Gallery).

This image of Pitt the Elder is known in several versions by William Hoare or from his studio and may date to 1754 or a few years later. The frame type is quite different from William Hoare's (see no.43) and, if original to the picture, was presumably chosen by the commissioner of the portrait. Unfortunately its history cannot be traced back with confidence earlier than the 2nd Baron Bridport in 1832.

40 [fig.60]
Georgiana Spencer, Duchess of Devonshire (1757–1806)
By Sir Joshua Reynolds, *c.*1761
Oil on canvas, 58.4 × 47 (23 × 18½)
NPG 1041

Carved and gilt pine, mitred and keyed, with working in the gesso as described below. 6 inches wide.

This sketch of the future Duchess of Devonshire and celebrated leader of Whig society as a young girl, was painted in about 1761. The elaborate rococo frame was probably made about the same time but was fitted to the picture by the Gallery in this century, replacing a mid-nineteenth century compo frame visible in an old photograph of the portrait.

This type of French-inspired heavily overloaded rococo frame is not commonly found, but was occasionally favoured for pastels and small portraits because of its richness of effect. In scale and detail the centres and corners are not unlike those on the much larger frame of Hudson's portrait of Handel (no.37), and the back edge is worked in the gesso in an identical manner. The carving, however, is less crisp and the top edge is scored in the gesso with lines and cross bands somewhat in the manner of the sight edge of two contemporary portraits by Francis Cotes (nos.38 and 42). Like them it may have been the work of a Huguenot maker.

41 [fig.61; before cleaning]
Sir Joseph Banks (1743–1820)
By Sir Joshua Reynolds, exhibited 1773
Oil on canvas, 127.3 × 101.9 (50⅛ × 40⅛)
NPG 5868

Carved and gilt pine, mitred, pinned and keyed, the ground punched. 4¼ inches wide. The cleaning and conservation of the frame kindly undertaken by Arnold Wiggins & Sons Ltd, 1996.

Reynolds's portrait of the explorer and botanist, Joseph Banks, was shown at the same Royal Academy exhibition as his double portrait of David Garrick and his wife (no.48), probably in a Maratta frame like the Garrick. The rococo frame now on the portrait was presumably chosen by a descendant of Sir Edward Knatchbull, 8th Bart, Banks's relative by marriage, in whose family the portrait remained until acquired by the Gallery in 1986. The frame probably dates to the 1760s but the coat of arms on the cartouche remains unidentified.[1]

1. The arms have been altered. They are not those of Sir Edward Knatchbull, 8th Bart, nor of his grandson, Lord Brabourne. The portrait can be seen in its present frame at Parham Park, Sussex, in *Country Life*, vol.CIX, 1951, p.1887 (repr.).

42 [fig.62]
Elizabeth Gunning, Duchess of Hamilton and later of Argyll (1734–90)
By Francis Cotes, signed and dated 1751
Pastel, 59.1 × 43.8 (23¼ × 17¼)
NPG 4890

Carved and gilt pine, mitred and keyed, much regilded but traces of burnished water gilding in the hollow behind the acanthus-and-tongue, on the top edge and in the back hollow. 3½ inches wide.

Cotes drew a number of pastel portraits of Elizabeth Gunning and her elder sister, Maria, the most celebrated beauties of the day. These pastels were engraved as a pair and helped to establish Cotes's reputation as a fashionable portraitist. They are found framed in the Maratta style, either as here with the acanthus-and-tongue carvings, or Carlo ornament, as it is also known, in the hollow, or with the ornament on the sight edge of the frame in the Italian manner. Cotes's use of the Maratta to frame his pictures is an indication of the style's growing popularity in the early 1750s. His taste in picture framing is discussed at greater length above on p.93.

This particular frame is densely carved with the acanthus-and-tongue completely filling the hollow and the tongues placed very close to the corners, rather like some other of Cotes's pastels of the period, such as that of Sir Edward Hulse, 1757 (Breamore House). Though undoubtedly the original, the frame on no.42 was replaced in 1972 by one in the rococo style, presumably because it was thought that a Maratta frame was not appropriate to such an early work. The frame has recently been restored to its rightful place.

43 [fig.92]
Alexander Pope (1688–1744)
By William Hoare, 1740 or later
Pastel, 60.7 × 45.1 (23⅞ × 17¾)
NPG 299

Carved and gilt pine, mitred and keyed, the ground extensively cross-hatched, the back edge worked in the gesso in the same manner as the portrait of Handel (no.37). 5 inches wide at the centre.

Hoare's pastel of Alexander Pope is difficult to date securely. The artist first painted Pope in oils in 1740 but produced other versions at a later date to satisfy the considerable demand for Pope's portrait.[1] Whatever the date of the pastel, this frame is a good example of the extravagant rococo frame type of French origin that Hoare used on many of his pastels of the 1750s and 1760s, occasionally on his oils, and even for prints.[2] A very similar frame can be found on François Boucher's oil of 1758, *Madame de Pompadour*, in the Jones collection at the

Victoria and Albert Museum. Hoare also used a Maratta type frame at the same period (see no.44).

At the National Portrait Gallery in 1921 the rococo frame on no.43 was removed from the pastel and swapped for the Maratta frame on John Russell's portrait of R.B. Sheridan.[3] The swap was reversed in 1993 so that once again both portraits are in the original frames chosen by their artists.

1. This portrait type is discussed by W.K. Wimsatt, *The Portraits of Alexander Pope*, New Haven and London, 1965, pp.279–98, and especially pp.287–9. See also John Kerslake, *Early Georgian Portraits*, 1977, pp.214–17. The National Portrait Gallery's portrait bears an inscription on the back by Hoare with the owner's name and the date 1784, but Kerslake suggests that it may have been drawn many years earlier and then kept to hand by Hoare as a model.
2. Examples of the frame type can be found on the pastel of an unknown lady (Victoria and Albert Museum, P.37–1936), a set of pastels of the Four Seasons (Christie's, 19 November 1985, lot 195, repr.), an oil of Mr Vann (Deene Park, photograph in National Portrait Gallery Archive) and a mezzotint of the Earl of Chatham after Hoare (Chevening).
3. National Portrait Gallery Archive, Duplicate of Accounts, vol.VIII, p.128, 'Refitting & pasting up 2 pastels Sheridan and Pope', 17 May 1921. An old photograph provides further evidence as to the framing of the Sheridan pastel before 1921.

44 [fig.93]

Thomas Pelham-Holles, 1st Duke of Newcastle (1693–1768)
By William Hoare, *c.*1752(?)
Pastel, 61 × 45.7 (24 × 18)
NPG 757

Carved and gilt pine, mitred and keyed, 3⅛ inches wide.

This pastel of the celebrated Whig statesman, the Duke of Newcastle, has a Maratta frame of fairly standard type, which can be found on some of Hoare's work of the 1750s and 1760s, including his portrait of Miss Gower in the Victoria and Albert Museum. Hoare later used a Maratta frame with the same motif of the acanthus-and-tongue ornament (but placed on the sight edge rather than in the scoop) for some of his portraits in oils such as that of Christopher Anstey and his daughter of *c.*1775 (National Portrait Gallery, on loan to Beningbrough Hall). For Hoare's taste in frames and his use of Isaac Gosset as framemaker, see above, pp.92–3.

45 [fig.99]

Arthur Young (1741–1820)
By John Russell, signed and dated 1794
Pastel, 61 × 45.5 (24 × 17⅞)
NPG 6253

Carved and gilt pine, mitred and keyed, the spandrels also mitred and keyed, the paterae on the spandrels water gilt lime, the main frame water gilt except for the carved ornament, with leaf overlap, creasing and faulting visible. 3¼ inches wide excluding spandrels.

John Russell, the leading pastel painter of the late eighteenth century, used this simple but elegant frame of Maratta profile for much of his work in the 1780s and 1790s. The National Portrait Gallery owns five pastels by him framed in this style.[1] The ornament is restricted to the pearl sight, the ribbon-and-stick beneath the top edges, and the stylised leaf back edge, with the occasional addition, as in this instance, of sanded spandrels decorated with crisply carved paterae or flowers.

A few of Russell's pastels of the 1770s are found in fluted frames, while his large-scale works of the late 1790s and early 1800s are framed in a heavier Maratta pattern with acanthus-and-tongue on the sight edge rather than in the main hollow. Evidence as to Russell's framemakers is sparse and inconclusive. Although he made a pastel of the carver, gilder and framemaker, Frederick Seaton, around 1790, this may indicate no closer link than a commission for a portrait.[2] In 1793 Solomon Hudson was paid for a pair of rich frames and glasses for Russell's pastels of the Prince of Wales and Mrs Fitzherbert.[3] In 1798 Russell provided a 'frame and glass by Charpentier', presumably Benjamin Charpentier, for a portrait of Mrs Jeans and her children.[4]

1. They are *Henry Venn*, 1787, *R.B. Sheridan*, 1788, *Francis Willis*, 1789, this pastel of Young, 1794, and *Colin Milne*, 1803.
2. Sold Sotheby's, 21 November 1984, lot 49. See also *DEFM*, p.793.
3. Oliver Millar, *The Later Georgian Portraits in the Collection of Her Majesty the Queen*, 1969, p.109.
4. G.C. Williamson, *John Russell*, 1894, p.90.

46 [fig.154]

John Ward (1679?–1758)
By Joseph Samuel Webster, *c.*1755–8
Oil on canvas, 59.7 × 47.7 (23½ × 18¾)
NPG 590

Carved and gilt pine, mitred and keyed. 3¾ inches wide

The frame and tablet are the originals made for the picture. Underneath the beautifully shaped tablet, which retains its original gilding and lettering, the curved moulding out of which the gadrooned sight edge was cut has been deliberately left untouched. In style, the frame, with its distinctive cabochon top edge, is not unlike some eighteenth-century Italian patterns of the Salvator Rosa or Maratta kind.[1]

As the tablet proclaims, John Ward was a Doctor of Law, Professor of Rhetoric at Gresham College, Fellow of the Royal Society and of the Society of Antiquaries and Trustee of the British Museum. The portrait was given to the British Museum on 5 January 1759, less than three months after Ward's death, by his friend and pupil, the 'republican', Thomas Hollis.[2]

As to the maker of the frame, his name is not known unless it be the obscure carver and gilder, Robert Tull, who made 'two frames carvd and Gilt in oile 4 book 21 leaves each' for a Mr Hollis at a cost of £5.5s in July 1756.[3] Tull did subcontract work for Gosset, Jean Antoine

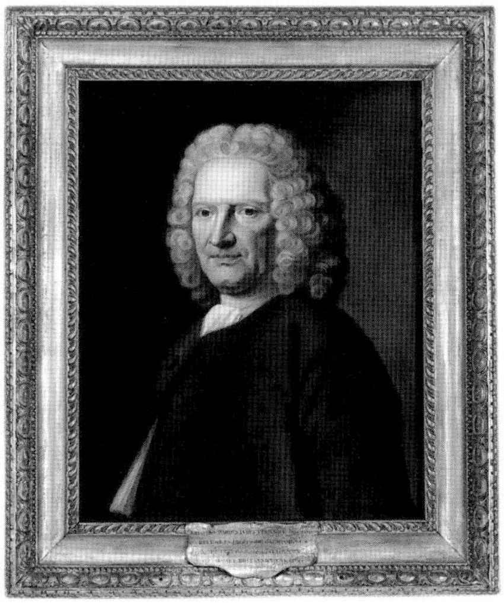

no.46; fig.154

Cuenot and Paul Petit and so is likely to have been a skilled carver. The portrait of Ward has recently been revealed to be by Joseph Webster, an artist almost as obscure as Robert Tull is a carver.[4]

1. See, for example, Paul Mitchell, 'Italian Picture Frames 1500-1825: A Brief Survey', *Furniture History*, vol.XX, 1984, pl.28b. Similar frames can be found on George Stubbs's four scenes of *Gentlemen Shooting* of 1767–70 at the Yale Center for British Art, New Haven.
2. British Museum, Committee Minutes, 1759.
3. Robert Tull's account book, 1753–8, collection of the Hon. Christopher Lennox-Boyd. For Tull, see p.143 above.
4. *Memoirs of Thomas Hollis, Esq*, 1780, vol.I, p.5.

47 [fig.94]

John Jervis, Earl of St Vincent (1735–1823)
By Francis Cotes, signed and dated 1769
Oil on canvas, 125.7 × 100.3 (49½ × 39½)
NPG 2026

Carved and gilt pine, mitred and keyed, the sight edge moulding with cross banding, the mitre leaves and the fluting worked in the gesso, the twisted ribbon-and-stick carved, the egg-and-dart back edge compo, the sight edge, tops of the fluting and the top edge burnished water gilding. 4¼ inches wide.

This distinctive fluted pattern was much used by Francis Cotes in the 1760s, and can be found on many of his oils and some of his pastels.[1] The earliest securely dated example belongs to 1764 but the type may have been in use a year or two before. While the profile is still that of a Maratta frame, the fluting is an early response to the more neo-classical taste which was taken up in framing in the 1760s. Much of the effect of the frame is inexpensively achieved by working in the gesso.

In 1768 Cotes was charging twenty-five guineas for his pastels and three guineas for their frames which he called 'Italian burnished frames'.[2] This description may have applied to this fluted pattern rather than to the Maratta frames (see no.42) which Cotes continued to use.

1. The following are examples of the type (references are to E.M. Johnson, *Francis Cotes*, Oxford, 1976): *Capt. Robert Nicholas*, *c.*1762 (no.110; Montacute), *Eleanor Burdett*, 1764 (no.150; private collection), *Mr and Mrs Crathorne*, 1767 (no.216; Huntington Art Collections, San Marino), and *Mr and Mrs William Welby* (no.287; private collection).
2. Johnson, op.cit., p.84. See also Oliver Millar, *The Later Georgian Portraits in the Collection of Her Majesty the Queen*, 1969, p.21.

48 [fig.96]

David Garrick (1717–79) *and his wife, Eva Maria* (1724–1822)
By Sir Joshua Reynolds, exhibited 1773
Oil on canvas, 140.3 × 169.9 (55¼ × 66⅞)
NPG 5375

Carved and gilt pine, mitred and keyed, the top edge water gilt on the top and right sides but regilt in oil on the bottom and left sides, the Carlo ornament applied to form the sight edge. 5 inches wide.

It is probable that the Maratta frame on this portrait of David Garrick and his wife is the original in which the picture was shown at the Royal Academy in 1773 since the canvas's unusual size makes it unlikely that the frame has subsequently been changed. The picture appears to have been commissioned by Garrick's very good friend, Thomas Fitzmaurice, who was the brother of the future Prime Minister, Lord Shelburne. Garrick wrote to Fitzmaurice on 19 January 1773 claiming to be going to Sir Joshua's 'for the last time', but in the event sittings were taking place as late as 17 April, only a week before the exhibition opened.[1] The frame was probably made in the early months of 1773 but may not have been included in Fitzmaurice's payment to Reynolds of £157.10s, that is 150 guineas, on 17 January 1775. Although Garrick is known for his interest in framing, it was probably Reynolds who chose the Maratta frame, his usual favourite, albeit differing in certain details (such as the placing of the enriched acanthus-and-shell ornament on the sight edge) from the more classic Maratta pattern he used in the same exhibition for his *Ugolino and his Children in the Dungeon*, now at Knole. Reynolds's taste in framing is described above on pp.94ff.

1. David Little and George Kahrl, *The Letters of David Garrick*, 1963, vol.II, p.851, no.739. Royal Academy Library, Reynolds's sitter book, 17 April 1773.

49 [figs.97, 189]

George Stubbs (1724–1806)
Self-portrait, signed and dated 1781
Enamel on Wedgwood plaque, oval, 67.6 × 51.1 (26⅝ × 20⅛)
NPG 4575

Carved and gilt pine, mitred, keyed and pinned, the fluted section fixed to the pine subframe, the back, top and sight edge moulding carved in box or another hardwood and applied, the oil gilding very friable leaving the gesso visible in many places, the working in the gesso at the mitre leaves also visible. 4⅜ inches wide, excluding the spandrels.

The influence of Josiah Wedgwood on Stubbs's choice of this frame style for his enamel paintings on Wedgwood plaques in the early 1780s is apparent from Wedgwood's correspondence with his partner, Thomas Bentley, which is quoted at length on pp.96–7. The type can be found on *Isabella Saltonstall* (Fitzwilliam Museum) and *The Farmer's Wife and the*

Raven (Lady Lever Art Gallery), both plaques of 1782, and in much the same form on *William Anderson with his Two Saddle-horses* (Royal Collection), an oil of 1793. Whether Stubbs used Wedgwood's framemaker, Thomas Vials, is not documented, but subsequently he seems to have used another framemaker, Thomas Allwood, who framed two of his pictures for Sir John Nelthorpe in 1785 and eight for the Prince of Wales in 1793 (the bill being endorsed by Stubbs).[1]

1. For Vials see p.132; for Allwood see *DEFM*, p.11 and Oliver Millar, *The Later Georgian Portraits in the Collection of Her Majesty the Queen*, 1969, p.122.

and the drawing of the actress Elizabeth Farren, Countess of Derby, dated 1787, retain their Downman frames. The pair to the latter, a portrait of Mrs Siddons, is to be reframed with a Downman frame recently acquired for the purpose.

It is possible that Downman used the firm of Foxhall to frame his work. His portrait of Mrs Hugh Watts of 1783 (sold Christie's, 10 July 1990, lot 87) bears the label of 'Foxhall & Sons, Carvers Gilders and Picture Frame Makers, No 19 Cavendish Street'. In 1799 Downman made drawings of Mrs Foxhall and her son (British Museum).

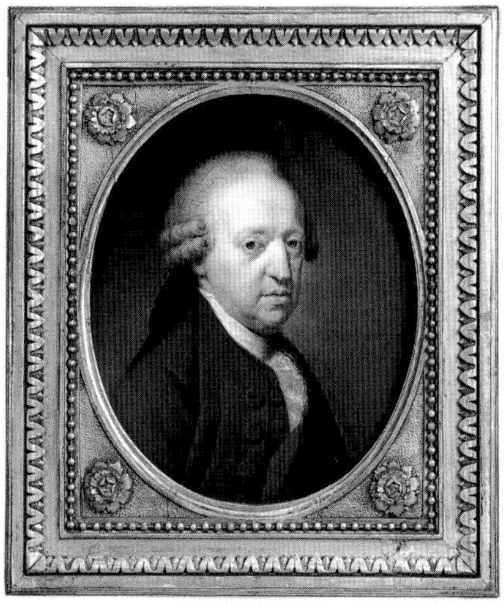

no.51; fig.155

50 [fig.87]

Benjamin West (1738–1820)
By John Downman, signed and dated 1777
Oil on copper, 21.6 × 17.8 (8½ × 7)
NPG 6264

Carved and gilt pine, mitred and pinned, the top edge, the top scoop and the sight-edge beading and tongue burnished water gilding on a plum bole, the oil gilding of the top waterleaf on a yellow base, the spandrels of oak, battens on the reverse on all four sides filling out the rebate, as found on some other Downman frames; the frame aperture marginally wider than the copper panel, hence the modern black slip. 1 5/16 inches wide (2¼ inches including the spandrels at the centre of each side).

John Downman used this distinctive frame pattern for almost all his small portraits from the late 1770s until the mid-1790s and on occasion thereafter until the early 1800s. This oil portrait of Benjamin West, 'my beloved teacher', as Downman described him on one of his studies now in the Fitzwilliam Museum, dates to 1777, some six or seven years after he had left West's studio. It was not with his oils, however, but with pretty, small-scale chalk-and-watercolour portraits, often in profile, that Downman was to make his name in the 1780s.

Of the small Downman portraits in the National Portrait Gallery only this one

51 [fig.155]

Prince Charles Edward Stuart (1720–88)
By Hugh Douglas Hamilton, *c.*1785–6
Oil on canvas, 25.1 × 22.2 (9⅞ × 8¾)
NPG 376

Carved and gilt poplar(?), mitred lap joints with wooden dowels, yellow ochred on the reverse, impression of old, perhaps original, hanging fixture on reverse at top centre, the pine spandrels coated with gesso on reverse. 1⅞ inches wide including spandrel at its narrowest.

The Dublin-born portrait painter, Hugh Douglas Hamilton, used three distinctive frame types for his small-scale oval portraits, each of which can be more or less closely associated with a different period of his life and a different city: London from about 1763 to 1779, Rome from 1779 to 1791 (including a few years in Florence), and Dublin again from 1792.

In London, where he had a very successful business drawing small oval portraits in pastels, he used a gadrooned oval frame with pearl sight, a common enough frame type for such portraits; among numerous dated examples of the early and mid-1770s are portraits of Lady Temple, dated 1770, and Samuel Ireland, dated 1776, in the National Portrait Gallery. By 1778 a husk top edge replaced the gadrooning on some of his frames.

In Italy Hamilton branched out into oil painting and large-scale pastels. Of his small portraits of this period the rectangular frame on this oval-format portrait of Bonnie Prince Charlie is typical: angular teeth inside a flat top edge, and inner spandrels with prominent rosettes on punched panels set within a string-and-pearl surround. This pattern is also found on the portrait of the Prince in the Scottish National Portrait Gallery and on various other Roman portraits by Hamilton, including dated paintings of 1787, 1789 and 1790. Somewhat similar frames are occasionally found on the work of other portrait painters of the period in Rome. A receipt for three frames for the Duchess of Albany suggests that Lorenzo Dolci may have been Hamilton's framemaker in 1785.[1]

In Dublin Hamilton reverted to an oval frame type with a husk top edge and pearl sight for the portraits he drew in 1793 and 1794 before abandoning small pastels altogether for life-size oils.

1. Royal Archives, Windsor, RA SP 510/157, dated 23 September 1785. The receipt is on the reverse of a note by Hamilton: 'Mr Hamiltons Compliments to Mr Stuart, the Bearer of this is the foreman of Sigr Dolci the Carver of the frames intended for the Duchess of Albany – they are very well executed. Friday morn' (quoted by gracious permission of Her Majesty the Queen).

52 [fig.98]
William Paley (1743–1805)
By George Romney, 1789–90
Oil on canvas, 149.9 × 119.4 (59 × 47)
NPG 3659

*Carved and gilt pine, the sub-frame lap jointed as can be seen by the vertical join in the flat frieze, the top mouldings mitred, the scoop water gilt. 5 inches wide. With the label: Saunders,/*CARVER, GILDER,*/ and/*PICTURE-FRAME MAKER*/ №10/ Great Castle Street / Cavendish Square.*

This fine neo-classical pattern is found on many of Romney's works of the late 1780s and early 1790s. It was made by Romney's framemaker, William Saunders, who worked at no.10 Great Castle Street, only a few hundred yards from the artist's studio in Cavendish Square. The frame still bears Saunders's trade label with its distinctive cut corners. The portrait was begun in July 1789 for John Law, a close friend of the sitter, the theological writer, William Paley; it was delivered on 24 January 1791 and so the frame may not have been made until 1790 or early in 1791. It has a ribbon-and-reeded sight edge and ribbed top edge, a type much used on Romney's portraits of the period. Romney's taste in frames and the working relationship between him and his framemakers are described in more detail above on pp.97–8.

53 [fig.64]
Charles Churchill (1731–64)
By J.S.C. Schaak, *c.*1763–4
Oil on canvas, 73 × 62.2 (28¾ × 24½)
NPG 162
Carved and gilt pine, mitred, the top edge perhaps originally water gilt. 2¾ inches wide without later slip.

This neo-classical frame with a large-scale open fretwork guilloche frieze and flat mitre leaves probably dates to the 1770s. It is of a type pioneered by Robert Adam in his designs for the Painted Breakfast Room at Kedleston in 1761. The frame apparently came to the Gallery on a Kneller studio portrait of the actor, Thomas Betterton, acquired in 1886 without provenance, and can be seen on an old glass negative of the picture. The frame has now for many years housed this portrait of the satirist, Charles Churchill, of the 1760s, albeit with the addition of a narrow sight slip.

54 [fig.121]
Mary Granville, Mrs Delany (1700–88)
By John Opie, *c.*1782
Oil on canvas, 74.9 × 62.2 (29½ × 24½)
NPG 1030

Carved and gilt pine, mitred; repaired and partly regilded by Francis Draper in 1896 including a new carved bow; restored by Arnold Wiggins & Sons Ltd, 1961, 1963, including renewal of the inscription on the palette. Much of the top trophy is a restoration based on Walpole's original design. 3¼ inches wide.

Horace Walpole designed this elaborate trophy frame as a memorial to his friend, Mrs Delany, within a few weeks of her death on 15 April 1788. The ornaments of musical instruments, flowers, easel, palette and brushes are emblematic of her accomplishments. The frame is in the French Louis XVI style, with straight sides, flat section and added ornament. It was designed by Walpole for his friend, Mary Wortley Montagu, Countess of Bute, who had commissioned the portrait in 1782.

Quite how the unusual decision was made to reframe the picture so soon after it was painted is not known. A younger member of Walpole's circle of friends, Mary Hamilton, later Mrs Dickenson, appears to have played a part; she had first met Walpole at Mrs Delany's in 1784 and was to become something of a favourite of his. She and her husband dined with him at Strawberry Hill on 13 May 1788, four weeks after Mrs Delany's death, and it was on this occasion that Walpole gave her the memorial inscription he had drafted for the palette on the frame of the portrait (fig.122).[1] Two days later Walpole wrote to her that he had 'had a note from Lady B'.[2] It would be nice to think that this was Lady Bute and that perhaps the scheme for the frame had been conceived on the occasion of the dinner at Strawberry Hill. The sheet with the inscription is annotated at the top by Mrs Dickenson, 'written & given to me by ye Honble Hor: Walpole at Strawberry Hill May 13th 1788' and at the bottom, possibly by another hand, 'The Frame was design'd & the Inscription was written out by the Honble Horace Walpole May 1788'.

The frame was first published by Lady Llanover, Mrs Delany's great-great-niece, in 1862.[3] In her book she reproduces a drawing of the frame which has the appearance of a commissioned illustration. It can hardly be by Walpole as is sometimes claimed. His original design is not known; it was probably in the nature of a sketch which would have been worked up by the framemaker, name unknown, to realise this magnificent memorial to Mrs Delany.

1. W.S. Lewis (ed.), *The Yale Edition of Horace Walpole's Correspondence*, vol.XII, 1944, p.229 for Walpole's visitor book recording the visit of the Dickensons.
2. Lewis, op.cit., vol.XXXI, 1961, p.263, where it is suggested that 'Lady B.' is Lady Browne.
3. Lady Llanover (ed.), *The Autobiography and Correspondence of Mary Granville, Mrs. Delany*, 2nd series, vol.III, 1862, pp.497–8.

55 [fig.66]
John Flaxman (1755–1826)
By Guy Head, 1792
Oil on canvas, 74.3 × 60.3 (29¼ × 23¾)
NPG 877

Carved and gilt pine, mitred and keyed, the top edge laurel leaf and berry set at an angle to continue the line of the curve of the back hollow (in the same manner as Head's portrait of the Duke of Sussex), the back edge finished at the corners with a berry. 4¼ inches wide.

Guy Head's portrait of the sculptor, John Flaxman, was painted in Rome where both artists were long resident. The frame's construction indicates that it was probably made in London rather than Rome, perhaps on Flaxman's return to England in 1794 or on Head's return in 1799. The portrait appeared in the Flaxman sale of 1862. The laurel top frame is a neo-classical type, perhaps of Roman origin, which became widely popular in the 1790s and 1800s for framing portraits and especially old masters. The pattern was used again for another portrait by Head in the National Portrait Gallery, that of the Duke of Sussex of about 1798, but with an additional heavy carved-leaf pattern in the hollow of the frame.

56 [fig.67]

Horatio Nelson, Viscount Nelson (1758–1805) *with a Midshipman*
By Guy Head, 1798–9
Oil on canvas, 223.5 × 169.0 (88 × 66½)
NPG 5101

Gilt compo on pine, mitred and keyed with corner blocks, the frame made in five sections, namely the back edge, the main section including the prominent hollow in which the Carlo ornament is planted, the top edge, the main flat and the sight edge, the flat areas and the hollows originally water gilt on plum bole but regilt in oil, the tooth sight edge applied in 4 or 5 inch lengths, the Carlo ornament in 12⅝ inch lengths. 8 inches wide, 6¼ inches deep.

Guy Head's portrait of Nelson at the Battle of the Nile was painted between Nelson's arrival in Naples in September 1798 and Head's departure for England in May 1799. The portrait was framed in England and given by Nelson to Lady Hamilton, as the apparently original tablet on the frame records.

Two letters written to Emma Hamilton suggest that the frame is likely to have been made by a Mr Brydon, presumably John Brydon, carver, gilder, print seller and looking-glass manufacturer, of no.7 Charing Cross. Nelson himself wrote on 8 February 1801, 'Pray, have you got any picture from Mrs Head's? I hope Mr Brydon has executed the frames to your satisfaction; the bill he is directed to send to me'.[1] This order may not have been completed for some years, perhaps due to Brydon's bankruptcy in June 1801, since a letter from Sir George Rose, Nelson's friend, on 17 November 1805, mentions 'a picture by Mr Head being framed at Brydons'.[2]

In style, the frame, with its heavy ribbon-and-reeded top edge and residual Carlo ornament in the deep hollow, is characteristic of the early years of the nineteenth century. It is an early example of a frame which is both very wide and very deep.

1. Harris Nicolas, *Nelson's Dispatches and Letters*, 1844–6, vol.IV, pp. 284–5.
2. Richard Walker, *Regency Portraits*, 1985, p.360.

57 [fig.65]

George Morland (1763–1804)
By John Raphael Smith, *c.*1792
Oil on canvas, 36.5 × 29.2 (14⅜ × 11½)
NPG 5931

Carved and gilt pine, mitred and pinned, the mitres reopened recently and the old fillets in the mitres removed, the corner ribbons on the top edge replaced, the top reeding and the narrow inner fillet water gilt and burnished, the scoop water gilt but left matt with faulting in the gold leaf visible, the sight edge lamb's tongue oil gilt with crazing revealing a yellow ground. 2¼ inches wide.

Precocious and dissolute, George Morland's career as a draughtsman and painter began early with his first exhibit at the Royal Academy in 1773 at the age of ten and ended with his premature death in 1804 after long spells in a debtors' prison. His name is remembered not only for his genre paintings and picturesque landscapes but also for the 'Morland' frame, though quite whether this familiar neo-classical type, with its ribbon-and-reeded top edge, wide, plain scoop and small-scale sight edge, originated with him is open to investigation.

This portrait of Morland by his friend and drinking companion, the engraver and painter, John Raphael Smith, was probably painted shortly before the exhibition of Morland's paintings held by Smith at his gallery in King Street, Covent Garden, in 1793. The frame has been altered but may still be the original.

58 [fig.69]

Thomas Hope (1770–1831)
By Sir William Beechey, exhibited 1799
Oil on canvas, 221.6 × 168.9 (87¼ × 66½)
NPG 4574

Carved and gilt with compo ornament on pine, mitred with butterfly keys in oak, the guilloche on the top edge set between burnished water-gilt fillets, egg-and-dart next to a similar fillet, the bole red with traces of a dark bole, the main hollow now plain but originally fluted as has been revealed at one corner, the compo acanthus mitre-leaves later, alterations to the back edge at the top perhaps associated with hanging the picture. 4 inches wide plus 1 inch slip.

This is the portrait of Thomas Hope which hung in the staircase hall of his celebrated house in Duchess Street, off Portland Place in London. Hope's pioneering neo-classical interiors and furnishings were the subject of his book, *Household Furniture and Interior Decoration*, published in 1807. The frame was originally fluted, as can be seen from the small area in one corner which has recently been stripped (see fig.69). At some stage in the nineteenth century the fluting was covered with a layer of gesso and strengthening linen tape, applied to give a smooth surface, and the hollow then regilded. The acanthus mitre leaves were added in compo at the same time, perhaps following the pattern of the original leaves which have not been uncovered. The frame has butterfly keys joining the corner mitres at the rear instead of the usual feather keys.

This French Louis XVI frame type, with a fluted hollow and a guilloche set between fillets on the top edge, was popular in England in the 1790s and again in the mid-nineteenth century. Was it Beechey who had Thomas Hope's portrait framed, probably early in 1799, shortly before its exhibition at the Royal Academy? At this stage Hope was yet to begin work on his Duchess Street house. Had the portrait been framed by Hope a few years later, one might have expected him to use a more severe neo-classical style, or even a 'Turkish' frame of the sort he illustrated as the frontispiece to his book, to match the Turkish costume he is wearing in his portrait. Moreover, the existence of a rather similar fluted frame on Beechey's half-length portrait of the Duke of Cumberland suggests that it was probably Beechey who was responsible for proposing the frame pattern for Hope's portrait.[1]

1. The Cumberland portrait is in a private collection; photograph in the National Portrait Gallery Archive. Beechey's framemaker in 1796 may have been G. Steevens; see Farington, *Diary*, pp.522–3, 9, 13 April 1796.

59 [figs.100, 190]
Sir Graham Moore (1764–1843)
By Sir Thomas Lawrence, exhibited 1792
Oil on canvas, 74.9 × 63.5 (29½ × 25)
NPG 1129

Carved and gilt pine, mitred and keyed. 5 inches wide.

An example of the hand-carved Maratta frames Lawrence was using in the 1790s, discussed in more detail above on p.99. The frame bears two labels, the one fixed to it when the portrait was sent to the Royal Academy exhibition in 1792, giving details of the picture, the other a damaged and largely illegible framemaker's label of the period. The portrait came to the Gallery with that of Sir Graham's brother, General Sir John Moore, likewise painted by Lawrence, but in the early 1800s and framed in the heavy style of the period exemplified by the artist's portrait of Lord Castlereagh (no.60).

60 [fig.101]
Robert Stewart, 2nd Marquess of Londonderry (Lord Castlereagh) (1769–1822)
By Sir Thomas Lawrence, 1809–10
Oil on canvas, 74.3 × 61.1 (29¼ × 24¼)
NPG 891

Gilt compo on pine, mitred and keyed, the ornament covered in bronze powder except in the hollow, the sight slip and back edge water gilt as probably are the other flat surfaces and possibly the gadroons. 5½ inches wide.

This compo version of a carved pattern popular in France in the late eighteenth century was widely used by Lawrence in the 1800s, as is discussed in more detail above on pp.99–100.

61 [fig.102]
George IV (1762–1830)
By Sir Thomas Lawrence, *c.*1814
Oil on canvas, 91.4 × 71.1 (36 × 28)
NPG 123

Gilt compo on pine, mitred with corner blocks, the inner section nailed in and fitted with blocks, the ground punched but much of the detail lost in regilding, the flat fillets water gilt (the leaf overlap clearly visible at the top), all the projecting centres and corners repaired, shrinkage in the frieze visible along the left side. 7½ inches wide.

An example of the compo frame type favoured by Lawrence in the 1810s, discussed in more detail above on p.100.

62 [fig.103]
George Canning (1770–1827)
By Sir Thomas Lawrence, 1825
Oil on canvas, 238.1 × 147.3 (93¾ × 54)
NPG 1832

Gilt compo on pine, mitred with corner blocks, the sight slip water gilt. 11 inches wide including slip.

The classic Lawrence frame of the 1820s on this portrait of the Foreign Secretary, George Canning, was probably made by George Morant, whose label is found on the almost identical frame on Lawrence's portrait of the Prime Minister, Lord Liverpool (National Portrait Gallery, on loan to the National Gallery). Both portraits formed part of Sir Robert Peel's gallery of statesmen, discussed on p.116; see also no.69. Lawrence's attitude to picture framing in the 1820s is discussed in detail above on pp.100–2.

63 [figs.68, 191]
Thomas Phillips (1770–1845)
Self-portrait, 1802 or 1803
Oil on canvas, 73.7 × 61 (29 × 24)
NPG 1601

Gilt compo on pine, mitred and keyed, the back of the frame with a chamfered outer edge; the rebate enlarged at the bottom, cutting into the keys (since the rebate is too large for the picture, the enlargement probably indicates that the frame was intended for another picture initially). 5 inches wide.

During his long career as a portrait painter Thomas Phillips used a limited range of frame types. Although close parallels can be drawn with Thomas Lawrence's frames, Phillips's own styles are quite distinctive and the frame on this self-portrait is more finely detailed than Lawrence's nearest equivalent (no.60). Very similar frames can be found on Phillips's *Lord Thurlow*, 1807 (Palace of Westminster), and on his *2nd Duke of Northumberland*, 1800 (Petworth), the latter with heavier corners in the Lawrence style. In one guise or another Phillips continued to use this type of frame for his portraits until the early 1810s.

Documentation relating to Phillips and framing is scarce but a letter of Lord Erskine's, instructing the artist to match the frames on portraits of Thurlow and Northumberland, versions of the portraits mentioned above, shows how one of Phillips's better patrons expected the artist to deal with matters of framing.[1]

1. A transcript of the Erskine letter, made by George Scharf, is in the National Portrait Gallery Archive.

64 [fig.105]

John Dalton (1766–1844)
By Thomas Phillips, signed and dated 1835
Oil on canvas, 91.4 × 71.4 (36 × 28⅛)
NPG 5963

Gilt compo on pine, mitred with corner blocks, the sharpness of the punched ground reduced by regilding. 6¼ inches wide including slip.

In the 1810s Thomas Phillips moved away from his early frame style (see no.63) to a much heavier, richer pattern in the manner of Lawrence's *George IV* (no.61). Phillips used this style, with slight variations, for the rest of his life as the many frames of the pattern in the National Portrait Gallery testify. Closest to Lawrence are the frames with prominent centres of shells and foliage set on a chequered ground as found, for example, at the National Portrait Gallery on Phillips's 1821 portrait of Sir Humphrey Davy and on other works of the 1810s and early 1820s. At the same time Phillips was using a similar pattern, but without centres, as on his portrait of Sir Francis Chantrey of 1818. The Chantrey frame is very like the one on this portrait of John Dalton of 1835 and other portraits of the late 1820s and 1830s where the Regency scroll-and-foliage pattern has been extended to fill the sides. A further variant, found on his portrait of Sir Francis Burdett of 1834 and other portraits of the 1830s and early 1840s, has slightly heavier corners. But while each of these types can be distinguished by their corner ornament, these are but variations on a theme established by Lawrence in the 1810s.

65 [fig.106]

Frederick, Duke of York (1763–1827)
By Sir David Wilkie, signed and dated 1823
Oil on panel, 59.1 × 52.1 (23¼ × 20½)
NPG 2936

Gilt compo on pine, mitred and probably pinned, the frame apparently made in three sections with the sight edge section pinned and rebated into the central section, oil gilt on a pale ground visible at various old damages, the gilding largely original except on the sight edge and at old repairs, the top of the coronet missing above the Garter ribbon. 5¾ inches wide including slip.

Wilkie's portrait of the Duke of York, a commission from General Sir Willoughby Gordon, was not finished until 1823 when it was exhibited at the Royal Academy. This frame, with its rather restrained centre and corner motifs and the all-over small-scale compo ornamentation, is of the type favoured by Wilkie in the 1820s and 1830s, discussed above on pp.102–3. To take two examples, both his *Chelsea Pensioners reading the Waterloo Despatch* of 1822 (Apsley House) and his late portrait of William IV of 1837 (National Portrait Gallery, on loan to Bodelwyddan Castle) have frames which, although differing in detail, conform to this taste. Wilkie used a number of framemakers including Benjamin Charpentier and David Ross in the early years of his career, Thomas Macdonald from *c.*1813–22,[1] and Francis Collins in the late 1820s.[2]

1. See H.A.D. Miles, *Fourteen Small Pictures by Wilkie*, exh.cat., The Fine Art Society Ltd, London, 1994, p.20. See also H.A.D. Miles and D.B. Brown, *Sir David Wilkie of Scotland (1785–1841)*, exh.cat., North Carolina Museum of Art, Raleigh, 1987, nos.17, 18, 20; see also no.13 where Wilkie refers to a 'flat French frame' made by Charpentier in a letter of 1811 to Sir George Beaumont.
2. See Oliver Millar, *The Later Georgian Portraits in the Collection of Her Majesty the Queen*, 1969, pp.137–42.

66 [fig.70]

Sir George Hayter (1792–1871)
Self-portrait, signed and dated 1820
Oil on mahogany, 51.4 × 52.1 (20¼ × 20½)
NPG 3104

Carved and gilt oak, mitred and keyed, the rebate enlarged at left and top and bottom; the veining of the sweeps and other fine surface details tooled in a thick coat of gesso in the traditional manner; heavily regilt and varnished but traces of water gilding are visible over a black bole, e.g. on the wavy high point of the sight edge. There are three holes vertically aligned in the back of the frame at top centre, perhaps originally used to hang the picture. 5¾ inches wide.

This fantastically encrusted carved French rococo frame is representative of the fashion in the Regency period for framing old masters and other pictures in elaborate French eighteenth-century frames. It is very similar to the more finely carved frame on Denys Calvaert's *Mystic Marriage of St Catherine* at Stourhead in Wiltshire, a French Louis XV frame of the 1740s or 1750s.[1] Like other French frames of the period it is made of oak. The arched top is of a sort fashionable in the eighteenth century for framing Dutch old masters.[2]

George Hayter painted this self-portrait on an old marbled board. The portrait at left and right does not cover the whole board but only extends as far as the frame sight edge, suggesting that Hayter may have painted it with this frame in mind. The use of such an extraordinary frame for an artist's self-portrait indicates that Hayter was something of a francophile. He had visited Paris in 1815 and was to work there for some years in the late 1820s.

1. Reproduced in *Country Life*, vol. CLXXXVIII, 8 September 1994, p.66, fig.4.
2. I owe this observation to Alastair Laing.

67 [fig.156]

Edward Littleton, 1st Baron Hatherton (1791–1863)
By Sir George Hayter, signed and dated 1834
Oil on millboard, 35.6 × 30.5 (14 × 12)
NPG 4658

Gilt compo on pine, mitred with butterfly keys. 3½ inches wide. With label, partly damaged: ...ment to Her Ma..../ Queen Adelaide & HRH the ..../W.THOMAS,/CARVER & GILDER,/ HOUSE AND ORNAMENTAL PAINTER,/ PAPER HANGER, DECORATOR &C./39, London Street, Fitzroy Square,/Workmen sent to any part of the kingdom.

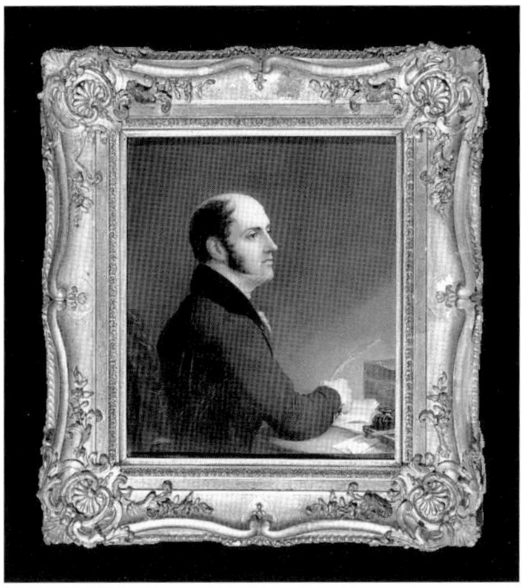

no.67; fig.156

This sketch, one of Hayter's studies for his large picture now in the National Portrait Gallery of the 1833 Reformed House of Commons, was framed by William Thomas, framemaker to Queen Victoria, probably between 1837 and 1851 judging from the text of Thomas's label on the back of the frame. There is no uniform framing style for Hayter's House of Commons sketches, suggesting that many of them may have been framed by their first owners. The Gallery owns a finished Hayter portrait of the same period, that of Thomas Waghorn, differently framed but with the identical Thomas label on the frame. Hayter would have come across Thomas in the course of his work for Queen Victoria but whether this framemaker worked for him personally remains to be established.

The construction of this frame is unusual, with butterfly keys used to join the mitres. The same feature is found on another William Thomas frame, that made for the portrait of J.G. Lockhart (Scottish National Portrait Gallery) by Francis Grant, another artist with links to Thomas (see no.72).

68 [figs.31, 32, 192]
Mary Shelley (1797–1851)
By Richard Rothwell, exhibited 1840
Oil on canvas, 76.2 × 63.0 (30 × 24¾)
NPG 1235

Gilt papier-mâché ornament on a pine framework with corner fillets. 6¼ inches wide plus replacement inner slip of 1⅛ inches. Probably acquired from the framemaker, R. Aldworth, Bournemouth, whose label is found on the other Shelley family portraits.

A papier-mâché frame made by Charles Frederick Bielefeld, the leading manufacturer of frames and ornament in papier-mâché in the first half of the nineteenth century.[1] The backs of the scroll leaves are stamped 'CF BIELEFELD London' (see fig. 32). This frame appears as pattern no.1117 in one of Bielefeld's published catalogues of papier-mâché ornament. The priced copy in the Victoria and Albert Museum, probably a working copy used by the firm, costs the main pierced foliage ornament at 1s.3d a foot, the large corner flowers at 1s each and the other ornaments at from 2d to 6d a foot.[2] The cost of the Mary Shelley frame would therefore have worked out very competitively at about £1.9s.9d for the ornament.

Mary Shelley, author of *Frankenstein* and wife of Percy Bysshe Shelley, was the daughter of the philosopher, William Godwin, and the author, Mary Wollstonecraft. Mary Shelley's portrait, together with earlier portraits of her parents, also in the National Portrait Gallery, were reframed in almost identical papier-mâché frames, probably for Mary's son, Sir Percy Shelley, who built the Shelley shrine, 'The Sanctum', at Boscombe Manor near Bournemouth in 1849.[3]

1. For Bielefeld see pp.43–4, 137. Papier-mâché frames by Bielefeld can also be found on Samuel Laurence's *Charles Babbage*, dated 1845 (National Portrait Gallery), and William Etty's *Britomart Redeems Faire Amoret* of *c.*1833 (Sotheby's, 9 June 1994, lot 178).
2. Victoria and Albert Museum, Print Room, E.166-1987, pressmark 95.C.104.
3. The portrait of William Godwin was lent to the 1868 National Portrait Exhibition in its present frame but that of Mary Shelley does not appear to have received its matching frame until later. See the photographs taken in 1868, in the Victoria and Albert Museum, Picture Library, Guardbook, nos.8290, 8260.

69 [figs.125, 193]
Edward Law, 1st Earl of Ellenborough (1790–1871)
By Frederick Richard Say, *c.*1846
Oil on canvas, 142.2 × 111.8 (56 × 44)
NPG 1805

Gilt compo on pine, mitred and pinned with corner blocks, the flat fillets and back scoop water gilt, the ogee sides with running arabesque foliage on a cross-hatched ground, large formalised shell corners and a plain flat as sight edge, with original lettering, THE EARL OF ELLENBOROUGH, BY SAY. *9 inches wide.*

To house his remarkable collection of portraits of his political contemporaries, the Tory Prime Minister, Sir Robert Peel, added a new gallery to his home, Drayton Manor in Staffordshire, to the design of Sydney Smirke. Two years later in 1847 the *Gentleman's Magazine* called the fifty portraits in the gallery, 'the matchless collection of portraits of eminent statesmen and men of celebrity in literature and the arts and sciences'.[1]

Peel's portrait collection – he was also a collector of old masters – was founded in the 1820s while he was serving in Lord Liverpool's administration as Home Secretary. He commissioned Sir Thomas Lawrence to paint full-lengths of both Liverpool and his Foreign Secretary, George Canning (both National Portrait Gallery; see no.62).

Peel's taste both in portraits and in frames seems to have settled on the Lawrence style. He used 'Sir Thos Lawrence's pattern' for framing a picture by Sir Joshua Reynolds in 1828.[2] When he resumed his portrait collection in the 1840s, he wrote of continuing 'the series of Eminent Men of my own time ... commenced by Sir Thomas Lawrence', and specifically requested John Lucas in 1843 to give Gladstone's portrait 'such a background as is in Sir Thomas Lawrence's portrait of Lord Liverpool'.[3]

Peel's other portrait painter of the 1840s was F.R. Say, who painted six portraits for him including those in the

National Portrait Gallery of Lord Ellenborough, Lord Derby and the Duke of Newcastle. Peel arranged his own framing, probably through his adviser John Seguier, ordering frames for portraits by Say from the framemaker Robert Thick on 21 August 1845, 11 December 1846 and 2 August 1848. This portrait of the First Lord of the Admiralty, Lord Ellenborough, was probably part of the 1846 order.[4] Peel adopted a uniform, straight-sided frame in the Lawrence manner for his portraits by both Say and Lucas (indeed 'Lawrence pattern frames' was the term used when the National Portrait Gallery's framemaker charged for undertaking repairs in 1919). Most of the frames were inscribed in capitals with the sitter's and artist's name along the bottom flat.

1. *Gentleman's Magazine*, vol.XXVII, 1847, p.289.
2. The picture was framed by John Smith; see Smith Day Book, vol.2, p.54 (Victoria and Albert Museum Library, 86.CC.2). Peel was also using Lawrence's framemaker, George Morant, for framing at this time, see Surrey Record Office, Goulburn Papers, letter from Geo. Morant & Son to Peel, 18 November 1828.
3. British Library, Peel papers, Add. MS. 40,536, ff.138–40.
4. Robert Thick, order ledger. The ledger belongs to the Duke of Wellington who kindly made it available for study. For Peel and John Seguier, see above, pp.116.

70 [fig.124]
Robert Vernon (1774–1849)
By George Jones and Henry Collen, inscribed and dated on reverse 1848
Oil on mahogany, 76.3 × 62.6 (30 × 24⅝)
NPG 4513

Gilt compo on pine. 4½ inches wide.

This portrait is the joint work of the miniaturist, Henry Collen, and the painter, George Jones, Keeper of the Royal Academy, who claimed to be Robert Vernon's chief adviser in forming his collection of modern British pictures, more than 150 of which he gave to the National Gallery in 1847. These are now mostly in the Tate Gallery. Constable, Turner, Wilkie, Etty and Mulready were among the artists Vernon patronised. His collection has been discussed in greater detail in Chapter 5.[1]

1. See pp.115–16. See also Robin Hamlyn, *Robert Vernon's Gift. British Art for the Nation 1847*, exh.cat., Tate Gallery, 1993.

71 [fig.74]
Lucie, Lady Duff-Gordon (1821–69)
By Henry Wyndham Phillips, 1851
Oil on canvas, 91.7 × 71.1 (36⅛ × 28)
NPG 5584

Gilt compo on pine, mitred and pinned with corner blocks, the sight slip and the inner and outer hollows water gilt, the outer one burnished, the inner one perhaps regilt in oil on a yellow ground. 5¾ inches including ½ inch slip.

Henry Wyndham Phillips painted this portrait of his close friend, the author Lady Duff-Gordon, as a gift to her husband while he was convalescing at their home. His frame style is in marked contrast to the massive frames favoured by his father, Thomas Phillips (see no.64). Running leaf-and-berry patterns of late seventeenth-century origins were particularly popular in the mid-nineteenth century, often as here with a very open pattern of leaves and an added sight slip. A similar frame can be found on H.W. Phillips's portrait of David Livingstone, painted in 1857 (Private Collection).

72 [fig.107]
George Bingham, 3rd Earl of Lucan (1800–88)
By Sir Francis Grant, 1855
Oil on canvas, 224.8 × 132.7 (88½ × 52¼)
NPG 6338

Gilt compo on pine, mitred and pinned with corner blocks, the top section planted on the base frame, the slip and the inner fillet water gilt on a dark grey bole, the S-scrolls at the corners and perhaps some of the strapwork originally burnished. 6 inches wide plus 1⅜ inches slip. On the back, two identical labels: By Appointment to Her Majesty the Queen./H.R.H. The Duchess of Kent [Royal coat of arms] & the Royal Family. /W.THOMAS./CARVER & GILDER,/HOUSE AND ORNAMENTAL PAINTER. /PAPER HANGER, DECORATOR &C./29, BERNERS STREET, OXFORD STREET,/(FROM 39, LONDON ST^{T} FITZROY SQUARE.) / *Workmen sent to any Part of the Kingdom.*

It was Lord Lucan who issued the order for the celebrated charge of the Light Brigade at Balaclava in 1854, so the appearance of Sir Francis Grant's portrait at the Royal Academy in 1856 stirred up bitter memories of failure.

In his long and successful career as an establishment portrait painter, which included the positions of President of the Royal Academy and Trustee of the National Portrait Gallery, Grant favoured a variety of frame types:

- a large-scale running pattern set in C-scrolls with centres and corners of baroque character, in use from at least 1844 to 1862, of which the frame on the 1857 full-length of John Nayler (Walker Art Gallery, Liverpool) is representative.

- the type represented here by *Lord Lucan*, current from at least 1850 to 1855, a Régence revival pattern but fussier and less bold in character than its French forerunners.

- a more classical frame found on his smaller portraits, with fluted hollow, acanthus mitre leaves and a narrow ribbon-tied laurel top edge, current from at least 1852 to 1862. In the National Portrait Gallery's collection the sketches of Sir Edwin Landseer, 1852, and Lord Macartney, 1853, have frames of this type. The type was widely used by other artists, for example by Sir George Reid (see no.89).

- most common of all, current from at least 1853 to 1873, a classical type of Maratta section but with a small cushion of overlapping leaves and berries next to the sight edge. Of this type, the National Portrait Gallery owns full-lengths of Lord

Russell, 1853, and James Grant, brother of the artist, *c.*1861, as well as a portrait of Sir Walter Scott by J.S. Gilbert which Grant had framed for the Gallery in 1867.

The frame on the Gallery's portrait of Lord Lucan was made by Grant's framemaker, William Thomas, a leading mid-nineteenth century maker with several royal appointments.

73 [fig.157]

Thomas Macaulay, 1st Baron Macaulay (1800–59)
By Edward Matthew Ward, 1853
Oil on canvas, 63.5 × 76.2 (25 × 30)
NPG 4882

Gilt compo on pine, mitred, pinned and with corner blocks, the slip with matt water gilding, the inner fillet burnished on a black and red bole, the plain top edge moulding on a red bole, the frieze finely sanded but badly crazed, the leaves of the cushion on a milky ground with the intervening husks on a warm ground. 4 inches wide plus $1\frac{3}{8}$ inch slip. With the label of Agnew's, Manchester, Liverpool and London (there is no trace of a Criswick & Dolman label).

This portrait of the historian, Thomas Macaulay, in his study in the Albany, Piccadilly, is one of a series of portraits of writers in their studies painted by E.M. Ward in the 1850s. The frame appears to be slightly later than the picture for it is recorded as having had the label of Criswick & Dolman, a leading framing partnership which lasted from about 1862 to 1876.[1] The frame perhaps was made for the 1868 National Portrait Exhibition at South Kensington. With its wide sight slip, sanded frieze and a main cushion ornamented with a classical leaf motif the frame appears to match the one shown in an old photograph of Ward's companion portrait of William Thackeray, painted in 1854, which has since been destroyed..

1. Richard Ormond, *Early Victorian Portraits*, 1973, p.568. For Criswick & Dolman, see above, p.133.

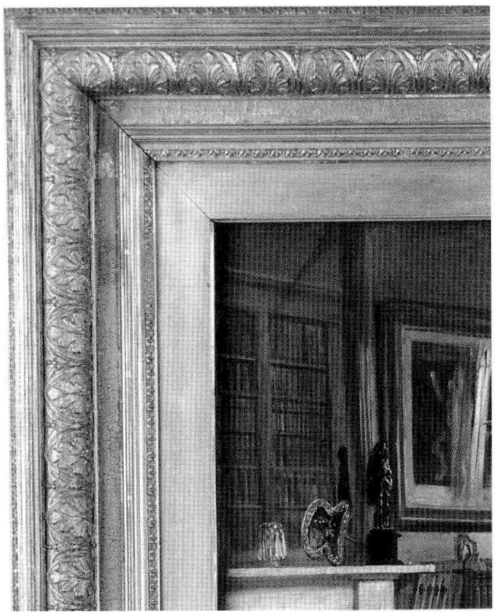

no.73; fig.157

74 [fig.158]

Sir Francis Grant (1803–78)
By John Ballantyne, signed and dated 1866
Oil on canvas, 71.1 × 92.1 (28 × $36\frac{1}{4}$)
NPG 5239

Gilt compo on pine, mitred and pinned, the small hollows on either side of the laurel-leaf top edge and next to the sight-edge ornament burnished on a red bole, the drying cracks in the compo clearly visible on the top edge and elsewhere. 4 inches wide plus $1\frac{1}{4}$ inch slip.

The Scottish artist, John Ballantyne, painted a series of pictures of artists in their studios between 1862 and 1867.[1] Most of them were exhibited at the Royal Scottish Academy in Edinburgh or at Henry Graves & Co. in London. They were probably framed in London where Ballantyne had settled in, or soon after, 1860. This portrait of Sir Francis Grant, President of the Royal Academy, is particularly richly framed in a laurel-leaf top frame with wide curving sides decorated with little flowers set within a diamond mesh of interlacing strapwork. It is identical to the frame on the portrait of David Roberts from the same series.[2]

1. See Richard Ormond, 'Artists in their Studios', *Christie's Review of the Season 1979*, 1979, pp.72–5. Two other portraits from the series belong to the National Portrait Gallery; *William Holman Hunt* has an unusual black ripple frame and *Sir Edwin Landseer* a gilt fluted frame of a type also found on the portrait of Erskine Nicol (Christie's, 7 June 1996, lot 642). Four of the series are at the Scottish National Portrait Gallery of which the portrait of Sir Noel Paton has a laurel-leaf top frame which is otherwise plain while the others have later plain gilt frames (information from Stephen Lloyd).
2. Exhibited at Graves 1865–6, according to Ormond, and recently exhibited at the Fine Art Society, *Spring '96*, 1996, no.3, repr. without frame.

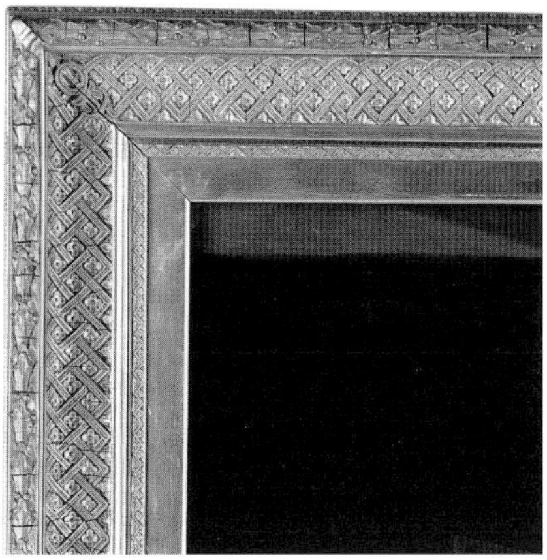

no.74; fig.158

75 [fig.73]

The Relief of Lucknow
By Thomas Jones Barker, signed and dated 1859
Oil on canvas, 105.4 × 181.3 ($41\frac{1}{2}$ × $71\frac{3}{8}$)
NPG 5851

Gilt compo on pine, mitred and pinned with triangular corner blocks, a diagonal pattern of strapwork and florettes in the scoop, Moresque ornament on the top and back edges, the two inner semi-circular fillets and the corner bosses burnished, the frame heavily restored on acquisition in 1985. $6\frac{3}{4}$ inches wide plus $1\frac{7}{8}$ inch slip.

The little-known Victorian history painter, Thomas Jones Barker, had a taste for elaborate frames, witness his *Spanish Officers surrendering Swords to Nelson* (Government Art Collection, on loan to the Admiralty) and *The Secret of England's Greatness* (no.76).

Some of his paintings were widely exhibited to promote the sale of the related engravings and for this purpose a spectacular frame was deemed necessary.

This picture of the relief of Lucknow, a key event in the Indian Mutiny of 1857, is appropriately housed in a frame decorated with trophies of flags and cannons. These were either modelled or cast in compo. If the trophies were removed, one would be left with a frame of Alhambra type (see no.78) with a scoop finished in a diaper pattern not unlike that of the frame on John Ballantyne's *Sir Francis Grant* (no.74).

76 [fig.72]

The Secret of England's Greatness

By Thomas Jones Barker, signed, *c*.1863

Oil on canvas, 167.6 × 213.8 (66 × 84$^{1}/_{8}$)

NPG 4969

Gilt compo on pine, mitred with corner blocks, much of the surface covered in bronze paint. 9½ inches wide. With the label (see fig.138): CRISWICK & DOLMAN, / Glass & Picture Frame Manufacturers, / AND / DECORATORS, / 6, New Compton Street, Soho. / THE TRADE SUPPLIED IN EVERY DEPARTMENT. / PICTURES REMOVED, PACKED, CLEANED, RESTORED AND WAREHOUSED. / Established 1818.

This scene of Queen Victoria presenting a Bible to a man wearing African dress was framed by Criswick & Dolman, who entered into partnership in 1862. The picture was exhibited to acclaim in Belfast in 1864, presumably as part of a wider tour, and engraved the same year as *The Bible: The Secret of England's Greatness*.

The broad sloping cushion of the frame, with a diaper pattern of gothic quatrefoils, contrasts with the inner frieze of intricate foliage and acorns, the former device a mid-nineteenth century style pioneered by J.R. Herbert, Pugin's protégé, for his medieval and biblical subjects, the latter Regency in origin, and exemplified in Thomas Lawrence's frames of the period (see fig.102).

77 [fig.8]

Charles Dickens (1812–70)

By Ary Scheffer, signed and dated 1855

Oil on canvas, 94.3 × 62.9 (37$^{1}/_{8}$ × 24$^{3}/_{4}$)

NPG 315

Gilt compo and gesso on an unidentified softwood, mitred, keyed, pinned and with corner blocks, adapted at the front by insertion of a removable glazed door, the back edge decoration in compo, the fine reeding of the main hollow combed in the gesso presumably in lengths before cutting and assembly, the back hollow and the top edge water gilt, the top edge on a red bole, and regilt in oil. 5 inches wide plus 1$^{1}/_{8}$ inches later slip.

Dickens sat to the Dutch-born painter, Ary Scheffer, in Paris in the winter of 1855–6. The frame of his portrait is an unusual one with fine horizontal banding on the curved sides, but from its similarity to frames on other Scheffers, and from the evidence of Dickens's correspondence, it has every appearance of having been chosen by Scheffer.[1] Dickens wrote to his old friend, the artist Daniel Maclise, from Paris on 6 February 1856 to ascertain the Royal Academy's regulations as to the width of the frame allowed.[2] The picture duly appeared at the Academy exhibition which opened on 5 May that year.

Scheffer's interest in frames remains to be explored in detail but his liking for heavy, elaborate styles is evident from views of his studio and from the surviving frames.[3] His portrait of Mrs Robert Hollond, one of his many British patrons, now in the collection of the National Gallery, has a broad frame ornamented with a series of neo-classical architectural motifs. In contrast the frame on *Charles Dickens* is rather simple and in its use of horizontal banding calls to mind Whistler's reeded frames of the 1870s.[4]

1. Similar frames can be found in the collection of the Dordrechts Museum on three works by Scheffer: *Sketch for 'The Bronze Age'*, 1852, *Margaretha* (part of a copy of *Margaretha at the Spinning Wheel*, 1831) and *Euterpe*. I am grateful to P.J.M. Deuss for supplying photographs of these frames. The three paintings came to the museum as a bequest from the artist's daughter, Cornelia, in 1899.
2. See above, p.20.
3. *Ary Scheffer 1795–1858*, exh. cat. with introductory essay by L.J.I. Ewals, Institut Néerlandais, Paris, 1980, pp.4–5; see also pp.107, 111. See also Anne-Marie de Brem, *L'atelier d' Ary Scheffer*, exh.cat., Musée de la vie romantique, 1991, p.9.
4. A somewhat similar frame can be found on George Inness's *Delaware Water Gap* (National Gallery), exhibited at the Royal Academy in 1859.

78 [fig.71]

Charles Kingsley (1819–75)

By Lowes Cato Dickinson, initialled and dated 1862

Oil on canvas, 91.2 × 91.2 (35$^{7}/_{8}$ × 35$^{7}/_{8}$)

NPG 2525

Gilt compo on pine, mitred at back, pinned and with corner blocks, traces of burnished water gilding on the sight edge beading, other traces of water gilding on the sight edge and top edge obscured by later regilding in oil, the front face of the frame also regilt more than once with a lacquer filling the crevices, the ornament of the spandrels attached to ⅓ inch thick pine board covered in linen and gessoed on the rear surface for stability. With the later label of A.W. Johnson, Gilder, Picture Frame Maker. Probably first regilt by Johnson in the 1880s or 1890s; repaired and regilt by Rowley, 1932, and subsequently by L.M. Helsen. 5¼ inches wide (including 1 inch flat), 15 inches wide diagonally into the corner.

The Moresque ornament in the spandrels of this spectacular Alhambra frame is very similar to some of the decorative details from the Alhambra at Granada published by Owen Jones in both *The Grammar of Ornament* of 1856 and in his earlier book devoted to the Alhambra.[1] The frame houses a portrait of the novelist and Christian Socialist, Charles Kingsley, commissioned by his publisher, Alexander Macmillan, from Lowes Cato Dickinson to join the painter's half-length portraits of F.D. Maurice and Tom Hughes who, like Kingsley and Dickinson, were also Christian Socialists.

Dickinson attempted an ambitious

composition for the Kingsley ('I really painted so much more important a picture', he told Macmillan, 'from the feeling that the subject deserved it').[2] In August 1863 Dickinson wrote to Macmillan offering him the portrait at the reduced price of seventy-five guineas 'not of course including the frame'. The portrait had just come from the Summer Exhibition at the Royal Academy and must therefore already have had a frame, almost certainly the present one. Some of Dickinson's other work of the period is framed in the Alhambra style, including one of the versions of his portrait of F.D. Maurice, painted in 1858, and his portrait of Lord Russell, completed in 1867.[3] By the 1870s Dickinson was using fluted frames like George Richmond's but with a richer leaf top edge; his frames of this period, again like Richmond's, were made by James Henry Chance.

1. Pascual de Gayangos, *Plans, elevations, sections and details of the Alhambra. From drawings by J. Goury, & Owen Jones*, 2 vols, 1842, 1845, published by Owen Jones.
2. This and subsequent quotations come from the Macmillan papers, British Library, Add. MS. 55, 253, ff.46, 50, letters of 6 and 10 August 1863.
3. The portrait of F.D. Maurice, not the Macmillan version, was in the collection of Revd D.B. Maurice. The portrait of Russell is in the National Portrait Gallery.

79 [fig.76]

Dame Ellen Terry (1847–1928)
By George Frederic Watts, *c.*1864
Oil on canvas, 48 × 35.2 (18⁷⁄₈ × 13⁷⁄₈)
NPG 5048

Gilt compo on pine, standard Watts frame construction with the inner and outer mouldings made separately from the middle flat frieze, the outer section mitred and pinned, the middle section keyed and originally fixed by nails to the outer moulding, the frieze gessoed, apparently water gilt in a lemon gold, punched and perhaps subsequently sized. 6¼ inches wide.

The characteristics and popularity of the Watts frame are described above on pp.73–4. The frame on Watts's portrait of his first wife, Ellen Terry, is one of the very earliest of the type and is exceptionally wide in relation to the size of the portrait; like his contemporary self-portrait and his portrait of Tennyson, both in the Tate Gallery, it is decorated with a punched leaf pattern. Rossetti used this type for *The Beloved*, 1865–6, and *Monna Vanna*, 1866, also both in the Tate Gallery, and Ford Madox Brown later termed it a 'Venetian' pattern when adopting it for his portrait of Henry Fawcett and his wife (no.82). In fact the frame is more akin to Emilian *cassetta* frames of the early seventeenth century, such as that found on Oswald Birley's portrait of George V (no.116).

80 [figs.77, 194]

Matthew Arnold (1822–88)
By George Frederic Watts, 1880
Oil on canvas, 66 × 52.1 (26 × 20½)
NPG 1000

Gilt compo on pine, standard Watts frame construction with the flat central frieze section fitted by nails to the inner and outer mouldings, the outer section mitred, the frieze of veneered oak on pine with butt joints, the gilding directly onto oak prepared with a warm-toned size. 6¼ inches wide. With the label printed in red including the image of a vase with plant and two birds, and the royal coat of arms: W.A. Smith, / Carver and Gilder, / Printseller & Publisher, / Restorer of Works of Art, / 20–22, MORTIMER ST., / REGENT ST., LONDON, W., / AND AT / VICTORIA ST. NOTTINGHAM.

This classic Watts frame with gilding applied directly onto the oak, in the manner commended by Charles Eastlake,[1] is found on all the Watts portraits in his 'Hall of Fame', his series of portraits of his illustrious contemporaries, some forty of which he gave to the National Portrait Gallery. The artist used the style for most of his other works (see fig.86). The Watts frame as a standard Victorian frame type is discussed more fully above on pp.73–4.

Watts used Joseph Green for framing his early work and stayed with Green's successor, William Augustine Smith, when the business changed hands in the early 1870s.[2] This portrait of Matthew Arnold bears Smith's distinctive framemaker's label. Watts was in the habit of using the nearest frame to hand so that the Arnold frame is not necessarily that in which the portrait was exhibited at the Royal Academy in 1881. When Watts gave the 'Hall of Fame' pictures to the National Portrait Gallery in 1895, he told the Director, Sir Lionel Cust, 'you will do what seems best about the frames.... If you do change the frames of any I should like the inappropriate frames back'. The Gallery, however, kept Watts's frames and had two Watts pattern frames made by Francis Draper for the portraits of Tennyson and Sir Henry Taylor, which had come in plain wooden frames.[3]

1. See above, p.46.
2. The work of both Green and Smith is discussed above on p.134. Smith was described by Watts's widow in 1912 as 'The head of the firm of carvers and gilders ... who gave Signor [i.e. Watts] service for sixty years' (*George Frederic Watts*, vol.I, 1912, p.329) and by George Williamson in 1898 as 'a somewhat illiterate maw ... in the Masters confidence' (letter to Spielmann, 11 February 1898, Watts Gallery Archive; I am grateful to Richard Jefferies for providing a copy). The business became Smith & Uppard in 1889 and was acquired by James Bourlet & Sons in 1899. Subsequently E.J. Uppard appears to have traded separately; Watts's *Three Heads* (Fitzwilliam Museum, no.1761) bears Uppard's label, with the date 1906. Watts also used a framemaker by the name of Lamm who is mentioned in his correspondence in 1899 and 1903.
3. National Portrait Gallery, Press Copy Book, no.1, p.282, letter of 6 December 1895.

81 [fig.159]

Stephen Lushington (1782–1873)
By William Holman Hunt, signed and dated 1862
Oil on canvas, 81.9 × 64.8 (32¼ × 25½)
NPG 1646

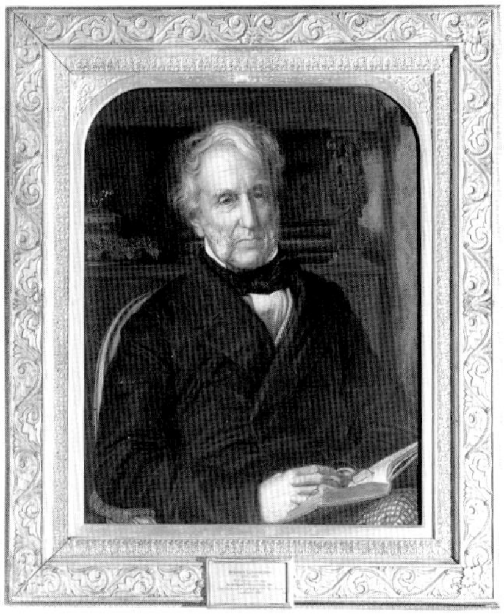

no.81; fig.159

Gilt compo on pine, mitred, arched top. 4¾ inches plus ¾ inch slip.

This portrait of the lawyer and reformer, Stephen Lushington, was commissioned in 1862 by his son, Vernon, a friend of Holman Hunt. It has a most distinctive frame which closely matches one made for the National Gallery in 1858 by Eliza and C. Foord to take two recently acquired panels, *Christ* and *The Virgin*, after Quentin Massys.[1]

The appearance of the Massys frame is intriguing. The National Gallery's Director, Sir Charles Eastlake, was closely involved in its choice for he wrote to the Keeper, Ralph Wornum, on 9 November 1857, 'I will see about a design for the frame – for the two should be in one frame'. It would seem likely that the pattern originated with Eastlake, or a member of his wide circle of acquaintances, rather than with Foord's the framemaker.

As to the frame on the portrait of Lushington, it was probably made by Foord & Dickinson, as the firm became known, since the similarities in profile and ornament with the National Gallery frame, even down to the use of an arched top, are so great as to make it unlikely that any other maker was involved. In design the frame has sufficient elements in common with Holman Hunt's own frames and frame drawings to make one ask if he could have been involved. At the very least he must have been aware of Lushington's choice of frame since the portrait was exhibited at the Royal Academy in 1863. Hunt may have directed his friend to Foord's, whom he was using to frame some of his own work.[2] The question remains as to whether Hunt actively approved of the design for he took a very strong interest in the framing of his pictures.

1. I am most grateful to Sarah Perry and David Carter for examining the National Gallery records on my behalf. The frame cost ten guineas; see the payment order to Eliza and C. Foord dated 1 March 1858.
2. A payment of twenty-five guineas to Foord & Co. appears in Hunt's bank account on 28 February 1861. Information from Judith Bronkhurst who has kindly corresponded with me over a period of time about this frame. In her opinion Hunt did not design it himself, but she points out similarities to Hunt's frame designs, including one in Birmingham Museum and Art Gallery (1985 P 86).

82 [fig.110]

Henry Fawcett (1833–84) *and Dame Millicent Fawcett* (1847–1929)
By Ford Madox Brown, signed and dated 1872
Oil on canvas, 108.6 × 83.8 (42¾ × 33)
NPG 1603

Gilt pine with compo mouldings, apparently of standard Watts construction. 6 inches wide.

This portrait of the blind political economist, Henry Fawcett, and his wife was commissioned by the politician, Sir Charles Dilke. On 2 July 1872, when it was nearing completion, Ford Madox Brown wrote to his patron about the frame, 'The time approaches when I shall want the frame for the Fawcett's picture; will you allow me to order it? I am particular as to the frames for my pictures & there is a Venecian pattern (much liked now by friends of mine for works of this description) – to be had at Messrs Green & Co 14 Charles St Middlesex Hospital. Should you have any particular taste for your own frames please let me know'.[1] Later Brown wrote to Sir Charles to inform him that the bill for the frame would be sent to him direct, which suggests that Brown's patron had left the choice of frame to him.

This Watts frame with its enriched flat is presumably the Venetian pattern 'to be had of Messrs Green', the framing business of Joseph Green who did so much work for the Pre-Raphaelites. It is a pattern used earlier by Watts himself (see no.79) and by Rossetti (the chief of the 'friends' to whom Brown refers in his letter).

1. British Library, Add. MS. 43,909, ff.281, 289–90.

83 [fig.109]

Christina Rossetti (1830–94) *with her mother, Frances Rossetti* (1800–86)
By Dante Gabriel Rossetti, 1877
Coloured chalks, 42.5 × 48.3 (16¾ × 19)
NPG 990

Gilt oak, reeded oak top section with inset corner squares, set on a pine carcass visible at the bevels, mitred and pinned, the back edge veneered in oak, the gilding directly onto oak prepared with a warm-toned size. 1¾ inches wide.

In addition to his 'thumb-mark' pattern and a Watts frame with a punched leaf frieze (see no.79), Rossetti's other favourite frame style of the 1860s was a reeded moulding with inset squares and roundels at intervals along the sides and at the corners, as described on p.105. In this small chalk of his mother and sister of 1877, the insets are restricted to squares at the corners. The picture, which is in a gold-bevelled green mount, copying the original, can be seen in Treffry Dunn's view of Rossetti's sitting-room at Cheyne Walk (fig.108). Similar frames are found on Rossetti's other chalks of the same date including the portrait of his mother (Birmingham City Museum and Art Gallery) and that of Christina Rossetti (Private Collection).

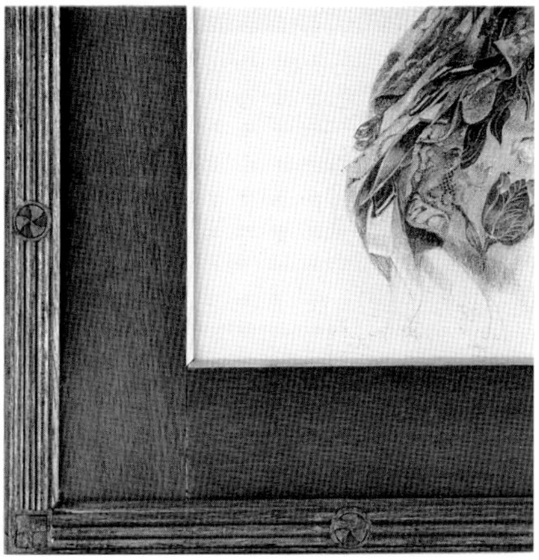

no.84; fig.160

84 [fig.160]

Margaret Oliphant (1828–97)
By Frederick Sandys, signed and dated 1881
Chalk on blue paper, 69.2 × 56.8 ($27^{1/4} \times 22^{3/8}$)
NPG 5391

Gilt oak, the reeded oak top edge, with circles cut in and squares applied, and the oak veneer on the back edge planted on a lap-jointed pine carcass, the inner flat oak-veneered with a bevelled gilt sight edge. 1⅝ inches wide, plus inner flat 4 inches wide. With the label: FOORD & DICKINSON,/Carvers & Gilders./129, ~~90~~ Wardour Street, W./DRAWINGS MOUNTED./PICTURES CLEANED AND RESTORED.

Frederick Sandys is best known for his highly finished portrait drawings. He studied under George Richmond and Samuel Laurence (see nos.85, 87) but it was the work of Dante Gabriel Rossetti (see no.83) which most influenced his style. This portrait of the prolific Scottish-born writer, Margaret Oliphant, has a standard Sandys frame which very closely follows the style pioneered by Rossetti in the 1860s but with the substitution of a plain oak flat for the gilt oak which Rossetti preferred.

Sandys's usual framemaker from about 1868 was Foord & Dickinson, also used by Rossetti. Some of Sandys's early Norwich pictures were framed by Boswell of Norwich from 1858 to 1870. After 1900 Sandys went to Foord's successor in business, George Minns & Co.[1] In 1903, the year before his death, he wrote to Ernest Brown of the Leicester Galleries about the framing of a portrait of Brown's daughter, Helen: 'I think the frame you name the Rossetti would be the best for the drawing – in oak – such as I generally use – with some of the mouldings gilded. I sometimes have the frame made without the circles and pateras. I am not sure it is not better and it is cheaper ... Minns 65 Berwick Street is the best man ...'.[2]

1. I am most grateful to Betty Elzea for information on Sandys's framemakers, which she has compiled in preparation for her catalogue raisonné.
2. Betty Elzea drew my attention to this letter, which is in the collection of Professor Toshiyuki Takamiya.

85 [fig.161]

Granville Leveson-Gower, 2nd Earl Granville (1815–91)
By George Richmond, 1876
Chalk on paper, 56.9 × 44.5 ($22^{3/8} \times 17^{1/2}$)
NPG 4900

Gilt pine, mitred and pinned, the surface detail worked in the gesso, water gilt (the leaf overlaps can be seen especially on the bottom side of the frame), mostly matt gilding on a red bole but the C-scrolls at the corners and the borders to the side panels burnished on a black bole. 3¼ inches wide with original stepped slip. Inscribed on the back in pencil: 35020, and with the label: J.H. CHANCE,/CARVER, GILDER AND/PRINT SELLER,/28, London Street,/FITZROY SQUARE,/Pictures cleaned & Restored./DRAWINGS MOUNTED/And COPIED IN PHOTOGRAPHY.

George Richmond was as well known in his day for his large portrait drawings in chalk, with their distinctive frames, as for his oil paintings. The frame on this portrait of the Liberal statesman, Lord Granville, is of the type Richmond used from the mid-1840s until he ceased making drawings of this kind in the late 1870s. The National Portrait Gallery has fifteen Richmonds in these frames. The scroll and leaf details and the cross-hatched corners are worked in the gesso, rather like some Italian seventeenth-century frames, the scrolls here being water gilt and burnished for effect in contrast to the matt water gilding of the ground.

Richmond's frames were usually made by his friend, James Henry Chance, whose label can often be found on his work.[1] This frame type was also occasionally used for the drawings of Alessandro Ossani and Lowes Cato Dickinson, both artists for whom Chance made frames.[2] It is also found in an undecorated version with the same ogee profile on some of the Richmonds bought by the National Portrait Gallery after Richmond's death and framed by Chance.

1. For Chance, see above, p.135. A few of Richmond's drawings were framed by Joseph Hogarth including his *John Bird Sumner*, *c.*1849 (NPG 2467), which has a frame with more elaborately incised corners than those made by Chance.
2. For example, *Frances Bodenham* by Ossani, 1890 (NPG 5586A), and *Jane Forster* by Dickinson (private collection, photograph in NPG Archive).

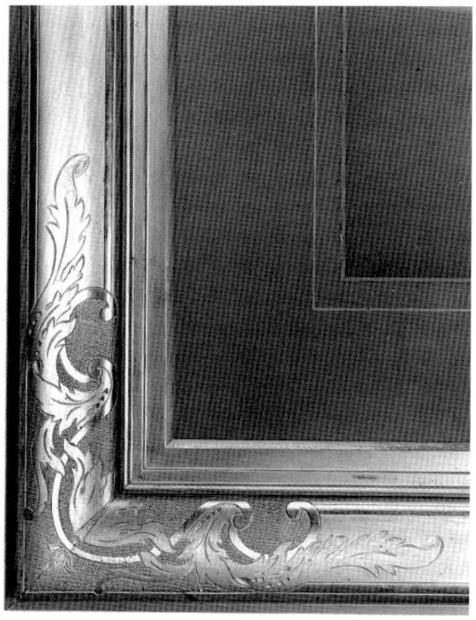

no.85; fig.161

86 [fig.75]

Charles Wood, 1st Viscount Halifax (1800–85)
By Anthony de Brie after George Richmond, *c.*1912
Oil on canvas, 91.4 × 70.2 (36 × $27\frac{5}{8}$)
NPG 1677

Gilt compo on pine, mitred and pinned with triangular corner blocks, the frieze section fixed by centre and corner blocks to the outer raised section, the hollow between the outer section and the frieze burnished as are the sight edge beads. $5\frac{1}{2}$ inches wide plus $\frac{3}{4}$ inch slip. With the label: CHAPMAN BROS. / Carvers, Gilders & Frame Makers. / 241, King's Road, / (Opposite Carlyle Square.) / LONDON, S.W. / N.B. ESTIMATES GIVEN FOR DECORATIVE GILDING. / TELEPHONE Nº 823 WESTERN. / TELEGRAMS, "FRAMBLE, LONDON."

This portrait of the Liberal statesman, Lord Halifax, is a posthumous copy by Anthony de Brie of George Richmond's original of 1873 at Oriel College, Oxford. It was framed by Chapman Bros, the Chelsea framemakers, in a renaissance-style frame, rather like those favoured by Richmond himself for his oil portraits but with a richer top and sight edge and a more open frieze. Examples of Richmond's frames, made by his framemaker, J.H. Chance, can be found on the large full-length of the Lord Chancellor, Lord Hatherley, 1872 (National Portrait Gallery, on loan to the Law Courts), and on the smaller portrait of Mrs W.F. Robinson, 1870 (Fitzwilliam Museum, Cambridge). For Richmond's frames, see also no.85.

87 [fig.78]

Anthony Trollope (1815–82)
By Samuel Laurence, *c.*1864
Oil on canvas, 59.7 × 50.2 ($23\frac{1}{2}$ × $19\frac{3}{4}$)
NPG 1680

Gilt compo on pine, standard Watts frame construction (see no.80), except for the use of keys in the frieze, the gilding of the oak in very good condition. $6\frac{1}{4}$ inches wide.

The portrait painter Samuel Laurence, best known for his work in chalk, used Watts frames for some of his oil portraits but with the gilt oak flats cut with fluting, perhaps in a search for a novel but inexpensive frame type. A fluted frame can serve to focus the eye on the portrait but here the fluting is primarily decorative, and the fussiness of the frame seems to distract attention both from the portrait and from the grain of the frame's oak flats.

Three portraits by Laurence using this frame style have been traced so far: this one of Anthony Trollope, probably of 1864, but perhaps kept by the artist and framed later, *F.D. Maurice* of *c.*1871 (National Portrait Gallery, on loan to King's College, London) and *William Bodham Donne* (London Library).

88 [fig.162]

Robert Gascoyne-Cecil, 3rd Marquess of Salisbury (1830–1903)
By Sir John Everett Millais, signed, 1883
Oil on canvas, 127.3 × 93.3 ($50\frac{1}{8}$ × $36\frac{3}{4}$)
NPG 3242

Gilt compo on pine, standard Watts frame construction (see no.80). 6 inches wide.

W.H. Smith, the founder of the firm of newsagents, took office in Disraeli's cabinet in 1877 as First Lord of the Admiralty. Between 1881 and his death in 1891 Smith acquired a series of portraits of his political colleagues in the Conservative party, commencing with the purchase of Millais's portrait of Disraeli himself from the Royal Academy in 1881. This was followed by Herkomer's *Lord Cross*, 1882, Edwin Long's *Lord Iddesleigh*, 1882, this portrait of Lord Salisbury by Millais, 1883, W.W. Ouless's *Duke of Rutland*, 1886 (with a frame made by James Bourlet), and apparently also Alma-Tadema's *Lord Balfour*, 1891. All these portraits, which were the same size, formerly hung at Smith's London home in Grosvenor Place. All have Watts frames,

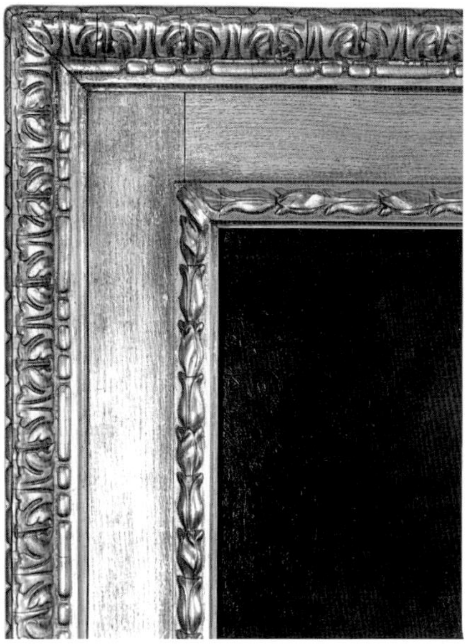

no.88; fig.162

presumably following the example set by Millais with his portrait of Disraeli (it can be seen in a Watts frame in W.P. Frith's view of the Great Room at the Academy in 1881, where it was added to the exhibition at Queen Victoria's request and hung on an easel). The Watts frame was common enough for portraits and was regularly used by Millais in the 1870s and 1880s. It was, however, a less obvious choice for artists such as Herkomer and Alma-Tadema, and this suggests that these frames were chosen by Smith to match those on Millais's portraits. Smith's son, Lord Hambleden, added two portraits by Arthur Cope to the series, *Lord Knutsford* and *Lord St Aldwyn*, in 1906, but these were differently framed.

89 [fig.112]

James Froude (1818–94)
By Sir George Reid, signed and dated 1881
Oil on canvas, 34.6 × 23.5 ($13\frac{5}{8}$ × $9\frac{1}{4}$)
NPG 4990

Gilt compo on pine, mitred and pinned, the appearance of fluting achieved by tooling the gesso, the stepped inner sight mouldings fixed with screws to the main frame, the gilding in original condition except for some regilding of the flat areas, the corner ribbons, fluting and fillet burnished on a plum bole with a further coat of black bole, the sight edge on a red bole. 4⅜ inches wide.

George Reid, the leading Scottish portraitist, landscape painter and illustrator, worked extensively in his native Aberdeen, in Edinburgh, and occasionally in London. Reid had most of his portraits framed in one of four standard styles, all of very high quality:

- an enriched fluted pattern of French origin, used from at least 1881 to 1892, with laurel leaf top and wide acanthus leaves at the mitres, of which this portrait of the historian and writer, James Froude, is a good example. Other examples are *Sir Henry Frere*, 1881, in the National Portrait Gallery, and *Dr John Brown*, 1881, and *Prof. J.S. Blackie*, *c.*1892, both in the Scottish National Portrait Gallery. The type is also found on some of Francis Grant's work (see no.72).

- an enriched leaf pattern, in use from at least 1881 to 1894, with elaborate laurel leaf top, rich ogee leaf sides, a row of pearls and a sanded flat, for example the *William Skene* of 1888 in the Scottish National Portrait Gallery with a frame made by John Kesson of Aberdeen.

- a Watts frame, with a flat husk sight, used on Reid's head sketches in the 1890s, including portraits of Samuel Smiles in the Scottish National Portrait Gallery and the National Portrait Gallery, the former with the framemaker's label of John Kesson, the latter with that of Kesson & MacDonald of Aberdeen.

- a Maratta frame of very high quality, used on commissioned and presentation portraits in the early 1900s, of which the portrait of the scientist, Sir Oliver Lodge (no.90), is typical.

90 [fig.24]
Sir Oliver Lodge (1851–1940)
By Sir George Reid, signed, *c.*1907
Oil on canvas, 73.7 × 55.9 (29 × 22)
NPG 3952

Carved and gilt pine, mitred with triangular corner blocks; the frame made of two sections, one for the top edge complete with compo egg-and-dart back edge and carved ribbon-and-stick, the other for the scoop and sight edge with oil gilt tongue-and-leaf planted in the highly burnished scoop which is water gilt on a dark bole. 6 inches wide including original slip.

This frame is finished to a high standard with burnished gold in the hollow and may perhaps have been made by the Edinburgh firm, Aitken Dott, whose label occurs on the almost identical frame of *Lord Kinross* (Scottish National Portrait Gallery). For Reid's taste in framing, see no.89.

91 [fig.111]
Sir William Schwenk Gilbert (1836–1911)
By Frank Holl, signed and dated 1886
Oil on canvas, 100.3 × 125.7 (39½ × 49½)
NPG 2911

Gilt pine, mitred and pinned with corner blocks, water gilt on a red bole, except for the oil gilt arabesque frieze and guilloche back edge in compo. 6½ inches wide plus 1 inch slip.

Frank Holl made his name in the 1870s with his dramatic social realist scenes. It was, however, his successful practice as a portrait painter which earned him enough money to build his own house in Hampstead to Norman Shaw's design. Holl often gave his larger portraits a substantial frame decorated with a flat frieze of renaissance-style arabesques set between a heavy reeded top edge and a roll moulding sight edge, as exemplified by the frame on this portrait of Gilbert (of Gilbert and Sullivan fame). There is an identical frame on the portrait of the judge, Sir J.W. Huddlestone, of 1888 (National Portrait Gallery, on loan to the Law Courts), and a similar frame on the portrait of the 3rd Lord de Tabley at Tabley House. Holl also used a distinctive Watts frame for some of his portraits (see fig.89).

92 [fig.113]
Horatio Kitchener, 1st Earl Kitchener of Khartoum (1850–1916)
By Sir Hubert von Herkomer, signed and dated 1890
Oil on canvas, 139.7 × 109.2 (55 × 43)
NPG 1782

Gilt oak, mitred, the main hollow, the back hollow and the planted reeded top edge in solid oak, the back frame in pine with carrying hand holes, oil gilding direct onto the oak allowing the grain of the oak to show through, the oak apparently sealed with a warm-toned size. 6¼ inches wide plus 1½ inch slip.

The Bavarian-born painter Hubert von Herkomer, son of a woodcarver, spent almost all his life in England, achieving great esteem as a graphic artist, subject painter and portraitist. It is not uncommon to find a successful portrait painter using more than one frame style but there can be no more marked contrast than between the two portrait frame types chosen by Herkomer: the one a massive unadorned scoop frame in solid oak with reeded top edge and sight edge, used by the artist with slight variations from 1887 to 1902, and the other a much lighter and narrower compo frame which has as its chief ornament a cushion decorated with large twisting leaves, without corner motifs, a style found on Herkomer's portraits from 1903 to 1913.

In 1885 Herkomer brought back from the USA plans for a monumental new house, Lululand, which was constructed on a site near Bushey in Hertfordshire with special fittings produced by his wood-carving relatives. His solid oak frames may have been influenced by his American experience and in any case are consistent with his interest in using the finest timbers. In addition to this portrait of Kitchener of 1890, the National Portrait Gallery owns seven other portraits by Herkomer framed in this style. The Gallery owns two works framed in the later cushion style, the portrait of Lord Baden-Powell, with a metal-leaf finish (no.93), and that of Admiral Lord Fisher of 1911, a gilt frame with surmounting coronet.

The limited evidence as to Herkomer's framemaker suggests that like Alma-Tadema (see no.94) he used R. Dolman & Son to frame some of his pictures, including *The Last Muster: Sunday at the Royal Hospital, Chelsea* of 1875 (Lady Lever Art Gallery, Port Sunlight) and the portrait of Sir George Goldie of 1898 (National Portrait Gallery). On the latter the label in red reads: 'This frame can be repeated at any time quoting the number 30.886 R. Dolman & Co. 6 New Compton St, Soho London W.C.'

93 [fig.114]

Robert Baden-Powell, 1st Baron Baden-Powell (1857–1941)
By Sir Hubert von Herkomer, signed and dated 1903
Oil on canvas, 141.9 × 112.1 ($55\frac{7}{8} \times 44\frac{1}{8}$)
NPG 5991

Compo on pine, mitred and pinned, finished in a lacquered Dutch or similar metal leaf on a deep red ground, the compo uncracked and so perhaps resin based. $4\frac{1}{8}$ inches wide plus later slip.

See no.92.

94 [fig.163]

Alfred Waterhouse (1830–1905)
By Sir Lawrence Alma-Tadema, signed, 1891
Oil on canvas, 66.5 × 53.6 ($26\frac{1}{4} \times 21\frac{1}{8}$)
NPG 6213

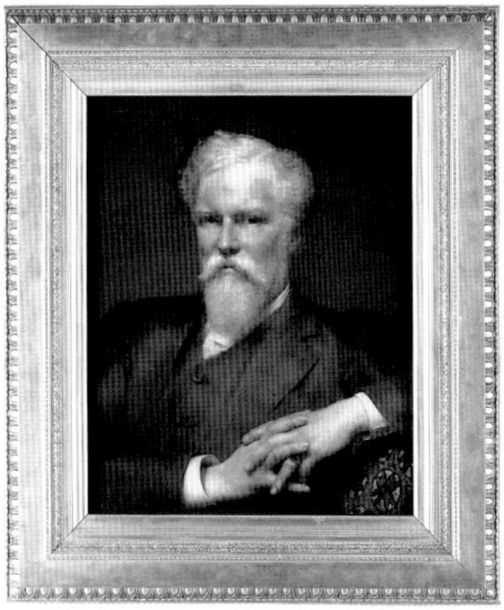

no.94; fig.163

Gilt pine, the ornament in compo, mitred, a wooden batten $1\frac{3}{4}$ inches thick planted to form the sloping back edge, the flat surfaces and the curved sight edge with matt water gilding on a warm bole. $5\frac{1}{2}$ inches wide. With the label printed in red: Dolman at New Compton Street 24697 *[the number added by hand to the label and frame].*

The frame on Alma-Tadema's portrait of his friend, Alfred Waterhouse, President of the Royal Institute of British Architects, was made by Alma-Tadema's framemaker, R. Dolman & Son, a firm which the artist had recommended to the National Gallery in 1880.[1] It is much plainer than the elaborate frames chosen by the artist for his imaginary Roman and Greek scenes, and in its use of a wide flat surface as the dominant element is more comparable to some of Lord Leighton's frames of the 1860s and 1870s.[2]

1. See p.133.
2. For a more detailed discussion of Alma-Tadema's frames, see Lynn Roberts, 'Nineteenth Century English Picture Frames, II: The Victorian High Renaissance', *International Journal of Museum Management and Curatorship*, vol.V, 1986, pp.275–8.

95 [figs.164, 195]

Sir Francis Seymour Haden (1818–1910)
By George Jacomb-Hood, signed and dated 1892
Oil on canvas, 74.3 × 50.2 ($29\frac{1}{4} \times 19\frac{3}{4}$)
NPG 1826

Pine base with an applied pine cushion ornamented with a frieze of overlapping oak leaves and acorns in compo, oil gilt except for water gilt inner flat, the base mitred and pinned. $3\frac{1}{2}$ inches wide including $\frac{3}{4}$ inch inner flat.

The last twenty years of the nineteenth century saw a fashion for these very deep rich cushion frames, often as here made up of oak leaves and acorns.[1] The type is sometimes found on large-scale works by Academicians such as Luke Fildes's *The Doctor* of 1891 (Tate Gallery), but rarely in so dominant a form on a portrait of this scale. The cushion is not unlike the '$2\frac{1}{2}$″ Acorn Stick Top' which features in the frame catalogue in the National Monuments Record for Scotland of an unknown framemaker of the 1880s, unidentified but for the initials 'RS' (see fig.35).

The portrait is one of two painted in 1892 by Jacomb-Hood of Sir Francis Seymour Haden, a fellow member of the Royal Society of Painter-Etchers, this one for Haden or his son, and the other for the Society.

1. A splendid laurel leaf example in the National Portrait Gallery can be found on Beatrice Bright's *Sir Samuel Canning* of 1897.

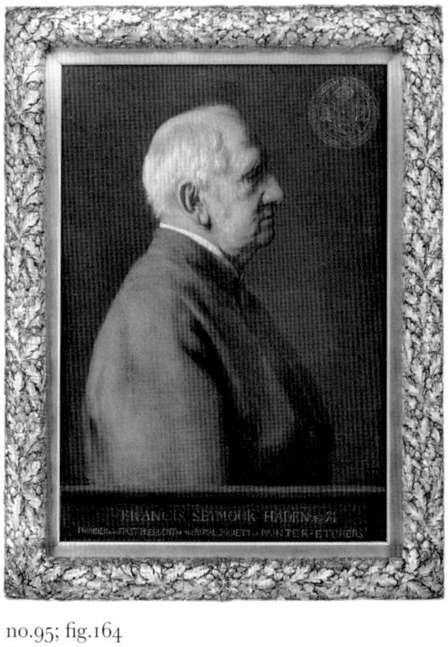

no.95; fig.164

96 [fig.37]
Victoria, Princess Royal (1840–1901)
By Joseph Mordecai, *c.*1900 or later
Oil on canvas, 35.6 × 30.5 (14 × 12)
NPG 4430

Rough sawn deal boards with applied compo laurel leaf cushion moulding, mitred and pinned, the rebate enlarged at left and right and the frame perhaps made for another picture, schlag or other imitation gold leaf over a warm-toned size; a later coating of bronze paint has now largely been removed. 4 inches wide.

Rough deal frames became popular in the 1880s and remained so until the First World War, either as plain deal boards or as here with a delicate leaf cushion moulding contrasting with the roughness of the deal.

This portrait of the Empress of Germany, eldest child of Queen Victoria, seems to have been painted from a photograph in about 1900 or perhaps posthumously a few years later. Its frame is a cheap commercial product, made from a single width of wood pinned close to the corners so allowing the mitres to open up with time. The frame corresponds very closely to one of the 'Best Quality Rough Gilt Ornamental Mouldings' in a commercial frame catalogue of 1910, that of H. Morell of 17 and 18 Great St Andrew Street, Bloomsbury.[1]

1. H. Morell, *Victorian Wooden Molding and Frame Designs. The 1910 Morell Catalogue*, Dover reprint edition, 1991, p.18, design no.1200, 4″ wide.

97 [figs.14–16]
William Shakespeare (1564–1616)
By John Taylor, *c.*1610
Oil on canvas, 55.2 × 43.8 (21¾ × 17¼)
NPG 1

Tortoiseshell veneer on pine(?), mitred and pinned, applied fruitwood sight and top mouldings. 4 inches wide.

Like some other celebrated pictures, the so-called 'Chandos Portrait' of Shakespeare has been reframed several times in its history. By chance, the National Portrait Gallery owns two of the previous frames, dating to the early 1800s and the 1860s; what we lack is the original frame, which was presumably a modest plain black moulding perhaps with a gilt sight edge.

It was the very modesty of the original frame which would have made it seem inappropriate to a later owner wanting something more conspicuous. The earliest recorded frame was a Maratta type (fig.14), which may have been fitted to the picture when it came to Stowe from the Chandos collection sometime in the early nineteenth century. The frame was probably made in the 1760s for a portrait measuring thirty by twenty-five inches, and was subsequently cut down (hence the off-centre reversal of the top edge ribbon-and-stick) and enriched with compo shells at the corners to suit an early nineteenth-century taste.

The portrait was the National Portrait Gallery's first recorded acquisition, and was given by the Earl of Ellesmere in 1856, the year of the Gallery's foundation. Its Maratta frame was regilded in 1858, only to be removed in 1864 at the wish of the Trustees who considered the portrait was 'seen to disadvantage in its present frame'. George Scharf, the Gallery's Director, records Mr Dickinson of Foord & Dickinson calling to discuss a new frame on 2 February 1864. It was intended that the cost of £4.10s should be partly offset by sale of the old frame, but in the event it was kept and fitted to a portrait of William Whiston.[1] A further eighteen shillings was spent in April 1864 altering and recolouring the new frame.[2] The rather horrific result (fig.15) echoes panel frames of the late seventeenth century but the dark background gives the frame a rather earlier feel.

In the 1950s or 1960s the portrait was put in a shadow box, a simple glazed box, with a velvet background, a fashionable solution at the time.[3] In 1983 an old mock tortoiseshell frame from store was dismantled and cut down, and the sight and back edges replaced by John Davies at a cost of £206.60 (fig.16).

1. The Whiston frame still bears the pink label of the 1857 Manchester Art Treasures exhibition to which the Shakespeare was lent as no.85.
2. Trustees Minutes 1 December 1863, 15 February 1864; Secretary's Journal (1861–65), 2 February, 26 and 30 March, 9, 19 and 23 April 1864; Duplicate of accounts vol.I, pp.18, 44.
3. Information from Robin Gibson.

98 [fig.120]
Elizabeth Talbot, Countess of Shrewsbury (1518–1608)
By an unknown artist, *c.*1600
Oil on canvas, 98.8 × 78.7 (38⅞ × 31)
NPG 203

Carved pine, mitred and keyed, polished black with applied gilt ornaments, the projections on back edge added. 4 inches wide.

This Elizabethan-revival frame of 1865 was conceived by George Scharf, Secretary and later Director of the National Portrait Gallery, in collaboration with Henry Critchfield, the Gallery's framemaker. It is an unusual instance of antiquarian framing by the Gallery in its early days.

The picture is an early copy of the portrait of 'Bess of Hardwick' at Hardwick Hall, Derbyshire. It was acquired for the Gallery at the Trustees' meeting of 9 December 1865. Six days later Scharf noted in his diary that Critchfield 'came for ... further instructions about the Elizabethan frames'; the previous day Critchfield's man had come 'for two frames and for patterns for ornaments to the frame of Css of Shrewsbury'. The profile of the frame and the foliage at the corners suggests that it may be eighteenth century in origins. All the rest of the applied gilt ornament, including the ribbon-twist sight edge, the unusual 'Elizabethan' bosses, lozenges and

no.99; fig.165

diamonds and the 'ES' monogram and coronet, would appear to have been made by Critchfield to Scharf's order. His bill, dated 8 January 1866, described it as an 'Old Frame French Polished Black & Gold with additional ornaments carved & gilt', the cost being £3.10s.

The result is quite different from the flat frames of Bess of Hardwick's day, as Scharf will have known since he was also commissioning much simpler 'Tudor' frames at this period (see no.102). Scharf had visited Hardwick in October 1865, and stayed there for four days sketching the pictures. He noted that the Hardwick original of the Gallery's picture was in a 'plain black moulded frame'. His visit must have so stimulated his imagination, however, that he looked to Elizabethan architecture for inspiration rather than to early frames, probably turning to one of the many available pattern books as well as to his Hardwick sketchbook, which includes some architectural details and several 'ES' monograms of the sort crowning the frame.

99 [fig.165]
George III (1738–1820)
Studio of Allan Ramsay, after 1763
Oil on canvas, 147.3 × 106.7 (58 × 42)
NPG 223

Gilt compo on pine, mitred and pinned with corner blocks, the slip water gilt, the narrow frieze sanded, drying cracks visible in the compo ornament. 4¾ inches wide.

The framemakers Foord & Dickinson are better known for their fastidious frames for Ruskin, Rossetti, Lord Leighton and Edward Lear than for their work at the National Portrait Gallery from 1857 to 1869. When this portrait of George III and its companion of Queen Charlotte were acquired in 1866, Foord & Dickinson made 'Two Ornamental Frames' at the considerable cost of £8.12s each. In type they are a throwback to the early eighteenth century (see for example no.32) but the large scale of the running ornament and the use of compo mark them out as Victorian imitations.

100 [fig.126]
Henry Hardinge, 1st Viscount Hardinge (1785–1856)
By Sir Francis Grant, 1876
Oil on canvas, 127.3 × 101.6 (50⅛ × 40)
NPG 437

Gilt compo on pine, mitred and pinned with corner blocks, the inner slip water gilt. 6 inches wide including slip.

This replica of Sir Francis Grant's 1849 portrait of the former governor-general of India, Lord Hardinge, was given to the Gallery by the artist in 1876. The frame was made by Henry Critchfield, the Gallery's framemaker, at a cost of £5.10s on 14 September 1876.

In type this running pattern of intertwining scrolls and foliage on an ogee section is not unlike the Lawrence frames used in the 1840s on F.R. Say's portraits for the Peel Gallery (see no.69). Critchfield made rather similar frames in the late 1870s and early 1880s for several early Victorian portraits, and it may be that this somewhat old-fashioned frame type was seen by George Scharf, the Gallery's Director, as appropriate for such pictures. In framing the portrait of Hardinge, however, Scharf must surely have been aware that Sir Francis Grant, a Gallery trustee, normally used rather different frames on his own pictures (see no.72).

The frame has been altered so that it is now a 'door frame' or 'front loader', with bolts at the top allowing the glass and canvas to be removed without taking the picture off the wall.

101 [fig.127]
Hugh Childers (1827–96)
By Emily Childers, signed and dated 1891
Oil on canvas, 90.2 × 69.9 (35½ × 27½)
NPG 1631

Gilt compo on pine, standard Watts frame construction (see no.80), oil gilt except for matt water gilding on some plain areas. 6¼ inches wide. With the label: FRANCIS DRAPER, 67 PARK ST GROSVENOR SQE.

The portrait painter, Milly Childers, daughter of Hugh Childers, Chancellor of the Exchequer in Gladstone's cabinet in the 1880s, worked mainly for patrons in her father's political circle. When this portrait of her father was first photographed by Emery Walker, before the addition of the signature and date, it was in a plain rough deal frame. Subsequently it was reframed temporarily, perhaps to send it to the National Portrait Gallery, and the artist then wrote to the Gallery's Director on 4 January 1912, with proposals for a permanent frame. But the Director, Charles Holmes, replied two days later, 'we had decided that a "Watts" pattern was the only one which would enable the portrait to be hung here harmoniously with the other pictures of the same period. If a portrait has an exceptional frame we find the greatest difficulty in making it suit the various positions which ... the pictures here have to take from time to time. Your friends work is exceedingly attractive but ...'.[1]

The Watts frame was made by Francis Draper, whose label is still on the frame, and billed on 20 May 1912 at a cost of £4.8s. The picture still retains its original picture tablet in a gilt lead holder. Interestingly, the husks of the sight edge of the frame run in one direction and do not reverse at the centres as normal.

1. National Portrait Gallery, Press Copy Book, vol.XXX, p.192.

102 [fig.166]
William Warham, Archbishop of Canterbury (1450–1532)
After Hans Holbein
Oil on panel, 82.2 × 66.3 (32 3/8 × 26 1/8)
NPG 2094

Ebonised and gilt pine, mitred and pinned, the cushion and the altered gilt sight edge beneath the glazing. 4 inches wide.

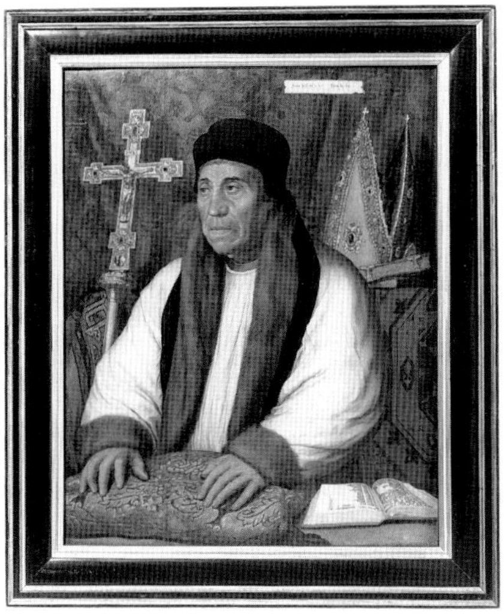

no.102; fig.166

This is one of two standard-pattern black-and-gold 'Tudor' frames the National Portrait Gallery used from the 1860s until the 1920s for almost all of its early portraits, with only the occasional variation in the mouldings. The simpler pattern has a flat frieze in place of this portrait's cushion and two gilt mouldings instead of three. Though the rather hard mouldings do not stand up to close scrutiny when compared to genuine sixteenth-century frames, these standard patterns have otherwise stood the test of time as can be seen from the number still in use. They were made by Henry Critchfield until his replacement as the Gallery's framemaker by Francis Draper in 1884.

This frame was made for the portrait on acquisition in 1925 by Draper at a cost of £6.18s: 'Making 4″ special pattern ebonized & gilt fillet top & ovolo door frame & black flat, door double gilt in matt & fitted up with brass thumb screws & velvet &c'. A 'door frame' of this sort allowed the panel to be removed from the front of the frame. Less than two years later in 1927 the frame was altered at a cost of £2.16s so that the picture could be glazed.

103 [figs.81, 196]
Thomas Hardy (1840–1928)
By William Strang, signed and dated 1893
Oil on panel, 43.2 × 38.1 (17 × 15)
NPG 2929

Gilt soft woods (the back frame pine, the main frame a closer-grained timber), mitred and pinned. 3 1/4 inches wide plus 3/4 inch slip.

The Scottish etcher William Strang studied at the Slade under Alphonse Legros in the late 1870s, only taking up painting seriously in the 1890s when he came under Whistler's influence. This small early sketch was bequeathed to the Gallery by Thomas Hardy's widow in 1938. It is framed in a small-scale reeded Whistler cushion frame of a type still being used by Whistler himself in the 1890s, but with variations such as the use of twelve reeds instead of the more usual fifteen on the inner face of the reeded cushion.

104 [fig.167]
Aubrey Beardsley (1872–98)
By Jacques-Emile Blanche, signed and dated 1895
Oil on canvas, 90.2 × 71.8 (35 1/2 × 28 1/4)
NPG 1991

Gilt oak, mitred and pinned, the gilding directly onto oak prepared with a warm-toned size. 3 1/2 inches wide.

Beardsley sat to the French portrait painter, Jacques-Emile Blanche, at Dieppe in the summer of 1895. In September he

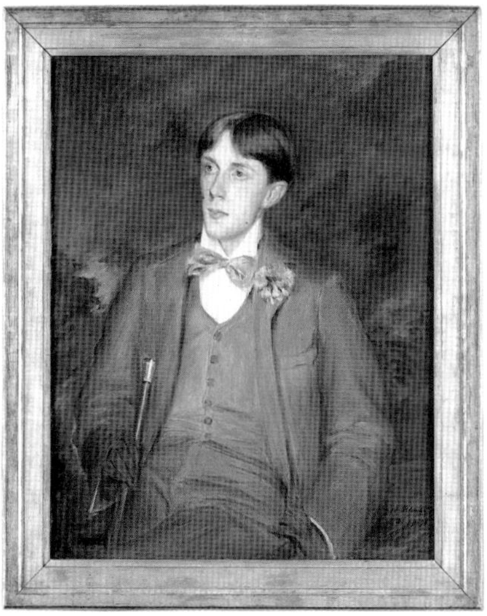

no.104; fig.167

wrote to William Rothenstein asking for help at very short notice with the frame: 'Dear Billy, J.E. Blanche is sending two pictures to the forthcoming exhibition of portraits [arranged by the Society of Portrait Painters] at the New Gallery. He has no time to get frames made in *Dieppe* so would you order Chapman to make frame AT ONCE ...'.[1] Beardsley enclosed four lengths of string, two to give the measurements for the larger picture, which in the event was not exhibited, and two smaller lengths for his own portrait. He penned a diagram for the large picture showing a frame with 'fluting' running along the sides and circular 'buttons' at the corners, to be of 'plain oak gilded', adding, 'The frame for my portrait an ordinary Watts frame – gilded (and glazed)'.

Beardsley's portrait was purchased by the National Portrait Gallery in its present gilt oak frame in 1923. Rothenstein may have ignored Beardsley's request for a Watts frame, preferring a simpler plain oak, or he may have found that it was not possible to get a Watts frame made to a non-stock size in the very limited time available. 'Chapman' is presumably Chapman Bros of 251 King's Road, Chelsea, a leading firm of framemakers in business from 1875 to 1922 or later, and widely patronised by artists.

1. Henry Maas, J.L. Duncan and W.G. Good (eds.), *The Letters of Aubrey Beardsley*, 1970, pp.100-1.

105 [fig.79]

Charles Haslewood Shannon (1863–1937)
Self-portrait, signed and dated 1897
Oil on canvas, 92.7 × 96.5 (36½ × 38)
NPG 3107

Gilt oak, reverse section, mitred and lap jointed, the gilding directly onto oak prepared with a warm-toned size, later sight fillet. 5¾ inches wide.

This self-portrait of the painter and lithographer, Charles Haslewood Shannon, and the portrait of his lifelong companion, Charles Ricketts, painted by Shannon a year later in 1898, have matching frames, albeit of differing construction. In his diary for 1898, the earliest of his diaries to survive, Shannon noted such events as the arrival of a frame at his studio, putting portraits into their frames, and taking drawings 'round to the framer'.[1] At this time he was still living in Chelsea, and he may have used a local framemaking firm such as Chapman Bros (see no.104). The use of a wide flat stepped reverse-section frame is characteristic of Shannon's frames of the late 1890s and early 1900s, although the precise profile occasionally varied from frame to frame. Later in life he used a much richer, more traditional Bolection leaf frame in compo, a revival of a late seventeenth-century fashion (see for example no.24).

1. British Library, Add. MS. 58,110.

106 [fig.80]

Coventry Patmore (1823–96)
By John Singer Sargent, signed and dated 1894
Oil on canvas, 91.4 × 61 (36 × 24)
NPG 1079

Gilt oak, mitred and pinned, the gilding directly onto oak prepared with a warm-toned size, the outer reeding of solid oak planted on a pine base with an oak edging applied to the outer edge, the central flat section of oak-veneered pine now held in place by blocks but originally pinned, the sight reeding again of oak on a pine base and now held by blocks, the slip of oak. 6 inches wide plus ¾ inch slip. With two identical labels: C.M. May,/Gilder & Picture Frame Manufacturer./ STEAMWORKS – 19, St Ann's Court, Soho./PICTURES CLEANED LINED AND RESTORED.

Sargent's portrait of the poet and author, Coventry Patmore, was given to the Gallery by Patmore's widow in 1897, a year after his death and within three years of the portrait being painted. The flat reeded Whistler frame, close to the type Whistler began using in the 1870s but slightly wider, was made by Charles Mitchell May, a framemaker used by Sargent in the period 1894–1922.[1] The frame contrasts with the richer, more traditional styles used by the artist for his society portraits and was evidently chosen to enhance the enlongated narrow format of the portrait and the upright, aloof character of the sitter.

1. May had set up as a framemaker in 1873 and was advertising his business in 1893 as 'Patronised by the leading artists of the day' (*The Year's Art*, 1893, p.26). He was used by Sargent for the framing of two other works in the National Portrait Gallery: *Sir Frank Swettenham*, 1904 (no.108), and *General Officers of World War I*, 1922.

107 [fig.115]

Octavia Hill (1838–1912)
By John Singer Sargent, 1899
Oil on canvas, 101 × 77.5 (39¾ × 30½)
NPG 1746

Carved and gilt pine, butt joint, the top cushion planted on the main frame which in turn is planted on the back frame, some of the fruit, the leaves at the corners and the tongues on the back edge punched. 4⅜ inches wide.

This portrait of the philanthropist, Octavia Hill, was given her by her friends on her sixtieth birthday. It has a fine carved frame of leaves and fruit not unlike some Italian mid-seventeenth century frames.[1] In a richer version in compo, made by Chapman Bros, the design was used both by Sargent, for example on his 1906 *Lord Roberts* (National Portrait Gallery), and by William Orpen, as on his *H.M. Butler* of *c.*1911 (anonymous loan to Fitzwilliam Museum, Cambridge).

1. For instance the slightly more elaborate frame reproduced in Franco Sabatelli, *La cornice italiana dal Rinascimento al Neoclassico*, Milan, 1992, pp.208–9.

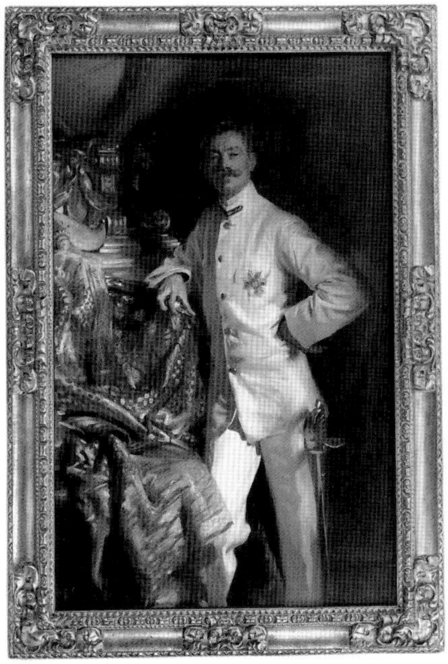

no.108; fig.168

108 [fig.168]

Sir Frank Swettenham (1850–1946)
By John Singer Sargent, signed and dated 1904
Oil on canvas, 170.8 × 110.5 (67¼ × 43½)
NPG 4837

Gilt compo on pine, mitred and keyed (the keys of oak, 1¾ inches wide, the main hollow water gilt and burnished on a red bole, the surface then punched with an ε-shaped punch, the drying cracks in the compo mouldings occurring at the joins in the castings. 6 inches wide. With the label: C.M. May & Sons,/Gilder & Picture Frame Manufacturer./STEAM WORKS – 18, St Anne's Court, Soho./PICTURES CLEANED, LINED AND RESTORED.

Sir Frank Swettenham, governor of the Malay States, commissioned this second version of his official portrait and bequeathed it to the National Portrait Gallery. The Spanish seventeenth-century style frame of reverse section with foliage centres and corners, made by Sargent's framemaker, C.M. May, is identical to the frame on Sargent's exactly contemporary portrait of Lady Helen Vincent, later Viscountess D'Abernon (Birmingham Museum of Art, Birmingham, Alabama).

Sargent used a wide range of revival frame styles but, like William Orpen, he experimented with Spanish-style frames, then quite a novelty. This taste had perhaps been encouraged by the first comprehensive exhibition of Spanish art at the New Gallery in 1895 but in any case Sargent was one of those portrait painters, like Whistler and Lavery, who had a deep-seated admiration for Velazquez and Spanish art.[1]

1. For the late nineteenth-century taste for Spanish art see Allan Braham, *El Greco to Goya. The Taste for Spanish Paintings in Britain and Ireland*, exh. cat., National Gallery, 1981, pp.35–44.

109 [fig.82]

Sir William Harcourt (1827–1904)
By Sir Arthur Cope, signed and dated 1904
Oil on canvas, 127 × 101.6 (50 × 40)
NPG 6212

Carved and gilt pine, mitred and plated with wide L-corner plates, the carving partly matt water gilt on a red bole, the flats oil gilt on a white ground. 6 inches wide.

This frame on Cope's portrait of the Lord Chancellor, Sir William Harcourt, takes up the spirit of the fantastic Italian auricular frames of the mid-seventeenth century, such as those in the Pitti Palace in Florence, though in execution it is broader and the forms more sweeping.

Cope had a substantial practice as a portraitist of men in positions of power. He favoured at least two main frame types: one an English seventeenth-century bunched leaf revival pattern, found in the National Portrait Gallery on portraits of Lords Knutsford, St Aldwyn and Chaplin, and formerly on the portrait of Sir William Perkin, all of the period 1906–8; the other a much more showy Italian revival style as exemplified by no.109, and also found on portraits of Admiral Sir Frederick Richards of 1900 (National Maritime Museum) and of the 3rd and 4th Marquesses of Bristol (Ickworth, Suffolk).

110 [fig.116]

Sir Lionel Cust (1859–1929)
By Sir John Lavery, signed and dated 1912
Oil on board, 35.6 × 25.4 (14 × 10)
NPG 6337

Machine carved with schlag metal and painted decoration on pine, lap jointed, the mitred back edge planted. 3¼ inches wide. With the label: SPECIALIST IN RESTORATION AND REPRODUCTION/OF ANTIQUE GILDING/ E. REMY,/Frame Maker and Furniture Gilder,/153, King's Road, CHELSEA, S.W./Near Town Hall./French Furniture Gilding, Enamelling and Decorating./ ARTISTS AND DEALERS SUPPLIED./Telephone: KENSINGTON 673. ESTIMATES GIVEN.

Lavery used this simple renaissance-style *cassetta* frame for some of his small portraits in the period immediately before and during the First World War. Another example in the National Portrait Gallery, horizontal rather than vertical in format, is the sketch of Sir Winston Churchill's wife, Clementine, with their daughter, Sarah, of about 1915. The frame on the portrait of Lionel Cust, Director of the National Portrait Gallery until 1909 and depicted in Court Dress of a Gentleman Usher, was made by Emile Remy, a specialist in French gilding. With its machine-carved moulding, schlag metal finish and simply painted frieze, it is designed rather successfully for maximum effect at minimum cost.

111 [fig.83]

The Royal Family at Buckingham Palace
By Sir John Lavery, signed and dated 1913
Oil on canvas, 340.3 × 271.8 (134 × 107)
NPG 1745

Carved and gilt pine, mitred and bolted, the top ogee carved section of 3½ to 4½ inches deep planted on the base frame and the carved centres and corners in turn planted on the ogee carved section, the corner shells fixed on with screws, oil gilt except for water gilding in the back hollow and on some of the highlights of the carving, with a red bole visible in places. 12 inches wide.

For this portrait of George V, Queen Mary, the Duke of Windsor and Princess Mary, a commission from the printer, W.H. Spottiswoode, for presentation to the nation, Lavery has used a very fine French-style rococo revival frame which is exceptionally bold in scale.

The picture was exhibited at the Royal Academy in 1913 and then at the Grosvenor Gallery the following summer, at which time Lavery's secretary wrote that the artist was 'desirous of trying one of two frames he has ready before finally deciding which one he leaves permanently on the picture. The frame that he prefers to use is now on the big canvas at the R.A.'.[1] This canvas was *The Artist's Studio* (National Gallery of Ireland), completed in 1911, which appears to be the only other painting on this scale painted by Lavery at the period. It is no longer in its original frame so it is not possible to understand the nature of the choice Lavery faced when framing such large pictures.[2] The royal group was finally fitted into its frame at some expense by the National Portrait Gallery's framemaker, Francis Draper, in December 1914. There is no record of who made the frame, but at the time Lavery was using Emile Remy to frame some of his smaller pictures, such as the portrait of Sir Lionel Cust (no.110), and Remy is mentioned by the artist in 1918 as having been responsible for packing the picture.[3]

1. Letter to Charles Holmes, 18 July 1914.
2. I am grateful to Michael Wynne for information about the Dublin picture.
3. Letter to James Milner, 6 January 1918.

112 [fig.85]

Sir Osbert Sitwell (1892–1969)
By Nina Hamnett, *c.*1915–18
Oil on canvas, 50.5 × 40.6 (19⅞ × 16)
NPG 5916

Painted pine, mitred with triangular corner plates, the gessoed ground coated in a white metal powder (clearly visible on the frame reverse) and an umber-coloured wash (visible on the back edge), broken by spattering with a solvent to create a pooled effect, and then stippled in pale grey and light and dark pink paint; the rear of the frame painted green. 5⅛ inches wide.

This delightful painted frame, with a stippled finish and a step in the otherwise flat profile next to the sloping sight edge, is old and perhaps original to the picture. Although Nina Hamnett worked for the Omega Workshops, the frame seems too pretty to be hers, however, and may possibly have been chosen by Osbert Sitwell himself in view of the fairly eclectic way the Sitwells' modern things were presented.[1]

1. I have benefited from the advice of Honor Clerk, Judy Collins and Charles Booth-Clibborn in considering this unusual frame.

113 [fig.118]

Francis Crittall (1860–1935)
By Augustus John, signed and dated 1919
Oil on canvas 76.2 × 63 (30 × 24¾)
NPG 6240

Ebonised pine, reverse section, with five applied ripple mouldings, the inner two of mahogany with gilding on the innermost, the outer three of ebony, mitred with a lap jointed back frame except at bottom left and top right where mitred and pinned, apparently where the original lap joint has been cut through, suggesting that the frame, although original to the picture, may have been cut down. 5¾ inches wide.

Augustus John's portrait of the metal window frame manufacturer, Francis Crittall, is one of a number of the painter's large portraits of the late 1910s and early 1920s which were framed in a modern black ripple moulding of Dutch or German seventeenth-century inspiration, a type also used by some of John's contemporaries. Very similar frames are found on John's portraits of Thomas Hardy (Fitzwilliam Museum, Cambridge) and Madame Suggia (Tate Gallery), both of 1923, William Nicholson's *Miss Jekyll's Gardening Boots* of 1920 (Tate Gallery), and William Orpen's *The Studio* of *c.*1911 (Leeds City Art Gallery).[1] A gilt compo variant of lesser quality was used for John's portrait of Sir Herbert Barker of 1916 (National Portrait Gallery).

John, Nicholson and Orpen were all three Chenil artists at one time or another, using the Chenil Galleries, a picture gallery and artists' material supplier set up by Orpen's brother-in-law, Jack Knewstub, in the King's Road, Chelsea, on the site of some studios John once occupied.[2] Both John and Orpen are known to have obtained white Whistler frames from Chenil and it is possible that these black ripple frames came from the same source.[3]

1. The frames on the Nicholson and Orpen seem to be identical to that on John's portrait of Hardy, but for the slightly smaller scale of the sight edge mouldings of the Nicholson.
2. For the Chenil Galleries, see Augustus John, *Finishing Touches*, 1964, p.137. As Charles Chenil & Co. Ltd, the business is recorded in Trade Directories from at least 1907 to 1928.
3. Two of John's 1910 sketches in the Fitzwilliam Museum have Chenil's label: *Woman with a Daffodil* and *Girl leaning on Stick*. For Orpen's 1918 order for white enamel Whistler frames, see above, pp.78–9.

114 [fig.117]

Jerome K. Jerome (1859–1927)
By Philip de Laszlo, signed and dated 1921
Oil on canvas, 91.4 × 71.1 (36 × 28)
NPG 4491

Carved and gilt pine, mitred and keyed, the keys visible from the front, water gilt on a red bole, burnished in part and finely stippled in black for effect. 4⅞ inches wide. With the label, largely obscured, of Emile Remy, apparently of the same form as that on Lavery's portrait of Sir Lionel Cust.

De Laszlo claimed that the frame was 'an integral part of the picture' and should be chosen before beginning a painting.[1] The reality may have been rather different on occasion, judging from the framing history of this portrait of the author, Jerome K. Jerome, painted in 1921. De Laszlo used a wide range of frame styles and when his photographer, Paul Laib, photographed this picture on completion it was framed in one of the artist's standard Italianate *cassetta* frames with gilt incised floral corner decoration on a black ground, of a type found, for example, on his *5th Marquess of Lansdowne* of 1920 in the National Portrait Gallery. The style sits heavily on a work of as pale a tonality as the Jerome portrait.

By 1926, however, the portrait had been reframed in its present Spanish reverse section frame.[2] The style was used by De Laszlo in the 1910s and 1920s either completely gilt as here or with the plain sides stained black.[3] The use of such Spanish frames had been popularised by J.S. Sargent (see no.108) and William Orpen in the early 1900s.

This particular frame has an incredibly thin outer edge so that the diagonal keys fitted across the rear of the mitres at each corner are visible as hairline cracks on the front face of the frame. It was made by Emile Remy, who was also responsible for the frames on two other pictures in the National Portrait Gallery, De Laszlo's *Sir William Pulteney* of 1917 and Sir John Lavery's *Sir Lionel Cust* of 1912 (no.110).

1. See above, p.108.
2. Reproduced with frame in a supplement to *The Bookman*, Christmas 1926. The frame is close in style to one in the Ashmolean Museum, Oxford, repr. Claus Grimm, *The Book of Picture Frames*, New York, 1981, pl.145.
3. Examples in one guise or the other are *Lady Leconfield*, 1913 (Petworth House), *Lady Lowther* and *Madame La Tamurin*, both of 1921 and recorded in old Laib photographs, and *Sir Walter Townley* (Foreign Office).

115 [fig.84]

Frederick Delius (1862–1934)
By Ernest Proctor, signed and dated 1929
Oil on millboard, 31.8 × 25.4 (12½ × 10)
NPG 3861

White hardwood, grained and polished to resemble rosewood, mitred and pinned, bronzed sight edge. 3 inches wide.

Ernest Proctor's study of Delius for his large picture of the blind composer at the Queen's Hall has a polished simulated rosewood frame which appears to be the original. The portrait was exhibited at the Leicester Galleries in 1929 and remained in the family of the purchaser, G.A. Balfour Gardiner, until acquired by the National Portrait Gallery with the frame in 1953. It is not clear who was responsible for framing the portrait, but polished wood frames of this sort had become increasingly popular since the relaxation of the Royal Academy's rule insisting on gilt frames in 1920.

116 [fig.11]

George V (1865–1936)
By Sir Oswald Birley, *c.*1935
Oil on canvas, 59.1 × 42.9 (23¼ × 16⅞)
NPG 4013

Carved and gilt poplar, lap jointed, the punched frieze water gilt and burnished over a red bole, the sight and top edge mitred and planted. 5 inches wide.

This is a case of putting the frame before the picture. Like some other twentieth-century artists, Birley had a fondness for carved frames and would have a canvas made to fit a particular antique frame.[1] Hence the non-standard measurements of this portrait. The frame is a very fine Italian *cassetta* frame of a type used in Bologna and elsewhere in Emilia in the first half of the seventeenth century. 'The hallmark ... of Emilian *cassetta* frames', Paul Mitchell has written, 'is the use of *granito* (punchwork) to create subtle arabesques, running flowers, blossom and leaves .... Also Emilian in character is the preference for foliate rather than architectural ornament'.[2] In the case of this frame, the punchwork frieze consists of an arabesque of running leaves set between a sight edge and top edge of overlapping leaves reversing at a central motif.

1. Information from Sir Oswald's son, Mark Birley, 14 February 1995, who also thinks that Bourlet may have made some frames for his father. For other artists' adoption of this practice, see above, p.23.
2. Paul Mitchell, 'Italian Picture Frames 1500–1825: A Brief Survey', *Furniture History*, vol.XX, 1984, p.22.

117 [fig.10]

Gluck (Hannah Gluckstein) (1895–1978)
Self-portrait, signed and dated 1942
Oil on canvas, 31 × 26 (12¼ × 10¼)
NPG CP4

Pine painted white, mitred and probably pinned, two layers of matt white paint possibly over a gessoed surface. 4¼ inches wide. With the damaged label of Rowley Frames, 140 Church Street, Kensington.

Gluck's passion for framing, and for white frames in particular, was apparent at her 1932 exhibition at the Fine Art Society, where all her paintings were shown in three-step white 'Gluck' frames against white walls (fig.9). 'The essential feature of the Gluck frame', according to a note in the catalogue of her 1937 Fine Art Society exhibition, 'is that it becomes part of any wall whatever its character, colour or period ... It can be painted the same colour as the wall, or covered with the same wall-paper, or made in any wall material'.[1]

This slightly later self-portrait is in a white Whistler frame, a type which dates back in its white form to the late 1880s, and in its original gilt form, as used by Whistler, to the early 1870s.[2] The portrait was given to the National Portrait Gallery by the artist following her exhibition at the Fine Art Society in 1973; she then wrote, 'I do so hope the Fine Art Society did not tint that frame, as they did others to go with the exhibition background, as the frame should be white'.

Like the similarly framed Gluck landscape, *Cottages below the Downs* (with the Fine Art Society, 1995), the self-portrait has the distinctive label in the Toulouse-Lautrec style of Rowley Frames of no.140 Church Street, Kensington.

1. Diana Souhami includes a chapter on the Gluck frame in her biography, *Gluck 1895–1978*, 1988, pp.102–11.
2. For the Whistler frame, see above, pp.76–7.

118 [fig.169]

Dame Edith Sitwell (1887–1964)
By John Banting, *c.*1944
Watercolour with white heightening, 55.9 × 75.6 (22 × 29¾)
NPG 5962

Pine, mitred and pinned, the sight edge and the inward sloping face of the frame covered in S2 or M2 grade glass paper in standard 11 inch lengths, the back of the frame apparently gessoed, with new pieces of wood planted to form a rebate and then painted with gloss black. 2½ inches wide. Inscribed on back of drawing: 'A Portrait of a bone-head/ For George Melly/ from John Banting/ 1970' and in another, probably earlier hand: 'Edith Sitwell May be'.

John Banting's 'portrait of a bone-head' is based on a bone he decorated with glass eyes and put on a plinth for a joke as a portrait of Edith Sitwell. The anarchic spirit which transforms a bone into a portrait is kept alive by a frame which takes a very ordinary material, glass paper, and exploits it for its decorative qualities. The frame seems to have been recycled and the glass paper added, perhaps relatively recently, so the frame is as likely to date to 1970, when the drawing was inscribed on the back, as to the 1940s.

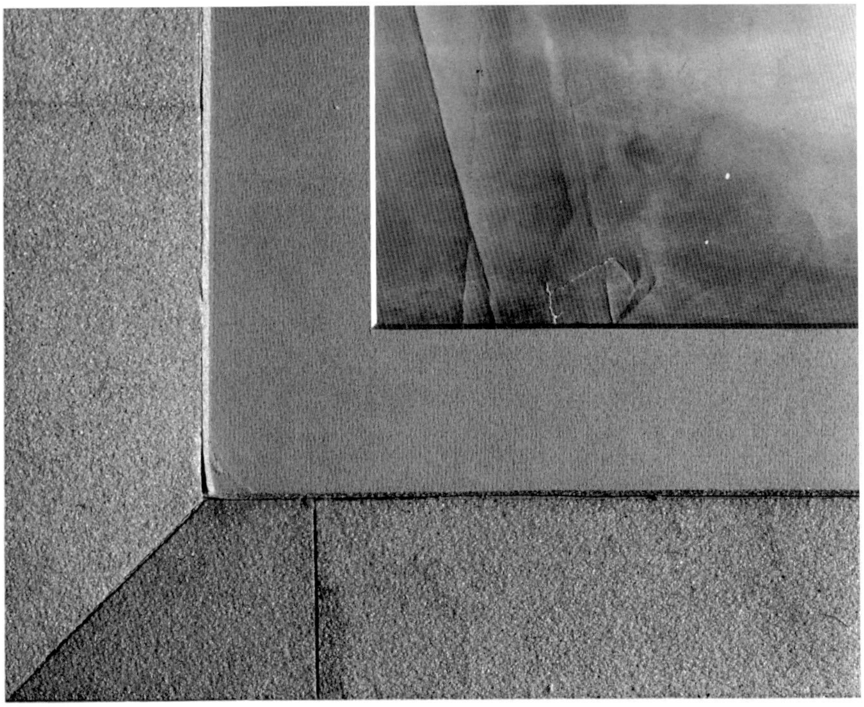

no.118; fig.169

119 [figs.22, 197]

Kenneth Clark, Baron Clark (1903–83)
By Graham Sutherland, signed and dated 1963–4
Oil on canvas, 54.6 × 45.7 (21½ × 18)
NPG 5243

Obeche(?), mitred and probably pinned, the sight edge planted and the top edge nailed onto the main flat frieze, burnished water gilding on a deep grey-blue bole, the outer face of the frame painted a deep grey-blue when the frame was built up by the National Portrait Gallery, probably repeating the existing colour. 3⅝ inches wide.

'Alfred Hecht, who liked describing himself as a picture frame-maker, was indeed a picture frame-maker, but in addition he had the gift of recognising genius before the general public came to recognise it'. So wrote Jennie Lee, like her husband, Aneurin Bevan, a Labour politician, who described evenings spent at Hecht's with artist friends, among them Henry Moore, Graham Sutherland, John Piper and Francis Bacon.[1] Hecht came to England in the mid-1920s and after the war set up business as a framemaker at no.326, King's Road, Chelsea, where he lived and worked for almost forty-five years.[2] He was Sutherland's framemaker from 1953 or before and was in the course of sitting for his portrait to Sutherland at the time of the artist's death in 1991.[3]

Sutherland's portrait of Kenneth Clark was exhibited in this burnished frame at the Sutherland exhibition at the National Portrait Gallery in 1977 and was presumably framed by Hecht in 1964. Such simple gold leaf frames, often making a feature of the overlapping sheets of gold, form a Hecht hallmark.

1. Jennie Lee, *My Life with Nye*, 1981 (Penguin edition), p.188.
2. Derek Granger, 'Alfred Hecht', obituary in *The Independent*, 12 January 1991. The 1947 Kelly's *Trade Directory* lists Hecht under art dealers.
3. Roger Berthoud, *Graham Sutherland. A Biography*, 1982, pp.163, 288.

120 [fig.170]

Graham Sutherland (1903–80)
Self-portrait, signed and dated 1977
Oil on canvas, 52.7 × 50.2 (20¾ × 19¾)
NPG 5338

Deal, the applied outer edge in fruitwood, the sight edge in an unidentified hardwood, mitred with dovetail keys (repaired) at two corners, cut down from a larger frame, originally ebonised and subsequently gessoed and largely water gilt on a red bole and distressed, the hollow of the reverse section given a green marbled finish. 6½ inches wide.

This frame, a most unusual choice for Graham Sutherland, appears to be a late

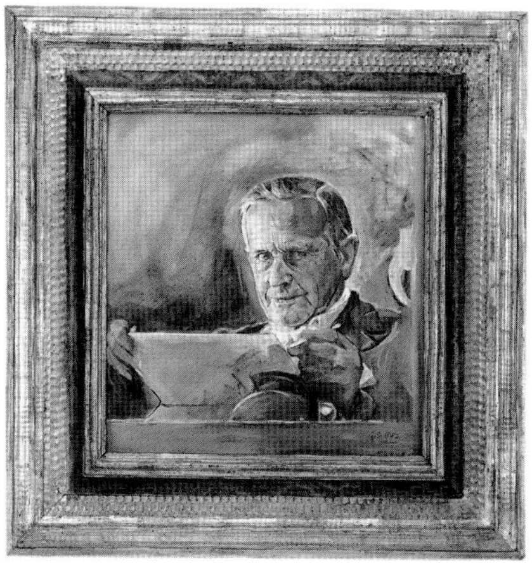

no.120; fig.170

nineteenth-century or early twentieth-century ebonised ripple moulding of continental origin, which has subsequently been cut down at two corners, then gilded and painted to suit Sutherland's self-portrait. It was presumably framed by Sutherland's framemaker, Alfred Hecht, for the National Portrait Gallery retrospective in 1977, and was given to the Gallery by the artist's widow in 1980. The inner green marbled band of the frame reduces the apparent bulk of the moulding to match the size of the portrait and at the same time picks up on one of the portrait's main colours in a way unique in Hecht's work for Sutherland.

121 [fig.13]
Brian Rix, Baron Rix of Whitehall (b.1924) *and his wife, Elspet Jeans* (b.1929)
By John Bratby, signed and dated 1967
Oil on canvas, 160 × 91.4 (63 × 36)
NPG 6159

Outer frame made by Paul Ferguson Workshop in 1992, the triangular top section in burnished water gilding on a plum bole with the leaf overlap clearly visible, 1½ inches wide. The canvas, without its Bratby battens, is fixed to the frame's backboard.

Some artists have rejected the idea of using a frame at all, among them. John Bratby, one of the leading members of the 'kitchen sink school' of the 1950s. Many of his earlier pictures, including this portrait of the actor Brian Rix and his wife, have detailed framing instructions on the back (see fig.13). This portrait has been framed by the National Portrait Gallery in order to protect it, respecting Bratby's wish that any frame should avoid encroaching on the picture surface. Later in life Bratby changed his approach and took to framing his pictures in cheap mouldings.

122 [fig.136]
Sir Giles Gilbert Scott (1880–1960)
By Reginald Grenville Eves, 1935
Oil on canvas, 61 × 50.8 (24 × 20)
NPG 4171

English oak, machined and polished, mitred with tongue joints, raised sight edge mouldings planted on a flat back frame. 4½ inches wide. Inscribed on the reverse, 'This frame made from House of Commons/ "Gilbert Scott" oak by direction of Sir Robert Cooke/ by E.A. NORTON District Works Officer D.O.E. 1979'.

This portrait of Sir Giles Gilbert Scott, architect of the House of Commons chamber as rebuilt after the Second World War, has been on loan to the Palace of Westminster since 1978. It was reframed in 1979 at the direction of Sir Robert Cooke, MP, then chairman of the House of Commons Advisory Committee on Works of Art, in House of Commons 'Gilbert Scott' oak of English origin specially cut for the rebuilding of the Chamber. The frame was made by parliamentary carpenters, Steve Tarpey and Fred Boileau, under the direction of Eddie Norton, District Works Officer, from original door frames which had been taken to store as a result of alterations to the building.[1] The double roll moulding was used for panelling, architraves and door frames in the Chamber and the surrounding offices, and is a standard Gilbert Scott interior motif.

1. Much of this information was kindly supplied by Jacqueline Riding, Assistant Curator at the Palace of Westminster, letter of 24 January 1996.

123 [fig.171]
Diana, Princess of Wales (b.1961)
By Bryan Organ, signed and dated 1981
Acrylic on canvas, 177.8 × 127 (70 × 50)
NPG 5408

Gilt ramin(?), mitred and pinned, flat-topped hockey section, burnished water gilding rubbed to show the orange bole, the overlap of the gold leaf creating a banding effect, faulting and creasing lines visible, the well of the float frame between the frame and the canvas lined in hessian. 1¾ inches wide.

'To framing ... in large hockey frame specially flattened and finished in English gold leaf lightly rubbed finish as discussed and agreed with the Artist ... £431.25'. Michael Carleton's frame, described in his bill of 31 July 1981, is one of three he made for portraits of the royal family painted by Bryan Organ for the National Portrait Gallery in the early 1980s. Its 'hockey' moulding (with a profile like a hockey stick) matches that on the slightly earlier portrait of the Prince of Wales, while the later portrait of the Duke of Edinburgh has a wider flat frame. As usual Michael Carleton sub-contracted the gilding, which had to be done very quickly to meet the deadline for unveiling the portrait.

The artist has spoken of his belief in showing the whole canvas as a visual flat image when framing.[1] The feel of space and of the picture can be changed

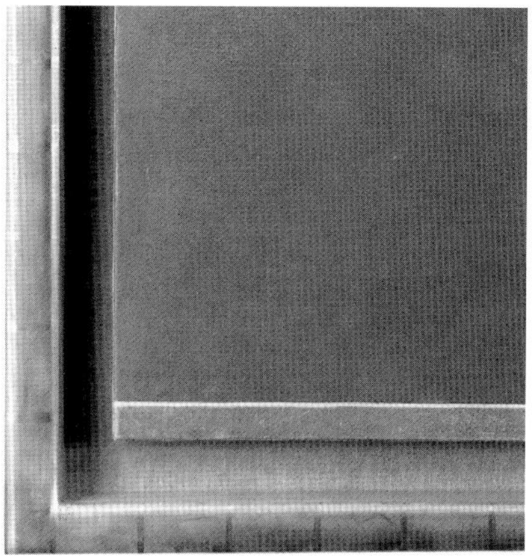

no.123; fig.171

dramatically by the frame. The use of a well round the canvas makes it possible to alter the interval and its colouring in relationship to the picture and the frame. Organ's feeling is that a fairly flat 'hockey' section, or even a flat frame such as on his portrait of the Duke of Edinburgh, suits a picture of this size; a D-section is more appropriate to a narrower picture. The gilding on the portrait of the Princess of Wales is of a lemon gold which he particularly likes, lightly rubbed to allow the underlayer to influence its tone.

Bryan Organ's interest in framing stems from his student days at the Royal College of Art in the 1950s when, like other students, he would go to Green & Stone in the King's Road, Chelsea, for frames. In the 1960s he used Dino de Biasi, a Venetian gilder and a great innovator, with premises in Tottenham Mews near Heals. Subsequently he turned to Michael Carleton, a framemaker who also ran a business hiring out antique furniture as props for film and television from a memorable shop on Haverstock Hill.[2] Since Carleton's death in about 1990 Organ has used John Jones Framing.

1. Much of this entry is based on a telephone conversation with the artist, 18 April 1996.
2. Carleton's framing business was one he took over from another framemaker. John Gill made many of the frames under his direction. Telephone conversation with Michael Francis, 18 April 1996.

124 [fig.172]
Sir Isaiah Berlin (b.1909)
By Lawrence Gowing, 1982
Oil on canvas, 94.6 × 86.4 (37¼ × 34)
NPG 5523

Gilt ramin, mitred and pinned, burnished water gilding on a plum bole, leaf overlap visible. 3½ inches wide.

'I always invoice the frames of the portraits, which have been fluctuating so wildly in price, separately to the purchaser and I now forward Mr Burns's bill for the rather beautiful frame that he provided

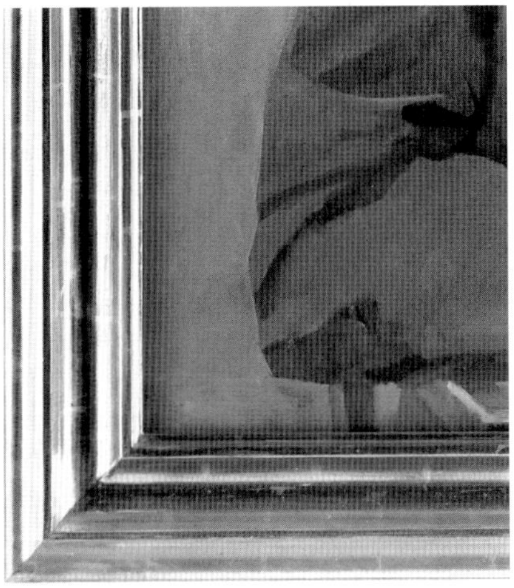

no.124; fig.172

for Isaiah'. So wrote Lawrence Gowing to the Director of the National Portrait Gallery in November 1982 about the frame for the portrait of Isaiah Berlin commissioned by the Gallery. The 'Gold Leaf Frame' was supplied by Terry Burns of J.T. Burns & Co Ltd, 'Fine Picture Framers & Gilders' of 20-24 Emerald Street, London WC1, at a cost of £181.70. It requires a highly burnished frame of recent date to show how striking a result can be achieved with a gilt frame, an effect which works well with a portrait painted as broadly as Gowing's in his late manner.

Gowing's framemaker at the time, Terry Burns, who did a lot of work for Royal Academicians, including Peter Greenham and Bernard Dunstan, recalls how Gowing's important commissions were usually gilded in a traditional manner.[1] Many of his works, however, were put into a cheaper, stained and waxed frame of a type much favoured by Academicians at the time.

1. Telephone conversation with Terry Burns, April 1996. Burns moved into framing in 1968 after selling his medical equipment business. He subsequently took on framing at the Royal Academy, and retired in 1991. I am grateful to Terry Burns for lending me his press cuttings file and his book, *Framing Pictures*, 1978.

125 [fig.173]
Paul McCartney (b.1942)
By Humphrey Ocean, signed and dated 1983
Oil on canvas, 85.4 × 49.5 (33⅝ × 19½)
NPG 5695

Steel, mitred and welded, an inverted flat U-shaped main piece contains a hidden ramin

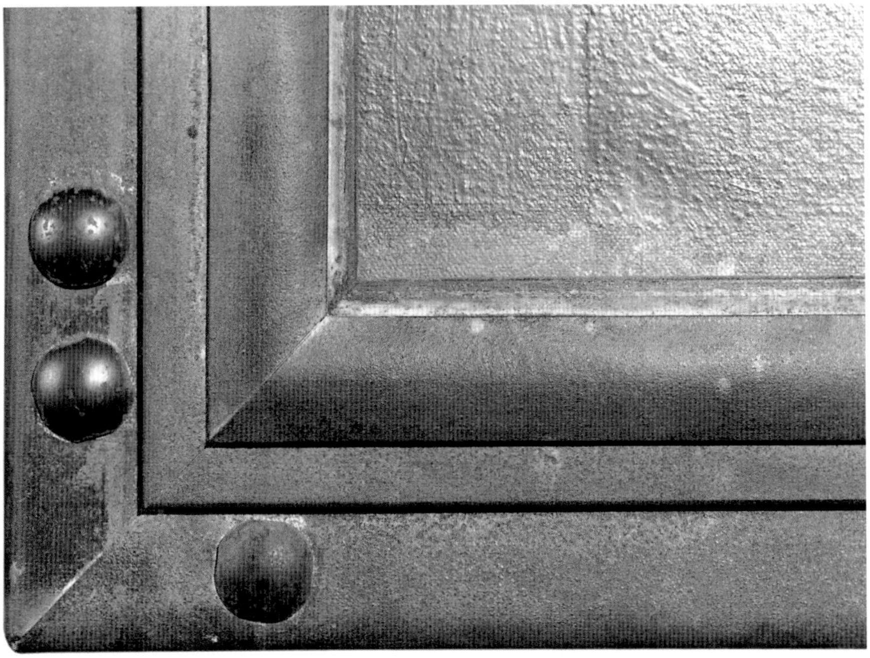

no.125; fig.173

under-frame held by the large domed corner bolts, and has a welded dome-shaped steel piece on a flat plate next to the sight edge. 2⅞ inches wide.

This frame of second-hand rusty steel was designed by the artist and made in collaboration with the sculptor, Chris Poulton, at a cost of £51.32 for the various parts.[1] The artist's bill, dated 15 November 1983, lists the frame's components of which the most expensive was the 'Roundel Angle' of the main steel framework at £29.38, supplied by Metal Fabrications Ltd. Other costs ranged from £8.65 for wood to £2.80 for bolts and 30p for washers.

Humphrey Ocean has always liked to be closely involved in the framing of his pictures. The portrait of Paul McCartney was both his first commission from the National Portrait Gallery, as prize winner of the John Player Portrait Award in 1982, and his first metal frame. Since then the artist has painted various other portraits for the Gallery, including Philip Larkin's in 1984 which has a recycled black Dutch ripple frame designed to reflect the domestic nature of the portrait, and A.J. Ayer's in 1985 in a flat white frame, intended to take up the idea of purity in intellectual thought. More recently Ocean has painted the portraits of Lord Whitelaw, which was given a traditional frame from store, and of Tony Benn, which has been framed in a more modern style.

1. Some of the information in this entry derives from a telephone conversation with the artist, 26 April 1996.

126 [fig.174]

Three Trade Union Leaders
By Hans Schwarz, signed and dated 1984
Oil on board, 183 × 183 (72 × 72)
NPG 5749

Painted hardwood, mitred and pinned, brass studs. 4½ inches wide.

Hans Schwarz's portrait of three former trade union leaders, Lord Gormley of the

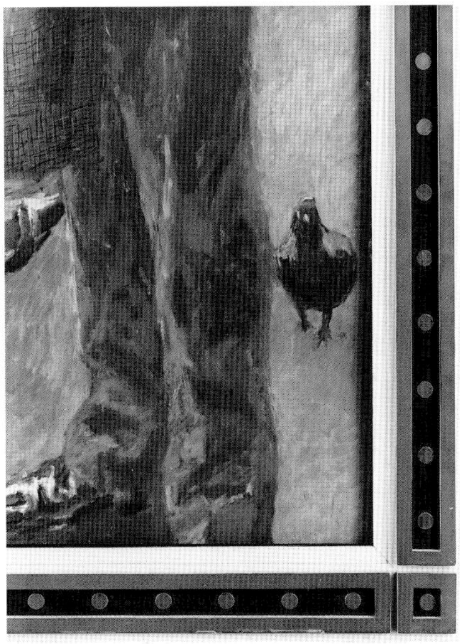

no.126; fig.174

National Union of Mineworkers, Sid Weighell of the National Union of Railwaymen and Tom Jackson of the Post Office Workers, was commissioned by the National Portrait Gallery in 1984. The painted wood and metal frame, designed by the artist, was made by the then Derby Carriage Works of British Rail Engineering Ltd. The artist thought it a good idea to involve a trade union in the work, and with Sid Weighell's support approached the railway coach builders at Derby where he met with an enthusiastic response. 'We've got cabinet makers, coach painters, metal workers, but with modern methods – plastics, spray paint, transfer lettering – they are sadly underused', Hans Schwarz recalls being told.[1] Schwarz chose the colours of the frame to suit the painting, and the brass studs to give life and sparkle, and to hint at the industrial theme, though the final result is not quite as bright and handmade in appearance as he had hoped.

1. Letter to the author, 19 July 1996.

127 [fig.38]

Sir John Summerson (1904–92)
By Leonard Rosoman, signed and dated 1984
Oil on canvas, 152.1 × 122 (60 × 48)
NPG 5730

Silvered obeche(?), mitred and underpinned, the reverse section moulding applied to a narrow underframe, the overlapping of the silver leaf visible, the leaf width the standard 3¾ inches, the silvering oxidised and varnished. 3⅛ inches wide.

'I hope that you approve of the frame', wrote Rosoman to the Gallery's Director in 1984 on completion of the portrait, 'Hawker has done a very good job, I think, and somehow has been able to give us an overall surface of oxidised silver at the reduced price'. The frame was made for £310.50 by Nick Hawker whom Rosoman has known for a very long time, ever since the days Hawker worked for Robert Sielle, Rosoman's framemaker in the 1960s.[1] Rosoman usually asks Hawker to come to his studio to discuss framing at some length: 'Usually we agree. It's a matter of trust. He knows the sort of thing I want'. Rosoman has used oxidised silver frames quite often, finding that solid gold frames do not suit the delicate colouring of his pictures.

1. Much of this entry is based on a telephone conversation with Leonard Rosoman, April 1996.

128 [fig.175]

Dame Iris Murdoch (b.1919)
By Tom Phillips, 1984–6
Oil on canvas, 91.4 × 71.1 (36 × 28)
NPG 5921

Painted ramin, mitred and pinned, both the frame and the canvas sitting on a back board. 2¾ inches wide.

In Tom Phillips's pictures important features (like the ginko leaf at the bottom left in *Iris Murdoch*) often press right up to the edge of the canvas, and in these cases a breathing space is required between

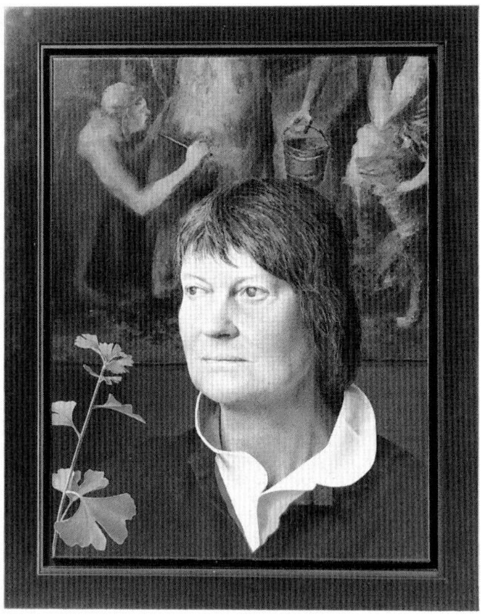

no.128; fig.175

picture and frame. Andy Gizauskas, Tom Phillips's assistant and framemaker for the past sixteen years, recalls trying out ideas: 'We decided you wanted to scan across the picture: the ginko did not want to go back or come forward'. The dark brown flat moulding is deliberately simple: 'If you can make the frame disappear from view it's been a success – we never do anything ostentatious'. If there are two rules of thumb, from Gizauskas's experience in framing Tom Phillips's work, they are to frame to the picture and to make the frame disappear. Because the picture floats – it is mounted on a board and separated from the frame – its edges can be seen. Sometimes Gizauskas ends up painting the edges to ghost what is on the front so that the canvas has the quality of an object in the frame rather than a flat picture; he uses a greyish tone or carries on the picture round the edge of the canvas.

Looking back to Phillips's pictures of the 1960s, framed before Gizauskas joined the studio, both artist and framemaker have mixed views about the metal frames of the time: dreadful through they now appear, they are of their time and may suit the pictures well.

1. Much of this discussion is based on telephone conversations with the artist and his framemaker, April 1996.

129 [fig.119]
Sir Michael Tippett (b.1905)
By Martin Rose, signed and dated 1989
Acrylic on canvas, 107 × 76.5 (42 1/8 × 30 1/8)
NPG 6043

Oak, mitred with hidden square corner tongues, apparently secured by the thick projecting corner pegs, the rebate enlarged to take the glazing slips revealing a cross-section of the thinner wooden dowels at the corners and the centre of each side. 4 inches wide.

It was Peter Cropper, leader of the Lindsay String Quartet, who suggested to Martin Rose that he should paint the composer Michael Tippett, and Rose recalls that the idea for the heavy oak frame came up in conversation with Cropper.[1] The use of old English beams embodies an idea of Englishness, a theme of a conversation Rose had had with Tippett. The framemaker, Edward Pontefract of Rochdale, found the old English oak for Rose and made the frame with projecting pegs, rather like the wooden pegs found in traditional beamed roofs (a feature of Cropper's stone-built Edale cottage). There was a lot of effort to place the timbers so that they best matched the workings of the portrait. The frame was made in 1986 for £385; the sight edge was subsequently altered at a cost of £87.50. 'Plain frames', reads Pontefract's trade card, 'Edward Pontefract makes frames and mounts to order, specialising in plain hardwood mouldings'.

1. Telephone conversation with the author, April 1996.

130 [fig.176]
Queen Elizabeth the Queen Mother (b.1900)
By Alison Watt, signed and dated 1989
Oil on canvas, 101.6 × 91.4 (40 × 36)
NPG 6042

Painted and gessoed obeche, reverse section, mitred, the main moulding planted on a flat back frame, chamfered fabric slip. 4 3/8 inches wide plus 3/4 inch slip.

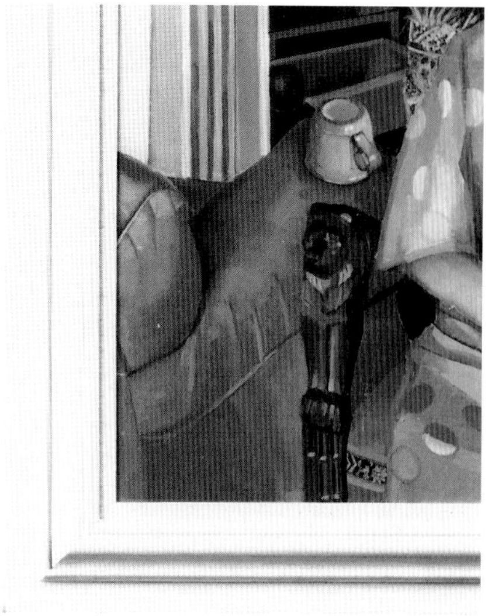

no.130; fig.176

This frame was made by Stephen Carruthers of Artworks the Framemakers, Glasgow, for Alison Watt in 1989 at a cost of £141.05 with the glass. She had come across his work as a framemaker at an exhibition in Glasgow while still a student at the Glasgow School of Art and liked the straightforward and sensitive way he spoke about what he did.[1] It was Carruthers who persuaded her to enter her *Self-portrait with Tea Cup*, a picture he felt had a humorous touch, in the John Player Portrait Award at the National Portrait Gallery in 1987. Her first prize brought her the commission for this portrait.

Alison Watt knows that gold or silver would kill the colour in her paintings and often uses this warm off-white for her frames. The paint mixture, says Carruthers, has a polish in it with a gold powder, and here has a brushed surface; the fabric slip picks up the texture of the canvas.

Many of Alison Watt's recent pictures have quite simple frames but for the portrait of the Queen Mother it was thought the frame should be slightly more formal and not too simple because of the nature of the sitter. Although the idea of the reverse section came from mouldings Stephen Carruthers showed her, he recalls not being allowed to see the portrait before making the frame owing to the confidentiality attached to the commission. The result, Alison Watt has suggested, is a frame which fell back and blended into the wall, but brought out the picture at the same time.

1. Much of this entry is based on telephone conversations with both Watt and Carruthers, 19 April 1996.

131 [fig.177]
A.J.P. Taylor (1906–90)
By Maggi Hambling, signed and dated 1988
Oil on canvas, 53.3 × 43.2 (21 × 17)
NPG 5988

Silvered ramin(?), mitred, the water silvering on a black bole with extensive leaf overlap (leaf width 3⅝ inches), treated with ammonium hydrosulphide and lacquered. Under reflected light a changing array of pink and green colours can be seen, a phenomenon caused by the reflection of light on the thin surface film. 2⅛ inches wide.

This is a silvered frame which has been artificially tarnished, rubbed back and lacquered. The silvering is distinguished by the overlapping of the silver leaf and by a thin surface film giving an unusual range of changing colours under reflected light. The frame is the work of Nick Hawker who has been responsible for Maggi Hambling's framing since her Serpentine show in 1987.[1] Much of her earlier work, including her portrait of Dorothy Hodgkin, commissioned by the National Portrait Gallery in 1985, was framed by Mattei Radev (he framed her Max Wall exhibition at the National Portrait Gallery in 1983).

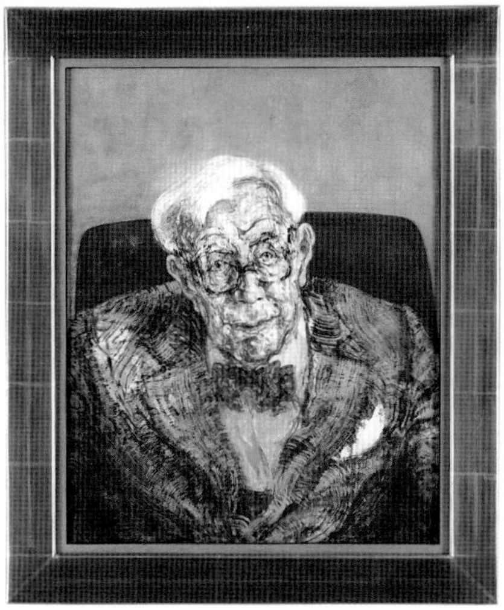

no.131; fig.177

1. The suggestion that she should go to Hawker for the framing of her Serpentine show came from Alister Warman, then the Serpentine's Director. Information from the artist.

132 [fig.178]
Antoinette Sibley (b.1939)
By Howard Morgan, signed and dated 1993
Oil on canvas, 111.8 × 101.2 (44 × 39¾)
NPG 6228

Carved and gilt obeche(?), mitred and keyed, the top leaf-and-berry carving applied, gilt in white gold over a red bole layered with yellow, the scoop burnished and sealed. 3¼ inches wide.

Howard Morgan's frames, which are distinguished by their high quality, have often taken late seventeenth-century bunched-leaf frames as their starting-point. Since 1987 Morgan has worked with Alexander George Ley & Sons, a London family firm of framemakers based in Kentish Town, who have produced both hand-carved and less expensive compo frames.[1] This particular frame, billed in October 1993 as a 'Carved & gilt reproduction Louis XIII berry and leaf frame. White gold', at a cost of £1880, was the result of discussion between the artist and Anthony Ley, who produced a trial frame section while the portrait was in progress, as a photograph in the National Portrait Gallery's files records.

This type of frame has an antecedent in an earlier portrait by Morgan owned by the Gallery, that of the conductor, Herbert Howells, painted in 1978, which was framed for the Gallery by John Davies in a silvered reproduction acorn-

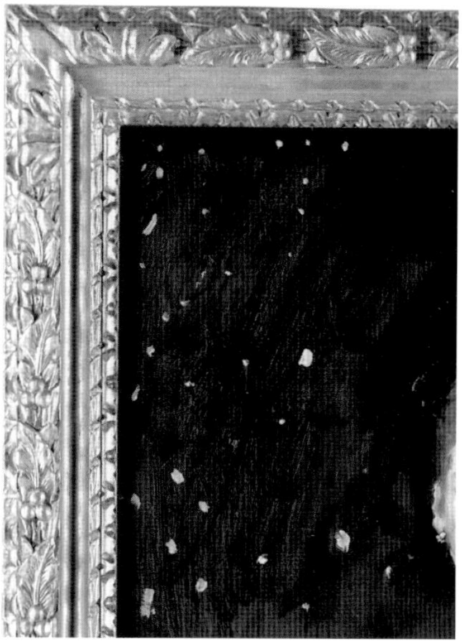

no.132, fig.178

and-leaf frame in the English style; this was chosen as a result of a conversation between the artist and the curator, Robin Gibson, who had just had a rather similar reproduction frame made for another portrait.[2]

1. Information from Howard Morgan and Anthony Ley, April 1996.
2. Information from Robin Gibson, May 1996.

Notes to Chapters 1 to 6

Unless otherwise stated, the place of publication for bibliographical sources and the location of exhibitions is London.

Abbreviations

DEF	Percy Macquoid and Ralph Edwards, 'Picture Frames', *The Dictionary of English Furniture*, 2nd edition, revised by Ralph Edwards, 1954, as reprinted by the Antique Collectors' Club, 1983, vol.III, pp.19–34 (including reproductions of sixteen framed pictures belonging to the National Portrait Gallery).
DEFM	Geoffrey Beard and Christopher Gilbert (eds), *Dictionary of English Furniture Makers 1660–1840*, Furniture History Society, 1986.
Farington	*The Diary of Joseph Farington*, ed. Kenneth Garlick and Angus MacIntyre (vols.I to VI), Kathryn Cave (vols.VII to XVI), New Haven and London, 1978–84.
Vertue	'Vertue Note Books', *Walpole Society*, vols.XVIII, XX, XXII, XXIV, XXVI, XXIX, XXX, Oxford 1930–55.
Trade Directories	Post Office London Directories, published by Kelly & Co.

Chapter 1: Attitudes to Picture Framing in Britain and Abroad

1. Jean André Rouquet, *The Present State of the Arts in England*, 1755, p.45, translated from the French edition of 1754.
2. Marcia Pointon, *Hanging the Head. Portraiture and Social Formation in Eighteenth-Century England*, New Haven and London, 1993, p.40. Pointon's estimate is based on Samuel Redgrave's *Dictionary of Artists of the English School*, 2nd edn. 1878. The figure of more than 800 painters produced by James Northcote in 1819 would seem to be no more than a turn of phrase.
3. Rouquet, op. cit., p.45.
4. W.A. Shaw (ed.), *Three Inventories of the Years 1542, 1547 and 1549-50 of Pictures in the Collections of Henry VIII & Edward VI*, 1937.
5. Susan Foister, 'Paintings and other works of art in sixteenth-century English inventories', *Burlington Magazine*, vol.CXXIII, 1981, p.275.
6. William J. Thoms, 'Pictures of the Great Earl of Leicester', *Notes and Queries*, 3rd Series, vol.II, 1862, pp.201–2.
7. The picture was by William Larkin. See *The Life of Edward First Lord Herbert of Cherbury*, ed. J.M. Shuttleworth, 1976, p.60.
8. Oliver Millar (ed.), 'The Inventories and Valuations of the King's Goods 1649–1651', *Walpole Society*, vol.XLIII, 1972, p.58.
9. Edward Croft-Murray, *Decorative Painting in England 1537-1837*, vol.1, 1962, pp.179, 193, 195.
10. O. Ter Kuile, 'Daniel Mijtens "His Majesties Picture-Drawer"', *Nederlands Kunsthistorisch Jaarboek*, vol.XX, 1969, p.25.
11. W. Noël Sainsbury, *Original Unpublished Papers illustrative of the Life of Sir Peter Paul Rubens*, 1859, p.45. See also p.52 for the importation of pictures with their frames.
12. H.M. Colvin (ed.), *The History of the King's Works*, vol.IV, part II, 1982, p.268.
13. Mary Edmond, 'Limners and Picturemakers – New Light on the lives of miniaturists and large-scale portrait-painters working in London in the sixteenth and seventeenth centuries', *Walpole Society*, vol.XLVII, 1980, p.174.
14. 'The Inventaire off divers Fyne picturs &c: At niubiging This First day of Januar 1665', typescript at Scottish National Portrait Gallery (original in the Scottish Record Office, GD18/1788).
15. *Mr Cartwright's Pictures*, exh. cat., Dulwich Picture Gallery, 1987–8, pp.20–7. By the late seventeenth century frames cease to be mentioned as a matter of routine in inventories of paintings.
16. The Duke of Montrose's order to a leading London maker for a 'Black and Gold' frame for a portrait in 1725 is an exception to his usual taste for gilt frames (Scottish Record Office, GD220/6/1356/20). Orders from the aristocracy for black frames for oil paintings after this date are difficult to find.
17. Jean-Claude Lebensztein, 'Framing Classical Space', *Art Journal*, vol.XLVII, 1988, p.37.
18. MIH in *The Builder*, vol.XV, 1857, p.609, quoted by John Gage, *Colour in Turner: Poetry and Truth*, 1969, p.163.
19. Charles Eastlake, *Hints on Household Taste in Furniture, Upholstery and Other Details*, 1878, p.193 (first published 1869; the 1878 edition as reprinted by Dover Publications, 1969, with an introduction by John Gloag, is used here).
20. Percy Fitzgerald, 'Picture Frames', *Art Journal*, 1886, p.325.
21. Philip Hamerton, 'Picture-Frames', *The Portfolio*, vol.II, 1871, p.179.
22. David Brewster, reviewing Eastlake's translation of Goethe's *Theory of Colours*, in *Edinburgh Review*, no.CXLV, October 1840, p.109. *Theory of Colours* was first published as *Zur Farbenlehre*, in 1810.
23. *Blackwood's Edinburgh Magazine*, vol.LXXVI, November 1854, pp.539–60. For Chevreul, see above, p.21.
24. Edward Rimbault, 'Sir Edward Dering's Household Book', *Notes and Queries*, 1st Series, vol.I, 12 January 1850, pp.161–2.
25. *Mr Cartwright's Pictures*, op.cit. in n.15, nos.96, 99, 158, 171.
26. Vertue, vol.I, p.108. Mrs Reginald Lane Poole, *Catalogue of Oxford Portraits*, vol.II, Oxford, 1925, p.262.
27. Exhibition at the Tate Gallery, 1995–6, *Dynasties. Painting in Tudor and Jacobean England 1530–1630*; nos.29, 35, 46, 55 and 144 retained their original frames and perhaps also nos.23, 52, 123, judging from an examination on the wall.
28. John Cornforth, 'Hardwick Hall, Derbyshire', *Country Life*, vol.CLXXXIX, 24 August 1995, pp.37–8. For the Tradescant pictures see 'Frames on the Tradescant/Ashmole paintings' in *Tradescant's Rarities*, ed. Arthur MacGregor, Oxford, 1983, pp.327–9. One of the Berkeley frames is repr. in James Ayres, *The Artist's Craft*, Oxford, 1985, p.124.
29. Charles Noble, 'Fashion in the gallery', *Apollo*, vol.CXXXVIII, 1993, pp.171–4. See also above, p.119.
30. Quoted in John Fowler and John Cornforth, *English Decoration in the*

Eighteenth Century, 1974, p.202.

31. John Cornforth, 'Houghton Hall, Norfolk – II', *Country Life*, vol.CLXXXI, 7 May 1987, p.106.
32. Brian Fitzgerald (ed.), *Correspondence of Emily, Duchess of Leinster (1731–1814)*, vol.I, Dublin, 1949, p.223.
33. W.T. Whitley, *Art in England, 1821–1837*, Cambridge, 1930, p.347.
34. Aymer Vallance, *William Morris*, 1897, p.14.
35. Letter to the *Morning Chronicle*, quoted by W.T. Whitley, *Artists and their Friends in England, 1700–1799*, vol.1, 1928, p.374.
36. Hugh Brigstocke, *William Buchanan and the 19th-century Art Trade*, 1982, p.181.
37. Sarah Uwins, *A Memoir of Thomas Uwins R.A.*, vol.2, 1858, p.131.
38. Geoffrey de Bellaigue and Pat Kirkham, 'George IV and the Furnishing of Windsor Castle', *Furniture History*, vol.VIII, 1972, p.17.
39. See above, p.116.
40. W.H. Pyne, *The History of the Royal Residences*, vol.II, 1819, p.83.
41. Ernest Fletcher (ed.), *Conversations of James Northcote R.A. with James Ward*, 1901, p.163. For Lawrence, see above, pp.99–103.
42. L. Parris, C. Shields & I. Fleming-Williams (eds), *John Constable: Further Documents and Correspondence*, 1975, p.274. The painting in question, *A heath-showry, noon*, now lost, was no.94 in the exhibition.
43. Sidney C. Hutchinson, *The History of the Royal Academy 1768–1968*, 1968, p.71; *Royal Academy*, exh. cat., 1837.
44. Royal Academy, Council Minutes, 29 January 1847.
45. Notice to exhibitors of Institute of the Fine Arts, Liverpool, March 1838 (copy in York City Library, William Etty letters, no.171); Royal Scottish Academy, exh. cat., 1839.
46. Fitzgerald, op.cit. in n.20, p.325.
47. 'The Fashion of Furniture', *Cornhill Magazine*, vol.IX, 1864, p.343 (published anonymously); *Hints on Household Taste*, op.cit. in n.19, pp.192–8.
48. John A. Mahey, 'The Letters of James McNeill Whistler to George A. Lucas', *Art Bulletin*, vol.XLIX, 1967, p.253.
49. 'La vie à Paris', *Le Temps*, 5 April 1881, quoted in Eva Mendgen, *et al., In Perfect Harmony: Picture and Frame, 1850–1920*, exh. cat., Van Gogh Museum, Amsterdam and Kunstforum, Vienna, 1995, p.132.
50. *In Perfect Harmony*, op.cit., p.132.
51. Jules Champfleury, *Journal*, 1882, p.37, quoted in Isabelle Cahn, 'Degas's frames', *Burlington Magazine*, vol.CXXXI, 1989, p.289.
52. *In Perfect Harmony*, pp.131–2, 142, 149. See above, p.17. See also Georges Roque, 'Chevreul and Impressionism: A Reappraisal', *Art Bulletin*, vol.LXXVIII, 1996, pp.26–39.
53. *Salon de 1884*, exh. cat., 1884, p.cxxv, Règlement, Peintures, Dessins, Aquarelles, Pastels, etc. Art. 2; kindly communicated by Robert Wenley.
54. Lloyd Goodrich, *Thomas Eakins*, Cambridge, Massachusetts, 1982, vol.2, pp.8–9.
55. Louisine Havemeyer, *Sixteen to Sixty. Memoirs of a Collector*, New York, 1961, p.251.
56. Apparently original are the flat white frame on Lavery's *Hokusai and the Butterfly (Mr & Mrs E.A. Walton)*, 1889 (Scottish National Portrait Gallery) and the white Whistler frame on Starr's *At the Café Royal*, 1888 (Fine Art Society).
57. Ira M. Horowitz, 'Whistler's Frames', *Art Journal*, vol.XXXIX, no.2, winter 1979–80, p.130; Horowitz claims that Whistler used white frames for his 1881 exhibition of etchings but without providing evidence.
58. D.M. Bendix, *Diabolical Designs. Paintings, Interiors and Exhibitions of James McNeill Whistler*, Washington, DC, 1995, p.253.
59. Vivien Hamilton, *Joseph Crawhall 1861–1913*, 1990, Appendix 3, p.170.
60. See the Sales Order Day Books of Alfred Stiles & Sons Ltd, Hammersmith and Fulham Archives, DD/76/25, for example the entry on 2 February 1934 for a 'stone grey & slight pink smooth finish' frame.
61. 'Frames of extravagant design or colour or unusual material should be avoided' became the advice to exhibitors in the Royal Academy catalogues; this advice continued to be given until 1963.
62. James Bourlet & Sons, catalogue, January 1921.
63. See n.60. Among the artists supplied with such frames were C.R.W. Nevinson, Mark Gertler, Edward Bawden and Gilbert Spencer. See also above, p.79.
64. Richard R. Brettell, 'The Problematics of Collecting and Display, Part 2: Modern French Painting and the Art Museum', *Art Bulletin*, vol.LXXVII, 1995, p.168.
65. Charles Merrill Mount, *John Singer Sargent*, 1957, p.174, quoting a letter of 22 March 1895 to Mrs George Whitin about the framing of a portrait of the actress, Ada Rehan (Metropolitan Museum of Art, New York). An example of a Sargent in the National Portrait Gallery in a period frame is his 1902 portrait of the 1st Earl of Cromer.
66. I. Hunter Donaldson, 'Picture Frames', *Journal of the Society of Arts*, vol.XLVII, 2 June 1899, p.597.
67. York City Library, Etty letters, no.36, dated 16 February 1832, referring to the *Destruction of the Temple of Vice*, exhibited RA 1832 (215). Payne gave Messrs Woodburn as the source of some of his carved frames.
68. Simon Jervis, 'Picture frames and picture hanging at Apsley House' in *Catalogue of Paintings in the Wellington Museum* by C.M. Kauffmann, 1982, p.17.
69. Information on Gunn from Chloë Blackburn, March 1995, including a copy of Arnold Wiggins & Sons' invoice of 25 May 1964 for eight Carlo Maratta and other period frames supplied to Gunn; information on Flint from Paul Mitchell, 22 November 1995.
70. One such frame on a 1936 portrait of McBey's wife, Marguerite, is reproduced in *James McBey*, exh. cat., Aberdeen Art Gallery, 1983.
71. Letter from Keith Christiansen, May 1995.
72. Information on Vannoni from Keith Christiansen, see n.71. Information on Remy from Shelley M. Bennett, letter of 3 July 1995. For Remy, see also above, p.119.
73. Information from Shelley M. Bennett, see n.72. Five other portraits in the collection of Lord Michelham, sold by Hamptons on the premises at 20 Arlington St, London, 24 November 1926, had matching frames to 'Pinkie'.
74. David Piper, unpublished autobiography, p.35, copy deposited in National Portrait Gallery Archive.
75. J.B. Manson, foreword to the trade catalogue of James Bourlet & Sons, 1938.
76. Tate Gallery Report 1964–5, p.3.
77. *Apollo*, vol.LXXXIII, 1966, p.327.
78. Information from William Drummond, 1 December 1995.
79. Information from David Alexander, 12 February 1996.
80. Address by René Varin, French Cultural Attaché in London, reported in *The Art Bulletin* of the Fine Art Trade Guild, no.57, summer 1956, p.6. Such an attitude goes back to revolutionary France where a decree in 1798 calls for gold to be recovered from old frames; see Isabelle Cahn, 'Cadres et cartels' in *La jeunesse des musées*, Musée d'Orsay, Paris, 1994, p.222, n.9.
81. For a wide-ranging survey of the attitudes of artists to framing in the twentieth century see *La cadre & le socle dans l'art du 20 éme siècle*, exh. cat., Université de Bourgogne, Dijon and Centre Georges Pompidou, Paris, 1987. See also *In Perfect Harmony*, op.cit. in n.49, pp.221–47.

82. 'Eleven Europeans in America', *The Museum of Modern Art Bulletin*, vol.XIII, no.45, 1946, pp.35–6, quoted in *In Perfect Harmony*, op.cit. in n.49, p.242.
83. John Elderfield, *Morris Louis*, exh. cat., Hayward Gallery, 1974, p.18.
84. Gertrude Stein, *Picasso*, Boston, 1970, p.38, quoted in *In Perfect Harmony*, op.cit. in n.49, p.221.
85. David Antin, 'Biography', *Representations*, autumn 1986, p.42, quoted in J.R.R. Christie and Fred Orton, 'Writing on a Text of the Life', *Art History*, vol.XI, no.4, 1988, p.554.
86. Roberto Aloi, *Musei: Architettura-Technica*, Milan, 1962, p.176, quoted in M. Kirby Talley, 'The 1985 Rehang of Old Masters at the Allen Memorial Art Museum, Oberlin, Ohio', *International Journal of Museum Management and Curatorship*, vol.VI, 1987, p.229.
87. Caterina Marcenaro, 'The Museum Concept and the Rearrangement of the Palazzo Bianco, Genoa', *Museum*, vol.VII, 1954, p.265.
88. Based on Susan Moore, *Framing Modern Masters. A Conversation with Heinz Berggruen*, 1991, p.6. Rubin's frames are already being replaced as his successor, Kirk Varnedoe, imposes his own aesthetic on the collection: 'Bill Rubin's framing radically emphasized the picture as object. I wanted to reconquer more of the picture as window' (*New York Times*, 5 May 1996, p.43).
89. Moore, op.cit., p.6.
90. Louis van Tilborgh, 'Framing Van Gogh 1880–1990' in *In Perfect Harmony*, op.cit. in n.49, pp.163–180.
91. Van Tilborgh, op.cit., p.176.
92. Gervase Jackson-Stops, 'English picture frames and their makers', *The Magazine Antiques*, vol.CXXXIII, 1988, p.233.
93. Giles Waterfield, 'Picture Hanging and Gallery Decoration', in *Palaces of Art. Art Galleries in Britain 1790–1990*, exh. cat., Dulwich Picture Gallery and National Gallery of Scotland, 1991–2, p.49.
94. Nicholas Penny, 'Back to the Wall', review of *In Perfect Harmony*, *London Review of Books*, 21 September 1995, p.12.
95. Germain Bazin, 'Renovation at the Musée du Jeu de Paume, Paris', *Museum*, vol.XIV, 1961, pp.25–35; P.J.J. van Thiel, 'The Framing of Paintings in the Rijksmuseum since 1800', Bulletin van het Rijksmuseum, vol.XXVIII, 1979, pp.159–79, 206–10; P.J.J. van Thiel, 'Framing Dutch pictures' in *Framing in the Golden Age. Picture and Frame in 17th-century Holland*, Zwolle, 1995, p.15–25.

Chapter 2: The Techniques and Practice of the Framemaker

1. John Ruskin, 'The Relation of Engraving to Other Arts in Florence', lecture delivered in 1872, in E.T. Cook and A. Wedderburn (eds), *The Works of John Ruskin*, vol.XXII, 1906, p.337.
2. Dillian Gordon, *Making & Meaning. The Wilton Diptych*, exh. cat., National Gallery, 1993, pp.74–5.
3. Repr. with frame in J. Alexander and P. Binski (eds), *Age of Chivalry. Art in Plantagenet England 1200-1400*, exh. cat., Royal Academy, 1987, no.711. It was used by Sir George Gilbert Scott as the model for the frame made for the portrait of Richard II in Westminster Abbey in 1872, repr. ibid., no.713.
4. The grooves have been cut away on portraits of Edward IV (fig.2) and Henry VIII (no.3) at the National Portrait Gallery, and of Henry VII at the Society of Antiquaries.
5. William Brenchley Rye, *England as seen by Foreigners in the Days of Elizabeth and James the First*, 1865, p.206.
6. Hélène Verougstraete-Marcq and Roger van Schoute, *Cadres et supports dans la peinture flamande aux 15e et 16e siècles*, Heure-le-Romain, Belgium, 1989.
7. The portrait of the 1st Earl, attributed to J. de Critz, hangs in the Great Hall. That of James I is reproduced in its frame in Gervase Jackson-Stops, 'English picture frames and their makers', *The Magazine Antiques*, vol.CXXXIII, 1988, p.232.
8. Oliver Millar, 'Abraham van der Doort's Catalogue of the Collections of Charles I', *Walpole Society*, vol.XXXVII, 1960, pp.27–8.
9. Ibid.
10. Mary Edmond, 'Limners and Picturemakers – New Light on the lives of miniaturists and large-scale portrait-painters working in London in the sixteenth and seventeenth centuries', *Walpole Society*, vol.XLVII, 1980, pp.173–4.
11. The Van Dyck is repr. with frame in Alastair Laing, *In Trust for the Nation. Paintings from National Trust Houses*, exh. cat., National Gallery, 1995, p.23.
12. Royal Society, manuscript Cl.P.III (i),1.
13. Edward Basil Jupp, *An Historical Account of the Worshipful Company of Carpenters of the City of London*, 1848, pp.295–9.
14. Pat Kirkham, 'The London Furniture Trade 1700–1870', *Furniture History*, vol.XXIV, 1988, pp.136, 144.
15. R. Campbell, *The London Tradesman*, 1747, p.174.
16. Ibid.
17. Butterfly keys are found at the National Portrait Gallery on portraits of Thomas Hope (no.58) and Lord Hatherton (no.67).
18. Robert Dossie, *The Handmaid to the Arts*, vol.I, 1758, p.372. My account of gilding and silvering owes much to the elegant and informative essay by Pippa Mason and Michael Gregory, *Of Gilding*, published by Arnold Wiggins & Sons Ltd to accompany an exhibition in 1989.
19. Charles Tomlinson, *Illustrations of Trades*, n.d. but *c.* 1858, p.54.
20. Ibid.
21. Dossie, op.cit. in n.18, p.368.
22. Tomlinson, op.cit. in n.19.
23. John Stalker and George Parker, *A Treatise of Japaning and Varnishing*, 1688, republished by Alec Tiranti, 1960, p.56.
24. Thomas Sheraton, *The Cabinet Dictionary*, 1803, p.223. A similar account of the 'better gloss' achievable using a thick oil is given by Stalker and Parker, op.cit., p.54.
25. Dossie, op.cit. in n.18, pp.374–5.
26. Ibid., p.375.
27. J. Douglas Stewart, *Sir Godfrey Kneller and the English Baroque Portrait*, Oxford, 1983, pp.194–5.
28. Sheraton, op.cit. in n.24, p.227.
29. Jean Felix Watin, *L'Art du peintre, doreur, vernisseur*, Paris, 1773. Cited in Mason and Gregory, 1989, op.cit. in n.18, unpaginated, at n.15.
30. Sheraton, op.cit. in n.24, p.228.
31. Dossie, op.cit. in n.18, p.381.
32. Victoria and Albert Museum Library, Box 86.AA.24, items 4 & 25.
33. Mason and Gregory, op.cit. in n.18.
34. Stalker and Parker, op.cit. in n.23, pp.60–1.
35. Christopher Gilbert, *The Life and Work of Thomas Chippendale*, 1978, p.177.
36. Stalker and Parker, op.cit. in n.23, p.59.
37. Ibid.
38. *The Carver and Gilder's Guide and Picture Frame Maker's Companion*, [1873], p.49. Published by Kent & Co (copy in British Library), this guide was re-issued by Brodie and Middleton in 1874 (copy in Victoria and Albert Museum Library) and in an amended version, as *The Gilder's Manual* in New York in 1876 (reprinted by the Society of Gilders, 1990).
39. Stalker and Parker, op.cit. in n.23, p.60.
40. Ibid.; Dossie, op.cit. in n.18, p.382.

41. John Barrow, *Dictionarium Polygraphicum*, vol.I, 1735, entry for gilding; this is derived from William Salmon, *Polygraphice*, 8th edn., vol.II, 1701, pp.922–3.
42. Reproduced in Mason and Gregory, op.cit. in n.18, pl.V.
43. *The Carver and Gilder's Guide and Picture Frame Maker's Companion* [1873] op.cit. in n.38, p.49.
44. Stalker and Parker, op.cit. in n.23, p.64.
45. I owe this observation to Mason and Gregory, op.cit.in n.18, *sub* Silvering.
46. R.T. Gunther (ed.), *The Architecture of Sir Roger Pratt*, Oxford, 1928, p.283.
47. Mason and Gregory, op.cit. in n.18, *sub* Silvering.
48. Pepys to Dr Charlett, 13 September 1702, see *Private Correspondence and Miscellaneous Papers of Samuel Pepys*, vol.II, 1926, p.269.
49. Dossie, op.cit. in n.18, p.429.
50. Stalker and Parker, op.cit. in n.23, p.57.
51. Campbell, op.cit. in n.15, p.174. See also Dimitri Shipounoff, 'La Reparure', *Museum Management and Curatorship*, vol.XIII, 1994, pp.431–4.
52. Duchy of Cornwall vouchers, Frederick Prince of Wales, vol.IX, pp.183, 236. See also David Buttery, 'The Picture Frames of Paul Petit, and Frederick, Prince of Wales', *Apollo*, vol.CXXVI, 1987, pp.12–15, and Peter Cannon-Brookes, 'An Addendum to Paul Petit: the Role of the Répareur', *Museum Management and Curatorship*, vol.XI, 1992, p.439.
53. Robert Boyle, *Some Considerations Touching the Usefulnesse of Experimental Naturall Philosophy*, vol.II, Oxford, 1671, Essay X, 'Of Mens Great Ignorance of the Uses of Natural Things', p.32.
54. The two best accounts of the use of papier-mâché in the eighteenth century are by Geoffrey Wills, *English Looking-glasses*, 1965, pp.138–42, and John Cornforth, 'Putting up with Georgian DIY', *Country Life*, vol.CLXXXVI, 9 April 1992, pp.54–6. The earliest definite dated reference to the use of papier-mâché in the eighteenth century occurs in a letter of 1742; see Alastair Laing, *The Rococo in England. A Symposium*, ed. Charles Hind, 1986, p.43.
55. *Letters written by ... Lady Luxborough to William Shenstone, Esq.*, 1775, p.223; the letter is dated to 1751 by Alastair Laing, op.cit., p.44.
56. Mrs Delany's letter to her sister, 17 December 1749, is in *The Autobiography and Correspondence of Mary Granville, Mrs Delany*, ed. Lady Llanover, vol.II, 1861, p.532.
57. Wills, op.cit. in n.54, p.141.
58. Ibid.
59. *Boddely's Bath Journal*, vol.XVIII, no.17, 27 April 1761; kindly communicated by Susan Sloman.
60. Wills, op.cit. in n.54, p.142.
61. Examples of papier-mâché frames are the three-quarter length by Thomas Hudson of Mrs Jonathan Midgley (Sotheby's, 12 April 1995, lot 44) and the half-length portraits of Viscount Curzon and his wife, attributed to Nathaniel Hone (formerly on loan to Commonwealth Relations Office). There is a half-length pair at Easton Neston of Sir Thomas and Lady Hesketh. Cornforth (op.cit. in n.54, p.56) refers to papier-mâché frames at Berkeley House, Somerset, and to the supply of such frames to Sir John Delaval of Doddington by Babell in 1766. For the pictures sent out in papier-mâché frames by Joshua Reynolds in 1757 and 1758, see Nicholas Penny, 'Reynolds and picture frames', *Burlington Magazine*, vol.CXXVIII, 1986, p.817. Rather different in feel are the papier-mâché frames found on Wright of Derby's Markheaton Hunt group; see Paul Mitchell, 'Wright's Picture Frames', in Judy Egerton, *Wright of Derby*, exh. cat., Tate Gallery, 1990, p.275, fig.5.
62. Peter Nicholson, *An Architectural Dictionary*, vol.II, 1819, p.556.
63. Thomas Martin, *The Circle of the Mechanical Arts*, 1813, pp.211, 213.
64. Henry Heydenryk, *The Art and History of Frames*, 1964, p.44.
65. Stalker and Parker, op.cit. in n.23, p.61; their account was plagiarised in the 1701 edition of William Salmon's *Polygraphice* and in John Barrow's *Dictionarium Polygraphicum* of 1735, suggesting the technique was widely known in the eighteenth century.
66. Supplied by Beckwith and France. See Anthony Coleridge, 'English Furniture and Cabinet-makers at Hatfield House, part II', *Burlington Magazine*, vol.CIX, 1967, p.205.
67. See William Millar, *Plastering: plain and decorative*, 4th edition, 1927, p.293 for the link to Liardet. See also Frank Kelsall, 'Liardet versus Adam', *Architectural History*, vol.XXIV, 1984, pp.118–26 for the stuccos used by the Adam brothers, and Judith Wetherall, 'The History and Techniques of Composition' in *Gilding and Surface Decoration*, ed. Sophie Budden, papers give at a conference held by the UKIC, 1991, p.28, n.9, for the nature of Liardet's composition.
68. The introduction of compo is barely discussed by Pat Kirkham in her chapter, 'New Materials and Techniques' in Kirkham, op.cit. in n.14, pp.117–23.
69. Martin, op.cit. in n.63, p.214.
70. Ernest Spon, *Workshop Receipts for the use of Manufacturers, Mechanics and Scientific Amateurs*, 1875, p.432.
71. *The Carver and Gilder's Guide and Picture Frame Maker's Companion* [1873] op.cit. in n.38, p.17.
72. Philip Hamerton, 'Picture Frames', *The Portfolio*, vol.II, 1871, p.178.
73. Hamerton, op.cit., p.179. Hamerton's words are echoed by D.G. Rossetti ('... it would be sure to come back with the frame knocked to pieces' and by L.C. Dickinson ('the injuries to the frame which always result from an exhibition at the RA'); see W.M. Rossetti (ed.), *Dante Gabriel Rossetti. His Family Letters*, vol.II, 1895, p.91; for L.C. Dickinson see National Portrait Gallery, Registered Packet for NPG 316.
74. *Ornaments in every style of design ... manufactured by Charles F. Bielefeld*, 1840 (to be found bound with the British Library copy of C.F. Bielefeld, *On the use of the Improved Papier Mâché in Furniture*, n.d.
75. Hugh Roberts, 'Royal Thrones, 1760–1840', *Furniture History*, vol.XXV, 1989, p.72, fig.20; 'Visits to British Manufactories. The Papier Mache Works of Mr C.F. Bielefeld', *Art Union*, vol.IX, 1847, pp.172–3; 'A Papier-Mache Village for Australia', *Illustrated London News*, vol.XXIII, 6 August 1853, p.80.
76. Edward T. Joy, *English Furniture 1800–1851*, 1977, pp.271–2.
77. F.H.W. Sheppard (ed.), *Survey of London*, vol.XXXVI, The Parish of St Paul, Covent Garden, 1970, pp.228–9.
78. Bielefeld catalogues can be found at the British Library and in the National Art Library and the Print Room at the Victoria and Albert Museum.
79. *Art Union*, vol.IX, 1847, p.176.
80. *Art Union*, vol.IV, 1842, p.257.
81. *The Carver and Gilder's Guide and Picture Frame Maker's Companion* [1873] op.cit. in n.38, p.37; *Workshop Receipts for Manufacturers and Scientific Amateurs*, published by E.& F.N. Spon Ltd, vol.III, 1909, p.323.
82. See Angela Hückel, 'Picture Frames in the Nineteenth Century' in *Gilded Wood, Conservation and History*, ed. Deborah Bigelow *et al.*, Madison, Conn., 1991, pp.121–3, for the extensive use of the process in Germany.
83. Charles Eastlake, *Hints on Household Taste in Furniture, Upholstery and Other Details*, 1878, pp.193–4.
84. For example, the catalogue of the London maker 'RS', belonging to the Royal Commission on the Ancient and Historical Monuments of

Scotland, Edinburgh.
85. Agnes Mackay, *Arthur Melville: Scottish Impressionist (1855–1904)*, Leigh-on-Sea, 1951, pp.62–4.
86. Royal Scottish Academy, Edinburgh, D.R. Hay's estimate, 11 January 1841. Information kindly supplied by Ian Gow.
87. *The Carver and Gilder's Guide and Picture Frame Maker's Companion* [1873] op.cit. in n.38, pp.17–8.
88. H. Morell, *Victorian Wooden Molding and Frame Designs*, Dover Publications reprint, 1991, of the 1910 Morell catalogue.
89. Hammersmith and Fulham Archives, Sales Order Books, DD/76/30 p.135, DD/76/30 p.34, DD/219/1 pp.318, 335.
90. *The Frame in America 1860–1960*, exh. cat., Federal Reserve Board Building, Washington, DC, 1995, p.11.

Chapter 3: The Development of the Picture Frame

1. Simon Thurley, *The Royal Palaces of Tudor England*, 1993, p.217.
2. The type is discussed by Timothy Newbery, 'European "Cassetta" Frames from the 15th to the 19th Century', *Museum Management and Curatorship*, vol.XIV, 1995, pp.103–8.
3. William J. Thoms, 'Pictures of the Great Earl of Leicester', *Notes and Queries*, 3rd Series, vol.II, 1862, pp.224–5.
4. W.A. Shaw, *Three Inventories of the Years 1542, 1547 and 1549-50 of Pictures in the Collections of Henry VIII and Edward VI*, 1937, pp.36–7, 51.
5. Oliver Millar, 'Abraham van der Doort's Catalogue of the Collections of Charles I', *Walpole Society*, vol.XXXVII, 1960, pp.27–8. These are associated by Millar with nos.6, 8, 10, 12, 14, 17 and 20 in his catalogue, *The Tudor, Stuart and Early Georgian Pictures in the Collection of Her Majesty The Queen*, 1963, but the portraits have long since lost their painted frames.
6. Vertue, vol.I, p.108. The frame was replaced in 1820; see Mrs Reginald Lane Poole, *Catalogue of Oxford Portraits*, vol.II, Oxford, 1925, p.262; see also above, p.17.
7. See Karen Hearn (ed.), *Dynasties. Painting in Tudor and Jacobean England 1530-1630*, exh. cat., Tate Gallery, 1995, p.92, no.46.
8. Millar, 1960, op.cit. in n.5, pp.65–6.
9. S.J. Barnes and A.K. Wheelock, Jr (eds), *Van Dyck 350, Studies in the History of Art*, vol.XLVI, National Gallery of Art, Washington, DC, 1994, pp.309, 312–14
10. Joseph Moxon, *Mechanick Exercises*, no.VI, 1678, p.103.
11. Peter Thornton and Maurice Tomlin, 'The Furnishing and Decoration of Ham House', *Furniture History*, vol.XVI, 1980, p.129.
12. National Portrait Gallery Archive, Joseph Wright of Derby account book, ff.52–4.
13. Lita-Rose Betcherman, 'The York House Collection and its Keeper', *Apollo*, vol.XCII, 1970, p.250.
14. Philip McEvansoneya, 'An unpublished inventory of the Hamilton collection in the 1620s and the Duke of Buckingham's pictures', *Burlington Magazine*, vol.CXXXIV, 1992, p.525.
15. Mary Edmond, 'Limners and Picturemakers – New Light on the lives of miniaturists and large-scale portrait-painters working in London in the sixteenth and seventeenth centuries', *Walpole Society*, vol.XLVII, 1980, p.173.
16. H.M. Colvin (ed.), *The History of the King's Works*, vol.IV, part 2, 1982, p.268. Extracts from the accounts are quoted by Edmond, op.cit., pp.173–6.
17. For example, Gerbier had some of the Duke of Buckingham's Italian purchases framed in Venice in 1621, whereas he had Titian's *Portrait of a Secretary*, bought in Paris in 1624, framed in London by his father-in-law. See Betcherman, op.cit. in n.13, p.252.
18. Both Colt and Stone produced innovatory church monuments which have elements in common with the sculptural vocabulary of contemporary picture frames. For Taylor and Goodrich's sub-contract work for Stone, see W.L. Spiers, 'The Notebook and Account Book of Nicholas Stone', *Walpole Society*, vol.VII, 1919, pp.43–4, and also Kent Record Office, Knole papers, U269 A462/5.
19. Betcherman, op.cit. in n.13, p.252.
20. W.N. Sainsbury, *Original Unpublished Papers illustrative of the Life of Sir Peter Paul Rubens*, 1859, p.45.
21. Notably on his picture of *Cain and Abel*, referred to in n.28. Both the Middlesex and the Hamilton frames seem to have had coloured backgrounds to the carved and gilt ornament.
22. Reproduced with frame in Alastair Laing, *In Trust for the Nation. Paintings from National Trust Houses*, exh. cat., National Gallery, 1995, p.23.
23. The Ham picture is reproduced with frame in Thornton and Tomlin, op.cit. in n.11, fig.20. Another frame of this type is at Claydon on the portrait of Nan Uvedale, Mrs Henslowe by Cornelius Johnson, painted in 1635.
24. For Italian frames of the type, see Paul Mitchell, 'Italian Picture Frames 1500–1825: A Brief Survey', *Furniture History*, vol.XX, 1984, plates 16A–16D, and Franco Sabatelli *et al.*, *La cornice italiana dal Rinascimento al Neoclassico*, Milan, 1992, pp.270-7.
25. The use of the animal skin as a framing device and more generally the introduction of the auricular style in England, and its relationship to developments on the Continent has still to be studied in detail. An indication of the international nature of the style can be found in the widespread use of elaborate frameworks to portrait prints engraved both on the Continent and in London. The earliest of these date to about 1615. Significant English examples dating from about 1617 onwards are reproduced in Arthur M. Hind, *Engraving in England in the sixteenth and seventeenth centuries*, vol.II, *The Reign of James I*, Cambridge, 1955, plates 13c, 61c, 68, 88d, 147, 151c, 155b, 157b, 160b and Margery Corbett and Michael Norton's continuation volume, vol.III, *The Reign of Charles I*, Cambridge, 1964, plates 3d, 4c, 5c, 7d, 103a, 110a, 139. Similar Dutch examples of the same period are reproduced in F.W.A. Hollstein, *Dutch and Flemish Etchings, Engravings and Woodcuts*, Amsterdam, 1949– , vol.I, p.23; vol.III, p.70; vol.V, pp.190, 221; vol.XX, p.63 and vol.XLIII, p.222.

   In silverware Paul van Vianen was using the auricular style in Holland by 1610 and his nephew Christian van Vianen in England in and after 1630; see *Zeldzaam Zilver uit de Gouden Eenw. De Utrechtse edelsmeden van Vianen*, exh. cat., Centraal Museum, Utrecht, 1984, and R.W. Lightbown, 'Christian von Vianen at the Court of Charles I', *Apollo*, vol.LXXXVII, 1968, pp.426–39. However, the influence of auricular silverware on English picture frames appears to be limited. A more fruitful area for research may lie in the study of the church monuments of the period, of which those of Nicholas Stone form an essential starting-point; see Spiers, op.cit. in n.18. The church monuments which make most use of the animal skin as a framing device tend to be later in date, for example those to John Wail (died 1666) in Christ Church Cathedral, Oxford, and Thomas Sacherell (died 1675) in All Saint's Church, Wroxton, Oxfordshire.
26. See no.14.
27. At Claydon the type can be found, slightly cut down, on the Van Dyck portraits of Sir Ralph and Lady Verney, and at Knole on the Larkin full-length of the 3rd Earl of Dorset (no.233); the frame is from the Van Dyck school portrait of Francis Cranfield, wife of the 5th Earl (no.232), as can be seen from a photograph of the portrait at the National Portrait Exhibition, South Kensington Museum, 1866, no.512. For the frame on the portrait of a youth, called Sir John

Suckling, in the Tradescant Collection, see the repr. in Arthur MacGregor (ed.), *Tradescant's Rarities*, Oxford, 1983, pl.141.

28. This was Cantarini's *Cain and Abel*, now in the Kunsthistorisches Museum, Vienna. A version of Teniers' painting is at Petworth.
29. See P.J.J. van Thiel and C.J. de Bruyn Kops, *Framing in the Golden Age. Picture and Frame in 17th-Century Holland*, Zwolle, 1995, pp.12, 41–2, 210–13, for a discussion of the introduction of the auricular style in picture framing in Holland, possibly as early as 1639. Whatever the case, there can be little doubt that the collecting activities of Charles I and his court meant that such frames were much more extensively used in England than in Holland.
30. For portraits by Johnson which appear to retain their original carved and gilt frames see those listed under nos.6 and 14; another example is at Ham House, *The Dukes of Hamilton and Lauderdale*, 1649. See also n.23.
31. The earliest mention known to me is George Scharf, 'Portraits of Judges in the Guildhall', *Archaeological Journal*, vol.L, 1893, p.272.
32. M. Kirby Talley, *Portrait Painting in England: Studies in the Technical Literature before 1700*, 1981, pp.299, 372. See also Elizabeth Walsh and Richard Jeffree, *'The Excellent Mrs Mary Beale'*, exh. cat., Geffrye Museum, 1975, p.18.
33. See H. Avray Tipping, *Grinling Gibbons and the Woodwork of his Age*, 1914, pp.39, 115, 123, and David Green, *Grinling Gibbons*, 1964, pp.77, 92.
34. Greater London Record Office, A/FH/B, *Book of Furniture*, under 13 November 1754; kindly drawn to my attention by Rica Jones.
35. Tipping, op.cit. in n.33, p.39.
36. Corbett and Norton, op.cit. in n.25, pl.4.
37. Van Thiel and De Bruyn Kops, op.cit. in n.29, pp.214–5.
38. The Tradescant portrait and its frame is reproduced as pl.132 in MacGregor, op.cit. in n.27.
39. Vertue, vol.II, p.11.
40. I am indebted to Nino Strachey for details of John Norris's account dated 24 May 1673 in the Ham papers. For Lely's executorship accounts, see Talley, op.cit. in n.32, p.372.
41. An example can be seen in Tipping, op.cit. in n.33, p.133, fig.121.
42. At Althorp frames of the type are or were to be found on portraits such as Carlo Maratta's *2nd Earl of Sunderland*, painted in about 1664, and Van Dyck's *Viscountess Andover and Lady Elizabeth Thimbleby*, acquired by the Earl at Lely's sale in 1682 and now in the National Gallery, London. At Dunham Massey the style seems to have been used by the 2nd Earl of Warrington from the 1690s until at least the 1720s; see Gervase Jackson-Stops, 'Dunham Massey, Cheshire', *Country Life*, vol.CLXX, 1981, p.18 and fig.5. At Lanhydrock the frame type may have been introduced with portraits which came from a Cheshire collection with links by marriage to the Earls of Warrington; see *Lanhydrock, Cornwall*, guidebook, 1993 (first published 1980), p.38; some of the frames at Lanhydrock were made in the nineteenth century. At Petworth there is a more elaborate version of the type of *c*.1690 bearing the crest and garter of the Duke of Somerset: see Gervase Jackson-Stops, 'Picture Frames at Petworth – I', *Country Life*, vol.CLXVIII, 1980, pp.798–9.
43. Austin Dobson (ed.), *The Diary of John Evelyn*, vol.III, 1906, p.141, 6 February 1685.
44. For *Ham House*, see Maurice Tomlin, Ham House, guidebook, 1986, p.15. For Castle Ashby, see H. Avray Tipping, *English Homes. Late Tudor and Early Stuart 1558–1649*, period III, vol.II, 1927, pp.175, 177. For Stapleford Park see *Country Life*, vol.XXIII, 1908, p.274.
45. Tomlin, op.cit., p.14.
46. Talley, op.cit. in n.32, p.299.
47. *Wren Society*, vol.VII, 1930, p.114.
48. Tomlin, op.cit., p.20.
49. See n.46.
50. Howard Colvin, 'Letters and Papers relating to the rebuilding of Combe Abbey, Warwickshire, 1681–1688', *Walpole Society*, vol.L, 1984, p.300.
51. Tessa Murdoch (ed.), *Boughton House. The English Versailles*, 1992, p.93, fig.92.
52. For West, see above, pp.98–9. Several of the Maratta frames supplied by Thomas Vials for Knole in the 1770s were enriched by gadrooning, notably Reynolds's full-length portrait of the 3rd Duke of Dorset. In 1775 Vials charged the Duke for three gold frames 'carv'd with gudroons att top' for other portraits by Reynolds; see Knole papers, U269 A243/5.
53. Murdoch, op.cit., p.92. Pelletier's bill is for a 'three quarter frame'; this would be for a picture size thirty by twenty-five inches, rather than for the full-length portrait of the Duchess of Mazarin, reproduced as figs. 30 and 93.
54. National Portrait Gallery Archive, Tonson papers, Gerrard Howard's account for 1736–7.
55. See above, pp.123, 125.
56. For John Howard, see *DEF*, p.31. For Arthur Pond, see Louise Lippincott, 'Arthur Pond's Journal of Receipts and Expenses, 1734–1750', *Walpole Society*, vol.LIV, 1991, p.238, November 1737 ('Architrave gold frame').
57. For Henry Flitcroft's measured drawing, inscribed by Lord Burlington, 'Tabernacle at The Vine', see John Harris, *Catalogue of the Drawings Collection of the Royal Institute of British Architects. Inigo Jones and John Webb*, 1972, fig.173. For Roger Morris's sketch for a niche frame at Combe Bank, Kent, see John Harris, *The Palladians*, 1981, fig.76. For John Green, Paul Petit and John Hele, all of whom were working for the Earl of Dysart, generally at Ham House, see Green's account of 4 April 1734 (copy in Victoria and Albert Museum Furniture Dept Archive), Petit's account of 1734–5 and John Hele's account of 1737 (copies of both kindly supplied by Nino Strachey). Chippendale uses the term in *The Director*. For Bradburn and France's account see Jacob Simon, 'Allan Ramsay and picture frames', *Burlington Magazine*, vol.CXXXVI, 1994, p.451. For Adam, see n.63 below.
58. A 'large Palladian frame' is included in an account rendered of the late Thomas Sharpe in 1826; see Guildhall Library, MS.546, account books of Thomas Sharpe and George Bishop, heraldic painters, kindly transcribed by Margaret Binnie.
59. Account of 13 January 1727, photocopy kindly supplied by Christopher Gilbert.
60. Helena Hayward and Pat Kirkham, *William and John Linnell: 18th Century London Furniture Makers*, 1980, pp.142–3. Exceptionally I have, in quoting this account, modernised Linnell's spelling.
61. For Langley's influence, see p.139.
62. Simon, op.cit. in n.57, p.450, fig.59.
63. Robert and James Adam, *The Works in Architecture*, 1778, pp.45–7. The book was published in numbers, commencing in 1773.
64. Jean André Rouquet, *The Present State of the Arts in England*, 1755, p.85, translated from the French edition of 1754.
65. See Michael Snodin, 'English Rococo and its Continental Origins', *Rococo Art and Design in Hogarth's England*, exh. cat., Victoria and Albert Museum, 1984, p.33.
66. Alastair Laing in a review of the Victoria and Albert Rococo exhibition (see n.65) dates the earliest use in English of the word rococo to 1822; see *Burlington Magazine*, vol.CXXVI, 1984, p.450.
67. Hayward and Kirkham, op.cit. in n.60, pp.143–4.

68. Pippa Mason and Michael Gregory, *Of Gilding*, exh. cat., Arnold Wiggins & Sons Ltd, 1989.
69. See n.65.
70. See Terry F. Friedman, 'Two Eighteenth-Century Catalogues of Ornamental Pattern Books', *Furniture History*, vol.XI, 1975, pp.66–75.
71. See above, pp.139–40.
72. For the Prince's frames, see also above, p.40.
73. Mitchell, op.cit. in n.24, p.24.
74. Timothy J. Standring, 'Some pictures by Poussin in the Dal Pozzo collection: three new inventories', *Burlington Magazine*, vol.CXXX, 1988, p.623, fig.58 *(Rebecca and Eliezer at the Well)*.
75. Jervas seems to have brought back his own frame style from Italy: see p.92. But Ramsay favoured the rococo, Hoare used a range of styles and it was only Reynolds, who returned to England after the style had been introduced, who preferred the Maratta.
76. More research is needed into the framing of Italian pictures imported into Britain before 1750, such as those at Burghley House, Lincolnshire. Most documented imports known to me date to after 1750, for example, the large picture by Maratta, *Marchese Pallavicini and the Artist*, at Stourhead, acquired by Henry Hoare II from the Arnaldi Collection in 1758, and apparently imported in its enriched Maratta frame.
77. Gervase Jackson-Stops, 'Picture Frames at Petworth – II', *Country Life*, vol.CLXVIII, 1980, p.1030. It is worth noting that the early Maratta frames on Joseph Goupy's copies of the Raphael cartoons cannot have been made by Paul Petit in 1740 as suggested in Tessa Murdoch (ed.), *The Quiet Conquest. The Huguenots 1685 to 1985*, exh. cat., Museum of London, 1985, p.203.
78. According to a report giving by the first owner, John Lane, to John Nichols in 1781 or 1782, the pictures were in 'elegant Carlo Maratt frames, which cost Mr. Hogarth four guineas apiece'. See J. Nichols, *Biographical Anecdotes of William Hogarth*, 2nd ed., 1782, pp.225–7. I am grateful to Judy Egerton for this reference.
79. I am grateful to Clare Lloyd-Jacob for her observations on Wootton.
80. Nicholas Penny, 'Reynolds and picture frames', *Burlington Magazine*, vol.CXXVIII, 1986, p.813.
81. Ibid. On 1 April 1771 Knight ordered an 'S. Rosa' frame from 'Brunet'.
82. Simon, op.cit. in n.57, p.448.
83. Kent Record Office, Knole papers, u269 a243/2. The picture is still at Knole.
84. *Letters & Papers of John Singleton Copley and Henry Pelham 1739–1776*, New York, 1970, p.181 (republication of *Collections of the Massachusetts Historical Society*, vol.LXXI, 1914).
85. Svend Eriksen, 'Marigny and *Le Goût Grec*', *Burlington Magazine*, vol.CIV, 1962, pp.96–101.
86. See n.63.
87. These are now in the Victoria and Albert Museum, repr. in John Hardy, 'Robert Adam and the furnishing of Kedleston Hall', *Connoisseur*, vol.CXCIX, 1978, p.199.
88. For the frame of Ramsay's portrait of Lord Coventry, see Simon, op.cit. in n.57, p.451, fig.63.
89. Christopher Gilbert, *The Life and Work of Thomas Chippendale*, 1978, pp.168, 182, 186.
90. Mention of a new pattern with reeds and ribbons crossing occurs in Romney's frame accounts in 1777. See Fitzwilliam Museum Library, Allwood's Carving Book, p.3.
91. See Gervase Jackson-Stops, 'Southill Park, Bedfordshire', *Country Life*, vol.CLXXXVIII, 28 April 1994, pp.62–7.
92. Victoria and Albert Museum Library, 86.cc.1, John Smith Day Book, 20 January 1812. See also Millar, 1963, op.cit. in n.5, nos.371 and 620. The portraits are now at Windsor.
93. John Smith Day Book, 30 June and 18 July 1812.
94. W.H. Pyne, *The History of the Royal Residences*, vol.II, 1819, p.83.
95. For accounts of the Louis Quartorze, see Edward T. Joy, *English Furniture, 1800–1851*, 1977, pp.144–153, and John Martin Robinson, *The Wyatts. An Architectural Dynasty*, pp.107–15.
96. Robinson, op.cit., p.109, for a mid-nineteenth century account of Crockford's, describing the interior decoration as deriving from Versailles and other examples of the periods of 'Louis Quatorze' and 'Louis Quinze'. For the White and Gold Room at Petworth, see Gervase Jackson-Stops, 'Living with the Louis', *Country Life*, vol.CLXXXVI, 1 October 1992, pp.72–3.
97. Art Union, vol.VI, 1844, p.49. Garbanati also supplied 'Handsome ornamented gilt Louis Quatorze window cornices'.
98. Victoria and Albert Museum Library, 86.cc.1, John Smith Day Book, 27 March 1812, 23 July 1817, 16 December 1819. The last two references come from notes kindly supplied by Robert Wenley. The taste for antique frames is more fully discussed above on pp.23–4.
99. *DEFM*, p.329.
100. For the influence of the regulations of the Academy, see above, pp.20, 21–2 and 23.
101. Windsor Royal Archives, pp2/98, 9474. Charles Noble kindly allowed me access to the notes kept by the Royal Collections Trust.
102. Royal Academy Library, E.W. Cooke Ledger, 1833–78.
103. The Alhambra in Granada became known in Britain through the publication of John Frederick Lewis's *Sketches and Drawings of the Alhambra* in 1835 and Richard Ford's *Handbook for Travellers in Spain* in 1845. The Alhambra, Leicester Square, opened its doors in 1854, becoming a celebrated music hall, while Owen Jones's *The Grammar of Ornament*, published in 1856, contains a series of plates of 'Moresque Ornament from the Alhambra'. For Jones's earlier book on the Alhambra, see no.78, under n.1.
104. The National Portrait Gallery's framemaker, Francis Draper, refers to both frame patterns in 1896: see Duplicate of Accounts, vol.III, under 25 February 1896. The terms were used by Alfred Stiles, the Hammersmith framemaker, as late as 1919; see Hammersmith and Fulham Archives, dd/76/3, p.280. The trade catalogue of H. Morrell in 1910 includes illustrations of Alhambra frames of a somewhat different kind.
105. Luther Hooper, 'On Picture Frames', *The Cabinet Maker and Art Furnisher*, 1 September 1883, p.45. I am grateful to Paul Mitchell for supplying me with a copy of this article.
106. Ibid.
107. *Retention of Important Pictures*, National Gallery Committee Report, chairman Lord Curzon, 1914, Appendix IV ('Note on Frames' by R.H. Benson).
108. See above, p.117.
109. National Portrait Gallery Archive, Duplicate of Accounts, vol.III, p.112; these bills are for the frames of Watts's portraits of Sir Henry Taylor and Lord Tennyson.
110. Lynn Roberts, 'Nineteenth Century English Picture Frames, I, The Pre-Raphaelites', *International Journal of Museum Management and Curatorship*, vol.IV, 1985, pp.158–9.
111. Charles Eastlake, *Hints on Household Taste in Furniture, Upholstery and Other Details*, 1878, p.195.
112. Phené Spiers, 'Picture Frames at the Royal Academy', *The Architect*, vol.I, 1869, pp.282–3, 296–7.
113. Christopher Newall, *The Grosvenor Gallery Exhibitions*, Cambridge, 1995, p.13.

114. T.R. Way and G.R. Dennis, *The Art of James McNeill Whistler*, 1905, p.104.
115. William Nicholson's frames can be seen to advantage at Fenton House, Hampstead, and the Fitzwilliam Museum, Cambridge.
116. Imperial War Museum, Dept of Art, volume 'First World War Frames'.
117. See above, p.47.
118. Hammersmith and Fulham Archives, DD/76/10, p.184; DD/76/20, pp.33, 272; DD/76/25, p.196.
119. Imperial War Museum, Dept of Art, GP/134A.
120. For Ocean's comments on the frame, which he called 'a kind of concession to football', see the picture file at the Scottish National Portrait Gallery. For John, see *The Tate Gallery 1980–82 Illustrated Catalogue of Acquisitions*, 1984, pp.145–6; the frame also incorporates images of a sexual motif, a pair of testicles and the base of an erect penis penetrating the vulva. For Morgan, see *Howard Morgan. The Golden Gate*, exh. cat., Agnew's, 1996.

CHAPTER 4: THE ARTIST AND THE PICTURE FRAME

1. See Marcia Pointon, *Hanging the Head. Portraiture and Social Formation in Eighteenth-Century England*, New Haven and London,1993, pp.36–52.
2. See above, pp.96, 102, 104.
3. See above, pp.108–9.
4. Jean André Rouquet, *The Present State of the Arts in England*, 1755, pp.42–3, translated from the French Edition of 1754.
5. Victoria and Albert Museum Library, Box 86.AA.24, item 4. Fitzwilliam Museum Library, Romney notebook, no.4, p.9. See also above, p.97.
6. *Morning Herald*, 17 April 1787 (British Museum Print Room, Whitley Papers, vol.X, p.1282). Romney took over Francis Cotes's house in Cavendish Square. Cotes's sale catalogue lists the contents of his showroom and provides a minimum size of twenty-two-and-half by fourteen-and-a-half feet for the room. The catalogue is reproduced in E. Mead Johnson, *Francis Cotes*, Oxford, 1976, Appendix II, pp.156–8.
7. James Northcote, *Memoirs of Sir Joshua Reynolds, Knt.*, 1813, p.53.
8. Richard H. Saunders, *John Smibert. Colonial America's First Portrait Painter*, New Haven and London, 1995, p.255.
9. Vertue, vol.III, p.109.
10. For Rymsdyk, see *Bath Chronicle*, 12 October 1786 (kindly communicated by Susan Sloman); for Boulton's Mechanical Paintings, see *Burlington Magazine*, vol.CXII, 1970, p.506, appendix with list from the Mint Inventory, taken in 1809.
11. Oswald Doughty and John Wahl (eds), *Letters of Dante Gabriel Rossetti*, vol.III, Oxford, 1967, p.1298.
12. See also above, p.55.
13. Louise Lippincott, 'Arthur Pond's Journal of Receipts and Expenses, 1734–1750', *Walpole Society*, vol.LIV, 1991, pp.220–333.
14. National Portrait Gallery Archive, George Romney Ledger. The year 1789 is a sample.
15. Jacob Simon, 'The Account Book of James Northcote', *Walpole Society*, vol.LVIII, 1996, p.25. After his first year Northcote ceased to use his account book to note framing details on a regular basis.
16. Royal Academy Library, James Ward Account Book.
17. Royal Academy Library, E.W. Cooke Ledger.
18. National Portrait Gallery Archive, photostat of Colvin Smith Ledger, 1833–44. My analysis is based on a sample of the first eleven pages.
19. Lynn Roberts, 'Victorian Picture Frames 1850–1890', unpublished M.Phil. thesis, Courtauld Institute of Art, 1984, p.124, letter of 26 August 1871.
20. Kent Record Office, Knole papers, U269 A252/27, letter of 13 July 1816. Mulready's picture, *The Fight Interrupted*, now in the Victoria and Albert Museum, was reframed at a later date.
21. York City Library, William Etty letters, no.326, 25 July 1846.
22. Tessa Murdoch, 'Courtiers and Classics. The Gosset Family', *Country Life*, vol.CLXXVII, 1985, p.1282.
23. British Museum, Standing Committee Minutes, vol.III, p.782, 6 August 1762. Mr Stone was commissioned to 'prepare a frame for the Picture of His Late Majesty according to the drawing laid before the Committee by Mr Shackleton'.
24. R.C.M. Colvin-Smith, *The Life and Works of Colvin Smith, R.S.A. 1796-1875*, Aberdeen, 1936, p.36.
25. E.K. Waterhouse, 'Reynolds's Sitter Book for 1755', *Walpole Society*, vol.XLI, 1968, p.129.
26. National Portrait Gallery Archive, George Romney Ledger, 24 March 1787.
27. Richard W. Goulding and C.K. Adams, *Catalogue of Pictures belonging to His Grace the Duke of Portland*, Cambridge, 1936, p.453.
28. Scottish Record Office, GD 152/104/21/1, Hamilton Bruce papers.
29. James Greig, *Sir Henry Raeburn, R.A.*, 1911, p.xliii.
30. York City Library, William Etty letters, no.167, 27 March 1838.
31. Mary Woodall (ed.), *The Letters of Thomas Gainsborough*, 1963, pp.135–9, as corrected when the letters were in possession of Raffael Valls Ltd, 1991.
32. Pine's letter from Bath, dated 22 February 1778, was sold at Phillips, 19 March 1992, lot 15; a partial transcript is in the National Portrait Gallery Archive.
33. Vertue, vol.III, p.85.
34. William Whitley, 'An Eighteenth-Century Art Chronicler: Sir Henry Bate Dudley, Bart', *Walpole Society*, vol.XIII, 1925, pp.45–6.
35. Jane Bayard, *Works of Splendor and Imagination: The Exhibition Watercolor, 1770-1870*, exh. cat., Yale Center for British Art, New Haven, 1981, p.29.
36. *The Year's Art*, 1901, p.6.
37. Ernest Fletcher (ed.), *Conversations of James Northcote R.A. with James Ward on Art and Artists*, 1901, pp.163–4.
38. W.T. Whitley, *Artists and their Friends in England, 1700–1799*, vol.I, 1928, p.247.
39. Farington, *Diary*, p.2667, 30 December 1805.
40. Philip Hamerton, 'Picture Frames', *The Portfolio*, vol.II, 1871, pp.178–9.
41. Royal Academy Library, 236/19/3/a-b, Thomas Miller papers.
42. See H.M. Cundall (ed.), *William Callow. An Autobiography*, 1908, p.104.
43. Jane Vickers in *Pre-Raphaelites, Painters and Patrons in the North East*, exh. cat., Laing Art Gallery, Newcastle upon Tyne, 1989, p.93.
44. National Portrait Gallery Archive, Watts Letterbooks, vol.XII, p.90.
45. British Library, Add. MS. 43,913, ff.172–3, letter of 29 December 1885. I am indebted to my colleague, Peter Funnell, for this reference.
46. National Portrait Gallery, Registered Packet for NPG 5523, Gowing's portrait of Isaiah Berlin.
47. Doughty and Wahl, op.cit. in n.11, p.1443.
48. Farington, *Diary*, p.4919, 4 November 1816. See also entries for 11 November and 30 December of the same year.
49. See n.47.
50. Wiltshire Record Office, Stourhead Archives, William Hoare to Henry Hoare, letter, 5 June 1760.
51. For Hoare see also John Kerslake, *Early Georgian Portraits*, 1977, p.292, where Warburton is quoted sending his picture by Hoare to London for a frame by Gosset. Gosset is mentioned in Gainsborough's correspondence in 1762 and 1768, see Woodall, op.cit. in n.31, pp.73, 139, 145. Payments to Gosset occur in Gainsborough's bank account

of £15 on 14 September 1762 and £39 on 13 September 1763 (information kindly supplied by John Hayes). Gainsborough on occasion went to a Bristol framemaker.

52. British Library, Add. MS. 35,636, p.252; Add. MS. 35,637, p.50.
53. J.C.B. Cooksey, *Alexander Nasmyth: A Man of the Scottish Renaissance*, 1991, p.127.
54. Charles Rowley, *Fifty Years of Work Without Wages (Laborare est Orare)*, n.d. but probably 1911, p.114.
55. R.B. Beckett (ed.), *John Constable's Correspondence*, 6 vols, 1962–1968, published by the Historical Manuscripts Commission and the Suffolk Records Society, vol.II, p.334.
56. Beckett, op.cit., vol.III, p.60. The frame mentioned by Constable was made for C.R. Leslie's *The Grosvenor Family* (The Duke of Westminster). It is entered in John Smith's Day Book in November 1831 as 'A large Frame 10^in^ Mg most splendidly enriched with ornaments in imitation of the most florid style of Louis 14th ...' at a cost of £30 (Victoria and Albert Museum Library, 86.CC.2).
57. Beckett, op.cit., vol.VI, p.112. 'Smith' is not the celebrated John Smith of Bond Street whom Constable also used.
58. This pastel has a Kent frame of the type used by William Hoare and found on Arthur Pond's portrait of Robert Walpole, 1st Earl of Orford (fig.55); it was sold at Phillips, 13 December 1994, lot 17.
59. See above, p.136.
60. Hammersmith and Fulham Archives, DD/76/73, letter of 10 April 1957. See also Bawden's letter of 1 July 1956.
61. *The Emma Holt Bequest, Sudley, Illustrated Catalogue and History of the House*, Liverpool, 1971, p.71, no.306.
62. Saunders, op.cit. in n.8, p.258.
63. Kensington and Chelsea Libraries, Central Library, Leighton letters, no.149, Leighton to J.S. Hodgson, *c*.1876, about the frame of *Daphnephoria* (Lady Lever Art Gallery). Leighton had proposed that Hodgson's architect, Frederick Pepys Cockerell, should design the frame, see letter no.146.
64. Doughty and Wahl, op.cit. in n.11, p.1444.
65. William James Smith, 'Letters from Michael Wright', *Burlington Magazine*, vol.XCV, 1953, p.236
66. National Portrait Gallery Archive, Charles Beale's notebook for 1681, under 9 and 11 June.
67. Royal Academy Library, William Beechey Account Book, entry under 18 July 1816.
68. Romney's four framemaking books are in the Fitzwilliam Museum library: Frame Book, 1783–5; Account Book with Allwoods, 1775–81; Account Books with Saunders, 1782–5 and 1786–93. Loose accounts with Saunders, 1783–96, are in the Victoria and Albert Museum Library, Box 86.AA.24. These records can be supplemented using the Romney Ledger, 1786–96, in the National Portrait Gallery Archive.
69. Lippincott, op.cit. in n.13. See also Louise Lippincott, *Selling Art in Georgian London. The Rise of Arthur Pond*, New Haven and London, 1983, pp.76–86, where Pond's considerable outlay on framing is discussed.
70. Farington, *Diary*, p.2736, 26 April 1806.
71. Victoria and Albert Museum Library, Box 86.AA.24, items 2, 6, 12, 15 and 16.
72. Victoria and Albert Museum Library, 86.CC.3, John Smith Day Book, vol.III, p.408.
73. Victoria and Albert Museum Library, 86.33.137–8. R. Brown Ledgers.
74. Sally A. Woodcock, 'The Roberson Archive: Content and Significance', in *Historical Painting Techniques, Materials and Studio Practice*, ed. Arie Wallert *et al.*, Preprints of a Symposium, University of Leiden. Getty Conservation Institute, Santa Monica, California, 1995, p.31.
75. See above, p.132.
76. Whitley, op.cit. in n.38, vol.II, p.247.
77. Chance bought William Blake Richmond's *Enid and Geraint* for £20 in 1859 and sat to him for his portrait in 1879 which was exhibited at the Grosvenor Gallery in 1883 as no.233; see Simon Reynolds, *William Blake Richmond*, Norwich, 1995, pp.24, 125. The George Richmond self-portrait is in the National Portrait Gallery (NPG 2509). In 1898 H. Montagu Butler, Master of Trinity College, Cambridge, wrote to Chance that 'when Mr George Richmond died, we both of us lost a dear and honoured friend'; see Royal Academy Library, R1/3/6, letter dated 28 January 1898.
78. Paul Mitchell, 'Italian Picture Frames 1500–1825: A Brief Survey', *Furniture History*, vol.XX, 1984, p.18.
79. Reproduced in Henry Heydenryk, *The Art and History of Frames*, 1964, p.45. Sadly the frame is separated from the picture.
80. Jean-Claude Lebensztein, 'Framing Classical Space', *Art Journal*, vol.XLVII, 1988, p.37.
81. Smith, op.cit. in n.65, p.234.
82. M. Kirby Talley, *Portrait Painting in England: Studies in the Technical Literature before 1700*, 1981, p.299.
83. W.H. Carpenter, *Pictorial Notices consisting of a Memoir of Anthony Van Dyck*, 1844, p.67.
84. Repr. Peter Thornton and Maurice Tomlin, 'The Furnishing and Decoration of Ham House', *Furniture History*, vol.XVI, 1980, fig.21. See also Alastair Laing and Nino Strachey, 'The Duke and Duchess of Lauderdale's pictures at Ham House', *Apollo*, vol.CXXXIX, 1994, p.9, fig.9.
85. Payments to Lely mentioning frames are recorded for the portraits of the Earl and Countess of Salisbury, 1654 (Erna Auerbach and C.K. Adams, *Paintings and Sculpture at Hatfield House*, 1971, p.167), Lady Percy, 1664 (S.J. Barnes and A.K. Wheelock, Jr (eds), *Van Dyck 350, Studies in the History of Art*, vol.XLVI, National Gallery of Art, Washington, DC, 1994, p.314), Lady Diana Russell, 1667 (Gladys Scott Thomson, *Life in a Noble Household*, 1937, p.293) and the Earl of Bedford, 1675, 1676, with payment for the frame being made to John Smith (Thomson, op.cit., pp.294–5).
86. Oliver Millar, *Sir Peter Lely*, exh. cat., National Portrait Gallery, 1978, nos.26 & 31.
87. A frame of this type on *The Cotton Family* is reproduced in Millar, op.cit., no.30.
88. Payments to Kneller mentioning frames are recorded by J. Douglas Stewart, *Sir Godfrey Kneller and the English Baroque Portrait*, Oxford, 1983, pp.191–5 under years 1679, 1681 (frame by John Le Sage), 1682, 1684, 1685 (frame by Le Sage), 1686, 1694, 1696 (frame by Mr Hugh) and 1699. Payments in 1716 and 1718 (frame by John Howard) are listed in R.W. Goulding and C.K. Adams, *Catalogue of the Pictures belonging to His Grace the Duke of Portland*, Cambridge, 1936, pp.xxxi, 229, 455. See also *DEF*, p.27 for a letter of Le Sage of 1685 referring to pictures by Kneller.
89. Mitchell, op.cit. in n.78, pp.24–5, pl.28D.
90. A frame of this type is reproduced and documented by Oliver Millar, 'Artists and Craftsmen in the service of Sir Stephen Fox and his family', *Burlington Magazine*, vol.CXXXVII, 1995, pp.522, 526–7, figs.51, 56, appendix item XIV. Sir Stephen Fox's portrait of 1713 cost £21 with a further £4.10s for the 'black & gold frame'; the signature of William Clarke on the receipt is not necessarily that of the framemaker. Other frames of this type can be found on the full-length of Ann, Countess of Sunderland and her daughter at Althorp

(no.312) and on the half-length of Adam Ottley at the National Library of Wales (fig.91).

91. Vertue, vol.III, p.109.
92. See n.13.
93. An example of Cotes's rococo frame pattern is repr. in Hermione Sandwith, 'National Trust Picture Frame Survey', *International Journal of Museum Management and Curatorship*, vol.IV, 1985, p.178. For Liotard's pattern see Paul Mitchell, *Frameworks*, 1996. Cotes began using his pattern before Liotard's visit to England.
94. Jacob Simon, 'Allan Ramsay and picture frames', *Burlington Magazine*, vol.CXXXVI, 1994, p.444, n.4. One hundred and fifty frames were examined either in the original or using photographs; this sort of time-consuming analysis in detail has yet to be carried out for most other artists.
95. Paul Mitchell, 'Wright's Picture Frames', in Judy Egerton, *Wright of Derby*, exh. cat., Tate Gallery, 1990, pp.272–88.
96. Nicholas Penny, 'Reynolds and picture frames', *Burlington Magazine*, vol.CXXVIII, 1986, p.810.
97. The full-size profile drawing by Edward Dayes of the frames of two of his most important watercolours of the late 1790s, *Lycurgus entering Athens* and *Theseus's Approach to Athens*, is exceptional. It may perhaps be a record of the frame as made for Dayes after discussion with his framemaker rather than a preparatory design by the artist but in any case it appears to be the earliest surviving drawing of its kind by a British artist. The drawing is in his sketchbook, sold Christie's, 30 March 1993, lot 29, now in the British Museum. The two watercolours, sold Christie's, 25 April 1995, lot 55, retain their original frames.
98. Penny, op.cit., pp.810–25.
99. Simon, op.cit. in n.94, pp.452–3.
100. See n.51.
101. The first of the two types is found on the Kenwood *Going to Market*, the Yale *Pastoral Landscape* (c.1772–4) and *Peasants Going to Market*, formerly at Royal Holloway College, with which a payment of eighty guineas in 1773 is linked. John Hayes, *The Holloway Gainsborough*, 1995, p.15, n.1, suggests the payment perhaps included the frame. The second type is found on the Kenwood *Greyhounds* and the Dublin *Cottage Girl with Dog and Pitcher*, 1785.
102. The correspondence is published by Basil Taylor, 'Josiah Wedgwood and George Stubbs', Proceedings of the Wedgwood Society, no.4, 1961, pp.209–22. The correspondence terminates with the death of Bentley on 26 November. While Stubbs appears to have adopted the frame type discussed in the correspondence for his enamels, Wedgwood himself chose a simpler narrower frame for his 'family piece' (Wedgwood Museum, Barlaston), repr. in Ruth Vincent-Kemp, *George Stubbs and the Wedgwood Connection*, Stoke-on-Trent, 1986, pp.32–2.
103. See n.68.
104. Mitchell, op.cit. in n.95, p.285.
105. W.H. Pyne, *The History of the Royal Residences*, vol.II, 1819, p.83.
106. For example, on Oliver Millar, *The Later Georgian Pictures in the Collection of Her Majesty The Queen*, 1969, nos.1154–5, 1157. Several of the pictures are currently on view at Spencer House, London.
107. For example, on two pictures of 1786, *St Paul shaking off the Viper* (Tate Gallery) and *Alexander III of Scotland rescued from the Fury of a Stag* (National Gallery of Scotland).
108. Ernest Fletcher (ed.), *Conversations of James Northcote R.A. with James Ward*, 1901, p.163.
109. Simon, op.cit. in n.94, pp.452–3.
110. See above, pp.41–3.
111. Hugh Honour, 'Sir Thomas Lawrence and Benjamin Gott', *Leeds Arts Calendar*, no.25, 1954, pp.13–19.
112. C.R. Leslie, *Memoirs of the Life of John Constable, Esq. R.A.*, 2nd edition, 1845, p.202.
113. British Museum Print Room, Whitley Papers, vol.V, p.547, letter to Sir George Beaumont: 'Charpentier has made a pretty frame, but I think he loads his work too much with little ornaments. I like a frame with rich corners & then more plain in the middle. Ross, although he did not finish them well, had an excellent pattern with shields at the corners. I have never seen frames set off pictures better'.
114. Beckett, op.cit. in n.55, vol.VI, p.127. For Constable and his frames, see also vol.IV, p.133.
115. Reproduced in Reg Gadney, *John Constable R.A. 1776–1837. A Catalogue of Drawings ... in the Fitzwilliam Museum, Cambridge*, 1976, no.25.
116. Martin Butlin and Evelyn Joll, *The Paintings of J.M.W. Turner*, London and New Haven, 1984, p.172, no.293.
117. Royal Scottish Academy, Etty correspondence files, Etty to William Nicholson, 1 November 1829. See also letters of 27 January and 7 May 1829 and 25 November 1831. The paintings, now in the National Gallery of Scotland, have been ruined by the effects of bitumen.
118. Richard James, 'Two Paintings by John Martin', *Burlington Magazine*, vol.XCIV, 1952, pp.234–7. The *Celestial City* was in the collection of Captain Sir Maurice Huntingdon-Whiteley Bart in 1952.
119. Royal Academy Library, 236/24/8/a–f, 236/24/10/a–d.
120. Miller's picture was sold at Christie's, 26 April 1946, lot 54, along with two other Herberts. The Tate picture is reproduced in its frame in Robin Hamlyn, *Robert Vernon's Gift*, exh. cat., Tate Gallery, 1993, p.29, no.32.
121. Royal Academy Library, 236/19/3/a–b.
122. National Portrait Gallery Archive, G.F. Watts Letterbooks, vol.XII, p.26.
123. Lynn Roberts, 'Nineteenth Century English Picture Frames, I, The Pre-Raphaelites', *International Journal of Museum Management and Curatorship*, vol.IV, 1985, p.157.
124. J.G. Millais, *The Life and Letters of Sir John Everett Millais*, vol.I, 1899, p.100.
125. Georgiana Burne-Jones, *Memorials of Edward Burne-Jones*, vol.II, 1904, p.20.
126. Roberts, op.cit., p.159.
127. A.M. Young *et al.*, *The Paintings of J.M. Whistler*, New Haven and London, 1980, p.32, no.56. The picture is now in the Freer Gallery of Art, Washington, DC.
128. John A. Mahey, 'The Letters of James McNeill Whistler to George A. Lucas', *Art Bulletin*, vol.XLIX, 1967, p.253.
129. A.L. Baldry, *Painting a Portrait. By De László*, London and New York, 1934, p.18.
130. See above, pp.23–4.
131. Diana Souhami, *Gluck 1895–1978. Her Biography*, 1988, p.103.

Chapter 5: Patrons and their Advisers

1. Sheila O'Connell, 'Lord Shaftesbury in Naples: 1711–1713', *Walpole Society*, vol.LIV, 1991, p.173. Shaftesbury was one of the first to recommend protecting pictures with glass 'especially in the smoaky Town of London'. *The Judgement of Paris* is now in the Ashmolean Museum, Oxford, in an elaborate later rococo frame.
2. Horace Walpole, *A Description of Strawberry-Hill*, 1784, pp.28–9, 51; see also W.S. Lewis (ed.), *The Yale Edition of Horace Walpole's Correspondence*, London and New Haven, vol.XXX, 1961, p.141 and vol.XXXV,

1973, pp.83, 174.

3. See above, pp.100, 102.
4. For the Hill Street gallery, see Peter Cannon-Brookes, *Paintings from Tabley*, exh. cat., Heim Gallery, 1989, pp.14–22. The role of Michael Tijou and his son, Henry, in the management of the Hill Street gallery requires further research but see Douglas Hall, 'The Tabley House Papers', *Walpole Society*, vol.XXXVIII, 1962, pp.109–10, for correspondence dating to 1824, and Peter Cannon-Brookes, *Tabley House*, guidebook, 1991, p.8, for Henry Tijou's responsibility for organising the 1827 sale.
5. The only collection to have been studied in some detail and published is that of the Duke of Wellington; see Simon Jervis, 'Picture frames and picture hanging at Apsley House' in C.M. Kauffmann, *Catalogue of Paintings in the Wellington Museum*, 1982, pp.17–20. It is worth noting of the Turner Bequest that the pictures were received by the National Gallery without their frames, with the frames coming later, while much of the Townshend bequest appears to have been framed in a standard laurel-leaf moulding on acquisition. There is a danger of the character of these collections being eroded at the hands of enthusiastic curators. While the Victoria and Albert Museum collections are remarkably intact, the Dulwich and Wallace collections have seen some of their finest pictures reframed since 1945 and the Vernon Collection has suffered relatively recently as frames in poor condition have been put aside rather than restored.
6. See John Gage, *Collected Correspondence of J.M.W. Turner*, Oxford, 1980, p.176.
7. See J.C. Horsley, *Recollections of a Royal Academician*, 1903, p.59. The picture is presumably *The Pride of the Village*, exhibited in 1839.
8. I am grateful to Robert Wenley and Colin Jenner for bringing Evans's accounts to my attention and for other information on frames at the Wallace Collection. Evans's bills are dated April 1857 and February 1859. The later bill includes a credit for the sale of old frames. See also John Ingamells, *The Wallace Collection. Catalogue of Pictures. British, German, Italian, Spanish*, 1985, p.432.
9. Vokins' label or stencil can be found on Frith's *The Village Merry-Making* (510–1882), Webster's *The Lesson* (509–1882) and Frederick Goodall's *The Irish Piper* (530–1882). Frith's *'Measuring Heights'* (479–1882) has an identical frame to the Goodall.
10. Jacob Simon, 'Allan Ramsay and picture frames', *Burlington Magazine*, vol.CXXXVI, 1994, p.448.
11. National Portrait Gallery, Registered Packets for NPG 1631, Hugh Childers, letter dated 6 January 1912 and NPG 3120, Lord Grey of Fallodon, letter dated 14 September 1942.
12. Scottish Record Office, GD 112/21/77–80, Personal account books of 3rd Earl of Breadalbane.
13. Scottish Record Office, GD 220/6/1132/19, 1155/18, 1226/60, 1230/2, 1235/42, 1256/41, 1356/20, 1363/28, 1743/11.
14. Their lack of frames was thought worthy of mention by Mary Berry in a letter to a friend in 1799; see Francis Haskell, *Rediscoveries in Art: Some Aspects of Taste, Fashion and Collecting in England and France*, Oxford, 1976, p.42.
15. See for example the dealer William Buchanan's remarks in 1804 about pictures selling better in rich frames, quoted above, p.19.
16. Alastair Laing, *In Trust for the Nation. Paintings from National Trust Houses*, exh. cat., National Gallery, 1995, p.216, no.58, n.6.
17. *The Manuscripts of the Earl of Carlisle preserved at Castle Howard*, Historical Manuscripts Commission, 15th Report, Appendix, Part VI, 1897, p.472.
18. *Gawthorpe Hall, Lancashire*, guidebook, 1992, p.47.
19. *Retention of Important Pictures*, National Gallery Committee Report, chairman Lord Curzon, 1914, Appendix IV ('Note on Frames' by R.H. Benson).
20. James Holloway, *William Aikman 1682-1731*, Edinburgh, 1988, p.13.
21. For the Duke of Buckingham, see n.36. For the Earl of Upper Ossory, see National Library of Ireland, Fitzpatrick Manuscripts, letters from Gavin Hamilton, Rome, to Lord Upper Ossory, 1767 to 1769.
22. *Kingston Lacy, Dorset*, guidebook, 1987, p.36.
23. National Gallery Archives, Trustees Minutes, vol.IV, p.5.
24. Ibid., p.118. It is possible that the importation of frames of this kind encouraged artists such as George Richmond to use tabernacle frames for their own work.
25. *The Emma Holt Bequest, Sudley, Illustrated Catalogue and History of the House*, Liverpool, 1971, p.71, no.306. See also Lynn Roberts, 'Nineteenth Century English Picture Frames, II: The Victorian High Renaissance', *International Journal of Museum Management and Curatorship*, vol.V, 1986, p.287.
26. Trade Directories give Emile Remy, carver, at 90 College Street, Chelsea, 1904–10, and as carver and gilder at 153 King's Road, Chelsea from 1911 until at least 1928.
27. National Gallery Archives, Trustees Minutes, vol.VIII, pp.331, 361. For Benson's report, see n.19.
28. For the use of antique frames, see above, p.23.
29. For the decision to purchase the Cassirer frames, see National Gallery Archives, Trustees Minutes, vol.XI, p.173.
30. See above, p.56; see also above, p.57, for the use of black-and-gold frames.
31. For Narford, see Andrew Moore, *Family and Friends; A Regional Survey of British Portraiture*, exh. cat., Norwich Castle Museum, 1992, p.33. See also David Piper, 'The Chesterfield House Library Portraits' in *Evidence in Literary Scholarship. Essays in Memory of James Marshall Osborn*, ed. by René Wellek and Alvaro Ribeiro, Oxford, 1979, pp.179–95; *Kingston Lacy, Dorset*, guidebook, 1994, pp.47–9; *Saltram, Devon*, guidebook, 1988, pp.32–4.
32. Charles Noble, 'Fashion in the Gallery', *Apollo*, vol.CXXXVIII, 1993, pp.171–4.
33. W.B. Pope (ed.), *The Diary of Benjamin Robert Haydon*, Cambridge, Mass., vol.III, 1963, p.453.
34. For Van der Doort and subsequent Surveyors of the collection, see Oliver Millar, *The Queen's Pictures*, 1977. Many holders of the post are listed in the index under 'Surveyors'.
35. 'Journaal van Constantijn Huygens, den zoon', *Werken Historisch Genootschap*, Utrecht, 2nd series, vol.XXV, 1877, pp.552, 555–6.
36. I.G. Philip, 'Balthazar Gerbier and the Duke of Buckingham's Pictures', *Burlington Magazine*, vol.XCIX, 1957, p.156; Lita-Rose Betcherman, 'The York House Collection and its keeper', *Apollo*, vol.XCII, 1970, p.252.
37. Robert Latham and William Matthews (eds), *The Diary of Samuel Pepys*, vol.IX, 1976, p.538. The context of the diary entry suggests that Pepys may have been looking for frames for prints rather than paintings.
38. See above, p.39.
39. *Report on the Manuscripts of the Earl of Egmont*, Historical Manuscripts Commission, vol.II, 1909, pp.144–5.
40. F.W. Hilles (ed.), *Letters of Sir Joshua Reynolds*, Cambridge, 1929, p.173.
41. Pope, op.cit. in n.33, p.455.
42. *The Dutch Connection. The Founding of the Fitzwilliam Museum*, exh. cat., Fitzwilliam Museum, Cambridge, 1988, p.6.
43. Jervis, op.cit. in n.5, p.18.

44. Surrey Record Office, Goulburn papers, letter dated 22 September 1848. See also above, p.116.
45. See n.43.
46. Robert Thick Account Book, 1839–47, p.8. The account book belongs to the Duke of Wellington who kindly made it available for study.
47. National Portrait Gallery Archive, Romney Ledger, 1786–96, under 6 October 1789. See also the entries for 5 August 1790 and 22 July 1791.
48. A series of revealing entries occur in Farington's diary between 1797 and 1799. See Farington, *Diary*, pp.836, 840, 905–7, 909; 1259, 1262.
49. Clive Wainwright, *The Romantic Interior. The British Collector at Home 1750–1850*, New Haven and London, 1989, p.120.
50. Helena Hayward and Pat Kirkham, *William and John Linnell: 18th Century London Furniture Makers*, 1980, p.147.
51. Geoffrey Beard, *Georgian Craftsmen and Their Work*, 1966, p.65.
52. R.T. Gunther (ed.), *The Architecture of Sir Roger Pratt*, Oxford, 1928, pp.282–3.
53. Geoffrey Beard, *Craftsmen and Interior Decoration in England 1660–1820*, Edinburgh, 1981, pp.129, 131.
54. Howard Colvin, 'The Rebuilding of Combe Abbey', *Walpole Society*, vol.L, 1984, p.292.
55. Michael Wilson, *William Kent*, 1984, p.106.
56. Ibid.
57. For the Gallery as rehung, see John Cornforth, 'Kensington Palace, London', *Country Life*, vol.CLXXXIX, 5 January 1995, pp.34–7. John Howard the framemaker was ordered to provide the frames on 12 March 1725; see Public Record Office, LC5/158, p.431.
58. Moore, op.cit. in n.31, pp.35–7.
59. Hayward and Kirkham, op.cit., p.148.
60. Ibid., p.145. Linnell's bill for the frames for Oakley survives; the more expensive of the two cost £9.6s: 'To a frame carved by drawing for over the chimney in the Library'.
61. Ibid.
62. Simon, op.cit. in n.10, p.450.
63. Christopher Gilbert, *The Life and Work of Thomas Chippendale*, 1978, p.162.
64. Hugh Roberts, '"Nicely Fitted Up": Furniture for the 4th Duke of Marlborough', *Furniture History*, vol.XXX, 1994, p.121.
65. Gilbert, op.cit. in n.63, p.260.
66. Arthur Bolton, *The Portrait of Sir John Soane, R.A.*, 1927, p.55; see also n.49 above.
67. *DEFM*, p.622; Howard Colvin, *A Biographical Dictionary of British Architects, 1600–1840*, 1978, p.619. See also Edward T. Joy, *English Furniture, 1800–1851*, 1977, p.180.
68. See above, p.44.
69. For the taste of the new collectors, see above, p.24.

Chapter 6: Framemakers and the Business of Framemaking

1. See above, p.33.
2. Joseph Collyer, *A Parent's and Guardian's Directory*, 1761, pp.150–1, 214.
3. Christopher Gilbert, *The Life and Works of Thomas Chippendale*, 1978, pp.186–7. Subsequently the frames were enriched by adding carved roses and other ornaments at a further cost of £35.
4. Helena Hayward and Pat Kirkham, *William and John Linnell: 18th Century London Furniture Makers*, 1980, p.145.
5. E.S. De Beer (ed.), *The Diary of John Evelyn*, Oxford, 1955, p.317, entry for 16 June 1683.
6. Geoffrey Beard, 'Some English wood-carvers', *Burlington Magazine*, vol.CXXVII, 1985, pp.690–1; *DEFM*, p.742.
7. David Buttery, 'The Picture Frames of Paul Petit, and Frederick, Prince of Wales', *Apollo*, vol.CXXVI, 1987, pp.12–15.
8. Beard, op.cit. in n.6, pp.693–7; Jacob Simon, 'Allan Ramsay and picture frames', *Burlington Magazine*, vol.CXXXVI, 1994, pp.450–1.
9. Nicholas Penny, 'Reynolds and picture frames', *Burlington Magazine*, vol.CXXVIII, 1986, pp.811, 821.
10. Edward Croft-Murray, *Decorative Painting in England 1537–1837*, vol.I, 1962, pp.178–80, 193–5, 198–201.
11. Mary Edmond, 'Limners and Picturemakers – New Light on the lives of miniaturists and large-scale portrait painters working in London in the sixteenth and seventeenth centuries', *Walpole Society*, vol.XLVII, 1980, pp.175–6; Croft-Murray, op.cit., p.202–4.
12. Philip McEvansoneya, 'Van Dyck and the Duchess of Buckingham's collection', *Apollo*, vol.CXL, December 1994, p.30; the Middlesex bill of 6 August 1639 is in the Kent Record Office, Knole papers, U269 A462/5.
13. Erna Auerbach and C. Kingsley Adams, *Paintings and Sculpture at Hatfield House*, 1971, pp.84–5.
14. Geldorp's account with the Earl of Middlesex is in the National Portrait Gallery Archive.
15. Jeremy Wood, 'Van Dyck and the Earl of Northumberland: Taste and Collecting in Stuart England', in *Van Dyck 350*, ed. Susan J. Barnes and A.K. Wheelock, Jr., *Studies in the History of Art*, vol.XLVI, National Gallery of Art, Washington, DC, 1994, pp.309–10.
16. Robert Wenley, 'William, Third Earl of Lothian', *Journal of the History of Collections*, vol.V, no.1, 1993, pp.31–2.
17. Oliver Millar, *The Queen's Pictures*, 1977, pp.60–9.
18. Wood, op.cit., pp.312–3.
19. Wood, op.cit., p.314.
20. Robert Latham and William Matthews, *The Diary of Samuel Pepys*, vol.IX, 1976, p.538, entry for 30 April 1669.
21. The prime source of information for Mary Beale's commissions to the Norris family are her husband's notebooks for 1677 in the Bodleian Library, Oxford, and for 1681 in the National Portrait Gallery. My interpretation of the position of Thompson Norris as a servant in the Beale household, based on entries for 23 February and 1 March in the 1681 Beale notebook, differs from that given by M. Kirby Talley, who calls him father of John Norris; see Talley's *Portrait Painting in England: Studies in the Technical Literature before 1700*, 1981, pp.299–301.
22. Millar, op.cit. in n.17, p.82; *DEFM*, p.654.
23. Vertue, vol.II, p.52, and III, p.42. Vertue also refers to Isaac Fuller's portrait of 'Norris the Kings Frame maker', presumably Henry Norris; see Vertue, vol.I, p.26.
24. Kent Record Office, Knole papers, U269 A7/25, A7/27, A192/9, A193/12, A195/2, from notes by Gervase Jackson-Stops held by the National Trust. Auerbach and Adams, op.cit., p.175. Oliver Millar, 'Artists and Craftsmen in the service of Sir Stephen Fox and his family', *Burlington Magazine*, vol.CXXXVII, 1995, pp.525–8.
25. See pp.58, 147 and Chapter 4, n.85, 88; see also *DEFM*, pp.280, 538, 687, and *DEF, p.27*.
26. Simon, op.cit. in n.8, p.454, n.64. The official title for the post was 'Joiner of the Privy Chamber'.
27. *DEF*, pp.30–1; *DEFM*, pp.453–4.
28. Simon, op.cit. in n.8, p.452.
29. Public Record Office, LC5/158, p.431. See also p.61, 125.
30. *London Evening Post*, 4–6 September 1746, transcript in Victoria and Albert Museum Furniture Dept Archive.
31. *DEFM*, p.947; see also Scottish Record Office, GD 112/21/77–8, 112/21/230/33.

32. Millar, op.cit. in n.24, p.526, item XIII. It is unlikely that Waters would have received payment in 1713 for a picture on behalf of Jervas if he had not also made the frame.
33. See also above, no.36, especially n.3. For Joseph Duffour and his son William, see Simon, op.cit. in n.8, p.454, n.66. Duffour's trade card is sometimes given to René Duffour, a shadowy figure who requires better documentation.
34. See Tessa Murdoch, 'Courtiers and Classics. The Gosset Family', *Country Life*, vol.CLXXVII, 1985, pp.1282–3. It is not possible to be sure that it was Isaac, rather than one of his brothers whom Hogarth knew. See also Simon, op.cit., in n.8, pp.447, 454. For Isaac Gosset's work for Hoare and Gainsborough, see Chapter 4, n.51. One of the brothers worked for Arthur Pond; Louise Lippincott, 'Arthur Pond's Journal of Receipts and Expenses, 1734–1750', *Walpole Society*, vol.LIV, 1991, p.323 suggests Gideon but this name does not appear in Pond's journal.
35. Vertue, vol.III, p.160. Gosset's customers included the Duke of Bedford and the Duke of Beaufort; see *DEFM*, p.359.
36. For Vials see *DEFM*, p.922. For Beaumont see *DEFM*, p.56 and for his trade card in the British Museum, see Ambrose Heal, *The London Furniture Makers*, 1953, republished by Dover Publications Inc., New York, 1972, p.5.
37. Ivan Hall, 'New Light on Yorkshire Craftsmen', *Country Life*, vol.CLIX, 1976, p.1478.
38. Kent Record Office, Knole papers, U269 A243/2. The bill for the frame on the portrait of the 3rd Duke is quoted on p.66.
39. Penny, op.cit. in n.9, pp.819–20. It is worth noting that Vials appears in Reynolds's sitter book in March 1776.
40. See above, pp.96–7.
41. Scottish Record Office, Seafield papers, GD 248/449/1/57.
42. Information kindly communicated by Alastair Laing.
43. Catherine Wills, 'Stable Ancestry', *Country Life*, vol.CLXXXIII, 9 March 1989, p.148. Vials packed up one of Gilpin's pictures after the 1771 exhibition to send it to Yorkshire; see M.E. Ingram, *Leaves from a Family Tree*, 1951, p.62.
44. Public Record Office, PROB 11/1079.
45. *DEFM*, pp.210, 296, 459. See also Penny, op.cit. in n.9, p.817.
46. National Portrait Gallery Archive, note made by George Scharf of a conversation with Critchfield. There is, however, no evidence in the Thick Order Ledgers and Account Book covering the years 1839–51 of Thick receiving much work from the Crown. The Duke of Wellington kindly made these documents available for study.
47. *DEFM*, p.210; Trade Directories. In 1919 the firm moved to no.110 Albany Street, the address of another framemaker, Francis Draper, who may have bought out the residual interest in the business.
48. National Gallery Archive, NG 1/9, p.147, Trustees Minutes, 21 June 1880.
49. *DEFM*, p.367.
50. York City Library, William Etty letters, no.147, Green to Etty, 3 October 1837, about acquiring a print of Landseer's *Bolton Abbey in the Olden Times* from Messrs Colnaghi. Maclise's *A Scene from 'Undine'*, dated 1843, in the Royal Collection has a frame by Green; see Oliver Millar, *The Victorian Pictures in the Collection of Her Majesty The Queen*, Cambridge, 1992, no.486. Maclise was using Green for packing pictures in 1856; see Royal Academy Library, 236/35/3/a–c. See also n.103.
51. Lynn Roberts, 'Nineteenth Century English Picture Frames, I: The Pre-Raphaelites', *International Journal of Museum Management and Curatorship*, vol.IV, 1985, p.159.
52. He is perhaps the Joseph Green whose will was proved 24 February 1870, giving his address as 6 Helmet Row, Old Street; his nephew German Green, a mathematical instrument maker, lived at no.7. I am grateful to Michèle Riley for locating and transcribing the will.
53. Trade Directories.
54. British Library, Add. MS. 43,909, f.281, Brown to Sir Charles Dilke, 2 July 1872. Mary Bennett, 'Footnotes to the William Holman Hunt Exhibition', *The Liverpool Bulletin*, vol.XIII, 1968–70, p.62.
55. Ibid., pp.62–3.
56. Bourlet's had begun as William Bourlet, carver and gilder, as early as 1808, and became one of the largest firms of framemakers between the two World Wars. The business, purchased by Sotheby's the auctioneers in the 1970s and subsequently resold, continues trading to this day. The firm still owns letters from G.F. Watts, dated 1905, and Edward Stott, dated 1891, to Smith & Uppard, and from artists as varied as Birket Foster, Laura Knight, Henry Lamb and Sir Gerald Kelly.
57. *DEFM*, p.308; Trade Directories; James Dickinson is named as partner by Ira Horowitz, 'The Picture Frame, 1848–1892: The Pre-Raphaelites, Whistler, Paris', unpublished thesis, Queen's College (CUNY), 1974, p.82. However two letters in the National Portrait Gallery Archive are signed by W. Dickinson.
58. *The Works of John Ruskin*, ed. E.T. Cook and Alexander Wedderburn, vol.XXV, 1908, p.484; see also vol.III, 1903, p.250, vol.XXXVI, 1909, p.39 and vol.XXXVII, 1909, p.270.
59. Christopher Newall, *The Grosvenor Gallery Exhibitions*, Cambridge, 1995, p.13.
60. *The Year's Art*, 1899, p.21; 1900, p.19.
61. C.M. May's advertisements can be found in *The Year's Art*, 1893, 1900, etc.
62. *Retention of Important Pictures*, National Gallery Committee Report, chairman Lord Curzon, 1914, Appendix IV ('Note on Frames by R.H. Benson').
63. Imperial War Museum, Dept of Art, GP/134. Memorandum, 18 April 1940.
64. Hammersmith and Fulham Archives, DD/76/1. See also n.95 below.
65. For Hecht, see above, p.186, under no.119; for Sielle see *The Art of Framing. An Exhibition of Pictures Framed by Robert Sielle*, exh. cat., British Crafts Centre, 1975.
66. Public Record Office, C104/146 Part 1, Cullen daybook, 8 July 1777.
67. British Museum Print Room, Whitley Papers, vol.VII, p.935, letter dated 6 December 1808.
68. Gilbert, op.cit. in n.3, p.22.
69. Hulton's trade card is among the Gordon papers in the Scottish Record Office, GD44/51/465/1/31. For Farley, Fletcher, Maskens and Merle, see *DEFM*, pp.289, 305, 583, 602.
70. *Art Union*, vol.II, 1840, p.87.
71. *Art Union*, vol.IV, 1842, p.114.
72. For Bielefeld, see above, pp.43–4.
73. *The Year's Art*, 1898, p.21.
74. *The Year's Art*, 1902, p.11.
75. Fitzwilliam Museum, Romney notebook, no.4, Allwood's carving book.
76. See also above, p.86.
77. Imperial War Museum, Dept of Art, volume 'First World War Frames', item 66.
78. See n.20.
79. Humberside County Record Office, Grimston papers, DDGR/42/5.
80. Helena Hayward, 'The Drawings of John Linnell in the Victoria and Albert Museum', *Furniture History*, vol.V, 1969, fig.133.
81. Gilbert, op.cit. in n.3, p.168, fig.310.

82. Hayward and Kirkham, op.cit in n.4, p.150.
83. See n.75.
84. Scottish Record Office, GD 220/6/1743/8.
85. Gervase Jackson-Stops, 'Picture Frames at Petworth – I', *Country Life*, vol.CLXVIII, 1980, p.799.
86. Hayward and Kirkham, op.cit. in n.4, pp.58, 61, 147.
87. See Ernest Enthoven (ed.), *Life and Works of Sir Christopher Wren. From the Parentalia or Memoirs by his son, Christopher, 1750*, 1903, p.106.
88. Another plate in the series is repr. in Pippa Mason and Gervase Jackson-Stops, *Designs for English Picture Frames*, exh. cat., Arnold Wiggins & Sons Ltd, 1987, no.3.
89. Eileen Harris, *British Architectural Books and Writers, 1556–1785*, Cambridge, 1990, p.273, no.413. See also p.210.
90. William Ince and John Mayhew, *Universal System of Household Furniture*, 1760–2, p.11, pl.88.
91. Morrison Heckscher in *Rococo. Art and Design in Hogarth's England*, ed. Michael Snodin, exh. cat., Victoria and Albert Museum, 1984, p.185. I am most grateful to Michael Snodin for lending me his notes on the Saint scrapbook.
92. Victoria and Albert Museum Library, 86.CC.1–3. I am most grateful to Charles Sebag-Montefiore for supplying me with a copy of his paper, *John Smith 1781–1855: Picture Dealer and Author*, given at the conference , 'The History of the Art Market in Europe 1500–1900', held at the National Gallery, London, 10 December 1994.
93. Hayward and Kirkham, op.cit. in n.4, p.45.
94. *DEFM*, p.555.
95. 'Framing Valuable Paintings', *Town and Country News*, 13 November 1931, pp.47–8.
96. P.A. Kirkham, 'Samuel Norman: a study of an 18th century Craftsman', *Burlington Magazine*, vol.CXI, 1969, p.502. The practice of sub-contracting is also discussed by Christopher Gilbert, op.cit. in n.3, pp.33–6.
97. I am most grateful to the Hon. Christopher Lennox-Boyd for the loan of the ledger and to Guy Shaw for his help.
98. Victoria and Albert Museum Library, 86.CC.1, entry for 17 March 1812, and 86.CC.2, entry for 3 August 1827.
99. Westminster City Archives, Gillow ledgers, 4 August 1796.
100. See n.79.
101. Dorothea Charnwood, 'Echoes of Great Artists', *Cornhill Magazine*, vol.LXV, 1928, p.156.
102. *DEF*, p.27. 'Neller' is, of course, Godfrey Kneller.
103. Green was acting for the York exhibition in 1836 and the Royal Scottish Academy in 1844; see York City Library, William Etty letters, nos.102–3, 274. For Tijou, see Trevor Fawcett, *The Rise of English Provincial Art: Artists, Patrons and Institutions outside London*, 1800–1830, Oxford, 1974, p.207.
104. Anthony Coleridge, 'Some Rococo Cabinet-Makers and Sir Lawrence Dundas', *Apollo*, vol.LXXXVI, September 1967, pp.216–7.
105. National Portrait Gallery, Duplicate of Accounts, vol.IV, p.113.
106. Scottish Record Office, GD 112/21/230/33.
107. *Gentleman's Magazine*, vol.XXXIV, 1764, p.535.
108. Farington, *Diary*, p.524, 15 April 1796.
109. Susan Chitty, *That Singular Person caller Lear*, 1988, p.173.
110. Humberside County Archive, DDGR 42/28/7.
111. Murdoch, op.cit. in n.34, pp.1282–3.
112. The frame costing £160 was probably the one for the portrait of the Prince by Jonathan Richardson at Warwick Castle, repr. Buttery, op.cit. in n.7, p.13.
113. Peter Cannon-Brookes, 'Robert Tournières, Lord Bateman and Two Picture Frames', *International Journal of Museum Management and Curatorship*, vol.IV, 1985, pp.141–5.
114. Anthony Coleridge, *Chippendale Furniture*, 1968, p.134.
115. Simon Jervis, 'Picture frames and picture hanging at Apsley House' in C.M. Kauffmann, *Catalogue of Paintings in the Wellington Museum*, 1982, p.47.
116. W.T. Whitley, *Thomas Gainsborough*, 1915, p.67.
117. See British Museum Print Room, Whitley Papers, vol.III, p.355 for the rumour in the *Oracle*, 9 July 1794, and Jules Prown, *John Singleton Copley in England, 1774 1815*, Cambridge, Mass., 1966, p.334, n.28 for the commission of the frame from James Brewer. On completion it was found the frame did not fit the room!
118. Talley, op.cit. in n.21, p.299.
119. Scottish Record Office, Montrose papers, GD 220/6/1356/20; National Portrait Gallery Archive, Joseph Wright of Derby account book.
120. Vertue, vol.II, p.11.
121. Simon, op.cit. in n.8, pp.446–7.
122. Penny, op.cit. in n.9, pp.812–3.
123. Jacob Simon, 'The Account Book of James Northcote', *Walpole Society*, vol.LVIII, 1996, p.26.
124. *Art Union*, vol.VI, 1844, p.49.
125. National Portrait Gallery Archive, G.F. Watts letters, book XII, p.90.
126. Imperial War Museum, Dept of Art, volume 'First World War Frames', item 7.
127. National Portrait Gallery Archive, Duplicate of Accounts, vol.VIII.
128. Hammersmith and Fulham Archives, DD/76/30, p.135, DD 219/1, pp.92, 335.
129. Letter to Clement Biddle, dated 28 May 1797, in *The Writings of George Washington*, p.455, quoted in William Adair, *The Frame in America 1700–1900*, exh. cat., The Octagon, Washington, DC, 1983, p.9.
130. See Chapter 4, n.102.
131. Penny, op.cit. in n.9, pp.812–3. Gilbert, op.cit. in n.3, pp.151–2 provides a useful account of the background to Knight's orders to Chippendale. I am most grateful to Nicholas Penny for lending me his files on Edward Knight.
132. *Wren Society*, vol.VII, 1930, p.121. See also pp.98, 104, 114–5 and vol.IV, 1927, p.44.
133. Simon, op.cit in n.8, p.451.
134. Basil Watson, *A Short Guide to the Chapel of St Peter and St Paul*, 1969, p.6.
135. National Portrait Gallery Archive, G.F. Watts letters, book XII, pp.84, 90.
136. Simon, op.cit. in n.123, p.6.

Glossary and Frame Sections

Cross-references are given in small capitals.
For line-drawings illustrating specific frame sections and construction techniques, see figs.180-201 on pp.210-16.

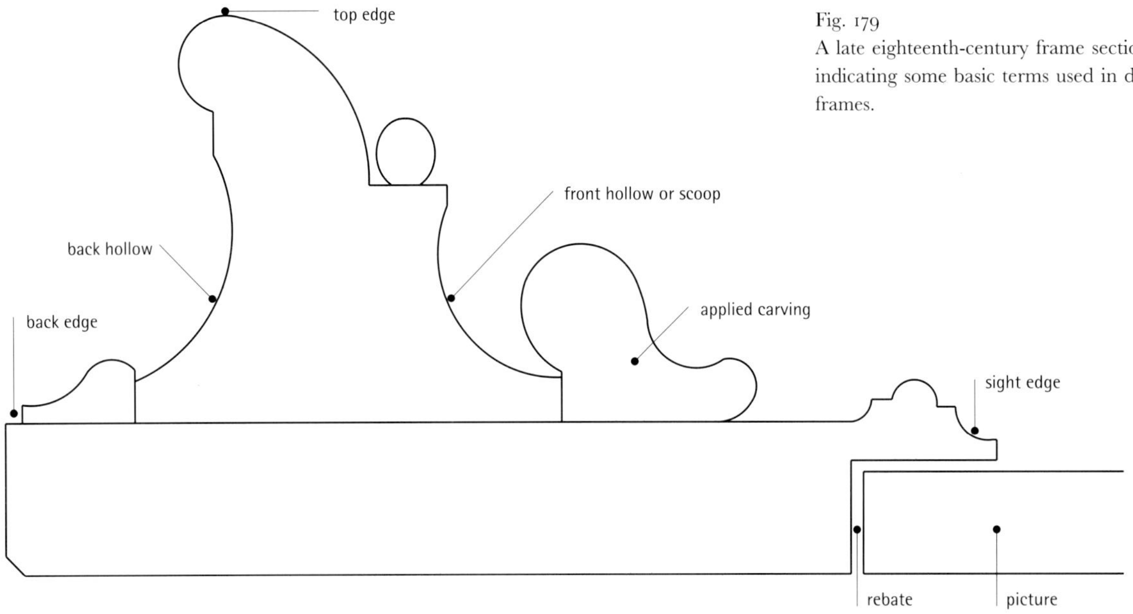

Fig. 179
A late eighteenth-century frame section, indicating some basic terms used in describing frames.

Basic terms

Back edge The outer edge of the frame furthest from the picture (see fig.179).
Chamfer A sloping or bevelled surface cut along the edge of a frame or panel (see fig.181).
Enrichment A run of carved or moulded ornament.
Fillet A narrow flat step between the mouldings of a frame (see fig.191).
Flat A wide flat area of a frame, often adjoining the picture (see figs.191, 194).
Frieze The flat central area between the inner and outer mouldings of a frame (see fig.181).
Hollow A concave section; often used to describe the main curve of a frame (see fig.179).
Moulding A shaped projecting or recessed band running along a frame, which may be plain or enriched.
Ogee A moulding with an S-shaped profile consisting of a double curve, half-concave, half-convex.
Rail The curving top edge of a rococo frame (see fig.188).
Rebate The recess beneath the sight edge designed to take the picture (see fig.179).
Reverse section A frame with the most prominent moulding nearest to the picture.
Running pattern Decoration running in a pattern along the sides of a frame.
Scoop The front hollow of a frame (see fig.179).
Section The profile of a frame cut at right angles to the sides (see figs.179–201).
Sight edge The inner edge of the frame nearest to the picture (see fig.179).
Slip An inserted flat or bevelled strip fitted in the rebate of a frame (see fig.192).
Spandrels The shaped additional inner structure filling the space between a rectangular frame and an oval or circular picture; in regular use from the second half of the eighteenth century (see fig.99).
Sweep The curving outer edge of a rococo frame (see fig.188).
Top edge The most prominent moulding of a frame (see fig.179).

Frame types

Alhambra A mid-nineteenth century frame type with a wide convex hollow decorated with MORESQUE or other intricate small-scale ornament, and a prominent rounded top edge on which the corner motifs of the frame are sometimes planted (see figs.71, 73); later used to describe a richly decorated frame of convex or ogee profile and ornamented top edge.

Architrave A frame taking its name from the architrave, an element of an entablature in classical architecture, but deriving more immediately from the use of the word to designate a door or window surround; a term used in the eighteenth century to designate a KENT frame (see figs.55, 187).
Auricular A frame in the auricular style (literally 'of the ear'), a highly stylised free-flowing interpretation of organic forms, usually animal or marine in nature, current from the 1630s to the 1680s (see fig.43).
Bolection A frame type, introduced in the late seventeenth century, with a distinctively shaped convex or OGEE moulding of REVERSE SECTION curving up from the picture and back to the wall (see fig.185), also known as a RAFFLE LEAF frame in the late seventeenth century.
Box A modern name for a CASSETTA frame, a frame of flat section with raised inner and outer mouldings (see fig.197).
Bunched leaf A late seventeenth-century frame type decorated with a repeated pattern of bunched leaves as its main feature, usually hanging from a rope, made up of bunches of oak leaves and acorns, leaves and berries or similar (see fig.184).
Carlo Maratta A frame with prominent curved top edge of distinctive profile, taking its name from the painter Carlo Maratta, current in Britain from the 1750s to the 1790s, usually ornamented with ACANTHUS-AND-TONGUE or acanthus-and-shell (see fig.190). Sometimes described as a SALVATOR ROSA frame.
Cassetta A frame of flat section with raised inner and outer mouldings, an Italian term for an internationally used type, literally a box or case (see fig.11); sometimes called a BOX frame.
Centre-and-corner An early eighteenth-century frame type with prominent centre and corner motifs; also applied to any frame with prominent centres and corners.
Collins A mid-nineteenth century frame type with a prominent cushion, decorated with a running ornamental foliage pattern, usually with wide, spreading flat shell or scroll corners, perhaps taking its name from the painter William Collins.
Cushion A frame of flattish rounded or convex section, a term used to describe the narrow cushion frames of the mid-seventeenth century (see figs.47, 183) and some frames of the nineteenth century (see fig.195).
Engaged An early sixteenth-century frame type with grooves into which the panel of the painting engages (see figs.20, 181).
Hockey A twentieth-century frame type of narrow but deep section, with a plain flat cushion or hockey top, sometimes literally called a hockey stick (see no.123).
Integral An early sixteenth-century frame type with the frame and the panel of the painting made from a single piece of wood (see fig.180).
Kent A BOX frame current from the 1720s to the 1760s, named after the architect William Kent, featuring projecting square corners, a flat frieze decorated with sand or architectural pattern, and a raised outer edge carved with EGG-AND-DART or other architectural motif (see figs.55, 187).
Lawrence A nineteenth-century frame type of broad OGEE section ornamented with a small-scale all-over foliage and scroll pattern, usually with restrained shell or foliage corners, named after the painter Sir Thomas Lawrence, current from the 1820s (see fig.193); also used more narrowly to describe any of the frame patterns actually used by Lawrence.
Leaf-and-berry A late seventeenth-century frame type ornamented with bunches of leaves and berries, a type of BUNCHED LEAF frame.
Leatherwork A frame in the AURICULAR style in some way resembling an animal skin.
Lely A term taking its name from the painter Sir Peter Lely used to describe a PANEL frame.
Maratta See Carlo Maratta.
Oak leaf-and-acorn A late seventeenth-century frame type ornamented with bunches of oak leaves and acorns, a type of BUNCHED LEAF frame.
Palladian A frame in the Palladian style, a term first used in the nineteenth century to describe a KENT frame.
Panel A late seventeenth-century and early eighteenth-century frame type with panels set between running foliage ornament as its main feature (see fig.53).
Raffle leaf A late seventeenth-century BOLECTION frame ornamented with raffle leaves (see fig.49).
Régence A frame in the late baroque style current in France in the period about 1710–1730, taking its name from the regency of Philippe d'Orleans.
Salvator Rosa A term used for a CARLO MARATTA frame, named after the painter Salvator Rosa, the term being more commonly used in Italy than Britain.
Sansovino A Venetian style named after the architect Jacopo Sansovino, current in the late sixteenth century and early seventeenth century, and reflecting the mannerist style of the period, characterized by the sculptural use of large-scale scrolls and volutes, often with cherub heads and festoons of fruit, the carving partially gilt (see fig.5).
Shadow box A late nineteenth-century and twentieth-century framing device in which the painting, either framed or unframed, sits within a shallow box lined with velvet or other material; the box is usually made up of polished hardwood mouldings.
Sunderland A frame in the AURICULAR style, current from the 1650s to the 1680s, named after the 2nd Earl of Sunderland (see fig.46).
Swept A rococo frame with swept sides, so-called for their sweeping curves (see fig.188).
Tabernacle In origins an ornamental niche above an altar and hence an architectural surround to a painting; a term used in eighteenth-century Britain to describe some KENT frames.

Trophy A frame with applied trophies, usually imposed upon and projecting from the main frame structure; the trophies are symbolic of the subject matter of the painting (see fig.73).
Watts A BOX frame, named after the painter George Frederic Watts, very common from the 1860s to the 1910s, the sight edge and top edge with leaf ornament in compo, the main flat frieze often gilt direct onto the oak (see figs.36, 194).
Whistler A reeded frame, named after the painter James McNeill Whistler, current from the 1870s onwards, found either as a flat frame with inner and outer reeded bands (see fig.80), or as a reeded cushion frame (see fig.196), usually gilt directly onto oak but later sometimes made of pine painted white (see fig.10).

ORNAMENT

Acanthus Stylized ornamental leaf based on the leaf of the acanthus plant.
Acanthus-and-tongue A running pattern commonly found applied to the hollow or sight edge of a CARLO MARATTA frame, made up of ACANTHUS leaves alternating with plain tongues (see figs.24, 190), sometimes found in the form of acanthus-and-shell with a shell replacing the tongue.
Appliqué Ornament which is applied to the surface of a frame (see fig.48).
Arabesque Intricate and stylized surface decoration made up of scrolling foliage, sometimes inset with animals, birds, ornamental objects or figures (see fig.111). See also GROTESQUE.
Bead-and-reel A thin convex moulding in the form of alternating circular and elliptical or elongated motifs, the beads usually in twos or threes (see fig.187).
Cabochon An egg or boss contained within a circular surround, colloquially an 'egg in a nest', often found in a series separated by a leaf or dart, sometimes used as a top or back edge ornament on mid-eighteenth century British frames (see no.46).
Carlo The characteristic ornament applied to the hollow or sight edge of a CARLO MARATTA frame, made up of ACANTHUS-AND-TONGUE (see fig.190) or acanthus-and-shell.
Clasp A flat leaf motif clasping or encircling the centre or corner of a frame, found on CUSHION and some other mid-seventeenth century frames.
C-scroll A scroll in the shape of a C, usually paired with a reverse-C scroll, partly overlaid by foliage and forming part of the corner or centre ornament of a rococo frame (see fig.188).
Diaper A repeated all-over surface pattern of small lozenges filled with florettes or quatrefoils (see fig.72).
Egg-and-dart An ornament of alternating oval and pointed motifs of classical origin used to enrich a convex moulding of about a quarter round; also called an egg-and-anchor or egg-and-tongue, a feature of KENT frames and some later classical styles (see fig.187).
Festoon A garland of interwoven leaves, fruit or flowers suspended in a curve between two points (see figs.4, 5).
Fluting A series of parallel concave grooves, generally cut across the hollow or frieze of a frame at right angles to the frame side, a feature of the neo-classical style (see fig.189).
Gadrooning A series of gadroons or convex shaped ridges, sometimes ornamented, set in a repeated decorative pattern (see figs.186, 187).
Grotesque Intricate and fanciful surface decoration made up of foliage inset with animals, birds, ornamental objects or figures (see fig.75). See also ARABESQUE.
Guilloche A continuous band of two interwoven spirals, forming a series of circles, often enclosing a rosette (see figs.64, 144).
Hazzling A fine zig-zag line scored in the gesso and used to animate flat background areas to the carving of frames in the late seventeenth and early eighteenth century (see fig.184).
Husk A short flat leaf, rather like an opening bud, or more generally, a line of such leaves.
Laurel leaf A laurel leaf, generally with berries, often run together in a series to decorate the top edge of a frame (see fig.189).
Leaf-and-tongue A small-scale running pattern made up of alternating leaves and tongues, commonly applied to the sight edge, back edge or another subsidiary moulding (see figs.186, 188, 189, 190).
Mitre leaf A large leaf, commonly an ACANTHUS leaf, covering the mitre at the corner of a frame (see figs.69, 189).
Moresque Intricate surface decoration of a sort found in Moorish architecture, often consisting of densely interwoven foliage, sometimes found as a stylized arabic script, a style used to ornament ALHAMBRA and some other nineteenth-century frames (see fig.71).
Patera A circular or oval ornament carved in low relief, often as a stylised flower with petals surrounding a small central circle (see fig.99).
Pearl A small round bead, resembling a pearl, often found repeated in a series along the sight edge or other moulding of a frame (see fig.190).
Raffle leaf A leaf with raffled edges, often found in the form of an ACANTHUS leaf on BOLECTION frames (see fig.49).
Raking knull A raking or angled pattern of ridges, normally used to ornament the top edge of a frame, frequently in the form of GADROONING.
Reeding A series of thin convex ridged mouldings set parallel with each other, somewhat resembling a group of bundled reeds, often found tied by a ribbon or a curling leaf (fig.67).
Ribbon-and-reed A band of carving made up of REEDING tied with ribbons, often found applied to the top edge or sight edge of frames in the neo-classical style (see fig.67).
Ribbon-and-stick A thin convex moulding or dowel in the form of a

ribbon twisted round a narrow stick, often found as an ornament next to the top edge or sight edge of MARATTA or neo-classical frames (see figs.24, 190).

Ribbon twist A thin convex moulding or dowel in the form of a twisted ribbon (see fig.184).

Ripple moulding A moulding with a fine ripple, commonly applied to a frame in one or more bands, a style originating with Dutch and German seventeenth-century ebony frames (see fig.42).

Rocaille A type of asymetrical decoration used on rococo frames, a French term meaning literally rock-work (see fig.188).

Sanding The sanded frieze found on eighteenth-century frames produced by applying sand to the sized frame surface before gessoing and gilding (see figs.133, 187).

S-scroll An S-shaped scroll often partly overlaid by foliage and used to ornament the sides of rococo frames (see fig.92).

Twisted ribbon See RIBBON TWIST.

Volute A spiral scroll (see fig.39).

Waterleaf A small veined leaf, used to enrich a subsidiary frame moulding, often found in the form of waterleaf-and-tongue where each waterleaf is followed by a plain tongue (see fig.189).

Technique and construction

Bole A fine clay mixed with SIZE, used in WATER GILDING to prepare a smooth surface for gilding and to serve as a GOLD SIZE; wetted immediately before gilding.

Burnishing A process of polishing WATER GILDING with a burnisher (see fig.21).

Butterfly key A butterfly or dovetail shaped key used on the rear side of a frame to secure a mitre joint (see fig.201).

Butt joint A joint with two closely abutting timbers.

Compo See COMPOSITION.

Composition A pliable mixture usually made of whiting, glue, resin and linseed oil, which can be pressed to make moulded ornament (see fig.30), known as compo.

Corner block A block used on the rear side of a frame to secure a mitre joint and to strengthen the inner and outer back frame, a technique used in the nineteenth century.

Double gilding The process in WATER GILDING of adding a second layer of gold leaf.

Dutch Metal An alloy of copper and zinc used in leaf form as a substitute for gold leaf but requiring a finishing lacquer to prevent tarnishing; also called Dutch gold.

Ebonised Stained or painted and polished to give the appearance of ebony.

Faulting The process of filling in small gaps or faults where the gilding has not adhered by resizing if necessary and regilding.

Gesso A mixture of WHITING and SIZE used as a ground for GILDING; the Italian word for gypsum.

Gilding The application of gold leaf to a prepared surface.

Gold size The adhesive used to fix gold leaf in place; in OIL GILDING oil-based, in WATER GILDING water-based. The water-based gold size is a mixture of clay and SIZE; see BOLE.

Key A shaped piece of timber used on the rear side of a frame to secure a mitre joint; usually of tapering shape with bevelled edges (see fig.200), sometimes called a feather key; see also BUTTERFLY key.

Lap joint A corner joint with the wood of one side overlapping the adjoining side (see fig.198).

Mason's mitre A corner joint where the visible joint and the structural joint do not coincide; used more generally to describe the stepped joint in AURICULAR and SUNDERLAND frames where the joint is secured by a back frame.

Matt gold Unburnished water gilding, usually protected by a coat of size or lacquer.

Mitre joint A diagonal joint used at the corner of frames with the adjacent sides abutting (see figs.200, 201).

Mortise-and-tenon A joint where a tenon or tongue of one timber is fixed through a matching shaped mortise or hole in another timber (see fig.199).

Obeche A fine-grained hardwood from West Africa.

Oil gilding Gilding using an oil-based GOLD SIZE as adhesive.

Papier-maché A material made of paper torn into strips or pulped, and soaked in a binder, used for moulded ornament; literally 'chewed paper' (see figs.27, 29, 32).

Punching A type of decoration achieved by using a fine punch to ornament a surface which has been gessoed and gilded (see fig.76).

Ramin A fine-grained hardwood from Indonesia or Malaysia.

Schlag leaf A thick leaf (literally a hammered or beaten leaf) usually made of an alloy of copper and zinc, and sometimes called DUTCH METAL.

Silvering The use of silver leaf to finish a frame, applied in the same manner as gold leaf but requiring a finishing lacquer to prevent tarnishing.

Size An adhesive used to make gesso and to protect unburnished WATER GILDING, traditionally made from animal skin or parchment clippings; the adhesive for the gold leaf is known as GOLD SIZE.

Water gilding Gilding using a water-based GOLD SIZE as adhesive, traditionally known as the BOLE requiring wetting immediately before gilding.

Whiting or Whitening An essential component of GESSO and COMPOSITION, made from natural chalk (calcium carbonate) in Northern Europe or gypsum (calcium sulphate) in Italy.

These sections are reproduced at 63.4 per cent or slightly under two-thirds actual size. The frames with more complex sections are shown with the depth of the carving or ornament indicated by a broken line. Later backing timbers, added to provide sufficient depth to glaze and back a picture, are not shown.

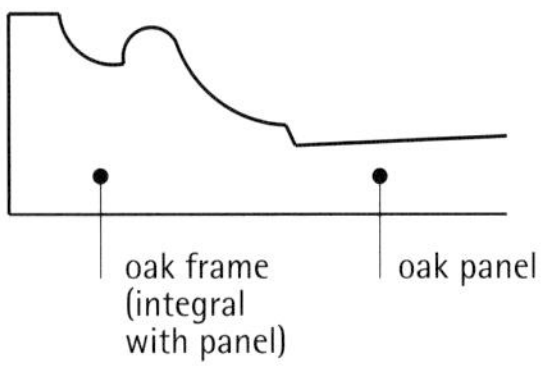

Fig.180
Henry VII (no.1; fig.18) by an unknown artist, 1505.
Oak frame integral with the panel, side section.

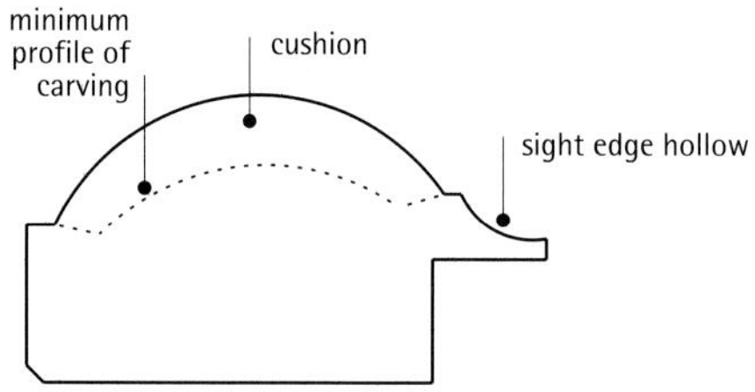

Fig.183
Sir Edward Nicholas (no.7; fig.47) by Sir Peter Lely, 1662.
Cushion frame.

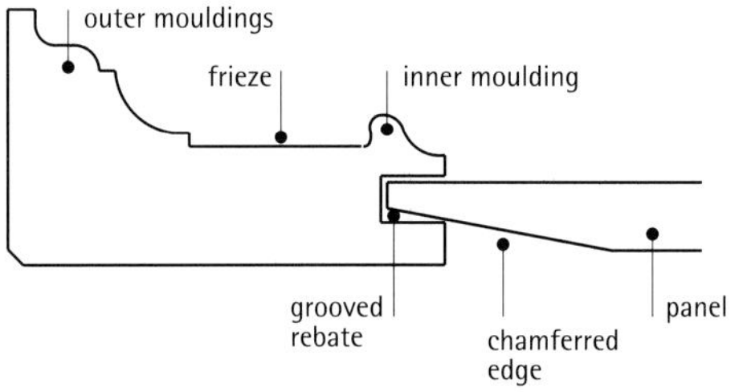

Fig.181
Henry VI (no.2; figs.19, 20) by an unknown artist, *c.*1540.
Oak frame engaged with the panel.

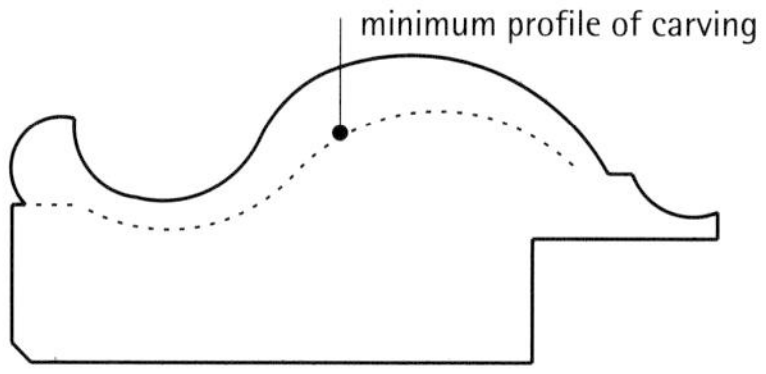

Fig.185
Dr Richard Mead (no.24; fig.49) by Allan Ramsay and studio, 1740.
Bolection frame, late seventeenth century.

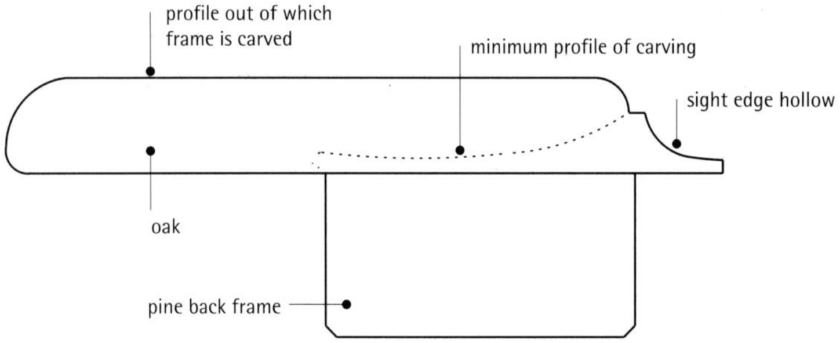

Fig.182
William Laud (no.12; fig.43), after Sir Anthony Van Dyck, *c.*1636 or later.
Auricular frame (with mortise and tenon joint, shown in fig.199).

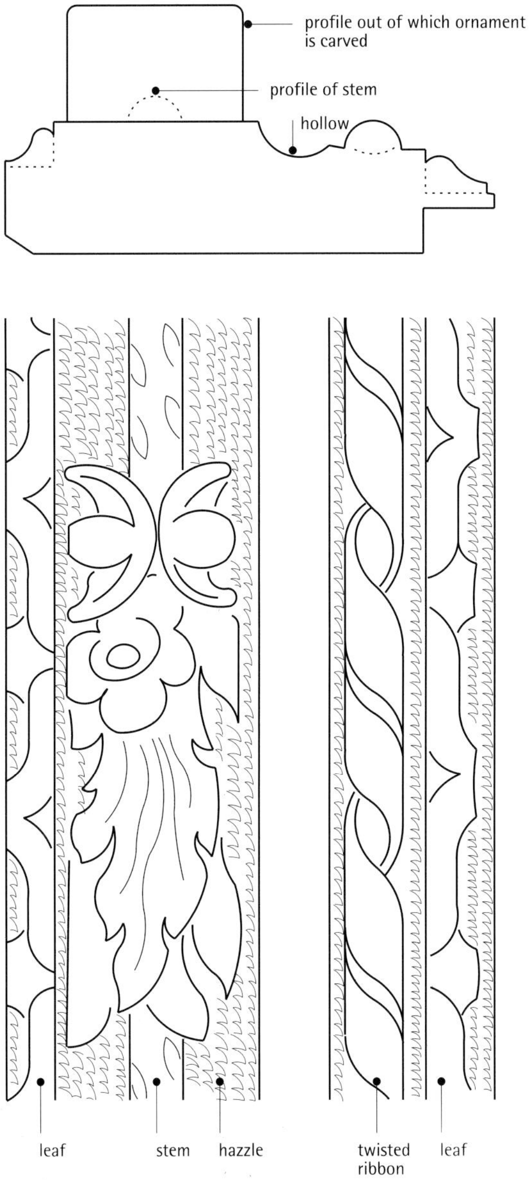

Fig.184
Samuel Pepys (no.18; fig.129) by John Hayls, 1666.
Bunched leaf frame, including side detail.

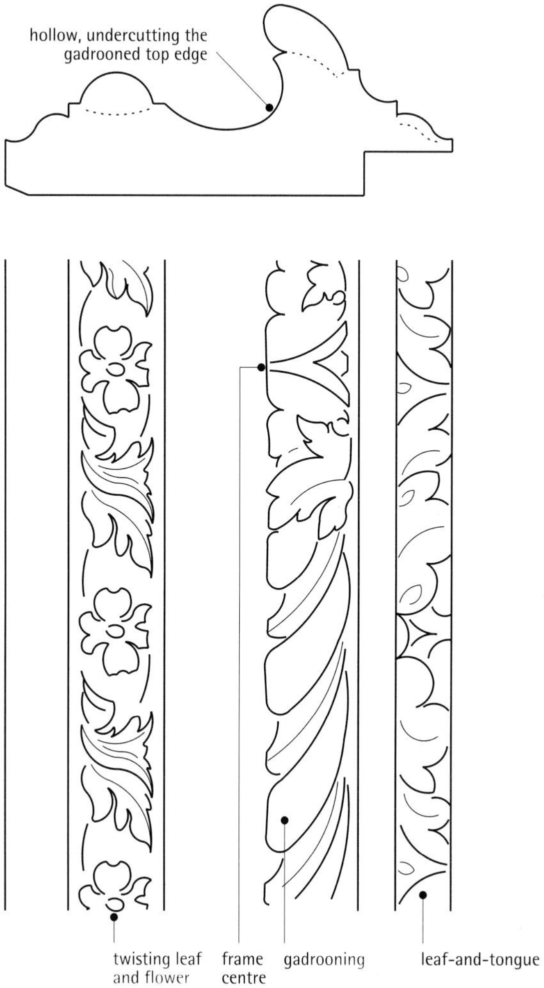

Fig.186
Sir Christopher Wren (no.25; fig.50) by Sir Godfrey Kneller, 1711.
Gadrooned frame, including side detail.

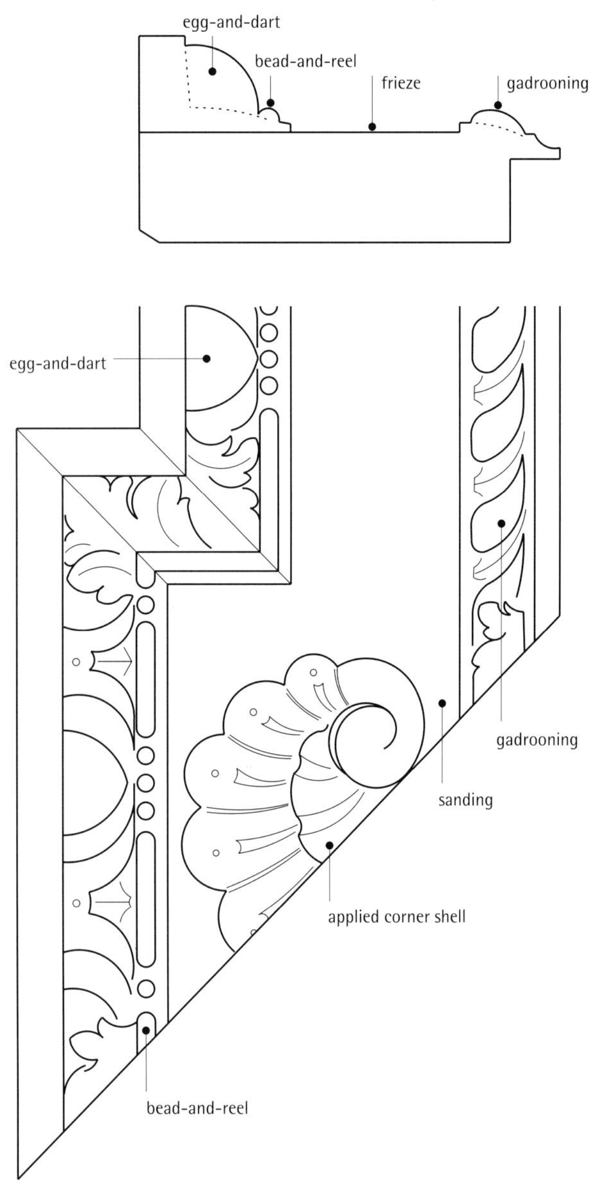

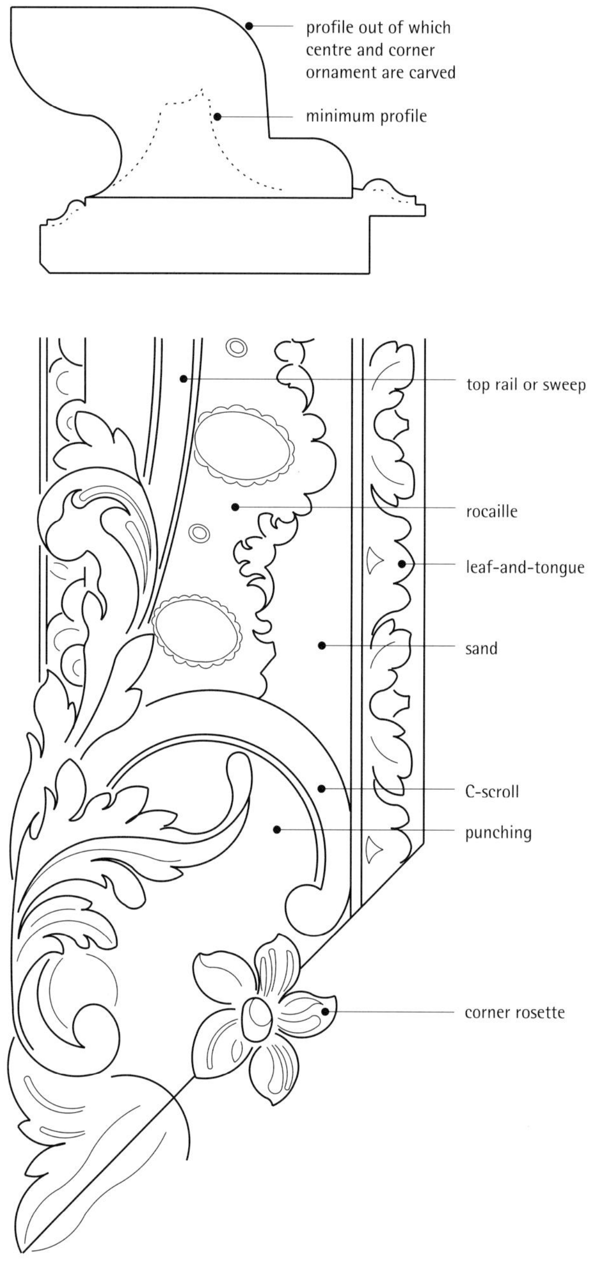

Fig.187
Robert Walpole, 1st Earl of Orford (no.28; fig.55) by Arthur Pond, 1742. Kent frame, including corner detail; the section shows the frame side rather than the corner.

Fig.188
Samuel Richardson (no.33; fig.153) by Joseph Highmore, 1750. Rococo frame, including corner detail.

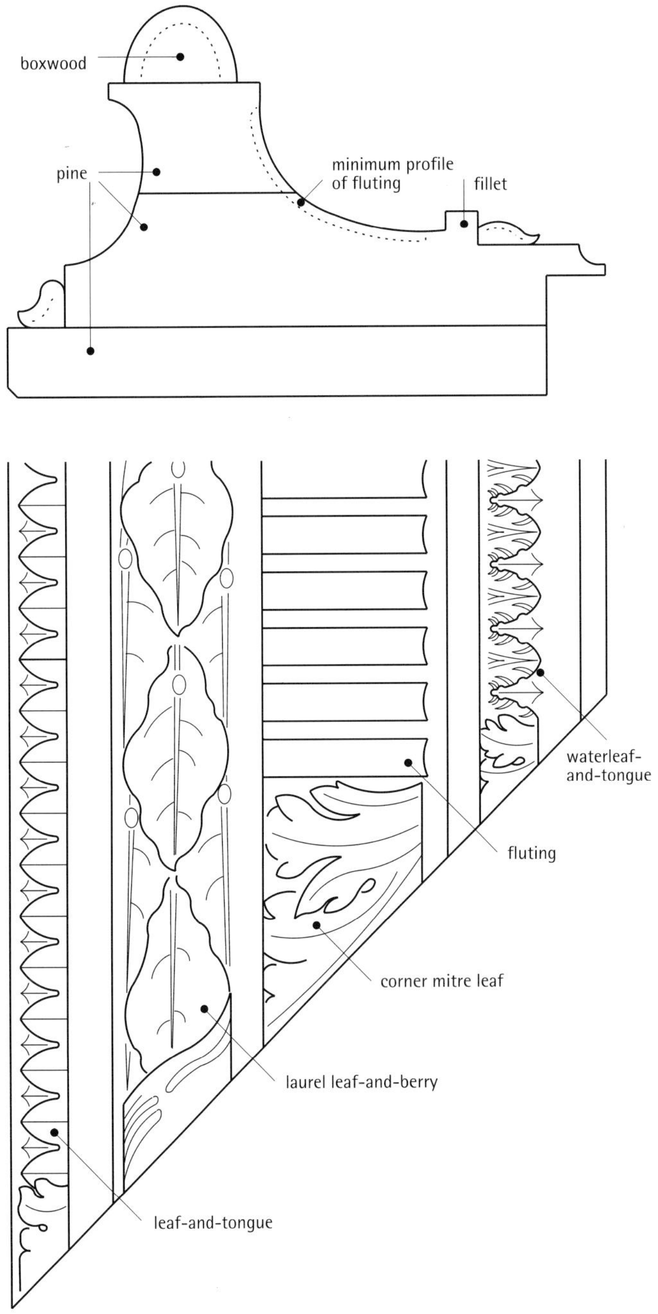

Fig.189
Self portrait by George Stubbs (no.49; fig.97), 1781.
Neo-classical frame, including corner detail.

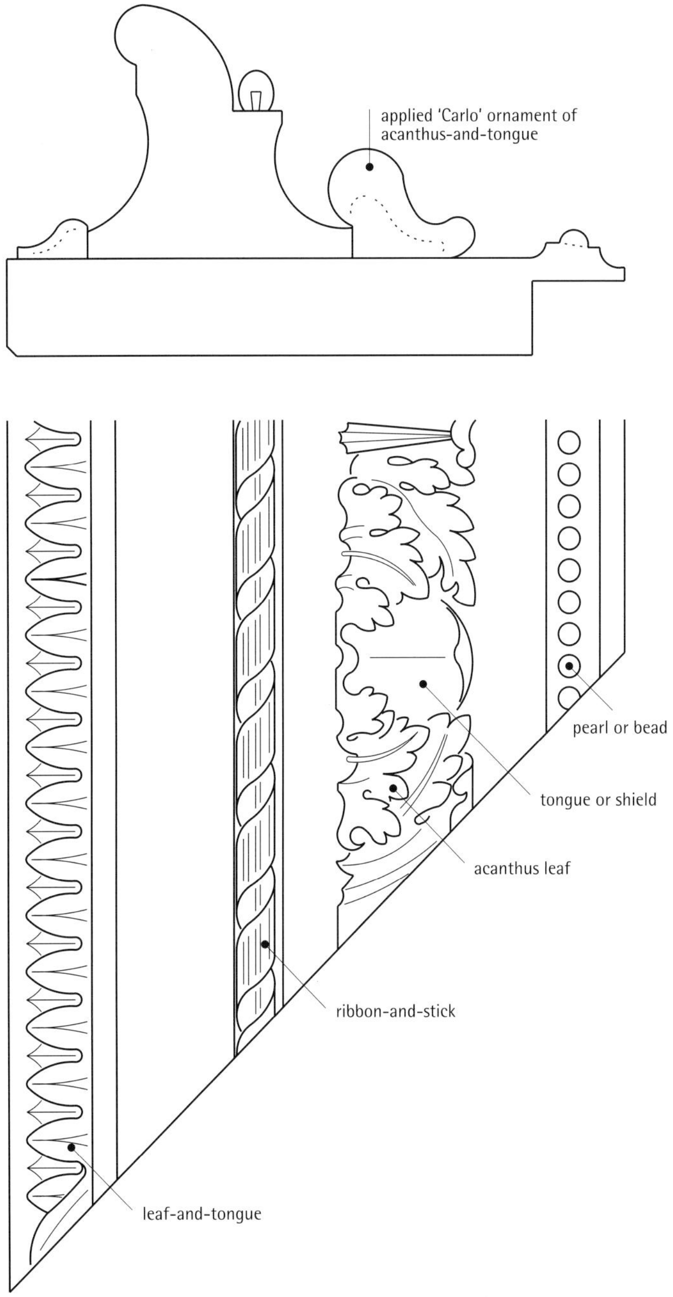

Fig.190
Sir Graham Moore (no.59; fig.100) by Sir Thomas Lawrence, 1792.
Maratta frame, including corner detail.

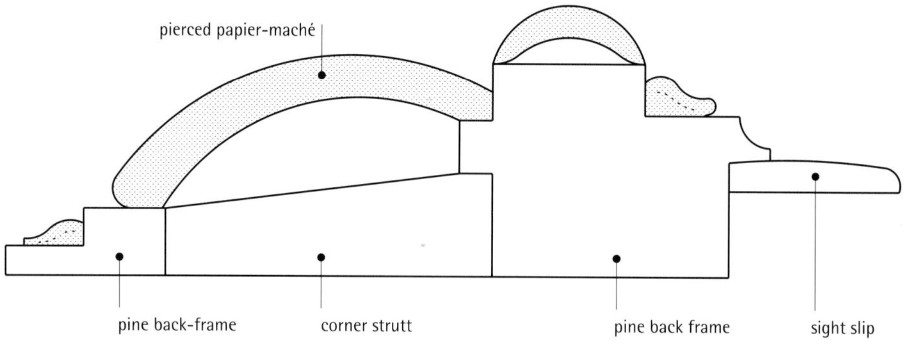

Fig.192
Mary Shelley (no.68; figs.31 and 32) by Richard Rothwell, exhibited 1840.
Papier-mâché frame, made by C.F.Bielefeld, the ornament in papier-mâché shaded.

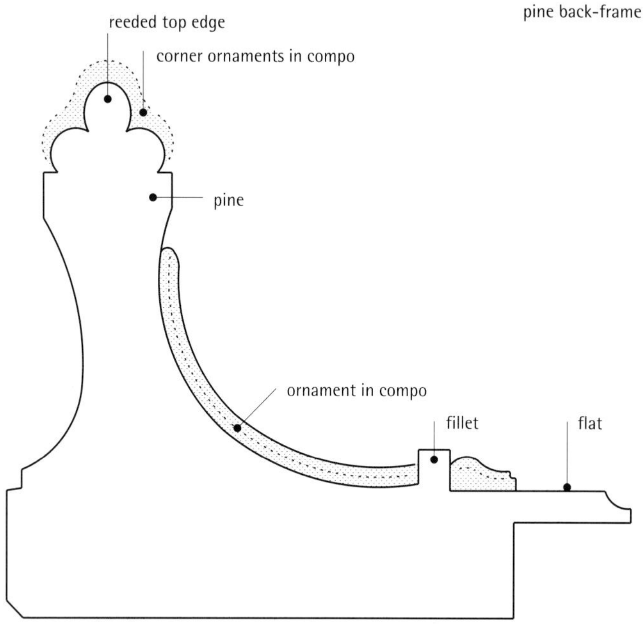

Fig.191
Self-portrait by Thomas Phillips (no.63; fig.68), 1802 or 1803.
Neo-classical frame, the ornament in compo shaded.

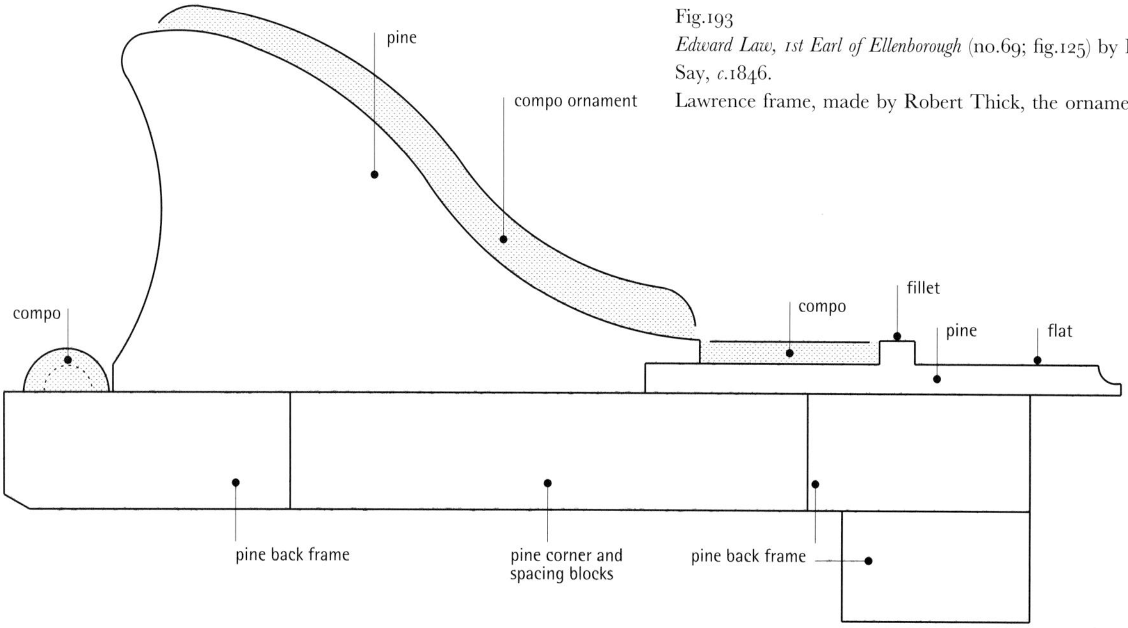

Fig.193
Edward Law, 1st Earl of Ellenborough (no.69; fig.125) by Frederick Richard Say, *c.*1846.
Lawrence frame, made by Robert Thick, the ornament in compo shaded.

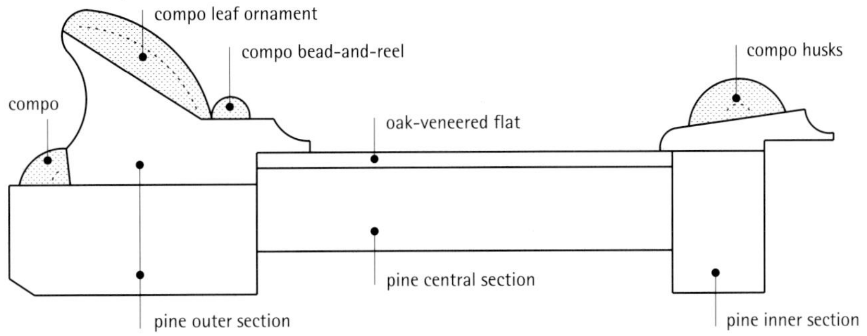

Fig.194
Matthew Arnold (no.80; fig.77) by George Frederic Watts, 1880.
Watts frame, made by W.A. Smith, the ornament in compo shaded.

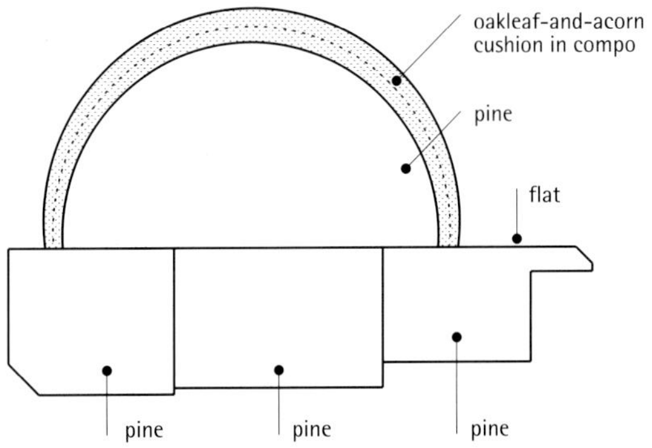

Fig.195
Sir Francis Seymour Haden (no.95, fig.164) by George Jacomb-Hood, 1892.
Cushion frame, the ornament in compo shaded.

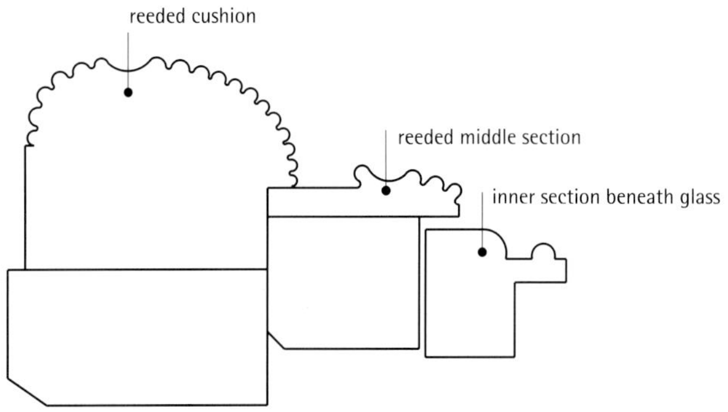

Fig.196
Thomas Hardy (no.103; fig.81) by William Strang, 1893.
Whistler frame.

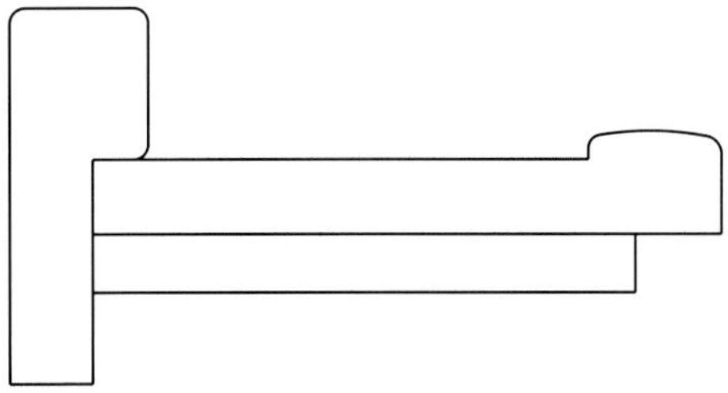

Fig.197
Kenneth Clark, Baron Clark (no.119; fig.22) by Graham Sutherland, 1963–4.
Cassetta or box frame.

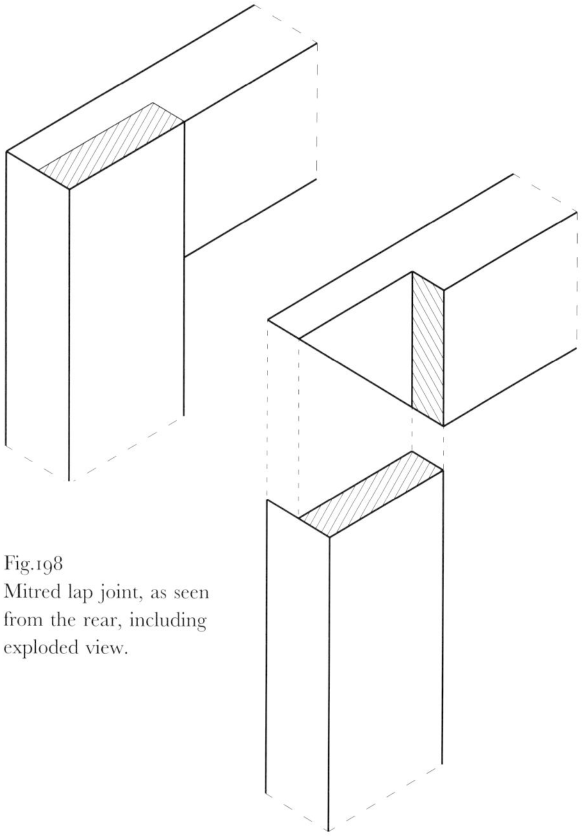

Fig.198
Mitred lap joint, as seen from the rear, including exploded view.

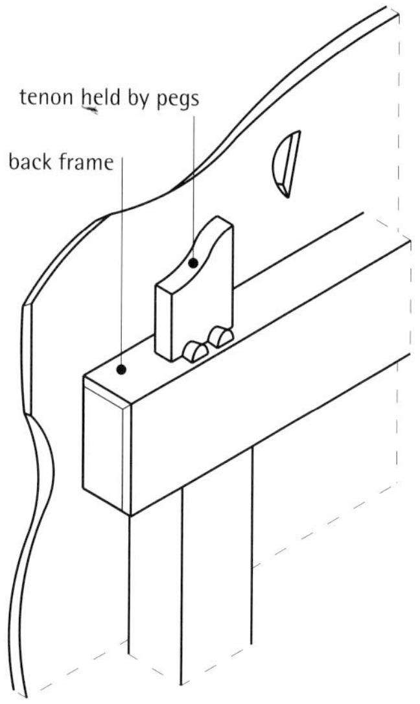

Fig.199
Mortise and tenon joint, taken from the portrait of William Laud (see fig.182), as seen from the rear.

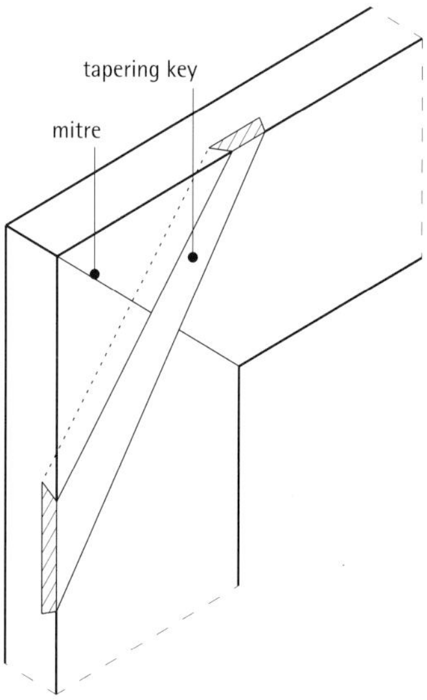

Fig.200
Mitre joint, secured by a tapering key, as seen from the rear of the frame.

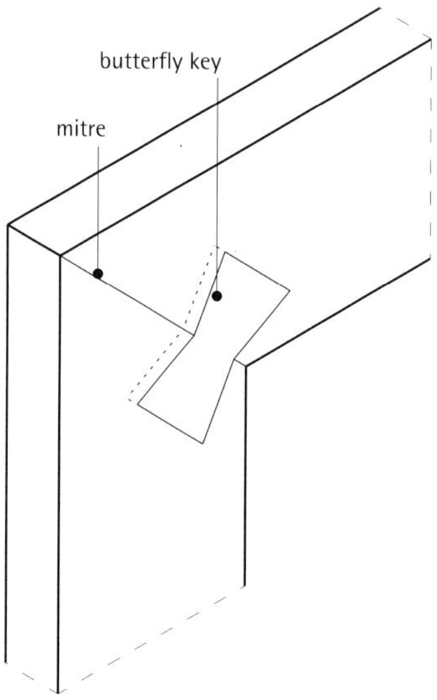

Fig.201
Mitre joint, secured by a butterfly key, as seen from the rear of the frame.

General Index

This index is to Chapters 1 to 7 and the catalogue section, and excludes the preliminary material, endnotes and glossary. There is a separate Index of Collections, Country Houses and Institutions on pp.223–4. Catalogue numbers for works included in the catalogue are given in square brackets (i.e. [no.1]). Numbers in italics refer to illustration page numbers.

Index of Collections, Country Houses and Institutions